Cooking Southern

Recipes and Their History

David G. Smith

David B. Hazelwood

Our other cookbooks:

Satsuma Fun for the Cook

Satsuma More Fun for the Cook

Cortner Mill: A Community Treasure

Easy on the Cook – Garden Vegetables

Easy on the Cook – Southern Breads

Easy on the Cook – Pies, Pies, Pies

Miss Lizzie's Heirlooms

Cooking Southern

Recipes and Their History

David G. Smith

David B. Hazelwood

WUFU3.com Publishing
Normandy, Tennessee

Copyright © 2021 WUFU3.com Publishing

All rights reserved.

Cover design by Anne Craig, Craig Communications

Published by:

WUFU3.com Publishing

Normandy, Tennessee

ISBN 978-1-7348305-2-1

Dedication

We devote this work, our labor of love, to our daughters
Lauren Elizabeth, Whitney Anne, and Sarah Kristen
Love of foods is their legacy.

We also dedicate this book to all past, present, and future generations
of Southern food lovers

"Thou shouldst eat to live; not live to eat."
-Cicero (106 BC-43 BC)

Contents

Our Beginnings	1
Meet the Authors	2
Satsuma Tea Room	7
Miss Arlene Ziegler	10
Cortner Mill Restaurant	12
Miss Lizzie Boswell	13
Recognitions	14
Bringing About a Gala Celebration	17
The South and Its Food	18

Our Tried and True Collected Southern Recipes

Appetizers	27
Beverages	39
Soups and Stews	57
Salads and Salad Dressings	81
Vegetables	116
Fruits	168
Chicken and Turkey	180
Pork	195
Barbeque	205
Beef	210
Lamb	219
Game	221
Old Terms Explained	226
Cheese	227
Seafood	229
Sauces	256
Over-the-Coals Cookery	280
Breads, Biscuits, and Stuffing	290
Sweet as Heaven Desserts	337
Pies and Tortes	338
Pastries and Icings	370
Cakes	382
Puddings and Souffles	416
Ice Cream, Sherbet, and Sorbet	447
Dessert Sauces	463
Cookies, Candies, and Confections	471
Breakfast and Brunch	508
Jams, Jellies, and Preserves	531
Pickles, Relish, and Canning	544
This and That	560
Bibliography	564
Index	567

OUR BEGINNINGS

Creating this book of historical Southern recipes and the stories behind them evolved from years of two friends and fellow restauranteurs sharing in delightful meals together along with the lively discussions that invariably followed those meals, often with a glass of wine or Bourbon neat. We worshiped at the temple of great food and there is none greater nor more steeped in tradition than Southern cookery. We are David Smith, a third-generation restaurant owner from Nashville and David Hazelwood, an entrepreneur-come-restauranteur from southern middle Tennessee. We are also cooks, weekend historians, and most important of all, proud sons of the South.

Our laid-back conversations always comprised a wide breadth of topics, but the discussions regularly had the suggestion of Southern foods and traditions. We discussed food in general while we also debated the origin and purpose of certain dishes and their role in Southern life. We discussed the history of the South and in so doing, because it was inevitable, we found the subjects of Southern cuisine, traditions, and folklore entwined.

We then made it our charge to collect an array of Southern recipes and dishes that represented our Southern historical past. These recipes were unearthed from our collections, personal experiences, and research. Our aim was to expose the "Old South," its customs and traditions as illustrated by its food. It should be noted that the most notable influences on Southern food were derived from African, English, Scottish, Irish, French, and Native American cooking.

An enormous amount of material was discovered to illustrate the premise of Southern food being a basis of clarifying what it was like being a Southerner. This unique trait of being a Southerner is continuously fluid and always evolving, but it became clearer to us how Southern cuisine, past and present—and the culture and the traditions that dictated these foods—were interlinked. It was and is our essence as a people. The Southern Personae.

We began to appreciate how the individuals from our historic past continue speaking to us through their writings, stories, and recipes, revealing to us their history represented by their foods and their way of life. Southern hospitality best illustrates this way of life. Food was a blessing, a means to survival, a way of sharing, a pleasure, a cause of celebration, an identity. In the South, the custom of hospitality continues to strengthen the very marrow of community, without which we as Southerners would not have survived. Throughout this book we point to how food has played such a dynamic role in this experience.

We were both focused on preserving our family histories and, in a much broader sense, passing on Southern food traditions and hospitality by sharing recipes and stories. David Smith had discovered boxes of his Aunt Arlene's hand notated cookbooks that were used from the 1918 founding of their Satsuma Tea Room. David Hazelwood had discovered an old memorandum book which had his grandmother, Miss Lizzie's, handwritten recipes from the 1930s.

We found the family recipes in the old cookbooks to be an amazing treasure trove of information. Their handwritten notes were stuck among the pages and written in margins of the books, recipe cards, and memorandum books, even on front and back leaves of the books themselves. Many times, they took a recipe and made it better, some they just left alone or dripped an ingredient onto the page, but over the years they had "cooked" and "blessed" every recipe in every book.

Verse which appeared in a 1762 Frontispiece of an English Cookbook:

"In cooking Fowl, or Flesh, or Fish
Or any nice or dainty Dish
With Care peruse this useful book
Twill make you soon a perfect Cook."

Each and every one of these resources, and much more, became core guides to our undertaking. As you read and use this book, you will find tasty dishes, and exceptional combinations of ingredients taken from many remarkable recipes. Carefully guarded secrets from years-gone-by are revealed in these pages. Each recipe is chosen from real Southern cooking that is delicious and tempting. The secrets are from accurate tried and tested recipes—all resulting in a total gastronomical delight.

Although we typically chose just one special recipe as an example of a really fantastic, wonderful dish to be included in these pages, there are hundreds of variations for cooking the very same dish which have been passed down through many families' lore and also those which can be found in countless cookbooks. Practically every recipe is just as good as the variations of recipes we have chosen to include in this book.

Each dish has a story to be told, a history to be recounted, and recipes to be shared. This is not a story of fast food trying to imitate Southern food. This is the story of Southern society, Southern people, the Southern Personae; people who lived, endured, and survived life's struggles; all of which are exemplified in their traditions, customs, and food.

Meet the Authors

I am a third-generation owner of the Satsuma Tea Room in Nashville. One of my earliest memories was filling water glasses at the restaurant around age four. For 86 years Satsuma was one of Nashville's most venerable restaurants and I honestly believe the reason we survived as a going business concern for as long as we did was because it was a family institution, a family business.

David G. Smith

At any point in time during our almost century-long existence, one would find numerous and extended combinations of family members working in the restaurant as cooks, wait staff, dishwashers, bussers, and kitchen workers. I am the oldest of six children and I often compared mom and dad having such a large family to the farmer having a similarly large family unit with many children to help on the farm. In both cases, a free steady labor force was realized and one that could always be counted on to show up and care about the caliber of work they performed. Is this obtuse thinking? Maybe, but I sure felt this way from time to time while I was growing up having to work in the restaurant.

You will want to utilize every one of your five senses when you partake of a marvelous meal. This assertion is even more spot on as you prepare that marvelous meal. This might sound peculiar to the lay cook, but when people ask me how I cook, my response is "by sense of feel, sense of smell and sense of sight, capped off by sense of taste." I use all my senses when I cook. I become one with the dish; no matter what I cook or how much I cook. A good cook does not depend just on measuring spoons or cups. She uses her instincts and her senses. She listens for just the right temperatures of frying oil; looks for the perfect color of biscuits; feels for textures and smells when the bread is just about ready; and tastes for the spot-on seasonings. A recipe, according to the dictionary, "is a set of directions for preparing something to eat."

David H and I are cooks first and foremost and restaurateurs second, so we totally appreciate the benefit of a good recipe. Remember that carelessness does not produce a good dish. All measurements must be level with no ingredient left out or passed over, and in-spite-of carefulness in seasoning; each dish must be always tasted and tested for flavor; during and after.

It became a yearly tradition for me, my youngest daughter, my wife, and niece to celebrate our birthdays as each occurred by dining at diverse, trendy, Nashville restaurants. In so doing, we were also sampling and experiencing the creations of the burgeoning local food scene. My daughter and niece are "card carrying" followers of this food scene in Nashville and both are very familiar with the constantly shifting and continuously fluctuating modern variations of foods, new drink and wine, distinct and unique combinations of ingredients and flavors, the farm-to-table movement, experimental cuisines, the colliding influences of different cultures to our local food experiences, cooking techniques, and ingredients for cooking from all over the world. To frame it another way or with a simpler, modern vernacular, the girls are "foodies." In Nashville, as in the world overall, there has been an awakening, a defining, if you will, of who we are by our food and drink. Is this development new?

There seems to be a resurgence, a trendy renaissance, in Southern customs and cooking within our mainstream society and culture. Southern cooking is now "hip." It is now "trendy" and quite "fashionable." People were now valuing Southern food for the pleasure of eating not just eating to survive. I began to speculate why?

While searching on eBay one day, my wife, Lisa, discovered that the two cookbooks/pamphlets authored by my great aunt for our restaurant—that she wrote in order to share some of our most asked for recipes with our customers—were now being sold as collector's items. Sometime later, while visiting an antique mall, she saw that these cookbooks were being sold in one of the many collector booths. The descriptions and acclaims of these small cookbooks on eBay were exceptional in their account of the quality of the included recipes and the food that resulted from following those recipes. People often tell me to this day that they still use those two cookbooks and the ensuing addendums religiously, and some have told me they have even made copies to pass on to their now-grown children or to give to their friends.

Case in point, one of my closest friends, Missy Porter, and I were discussing this cookbook project. Remember the year is presently 2021. I was sharing with Missy all the unbelievable resources that were at our disposal, but during the conversation, I mentioned that one of the cookbook addendums of the Satsuma was apparently non-existent. It had vanished close to 50 years ago and no one knew anything. Two hours after our conversation, I received an email from Missy. Attached to the email was a photo she had taken of all the various Satsuma publications that the restaurant had sold to the public over the years, including the missing addendum. Her family before her had bought, used, and cherished all the Satsuma cookbooks. Southern food endures. Tradition.

I remembered that large box of cookbooks of my Aunt Arlene's that was still stored away deep in the back of my closet, where I had left it. On a lark, I went to the box and began to study the contents, and it was as if I were in a machine traveling back in time. The answers to "why" were starting to become obvious. Southern cooking was unique, diverse and quite noteworthy. Also, timeless. I began to see the direct correlation, the parallel between Southern cooking today and Southern cooking of the past. Heritage and tradition. Our food defines us.

Meet the Authors

David B. Hazelwood

I was born hungry and in the first hours of my life I was satisfied with a sumptuous meal. So, from the start I have been drawn to food. Many a cook has answered the question of why they started cooking by saying, "I was hungry." While basic enough, the drive of hunger is also complimented with the cook's pleasure of satisfying the hunger of others. The quest to always make food better deepens the pleasure for both the cook and the guest. Adding a story at mealtime about what is in it, how the dish was made and where the recipe came from makes it even more special. The first taste and compliment are only exceeded by a request for and the sharing of the recipe.

A love of farm life led me to college and a degree in animal science. After twenty years of consulting, traveling among all fifty states and eating at a lot of fine dining restaurants, I had a career change and found myself directly involved in the food and hospitality business. I bought a country inn, a fine dining restaurant, along with a three hundred-acre farm. My ability was wide, but also thin. The thinnest part of my resume was the fine dining restaurant. It would take more than sitting at white cloth tables and being served gourmet food to equip me to own and operate a one-hundred-seat fine dining restaurant. I was lucky enough to get a call from Isabel Woodlee, a local woman with forty years of restaurant ownership and operating experience. I had the good sense to hire her right away without even considering anyone else.

One of my personal qualities is curiosity, which is an essential quality in order to be a good cook. "What if I add a little bit of this? What if I add a little more or less of that? I don't have an ingredient in the recipe. What if I substitute this?" Answers to these questions led me down twenty-five years of adventuresome roads to both successes and failures.

David Smith honored me as co-author of this cookbook. I am honored by my title because he did almost all of the research, collecting, organizing, and writing. Contributor may be a better title for me. I contributed a lot of recipes from my *Cortner Mill* and *Miss Lizzie's* cookbooks. Contributing recipes was easy because they fit the Southern cooking theme and it was the policy at our Cortner Mill Restaurant to give a recipe to guests when they asked for it. I have never been a believer in secret recipes. Give me a few tries and I will figure out what ingredients and methods are in your secret recipe. Or, I will be so close, few would know the difference. But the biggest reasons for sharing our recipes were accepting the compliment and knowing guests would spread the word about us when they made the dish and told their friends where they got the recipe. We didn't even leave out a key ingredient so you couldn't get it right.

Here's what David Smith said about me: "David B. Hazelwood is entrepreneur, connoisseur of all things Southern, and an accomplished "foodie." He is a son of the South but would rather be known first and foremost as a son of Kentucky. Kentucky natives are funny that way. In many ways David Hazelwood is reminiscent of the man sitting on the porch of a country store rocking away, whittling, regaling anyone who will listen to his stories. (It is perhaps the preacher in him. I'm positive it is the Kentuckian in him.) I can personally attest to hearing close to fifty years of his stories, many of them multiple and numerous times. We are all truly blessed as the beneficiaries of his narratives."

Sharing recipes has been just a small part of my relationship with David Smith. I first met him in 1973, when I came to Nashville and started eating lunch at his family's Satsuma Tea Room. Pretty soon after that I made it my daily choice for lunch. My friends would ask, "How can you eat lunch at the same place every day? Doesn't it get boring?" Not when the food is that good, the menu changes every day, and choices vary as the market's fresh foods change with the seasons. David Smith and I became hard and fast friends as I ate daily in his restaurant while David served as the lunch host. After fifteen years of our friendship, he introduced me to one of his friends who would become my wife. What more could I expect from a restaurant and a friend? I know, of course, he could publish any of my recipes!

"People who love to eat are always the best people."
-Julia Child (1912-2004)

Satsuma Tea Room
David Smith

Satsuma is a variety of the mandarin orange that is found readily growing in the southern United States, especially along the Gulf of Mexico coast. It is the name of a town in Alabama near Mobile Bay. Satsuma is the name of a province located in Southwest Japan which is world famous for its porcelain ware. It was also the name of our family's restaurant, Satsuma Tea Room.

> **SATSUMA**
>
> In 1918, Miss Ward and Miss Ziegler began this fine eating establishment and named it after the Satsuma Orange from Miss Ward's birthplace in Mississippi. Satsuma, now owned and managed by Betty and Truman Smith and two of their five children, was passed down from Mrs. Smith's aunt, Miss Ziegler. All items on the menu are made from scratch including salad dressings, breads, casseroles, vegetables, wonderful desserts and the award winning ice cream. Satsuma also specializes in box lunches for any of your catered affairs. The pleasant atmosphere, complete with flowers on the tables and a men's and women's table (so you won't have to eat alone), offers one of the best lunches in Nashville.
>
> **Satsuma   417 Union Street   256-5211**
> Monday--Friday 10:45 a.m.-2:00 p.m.
> No Credit Cards--Checks Accepted

1968 Newspaper Print Ad

Two young home economics teachers, forerunners of their time, Miss Arlene Ziegler and Miss Mabel Ward, opened the Satsuma in October of 1918. They had met at South Dakota State University where Miss Ziegler was a home economics student and Miss Ward was her teacher. Ultimately these two spirited and adventurous young ladies, both in their twenties, decided to open a restaurant. They embraced a conviction and the belief that they could serve excellent food in attractive surroundings at a reasonable cost to the customer.

They chose to open this restaurant in the small, at the time, city of Nashville, Tennessee, where Miss Ward had attended Peabody College as a student. Their dream commenced as they drove a Model T Ford, journeying from South Dakota to Nashville, camping in their tent all along the way.

No banks or suppliers would provide these two single, twenty-something women any type of support in 1918, but the young women stubbornly forged ahead with their plans to open a tea room (high tea was served every afternoon during the early years of the restaurant's operation). They even used wooden packing crates as kitchen furniture due to lack of funds for purchasing real kitchen furnishings. Thus, an eatery with a quaint tearoom atmosphere was launched, becoming an instantaneous Nashville success surviving two World Wars, a Great Depression and the event-packed history of the entire twentieth century.

Calvary Troops Returning from World War I in Front of Satsuma, 1920

The extensive variety of menu items offered was surpassed only by the number of customers that were served daily at the restaurant—approximately five to six hundred people for lunch—which was the only meal served five days a week. Over the decades, the Satsuma Tea Room enjoyed and took great pride in the fact that year after year the same people continued to eat with them—in many or most cases also their children, grandchildren, and great grandchildren. Generation upon generation of Nashville inhabitants were customers of Satsuma. Some families boasted as many as six-plus generations represented through the years as being our regular customers, "our family." This is Southern Tradition. Good food and hospitality—the Southern Way.

In their 2002 edition of *Roadfood,* published by Broadway Books, Jane and Michael Stern wrote in their review of Satsuma, "... Captains of industry, politicians, shoppers, and even blue-collar types (who are willing to wash their hands and comb their hair) crowd into the vestibule around eleven every weekday morning, to eat meals that always include cupcake-shaped (yeast) rolls and/or corn sticks, and entrees that range from southern fried chicken to American style spaghetti. ... Dining at Satsuma is a unique experience. Once you are seated, you look over the menu (printed every day) and write your own order on a small (yellow) pad set upon the table. The waitress, in white uniform and red apron, looks over the list (order ticket) and doesn't blink if you order six good vegetables and four desserts for two people."

In 2004, Satsuma Tea Room closed its doors as a Nashville eatery, a true Nashville institution. It was indeed the end of an era. Our establishment was born in October 1918 with the austere of foundations for a restaurant. Placing this time frame in the narration of the twentieth century, the Satsuma opened one month prior to Armistice Day ending World War I and one year after the October Revolution of the 1917 Russian Civil War that resulted in the formation of the Soviet Union (1922-1991). As a child of the 1950's, it was always with great pride that I shared that Satsuma started before the Soviet Union began and ended long after the Soviet Union fell.

Satsuma was an incredibly popular restaurant right up to the day the doors were closed. I am often asked why we closed. The answer, if I'm being perfectly honest with myself, was that holding the quality of food and customer service to the pinnacle of perfection was hard and at times seemingly impossible.

Dan Smith (brother) Truman Smith (father),
Working During a Busy Lunch. Circa 1982

I am establishing the principal fact of why we closed. We were respected for and expected to offer constantly great food and service. We never wanted this stellar reputation to diminish—so we chose to bring to a conclusion our long and successful run as a restaurant while we were still at the top of our game. For readers who enjoy pop culture, much like *Seinfeld* signing off at the top with the highest of network TV ratings.

Do I miss the business? Absolutely. Looking back, what I miss the most are the customers, the people that we grew to know so well as we fed generations upon generations of the families of Nashville. Our customers became our family and serving them day in and day out was our reward for a job well done.

I do miss the accolades and fame that went along with the notoriety of being such an integral part of Nashville's history. My wife is a native of South Carolina and thus was not familiar with the history and people of Nashville. She was constantly amazed that I was recognized by people anywhere we traveled, as well as whatever we did and wherever we went in the area, as being a part of Satsuma.

Satsuma in Downtown Nashville, 1968

Satsuma was always known for its fresh food and ingredients, known for always having its dishes prepared as if they were home cooked from the many hundreds of our traditional recipes and cookbooks. Satsuma was well known for always offering food cooked without any doubt as to the recognized excellence and standards expected by our guests—guests who were always greeted with a welcoming smile and a handshake. Our restaurant mirrored the South, its foods, hospitality, customs, histories, and traditions.

Miss Arlene Ziegler

Miss Arlene Ziegler was my maternal great-aunt. Her love of food, love of the South, love of gardening, love of reading and art, and her constant capacity to strive for quality and excellence in all endeavors, are things that I like to think are my birthright and my legacy bequeathed from her. She was a great role model.

Arlene Ziegler, Circa 1925

Arlene was unwavering from the very beginning that the restaurant she created be regarded with the highest of distinctions. As an expert gardener and horticulturist, she made sure that each of the customers' tables in the tearoom displayed daily fresh cut flowers from her gardens. Nonetheless, she was known to say with the firmest and the utmost of conviction, "All the freshest, most beautiful and exceptional flowers in the world don't count if you don't have outstanding and extraordinary food to serve the customers." Miss Ziegler's vitality and enthusiasm for food is evident in that the restaurant had such varied menus. In fact, the menu was changed daily, contingent on the freshest of ingredients attained that day. The menu was composed and printed a few hours before each meal was to get underway. She constantly updated and added new food selections to the tea room's menu, using recipes uncovered from her never-ending perusal of current and past cookbooks.

Arlene Ziegler, with 'Satsuma,' Is Dead At 85
by Tom Normand, staff writer, The Nashville Banner

"Miss Arlene Ziegler was a local gastronomic institution, and she will be missed by one of the largest followings a restaurateur ever enjoyed. ... Miss Ziegler, 85, a partner in the unusual landmark restaurant called the Satsuma Tea Room. ... Just reading her menus is a culinary adventure: cherry wine salad with pumpkin bread, deviled fresh crabmeat baked in the shell, Canadian cheese soup, corn light bread 'from an old recipe,' turnip greens and hog jowl, rhubarb pie, etc. ... And the surroundings: fresh linen laid out for each customer, sturdy pottery china, arrangements of flowers and vegetables fresh from her garden, richly bursting with each season's theme. ... And the clientele: state supreme court judges, secretaries, lawyers from the nearby courthouse square, stockbrokers, and bankers from the nearby financial district, merchants, society ladies, governors, mayors and legislators, and whoever from the general population appreciates fine food at un-prohibitive prices. Meals served, Monday through Friday."

When we wrapped up her possessions, as we closed her home upon her death, we found cookbook after cookbook after cookbook, going back to the early 1920's, which were used for the restaurant. I just packed the books not really knowing why, but they were part of her, and I just could not give or throw them away, so the cookbooks were boxed and stored.

In 1968, at the insistence of the customers of the restaurant, Arlene had compiled a small pamphlet/cookbook to sell in the restaurant. The front cover read, *Fun for the Cook; 110 Prized Recipes Collected Over 50 Years; From Satsuma Tea Room*. It was an instant success, selling out printing after printing. Because of this huge demand, the first cookbook was quickly followed by another pamphlet/cookbook in 1974 titled, *More Fun for the Cook; A Personal Collection from Home and Tea Room; The Satsuma Tea Room*. This second cookbook also proved to be a huge success. These two cookbooks were soon followed by individual booklets, addendums if you will, of additional recipes for each category: *Easy on the Cook-Garden Vegetables, Easy on the Cook-Southern Breads*, and *Easy on the Cook-Pies, Pies, Pies*.

All these publications contained recipes of dishes the restaurant was known for, was famous for. These recipes represented Southern cooking at its best; but also, the recipes epitomized Southern tradition at its best, by way of its food.

At this point in the twentieth century, the term "foodie" was still decades away from being coined in our culture and lexicons; yet in the South, food, the love of food, love of cooking, love of drink, our famous hospitality, home grown and fresh ingredients, generational family food recipes, were just a fact of everyday existence to a Southerner. These characteristics identify our lifeblood as people of the South. They were/are rejoiced and celebrated.

Cortner Mill Restaurant

David B. Hazelwood

Many of the recipes in this cookbook came from the *Cortner Mill Restaurant Cookbook* and *Miss Lizzie's Heirlooms*, a cookbook including recollections and recipes of my maternal grandmother, Miss Lizzie Boswell, collected from her life in the farm country of Western Kentucky during the 1920s and 30s. When David Smith asked if we could incorporate recipes from these cookbooks into the collaborative cookbook that we were researching and writing, it was quite easy to share them. Sharing a recipe is the right thing to do, and besides, a lot of mine came from him anyway.

Cortner Mill Restaurant Cookbook

When I started operating Cortner Mill Restaurant, the best inspiration came from Satsuma with their practice of utilizing fresh fruits and vegetables and also cranking their own ice cream. This led us to make all of our dishes in-house from fresh ingredients. We were quick to share our recipes and didn't want to have to respond to a request with "We get ours ready-made from the food distributor." If you open a restaurant and can't make but one thing from scratch, make your own ice cream. First, everyone knows the difference in store-bought and fresh churned. Second, you already have all of the ingredients you need except rock salt.

With the establishment of the Cortner Mill Restaurant, chefs were not clamoring, knocking on the door, seeking employment in Normandy, Tennessee with its total population of only 161 and located in the rural outskirts of Nashville. Even though we were doing white tablecloth, china, and fine dining, there were no chefs. I began with country cooks like Isabel, Bettie, Ethel, and the other Ethel. This is the biggest reason so many of Cortner Mill Restaurant's recipes appear in this cookbook. They are tradition and family-based, tried and true recipes.

I learned a lot from these ladies. One of the Ethels told me that an apple didn't just have a bad spot on it. The whole apple was bad. You don't just cut out the bad spot and use the rest. "Get another apple," she said. She also told me that her favorite thing to make was chicken noodle soup. When I asked her why, she said, "Because people like it." "Why do they like it?" I asked. "Because it's good," she said. "Why is it so good, Ethel?" "I put chicken in it!" Now that's a Southern country cook.

Bettie also typified the Southern country cook. I asked her for the recipe for her delicious chocolate meringue pie. "I don't have one,'" she replied. I asked her to write down the recipe from her memory. A couple of weeks later she handed me a sheet of lined notebook paper on which she had written the pie recipe with a dull pencil. The first ingredient on the notebook paper was a large glass of milk. When I asked what she meant by large, she replied, "You know, a big one." Seeing I wasn't getting anywhere, I went to the other ingredients on the list and the amounts of every ingredient written were just as vague. I won't bore you here with my intricate investigative powers, but I was finally able to pin Bettie down so I could piece together her beautiful chocolate meringue pie recipe.

Sarah "Miss Lizzie" Boswell

Sarah Elizabeth (Lizzie) Reid was born in Hebbardsville, Kentucky. on September 8, 1893 as the fourth of six children to her parents, Henry and Rosa Lee Reid. She married John Hubert "Pop" Boswell on January 25, 1911. In their log cabin built on Pop's father's farm, they started a family and when they were done twenty-two years later, there were six girls and two boys. Learning to cook was a necessity and needless to say, there was plenty of opportunity for practice, with resourcefulness, ingenuity, and inventiveness as the main ingredients.

Most everything Miss Lizzie cooked came in combinations of just four basic ingredients. Flour and sugar were bought at the store, but the milk came from a family cow or goat, and eggs from the chicken house. From the whole milk, butter was churned, and buttermilk remained. Hog killings provided meat and lard. Chickens were killed and plucked. There were cured hams, shoulders, bacon, sausage and seasoning meat in the smokehouse. After plowing the garden with a mule, came green beans, tomatoes, cucumbers, peppers, beets, corn, potatoes, onions, cabbage, lettuce, okra, and many other vegetables. Strawberries were picked in the garden and wild blackberries picked from the fields. Fruit trees provided bushels of apples, peaches, cherries, plums, and pears to be stored, dried or canned. In the summer of 1930 Lizzie set a goal of canning 100 gallons of fruit and vegetables. In July she stepped on a nail and got blood poisoning, but the whole family pitched in to help her reach her goal.

Water was carried from a spring or drawn from a well on the enclosed back porch. Coffee beans went through the hand turned coffee grinder. From a 21st century perspective, all the many tasks to put food on the table gave new meaning to "homemade from scratch." We don't have Grandmother's cooking anymore, but we will always have sweet memories of her and her good food.

Recognitions

For centuries recipes have been passed along verbally from generation to generation, if for no other reason than there was an inability to read and write by most. The historic Southern cooks were such good cooks that "you just put them in front of the stove or fire with the fixin's and they created somethin' grand, even if they couldn't "always 'splain you jus' how." Generational verbal recipes evolved into a written form as the ability to read and write became more widespread. Written recipes and cookbooks became significant, often viewed as hallowed works of the Southern food tradition. The early American cookbooks give one a deeper appreciation for the homemakers of old and their stories; their abilities in food preparation, and their nurturing of their families. Cookbooks are part of the histories and customs of our country and permit us to study the many changes of our lives—our history.

Many of the recipes included in this book represent numerous and delightful dishes, all using countless and varied mixtures of ingredients. Most of these particular recipes, however, had been collected much later than the introduction of the original underlying dishes or the induction of their foundational ingredients into our Southern heritage and culture. With the passage of time, much has been amended as the recipes evolved from their "passed down" form to their "written" form.

As we began this project, at our disposal were all the boxed and stowed-away, many quite-old cookbooks collected and used by David Smith's Aunt Arlene beginning in the early 1920's for the Satsuma restaurant. Also, we found the now out-of-print, but still popular cookbooks/pamphlets written for Satsuma's customers of old, needing to be republished.

David Hazelwood had chosen recipes from the *Cortner Mill* cookbook and from *Miss Lizzie's Heirlooms*, collected from his grandmother's life in the farm country of Western Kentucky during the early years of the twentieth century. All of these resources and many more became the core guides to our undertaking.

Arlene Ziegler's heavily marked-up copy of *The Southern Cook Book of Fine Old Recipes*, by Lustig, Sondheim, and Rensel was published before 1935 and was an invaluable source of recipes for us. She was equally inspired, as were we, by the *Farm Journal's Country Cookbook*, edited by Nell Nichols and published in 1959.

We have included below pictures of just a few of the many cookbooks we used in our restaurants and again used as we were writing this book of Southern foods and the Southern personae. We had boxes of these old cookbooks, our oldest originating in 1922 was the well-worn copy of *The Times-Picayune Creole Cookbook*. These cookbooks were like the yellow pads or Post-Its of today. When a recipe comment or change was to be considered, what better place than to note these thoughts on the pages themselves or even on the front and back book covers.

Why not stick a piece of paper or a used envelope with the observations of the recipe in the book? We discovered many such slips of paper in the books as we began our research. These cookbooks were constantly sourced for food recipes used for the restaurant and these cookbooks that were used were so good in their content that book wear and tear was the order of the day. The *Farm Journal Country Cookbook* mentioned above was quite helpful and was referenced over the years constantly, so much so that the spine of the book now has to be held together by duct tape. The *Times-Picayune Creole Cookbook* was used repeatedly which caused the front cover to separate itself from the rest of the book. *The Southern Cookbook* as a result of its continual appraisal and usefulness, now has no cover what-so-ever with its pages held together by scotch tape. There are even a number of cigarette burns scattered among the pages as a result of years of constant use beginning in the 1930's.

What we discovered or at least had reaffirmed is that history not only just evolves but also repeats. Working with the wealth of cookbooks at hand both in the restaurant and again in our research was such a godsend. The recipes seemed almost timeless, ageless in their generational intricacies. They were just that good! Every time we used a recipe it was almost with an untold reverence that we noted the place and date of their beginnings. Each recipe gave us a direction and a focus and we are truly blessed. Thanks to all those in our past who put these cookbooks together; wrote those wonderful recipes. We are the better for their amazing work.

"... No book of receipts (recipes) can boast originality, since by the very nature of things, the good dishes get copied, and the receipts (are) swapped about until it is very hard (next to impossible) to know when and how they originated. Her receipts along with the countless other recipes found in these pages, have been taken from countless other cookbooks comprised over many different eras and from many different places of the Southland ... have been taken, verbatim, from family culinary albums—old manuscripts written in fine lady-like hands—many of them including identical directions which have been passed among friends."   - Harriet Ross Colquitt, *The Savannah Cook Book*,

You will also find among these pages modern recipes that were chosen from the 2006 church cookbook, *Fruit of the Spirit, A Collection of Recipes by Friends in Faith Evening Circle,* Mt Bethel United Methodist Church, Marietta, Ga. Our intent in doing so was to illustrate some Southern recipes that are still used in our present day and perhaps demonstrate to the reader just how little Southern food and tradition has changed from our historical past. The Southern personae lives on.

"Community cookbooks, those clunky, spiral-bound, gravy-splattered volumes, are as Southern as sweet tea. They may get comparatively little critical respect, but they are much relied upon in Southern kitchens. Community cookbooks are a voyeur's treat, a window into everyday life and foods of a group of churchgoers, a clutch of quilters, or a league of ladies inclined towards service. At first glance, the books are almost formulaic in their intent, organization, and content. Yet a closer look at the foods selected for inclusion, the names ascribed to the dishes, and the tales told of the meals past reveals as much about the history of the compilers as any local history could."   -John T. Edge, *A Gracious Plenty*

Bringing About a Gala Celebration

After devoting nearly five years to researching and recording this narrative, we are now able to find ourselves envisioning all the Southern personages we have encountered along our long journey, sitting at a fantastically huge table. Our labor has turned into a pilgrimage through time. Seated at the table are those of our past, our present, and our future, but who are first and foremost Southerners. Everyone is eating, drinking, and sharing their stories and tales. They are just having a downright good ole time.

Accepting a seat at the table is Harriet Ross Colquitt of Savannah, Georgia, who compiled a local cookbook during the dawning of the twentieth century. She had a true reverence for Southern food and culture and a sense of humor that many of today's humorists would love to possess. Also enjoying themselves at the table are the now-deceased John Egerton and the very much alive John T. Edge, who are in our estimation two of the finest historians and experts of Southern food and culture.

The native Americans who introduced us to their foods, the Africans who were enslaved and transported to the American South, and the early European pioneers settling in our region, all interwove their food experiences to form the foundations of Southern cooking. All, of these people are full of merriment and embracing a celebration for food. Christina Regelski is in the middle of them confirming her research on *The Soul of Food* as it pertains to the Southern personae.

There is Helen Smith Rhett, who from the last decades of the 1800s onward was matron of Charleston, South Carolina's high society and who, with her fellow ladies of Charleston society, accumulated and rescued the cooking traditions of the Low Country past. Also worthy of a seat at the table is William Deas, Mrs. Rhett's butler and cook, just one generation removed from slavery. Mr. Deas was singled out in the early 1900s as "one of the great cooks of the world." The famous She Crab Soup was just one of his creations.

Ann Williams-Heller is such an interesting table guest. Starting in the 1920s, she applied her own life and writings to vegetarianism. She theorized and demonstrated how all food diets, including our Southern diets, needed to be changed or at least supplemented. Although her ideas seemed alien and extreme at the time, future generations have made them quite established. As Southerners, we are her rightful beneficiaries.

Bill Neal is seated at the table, alongside his peers at The Southern Foodways Alliance and the multitude of other Southern food authors and historians on whom we relied heavily in our writing. The generations upon generations of family members who cooked for their household, and the congregations and communities across the South who shared their priceless recipes in those spiral-bound, money-raising cookbooks are all at the table.

We see David Smith's great aunt Arlene, owner of the Satsuma Tea Room and a pioneer of the Nashville food scene. Seated next to her is David's grandmother, Pearl Janssen, a full professor of home economics in the field of food experimentation at the University of Illinois. She and her students developed many avant-garde food recipes that today are praised and accepted as mainstream. These women are taking deserved seats at the table.

There is David Hazelwood, reunited with his grandmother, Lizzie Boswell, and his mother, Jeanette Hazelwood, all enjoying foods from their rural Kentucky heritage. David Smith glimpses sitting at the table Louella Johnson, his black "mama," the rudder and anchor of Satsuma Tea Room's kitchen for fifty-plus years. A cook extraordinaire, she performed her daily duties guided by the lessons she absorbed from experiences and skills acquired amid her family and the narratives they shared.

As Southerners, we owe all these individuals and the Southern people they epitomize such a huge debt. That is why they have been invited to sit at the table celebrating all Southerners and their culture. They are part of our community and its history. Can you feel, acknowledge, and taste by way of the foods of the past and present the continuous fluid motion of our change and evolution as a Southern people? We sure can.

Anybody and everybody—those people from centuries past, those people that are entrenched in our present day, and the people awaiting and anticipating our future foods— all have a seat at the table. As Southerners, we are Southerners in a very large part due to our food, hospitality and sense of community. This seems to be the actual blood that courses through our bodies. It is at the root of our true soul. It is our history. It is our custom. We all belong at the table. Every one of us. Come to the table and celebrate; eat, drink, and be merry! Laissez les bon temps rouler! We are truly glad y'all are here!

The South and Its Food

Southern landscape, Southern folklore, Southern culture, Southern history, and the character and reputation of Southern people, are all puzzle pieces that fit together attempting to suggest the definition of Southern tradition. We find too, that food is continuously at the heart and soul of all our Southern customs, our culture and heritage. Hospitality was and is the underpinning of all Southern cooking. Southern pride, and our history of being of and part of the South. It is a notion revealed more than anything else by its food and drink. John Egerton maintained in his *Southern Food*, "Food was a blessing, a pleasure, a cause for celebration. The tradition of hospitality, of serving large quantities of good things to drink and to eat to large numbers of hungry people, of sharing food and drink with family, friends and even strangers proved to be a durable tradition in the South, outliving war and depression and hunger." Southern cooking is about culture and community as much as it is about our need to just survive. Southern food summons the region's difficult past, but Southern food also helps us as Americans to understand and respect this past with absolute deference.

Christina Regelski wrote, "While many American regions and cities have famous fare, few will argue against the fact that the South wears the culinary crown. Southern identity is strongly linked to its cuisine and food has long been enticing for tourism in the South. Southern food has inspired songs, books, television shows, websites, trails, and movies." Fried Green Tomatoes, anyone?   —http://ushistoryscene.com/author/christina-regelski/

Our food defines us. John Egerton wrote in his *Southern Food: At Home, On the Road, In History,* "Within the South itself, no other form of cultural expression, not even music, is as distinctly characteristic of the region as the spreading of a feast of native food and drink before a gathering of kin and friends. For as long as there has been a South, and the people who think of themselves as Southerners, food has been central to the region's image, its personality, and its character."

During an oral history for the Southern Foodways Alliance (SFA), John Egerton recalled meeting a woman living outside the South at that organization's annual conference. He later learned during a chat with the woman that her home was in California. He said to her, "Well it's a long way to come just for supper." And then she said, "Yeah, but it's so Southern and you know being Southern is kind of like being Catholic. It is almost impossible to get away from it. You cannot outgrow it or give it up or renounce it. It's just part of you."   -www.southernfoodways.org

Many imagine the Southland as a place where the sun shines brighter, the breezes are gentler, the birds sing sweeter and the flowers are fairer. Honeysuckle and honey. One can almost hear bars of a Stephen Foster ballad wafting in the trees as the smells of food cooking, food that is the backbone and mainstay of the Southland tradition, drift along.

Some can even envision Scarlett O'Hara standing on the portico of Tara, eyes and fist pointing to the sky. This is the South of our dreams, but these imaginings, our imagination, is founded in fact and tradition. But one quickly comprehends that most of our time-honored traditions are not all "honeysuckle and honey" as would be claimed in the Southern folklore of old. Our Southern traditions have been romanticized and idealized, but they are founded in truth; the pain, joy, family, heritage, suffering, and hardship, is the reality represented in our Southern cooking.

When the European settlers and explorers first arrived in the New World, there were many groups of Native Americans living here. Many of these native groups were friendly and helpful towards the new arrivals, teaching them the skills needed to help them survive in this unfamiliar world. The southern Native American tribes were also farmers and they cultivated three main foods predominately. They raised squash, beans, and corn; often called "the three sisters."

"The most important foodstuff for the white European settlers and the most meaningful lesson taught by the Native Americans, was how to grow, prepare, and use corn, or as the natives called it, maize. Corn proved to be the basic staple for these early Americans, and it established a deep-rooted and a markedly staunch grip on the South and its culture. The capability to grow corn, in our estimation, was the greatest lesson that the Native Americans ever imparted to the Europeans. Corn, and its byproducts, have occupied every Southern table in some form or fashion since its early introduction into the culture of the South. Corn could be eaten fresh or dried, and dried corn could be stored for months. The dried kernels were often ground into a flour or meal. In this form, it was boiled for puddings or made into bread." —*americanfood.net/history-of-southern-food*

Squash, tomatoes, corn, along with deep pit barbecuing are contributions to Southern cuisine from the Native American tribes of the Southeast. Use of sugar, flour, milk, eggs came over to the New World by way of Europe. The Southern affection of all things fried is of Scottish derivation. Black-eyed peas, okra, rice, eggplant, benne (sesame) seed, sorghum, melons of all kinds, and most of the spices that we find used in Southern cooking, past and present, came from Africa carried by enslaved people that were brought to our shores. Enslaved African and African Americans advanced a distinctively African American culture, presence, and influence on the South, which is strongly supported by the Southern cuisine of today. Many of the Southern foods we celebrate and enjoy today have their deep roots in enslaved peoples' toil, tradition, and creativity.

Southerners knew how to cook their vegetables. It seemed to be in in their genetic makeup. In the past, if vegetables were not flavored with meat, animal fat or butter, then more often than not, they were fried. One such vegetable, which is native to Ethiopia, is okra. It is one of the South's most celebrated vegetables and one that is most often associated with the African culture. Even the word okra is derived from an Igbo (an African people) word for vegetable, okuru.

In West Africa, okra was often used as a thickening agent for soups or in one pot meals like a gumbo. Okra spread into North America by way of the Caribbean with the migration of enslaved people during the 16th, 17th, and 18th centuries, as did the widespread use of okra in their cooking. Okra was often found growing in the gardens of these people as one of their fundamental food staples.

"We must credit the enslaved people for their cooking creativity, not because they were trying to create new dishes, but because they were cooking with what they had in order to survive. The masters fed the enslaved people as cheaply as possible. While they were given a lot of pork meat, they never lived high on the hog. At butchering time, the masters kept the best cuts of meat for themselves and disposed of the remaining waste by giving it to the enslaved. They got the head, snout, ears, fat back, and intestines, i.e., chitterlings aka chitlin's. It wasn't a healthy diet, but they were able to survive. The saying 'we used all of the hog except the squeal', could have originated with the enslaved people or other poor Southerners." – *Sylvia Boyd*

Much like pork, corn was widely eaten by both free and enslaved people, but the enslaved were predominantly reliant on corn. Corn was the constant, everyday food provision for these Southerners. Cornbread, a resulting offshoot of cooking with corn, is often associated to the cruelties of forced slavery. The enslaved were given only limited rations of food and limited time to eat and prepare their meals and thus they became heavily dependent on cornbread. Cornbread and all its different varieties were just the thing for the enslaved workers in the fields, because it didn't require utensils, was easily carried, and kept a long time.

Gardening was a means that provided the enslaved with personal choices for their individual diets while supplementing these diets with meat from hunting and fishing. After working on the plantation, a full day for the "master," which was excruciating and backbreaking labor, more often than not, the gardening or obtaining their food by other means was done on the enslaved's own time, at night.

The natural geographic and climatic advantages of the different sections of the sunny South have played an important part in Southern cooking. The fertile fields, plentiful fruit trees and waterways within a region have each contributed amply. Just as territorial and as local as defining terrain changes, Southern foods are also locally and regionally classified by their own distinctive ingredients, taste, and features of their cooking traditions. What are red beans and rice in Louisiana will doubtless be Hoppin' John (peas, generally black eyed, and rice) in South Carolina, while in Florida you will most likely find black beans and rice. Fresh water crabs are steamed in Maryland and Virginia and then seasoned afterwards, while along the Gulf Coast they are boiled in highly seasoned water.

As Southerners, we like to point out that when a person views us as one people, that person is in fact a non-Southerner. In reality, every part of the South has its own individuality and distinctiveness. We do find one fact to be universally true: as extensive and diverse, connected and comparable the different sections of the South are, we discover that every locality in every region is famous for its own version of distinct recognizable cookery. The food defines us. As Henry Higgins championed in the play *My Fair Lady*, accent and vocabulary defined where and how someone was raised in England. So too can a Southerner's specific region be recognized by the food for which that region is known and treasured by its inhabitants.

The creole dish of New Orleans has nothing to do with the ethnic origin of the cook, but rather indicates the use and incorporation into a meal of red and green peppers, onion, and garlic. Oranges, grapefruit and avocadoes play an important part in Florida cookery. Maryland is famous for its fried chicken and seafood recipes. Virginia conjures thoughts of sugar-cured hams and its hot breads. Kentucky is known for its corn "likker", its flannel cakes, and its truly amazing and identifiable Kentucky burgoo. Although many Southerners do not accept Texas as a true Southern state, we have never experienced smoked or barbequed brisket anywhere in the world to equal what we have eaten in Texas.

As noted earlier, the most notable influences on Southern food were derived from African, English, Scottish, Irish, French, and Native American cooking. The different assortments of foods, the varied ways of preparing these foods, and the regions in the South from which the foods originated, all combine to give Southern cuisine its own distinctiveness. Each region of the South is defined by its foodstuffs, as well as by its terrain. Tidewater, Appalachian, Creole, Low Country, Floribbean, Delta, are some of the many examples of the topographical differences that are used to classify Southern regions.

From the beginning of the Civil War through the darkest periods of the Great Depression, the South was the "red-headed step-child" of the United States. The economic environment in the South was of such disarray that its cooks learned to "make do" with the most common and cheapest of foods—yet loving hands still created good home cooking. The Confederate Commissary put heavy levies on certain foodstuffs. Flour became so scarce and expensive that cornbread was universal instead of biscuits, rolls, or waffles. The Yankee blockades of Southern ports made luxuries of items such as tea and coffee. There was almost no beef and very little mutton, so only the rich could afford them. Hominy and dried peas became such standard fare that some swore never to eat them again. Yet there was plenty of hog meat, chickens, and wild game to provide protein. Gardens produced such vegetables as potatoes, squash, snap beans, okra, and collard greens to be cooked with pot liker. Milk was available if you were fortunate enough to still have a cow. Pork fat and flour made rich gravy. Leftovers made good stews and gumbos. When cane sugar could be obtained, three desserts were common- pound cake topped with whipped cream, vanilla blanc mange, or chocolate layer cake. Stale bread became a sweet dessert.

"Reports of foods eaten during the slave centuries indicate that planters may have attempted to reproduce the cuisine of their mother countries, but a transformation took place. In African hands, the enslaved people cooked food that had been modified by means of ingredients they found locally and cooking methods that they brought from Africa.

Spices were being used more intensively. In the warmer climates of the South, this practice served the purposes of helping to disguise spoiled meats and to enhance the flavors of the meals. Foods began to be grilled and vegetables were being added to daily diets of what in Europe had been mainly a protein and carbohydrate diet. One historian has gone so far as to acknowledge enslaved people "for adding greens and green vegetables to the slave holder's diet, thereby saving countless numbers from nutritional deficiencies."

-Jessica Harris, *Iron Pots and Wooden Spoons*

After the end of slavery, and with the slow migration away from the conditions of bondage, Blacks, particularly Black women, continued to hold dominion in the kitchen as they found work as housekeepers, cooks, or in other forms of domestic service. Throughout the country, these women fed their charges with freshly made African American foods from their own family recipes handed down through oral tradition. By way of plentiful, good and tasty food, combined with love, these women, descendants of enslaved people, served as domestic glue to soldered together countless white families.

The very representation of Southern cuisine, or should we just say Southern "cookin", seems to conjure up visions of the old, jovial, stout, wholesome black woman, head wrapped with a bandana to help control the heat radiating from the oven as she cooked her delicious meals. This fantasy image originated in fact. We hold in the highest regard this much admired personality as a person of remarkable abilities in the art of creating savory, appetizing dishes from just plain everyday ingredients.

It should be remembered and understood that not all the good cooks of the Southland were Black women or, for that matter, even folks who lived on plantations. Southern "city folks" and "country farmers" were also lauded for their food and hospitality; praised for their entertaining talents and acclaimed for magnificent palate-tickling culinary efforts.

"In America's recent history, features of Southern cookery have spread to the North and the West; to the four corners of our country, these fundamentals had a decisive influence on the development of many other styles of American cuisine. Even still into our present day, these African Americans, as they migrate in search of better lives, maintain their ways of eating and cooking which are constantly influencing the broadening tastes of our nation. Their culinary talents not only have a major influence on the cooking and food of today, but there was proof of these skills, talent, and culinary knowhow found in the very primitive community cookbooks.   —Jessica Harris, *The Welcome Table*

"The sad theme of loss runs through all of southern culture from way back. The Black spiritual and blues are its musical expression. But, its counter-theme is endurance. Today Southerners are more and more aware of their traditional foods as the rest of their culture blends into the nation as a whole. Certain Southerners choose to ignore our humble foundations of ignorance, slavery, and extreme poverty which was accurately a major part of the account of the privileged few building a civilization on the backs of others, yet these are the stimuli that have given us our story, our history, and our traditions. These occurrences should not be ignored but ... When we no longer appreciate those foods of our past, we will no longer be Southerners."   —Bill Neal, *Southern Cooking*

In sharing an excerpt taken from the journal of George Wymberly Jones De Renne titled "An Old-Fashioned Picnic" (written in 1878 with an additional entry written in 1880), Harriet Ross Colquitt recorded in her *1933 The Savannah Cook Book:* "Half a century (our present day has the overall number of years at around 140 years) has rolled by, and although we do not do things in so grand a manner these days, many of the old traditions which are observed still give an atmosphere of leisure and grace to our Southern customs which have persisted in standing out against progress and its devastating hand. Some of these old receipts (recipes) may seem complicated when compared to modern makeshift dishes, but they have stood the test of time; and are still used in many Southern homes where good cooking is considered so important a part of good living."

Today, cookbooks continue to play an important role in maintaining Southerners' sense of identity. In times of tragedy and hurt, Southerners are drawn to their food, which is their salvation, identity, and tradition. *The Washington Post* journalist Julia Cass reports, "This was especially visible, when (New Orleans) bookstores began opening after Hurricane Katrina's floodwaters receded, the first volumes residents bought to replace their waterlogged, moldy collections were often beloved cookbooks. Philipe LaMancusa, owner of the Kitchen Witch bookstore in the French Quarter, said 70 percent of his sales since reopening in November (2005) came from customers whose recipe books were among Katrina's causalities. 'People are replacing their cookbooks first,' agreed Tom Lowenburg, owner of Octavia Books. 'Cooking is so tied in with people's comfort and quality of life, especially in New Orleans. Making familiar foods helps people with the heartbreak of loss." —"After Katrina, Cookbooks Top the Best-Seller List", March 22, 2006

We are writing this book in the years 2015-2021. Present day 21st century culture is fast becoming one that demands that we label all facts and issues as "politically correct," or at the very least needing to be. Our contemporary place in social history is exemplified by such events as electing the first black United States president, the "Me Too Movement," our concerns and fears of climate change, Black Lives Matter, democratic protests and uprisings against worldwide authoritarian and dictatorial regimes that strive to disintegrate their people in order to retain power, amass their fortunes, and to keep their populaces subjugated. Tectonic, shifting plates colliding, each representing old versus new perceptions of society. There are numerous other illustrations of why we need to embrace political correctness. We prefer the concept of social acceptability.

These instances and circumstances of acceptability, of correctness, would have been regarded as completely alien and totally unfamiliar to the people living in the South during the late 19th and early 20th centuries. This was the South that had just been ravaged by a devastating Civil War and a South that saw their entire economic model and social strata turned upside-down. All these events did not happen in the history of their past but directly, firsthand to these Southerners as they saw their way of life shattered completely.

A punishing Reconstruction; an invasion of the South from the North by self-serving carpet baggers; penalizing economic restrictions; the birth and growth of the repressive Ku Klux Klan; inferior, impoverished, substandard education for blacks and for whites; the Jim Crow era; lynching; voter repression; land ownership suppression; segregation to keep the whites and people of color totally separated; the Negro, who from the days of slavery that preceded the Civil War to the years following, was generally believed by many whites to be second class citizens; these were all Southern realities and attitudes that prevailed following the Civil War and up to and including our present day.

Dealing with these attitudes and realities provided tremendous angst for us as we researched and wrote. The majority of the Southern resources we used were written between the 1910s to the 1980s. Political correctness is a fact of life today but it was not during the time frame of this book's subject matter. Our anguish comes from the fact that it was very difficult to offer real time instances of the Southern personae while remaining true to the need of being politically correct and reflect the need for all people to be equal. There proved to be no way to proffer an explanation of the ugliness being the true reality and the sociality norm of the time.

It was not our intention in any way to make frivolous and insubstantial the plight of the Negro, the African American, or enslaved people. We apologize to all whom we have insulted or offended with quotes in Pidgin English or stories and sayings that were attributable to the Negro, but offered by the whites of the period. These were whites who viewed themselves as superior to the people of color. These were behaviors of Southerners of old. We cannot rewrite history, try as we might, although we sure wish we could.

The influences for many of the Southern foods we now enjoy came directly from the colonial and antebellum slave quarters. Southern food was often perceived as the model for American cuisine, but this cuisine is actually derived from a complex blend of European, Native American, and African origins that found recognition at the hands of an enslaved people. Southern food has evolved from sources and cultures of diverse regions, classes, races, and ethnicities.

Our Southern traditions have been romanticized and idealized. We choose to ignore our humble foundations of ignorance, slavery, extreme poverty, with the elite few building civilization on the backs of others, yet these are the stimuli that gave us our story, our history, and our traditions. These occurrences should not be ignored but embraced in context as the mechanisms that have molded who we are today. We are founded in the pain, joy, family, heritage, suffering, and hardship that is the true reality represented in our Southern cooking.

When more wealth recovered in the South and life seemingly improved for whites, most of the African American citizens still found themselves quite left out; but the old constant known as Southern cooking endured and became the "makings" and "basics" of what we now recognize as Soul Food. Soul Food was to be shaped, enjoyed, and experienced with all our senses. Cooking soul food became absolutely a sensory happening.

You will find tucked among these pages some carefully guarded secrets and gems of real Southern cooking; unlocked, palatable, and tempting to the eye. Southern food originally crucial just for survival has now become a gastronomical delight. It has also become the yardstick of our body and our soul as Southerners. It describes and defines us. It is the lifeblood that courses through our veins even now, just as it once ensured survival among those who came before. Tradition? Heritage?

Perhaps you will discover from this narrative, nuggets of meticulously treasured secrets of real Southern cooking. Southern food that has become Southern tradition, developed from more than 400 years of change, innovation, and resilience—and this journey is not over. Our culinary traditions will continue to draw inspiration from generation to generation and take on new characteristics as we continue to discover who we are through our food.

Sociologist William C. Whit in *Soul Food* predicts that, "The next transformation in Southern cuisine will be reconciling the traditional rich flavors of the food (we love) with our now contemporary lifestyles. This adaptation already has begun. The enslaved people's diet hinged on salty, fatty foods in order to survive the severe labor that they had to endure day in and day out. Today, we no longer have to engage in that level of physical activity and we no longer are enslaved, totally dependent on the "master" for the mere subsistence and continuation of life. The trend in this day of nouveau Southern food now is creativeness towards protecting the tastes we love while safeguarding our health and our modern-day existence."

We can't wait to see what comes out of our Southern kitchens next, most assuredly being guided along the way by our history, traditions, and our customs—our food!

"There is no sincerer love than the love of food."
-George Bernard Shaw (1856-1930)

APPETIZERS

Some say that it scarcely seems necessary to whet the appetites of hearty-eating Southerners. Nevertheless, there is a growing tradition (there is that word again) of serving a "little something to start with" particularly when the occasion is a special one. There is now even a word that "foodies" and "gourmets" are using to label the appetizer or hors d'oeuvre; to give their acceptance for the significance that has now been associated with this part of a very special occasion or meal. That word is *amuse bouche*, which is French for "amused mouth". I can't think of a more playful way to illustrate the appetizer, such an important, yet overlooked part of the meal.

Appetizers start off a meal in grand style. They often turn a party lull into a time of easy conversation and pleasant hospitality. These delectable tidbits awaken our taste buds for more good things to come as the evening progresses.

"The food eaten first lasts longest in the stomach."
Kikuyu (African) Proverb

THE DELICIOUS APPETIZER

1/2 pound freshly-sliced dried beef
2 packages cream cheese
1 1/2 Tablespoons onion juice
2 teaspoons Worcestershire sauce

Blend the onion juice and Worcestershire sauce into the cream cheese and roll into small balls; add a bit of cream to thin the mixture if necessary. Place the cheese ball on the edge of a slice of dried beef and roll, tucking the edges in as you go. If this does not hold, it can be fastened with a toothpick.
The Southern Cook Book, 1939

PARMESAN CHEESE BALL

1 package (8 ounces) cream cheese
1/2 cup grated Parmesan cheese
1/4 teaspoon garlic salt
2 Tablespoons finely chopped green pepper
2 Tablespoons finely chopped pimento, chopped parsley, or nuts

Combine cheeses and garlic salt until well blended. Add green pepper and pimento. Mix well and chill. Form into desired shapes and desired sizes. May even form into log shape if desired. Roll in parsley. One could even form into cone shape and insert nuts in pine-cone pattern.
Ann C. Cox. The Nashville Cookbook, 1977

CHEESE BALLS

2 pounds uncured (mild or spongy) cheese
8 ounces cream cheese
6 ounces moldy-type (bleu) cheese
10 ounces "sharp" or "aged" cheese
½ cup prepared mustard
1/3 cup lemon juice
2 Tablespoons horseradish
dash of Tabasco
dash of Worcestershire Sauce
dash of onion juice or onion salt
1 1/2 cups nuts, chopped (optional)
chopped parsley (optional)

Make sure your cheeses are at room temperature. Combine mustard, lemon juice, horseradish, tabasco, Worcestershire sauce and the onion juice or salt. Add slowly to the cheeses in a mixing bowl of an electric mixer. When thoroughly blended, shape into a large ball, oblong roll, or smaller balls. Cover loosely with wax paper and store in the refrigerator. Let age several days and when ready to serve, coat with nuts and parsley for flavor, texture, and color.
Yield: 4 pounds of cheese balls or rolls

NOTE: Cheese is always a hit with any party or just as an appetizer. So easy. Serve on a plate accompanied with crackers. Everyone has encountered the quandary of what to give as teacher gifts or the need to give a very special gift to someone to say thanks in an out of the ordinary way. Look no further than the cheese ball.
Clareta Walker, University of Illinois Home Economics Faculty Favorites, 1965

CHEESE-SAUSAGE BALLS

1 pound sharp cheese, grated
1 pound sausage, mild or hot
3 cups biscuit mix

Heat oven to 350 degrees. Bring cheese to room temperature. Mix cheese and sausage with the biscuit mix, using fork. Shape into 1-inch balls and place on ungreased baking sheet. Bake 12 to 15 minutes. Serve hot or cold. Makes 40 balls.

NOTE: These balls may be frozen. Thaw slightly before baking and increase cooking time.
Bebe King, The Nashville Cookbook, 1977

SAUSAGE BALLS

2 pound sausage
2 cups soda crackers, crushed
1 egg
1/4 cup parsley flakes

Mix all ingredients well and shape into 1-inch balls. Place on baking sheet and bake at 350 F for 20 minutes. Makes 5 dozen balls.
Cortner Mill Restaurant cookbook, 2009

DATE BALLS

1 stick butter	½ cup finely chopped nuts
1/2 pound chopped dates	1/2 cup flaked coconut
1/2 cup sugar	2 cups crisp rice cereal

Heat butter, dates, and sugar over low heat, stirring constantly until the dates are soft. Cool and add remaining ingredients. Mix well and roll into balls.

NOTE: Roll balls in powdered sugar if desired.
Edna T. Matthews, The Nashville Cookbook, 1977

SPINACH BALLS

1 package frozen spinach, cooked and drained	1 cup Parmesan cheese
1 cup Pepperidge Farm Herb Stuffing (not cubed)	1/2 medium onion, chopped
	2 eggs, slightly beaten
	6 Tablespoons butter, melted

Mix ingredients together. Make into small balls. Place on cookie sheet. Bake at 350 for 15 minutes; or freeze, bag and bake as needed. Makes roughly 24-36 spinach balls.
Pam Gillespie, Fruit of the Spirit, Mt. Bethel United Methodist Church, Marietta, GA

FROZEN ORANGE BALLS

1 box (12 ounces) vanilla wafers	1/2 cup butter
3 cups confectioner's sugar	1/2 cup chopped pecans
6 ounces frozen orange juice concentrate	1/2 cup flake coconut

Crush the vanilla wafers. Mix all the ingredients except coconut. Shape into small balls and roll into coconut. Freeze and serve frozen. Makes 3 dozen.

NOTE: This is a nice party item to make ahead and freeze.
Sharon Turner, The Nashville Cookbook, 1977

APRICOT STICKS

20 large dried apricot halves	1/4 cup candied pineapple, chopped fine
1/2 cup flaked or shredded coconut	sugar

Wash apricots and cover with boiling water and let stand 5 minutes or until softened. Drain and dry on paper towels. Combine the pineapple and coconut and mix well. Flatten each apricot half, skin side down. Spread portion of the coconut pineapple mixture over apricot surface. Roll these, jelly roll fashion. Place on a tray to dry at room temperature. Roll in sugar. Store in loosely covered container at room temperature. Makes 20 apricot candies.
Farm Journal's Country Cookbook, 1959

AVOCADO CANAPES

Cut small rounds of bread, and then toast both sides. Spread each with the following mixture: Peel the avocados and put through the ricer (processor). Add 1 Tablespoon of onion juice, 1 Tablespoon lemon juice, cayenne, salt and pepper to taste. Mix with just enough mayonnaise to hold together. Press half a plain or stuffed olive on each canape before serving.
The Southern Cook Book, 1939

BROWN SUGAR BACON

1 pound sliced bacon   1 1/2 cups brown sugar

Arrange bacon in single layer on a foiled baking pan. Cover evenly with brown sugar. Bake at 425 for 25 minutes until done. Quarter each slice. Let stand 2-3 minutes until sugar is set.
Kristin Burrows, Fruit of the Spirit, Mt. Bethel United Methodist Church, Marietta, GA

CHEESE APPETIZER FOR COCKTAILS

2 egg whites   1/4 cup grated stale bread crumbs
1 cup grated cheese   dash of cayenne

Beat whites of two eggs to a very stiff froth, and add one cup of grated cheese, cayenne and 1/4 cup bread crumbs. Pat/roll into small balls and fry in deep fat.
The Southern Cook Book, 1939

CHEESE STRAWS

1 cup flour   1 egg
1 cup grated cheese   1/2 teaspoon salt
1/4 cup butter   1/4 teaspoon red pepper

Mix together the flour, cheese, salt, and pepper. Cut in the butter as for pastry and add the beaten egg. If more liquid is needed, add a few drops of water. This should feel and look like pastry. Roll out thin. Cut in strips and bake in quick oven (425 F.) until lightly browned. This makes about 5 dozen straws.
Mary Leize Simons, 200 Years of Charleston Cooking, 1930

CHEESE TOAST

8 rounds buttered bread   1/4 teaspoon paprika
1/2 pound American cheese   1/2 teaspoon Worcestershire sauce

Make a paste of the cheese which should be fresh and add the seasonings. Spread the rounds generously with the cheese mixture and set in a hot oven until brown. Serve hot. The cheese toast is good as a party opener and is especially nice for a light Sunday night party.
William Deas, 200 Years of Charleston Cooking, 1930

CHEESE WAFERS

1 cup margarine	1/2 teaspoon cayenne pepper
2 cups flour	1/2 teaspoon salt
2 cups sharp cheese, grated	1 cup crisp rice cereal

Cut margarine into flour. Blend in cheese, cayenne, and salt; mix with cereal. Roll into marble size balls. Press with a fork and place on ungreased cooky sheet. Bake at (350 F.) for 15 minutes. Makes about 60.
Nancy Smith, The Nashville Cookbook, 1977

CHICKEN LIVER TURNOVERS

1 pound chicken livers	1/4 cup chopped onions	Parmesan cheese
flour, salt, and pepper	1/8 teaspoon A-1 Sauce	paprika
1/4 cup butter	pie dough	

Dust the chicken livers with flour. Sauté in butter with the onions and A-1 sauce. Season with salt and pepper. Remove from heat and chop. Cut pie dough in 2 inch rounds. Put a teaspoon of the mixture on half of the round. Fold over the upper half. Press together with the prongs of a fork. Brush with melted butter and sprinkle with parmesan cheese and paprika. Bake at 350 until light brown. Serve hot.

NOTE: These take some work, but so wonderful to serve and eat. Makes 60. They can be frozen before baking.
Satsuma Tea Room, Fun for the Cook, 1968

WARM DATE APPETIZERS

pitted dates	whole almonds
Feta or goat cheese, crumbled	1/2 strip bacon

Fill the pitted dates with crumbled cheese and almond. Wrap 1/2 bacon strip around each date and secure with a toothpick. Place on cookie sheet. Bake at 375-400 until crisp (10 minutes).

NOTE: The amounts made depend on how many dates are being used.
Gail Lightfoot, Fruit of the Spirit, Mt. Bethel United Methodist Church, Marietta, GA

SURPRISE ASPARAGUS DIP

1 can (14 1/2 ounces) asparagus spears, drained	1/4 teaspoon hot sauce
	1/2 teaspoon dried dill weed
1/2 cup dairy sour cream	1/2 teaspoon seasoned salt

Place all ingredients in container in a blender. Chill. Serve with chips. Makes 1 cup.
Sarah Long, The Nashville Cookbook, 1977

AVOCADO DIP (Guacamole)

1 cup mashed avocado
1 Tablespoon fresh lime juice
1 teaspoon salt
1 1/2 teaspoon grated onion
1 teaspoon Worcestershire sauce
1/4 cup Roquefort or bleu cheese (mashed)

Beat all ingredients together until smooth. Good on potato chips, corn chips, melba toast, or crackers.
Satsuma Tea Room, Fun for the Cook, 1968

CRABMEAT DIP

1/2 cup butter
1 bunch shallots, chopped fine
1/2 cup fresh parsley, chopped fine
2 Tablespoon flour
1 pint heavy cream
1/2 pound Swiss cheese grated
1 Tablespoon dry sherry
1/4 teaspoon red pepper
salt
1 pound white crabmeat

Melt butter in heavy pot and sauté onions and parsley. Blend in the flour, cream, and cheese until the cheese is melted. Add the other ingredients and fold in the crabmeat. Makes 2 quarts.

NOTE: With David H's wife, Claudia, being a native of New Orleans, it would be a given that we'd call on her mom for some recipes. When people ask where is the best place to eat in New Orleans, we always answer "The 401". It's the Manson house.
Nadyne Manson (David H's mother-in-law), Cortner Mill Restaurant cookbook, 2009

SHRIMP DIP

1 cup shrimp, deveined and chopped
1 package (8 ounces) cream cheese
1 small onion grated
1/2 cup tomato catsup
1/2 cup mayonnaise
pinch of salt
1/2 lemon, juice of
1/4 teaspoon Worcestershire sauce

Mix well with beater or by hand. Makes 3 cups.
Martha T. Smith, The Nashville Cookbook, 1977

SMOKED OYSTER DIP

3 ounces smoked oysters, undrained
16 ounces cream cheese, softened
1 teaspoon Worcestershire sauce
2 teaspoons lemon juice
1 cup sour cream

Thoroughly blend the oysters and cheese. Mix well. Serve with corn or potato chips.
Virginia Kendall White, The Nashville Cookbook, 1977

SMOKED EGG DIP

12 hard cooked eggs, riced and sieved
2 Tablespoons soft butter or margarine
1 1/2 teaspoons liquid smoke seasoning
1 Tablespoon lemon juice or vinegar
2 teaspoons prepared mustard
2 teaspoons Worcestershire sauce
2 drops Tabasco

1 teaspoon salt
1/4 teaspoon ground pepper
3/4 cup mayonnaise or salad dressing
radish slices
potato chips
tiny rolls

Combine all the ingredients except radishes, potato chips, and rolls. Beat until smooth. If desired, more quantities of the seasonings may be added. Just make sure the consistency is soft enough to permit potato chips or other type of dipping chip to be dipped into dip easily. About 30 minutes before serving, remove from refrigerator and beat dip to fluff and soften it. Garnish with radish slices. Serve with potato chips, other chips, or tiny rolls. Makes 1 quart.

NOTE: Smoked Egg Dip makes an excellent sandwich filling. Whether it is made as a dip or as a sandwich filling, it can be prepared the day before serving.
Easy-on-the-Cook Book, 1960

SPINACH DIP

20 ounces frozen chopped spinach
1/2 cup mayonnaise
2/3 cup onion, chopped

1/3 cup parsley, chopped
1/2 cup sour cream
1 Tablespoon garlic, minced

Thaw and drain spinach. Squeeze all excess liquid out of spinach. Combine all the ingredients and mix thoroughly. Refrigerate overnight. Makes 4 cups and serves 25.
Cortner Mill Restaurant cookbook, 2009

SPINACH ARTICHOKE DIP

20 ounces frozen spinach chopped
1/2 cup butter
1/2 onion
14 ounces artichoke hearts, canned

8 ounces cream cheese, softened
1/2 cup Parmesan cheese
8 ounces Monterey Jack cheese
1 cup sour cream

Cook and drain spinach. Sauté onion in butter until clear, about 5 minutes. Remove from heat. Drain and mash artichokes. Add spinach, artichokes, sour cream, and cheeses to onions and butter. Blend well. Microwave on high for 5 minutes. Serve with tortilla chips, salsa, and sour cream.
Cortner Mill Restaurant cookbook, 2009

WEST INDIES DIP

3 ounces cream cheese, softened
1 Tablespoon finely chopped chutney
3/4 teaspoon curry powder
1 teaspoon lemon juice
1/2 teaspoon grated onion
2 to 3 Tablespoons cream
potato chips, or corn chips, or pretzel sticks

Combine cheese, chutney, curry powder, lemon juice and onion; blend well. Add enough cream to thin mixture to dripping consistency. Serve with potato chips, corn chips or pretzel sticks. Makes about 1/2 cup.

NOTE: For a more pronounced curry flavor add additional curry to taste.
Easy-on-the-Cook, 1960

CUCUMBER DIP

1 cucumber
1 teaspoon onion, grated
1/2 teaspoon horseradish
6 ounces cream cheese
2 teaspoon mayonnaise
1 pinch seasoned salt
1/2 teaspoon sugar
1 drop green food coloring

Quarter the cucumber lengthwise and remove seeds. Finely grate the cucumber and onion. Drain juice from the vegetables. Blend vegetables with remaining ingredients. Chill and serve with fresh vegetables. Makes 1 cup.
Nadyne Manson, Cortner Mill Restaurant cookbook, 2009

BEEF FONDUE

3/4 inch cubes sirloin steak
1 cup butter
2 cups salad oil

SAUCE

1 cup sour cream
1/2 teaspoon curry
1 teaspoon horseradish
1/4 teaspoon sugar
1/8 teaspoon salt

Cut sirloin steak in 3/4 inch cubes. Fry in hot salad oil and butter. To serve, dip in the sauce (not cooked). This dish is simply marvelous. Chafing dish cannot be used. An electric skillet or fondue dish will get the fat to the right temperature.

NOTE: This recipe comes from Europe, but it is such a huge hit here.
Satsuma Tea Room, Fun for the Cook, 1968

GOAT CHEESE APPETIZER

scallions, chopped
sundried tomatoes, chopped
herbed flavored goat cheese- (Chavira with basil and roasted garlic)
olive oil

Sprinkle lots of chopped scallions and chopped sundried tomatoes on top of the goat cheese. Cover with olive oil. Serve with crackers, pieces of bread, or bagel chips.
Pat Almy, Fruit of the Spirit, Mt. Bethel United Methodist Church, Marietta, GA

MACAROON MERINGUES

1 cup sugar
1 Tablespoon cornstarch
3 egg whites, beaten
2 cups shredded coconut
1 teaspoon almond extract

Heat oven to 300 F. Mix sugar and cornstarch. Beat gradually into egg whites until sugar is dissolved. Stir in the coconut and almond extract. Drop small spoonful onto oiled (greased) baking sheet. Bake for about 30 minutes or until delicately browned and dry. Remove from pan while hot. Makes about 30.
Anita Wherry, The Nashville Cookbook, 1977

PARTY MINTS

5 Tablespoons butter, melted
2 1/2 Tablespoons evaporated milk
1 teaspoon mint extract
food coloring, few drops
16 ounces powdered sugar

Melt butter and then add milk, extract, and coloring. Mix sugar in slowly. Knead the mixture and press into rubber molds. Makes about 60 small mints.
Eva Redmon, The Nashville Cookbook, 1977

STUFFED MUSHROOMS

3 pounds fresh mushrooms, medium
6 Tablespoon butter, melted
3/4 cup hot water
1 cube chicken bouillon

Combine butter, water, and bouillon cube. Stir until cube is dissolved. Pour over croutons and mix thoroughly. Remove stems from the mushrooms and stuff each with the mixture. Bake at 325 for 20 minutes. Serve warm.
Cortner Mill Restaurant cookbook, 2009

"The discovery of a new dish does more for the happiness of mankind than the discovery of a star."
-Brillat-Savarin (1755-1826)

STUFFED MUSHROOMS (A Variation)

16 ounces fresh mushrooms
12 ounces breakfast sausage

8 ounces cream cheese, softened

Clean mushrooms and remove the stems and set aside. Brown the sausage until crumbly and drain. Mix the sausage with the softened cream cheese. Place 1 teaspoon of sausage mixture in each mushroom cap. Place on cookie sheet and bake at 350 for 10 to 15 minutes.
Mary Ettel, Fruit of the Spirit, Mt. Bethel United Methodist Church, Marietta, GA

OLIVE SURPRISE

1/2 cup flour
2 dozen stuffed green olives, medium size

1/4 cup soft butter or margarine
1 cup grated sharp Cheddar cheese

Cream butter and cheese until blended, add flour and mix well. Chill dough 15 to 20 minutes. Drain olives and dry with a paper towel. Shape small portion of dough around each olive. Place olives on a cookie sheet and bake at 375 for 15 minutes. Serve hot or cold. Makes 36.

NOTE: To freeze, roll dough around the olives, place on cookie sheet and freeze. After freezing, store in a plastic bag until ready to use. When ready to use, bake at 350 for about 15-20 minutes.
Irene Burbs, The Nashville Cookbook, 1977

ORANGE SUGARED NUTS

3 cups sugar
1/2 cup water
1/2 cup orange juice

1 teaspoon grated orange rind
1 teaspoon grated lemon rind
1 pound nuts (walnuts or pecans)

Dissolve sugar in water and orange juice. Cook to soft ball stage when tested in ice water or to 238 F. and remove from heat and add grated rind and nuts. Stir quickly until mixture looks chalky but is hardened. Drop by teaspoons onto oiled (greased) surface. Separate into small pieces when firm.
Lucy F. Dye, The Nashville Cookbook, 1977

PARMESAN BITS

1 cup sifted flour
1/2 teaspoon salt
1/16 teaspoon pepper

3 ounces grated Parmesan cheese
1/2 cup soft butter

Heat oven to 375 F. Combine first four ingredients. Cut in the butter until the particles are the size of small peas. Knead and work with hands or spoons until a smooth ball is formed. Roll out on floured pastry cloth or board to ½-inch thickness. Cut into ½-inch cubes. Place on greased baking sheet. Brush with slightly beaten egg or milk. Bake 20 to 25 minutes. Cool and store in tightly covered container. Makes 4 dozen.
Peggy Pennington, The Nashville Cookbook, 1977

PIGS IN BLANKETS (Oysters and bacon-yum!)

| 12 large oysters | 1 pimento | dashes of cayenne |
| 12 slices bacon | 1/2 teaspoon salt | pinch of pepper |

Season the oysters with salt and pepper. Slice pimento into 12 strips, placing one strip on each oyster. Wrap each oyster with a slice of bacon, closing the bacon with a toothpick or skewer. Broil about 8 minutes, browning bacon to a golden crisp.
The Southern Cook Book, 1939

SPICY PIMENTO CHEESE

24 ounces sharp shredded cheese
8 ounces cream cheese, softened
8 ounces Monterey Jack cheese with peppers
2 cups lite mayonnaise
1 1/2 Tablespoons ground red pepper
9 ounces pimentos, chopped
1 Tablespoon onion, grated

Let cheeses get to room temperature, then add other ingredients and mix well. Great as an appetizer on crackers. This will last in the refrigerator for approximately 2 weeks.
Mary Bosworth, Fruit of the Spirit, Mt Bethel United Methodist Church, Marietta, GA

SHRIMP AVOCADO COCKTAIL (From the Heart of the Southland)

Take an equal portion of shrimp and alligator pears (avocado), cut into small pieces and serve with a sauce made by stirring together 2 Tablespoons of mayonnaise, 2 Tablespoons ketchup, 1 Tablespoon each of finely-chopped green peppers and chili sauce.
The Southern Cook Book, 1939

SHRIMP PUFFS

| 16 small round crackers | 1 cup mayonnaise |
| 16 cooked shrimp, well drained | grated Parmesan cheese |

Place crackers on cookie sheet and top each with shrimp. Put 1 Tablespoon mayonnaise on each shrimp, sprinkle with cheese. Broil until lightly browned and puffy. Serve hot at once.
Satsuma Tea Room, Fun for the Cook, 1968

SUN DRIED TOMATO BASIL IN FILO

1 cup sun dried tomatoes, minced	1/4 teaspoon salt
6 ounces cream cheese softened	1/8 teaspoon black pepper
1/4 cup Parmesan cheese	1 1/2 teaspoons butter
2 1/4 teaspoons extra virgin olive oil	50 filo cups

Melt butter and add remaining ingredients. Heat through. Put into filo cups. Makes 50.
Jim Long, Cortner Mill Restaurant cookbook, 2009

SOUTHERN CAVIAR (A very good and zesty party dip)

1 can black-eyed peas, drained
1 can white shoe peg corn, drained
1 small onion, chopped
1 small green bell pepper, chopped
2 tomatoes, chopped
1 small jar *Braswell's Sweet Red Pepper Relish*
8-ounces *Kraft Zesty Italian Dressing*
chips- *Scoops*, dip size

Drain black-eyed peas and corn in colander. Rinse well. Chop onion, bell pepper and tomatoes. Combine all the ingredients. Mix well and chill two hours before serving. Serve using *Scoops*.
Millie Atkinson, Fruit of the Spirit, Mt Bethel United Methodist Church, Marietta, GA

SPICED NUT TRIANGLES

1 cup butter, softened
1 cup sugar
1 egg, separated
2 cups flour
1 teaspoon cinnamon
1 cup chopped nuts

Heat oven to 250 F Cream butter and sugar together. Add egg yolk. Add flour and cinnamon. Stir well. Spread dough evenly in 15 x 10-inch ungreased pan. Beat the egg whites slightly and brush over the top of the dough. Smooth the surface of the dough with fingers. Sprinkle nuts over the top of the dough and press in. Bake for 1 hour. While still warm cut into long strips, then cut crosswise. Cut each piece in half diagonally to make triangles. Makes 6 dozen and cookies freeze well.

NOTE: Variations can be made by omitting cinnamon and adding 1 Tablespoon grated orange or lemon peel; or omitting cinnamon and substituting brown sugar for white sugar and substituting salted peanuts for other nuts; or substituting brown sugar for white sugar, omit the nuts and add 1 1/2 teaspoons cinnamon, teaspoon nutmeg, and 1/4 teaspoon ground cloves.
Martha Schiffman, The Nashville Cookbook, 1977

WATER CHESTNUTS IN BACON

1 pound bacon
8 ounce water chestnuts

Cut bacon strips in half. Wrap water chestnut in bacon. Stick a toothpick in center of bacon to hold it together. Cook in deep fat 2 to 3 minutes or until the bacon is done. Serve warm.
Cortner Mill Restaurant cookbook, 2009

WATER CHESTNUTS

1 can whole water chestnuts
1/2 cup ketchup
1/2 cup brown sugar
bacon

Roll water chestnuts in bacon, about 1/4 of a strip to each chestnut. Secure with toothpick. Place on baking sheet. Bake at 350 F for 30 minutes. Drain off grease. Mix ketchup and brown sugar and pour over chestnuts and bake at 350 F for 30 minutes more.
Martha Ward, Fruit of the Spirit, Mt. Bethel United Methodist Church, Marietta, GA

BEVERAGES

*"Taking food and drink is a great enjoyment for healthy people,
and those who do not enjoy eating and drinking
rarely have much capacity for enjoyment or usefulness of any sort."*
-Charles W. Eliot (1834-1926)

No matter what kind of party you throw, be it a large group or a small intimate gathering, from the most formal reception to a spontaneous get-together, you will want to offer your guests something to drink. Let the thermometer help you decide the choice of drink you offer. A long, cool drink and the clink of ice in their glasses will help your summer guests forget the heat. On a frigid day, a steaming beverage is as inviting and heart-warming as a blazing fire in the fireplace.

One of the images of Southern myth which has become deep-rooted in the history of the South is a flamboyant and powerful example of "Southern Hospitality". This symbol is the drink we know as *Mint Julep*. The following article and recipe are taken from an old Southern cookbook of the 1930's.

MINT JULEP

"Few folks agree as to what should constitute a really good mint julep. The controversy dates back to Captain Marryat who contended that he had learned how to make the real julep with fair success. Following his instructions, we do not crush the sprigs of tender mint shoots, we do use a little sugar and equal portions of peach and common brandy, and we fill our glass with shaved ice. 'Stalactites' of ice will form on the tumbler; and as the ice melts, we drink.

A Georgia writer of fifty years ago (the 1880's) summed up the matter thus: "The mint julep still lives but is by no means fashionable. Somehow the idea had gotten abroad that the mint ought to be crushed and shaken up with water and whisky in equal proportions. No man can fall in love with such a mixture."

Then there is the Kentucky Colonel who advises crushing the mint within the glass until no place has been left untouched. We are then to throw away the mint; in so doing 'it is a sacrifice.' This is 'the only way of perfection' in concocting this 'most delectable libation of man.' The Colonel's road map to creating this enticing libation is as follows:

"For each glass of mint julep, dissolve two lumps of sugar in enough water to form a sort of oily syrup. In a glass crush a few sprigs of tender mint shoots until most of the mint essence has been extracted. Remove the mint from the glass; fill the glass with cracked ice and pour in the quantity of Bourbon desired. Allow the Bourbon to become thoroughly chilled and then add the heavy sugar syrup. Let the glass stand for a few minutes, not stirring it at all. Place sprigs of fresh mint around the rim of the glass; serve immediately."
The Southern Cook Book, 1939

ORANGE JULEP

1 quart orange juice	6 limes (juice)	1 pint charged water
1 cup sugar	1/2 cup minced mint	ice

Mix orange juice, sugar, lime juice and minced mint. Place on the ice one hour. Half fill glasses with ice, add prepared juice and sprigs of mint.

SOUTHERN SWEET TEA

There are certain foods that when you hear their names, you inevitably think of the South and Southern food. There are many dishes that fit this category, but I'll list just a few and they will automatically be recognized as a Southern dish or associated with Southern cooking; grits, fried chicken, black-eyed peas, "greens", corn bread, mint juleps and of course "sweet tea".

The Southern Cook Book, 1939 says sweet tea began as a luxury item due to the expensive nature of its ingredients; tea, ice, and sugar with ice being the most treasured of the three because of its rarity (pre- refrigerator/freezer days). The oldest recipe for sweet tea was published in 1879, and at that time sweet tea was drunk as a punch mixed with hard liquor flavored with mint and cream; very similar to what we know as a mint julep.

The general thinking by people a number of years ago, was that if you went into a restaurant and ordered a glass of sweet tea and that restaurant was located elsewhere other than the South; you would not be able to get a glass of "exact sweet tea," because no one would know what you were talking about. If you did get lucky and a glass of sweet tea was brought to you, the odds were very good that it just wasn't made correctly. As Southern foods have become more popular and more in vogue these days, when you go into a restaurant and order iced tea, the follow-up question from the wait staff is *sweet or un?*

The following recipe is a very good sweet tea recipe:

SOUTHERN SWEET TEA

6 regular tea bags	1 1/2 -2 cups sugar
1/8 teaspoon baking soda	6 cups cold water
2 cups boiling water	

In a large glass measuring cup, place the tea bags and add the baking soda. Pour the boiling water over the tea bags. Cover and steep for 15 minutes. Take out the tea bags and do not squeeze them. Pour the tea mixture into a 2-quart pitcher; add the sugar. Stir until the sugar is dissolved. Add in the cold water. Let cool; chill in refrigerator and serve over ice.
The Nashville Cookbook, 1977

DIXIE TEA

8 cups boiling water	juice of 6 oranges	1 teaspoon whole cloves
5 Tablespoons tea leaves	2 cups sugar	
juice of 1 lemon	8 cups water	

Add the boiling water to the tea, let stand five minutes and pour the tea off the leaves. Add the fruit juice and a syrup made by boiling the sugar, water and cloves to the tea. This recipe makes about 18 cups.
Mrs. Cornelius Youmans Reamer, 200 Years of Charleston Cooking, 1930

CAROLINA MINT TEA

2 cups sugar
1/2 cup water
grated rind of 1 orange
juice of 6 oranges
6 glasses of very strong orange pekoe tea
several sprays of mint

Boil the sugar, water, and orange rind about 5 minutes to make a syrup. Remove from the fire, add the crushed leaves of mint and let cool. Make the tea, strain, add the orange juice. Half fill the glasses with crushed ice; add the tea and sweeten to taste with the mint syrup.

NOTE: A fresh spray of mint in each glass or a slice of orange as a garnish adds to the attractiveness of the drink.
Mrs. Cornelius Youmans Reamer, 200 Years of Charleston Cooking, 1930

MINT TEA

2 cups sugar
1/2 cup water
grated rind of one orange
juice of 6 oranges
6 glasses very strong tea
several sprays of mint

Boil the sugar, water, and orange rind about 5 minutes. Remove from the fire and add crushed leaves of mint and let cool. Into the tea put the orange juice. Half fill the iced tea glasses with crushed ice, add the tea and sweeten to taste with the mint syrup. A sprig of mint or a slice of orange may be added to each glass as a garnish.
The Southern Cook Book, 1939

HOT SPICED TEA

1 teaspoon whole cloves
3 inch stick cinnamon
3 quarts water
2 1/2 Tablespoons tea
juice of 4 oranges
juice of 3 lemons
1 cup sugar

Tie spices in a bag. Place in the water and bring to a boil. Place tea in bag. Drop in the hot water. Boil 5 minutes. Strain, add juices and sugar. Keeps for weeks in the refrigerator and can be heated as desired. This recipe is a blessing if you like to serve tea. So easy to heat and so good. Makes 25 cups.
Satsuma Tea Room, Fun for the Cook, 1968

DAVID'S FRESH LEMONADE

3 cups sugar
1 quart hot water
3 quarts cold water
1 1/2 cup fresh lemon juice (4-7 lemons)
1 lemon, sliced for garnish

Dissolve sugar in hot water. Add lemon juice and stir. Add cold water and stir. Put lemon slices in pitcher over ice. Makes 35 eight ounce servings.

NOTE: This is so easy to make and so good to drink. I can't imagine why anyone would use a powdered lemonade mix.
David Hazelwood, Cortner Mill Restaurant cookbook, 2009

BUTTERMILK

Buttermilk was once an everyday drink in the South. Originally, it was just the liquid left behind after the churning of the butter, (the making of butter out of cultured cream). In his *Classical Southern Cooking*, Damon Lee Fowler shares, "In the warm climate of the South (and with the absence of any refrigeration) sweet (fresh) milk would sour quickly, but buttermilk would keep for days. Therefore, buttermilk was not only drunk, it also became a staple in most Southern kitchens, adding tenderness to the crumb of breads and cakes, and when combined with soda, also provided leavening."

I can remember as a young child my father "purposely" drinking buttermilk on many occasions, even going so far as sometimes ordering it in restaurants. I can truthfully say after trying to drink buttermilk just once, that I had included drinking and enjoying buttermilk as a mystery of the universe. Why would anyone ever want to attempt this feat?

"Buttermilk has a tart flavor and this tartness is due to the acid found in the milk. The increased acidity is primarily due to the lactic acid that is created by the fermenting of lactose, the basic sugar found in milk." Many, many recipes in this book, especially most of the older recipes, call for buttermilk or sour milk. When making breads, biscuits, or cakes, the acid in the buttermilk reacts when a rising agent, like baking soda, results in carbon dioxide which then acts as a leavening agent. If more acidic taste (less sweet) in a dish is preferred, like a Buttermilk pie versus a Chess pie, the use of buttermilk is usually suggested. Buttermilk also makes a great marinade, especially for chicken and pork. The acid in the buttermilk helps to tenderize the meat and helps to retain moisture, especially chicken and pork, and allows added flavors to infuse throughout the meat as it marinates."

"Buttermilk"-Wikipedia

Sour cream, the stepsister (an "orphaned byproduct") to butter and cream, obtains a much greater respect and popularity with each passing year. Once thrifty country women regarded it only as a byproduct, something to salvage after a hot day, and with refrigeration not widespread or even nonexistent, sour cream just made sense; it was a necessity. In our present time, we find that sour cream cookies, biscuits, cake, pancakes, candies, superb dressings made to accompany our home-grown garden produce, etc., gave rise to us as Southerners making us the fortunate beneficiaries of these accomplishments.

HOW TO MAKE MEAD

We feel reasonably certain that no one will try this recipe but we cannot resist. These are the directions given in *The Southern Gardner and Recipe Book* published in 1845.

"Take ten gallons of water, two gallons of honey, and a handful of raced ginger; then take two lemons, cut them in pieces and then put them into it; boil it very well; keep skimming it; let stand all night in the same vessel you boil it in. The next morning barrel it up with two or three spoonsful of good yeast. In two or three weeks after this, you may bottle it."

NOTE: The old saying, "What goes around, comes around" holds true for Mead. Once considered a drink of the Middle Ages, is now making a select resurgence in our present day and time.
200 Years of Charleston Cooking, 1930

SYLLABUB

Syllabub was frequently served on festive occasions in early Nashville. It is a drink that resembles eggnog and was by tradition made with Madeira wine and was enjoyed by all ages. Most recipes included cream, lemon juice and rind, beaten egg whites, sugar and wine.

SYLLABUB

Whisk 1 quart of cream while gradually adding 1 cup of sugar, and the juice and the rind of 3 lemons. When light and frothy, add 1 cup of Madeira wine or sherry, continuing to whisk. Beat 4 egg whites, gradually adding 1/2 cup sugar, until stiff. Spoon syllabub into punch cups and top with beaten egg whites or fold egg whites into cream mixture, then spoon into cups. Sprinkle with nutmeg or grated lemon rind.

NORTH CAROLINA SYLLABUB

1 pint of cream, a day old	1/2 teaspoon vanilla
1/2 cup fresh milk	1 cup sugar
1/2 cup sweet cider	a little nutmeg

Chill the ingredients and make shortly before you are ready to serve. Mix all the ingredients in a mixing bowl except the cream, which should be beaten lightly. Add cream and beat again. Sprinkle a little nutmeg on top and serve. Whiskey or brandy may be used in place of cider. A teaspoon of sherry may be added if desired.

NOTE: They call this drink "A Builder-Upper." You can understand why.
The Southern Cook Book, 1939

PLANTATION TODDY

1 loaf sugar	small piece lemon skin
2 cloves	1 pony rye whiskey

Pour into toddy with a little cracked ice. Add a shake of nutmeg.
William A. Hutchinson, 200 Years of Charleston Cooking, 1930

IRISH COFFEE

CREAM: Rich as an Irish brogue	SUGAR: Sweet as the tongue of a rogue
COFFEE: Strong as a friendly hand	WHISKEY: Smooth as the wit of the land

In an Irish coffee glass place one teaspoon sugar, cover with Irish Mist (Irish whiskey). Fill glass with hot coffee within one inch of top. Add a generous dollop of whipped cream; do not stir. Serve.

NOTE: Rinse glass with hot water; place a spoon in the glass before adding the coffee, to prevent breaking.
Larry Bowles, The Nashville Cookbook, 1977

SCOTCH SLING

2 ounces whiskey
1 lump sugar
1 piece lemon rind
hot water

Place the first 3 ingredients in a whiskey glass, add hot water until glass is 3/4 full. Serve with grated nutmeg on top.
The Settlement Cook Book, 1940

BARCARDI RUM PUNCH

4 1/2 dozen oranges, diced
5 dozen lemons
3 quarts maraschino cherries
6 large cans sliced pineapple, diced (in own juice)
3 large cans grated pineapple
4 quarts tea (green tea: use 1 teaspoon tea per 1 cup water)

The Savannah Cook Book, 1933

HOT TODDY

2 Tablespoons Cognac
1 teaspoon sugar

Fill toddy glass with very hot water and stir briskly as the ingredients are added. Add a shake of freshly grated nutmeg.
Alicia Rhett Mayberry, 200 Years of Charleston Cooking, 1930

SPECIAL HOT CHOCOLATE

1 cup sugar
1 cup cocoa (Droste's, if possible)
1 cup boiling water
1 quart whipping cream
2 quarts milk
1 teaspoon vanilla
1/4 teaspoon salt

Mix sugar and cocoa. Stir to smooth paste with boiling water. Then cook in double boiler about 20 minutes. Whip the cream, fold into cocoa paste. Scald milk in double boiler, add salt and vanilla. To serve, put chocolate mixture in bowl and hot milk in a pitcher. Put large spoon of chocolate in cup, add hot milk. Absolutely delicious and full of calories.
Satsuma Tea Room, Fun for the Cook, 1968

MEXICAN CHOCOLATE

1 quart milk
1 inch stick cinnamon
3 Tbl instant coffee
2 ounces sweet chocolate
1/2 cup boiling water
1/2 teaspoon vanilla
1/8 teaspoon salt
whipped cream

Scald milk; add the cinnamon and coffee. Melt chocolate in boiling water. Heat again. Add vanilla and salt and serve hot. Top with whipped cream, if desired. Serves 4-6.
Elnora Culbert, The Nashville Cookbook, 1977

SANGRIA

1/2 lemon, cut into 1/4 inch slices	1 bottle dry red wine, preferably Spanish
1/2 orange, cut into 1/4 inch slices	2 ounces brandy
1/2 large apple, cut into thin wedges	club soda, chilled
1/4 to 1/2 cup superfine sugar	ice cubes (optional)

Combine the lemon, orange, apple and sugar in a large pitcher. Add the wine and brandy and stir until well mixed. Add sugar to taste. Chill for at least 1 hour. Add chilled club soda to taste just before serving. Serve in chilled wine glasses. Ice may be added. Serves 4 to 6.
Lalah Gee, The Nashville Cookbook, 1977

CHARLESTON EGGNOG

NOTE: The friends of Mr. and Mrs. Waites Waring look forward yearly to the New Year's reception, at which this -*Charleston's Best Eggnog*- is always served.

10 egg yolks	1 pint rye whiskey or	1 quart heavy cream
3/4 cup granulated sugar	well-cured corn whiskey	10 egg whites

Cream the ten egg yolks and granulated sugar thoroughly. Slowly add the whiskey, stirring constantly, then the heavy cream (not whipped), and lastly add the egg whites beaten stiff.
Annie Gammell Waring, 200 Years of Charleston Cooking, 1930

EGGNOG

1 dozen eggs separated	1 1/2 cups sugar	nutmeg (optional)
1 quart whipping cream	1 pint Bourbon	

Beat egg yolks until light and smooth; add sugar and whip until creamy. Slowly add Bourbon, stirring constantly. This part of the mixture may be made several hours before serving. At serving time, whip the cream and fold into the first mixture. Beat egg whites until stiff and add before serving. Serve with sprinkling of nutmeg if desired. Serves 10-12.

NOTE: Vanilla ice cream is sometimes added to eggnog at serving time.
Nancye Shannon, The Nashville Cookbook, 1977

EGGNOG WITH ICE CREAM

12 egg yolks	1 pint heavy cream, whipped
1 cup sugar	1/2 pint cream, not whipped
1/2 pint rye whiskey	12 egg whites, beaten stiff
1/2 cup Cognac	1 quart vanilla ice cream

Mix together the egg yolks and the sugar, add whiskey and Cognac slowly, stirring well. Fold in the whipped cream; add the plain cream and then the beaten egg whites. When ready to serve, add 1 quart vanilla ice cream, cut up in small portions.
Mrs. E. F. Daniels, 200 Years of Charleston Cooking, 1930

HOT EGGNOG

1 quart milk	1/4 teaspoon salt	1/2 cup Bourbon or rum
4 egg yolks	4 egg whites	grated nutmeg
1/3 cup sugar	1/4 cup sugar	

Scald milk. Beat egg yolks with sugar until light and fluffy. Add salt and hot milk and mix well. Place over low heat or hot water and cook, while stirring, until mixture thickens (Excess heat and long cooking will cause mixture to curdle). Beat egg whites until stiff, gradually adding the 1/4 cup sugar. Fold whites into the hot milk mixture. Stir in the Bourbon or rum. Serve hot with a dash of nutmeg. Serves 8-10.
Annie L. Foster, The Nashville Cookbook, 1977

HOT APPLE PUNCH

2 1/4 cups sugar	1 whole piece ginger root (size of quarter)
4 cups water	4 cups orange juice
2 (2 1/2 inch) sticks of cinnamon	2 cups lemon juice
8 whole spice berries	2 quarts apple cider or apple juice
10 whole cloves	

Combine sugar and water and boil 5 minutes. Remove from heat; add spices. Let beverage stand, covered, 1 hour. Strain. Just before serving, combine syrup, fruit juices and cider; bring quickly to boiling. Remove from heat and serve at once. Makes 4 1/2 quarts.
Farm Journal's Country Cook Book, 1959

HOT BUTTERED TOMATO JUICE

5 3/4 cups tomato juice	1/2 teaspoon oregano
1 teaspoon Worcestershire sauce	4 cloves
1/2 teaspoon salt	1/4 cup butter

Combine the ingredients in 2-quart sauce pan. Heat slowly until butter is melted. Do not boil. Serve immediately. Serves 8.
Easy-on-the-Cook Book, 1960

TEA PUNCH

1 quart boiling water	1 can (12 ounces) frozen orange juice
5 tea bags	1 quart ginger ale
2 1/2 cups sugar	fresh mint leaves
12 ounces frozen lemonade	

In a gallon container pour boiling water over tea bags. Cover and steep 5 minutes. Add sugar and stir until dissolved. Add orange juice and lemonade and mix. When ready to serve add ginger ale and water to make 1 gallon. Serve over ice and garnish with mint leaves. Makes 1 gallon.
Jo Ellen Hunter, The Nashville Cookbook, 1977

CORN LIKKER

Corn all through our history and into our present day was not just eaten but also imbibed because whiskey is another well-known, liquid byproduct of corn. "Corn likker" was a very useful and expedient way to store and transport corn by the first settlers. In reality, Tennessee whiskey and Bourbon are basically the same product. By law they both must contain at least fifty one percent corn.

Being a Tennessee native, my answer to the question of the difference between whiskey and Bourbon is that Tennessee whiskey remains generally recognized as having been distilled only in Tennessee and Bourbon is often acknowledged as being distilled only in Kentucky. They are that similar in character and other than a few differences in their production, they are basically the same. Which is the better product? I won't weigh in on that question, because duels have been waged over the countless answers that have been offered over the years.

> "Kentucky, oh Kentucky,
> How I love your classic shades,
> Where flit the fairy figures
> Of the star-eyed Southern maids;
> Where the butterflies are joying
> 'Mid the blossoms newly born;
> Where the corn is full of kernels,
> And the Colonel Full of Corn!"
> Will Lampton (1850-1917)

PLANTER'S PUNCH

Dissolve a Tablespoon of sugar in a large glass; add one wineglassful of Jamaica rum, one-half wineglassful of good brandy. Squeeze into this mixture the juice of one-half lemon and a little pineapple juice. Pour into a tall glass with shaved ice and mix thoroughly with a spoon. The glass should be frosted when the drink is served.

NOTE: See the world through rose colored glasses!
The Southern Cook Book, 1939

IDLE HOUR COCKTAIL

2/3 gin
1/6 Italian vermouth
1/6 grapefruit juice

Mix all the ingredients, stir well, but do not shake.
The Southern Cook Book, 1939

SAZERAC COCKTAIL (one portion)

1/3 pony (pony glass about 1 ounce) Bacardi rum	1/3 pony rye whiskey 1/6 pony anisette 1/6 pony gum	1 dash angostura bitters 1 dash orange bitters 3 dashes absinthe

Put all the ingredients in a cocktail shaker with some ice. Shake well, strain, pour in a glass and serve.
The Southern Cook Book, 1939

PLUM CORDIAL

Half fill a stone or glass jar with August plums. Perforate each plum with a silver fork before placing them in a container. Fill the jar with good whiskey, allow to stand for 6 weeks and then strain through a fine cloth. Add sugar syrup to taste and bottle.
Edward A. Simons, 200 Years of Charleston Cooking, 1930

NOYAN

Take of peach kernels, two ounces. Alcohol and water each a half pint. White sugar eight ounces. Blanch your kernels first, then beat with the sugar to a paste. Add the diluted alcohol and suffer it to stand for a week, then filter. You now have a delightful cordial.

NOTE: Mary A. Sparkman, who contributed this recipe wrote, "Noyan must have been a favorite beverage, judging from the frequency with which the recipes for it appear in the old books. The quaint wording of this recipe and the writing itself indicate its age, as well as the dates in the book, the earliest of which is 1773. The book was handed down to my grandmother, Mrs. P.C. Kirk of Loch Dhu Plantation, Upper St. John's, Berkeley County, S.C."
Mary A. Sparkman, 200 Years of Charleston Cooking, 1930

SOUTHERN WHIP

1/2 pint of cream	peel of 1 orange	1/2 cup sugar
juice of 1/2 orange	1/2 cup sherry	3 egg whites

Mix the sugar and orange juice together and then pour over the whole orange peel. Use a wooden spoon and crush the peel in the juice and then let stand one hour and strain. Whip the cream and add the strained orange juice. Add the wine and then fold in the stiffly beaten egg whites. Serve at once.
The Southern Cook Book, 1939

SPICED CIDER

1 quart sweet cider	8 short pieces of stick cinnamon	8 whole allspice
1/4 cup sugar	12 whole cloves	pinch salt

Mix all the ingredients in a pot and heat to a boiling point. Let stand for several hours. Reheat, remove the whole spices and serve hot with cookies or cake.
The Southern Cook Book, 1939

MULLED CIDER

1 quart cider	dash of mace and allspice	1/2 tsp. whole cloves
1/2 cup brown sugar	2 sticks cinnamon bark	1/4 tsp whole nutmeg

Combine-heat-strain-serve hot. Serves 6-8.
Satsuma Tea Room, Fun for the Cook, 1968

MULLED APRICOT NECTAR

1 (46 ounce) can apricot nectar
1/2 lemon, sliced
2 (2 1/2 inch) sticks cinnamon
15 whole cloves
8 whole allspice berries

Combine all the ingredients in a heavy saucepan and bring to a boil then simmer gently 5 minutes. Remove from the heat; cover; and allow to stand 30 minutes. Strain. If you wish, you may sweeten to taste with honey or sugar. Heat before serving. Makes about 5 cups.

NOTE: Heat this spiced drink after the guests arrive. They will enjoy the aroma and the taste. By the way, it will be a good idea to pass a plate of fudge.
Farm Journal's Country Cookbook, 1959

HOT MULLED PINEAPPLE JUICE

1 pint 2 ounce can (2 1/4 cups) pineapple juice
1/2 cup sugar
4 sticks cinnamon
1 teaspoon whole cloves
1/4 cup lemon juice

Simmer first 4 ingredients together for about 10 minutes. Add the lemon juice and then strain. Serve in mugs with a cinnamon stick for a stirrer. Serves 4.
Easy-on-the-Cook Book, 1960

HOMEMADE APPLE CIDER

10 apples, quartered
3/4 cup white sugar
1 Tablespoon ground cinnamon
1 Tablespoon ground allspice

Place apples in a large stockpot and add enough water to cover by at least 2 inches. Stir in sugar, cinnamon, and allspice. Bring to a boil. Boil uncovered for 1 hour. Cover pot, reduce heat, and simmer for 2 hours. Strain apple mixture through a fine mesh sieve. Discard the solids. Now drain cider again through a cheesecloth-lined sieve. Refrigerate until cold.
The Nashville Cookbook, 1977

THIRST QUENCHER

32 ounce can or bottle apple cider
18 ounce can grapefruit juice
18 ounce can orange juice
iced water
sugar to taste

Pour cider, grapefruit juice, and orange juice into a 10-quart utensil. Fill with ice water. Add sugar sparingly. Makes 10 quarts.

NOTE: Perfect hot-weather treat!!
Farm Journal's Country Cookbook, 1959

SHRUB

Shrub is the name of two different but related acidulated (slightly acidotic) beverages. One type of shrub is a fruit liqueur popular in 17th and 18th century England; much like medicinal cordials of the 15th century. This drink was typically made with rum or brandy mixed with sugar and the juice or rinds of citrus fruit.

Shrub can also refer to a cocktail with alcohol or a beverage that is a non-alcoholic drink, both fashionable in America's colonial era. This shrub was derived by mixing vinegary syrup with spirits, water, or even carbonated water.

Today shrub vinegar is often infused with fruit juice, herbs and spices for use in the mixed drinks of those that are now known in restaurants and bars as "shrubs" and have become ever more popular again. The sweetened vinegar-based syrup from which the cocktail is made is known as "drinking vinegar". The acidity of the shrub makes the drink very well-suited as an aperitif or can even be used as an alternative to bitters in cocktails
.

-*"Shrub"-Wikipedia*

CHERRY SHRUB

"....Men from all nearby places came together for deer hunting and each plantation supplied its own special dish. These dishes were either brought all prepared or else servants skilled in their preparation came along to do the work. Very popular was a mixture called Shrub, that came originally from the West Indies. Sometimes this Shrub was made of strawberries, sometimes of raspberries, or sometimes like this one, cherries."

Gather ripe Morello cherries (common black cherries). Put them in an earthen pot which must be set into an iron pot of water; make the water boil but take care that none of the water gets into the cherries. When the juice is extracted, pour it into a bag of tolerably thick cloth (thick cheese cloth) which will permit the juice but not the pulp of the cherries to pass. Sweeten to your taste, and when it becomes perfectly clear, bottle.

Put a gill (4 US fluid ounces) of brandy in each bottle before you pour the juice in. Cork and then cover the corks with rosin or paraffin. It will keep all summer in a dry, cool place, and is delicious mixed with water.
200 Years of Charleston Cooking, 1930

RHUBARB SHRUB

2 pounds fresh rhubarb	dash red food coloring (optional)
3 cups water	1 pint lime sherbet
2/3 cup sugar	

Clean and cut rhubarb into 1-inch pieces. Cook in water until tender. Strain well through sieve but do not push pulp through. Add sugar to the juice; stir until sugar is dissolved. Cool to room temperature; add dash of food coloring if desired. Cover, chill, serve in cocktail glasses, topping each with a scoop of sherbet. Serves 8.
Easy-on-the-Cook Book, 1960

FRUIT JUICE SHRUB

2 1/4 cups (1 pint, 2 fluid ounce can) pineapple juice, chilled
6 ounces frozen orange juice
1 1/2 cups cold water

14 ounces ginger ale, chilled
1 pint orange sherbet
1 orange cut into slices

Combine pineapple juice, orange juice, and water. Mix well. Add ginger ale. Spoon sherbet into 6 tall glasses. Fill with fruit ginger ale mixture. Garnish with orange slices. Makes 6 tall glasses.
Easy-on-the-Cook Book, 1960

FRUIT PUNCH COMBINATIONS

PUNCH FOUNDATION

1/2 cup lemon juice
1 cup orange juice
grated rind of one orange
grated rind of 1 lemon
1 quart water
1 cup sugar

Cook sugar and water for 5 minutes, cool, add juices, grated rinds and any of the following combinations:
- 1 quart ginger ale; 1/4 cup preserved ginger, cut fine.
- 1 quart tea; 1/2 cup maraschino cherries, cut fine.
- 1 cup grated pineapple; 1 pint charged water .
- 1 Tablespoon grated cucumber rind; 1 pint loganberry juice; sugar to sweeten.
- 1 pint raspberry juice; 1 pint charged .
- 1 glass currant jelly dissolved in 1 cup hot water; cook. Chill, and add 1/4 cup mint, finely minced.   Garnish the pitcher with mint sprays.
- 1 quart grape juice, 1 quart ginger ale, 1 quart charged water .
- 1/2 pint loganberry syrup, 1 1/2 pints fresh water, 1 quart ginger ale.
- 1 quart grapefruit juice and pulp, 1 quart mock champagne.
- Strained, sweetened juice of 1 quart strawberries and 1 quart raspberries.
- 1 quart cider, 1 quart grape juice, 1 quart mock champagne.

The Settlement Cook Book, 1940

MILK PUNCH

3/4 cup rum, brandy, whiskey, or sherry
1 quart milk or milk and cream
4 eggs

5 Tablespoons sifted confectioners' sugar
nutmeg

Pour all ingredients except nutmeg into blender; blend just a few seconds. Pour into glasses. Top with a sprinkling of nutmeg. Serves 4.
Easy-on-the-Cook Book, 1960

CREAMY SHERRY PUNCH

2 cups mashed bananas
2 cups dry sherry, chilled
2 cups milk
1 qt softened coffee ice cream

In a large mixing bowl beat the mashed bananas and milk together until blended. Add the chilled sherry. Spoon in ice cream and beat slowly until smooth. Pour into a chilled punch bowl. Makes about 20 1/2- cup servings.
Sarah Long, The Nashville Cookbook, 1977

CHAMPAGNE PUNCH

12 oz. frozen cranberry juice concentrate
1 liter club soda, chilled
2 bottles Champagne
1 orange, sliced and chilled

In a punch bowl, gently stir together club soda and cranberry juice concentrate that has been thawed. Add the Champagne. Garnish with orange slices. Serve immediately in ice-filled glasses. Makes 3 quarts. Serves 15.
Cortner Mill Restaurant cookbook, 2009

CHAMPAGNE PUNCH

Mix juice of 6 lemons and juice of 6 oranges with sugar enough to make thick syrup. Add 2 bottles of Apollinaris (a German natural sparkling water) and let stand until sugar is dissolved. Add crushed ice and just before serving, 3 bottles of Champagne and one of Sauterne. This is enough for 25 people.
The Savannah Cook Book, 1933

HALF-AND-HALF COOLER

6 ounces limeade concentrate
4 cans cold water
1 quart cold ginger ale
1 lemon or lime, thinly sliced

Combine concentrate with water according to the can directions. When ready to serve, add ginger ale and lemon. Makes 8 servings.

NOTE: Use any flavor frozen or canned juice instead of limeade. Combine with equal amount chilled ginger ale.
Farm Journal's Country Cookbook, 1959

CHABLIS ORANGE PUNCH

1 bottle white wine
1 gallon orange juice
1 cup grenadine
1 liter ginger ale

Mix all ingredients and chill. May be served with ice. Makes 1 1/2 gallons. Serves 32
Cortner Mill Restaurant cookbook, 2009

STRAWBERRY PUNCH

5 quarts strawberries	6 oranges (juice)	3 quarts carbonated
1 pound sugar	1 can pineapple	water
1 quart claret	a few sprigs of mint	
1 pint Burgundy	2 quarts Champagne	

Melt the sugar in a quart of hot water and pour it over the strawberries. Let it cool, then add the other ingredients all together, and at the last moment add the 3 quarts of carbonated water and the Champagne with a lump of ice in the bowl.
Mrs. W. Alston Pringle, 200 Years of Charleston Cooking, 1930

CRANBERRY-GINGER ALE COCKTAIL

2 1/2 cups cranberries
2 cups water
1/2 cup sugar
1 Tablespoon lemon juice
1 1/2 cups ginger ale

Cook cranberries in water until skins pop. About 5 minutes. Put them through sieve to get juice. Bring juice to boiling point. Add sugar. Cool, add lemon juice. Add ginger ale just before serving. Serve on crushed ice. Serves 8.
Satsuma Tea Room, Fun for the Cook, 1968

SPICED TOMATO JUICE

46 ounces tomato juice	2 (2 1/2 inch) sticks of cinnamon
6 Tablespoons brown sugar	1/2 lemon sliced
6 whole cloves	

Combine all the ingredients in a heavy saucepan. Bring to a boil and simmer 5 minutes. Strain and heat before serving. Makes about 5 cups.

NOTE: Great idea! Serve with a homemade grilled cheese sandwich.
Farm Journal's Country Cookbook, 1959

TOMATO JUICE COCKTAIL

2 cups tomato juice	1 teaspoon Worcestershire sauce
2 teaspoons vinegar	2 teaspoons chopped onions
1 Tablespoon sugar	1/2 cup diced celery
1/2 bay leaf	

Mix ingredients. Let stand in the refrigerator one hour. Strain. Serve cold. Excellent served with crackers and cheese. Serves 6.

NOTE: Perfect as a stand-alone beverage. It could also be used as a mix.
Satsuma Tea Room, Fun for the Cook, 1968

RAW APPLE FLOAT

3 apples
4 Tablespoons sugar
5 egg whites
nutmeg

Peel and grate the apples and then drain off the liquid. Beat the whites of eggs stiff and gradually add the sugar. Fold in the grated apple slowly, beating all the time. Pour into a serving bowl and sprinkle nutmeg on the top. Place in the ice box until very cold and serve.
The Southern Cook Book, 1939

EGG NOG-INDIVIDUAL PORTION

1 egg
2 teaspoons sugar
cold milk
dash vanilla
nutmeg, grated
2 Tablespoons cream
1 whiskey glass of brandy, or Bourbon

Separate egg. Beat yolk until very light with sugar, add white, beaten stiff. Add 2 Tablespoons sweet cream, brandy or whiskey, vanilla; fill glass with cold milk. Grate nutmeg on top.
The Southern Cook Book, 1939

CRANBERRY SPIKE

1 pint cranberry juice cocktail
12 ounce can apricot nectar
2 Tablespoons lemon juice

Combine chilled juices. Ice and serve. Makes 1 quart.
Farm Journal's Country Cookbook, 1959

CRANBERRY MULLED PUNCH

1 pint cranberry juice
2 1/4 cups pineapple juice
1/2 cup water
1/3 cup brown sugar
1/4 teaspoon cloves
1/4 teaspoon cinnamon
1/4 teaspoon allspice
1/8 teaspoon nutmeg
1/8 teaspoon salt
Cinnamon sticks (optional)

Combine the liquids in a pouring pot. Combine the dry ingredients in a small bowl and pour in top of pot. Heat. Serve piping hot, with cinnamon sticks if desired. Serves 6.
Charmaine Jamieson, The Nashville Cookbook, 1977

MAPLE SNAP

1/2 gallon maple walnut ice cream
1 to 2 cups maple or maple flavored syrup
1 gallon cold milk

Scoop ice cream into a punch bowl. Add syrup and milk. Stir gently. Serves 50
Ann C. Cox, The Nashville Cookbook, 1977

TIPSY PUNCH

3 cups apple juice
3 cups reconstituted frozen orange juice
3 cups reconstituted frozen grapefruit juice
1/3 cup lemon juice
1 1/2 cups gin
3/4 cup Grand Marnier
3/4 cup grenadine

Chill and mix all the ingredients. Pour over a block of ice in a punch bowl. Serves 10.
Virginia Kendall White, The Nashville Cookbook, 1977

ORGEAT

2 quarts milk
1 stick cinnamon
1/4 pound almonds
2 Tablespoons rosewater
1/4 cup sugar

Add cinnamon to milk and bring gently to boiling point. Remove cinnamon and let milk cool. Blanch almonds and "pound them in a marble mortar," but since this isn't possible for most of us, chopping them very fine will do. Add rosewater to chopped almonds and then put all into milk, mixing well. Sweeten milk to taste (we used 1/4 cup sugar for a sweet drink), and let milk boil for a minute or two. If this is cooked too long, almonds will make it oily. Strain the drink through a very fine sieve or a piece of cheesecloth to remove the almonds and "serve either cold or lukewarm in glasses with handles."

NOTE: We preferred this drink icy cold. The cinnamon, rosewater and almond flavors are blended such that it is difficult to tell just what flavor the drink really has.
Carolina House Wife recipe recounted in 200 Years of Charleston Cooking, 1930

TOMATO CREAM FROSTY

4 cups milk, chilled
2 cups tomato juice, chilled
1/2 teaspoon salt
2 teaspoons onion salt
2 teaspoons Worcestershire sauce
dash salt
minced chives or parsley

Combine ingredients, except the chives, and blend thoroughly. Pour into glasses. Garnish with chives or parsley.
Easy-on-the-Cook Book, 1960

ORANGE PUNCH

4 Tablespoons tea leaves
3 cups boiling water
2 1/4 cups sugar
6 cups orange juice
1 1/2 cups lemon juice
1 1/2 cups pineapple juice
3 quarts ginger ale

Let tea stand in boiling water 5 minutes, strain. Dissolve sugar in hot tea. Cool and add juices. Just before serving, add ginger ale. Orange sherbet can be added. 50 small glasses.
Satsuma Tea Room, Fun for the Cook, 1968

RASPBERRY FLOAT

4 ounces raspberry flavor gelatin
4 cups boiling water
1 1/2 cup sugar
4 cups cold water

1/2 cup lime juice
2 1/4 cups orange juice
1 1/4 cups lemon juice
1 quart ginger ale
20 ounces frozen raspberries

Dissolve the gelatin in boiling water. Then add the sugar, cold water and juices; cool, but do not chill or the gelatin will congeal. If you let it congeal, heat it just enough to bring it back to its liquid state. When it is time to serve, pour the punch into a punch bowl. Add ginger ale and frozen raspberries. Stir until the raspberries break apart and are partially thawed. Makes about 4 quarts.
Farm Journal's Country Cookbook, 1959

TOM AND JERRY, SOUTHERN STYLE

Beat 12 eggs very well and slowly add 1 pound 4x sugar, while continuing to beat. For each serving pour a jigger of whiskey into a cup. Fill each cup 2/3 full of boiling water; put spoonful of egg mixture on top and a dash of nutmeg and serve. WOW!

NOTE: "Beware! A sudden jolt of this has been known to stop a victim's watch, snap both of his suspenders, and crack his glass eye right across….all in the same motion." -Cobb
The Southern Cookbook, 1939

BLACKBERRY WINE

Possibly after this recipe is published, the consumption of blackberries will be greatly increased! Wash the berries well, and for every gallon of fruit allow two quarts of boiling water. Let water stand on the fruit for 10 to 12 hours; then strain off pressing the pulp well. To each gallon of the liquid add two pounds of brown sugar. Put in a cask or jug but do not cork tightly until the fermentation is over, which will take about 10 days. Then you may seal the wine up and put it away for future use.
Mrs. Bennett, 200 Years of Charleston Cooking, 1930

HEAVENLY NECTAR PUNCH

46 ounces apricot, peach, or pear nectar
3/4 cup lemon juice
1 quart ginger ale

ice cubes
dash food coloring

Pour nectar, lemon juice, and ginger ale over ice in a punch bowl. Tint with a dash of food coloring, red for peach or apricot, green for pear. Makes 2 1/2 quarts.
Easy-on-the-Cook Book, 1960

*"If more of us valued food and cheer and song above hoarded gold,
it would be a merrier world."
-J.R.R. Tolkien (1892-1973)*

SOUPS & STEWS

"A rich soup; a small turbot;
a saddle of venison; an apricot tart:
this is a dinner fit for a king."
-Brillat-Savarin (1755-1826)

Soup belongs at any dinner or party, be it an elaborate dinner or just an informal get together. Bowls of savory consommé or bouillon are a delightful, exciting opening to an hour of good eating. Throughout the ages, soups and stews have been enjoyed universally. Recipes, written or verbal, have been wide-ranging for soups or stews based on the necessities available; depending on time, place, and on the ingredients at hand.

Soup is cookery's most caring course. It seems to breathe reassurance; its steam emitting from the bowl offers consolation. After a weary day, a good soup promotes dinner geniality as much as the evening cocktail or an afternoon tea. Every nation, every known and forgotten corner of the world has its own special soup recipe.

In our own historic past, soup was often the only sustenance of the day available to our forefathers. Even today, a bowl of rich, hearty soup can make an intimate, highly easy supper by itself. A modern-day version of an old Southern staple is presented here, Pioneer Corn Stew.

PIONEER CORN STEW

1 medium onion, chopped	17 ounces whole kernel corn
1/2 cup diced green pepper	1 or 2 cans (10 3/4 oz. each) tomato soup
2 Tablespoons butter	2 teaspoons sugar
1 pound ground lean beef	1 teaspoon salt

Sauté onion and green peppers over low heat until tender. Add beef and cook slowly until beef browns slightly. Add corn, 1 can tomato soup, sugar, and salt. Simmer gently until the stew is thoroughly heated. A second can of soup may be used to increase number of servings without altering the quality of the soup.
The Nashville Cookbook, 1977

MARYLAND CREAM OF CRAB SOUP

1 Tablespoon flour	1 pint crab meat	chopped parsley, celery,
2 Tablespoons butter	1/2 onion sliced	salt and pepper
2 quarts milk	1/2 pint heavy cream	

Melt butter in top of double boiler, add flour and blend. Gradually add the milk, onion, parsley, celery, and season to taste. Cook slowly until the soup thickens a little and then add the crab meat. Serve in individual dishes with a spoon of whipped cream on top.
The Southern Cookbook, 1939

FRESH TOMATO SOUP

1/4 cup butter	1 1/4 teaspoons salt
1/2 cup chopped onion	1/4 teaspoon black pepper
1/4 cup flour	1 teaspoon sugar
1 cup water	1/2 teaspoon thyme leaves
6 medium tomatoes	1 bay leaf
1 Tablespoon minced parsley	4 lemon slices

Cook onion in butter over medium heat until tender. Stir in flour until blended. Blanche, peel, seed, and dice tomatoes. Gradually add water, tomatoes and all other ingredients to onions and heat until boiling. Reduce heat to low, cover and simmer 30 minutes, stirring frequently. Add more water if soup is too thick. Discard bay leaf and serve with lemon slices. Serves 4.
Cortner Mill Restaurant cookbook, 2009

ALMOND CHICKEN SOUP

1/2 cup blanched almonds	3 Tablespoons butter
6 bitter almonds	3 Tablespoons flour
3 cups chicken broth	2 cups milk
1 teaspoon onion juice	1 cup cream
1 bay leaf, crushed fine	salt and pepper to taste

Chop almonds fine, adding the bitter almonds for a more pronounced flavor. Add the chopped almonds to the chicken broth, seasoned with onion juice and bay leaf. Simmer slowly. Melt the butter and stir in the flour; when smooth add to the broth, stirring constantly until the boiling point is reached. Add the milk and cream and season to taste with the salt and pepper.
The Southern Cookbook, 1939

AUNT LINDA'S CREOLE BEEF STEW

1 1/2 pounds lean beef	1 cup string beans	Worcestershire sauce
2 cups tomatoes	3 ears or 1 can corn	potatoes as indicated
1 large onion	2 carrots sliced	
1 green pepper	flour	

Place 1 1/2 pounds of lean beef in a casserole or deep iron skillet. Around the beef, place as many potatoes as needed, tomatoes, onion, green pepper, string beans, corn, carrots. Sprinkle well with salt and pepper, partially cover with water, and place in a slow oven to cook until the meat is done. More water may be added to prevent meat from drying out too much. Remove from pan and place on serving platter and garnish with the vegetables. Add flour to thicken the meat juices and make gravy, using chopped parsley and Worcestershire sauce for the final flavoring.
The Southern Cookbook, 1939

OLD-TIME BEEF STEW

2 Tablespoons fat	1 Tablespoon lemon juice	paprika as desired
2 pounds beef chuck	1 teaspoon sugar	1 or 2 bay leaves
1 large onion, sliced	1 teaspoon Worcestershire sauce	dash of allspice or cloves
1 clove garlic		6 small potatoes
4 cups boiling water	1/2 teaspoon black pepper	6 small onions
1 Tablespoon salt		
1 cup 1-inch cut carrots		

Heat fat in Dutch oven. Cut beef into 1½-inch cubes, add to fat and brown on all sides. This will take about 20 minutes. Add onion, garlic (stuck on a toothpick), boiling water, salt lemon juice, sugar, Worcestershire sauce, pepper, paprika, bay leaf, and spice. Gentle cooking makes the meat tender, cover and simmer (do not boil) for 2 hours. Stir occasionally. When meat is almost done, add vegetables. Simmer the stew about 30 minutes longer or until vegetables are tender. Discard any bay leaf and garlic.
Serves 6-8.

GRAVY

Pour 1/2 cup cold water into a shaker and add 1/4 cup flour; shake hard to blend. Remove stew from heat. Push meat and vegetables to one side of container; stir in the flour mixture. Cook and stir until gravy thickens and boils. Cook gently for a few minutes.
Marilyne Burgess, The Nashville Cookbook, 1977

ZUCCHINI SOUP-HOT OR COLD

2 cups zucchini	1 medium onion, diced	2 Tablespoons butter
21 ounces chicken broth	2 cups milk	

Add onion to melted butter and cook until the onions are yellow. Slice the zucchini with the skin on and add half the broth to the onions. Cook until the zucchini is tender. Put mixture into a blender to puree. Return mixture to a pan and add the remaining milk and broth. Salt and pepper to taste and cook over medium heat for 10 minutes. Remove from the stove and serve in hot bowls or allow to cool if you wish to serve cold. Place in refrigerator until chilled. Serve in cold bowls.

NOTE: We keep this soup on hand at all times. We make it fresh in the summer, when we are overwhelmed with zucchini. Served cold, it makes a refreshing start to a summer meal. We freeze any extra for a hot winter warm up.
David Hazelwood, Cortner Mill Restaurant cookbook, 2009

GUMBO

Gumbo is a soup-like dish often associated with Louisiana and contains combinations of different food varieties; shrimp, chicken, crab, ham, or oysters. Most vegetables can be used. Tomatoes and tomato base are most often found in a seafood gumbo other than a poultry gumbo. Gumbo begins with a roux, generally a brown roux, for flavor and body. The thickening of a gumbo is from okra being cooked in the gumbo or from file powder added at serving time.

"..... Excellent way of utilizing left-over..." This statement is so Southern. Every Friday in our restaurant, *Satsuma Tea Room,* we served our most popular dish. A different menu was created daily, each menu included a poultry, beef, ham, and seafood entrée. We served new vegetable dishes every single day that were prepared and served fresh; depending on the growing season and what produce we were able to purchase each morning at the local Farmer's Market.

Now as I was saying about our most popular meal on Friday; this was the meal in which I was constantly questioned about the recipe. This was a meal that generated Friday business to become our busiest day of the week because one and all appeared to come into the restaurant just for this dish. The dish was New Orleans Creole Gumbo served with fresh-baked corn sticks. It was absolutely delicious. What our customers did not realize was there was no recipe and the gumbo deviated in composition week to week. It was not a drastic change. It was very slight and subtle, but we as the cooks knew it wasn't the same. The roux, shrimp, okra and rice were the same. But all the other ingredients were different week to week. That is because this was our "leftover" dish. We were able to use leftovers from menu items "left-over" during the week, frozen daily, and as with any gumbo, an incredible meal was created.

This is not to say that you can't make gumbo if you don't have leftovers. You can, and quite successfully cook gumbo from scratch. Not all leftovers will enable you to create a masterful and tasty gumbo, but this practice is so Southern.

FILE POWDER

File powder is made from the dried leaves of the sassafras tree. The making of file was a practice that early settlers had adapted from the Choctaw Indians. Sassafras is an indigenous bush/tree found throughout the South and is best known for the sassafras tea, which is made from its leaves or the bright red fall color of these leaves. It is also known for file powder which is ground and powdered from dried sassafras leaves which is then used in gumbo file.

FILE POWDER
To make file powder, clip green and tender sassafras leaves and lay them in the sun for 2-3 days until dry. Turn the leaves to enable drying on both sides. Remove the stems and pulverize the dried leaves. Store the resulting dried leaves in an airtight container. File flavors, as well as thickens gumbo.

SOUTHERN GUMBO

2 Tablespoons butter, melted
1 onion chopped
2 cups tomatoes
2 cups okra, cut fine

1 cup chopped green pepper
2 cups hot water
1/2 teaspoon celery seed
salt and pepper

Fry the onions in the melted butter until brown; add the vegetables, hot water and seasonings. Cook slowly until quite thick.
The Southern Cook Book, 1939

SHRIMP GUMBO

2 quarts fresh shrimp	4 cups okra, finely cut
3 onions	1 cup cooked rice
1/2 cup vinegar	6 large tomatoes blanched and skinned
salt	(canned tomatoes can be used)
2 quarts water	2 bay leaves
1 Tablespoon butter, melted	pinch of sugar and pepper
1 Tablespoon flour	

Make sure the shrimp is washed and cleaned. Boil the shrimp, 2 of the onions, the vinegar and salt in the water about 20 minutes. Drain off the stock with strainer and save. Shell the shrimp (if not already shelled). Chop the remaining onion and brown in the melted butter. Stir in the flour and slowly add the strained broth, stirring constantly. Add the okra, rice, tomatoes, seasonings and shelled shrimp. Let simmer a short time before serving in order to cook the okra and tomatoes.
The Southern Cook Book, 1939

CHICKEN GUMBO

1 small stewing chicken	2 cups tomato pulp
2 Tablespoons flour	few sprigs parsley, chopped
3 Tablespoons butter, melted	4 cups water
1 onion, chopped	salt and pepper to taste
4 cups okra, sliced and chopped	

After chicken is cleaned and dressed, cut the chicken into serving portions. Dredge lightly with the flour and sauté in the butter, along with the chopped onion. When the chicken is nicely browned, add the okra, tomatoes, parsley and water. Season to taste with salt and pepper. Cook very slowly until the chicken is tender and the okra is well-cooked (about 2 1/2 hours). Add water as required during the slow cooking process. If thin soup is preferred, the quantity of water may be increased.
The Southern Cookbook, 1939

CHICKEN OYSTER GUMBO

1 small chicken	3 pints water
1 pound of beef cut up for stewing	2 dozen oysters
1 cup diced okra	1 1/2 teaspoons sassafras leaves
1 Tablespoon butter and 1 onion	salt and pepper

Cut up the chicken and stew it with the beef and 1 cup okra in 3 pints of water. When a strong broth has been obtained and the meat is tender, remove the chicken bones and cut the meat into small pieces. Add the oysters with their liquor and season to taste with salt, pepper and onion browned in butter. Add the sassafras leaves. Cook until the edges of the oysters curl.
The Southern Cookbook, 1939

CHICKEN GUMBO & GUMBO FILE

1 large hen (around 5 pounds), disjointed
1/2 cup cooking oil
6 Tablespoons cooking oil
6 Tablespoons flour
1 1/2 cups chopped onions
1 Tablespoon salt
1 1/2 teaspoons black pepper
2 Tablespoons chopped parsley
2 Tablespoons chopped onion tops
1 pint oysters (optional)
file powder

Lightly brown the chicken pieces in cooking oil. Set aside. Make a roux of 6 Tablespoons cooking oil and 6 Tablespoons flour in heavy skillet. Cook over low heat, stirring constantly, until the mixture is a rich brown, taking care not to burn. Add the chopped onion to hot roux and stir one minute. Transfer the roux-onion mixture to a large pot (6-8 quart capacity). Add 2 ½ - 3 quarts cool water, chicken, salt, and pepper and mix well. Simmer gently until meat is very tender, about 2 hours. Stir occasionally. Oysters may be added during last 10 minutes of cooking if desired. About 5 minutes before serving, add chopped parsley and onion tops. Serve gumbo over rice mounded in soup plates. Add about 1/4 teaspoon gumbo file to edge of each plate for serving. File should be added to gumbo slowly as one is eating. File is stringy if heated prior serving. Serves 8.
Brenda Broussard, The Nashville Cookbook, 1977

SPINACH SOUP

2 pounds fresh spinach
2 Tablespoons butter
1 onion, finely chopped
1 1/2 Tablespoons flour
2 pints chicken stock
1/2 pint cream
salt, cayenne pepper,
grated nutmeg as desired

Strip the spinach leaves from the stems and wash thoroughly. Heat butter; add onion and simmer 3 to 4 minutes. Add flour; stir and cook until mixture is golden. Add the spinach and stir. Then gradually add the stock. Cook gently until spinach is tender. Put through a sieve or puree in a blender. Return soup to pan and dilute with additional stock if necessary. Stir in cream, salt, pepper, nutmeg and reheat. Soup may be garnished with finely chopped parsley, croutons or paprika. Serves 4-6.

NOTE: A very delicious luncheon dish.
Irene Burba, The Nashville Cookbook, 1977

CREOLE SOUP A LA MADAME BEGUE

1 Tbl butter, melted
1 Tablespoon chopped green pepper
1 Tbl chopped red pepper
1 Tablespoon flour
1 1/2 cups soup stock
1 cup tomato pulp
1/2 cup corn
salt and pepper

Lightly brown the peppers in the melted butter; blend in the flour. Slowly add the soup stock and tomato pulp; place over the fire and continue to stir until soup boils. Reduce the heat, cover and let cook slowly for another 20 minutes. Strain into another pot, add the corn and season to taste with salt and pepper.
The Southern Cookbook, 1939

CREAM OF POTATO SOUP

Scald 2 cups milk with 1 sliced onion. Add 1 cup mashed potatoes. Beat together with a wire whisk. Strain and pour into hot bowls. Put piece of butter into each bowl and sprinkle with chopped parsley. Can be chilled.

VICHYSSOISE

For Vichyssoise, chill soup and mix with 1/2 cup heavy cream and sprinkle chopped parsley on top.
Satsuma Tea Room, More Fun for the Cook, 1974

MOCK TERRAPIN STEW

Boil two chickens until tender, cut the meat from the bones and dice it. Beat the yolks of 6 eggs and set aside. Blend two tablespoons of flour with 1/4 pound of melted butter and add 1 pint of milk heated to the boiling point. Add the beaten yolks, season with salt and pepper. Put back on fire, adding diced chicken and 1 large glass wine just before serving.
The Southern Cookbook, 1939

FRESH ASPARAGUS SOUP

2 pounds fresh asparagus, chopped	1/4 cup butter
3 cup chicken broth	5 Tablespoons flour
1 medium onion	3 cups half and half

Cook asparagus and onion in broth until tender. Puree in food processor. Melt butter in medium saucepan, stir in flour, and cook for 3 minutes, stirring regularly. Stir asparagus and half and half into the butter. Season with salt and pepper to taste. Cook over medium heat for 10 minutes and serve in hot bowls.

NOTE: In April and May the asparagus from the garden is abundant. Now that is fresh!
Cortner Mill Restaurant cookbook, 2009

SOUTHERN JUGGED SOUP

6 potatoes, sliced	1/4 cup rice
1 onion sliced	3 quarts water
6 tomatoes or two cups canned tomatoes	1 Tablespoon salt
1 turnip, diced	1 Tablespoon sugar
1 can peas	1/2 teaspoon pepper
1 grated carrot	1 pinch allspice

Arrange vegetables, rice and seasonings in alternate layers in the bottom of a stone crock with a cover. Boil any carcasses of cold chicken, bones of roast meat or steak with trimmings in three quarts of water until the water is reduced to two quarts. Strain, cool and remove. Pour the broth over the vegetables. Put on the cover and seal (using tape or muslin or any other methods as long as the steam is kept in). Set crock in a pan of hot water. Place in oven and cook from 4 to 6 hours.
The Southern Cookbook, 1939

PLANTATION SOUP

1 carrot, diced	4 Tablespoons butter
1 stalk celery, cut fine	2 Tablespoons flour
1 small onion, chopped fine	2 cups milk
2 cups soup stock	1/3 cup grated cheese

Cook carrot, celery and onion in the stock until very tender; strain; make a thin white sauce by melting the butter, stirring in the flour and slowly adding the milk. Combine the stock with white sauce and simmer until blended. When ready to serve, add grated cheese.
The Southern Cookbook, 1939

ONION SOUP AU GRATIN

2 quarts meat broth	1 teaspoon	toast
8 medium sized onions	Worcestershire sauce	grated Parmesan cheese
2 Tablespoons butter	salt and pepper	

Slice onions thin and brown in butter. Add the broth, Worcestershire sauce, salt and pepper to taste, and simmer until the onions are tender. Pour soup into an earthen jar or oven-glass casserole. Arrange toast on top of soup, sprinkle with grated parmesan cheese and place under the broiler until the cheese melts and browns.
The Southern Cookbook, 1939

CRAB SOUP

To a white sauce made of 2 Tablespoons of flour, 2 Tablespoons of butter, and 1 cup of milk; add a paste made of 1 teaspoon dry mustard and 1 Tablespoon of Worcestershire Sauce and then salt and pepper to taste.
Thin this mixture out with 2 more cups of milk. Just before serving add 2 cups of crab meat and a few slices of sliced lemon.
The Savannah Cook Book, 1933

CHICKEN CUSTARD (Hot or Cold)

1 cup strong chicken broth	3 egg yolks
1 cup thin cream	salt to taste

Scald together the chicken broth and cream. (If a thicker broth is preferred, use heavy cream.) Pour the scalded mixture over the well-beaten egg yolks and cook in a double boiler stirring constantly until slightly thickened. Salt to taste and serve in custard cups.

NOTE: While this delicately flavored custard could be served hot or cold, we think it would be especially attractive served in green custard cups very thoroughly chilled and served as the beginning to a summer luncheon.
200 years of Charleston Cooking, 1930

CREAM OF CUCUMBER SOUP

2 cups peeled and chopped cucumbers
1/4 cup chopped onion
1/4 cup chopped celery
1/4 cup chopped green pepper
3 sprigs parsley

3 Tablespoons soft butter
2 Tablespoons flour
salt and pepper as desired
1 cup chicken broth
1 cup light cream

Combine vegetables in blender until smooth. Make a white sauce by melting butter in saucepan, add flour, and stir until golden; add broth and cook while stirring until thickened. Add the blended vegetables to white sauce. Season with salt and pepper. To serve hot, garnish with a small amount of dill weed. To serve cold, garnish with finely chopped cucumber and grated lemon rind. Serves 4-6

NOTE: This recipe is perfect for making use of all those excess cucumbers and green peppers from the garden. Prepare the cucumbers, onion, green peppers, celery leaves, and parsley in blender/processor. Pour into container and freeze. At the time of serving, make the white sauce and continue as above.
Ruth Fay Kilgore, The Nashville Cookbook, 1977

CANADIAN CHEESE SOUP

2 Tablespoons butter
1/4 cup chopped onion
2 Tablespoons flour
1 Tablespoon corn starch
1/8 teaspoon paprika
1/2 teaspoon salt
dash of white pepper

2 cups milk
2 cups chicken stock or consommé
1/4 cooked diced carrots
1/4 cup diced celery
1/2 cup diced sharp Cheddar cheese
2 Tablespoons chopped parsley

Melt butter in a double boiler. Add flour and cornstarch, and blend into the butter. Add the seasonings. Stir in milk and chicken stock; cook until thickened. Add vegetables and more seasoning if desired. Cook in double boiler for 15 minutes. Just before serving, add cheese cubes and blend into soup. Add chopped parsley last. Serve hot. Makes 6-8 servings.
The Settlement Cookbook, 1952

NOTE: There are as many cheese soup recipes as there are grains of sand on the beach. This was the most popular soup that was served at *Satsuma*. The soup was paired with a baked ham sandwich and was a much-desired dish. The above recipe was adapted to serve hundreds of people eating in the restaurant. There is one adaptation that we made different from the above recipe and one I think was a beneficial adaptation because of the taste of the soup and ease in making the soup. This recipe was written before the widespread use and availability of food processors to the general public. I would recommend chopping all the vegetables in a processor and then sauté the result in the butter and add the flour, etc. You now have the "makings for the soup" to add with the milk, cheese and stock in the double boiler.

ZUCCHINI SOUP

1 medium onion, chopped
2 Tablespoons butter
2 cans (10 3/4 oz.) each of chicken broth
salt and pepper to taste
2 cups thinly sliced zucchini (with peel)
1/2 pint whipping cream
Parmesan cheese
chopped chives or parsley

Sauté the onion in butter. Add broth, salt, pepper, and zucchini. Simmer until tender, about 15-20 minutes. Put in blender and puree. Stir in the cream. Serve hot or cold. Top each bowl with Parmesan cheese and chives or parsley flakes. Serves 6.
Mary Ann Gibson, The Nashville Cookbook, 1977

EGG SOUP

NOTE: This is an old German recipe taken from the *Carolina Housewife*, a little old book, long out of print, of which the remaining few copies are guarded like jewels by Charleston ladies. The last of the recipe reads, "If the bouillon be of chicken, you may put it back into the bouillon; you may also add asparagus and green peas, both being already boiled." The time of year when we tested this recipe prevented our having the fresh vegetables on hand; but they would undoubtedly be a delicious addition.

4 eggs
1/8 teaspoon nutmeg
2 quarts bouillon
4 ounces breadcrumbs
1 Tablespoon chopped parsley

Beat the eggs, add the nutmeg, parsley and bread crumbs and mix well together. Add the bouillon carefully, stirring constantly. If bouillon cubes are used- no salt will be required, otherwise add salt to taste. This will serve 8.
Carolina Housewife, recipe offered by 200 years of Charleston Cooking, 1930

FISH CHOWDER

NOTE: Wine is added to this chowder; the amount may be varied according to taste.

2 pounds fish
2 large onions
3 slices salt pork
4 sailor's biscuits (pilot biscuit)
cayenne pepper and spices
2 Tablespoons tomato catsup
1 pint wine or cooking sherry

Fry the pork and in the resulting fat cook the chopped onions. Cut the fish into pieces and wash well. Put the fish into a saucepan with sufficient water to cover. Add the onions and thicken with the pilot biscuits, broken into pieces. Season to taste with cayenne and spices (nutmeg and allspice are usually used). Cook for about 3/4 of an hour and then add the catsup and wine. About an hour is used for the entire cooking.
Carolina Housewife, recipe offered by 200 years of Charleston Cooking, 1930

CLAM CHOWDER

18 fresh clams, run through grinder (processor)	1 egg
2 large boiled potatoes, diced small	1 bay leaf
1 pint cream	1 onion, ground fine
1/2 teaspoon thyme	dash of red pepper
	2 Tablespoons chopped parsley

Cook clams five or 10 minutes in own liquor with seasoning, add potatoes and let cool. Then add yolk of egg, and cream, and if not thick enough, thicken with a little flour rubbed smooth in water.
The Savannah Cook Book, 1933

CORN CHOWDER

3 cups whole kernel corn	2 cups milk
2 cans cream style corn	3 quarts chicken stock
1/2 onion, chopped	3 Tablespoons flour
1/2 green pepper, chopped	1/2 teaspoon salt
2 Tbl. butter or extra virgin olive oil	1/2 teaspoon black pepper
1 potato cubed	1/2 cup cooked bacon

Sauté onion and green pepper in butter or oil. Add chicken stock, potato, milk, corn. Bring to a boil and reduce heat, cover and simmer for 10 minutes or until tender. Combine flour, salt, and pepper to make paste. Add to soup mixture to thicken. Add bacon and simmer 10 minutes. Serve in hot bowls. Makes 1 1/2 gallons. Serves 24 but does keep for that second or third later serving.
Jim Long, Cortner Mill Restaurant cookbook, 2009

TOMATO-CORN CHOWDER

2 slices bacon, diced	1/8 teaspoon pepper
1/4 cup grated onion	1 cup drained whole kernel corn
2 cups cubed raw potatoes	2 cups tomato juice
1 cup cold water	1/4 cup flour
1 1/2 teaspoons salt	1/2 cup milk

Cook bacon and onion until bacon is crisp. Add potatoes, water, and seasonings. Cover; simmer about 30 minutes or until potatoes are tender. Add corn, tomato juice, and flour which has been mixed with milk. Cook over low heat, stirring occasionally until thickened.
Easy-on-the-Cook Book, 1960

CRAB SOUP BALTIMORE

2 Tablespoons butter	1 cup crab meat	dash Tabasco sauce
1 onion, finely chopped	1/4 cup chopped celery	3 cups scalded milk
1 Tablespoon flour	chopped parsley	
2 cups warm water	salt and pepper	

Melt the butter, add the onion and brown. Blend in the flour and slowly add the warm water; allow to cook until slightly thickened. Add the crab meat, celery, parsley and seasonings. Allow to simmer for 30 minutes. Just before serving, add the scalded milk.
The Southern Cookbook, 1939

CRAYFISH BISQUE

2 dozen crayfish	4 branches parsley	3 Tablespoons butter
1 quart water	1/4 teaspoon thyme	2 Tablespoons flour
2 onions	6 Tablespoons cracker crumbs	salt and pepper
2 carrots	milk	1 egg, beaten
2 stalks celery		

Prepare crayfish for soup by soaking in cold water for 30 minutes. Wash carefully; use a brush to remove all the dirt. When cleaned, place in a soup pot with the water, 1 onion, the carrots, celery, half the quantity of parsley and thyme. Allow to come to a boil and continue to cook for 25 minutes. Drain off the water from the crayfish and set aside for later use. Remove all the meat from the heads and bodies of the crayfish; set aside the heads which are to be stuffed.

Moisten the cracker crumbs with the milk. Chop the crayfish meat and add to the moistened crumbs. Mince the remaining onion; melt the butter, add the onion and 1 Tablespoon of flour. Add 1 Tablespoon of the fish broth and the remainder of the parsley. Season with salt and pepper to taste. Simmer slowly for a few minutes; add the crayfish and bread crumb mixture and cook 2 minutes longer. Remove from the stove and let cool slightly. Stir in the beaten egg. Fill the crayfish heads with this mixture. Dredge the heads in flour and fry in butter until nicely browned.

Drain on paper and keep warm while preparing the stock. Melt the balance of the butter; add the remainder of the flour and stir until smooth. Strain reserved stock in order to remove celery and carrots. Add the broth to the butter and flour. Cook slowly for 12 minutes; season with more salt and pepper if desired. Before serving, add the stuffed crayfish heads.
The Southern Cook Book, 1939

OYSTER BISQUE

1 quart oysters	1 Tablespoon butter	Worcestershire sauce
1 quart milk	1/2 cup chopped celery	salt and pepper
1 Tablespoon flour	1 green pepper	

Put oysters in a meat grinder/food processor. Make a cream soup with milk, thickened with flour and seasoned with butter, salt, pepper, chopped celery and green pepper. Add the oysters and keep the soup hot, but do not allow it to boil as it may curdle. Add Worcestershire before serving.
The Southern Cookbook, 1939

SHRIMP STEW

Make a thick stew as follows: Melt 1 heaping Tablespoon of butter. Remove this butter from the stove and mix gradually with 2 Tablespoons of flour; then 1 cup of milk, stirring all well so that there are no lumps. Then add another cup of milk and put back on the stove. Stir until the mixture is the right consistency; then add 1 pint of picked shrimp. Heat thoroughly and flavor with sherry.
The Savannah Cook Book, 1933

SHRIMP NEWBURG

This receipt is the same as above receipt except that a paste is made of the yolks of 2 hard-boiled eggs and 1 cup of cream. This is added to the above white stew before adding shrimp
The Savannah Cook Book, 1933

TURNIP SOUP

1 pound "scrag of mutton"	1 large onion	pepper and salt to taste
	1 head of celery	2 large turnips

Have a pound of lamb or mutton cut into pieces and add about 3 pints of water to it. Slice the onion, cut the celery into small pieces and add salt and pepper to taste. Cook these ingredients together until a strong broth is obtained (about 1 to 1 1/2 hours). Meanwhile peel the turnips, cut them in pieces and boil them until tender enough to put through a sieve. Add sufficient turnips to the broth to make it thick (the amount used depends, of course, upon the size of the turnips) and boil the turnips in the broth for about 5 minutes. Add more salt and pepper if needed and serve very hot. A little cream may be added, if desired.

NOTE: I personally use a little sugar when I cook this soup or when I cook just regular mashed turnips. Then, don't forget the butter! You can't have too much.
200 Years of Charleston Cooking, 1930

BURGOO

If I might be allowed a divergence at this point, Kentucky Burgoo is a dish mentioned as truly Southern and a dish that is defined as a Kentucky original. A dish much steeped in tradition. Now being a Tennessee native and Tennessee being a neighboring state to Kentucky, I should have at least heard of the burgoo stew but I had never once heard the name burgoo uttered much less had I ever eaten this traditional dish. The word burgoo seems as if it is derived from a foreign language.

My oldest daughter at the age of seven tasted her first burgoo. She had come from her friend's home (a young girl of Kentucky parentage) one fall evening and I asked how the day had gone and she proudly said that she helped cook and eat "bird do".

It was only after decades of association and friendship with my co-author, a true native of the Commonwealth of Kentucky, that I savored burgoo after an all-day-long backyard cooking event of the soup/stew over an open fire; by means of a very large cast iron kettle and using a wooden paddle to stir.

The day-long cooking event along with the essential continuous stirrings of the pot with the above-mentioned large wooden paddle culminated in a fabulous potluck dinner with all in attendance bringing a homemade dish to share. What could be more Southern?

Looking up the definition or a recipe for burgoo, one finds that an exact definition and recipe doesn't exist. It is literally a soup composed of many vegetables and meats delectably combined together in an enormous iron kettle. About the only point on which burgoo experts agree is the consistency of the soup. A good burgoo should be thick, but still soupy. This is the reason for a long, slow cooking time. It gives the burgoo an opportunity to thicken naturally. After that, more or less anything and everything was put into the pot as a burgoo ingredient. Cooking burgoo was a community event. Each person or family contributed a food item to the pot. Every village, town, and event in Kentucky has turned out to celebrate and contribute to their traditional version of burgoo. This was a Southern thing to do. Our food defines us.

(It's interesting that the Tennessee native, not the Kentucky native got the writing assignment for Kentucky burgoo.)

BURGOO FOR SMALL PARTIES

Meat from any domestic beasts or barnyard fowls may be used, along with any garden vegetables desired. Burgoo was first made from wild things found in Kentucky woods.

Cut the meat into one-inch cubes; do not throw away any bones; add them to the meat cubes. Add any dried vegetables which will enhance the flavor of the stew. Put all the ingredients into a large stewing kettle, unless beans and potatoes are being used. If this is the case, cook meats first and add beans and potatoes about an hour before serving.

Fill a kettle half full of water and place over fire to come to a boil. Prepare other vegetables for stew. Peel and half onions, scrape and dice carrots, chop the cabbage, open cans of corn, open cans of tomatoes and tomato puree, pare and cube potatoes. When the liquid in the kettle is boiling, add the vegetables. Lower heat and continue to simmer stew until vegetables are tender. Add salt and seasonings when stew is almost cooked. There should always be enough water to cover the vegetables. Canned tomatoes and a little puree will add to the flavor of the broth. In a real burgoo, no thickening like meal or rice is used, because the broth is to be strained and served clear. Likewise, sweet vegetables were not used in the real burgoo.

NOTE: As an editorial comment, not using sweet vegetables in the burgoo is because of their high sugar content causing a tendency to burn or stick and also will cause the dish to be too sweet. Constant stirring does help. It is pretty much a necessity after everything has been put in the pot to cook.

The Southern Cook Book, 1939

KENTUCKY BURGOO

7 pounds chicken thighs	2 gallons tomatoes, diced
4 pounds beef chuck	2 quarts whole kernel corn
1 pound beef soup bones	2 quarts lima beans
8 pounds potatoes, diced	2 quarts mixed vegetables
5 pounds onions, diced	½ cup salt ¼ cup black pepper

Build an open fire under a 20 gallon iron kettle and fill kettle half with water. Bring to a rolling boil and add beef chuck and soup bones. Cook for two hours and tell Hebbardsville stories while you wait. Add chicken thighs and more water to cover as needed. Cook for one and a half hours and tell more Hebbardsville stories while you wait. Remove meats from kettle, when they are tender enough to be pulled apart. Add potatoes and onions to the remaining water and let them cook while you debone and pull meat apart into small pieces. Return meat to kettle and cook for another thirty minutes. Add vegetables, salt, and pepper and stir constantly from the bottom of kettle to prevent corn from sticking. If more water is needed, add it now, not later. Cook for about two more hours. Pour into quart jars for giving to family and neighbors you have invited. Serve them a bowl of burgoo with crackers and the potluck of pies they have brought.

NOTE: The Burgoo Supper was a beginning of the year community fund raiser at Hebbardsville School. Families would donate old hens, bushels of potatoes, and jars of vegetables they had canned from their gardens. Cousin Hugh Allen Boswell was the master cooker for a number of years. Their kettles were 300 gallons and stirred with boat oars.
David Hazelwood, Cortner Mill Restaurant cookbook, 2009

BOUILLABAISSE

1 1/2 quarts water	2 large onions, chopped	1 cup grated cheese
1 Tablespoon salt	2 buds garlic	1/2 cup sherry
1 lb. fresh shrimp	2 cups tomato pulp	2 pounds fish fillets
12 cloves	2 cups water	(haddock works well)
½ lb. fresh mushrooms	3 bay leaves	1 pound scallops
2 Tablespoons butter	1 1/2 tsp. curry powder	2 Tablespoons flour

Add shrimp, 4 cloves and salt to 1 1/2 quarts of water and bring to a boil. After boiling for 10 minutes remove the shrimp from the pot, saving the broth for later use. Shell the shrimp and cut in half lengthwise. Cut mushrooms into thin slices, add to the shrimp and allow to stand until needed. Melt the butter and fry the onions and garlic in the butter until golden brown; add the tomato pulp and 2 cups of water, 4 cloves, the bay leaves, curry powder, cheese and 1/4 cup of sherry. Allow this mixture to cook slowly for 30 minutes. Season with more salt if desired. Meanwhile bring shrimp broth to boiling point, add the fish filleted, scallops, 4 cloves and 1/4 cup sherry, lower the flame and simmer until fish is sufficiently cooked (about 15 minutes). Combine the shrimp and mushroom mixture with the fish and cook for 5 minutes. Moisten the flour with a little cold water and add to the boiling liquid as a slight thickening. Cook another 5 minutes. Remove pieces of fish from the sauce, place on buttered slices of toast on large platter. Pour sauce over fish and serve.
The Southern Cookbook, 1939

THE BALLAD OF BOUILLABAISSE

"This bouillabaisse a noble dish is-
a sort of soup, or broth, or stew,
or hotchpotch of all sorts of fishes,
that Greenwich could never outdo;
green herbs, red peppers, mussels, saffron,
soles, onions, garlic, roach, and dace:
All these you can eat at Terre's Tavern
in that one dish of Bouillabaisse."
-William Makepeace Thackeray (1811-1863)

BRUNSWICK STEW

2 Tablespoons bacon grease
1 frying chicken (about 2-2 1/2 pounds)
2 onions
3 cups of water
3 tomatoes, peeled and quartered
1/2 cup sherry
2 Tablespoons butter
1/2 cup breadcrumbs
2 teaspoons Worcestershire sauce
1 pound fresh lima beans
salt and pepper
1/2 cup okra
3 ears green corn

Brown the onion in the bacon grease; then add the chicken which has been cut in small pieces and seasoned. When the chicken is done, pour off the grease and put chicken and onion in a Dutch oven. Add the water, tomatoes, sherry wine and Worcestershire sauce. Cook slowly over a low flame for 1/2 hour, then add the lima beans, okra and corn cut from the cob. Let simmer 1 hour. Then add the butter and breadcrumbs and cook 1/2 hour longer.
The Southern Cookbook, 1939

LEMON SOUP

2 cans condensed chicken broth
2 cans water
1/3 cup rice
4 eggs
4 Tablespoons lemon juice
lemon slices
parsley

Bring broth and water to a boil. Add the rice and cook over medium heat until rice is tender. Remove from the heat. Beat eggs until frothy light. Add lemon juice and 1 cup of broth mixture to eggs. Beat this egg mixture back into the remaining broth. Heat slowly. Do not boil. Serve in bowls garnished with lemon slices and parsley.

NOTE: This light and refreshing soup can be served year round. It is a fantastic meal starter.
David Hazelwood, Cortner Mill Restaurant cookbook, 2009

OYSTER SOUP

1 quart oysters	dash of onion salt or
1 quart rich milk	1 teaspoon onion juice
2 Tablespoons butter	salt and pepper to taste
1 Tablespoon finely chopped parsley	

Strain the oysters. Put this oyster broth in a saucepan. Pour milk into double boiler and heat. Heat the oyster broth, but do not boil. When both are hot, add broth to milk, stir. Add the butter and seasoning, then gradually one by one, put the oysters in and heat until hot, but never let it boil. When the oysters puff and the edges crinkle, serve at once.
The Southern Cook Book, 1939

CHICKEN OR TURKEY STEW

2 cups cold diced chicken or turkey	a little grated nutmeg
2 hard-boiled eggs	a little lemon juice and rind of 1/4 lemon
1 Tablespoon butter	1 teaspoon Worcestershire sauce
2 Tablespoons flour	chicken or turkey stock
1 can mushrooms	

Rub the yolks of the eggs and butter together and then add flour and chicken or turkey stock, the liquor from the mushrooms and the seasoning. Add chicken or turkey and mushrooms, and the chopped whites of the eggs just before serving. The mushrooms may be omitted.
The Savannah Cook Book, 1933

VEGETABLE CHOWDER

3 cups diced or sliced raw vegetables: beans, carrots, cauliflower, celery, corn, parsnips, peas, peppers, potatoes and tomatoes.	1/2 cup sliced okra
	2 slices salt pork
	6 to 8 cups water
	salt and pepper to taste
2 medium onions	

Slice or chop onions; slice or cube pork. Pan all vegetables in hot fat for 5 minutes. Add water and let come to a quick boil; cover, simmer over a low flame for about 35 minutes or until vegetables are tender. Season.
Cooked to Your Taste, 1945

CREAM OF SPINACH SOUP

1 cup milk	1 onion, sliced	salt and pepper
1 cup chicken stock	3/4 cup cooked spinach	

Cook all together in a double boiler. Heat for 20 minutes and strain.

NOTE: Ideal when served with Parmesan cheese or croutons.
Satsuma Tea Room, More Fun for the Cook, 1974

FRENCH ONION SOUP

1/2 pound onions, small or large
4 thin slices white bread
1 small bay leaf
5 cups vegetable stock, or water
3 Tablespoons butter
salt
4 to 5 Tablespoons grated cheese, preferably Parmesan

Slice the onion very fine and pan in hot butter until tender and slightly brown. Add vegetable stock, salt, and bay leaf; cover and simmer for about 10 minutes over a very low flame. Remove the bay leaf and proceed to simmer for an additional 15 minutes. Toast the bread, place in the soup plates. Sprinkle each slice with 1 Tablespoon of cheese and pour soup over it. If desired, serve additional grated cheese in a separate bowl.
Cooked to Your Taste, 1945

ONION SOUP

6 white onions, 1 pint of milk, 4 eggs, 1 cup sweet cream, and seasoning. Onions should be peeled, cut in very thin slices and then fry to a light brown in a Tablespoon of butter. Add to the fried onions 1 pint sweet milk, 1 quart boiling water, 1 salt spoon (1/4 teaspoon) white pepper, 1 teaspoon white sugar and a pinch of mace.
Cook slowly for 1 hour- strain and add 4 eggs beaten to a froth. Add a cupful of cream, and 1 Tablespoon of cornstarch moistened with cold water. Stir until the soup comes to a boil. Serve with croutons.
The Savannah Cook Book, 1933

CLEAR OR JELLIED CONSUME

3 to 4 cups raw vegetables (any of the following alone or in combination: carrots, cauliflower, celery, lima beans, peas, snap beans, turnips.
4 to 5 small onions
1 to 1 1/2 quarts water
1/2 cup tomato juice
1 Tablespoon oil or vegetable shortening
1 egg white
1 Tablespoon lemon juice or vinegar
salt, marjoram, and savory to taste

Cut all vegetables into small pieces; chop onion. Pan onion in hot fat until tender. All the remaining vegetables and brown for 5 minutes.
Add cold water, let come to a boil, season, cover, and let come to a quick boil. Strain through a fine sieve. Add tomato juice, season to taste, and serve.

FOR JELLIED CONSUME

2 to 3 Tablespoons unflavored gelatin

Measure liquid. Use 1 Tablespoon gelatin for every 2 cups liquid. Dissolve gelatin in 1/3 of cold liquid; heat the remaining liquid to boiling, add the gelatin and stir until dissolved. Pour into a mold or individual cups; chill until set. Garnish with sprigs of parsley and lemon slices and serve.
Cooked to Your Taste, 1945

VEGETABLE BOUILLON (General Lee's favorite soup)

4 cups tomatoes	1 bay leaf
1 stalk celery, chopped	2 teaspoons onion juice
2 carrots, chopped	salt and pepper to taste
2 sprigs parsley	1 wineglass sherry wine
1/4 green pepper, chopped	2 cups water

Put the tomatoes in a saucepan with the water, add all the vegetables and seasoning and let boil for 30 minutes. Strain. Add the sherry wine. Serve piping hot.
The Southern Cookbook, 1939

BLACK BEAN SOUP

2 cups black beans	1 carrot, diced	3 hard cooked eggs, sliced
12 cups water	3 small onions, minced	1 lemon, sliced
1/4 pound salt pork	3 cloves	1 wineglass of sherry
1/2 pound lean beef, cut into small pieces	1/4 teaspoon mace	
	dash of red pepper	

Wash and clean beans and soak overnight. In the morning, sort carefully and add to the water the salt pork, the lean beef, the carrot, the onion, and the seasonings. Cover and cook slowly for 3 hours, or until the beans have become very soft. Rub through a sieve, place in a tureen; add the sliced eggs, the lemon and the glass of sherry.
The Southern Cookbook, 1939

BLACK BEAN SOUP

NOTE: This soup is considered to rank next to Mock Turtle Soup, the beans also being known as Turtle Beans.

1 pint of black beans	3 cloves, and a little mace	2 onions
4 ounces salt pork	1 lemon	1 salt spoon cayenne
1 carrot	3 quarts water	3 eggs
1 Tablespoon salt	1/2 pound lean beef	1 glass sherry

Soak beans overnight. In the morning put in water over the fire; which as the water boils away, must be added to preserve the original quantity as the water boils away (3 quarts). Add salt pork, the lean beef cut in bits, the carrot and onions cut fine, and the seasoning. Close cover tight and boil for 4 hours. Rub through a sieve and put in a tureen on top of the soup 3 hard-boiled eggs (sliced), 1 lemon cut in thin slices and 1 glass of sherry.

NOTE: The person who contributed this delectable receipt copied it from an old yellowed leaved notebook in which her mother and grandmother had kept their favorite "prescriptions." It was the first time, she said, that she had ever realized that there was such a thing as "rank" among soups but that she would not hesitate to place it among any company.
Harriet Ross Colquitt, The Savannah Cook Book, 1933

TOMATO SOUP

1 pint can of tomatoes	pepper and salt
2 potatoes	1 Tablespoon butter

Boil the tomatoes and run through strainer. Boil the potatoes, mash and add to tomatoes with salt, pepper and butter.

NOTE: A simple and very delicious quick soup.
The Savannah Cook Book, 1933

TOMATO BISQUE SOUP

14 ounce can tomato soup	1 pinch celery seed	3 Tablespoons heavy cream
1 medium fresh tomato	1 pinch thyme	3 Tablespoons celery hearts, chopped
1 dash white pepper	1 pinch nutmeg	
1 dash black pepper	1 pinch garlic powder	
	1 pinch salt	

Bring soup, tomatoes, and seasonings to boil. Reduce heat and simmer 2 minutes. Ladle into hot bowls. Pour warm cream onto top of soup. Do not stir. Garnish with celery hearts.
Cortner Mill Restaurant cookbook, 2009

CLEAR TOMATO SOUP

2 1/2 cups tomato juice or V-8	2 cans beef bouillon	1/2 teaspoon sugar
	1/2 teaspoon salt	2 lemon slices

Simmer all ingredients 5 minutes. Serve with slice of lemon and sliced parsley, or Parmesan cheese, or croutons, or crumbled bacon. Dot with sour cream. Very easy. Very delicious. Can be kept in refrigerator several weeks. Wonderful to have on hand.
Satsuma Tea Room, More Fun for the Cook, 1974

SOUTHERN BEAN SOUP

1 cup dried beans	1 cup chopped celery	3 Tablespoons flour
cold water	1/2 onion, minced	salt and pepper
6 cups ham broth	3 Tablespoons butter	

Cover the beans with cold water and let stand overnight or at least 6 hours. Drain off the water and add the beans to the ham broth. Add the celery and onion and let cook slowly until beans become quite soft. Strain the bean broth; press the beans through a sieve and add the pulp to the strained broth. If necessary, add more water in order to have five cups of broth. Melt the butter, stir in the flour, salt and pepper; slowly stir in the hot bean broth and simmer until thickened (I have found it to be beneficial at this stage, and even before, to lower the heat and stir a fair amount to keep the beans from sticking and burning). Serve hot with slices of lemon and hard cooked eggs.
The Southern Cookbook, 1939

GREEN SOUP

1 pound greens, 1 kind or mixed
1 egg yolk
4 Tablespoons grated cheese

3 Tablespoons butter
1 quart water, or vegetable stock

Chop the greens coarsely and pan in hot fat for about 5 minutes. Add liquid, let come to a quick boil, cover and simmer over a low flame for about 20 minutes. Season and drop well-beaten egg into soup, stirring with a fork so as to form shreds. Serve accompanied by a bowl of grated cheese and one of fried bread croutons.
Cooked to Your Taste, 1945

"In mid-summer, a thick okra soup generously supplemented with rice and corn bread- proceeded with a long mint julep- and then followed by a slice of iced watermelon were happiness enough in the old days for any cotton factor or rice planter who strolled out in mid-afternoon for a heavy luncheon at 3:00 and an hour's siesta after. And today, it is considered a real meal- minus the mint julep- and a very popular one during the okra and watermelon season."
—Harriet Ross Colquitt, *The Savannah Cook Book, 1933*

OKRA SOUP

1 soup bone
4 cups cold water
4 cups okra, cut fine

2 cups tomato pulp
salt and pepper

Cover soup bone with cold water and allow to come to a boil; cook about 1 hour. Add the okra which has been cut fine and the tomato pulp. Simmer all together for 2 hours until thick. Rice is invariably served with this soup and sometimes corn and buttered beans.
The Southern Cookbook, 1939

OKRA SOUP

1 soup bone
1 pint tomatoes

2 quarts okra
salt to taste

Put soup bone into large pot with just enough water to cover it well. Boil 1 hour and add okra, which has been cut into small pieces and 1 can tomatoes. Boil 3 hours or until well blended and thick. Rice is invariably passed with soup and sometimes corn or butterbeans.
Harriet Ross Colquitt, The Savannah Cook Book, 1933

THE RITUAL OF THE BIRD'S-EYE PEPPER

"The ritual of the bird's eye pepper is still observed in the old-fashioned households where the soup comes to the table steaming in the big (soup) tureen; and the host helps it at the table. He asks each guest if he will have one or two of the little green peppers which are picked fresh right before the meal. He mashes it (or them, if the guest has a hearty palate) in the plate bowl before putting in the soup. This is so the peppers permeate the dish.

But woe be to the guest who fails to remove the innocent looking little green condiment because its trail is hot enough for the 'highest' taste and just a touch of the pepper itself is purgatory undiluted."
-Harriet Ross Colquitt, *The Savannah Cook Book, 1933*

CREOLE GOULASH

2 cans red kidney beans
1/2 pound sliced bacon
1 quart can of tomatoes
1 teaspoon baking powder
1/4 pound cheese
salt and pepper to taste

Cook the bacon crispy, then lift it from the pan. Add the kidney beans to the bacon fat. Then add the tomatoes to which baking powder has been added. Stir all together. Season to taste with salt and pepper, then put in a casserole. Cover closely, set in moderate oven and cook slowly for 1 hour. Then remove the cover and sprinkle with grated cheese, arrange the bacon strips overall and cook for 10 minutes longer. Serve in the casserole.
The Southern Cookbook, 1939

CHICKEN CREAM SOUP

3 cups chicken broth
3 Tablespoons rice
1/2 cup diced celery
2 cups hot milk

Cook the rice and celery until soft. Strain and rub through a strainer and add to the stock. Add 2 cups of hot milk, season with salt and pepper to taste. When ready to serve, sprinkle chopped parsley over the top.
The Southern Cookbook, 1939

VEGETABLE STOCK

There is practically no limit to the combinations of vegetables which can be used to make a soup. For that very reason, soup is one of the best ways for using up all the little bits of left-over, raw or cooked vegetables. There is really only one important rule to follow and that is to use only vegetable stock or water when making vegetable soups. Never use meat stocks.

Once you understand this one rule, then it is only with the imagination and ingenuity of the cook to take a basic recipe for plain, creamed, and pureed vegetable soups or bisques as mere suggestions that can be varied indefinitely; so, create!

VEGETABLE SOUP STOCK

3 to 4 cups raw vegetables (any of the following alone or in combination: asparagus ends, beet tops, broccoli leaves and stems, cauliflower leaves, mushroom stems, potato peelings, turnip tops, carrots, leeks, greens, lima beans, parsnips, peas, snap beans, turnips).

1 large or 2 small onions
1 to 1 1/2 quarts water
1 bay leaf
1 clove
1 egg white
1 Tablespoon oil or vegetable shortening
1 Tablespoon lemon juice
salt and pepper

Cut all vegetables into small pieces; chop onion. Pan the onion in hot fat until tender; add vegetables and brown 5 minutes. Add cold water, let come to a boil, season, cover, and simmer over a low flame for about 45 minutes. Strain through a sieve. Add beaten egg white and lemon juice, cover, and let come to a quick boil; strain through a fine sieve.
Cooked to Your Taste, 1945

VEGETABLE SOUPS

2 cups sliced or diced raw vegetables
4 to 6 cups vegetable stock or water
2 to 3 Tbl. butter or vegetable shortening
salt
chopped parsley or chives

Pan the vegetables in hot fat for about 5 minutes, stirring occasionally to prevent scorching. Cover with boiling water and then cover pot and simmer over a low flame for about 1 hour or until the vegetables are tender. Add salt after 20 minutes cooking. Serve sprinkled with parsley or chives.
Cooked to Your Taste, 1945

VEGETABLE SOUP

soup bone
soup bunch (seasonings)
3 or 4 small onions
5 or 6 small potatoes
1 quart tomatoes
salt and pepper to taste

Put the bone on to boil with a little water and add all the ingredients except tomatoes letting them boil for 20 minutes. After tomatoes are added, cook for 2 hours. Strain before serving.

NOTE: Rice is passed around the table in the South with vegetable soups, just as grated cheese is passed in Italy with the clear soups.
The Savannah Cook Book, 1933

PUREED VEGETABLE SOUPS AND BISQUES

2 cups cooked or pureed vegetables
2 to 2 1/2 vegetable stock or water
4 Tablespoons cream
or thin white sauce or butter sauce
salt
parsley sprigs or chopped chives

BISQUES

1/2 cup milk
1 Tablespoon flour instead of vegetable stock

Heat pureed vegetable and vegetable stock in top of double boiler. Add cream or cream sauce, beat well with rotary eggbeater (electric mixer), and heat thoroughly. Season.

If bisque is served, use milk blended with flour instead of vegetable stock.
Serve garnished with parsley or chives.
Cooked to Your Taste, 1945

CREAMED VEGETABLE SOUPS

2 cups sliced or diced raw vegetables
3 to 4 cups vegetable stock, or water
1/2 cup milk and/or cream
(sweet or sour), or thin white sauce or
butter sauce.

1 egg yolk
2 to 3 Tbl. butter or vegetable shortening
salt
chopped parsley or chives

Pan vegetables in hot fat about 5 minutes, stirring occasionally to prevent scorching. Cover with boiling liquid, cover pot and simmer over low flame about 1 hour or until vegetables are tender. Add salt after 20 minutes of cooking. Stir egg yolk into milk, then stir this gradually into soup. If cream, or white sauce, or butter sauce is used, stir constantly while adding. Bring to quick boil once. Season. Serve sprinkled with parsley or chives.
Cooked to Your Taste, 1945

"Food is our common ground, a universal experience."
-James Beard (1903-1985)

NOTES

SALADS & SALAD DRESSINGS

*"Let the salad maker be a spendthrift for oil, a miser for vinegar,
a statesman for salt, and a mad man for mixing."*
-A Spanish Proverb

The South is an ideal place for the growing of salad greens. Uncultivated as well as garden-grown greens are all valued, including crisp beautiful water cress growing next to streams and the dark green dandelions leaves found in spring. Delicious tender leaf lettuce from the vegetable garden plot is a seasonal pleasure found among the many other edible greens.

Numerous groups of food enthusiasts adhere to these varied notions about salads. There are those who say salads must be eaten *before* the main course to be enjoyed to their fullest. A similarly staunch group insists that salads offer the fitting finale to the meal and must come *after* the "meat and potatoes" and before the luscious dessert. Still a third group of food lovers firmly hold to eating salads *with* their meal. Just to further muddy the water; in recent times, different kinds of salads are now stand-alone as the principal dish and have become the entire meal, changing our eating traditions.

So, take your choice as to when to eat salads, but today, more than ever, salads are deemed to be highly desired, satisfying, delicious, and health-giving. Go for it and enjoy!

A TOUCH OF GREEN

"No salads are included in this book (The Savannah Cook Book, 1933) because they are not especially Southern, and because we agree with the French that nothing can improve the simple method of marinating with good dressing lettuce, escarole or endive, and letting it go at that. Adding anything to this is but painting the lily. Given a head of lettuce and a dash of imagination, a salad may be made from anything in the vegetable kingdom. Receipts (recipes) for these are legion."

-Harriet Ross Colquitt, The Savannah Cook Book, 1933

SPINACH SALAD

1 pound young spinach
1/2 cup light cream
1/2 cup Roquefort dressing

2 firm tomatoes
2 hard-cooked eggs

Chop cleaned raw spinach fine, put in salad bowl, and toss lightly with dressing. Garnish with alternate egg and tomato slices.
Cooked to Your Taste, 1945

SALAD DRESSING FOR SPINACH

1 teaspoon salt
1/2 teaspoon white pepper
1/2 teaspoon cayenne pepper
1/2 teaspoon celery salt
1/4 teaspoon dry mustard

2 Tablespoons vinegar
2 Tablespoons tomato juice or ketchup
1 cup salad oil
1 clove garlic, minced
1 onion (small), chopped

Shake together. Makes 1 1/2 cups

NOTE: May be used with/on other vegetables.
Margaret Ussery, The Nashville Cookbook, 1977

SPINACH SALAD WITH EGG AND BACON DRESSING

Boil 10 ounces of chopped spinach for 10 minutes in 1/2 teaspoon salt and in 1/2 cup water. Drain well. Top with the following dressing:

DRESSING

2 hard- boiled eggs chopped fine
2 strips bacon, fried crisp and crumbled
fat from the bacon

1 Tablespoon mayonnaise
1/2 teaspoon grated onion
1/2 teaspoon salt

Mix lightly with spinach and serve hot. Serves 3-4.
Satsuma Tea Room, More Fun for the Cook, 1974

WILTED SALAD

Wash and dry tender leaves of lettuce. Tear into pieces and put in a large warm bowl with sliced radishes, spring (green) onions, and crisp bits of bacon. Drizzle with seasoned warm bacon drippings and toss the salad lightly to coat all the ingredients. Some families add hot vinegar and a little sugar to the bacon drippings before tossing the salad. Others add hard cooked eggs. The dressing must be warm enough to wilt the lettuce but not cook it or make it limp.
The Nashville Cookbook, 1977

POINSETTIA SALAD

Place a lettuce leaf on a salad plate and a slice of canned pineapple in the center. Cut a pimiento into 1/2 inch strips and place one end in the center of the pineapple and letting the other end extend to the rim. Arrange the strips all around like the spokes of a wheel, make a soft paste of cream cheese moistened with French dressing and season with salt and paprika. Place a small ball of this mixture in the center of the pineapple and thus you have the effect of a poinsettia flower. Serve with French dressing.
The Southern Cookbook, 1939

ROYAL SALAD

1 small head of cabbage
1 cup shredded pineapple
1 cup chopped blanched almonds

mayonnaise
watercress or lettuce

Cut the top of the cabbage and hollow it out, leaving a shell of the outer leaves. Soak the cabbage in cold salted water for about a half hour. Drain the small pieces well and chop them. There will be around 2 cups. Mix this with the pineapple and almonds and add enough mayonnaise to moisten. Fill the shell and top with mayonnaise. Arrange on a bed of watercress or lettuce. Serves 6.
May Salley of Columbia, South Carolina, 200 Years of Charleston Cooking, 1930

DRESSING FOR COLE SLAW

2 eggs
1/2 cup sugar
1/2 teaspoon salt
pinch of cayenne

1/4 teaspoon dry mustard
1/2 cup vinegar
1 small teaspoon cornstarch
lump of butter

Mix all the ingredients and cook slowly in double boiler. Thin it with a little cream or milk. The cabbage should be shredded and plunged in iced water, then dried before mixing with the dressing.
The Savannah Cook Book, 1933

MISSISSIPPI COLE SLAW

1 cup mayonnaise
1 head solid cabbage
1 cup cold chopped ham
1 cup cold chopped lean beef *or* veal

1 green pepper
1 red pepper
1/2 chopped onion
1 egg white

Slice cabbage as for coleslaw. Mix all the ingredients together and add to the cabbage. Thin the mayonnaise with the beaten white of one egg and add to the cabbage slaw. Sugar may be added if not sweet enough.
The Southern Cookbook, 1939

COLE SLAW

1 cup sugar
1 egg

1/2 cup vinegar
1 head cabbage, chopped

Combine sugar and vinegar in a saucepan. Add beaten egg. Blend over medium heat until sugar dissolves. Remove from heat and allow to cool. Pour mixture over cabbage and stir well. Refrigerate until chilled. Dressing may be stored in refrigerator for up to one week. Serves 8.

NOTE: This is one of the first recipes my grandmother passed on to me. The sweet and sour dressing is a change from the typical mayonnaise-based dressing and even a favorite of those who don't normally like slaw.
Irene Hazelwood, Cortner Mill Restaurant cookbook, 2009

RED CABBAGE SALAD

1 pound red cabbage
4 to 6 Tbl. horseradish/mayonnaise

2 Tablespoons grated cheese,
preferably Parmesan

Shred cabbage fine, place in dry dish towel and beat with something heavy (rolling pin, wooden mallet, or milk bottle); this makes the cabbage very tender. Mix with dressing and toss lightly. Sprinkle with grated cheese and serve.
Cooked to Your Taste, 1945

HOT SLAW

3 cups shredded cabbage, green or white
1 small carrot
5 Tbl. well-seasoned French dressing
4 Tablespoons chopped nutmeats

Shred carrot. Heat the French dressing in the top of a double boiler; add cabbage, carrots and nutmeats. Blend well and heat thoroughly.
Cooked to Your Taste, 1945

BUTTERMILK SLAW

1/2 cup buttermilk
1/2 cup mayonnaise
1 1/2 Tablespoons vinegar
1/2 teaspoon prepared mustard
4 cups shredded cabbage
1 cup grated carrot
1/4 cup sugar
1/2 teaspoon celery seed
1/2 teaspoon salt
1/2 teaspoon paprika
1 teaspoon Worcestershire sauce

Blend buttermilk and mayonnaise. Add the other seasonings. Mix well. Toss with cabbage and carrots.
Satsuma Tea Room, More Fun for the Cook, 1974

BROCCOLI SLAW

10 ounces broccoli slaw
3 ounces dried cranberries
3/4 cup or less Marzetti coleslaw dressing
1 cup cashews
salt to taste (optional)

In a large mixing bowl, combine the broccoli slaw mix, cranberries, and dressing. Chill for at least 1 hour before serving. Add the cashews just before serving. You can double the recipe to fill a salad bowl.

NOTE: Everyone has a favorite go-to recipe to make and take to a pot luck dinner. This recipe is definitely in my wife's top five repertoire. -David S.
Dorothy Ball, Fruit of the Spirit, Mt Bethel United Methodist Church, Marietta, GA, 2006

CHINESE SLAW

#1 can bean sprouts
#1 can Del Monte seasoned green beans
#1 can water chestnuts, 5 ounces- sliced
#1 can tiny peas
1 1/2 cups celery, chopped thin
1 onion, cut into rings
salt and pepper to taste
Stir all together and add:
1 cup sugar
3/4 cup vinegar

Let stand over night after mixed. The longer it stands, the crisper it will be. Be sure to keep it in the refrigerator.
Satsuma Tea Room, More Fun for the Cook, 1974

EGGS – STUFFED, DRESSED, OR DEVILED?

A distinctive food that conjures up images of Southern cuisine and Southern hospitality is the *Deviled Egg* or as many true hard-core Southerners call them, *Dressed Eggs*. One would be hard-pressed to attend any church "dinner on the grounds", attend a summer picnic or patio luncheon, attend any type of potluck gathering among friends or family, and not find *Dressed Eggs* or *Deviled Eggs* or *Stuffed Eggs* being served. It is inevitable. This is almost the unwritten law of the land, or at least of the South. This is a food that when served, screams to the recipient, "YOU ARE SPECIAL!"

STUFFED EGGS

6 hard-cooked eggs
2 Tablespoons sweet pickle juice

1 Tablespoon butter
salt and pepper

Cut the hard-cooked eggs in half lengthwise, take out all the yolks keeping the whites carefully in shape. Mash the yolks, add the butter and pickle juice and season to taste with salt and pepper. Put this yolk mixture back into the whites of the eggs; set in a buttered pan and bake for 15 minutes in a slow oven (300 F) to brown the uneven points of the egg yolks. These stuffed eggs can be eaten warm or cold.

NOTE: The recipe may be varied in many ways. Indeed, it is most convenient since anything spicy may be used. For instance, mayonnaise can be substituted for the butter, and mustard for the sweet pickle juice. A little caviar is also good in the mixture. The secret of the success of this recipe is that the eggs are baked after they are stuffed.
Helen Woodward, 200 years of Charleston Cooking, 1930

DRESSED EGGS

Go to the hen house and gather a dozen eggs. If you discover a setting nest of unknown age, put the eggs in a bowl of water. Eggs that float are not fresh. Eggs two or three days old are best for this recipe since fresh eggs are harder to peel. Hard boil your eggs by placing them in a large saucepan and covering them with cold water. Put the pan over medium heat and bring the water to a boiling point. Reduce the heat to below the boiling point and let the water simmer. For large eggs that were at room temperature let them simmer for 15 minutes. For smaller eggs, reduce the simmering time. For eggs taken out of the refrigerator, increase simmering time by 2 minutes. Plunge the finished eggs at once into cold water to arrest further cooking and prevent the yolks from discoloring. Peel the shells from the eggs and cut the eggs in half length-wise. Remove the yolks carefully so as not to damage the whites. Crush the yolks without packing the yolks together, loose. Stir in mayonnaise and relish. Add salt and pepper to taste. Stuff the empty whites with yolk mixture and sprinkle each egg with a dash of paprika. Chill, but remove from refrigerator 1/2 hour before serving for improved flavor and texture.

NOTE: My mom, Polly, learned to dress eggs from her grandmother, Granny Reid. She took them to an all-day church and dinner on the grounds. She was so proud, when many people there asked her how to make the eggs. I guess I need to also teach my granddaughter how to dress eggs.
Marilyn Harrison Holland, Miss Lizzie's Heirlooms, 2009

DRESSED EGGS

12 hard-boiled eggs	1/3 cup sweet pickle relish
5 teaspoons mayonnaise	salt, pepper, paprika

Peel shells from the eggs and cut in half, length-wise. Remove yolk from the white and put into bowl. Use whisk to break yolks into small pieces. Stir in mayonnaise and relish. Add salt and black pepper to taste. Stuff the white halves with this yolk mixture and sprinkle each with a dash of paprika. Serve chilled.

NOTE: We are always in trouble with some of our guests, if dressed eggs aren't served on our buffet. They come to the kitchen and ask, "Where are the dressed eggs?"
Ethel Leverette, Cortner Mill Restaurant cookbook, 2009

DEVILED EGGS

4 hard-cooked eggs	1/2 teaspoon dry mustard
1/4 teaspoon salt	1/4 teaspoon cayenne pepper
1 tablespoon melted butter	1 teaspoon vinegar

Take the eggs when cold, remove the shell and cut each in two, lengthwise. Remove the yolks and set the whites aside. Rub the yolks smooth and mix thoroughly with the rest of the ingredients and create balls the size of the original yolk. Place a ball (spoonful) into each half white of the egg and send them to the table, plated on a bed of crisp lettuce leaves.
The Settlement Cookbook, 1940

HOT DEVILED EGGS (Modern take on a traditional recipe)

12 eggs, hardboiled	1 teaspoon salt
3 Tablespoons mayonnaise	1/2 teaspoon dried mustard
1/2 cup crumbled cooked bacon	dash of chili powder
1/2 stick butter	2 cups milk
1 Tablespoon flour	8 ounces Cheez Whiz

Cook eggs and peel. Cut eggs in half lengthwise. Remove the yolks and mix with mayonnaise. Stir in crumbled bacon bits and stuff this mixture back into the shells. Place in a 13 x 9 x 2 inch pan sprayed with Pam. Melt the butter on the stove and mix in flour, salt, mustard, chili powder, milk and Cheez Whiz. Cook over low heat, stirring frequently. Cover the eggs with mixture. Bake at 350 degrees until the mixture bubbles.

NOTE: Great for brunch with an unusual take on the traditional deviled egg.
Mae Smith, Fruit of the Spirit, Mt. Bethel United Methodist Church, Marietta, GA

POTATO SALAD

6 medium potatoes
1 pint Old Fashioned Boiled Dressing
Salt, pepper, paprika

12 hard cooked eggs, peeled and sliced
1 large sweet onion, scraped or minced
leaf lettuce

Cook the potatoes in skins; drain. Cool potatoes just enough to handle easily; peel; slice thinly. Spread dressing (page 107) over the bottom of the bowl. Fill bowl with alternating layers of sliced potato, spread of salad dressing, sliced eggs, onion, and a sprinkling of salt and pepper. Finish with carefully arranged layer of egg slices and sprinkling of paprika. Do not stir. Chill. Just before serving, tuck lettuce around eggs of bowl. 6 to 8 servings.
Easy-on-the-Cook Book, 1960

TOMATO SALAD

6 tomatoes
4 hard-cooked eggs

mayonnaise dressing
lettuce

Select firm tomatoes, dip into boiling water, drain and slip off the skins. Set in the refrigerator to chill. Chop the hard-cooked eggs in large pieces and mix with the mayonnaise dressing. Hollow out the centers of the tomatoes, fill with the egg stuffing and serve on lettuce; topping each tomato with a spoon of mayonnaise.

NOTE: We made this salad and many more tomato salads with different salad fillings at *Satsuma*. We would start each lunch with beau-coup tomatoes; blanched and peeled, and ready to serve as needed. Because we were so busy during lunch, there really wasn't time to "hollow out" each tomato for the fillings. We made eight partial cuts in the tomatoes.
Helen Rhett Simons, 200 years of Charleston Cooking, 1930

TOMATO SALAD DRESSING

Into a quart jar put the following ingredients in the order given:
1 can of tomato soup, 3/4 cup of vinegar, 1/2 cup of oil, 1/4 cup of sugar, a Tablespoon of Worcestershire Sauce, and 3 Tablespoons of grated onion.

Mix together 1 teaspoon of salt, 1 scant teaspoon mustard, and 1 teaspoon paprika. Add all this to ingredients in jar. Seal, shake well, and put in refrigerator. Will keep indefinitely.
The Savannah Cook Book, 1933

STUFFED TOMATO SALAD

Chill 4 large or 8 small firm tomatoes. Cut thin slice at blossom end and scoop out the pulp, leaving the firm shell. Salt the inside lightly. Fill with stuffing and top with an olive or sprig of parsley.

NOTE: Suggestions for stuffing could be *Cottage Cheese Stuffing, Pea Salad, Cole Slaw Stuffing, Potato Salad Stuffing, etc.* Just about anything you can imagine. Use the scooped-out pulp in soups, stews, or sauces.
Cooked to Your Taste, 1945

TOMATO AND CHEESE ASPIC

1 small onion, chopped
1/4 green pepper, chopped
2 whole cloves
1/4 teaspoon salt
1/4 teaspoon Worcestershire sauce
1 sprig parsley, chopped
1 teaspoon sugar
pepper to taste
2 cups stewed tomatoes
1 cake cream cheese
1 1/2 Tablespoons gelatin
1/4 cup water

Add the onion, green pepper, parsley and seasonings to the tomatoes and cook together for 5 minutes. Soak the gelatin in the cold water and dissolve it in the hot liquid. Then add the cream cheese, breaking it up and stirring until it is almost dissolved. Turn the mixture into a mold and let it stand in the refrigerator until firm. Serve on lettuce with mayonnaise dressing. Serves 6.
Mrs. Rhett, 200 Years of Charleston Cooking, 1930

COPPER PENNIES

5 cups carrots, sliced
1 medium onion, sliced into rings
1 green pepper, in rings
10 ounces condensed tomato soup
1 teaspoon dry mustard
1 teaspoon Worcestershire sauce
1 teaspoon salt
1 teaspoon black pepper
1 teaspoon horseradish
1 cup sugar
3/4 cup vinegar
1/2 cup vegetable oil

Cook carrots until tender and drain. Blanche onion and green pepper and set aside. Combine remaining ingredients and pour over carrot mixture. Keep refrigerated. This dish is better if made a day before serving.
Cortner Mill Restaurant cookbook, 2009

THREE BEAN SALAD

#2 can Blue Lake beans
#2 can wax beans
#2 can kidney beans
1 red Italian onion, sliced thin
1 green pepper, slivered
1/2 cup salad oil
2/3 cup vinegar
1/2 teaspoon Worcestershire sauce
1/2 cup sugar
1 teaspoon salt
1/8 teaspoon pepper

Mix together the beans, onion, and pepper. Mix the other ingredients and pour over the beans. Let stand at least overnight in refrigerator. Longer is even better. Salad will keep for some time if refrigerated. It may even be frozen. Serves 8-10.

NOTE: You can serve in lettuce cups if desired. This salad is ideal for picnics, but it is equally good with an indoor menu whenever the meat served would be enhanced by the tart contrast of the salad. This recipe can be used with Blue Lake beans without the other beans.
Satsuma Tea Room, Fun for the Cook, 1968

SPICY BEET SALAD

2 cups cooked diced beets
2 hard-cooked
5-6 black olives
3 Tablespoons chopped nut meats
1 Tablespoon caraway seed
1 Tablespoon grated horseradish
1 teaspoon sugar or honey
lemon juice

Mix beets with lemon juice. Core and shred unpeeled apple, mix well with caraway seed, horseradish, and honey. Mix with beets and nut meats. Garnish with sliced eggs and sliced olives.
Cooked to Your Taste, 1945

TROPICAL FRUIT SALAD DRESSING

½ cup orange juice
2 Tablespoons sugar
2 Tablespoons honey
¼ cup lemon juice
¼ teaspoon salt
½ cup salad oil

Combine juices. Add sugar, salt, and honey; stir until dissolved. Blend in oil. Chill. Beat before serving. Serve on any variety of fruits. Makes 1 ¼ cups.
Easy -on-the Cook Book, 1960

MARINATED SLICED TOMATOES

4 large, ripe tomatoes
1/4 cup salad oil
1 Tablespoon lemon juice
1/2 teaspoon minced garlic
1/2 teaspoon salt
1/2 teaspoon oregano

Peel and slice the tomatoes (each tomato should yield 4 to 5 slices). Combine remaining ingredients and mix. Pour over tomatoes. Cover and chill thoroughly. Thin cucumber slices may be added. Serves 8 to 10.

NOTE: Summer vegetable growing is just around the corner.
Betty Forsythe, The Nashville Cookbook, 1977

ARTICHOKE SALAD

1 pint cold, boiled Jerusalem artichokes
1 teaspoon vinegar
1 teaspoon chopped parsley
French dressing

Boil artichokes. When cold, peel and cut into quarters. Mix and serve very cold.

NOTE: Today, canned artichokes can be used.
The Picayune Creole Cook Book, 1922

GREEN PEPPER SALAD

1 tomato
1 large onion
2 green peppers
French dressing, plain

Slice tomato, onion, and green peppers very thin. Arrange them on a dish, putting a large layer of tomatoes with alternate layers of onions, green pepper, and tomatoes mixed. Dress with French dressing, either before bringing to the table or at the table.

NOTE: This is a great Creole family salad and a very beautiful one.
Picayune Creole Cook Book, 1922

TOMATO ASPIC

1 quart tomato juice
3 Tablespoons sugar
2 ribs (stalks) of celery
1 onion, cut up
juice of 1 lemon
salt and pepper to taste
2 Tablespoons gelatin in
1/2 cup cold water

Soak gelatin in cold water. Combine other ingredients. Cook slowly for 10-15 minutes. Pour over gelatin. Stir until dissolved. Strain and pour into 8 molds for 8 Servings.
Satsuma Tea Room, More Fun for the Cook, 1974

BUTTER BEAN SALAD

4 cups butter beans, cooked
1/2 cup celery, chopped
2 cups green onions, chopped
2 cups hard-boiled eggs, chopped
1/4 cup green pepper, chopped
2 ounces pimiento, diced
2 Tablespoons fresh parsley, chopped
1/2 cup mayonnaise
lettuce leaves

Combine ingredients and toss gently. Cover and refrigerate several hours. Serve chilled salad on lettuce leaf. Serves 6.
Cortner Mill Restaurant cookbook, 2009

SNAP OR WAX BEAN SALAD

1 pound cooked snap or wax beans
1/2 cup Roquefort dressing
or sharp mayonnaise dressing
red pepper and onion juice
1 green pepper

Cut the beans into bite size pieces. Marinate in dressing for at least 30 minutes. Chop green pepper fine and season with pepper and onion juice. Garnish the beans with green pepper and serve.
Cooked to Your Taste, 1945

CUCUMBER AND ONIONS (Salad or vegetable)

6 cucumbers, medium	4 Tablespoons sugar
1 red onion	1/2 cup white vinegar
2 teaspoons salt	1/2 teaspoon black pepper

Slice cucumber and onions. Separate onion slices into rings and toss with the cucumbers. Mix the remaining ingredients in saucepan and cook over medium heat until sugar dissolves. Pour over cucumbers and onions. Cover and refrigerate four hours before serving. Will hold a week in refrigerator.

NOTE: Instead of a red onion, use yellow onions. Just a different flavor which is not as strong, could work well in the spring and summer onion growing season. Vidalia onions are amazing in this dish.
Isabel Woodlee, Cortner Mill Restaurant cookbook, 2009

FLORIDA GUSPACHY SALAD

4 tomatoes	salt, pepper, paprika
1 cucumber	1/4 teaspoon dry mustard
2 green peppers	1 teaspoon sugar
1 tablespoon onion, finely chopped	1 pilot cracker (hard tack)
1/2 teaspoon Worcestershire sauce	2 Tablespoons sour cream
1/2 teaspoon A-1 sauce	

Peel cucumber and tomatoes and slice thin. Also slice the green pepper very thin. Drain off their juices. Soak the cracker in cold water for about 3 minutes and squeeze dry. Place a layer of the vegetable mixture in a bowl and sprinkle with the chopped onion and cracker. Spread with sour cream to which all the above spices have been added. Repeat until all the ingredients are used. Place on ice for about 3 hours; serve on crisp lettuce leaves.
The Southern Cookbook, 1939

MARINATED ASPARAGUS

2 pounds fresh asparagus	2 Tablespoon garlic, minced
2/3 cup white wine vinegar	1/2 teaspoon black pepper
3/4 cup salad/olive oil	1 teaspoon salt

Trim and lightly steam asparagus. Combine remaining ingredients and pour over asparagus. Refrigerate overnight. Drain marinade and serve over lettuce leaves. Serves 6.
Jim Long, Cortner Mill Restaurant cookbook, 2009

ASPARAUS SALAD

1 can asparagus tips	1 Tablespoon gelatin	juice of 1 lemon
2 Tablespoons butter	2 Tablespoons cold water	1 cup cream, whipped
2 Tablespoons flour	4 egg yolks	

Make a sauce of the butter, flour and liquid drained from the asparagus. (There should be one cup of liquid. Add enough water to make up the water if there is not one cup in the can.) Pour the sauce over the beaten egg yolks, return to the fire and cook 1 minute, stirring constantly. Soak the gelatin in the cold water and add to the hot sauce, stirring until the gelatin is dissolved. When the mixture is cool, add the lemon juice, whipped cream and salt and pepper to taste. Line a mold with a layer of asparagus, pour over half with sauce, then add another layer of asparagus and then the rest of the sauce. This will serve 8. Garnish with mayonnaise and strips of pimiento.

NOTE: Delicious as this salad is when made with canned asparagus, we feel it would be even better if steamed fresh asparagus is used.
Mrs. F.S. Munsell of Columbia, South Carolina, 200 Years of Charleston Cooking, 1930

ASPARAGUS VINAIGRETTE SALAD

1 can asparagus tips	deviled eggs
1/2 cup French dressing	rings of Italian onions
3 Tablespoons pickle relish	strips of pimiento
1 teaspoon finely chopped parsley	lettuce

Drain asparagus. Put in shallow dish. Pour French dressing mixed with pickle relish and parsley on top. Let chill at least an hour. To serve, arrange about 6 tips on lettuce, pour sauce on. Garnish with deviled eggs, pimiento and onions.
Satsuma Tea Room, Fun for the Cook, 1968

AVOCADO SALAD

2 3-ounce packages of lime gelatin	2 avocados- mashed
2 cups boiling water	1 cup crushed pineapple
1 1/2 cups cold water	6 ounces cream cheese, beaten smooth

Dissolve gelatin in boiling water. Add the cold water. Cool and chill until thick but not set. Whip until light and fold in other ingredients. Place in molds and refrigerate. Serves 6-8.
Satsuma Tea Room, Fun for the Cook, 1968

ALLIGATOR PEAR (AVOCADO) SALAD

Chill 3 alligator pears (avocado). Peel and cut in halves and remove stones; then cut in cubes. Marinate in French dressing. Serve on crisp lettuce. Sprinkle with chopped almonds.
The Southern Cookbook, 1939

GUACAMOLE SALAD

2 large ripe avocados
1/2 teaspoon salt
1/4 teaspoon garlic powder
2 Tablespoons finely chopped onion

2 Tablespoons chili sauce
or hot tomato sauce
1 Tablespoon lemon juice
1 Tablespoon salad dressing

Peel avocados and mash well. Mix well with remaining ingredients. Serve on lettuce leaves with corn chips.

NOTE: May also be used as a dip. Cottage cheese may also be added as an extender for dip.
Kathy Shaw, The Nashville Cookbook, 1977

RAW BEET AND APPLE SALAD

2 to 3 young raw beets
1 medium tart apple

1 Tablespoon light cream
1 teaspoon caraway seeds

pinch of sugar
lemon juice

Scrape the beets and shred on fine shredder. Core and shred the apple; mix lightly with beets, cream, and seasoning and serve.
Cooked to Your Taste, 1945

WALDORF SALAD

3 stalks celery
3 medium tart apples
8 ripe olives
1/2 cup chopped nutmeats
1/2 cup mayonnaise

3 Tablespoons fruit juice (lemon, grapefruit, or pineapple)
1 Tablespoon grated horseradish
salt, red pepper, and nutmeg to taste
lettuce leaves

Quarter and core apples and slice crosswise. Do not peel. Sprinkle with a little juice. Chop the celery fine, and mix with the apples, mayonnaise, nutmeats and seasoning. Add the horseradish and mix well. Chill for at least 30 minutes. Serve garnished with olives in lettuce cups.
Cooked to Your Taste, 1945

MOLDED WALDORF SALAD (Apple, Cherry, Celery, & Nut Salad)

1 Tablespoon gelatin
1/3 cup sugar

1/2 teaspoon salt
1 1/2 cups water
1/2 cup celery, diced

1/4 cup vinegar
2 cups tart apples, diced
1/4 cup pecans, chopped

Mix gelatin, sugar, and salt thoroughly in small saucepan. Add 1/2 cup of the water. Stir over low heat until gelatin is dissolved. Remove from heat. Stir in remaining water and vinegar. Chill until thickened. Fold in celery, apples, and nuts. Chill until firm. Serves 6.
Satsuma Tea Room, More Fun for the Cook, 1974

CINNAMON APPLE SALAD

2 cups sugar
1 cup water
8 medium sized firm apples
1 cup cinnamon drops (candy)

Peel the apples, leaving a little of the peel around the stem and core. Put the apples in an open pan on top of the stove; pour over them the water, sugar, cinnamon drops. Cook slowly, turning the apples frequently in the syrup; until done. Cool and place on lettuce leaves, filling the centers of the apples with nuts and cream cheese or with cream cheese and mayonnaise.

NOTE: The apples are delicious as baked apples with the middle filled with jellied juice in which they were cooked. If you wish a less deep rose color, use less of the cinnamon drops.
Mrs. Cornelius Youmans Reamer, 200 Years of Charleston Cooking, 1930

APPLE CHIP SALAD

6 ounces apple flavor gelatin
2 cups hot water
2 cups apple cider
2 cups diced, unpeeled apples
3/4 cup coarsely broken nuts

Empty gelatin into bowl. Add water; stir to dissolve; add cider. Chill until mixture thickens slightly. Fold in apples and nuts; pour into 8 x 8 x 2 inch pan. Makes 8 servings.
Farm Journal's Country Cook Book, 1959

SEPTEMBER APPLE SALAD

2 cups diced unpeeled apples
2 cups diced peeled cucumbers
1/2 teaspoon salt
1/4 cup lemon juice
1/2 cup salad dressing (Miracle Whip)
1/4 cup chopped nuts (optional)
lettuce

Toss apples and cucumbers with salt; sprinkle with lemon juice. Mix in the salad dressing and nuts. Serve chilled on lettuce. Makes six servings.

NOTE: Great way to pair off apples and cucumbers in a wonderful dish.
Farm Journal's Country Cook Book, 1959

BLACK CHERRY WINE MOLD SALAD

2 lbs. canned dark sweet cherries, pitted
6 ounces cherry flavored gelatin
1 cup red wine
water

Drain the cherries, saving the syrup. Add enough water to make 2 1/2 cups liquid. Bring to a boil. Add to the gelatin, stirring until gelatin is dissolved. Add wine. Chill and when slightly thickened, add the cherries. Mold. Serves 8.

NOTE: An outstanding cherry salad. Serve with our Sour Cream Dressing, page 108.
Satsuma Tea Room, Fun for the Cook, 1968

CRANBERRY GELATIN SALAD

2 cups raw cranberries	1 1/2 cups sugar	2 cups hot water
3 apples, cored unpeeled	1/2 to 1 cup nuts chopped	1/2 cup sugar
1 orange unpeeled	2 pkgs. raspberry gelatin	lettuce leaves, dark green

Grind cranberries, apples, and orange. Add 1 1/2 cups sugar and let stand for 1 ½ hours. Add nuts. To the two packages of gelatin, add the hot water and the 1/2 cup sugar. Let cool until the substance starts to gel. Add to the ground mixture. Blend well and pour into a 9-inch square pan. Serve on lettuce leaves. Yields 9 to 12 servings.

NOTE: I think it looks and tastes better with a touch of mayonnaise on the side.
Dr. Shirley Clark, University of Illinois, Home Economics Faculty Favorites, 1965

JELLIED STRAWBERRY SALAD

6 ounces strawberry Jell-O	#2 can crushed pineapple
1 1/4 cups, hot water	3 mashed bananas
1 pint frozen strawberries	1 cup sour cream

Pour boiling water on Jell-O. Cool, add other ingredients. Put 1/2 in pan and jell. Spread sour cream over it. Pour other half on top. This is really a salad/dessert, but very good. 10 to 12 servings. The salad will keep several days in the refrigerator.
Satsuma Tea Room, More Fun for the Cook, 1974

MOLDED CRANBERRY RELISH SALAD

3 ounces cherry Jell-O	1 1/2 cups cranberry relish
1 1/2 cups boiling water	

Dissolve Jell-O in boiling water. Cool, stir in relish. Chill until set

NOTE: Excellent and so easy to make, plus so versatile. Serves 6.
Satsuma Tea Room, More Fun for the Cook, 1974

FROZEN FRUIT SALAD WITH TOPPING

8 ounces cream cheese	2 bananas
3/4 cup sugar	1/2 cup pecans
16 ounces strawberries or cherries	9 ounces Cool Whip
20 ounces crushed pineapple, drained	

Beat cream cheese and sugar well. Add remaining ingredients and blend well. Pour into a 9 x 13 dish and freeze. Can be frozen in muffin tin for individual servings.

NOTE: Stiff whipped cream can be substituted for the Cool Whip. It will give a richer flavor.
Jeanette Hazelwood, Cortner Mill Restaurant cookbook, 2009

FROZEN FRUIT SALAD

2 firm bananas (sliced round)
2 Tablespoons lemon juice
1 can crushed pineapple, undrained
3/4 cup sugar
1 pint sour cream

1/2 cup maraschino cherries, chopped
1/2 teaspoon salt
1/2 pecans, chopped
cupcake liners

Toss bananas in lemon juice. Mix crushed pineapple and sugar together until blended well. Then combine bananas, pineapple mixture and the rest of the ingredients together. Line muffin pan with cupcake liners. Pour mixture into each of the liners. Then freeze. When serving, remove the paper liner and place each frozen fruit cup upside down on a lettuce leaf and a dollop of homemade mayonnaise on the side. Serves 12.
Sandra Skinner, Fruit of the Spirit, Mt. Bethel United Methodist Church, Marietta, GA

FROZEN CREAM CHEESE AND CRANBERRY SALAD

6 ounces cream cheese
1 cup cream, whipped
1/2 cup mayonnaise

½ cup blanched almonds
1 small can grated pineapple with juice
1 can whole cranberry sauce

Soften cheese- beat and add whipped cream and mayonnaise. Break up the cranberry sauce. Combine ingredients. Freeze. Serves 6-8.

NOTE: Also, very good made with our cranberry relish.
Satsuma Tea Room, More Fun for the Cook, 1974

FROZEN CRANBERRY SALAD

6 ounces cream cheese, softened
2 Tablespoons sugar
2 Tablespoons mayonnaise
16 oz. jellied whole berry cranberry sauce
(At *Satsuma* we used our homemade
cranberry relish.)
8 ounces crushed pineapple, drained

1/2 cup pecans, chopped
1 cup whipping cream
1/2 cup powdered sugar, sifted
1 teaspoon vanilla
lettuce leaves
fresh cranberries (optional)
mint sprigs (optional)

Combine first 3 ingredients, stirring until smooth. Stir in cranberry sauce, pineapple and pecans. Beat the whipping cream until foamy; gradually add powdered sugar, beating until soft peaks form. Stir in vanilla. Fold whip cream mixture into cranberry mixture; spoon into an 8-inch square dish. Cover and freeze until firm, or freeze in individual tins (lightly oiled) Cut into squares and serve on lettuce leaves. Garnish, if desired, with fresh cranberries or fresh mint sprigs. Makes 9 servings.

NOTE: *So, Refreshing!*
Nellie Reaves, Fruit of the Spirit, Mt. Bethel United Methodist Church, Marietta, GA, 2006

APPLE-GRAPEFRUIT SALAD

3 ounces lemon flavor gelatin
3 1/2 cups boiling water
1 apple
3 ounces lime flavor gelatin

1 cup diced unpeeled apples
1/2 cup coarsely chopped nuts
20 ounces grapefruit sections, well-drained

Dissolve lemon gelatin in 1 1/2 cups water. Cool. Pour about 1/2 cup into 2-quart mold; let set. Chill remaining lemon gelatin until syrupy. Core the apple; cut into narrow wedges and arrange in pattern, skin side down, on top of the gelatin in bottom of the mold. Pour remaining lemon gelatin into mold. Let set until firm. Dissolve lime gelatin in remaining 2 cups water. Cool until syrupy. Add diced apples, nuts and grapefruit. Spoon over set layer in mold. Chill until firm. Unmold on platter; surround with crisp salad greens; serve with mayonnaise. Makes 10 to 12 servings.
Farm Journal's Country Cook Book, 1959

JELIED GRAPEFRUIT SALAD

2 1/2 Tablespoons unflavored gelatin
1/2 cup ice water
1 cup boiling water
6 Tablespoons sugar
1/2 teaspoon salt

1 1/2 cups grapefruit juice
2 Tablespoons lemon juice
2 pimientos
1 cup grapefruit sections

Soak gelatin in cold water. Dissolve in boiling water. Add salt, sugar, and juices. Cut pimiento into strips and arrange with grapefruit sections in bottom of mold. Pour in gelatin mixture to cover. Chill. Add another layer of grapefruit and pimento. Turn out onto lettuce leaf and serve with mayonnaise and tiny cream cheese ball.

NOTE: When we make this recipe, we like to make the color pale green.
Satsuma Tea Room, Fun for the Cook, 1968

GRAPEFRUIT ASPIC WITH ALMONDS

2 grapefruit
2 ounces chopped blanched almonds
1 package of lemon gelatin

1 cup grapefruit juice
3/4 cup boiling water
1 Tablespoon sugar

Cut the pulp of the grapefruit out, dice, and drain. Add the chopped almonds to the grapefruit. Dissolve the gelatin and sugar in the boiling water and add the grapefruit juice. When this is cool and beginning to thicken, add the grapefruit and almond mixture. Pour into a mold and put in the refrigerator to harden.

NOTE: Serve as a salad with mayonnaise dressing or as a dessert with whipped cream. This recipe makes 6 servings and is a favorite dish for Sunday night supper in Charleston.
William Deas, 200 years of Charleston Cooking, 1930

NUT SALAD

This salad is decidedly kin to our old friend, the Waldorf salad. The boiled dressing, however, is very good and gives a somewhat different taste to the apple, nut and celery combination. For the salad use equal parts of celery, apples, and nuts; having chopped them coarsely. Walnuts may be used, but pecans give a better flavor.

NUT SALAD DRESSING

1 teaspoon ground mustard	2 egg yolks
1/2 teaspoon salt	1/2 cup vinegar
1 teaspoon cornstarch	1/4 cup milk
1 teaspoon sugar	

Mix the dry ingredients together thoroughly and beat in the eggs. Then add in the vinegar and cook in the upper part of a double boiler until it begins to thicken. Then stir in the milk. Keep stirring until thick, remove from the fire and allow to cool. Mix with the celery, apples and nuts and serve on lettuce. If one cup of each of the chopped ingredients is used, then 6 will be served.
Miss May Salley of Columbia, South Carolina, 200 Years of Charleston Cooking, 1930

MOLDED PINEAPPLE AND BANANA SALAD

2 small packages lemon Jell-O	1 Tablespoon butter, melted
1 cup hot water	1 Tablespoon flour
1 cup cold water	1 cup heavy cream, whipped
2 cups 7-Up or ginger ale	1/2 cup sugar
20 ounces crushed pineapple, drained	1 cup pineapple juice
1 cup miniature marshmallows	1 egg, beaten
2 bananas, mashed	1 cup heavy cream, whipped

Dissolve Jell-O in hot water. Add cold water and 7-Up. Chill until slightly thickened. Add pineapple, marshmallows and bananas. Pour into a 10 1/2 x 15 1/2 x 2-inch pan. Chill until firm. Blend butter, flour, sugar, pineapple juice and egg. Cook until thickened. Cool. Fold cream into mixture. Spread over Jell-O. Chill. Yields 24 servings.
Specialty of the Spice Box, University of Illinois, Home Economics Faculty Favorites, 1965

OVERNIGHT PINEAPPLE SALAD

2 eggs	#2 can sliced pineapple,
1/3 cup lemon juice	drained and diced
40 large marshmallows	1 pint heavy cream, whipped
1 cup pecans, chopped	lettuce leaves

Beat eggs thoroughly. Gradually stir in lemon juice. Cook until thickened. Add marshmallows. Heat slowly until marshmallows are melted. Cool. Blend in pineapple, nuts, and cream. Pour into 8 1/2 x 13 x 2-inch pan or 18 (1/2 cup) individual molds. Serve on lettuce. Yields 16 to 18 servings.
Mrs. Frances La Font, University of Illinois, Home Economics Faculty Favorites, 1965

ORANGE SALAD

6 fine Louisiana oranges
3/4 pound of powdered sugar

Peel the oranges whole, removing the rind entirely down to the tips of the skin end. Cut in slices and cut out the seeds. Pile the oranges in a neat heap in a dish. Sprinkle with powdered sugar. Boil some sugar into a syrup using about 1/2 pound to 1 pound oranges. When cold, pour it over the fruit.
The Picayune Creole Cook Book, 1922

ORANGE SHERBET SALAD

2 cups orange juice
2 packages orange gelatin
1 pint orange sherbet
5 1/2 ounces Mandarin oranges, drained
18 ounces crushed pineapple, drained
lettuce leaves

Heat orange juice to simmering temperature. Dissolve the gelatin in the orange juice. Cool slightly and add sherbet broken into small pieces. Blend until sherbet dissolves. Add pineapple and oranges. This can be completed in 1 operation. No need to wait for gelatin to begin to set before adding fruit. Rinse a 9 inch square pan with water and pour in the salad mixture. Chill. Serve on lettuce. Yields 9 servings.
Mrs. Trudy Gobbel, University of Illinois, Home Economics Faculty Favorites, 1965

FROZEN CREAM CHEESE AND CRANBERRY SALAD

6 ounces cream cheese
1 cup cream, whipped
1/2 cup mayonnaise
½ cup blanched almonds
1 small can grated pineapple with juice
1 can whole cranberry sauce

Soften cheese- beat and add whipped cream and mayonnaise. Break up the cranberry sauce. Combine ingredients. Freeze. Serves 6-8.

NOTE: Also, very good made with our cranberry relish.
Satsuma Tea Room, More Fun for the Cook, 1974

MANDARIN ORANGE COCONUT SALAD

1 small package miniature marshmallows
1/2 pint sour cream
1 can Mandarin oranges, drained
1 small can pineapple tidbits, drained
1/2 can shredded dry coconut

Mix coconut, marshmallows, and well-drained fruit. Fold in the sour cream and mold. Serves 6-8.

NOTE: You may like more sugar and it can be added. This salad is so easy to do and surprisingly good.
Satsuma Tea Room, Fun for the Cook, 1968

APRICOT NECTAR SALAD

2 cups apricot nectar and pineapple juice
1 package lemon Jell-O, 3 ounces
1 small can, crushed pineapple (1 cup)

Dissolve Jell-O in hot apricot liquid. Chill until nearly firm. Add drained crushed pineapple. Add can of mandarin oranges if desired. When firm, frost with cream cheese to which a little apricot nectar has been added.
Satsuma Tea Room, More Fun for the Cook, 1974

SPECIAL COTTAGE CHEESE AND OTHER SECRETS

This recipe was one of our "secret recipes," one that we just didn't reveal; not to anyone. Some of the Satsuma recipes we just didn't share. Some recipes were withheld from the public so the customer would continue to come eat with us and just wonder, "How is this made?", "What is that unique flavor?" Special Cottage Cheese was one of those recipes. I was not in the know as to the composition of the recipe. I understand in this day of constant information overload and instant gratification, all our "unrevealed recipes" sounds selfish and bizarre, but a little secrecy in food always makes the dish more mysterious and enjoyable.

You either love cottage cheese or not. We offered this particular dish at our restaurant and named it Special Cottage Cheese. We served it as a sandwich with a garnish. We also served it as a salad, placing a large scoop of the Special Cottage Cheese atop an iceberg lettuce leaf with a dash of our homemade mayonnaise, along with a garnish on the side. We also served a large scoop of the Special Cottage Cheese within a whole, peeled, fresh tomato, again on lettuce and accompanied with our homemade mayonnaise. It was one of our most requested and successful of our sandwiches and salads. It was just that GOOD. You could eat healthy cottage cheese and not be turned off by the unremarkable nature and taste of regular, plain cottage cheese by ordering our special cottage cheese.

This was a recipe that was developed for the restaurant. I never was privy to exactly how this dish was made. Since all our salad dressings, our salads, and even our mayonnaise were made from scratch our salad cooks made everything associated with the salads, the sandwiches, and the dressings for the restaurant. I roughly knew the ingredients included in this dish, but I did not know the proportions since I had never put the dish together completely. I discovered this hidden recipe written on a sheet of paper folded and tucked between the pages of a 510-page cookbook, dated 1952. The recipe was in my great-aunt's handwriting. Apparently, by trial and error, she had created this formula and boy did it ever become a hit with our daily lunch customers.

I dedicate this recipe to Ann Humbracht, a family friend. She had arrived in Nashville during the early 1970's. Ann ate lunch in our restaurant often and ordered the Special Cottage Cheese consistently. She asked and asked and asked me and my wife for the recipe. I never knew it, so I couldn't give it to her. With what I consider to be a truly historic discovery of the Special Cottage Cheese written recipe in my great-aunt's handwriting tucked among the pages of an old cookbook, I can now say with all honesty, "Here you go Ann, ENJOY!

-David Smith, Satsuma Tea Room

Fast forward 50 years. It was the policy at our Cortner Mill Restaurant to give a recipe to guests when they asked for it. I've never been a believer in secret recipes. Given a few tries and I'll figure out what ingredients and methods were in your secret recipe or I'll be so close, few would know the difference. But the biggest reason for sharing our recipes was accepting the compliment of a dish well-cooked and knowing guests would spread the word about us when they made the dish and shared with their friends where they got the recipe. We didn't even leave out a key ingredient so you couldn't get the dish right as you made it. I contributed a lot of recipes from my Cortner Mill and Miss Lizzie's cookbooks as we put together this cookbook. I told David Smith, when he proposed we work together on our cookbook project, "You can publish my recipes! Besides, a lot of them came from you and Satsuma anyway."

-*David Hazelwood, Cortner Mill Restaurant*

SPECIAL COTTAGE CHEESE

2 cups chopped pecans or walnuts
3 large onions, chopped
2- 5 pounds tubs cottage cheese
2 cups mayonnaise
1 Tablespoon paprika
1 Tablespoon salt

Miss Arlene Ziegler, Satsuma Tea Room, 1955

NOTE: To modify this recipe for personal use, decide how much cottage cheese you want to use and adjust percentages of the other ingredients to the cheese quantity you are using.

COTTAGE CHEESE DRESING

1/2 cup cottage cheese, sieved
1 Tablespoon honey
1/4 cup orange juice
1/2 teaspoon grated lemon rind
1 Tablespoon lemon juice
1/2 teaspoon salt
dash of paprika

Mix cottage cheese with honey and orange juice. Add remaining ingredients. Mix well. Chill before serving. Makes 3/4 cup.

NOTE: For fruit and melon salads, a combination of honey and cottage cheese.
Farm Journal's Country Cook Book, 1959

PINEAPPLE CREAM CHEESE DATE SALAD

1 pound cream cheese
1 cup nuts
1/2 pint cream, whipped
1 1/2 cups crushed pineapple
1 cup maple syrup

Mix cheese and syrup. Add other ingredients. Mix well. Store in refrigerator overnight. Serves 8-10. Can be kept several days.
Satsuma Tea Room, More Fun for the Cook, 1974

CREAM CHEESE SALAD

2 cakes cream cheese
1 cup thin cream
1/4 cup chopped almonds
1/2 teaspoon salt

1 teaspoon tarragon vinegar
1 cup whipped cream
2 Tablespoons gelatin
1/4 cup milk

Warm the thin cream and dissolve the cream cheese in it. Add the chopped almonds, salt and vinegar. Soak the gelatin in the milk and heat over steam, stirring until the gelatin is dissolved. Add to the first mixture and fold in the whipped cream. Mold in a ring mold and when firm, turn out onto lettuce leaves. This salad is especially good when fruit salad is heaped in the center of the ring.

NOTE: William's cream cheese salads are delicious, but they are very rich and the portions served should be small.
William Deas, 200 years of Charleston Cooking, 1930

LIME, PINEAPPLE AND CREAM CHEESE SALAD

1 package lime Jell-O
1 3/4 cups pineapple juice or water
3 Tablespoons lemon juice
1/2 cup whipping cream
1/2 cup cream cheese (3 ounce package)

2 Tablespoons mayonnaise
1/2 cup drained crushed pineapple
1/2 teaspoon salt
1/2 cup slivered blanched almonds

Drain pineapple of the juice and add water to make 1 3/4 cups. Dissolve Jell-O in boiling water or fruit juice. Add lemon juice. Beat cream cheese smooth. Whip in cooled gelatin. Fold in whipped cream and other ingredients. Pour into individual molds and let stand until set. Serves 8-10.
Satsuma Tea Room, Fun for the Cook, 1968

ALMOND CREAM CHEESE DRESSING

3 ounces cream cheese
juice of 1/2 lemon
1/2 cup mayonnaise

2/3 cup whipping cream, whipped
1/3 cup toasted slivered almonds
1/6 pound marshmallows

Beat cream cheese smooth. Blend with lemon juice. Add mayonnaise and fold in the whipped cream. Add marshmallows and almonds.

NOTE: Extra good on congealed salads.
Satsuma Tea Room, Fun for the Cook, 1968

CRAB SALAD WITH MAYONNAISE

1 pint of crab meat (hard shell)
mayonnaise
hard-boiled eggs
garnishes

Boil and pick crabs sufficient to give a pint of meat. Season well with salt and pepper. Place in a dish on a bed of crisp lettuce leaves, spreading over them the mayonnaise sauce. Garnish nicely with hard boiled eggs, sliced beets and tips of celery.
The Picayune Creole Cook Book, 1922

DRESSING FOR CRAB SALAD

Use one part Worcestershire sauce to two parts mayonnaise for a distinctive dressing for crab salad.
The Savannah Cook Book, 1933

SHRIMP SALAD LOUIS

1 cup mayonnaise
1/4 cup French dressing
1/4 cup catsup
1 teaspoon horseradish
1 teaspoon Worcestershire sauce
1 teaspoon salt
Tabasco to taste
1 pound cleaned cooked shrimp

Combine all the ingredients except the shrimp. Arrange the cooked shrimp on shredded lettuce. Serve with Shrimp Louis Dressing. Serves 4.
Satsuma Tea Room, Fun for the Cook, 1968

SHRIMP LOUIS DRESSING

If you add chopped celery and pimientos to the mayonnaise you use for shrimp salad, it will taste like lobster.
The Savannah Cook Book, 1933

CHICKEN SALAD

3 cups diced chicken
1 1/2 stalks diced celery
1 1/2 cups seedless grapes, cut in half
3/4 cup almonds, cut up, toasted
3 Tablespoons lemon juice
1 cup mayonnaise
1/4 cup cream
1 1/2 teaspoons salt
1 teaspoon mustard

Combine chicken, celery, and lemon juice. Chill- add other ingredients. Serves 8-10.

NOTE: It is better to make this dish the day it is ready to be used.
Satsuma Tea Room, More Fun for the Cook, 1974

SALMON SALAD

1 cup fine chopped cabbage and marinated in tarragon vinegar with ice until the cabbage is crisp. Add the flaked salmon to the well-drained cabbage and mix with mayonnaise. Serve topped with mayonnaise and garnish with a dash of paprika. Yields 4 small servings.
Emma Salley, recipe from the Pirate House Inn and Restaurant as recounted in
200 Years of Charleston Cooking, 1930

JELLIED CHICKEN

Soak 2 Tablespoons of gelatin in a little cold water and dissolve in a small quantity of hot water. Stir into this 1/2 cup mayonnaise, 1/2 cup of whipped cream, 1/3 cup of minced celery, 3/4 Tablespoon lemon juice, 1 1/2 cups of minced chicken, and 1/4 cup of stuffed olives, chopped fine. Transfer into small molds and set aside to congeal. Turn out onto thick slices of tomato.
The Savannah Cook Book, 1933

JELLIED MELANGE

2 Tablespoons gelatin	1 cup chopped cooked chicken
1/4 cup cold water	1/2 cup chopped cooked ham
4 cups hot chicken broth	1/2 cup chopped celery
2 Tablespoons onion juice	1 pimiento, chopped fine

Soak the gelatin in the cold water for 5 minutes. Add to the hot chicken broth with the onion juice until it dissolves. Set aside to cool; when it starts to congeal, stir in the other ingredients and put in small molds. Chill. Serve on lettuce garnished with mayonnaise and parsley.
The Southern Cookbook, 1939

RUSSIAN SANDWICHES

1/2 cup chopped tomatoes	salt and pepper to taste
1/2 cup chopped celery	mayonnaise
1/2 cup chopped olives	1 Tablespoon minced onions

Mix the tomatoes, celery, olives and onions together and season to taste with salt and pepper. Add enough mayonnaise to make it smooth enough to spread, and then spread between layers of whole wheat bread.
Emma Salley, recipe from the Pirate House Inn and Restaurant as recounted in 200 Years of Charleston Cooking, 1930

CHICKEN AND FRUIT SALAD

3 cups white meat of chicken from a boiled fowl	1 orange 1 apple 1 cup mayonnaise	15 large grapes 15 salted almonds 1 banana

Cut chicken into small pieces. Remove seeds from the orange sections and cut in half. Cut grapes in half, removing seeds. Split the almonds. Slice banana. Add the mayonnaise and mix all the ingredients slowly but thoroughly. Serve chilled on a lettuce leaf.
The Southern Cookbook, 1939

SHRIMP SALAD WITH PEAS

1 can of shrimp or 1 cup of fresh shrimp 1/2 cup diced celery	2 hard cooked eggs 1/2 cup of peas

This may be served as a cold plate for five with 1 Tablespoon each of celery, chopped eggs and peas placed around the Tablespoon of shrimp; in which case you would need almost a whole cup of celery. Or you may mix all the ingredients lightly together with mayonnaise, cream, and seasoning and serve as salad on crisp lettuce.

NOTE: This was a popular salad in our household and so easy to make. The key ingredients that make this salad happen are the celery and the peas. I suggest frozen baby peas. See the pattern? It's the crunch that makes this dish work.
The Southern Cookbook, 1939

> "The old order changeth; yes, but we ought to be able to preserve beauty and dignity and the sense of service and manners, things that have come very slowly, and can be made to vanish very fast if we aren't set on preserving them somehow."
> -Galsworthy (1867-1933)

SALAD DRESSINGS

SALAD DRESSING (A very old recipe)

3 hard-cooked eggs
1/4 teaspoon salt
1 teaspoon mustard
1 Tablespoon vinegar
3 Tablespoons oil

Separate the yolks and the whites of the hard-cooked eggs and mash the yolks. Add the salt and mustard to the yolks and mix well. Then add the oil and vinegar and stir until thoroughly mixed.
Cut up the whites of the eggs finely and add to the dressing. If this dressing is served with lettuce, it makes almost an egg salad. The dressing is also delightful with finely chopped cabbage. This recipe makes about 1 cup dressing.

NOTE: "OLD" is the note in the margin of the book in which this recipe is originally written and after tasting this dressing, we are very glad that it has been preserved for our later use.
Mrs. Shackelford, 200 Years of Charleston Cooking, 1930

CREAM DRESSING

1 cup light cream
2 Tablespoons oil
1 teaspoon lemon juice
2 pearl onions
salt, dry mustard and red pepper, to taste
chopped parsley

Chop the onion and parsley very fine. Blend cream with oil, add onion and parsley and season. Mix well and chill for 20 minutes. Add lemon juice and blend well before serving.
Cooked to Your Taste, 1945

BUTTERMILK DRESSING

3 Tablespoons flour
3/4 teaspoon salt
1/4 teaspoon dry mustard
dash cayenne pepper
3 Tablespoons sugar
3/4 cup buttermilk
1 egg, slightly beaten
1 Tablespoon butter or margarine
2 Tablespoons lemon juice
1/4 cup orange juice

Combine flour, salt, mustard, pepper and sugar. Gradually stir in buttermilk and egg. Cook over hot water, stirring constantly until thickened. Remove from heat. Stir in butter, lemon, and orange juices. Chill. Makes 1 1/4 cups.
Easy-on-the-Cookbook, 1960

SIMPLE SALAD DRESSING

1/2 cup oil
juice of 1 small lemon
salt, celery salt, red pepper and basil to taste

Mix all the ingredients and chill before using.
Cooked to Your Taste, 1945

OLD FASHIONED BOILED DRESSING

7 Tablespoons sugar	1/8 teaspoon pepper	3/4 cup vinegar
2 Tablespoons flour	1/8 teaspoon paprika	1 Tablespoon butter
1 Tbl. dry mustard	3 eggs or 6 egg yolks	
1 teaspoon salt	3/4 cup water	

Blend dry ingredients (sift if lumpy) in a double boiler or heavy saucepan. Add eggs. Mix until smooth. Add water; stir in vinegar. Cook over low heat, stirring constantly, until thickened. Stir in butter. Cool before serving. Makes 3 ½ cups.

NOTE: The secret of superior flavor in potato salad is in using boiled dressing and putting together while the potatoes are warm. They absorb the flavor of the dressing as they cool. Retail salad dressing, like Miracle Whip, can be used instead of the Old-Fashioned Boiled Dressing.
Easy-on-the-Cook Book, 1960

SOUR CREAM DRESSING

1/2 teaspoon mustard	1 Tablespoon flour	1/4 cup water
2 Tablespoons sugar	1 Tablespoon butter	1 cup sour cream
dash of paprika	1/4 cup vinegar	1 egg yolk

Mix the seasonings, add the flour and sugar, add the vinegar and water, cook in a double boiler until thickened, stirring constantly. Add the egg yolk and butter, cook a few minutes longer. Cool. Whip the sour cream and add to the above mixture.

NOTE: Serve on lettuce, dandelion salad, asparagus, cucumbers, or fish. A little dash of Tabasco mixed never hurts either.
The Southern Cookbook, 1939

RICHMOND SOUR CREAM DRESSING

3 Tablespoons vinegar	1/2 pint sour cream	1 teaspoon salt
1 1/2 Tablespoons sugar	dash of paprika	1 teaspoon dry mustard

Partly whip the cream, mix together the other ingredients and slowly add to the whipping cream and then beat until stiff.

NOTE: Serve on tomatoes. This dressing is really good on chopped cabbage too.
The Southern Cookbook, 1939

SOUR CREAM DRESSING

1 cup sour cream	1/4 teaspoon salt	4 marshmallows- cut very fine
1 Tablespoon lemon juice	1/2 teaspoon sugar	

Mix all the ingredients together- chill. Makes 1 1/3 cups.

NOTE: Especially good on Black Cherry Wine Mold.
Satsuma Tea Room, Fun for the Cook, 1968

SOUR CREAM FRUIT SALAD DRESSING

1 teaspoon grated orange peel	1/2 teaspoon dry mustard
2 Tablespoons orange juice	1 cup dairy sour cream
2 Tablespoons lemon juice	dash salt
1 Tablespoon honey	dash pepper

Fold orange peel and juice, lemon juice, honey and dry mustard into sour cream. Season with salt and pepper. Chill. Serve on fruit salad. Makes 1 cup.
Easy-on-the-Cook Book, 1960

LOW CALORIE SALAD DRESSING

1 cup buttermilk	red and black pepper to taste
1/2 teaspoon dry mustard	lemon juice or vinegar
1/2 teaspoon salt	

Mix all the ingredients and chill before using.
Cooked to Your Taste, 1945

PENNSYLVANIA DUTCH HOT BACON DRESSING

6 slices bacon	dash of pepper
1/4 cup minced onion	1/2 teaspoon sugar
3/4 cup vinegar	1/2 teaspoon prepared mustard
1/4 teaspoon salt, or to taste	2 hard cooked eggs, diced

Cut bacon into small pieces with scissors. Put into skillet. Cook slowly until crisp. Strain to remove bacon; add onion to bacon fat and sauté until golden in color. Add vinegar, seasonings, and prepared mustard; bring to a boil. Cool slightly and pour over the salad. Sprinkle crisp bacon pieces on top and diced eggs overall. Use with lettuce or any green salad. Makes about 1 cup.

NOTE: For added zest to any meal, serve this peppy, tart bacon dressing on potato salad. This dressing complements dandelion greens, chicory, or romaine. This dressing makes those mealtime salads totally delightful in the winter.
What to Cook for Company, 1953

RUSSIAN DRESSING

1 cup mayonnaise
2 Tablespoons finely diced celery
2 Tablespoons diced green pepper
2 Tablespoons pickle relish

1 Tablespoon chopped pimiento
2 Tablespoons chili sauce
1 Tablespoon catsup

Mix all ingredients together.

NOTE: Very good on a head lettuce salad.
Satsuma Tea Room, Fun for the Cook, 1968

LEMONADE DRESSING

2 eggs
2 Tablespoons sugar

1 cup heavy cream, whipped
6 ounces lemonade concentrate

Beat eggs until lemon colored. Stir in sugar and lemonade concentrate. Cook over low heat, stirring constantly, until thickened. Cool. Fold in whipped cream. Chill. Makes 2 cups.

NOTE: A good dressing for fresh mixed fruits.
Margaret Putman, The Nashville Cookbook, 1977

A DELICIOUS FRENCH DRESSING FOR FRUIT SALAD OR TOMATOES

To 1/2 cup of confectioner's sugar, add two teaspoons of paprika, 4 Tablespoons of lemon juice, 2 teaspoons salt, and stir in slowly 1 cup of olive oil. This all should be almost the consistency of mayonnaise.
The Savannah Cook Book, 1933

OLIVE OIL AND WINE VINEGAR (French Dressing)

2 Tablespoons minced celery
1 Tablespoon finely chopped parsley
1 Tablespoons chopped chives or onions
1 clove garlic

1 teaspoon salt
1/8 teaspoon pepper
3 Tablespoons wine vinegar
3/4 cup olive oil

Mix all ingredients except the oil. Let stand 10 minutes before adding the oil. Mix well. This is an excellent dressing that we often send out for parties we are catering.
Satsuma Tea Room, Fun for the Cook, 1968

FRENCH DRESSING

1 cup oil
1/3 cup vinegar
dash of pepper, red or black

½ teaspoon salt
1 teaspoon prepared mustard

Mix vinegar, salt, mustard, and pepper well; add oil and beat until smooth.
Cooked to Your Taste, 1945

FRENCH DRESSING

1 cup olive oil or salad oil	dash pepper
1/2 cup lemon juice or vinegar	dash cayenne pepper
1/2 teaspoon salt	1 teaspoon paprika

Combine and beat or shake thoroughly before using. Add 1 teaspoon sugar if desired. Serve with heads of lettuce or tossed salad. Makes 1 1/2 cups.
What to Cook for Company, 1953

FRENCH DRESSING

4 Tablespoons pure olive oil	1/4 teaspoon salt
in which a garlic clove has been soaked	1/8 teaspoon white pepper
1 1/8 Tablespoons tarragon vinegar	

Mix the salt and pepper together; add some of the oil and stir. Add vinegar and then remaining oil.
The Southern Cookbook, 1939

FRENCH DRESSING VARIATIONS

The French Dressing above combined with:
- Horseradish
- Roquefort or bleu cheese
- Worcestershire sauce
- Finely chopped hard-cooked eggs, olives, parsley, pimento, onion
- Finely chopped red and green peppers, onion juice

What to Cook for Company, 1953

CREOLE FRENCH DRESSING

3 Tablespoons of the best olive oil	yolk of hard-boiled egg
1 Tablespoon of vinegar	salt and pepper to taste
1 teaspoon mustard	

Blend the oil and salt and pepper in the manner above indicated, and then add these to the mustard, drop by drop, alternating with the vinegar. When well blended add the well mashed yolk of a hard-boiled egg. Stir well, and serve with lettuce, celery or potato salad.
The Picayune Creole Cook Book, 1922

THOUSAND ISLAND DRESSING

1 cup homemade mayonnaise
1/4 cup chili sauce
2 hard-cooked eggs, chopped
2 Tablespoons chopped pimiento
1 teaspoon grated onion
1/4 teaspoon Worcestershire sauce
1 Tablespoon chopped stuffed olives

Combine all the above ingredients. Makes about 1 1/2 cups.

NOTE: Serve on head lettuce or tomato salad.
What to Cook for Company, 1953

BLEU CHEESE DRESSING

4 ounces bleu cheese
1 cup mayonnaise
1/4 cup commercial sour cream
1/4 cup salad oil
1/4 cup buttermilk
1 Tablespoon white vinegar
1/4 teaspoon salt
1 teaspoon garlic powder

Put bleu cheese into mixing bowl. Add mayonnaise and salad oil. Blend. Add sour cream. Blend. Add buttermilk, vinegar, salt and garlic powder. Blend. Store in refrigerator 24 hours before serving. Makes 2 cups.

NOTE: This dressing is delightfully different and so tasty.
Mary Jo Work, The Nashville Cookbook, 1977

HONEY MUSTARD DRESSING

1 cup mayonnaise
1/4 cup Dijon mustard
1/4 cup cider vinegar
1/4 cup honey
2 Tablespoons parsley, minced
3 Tablespoons onion, minced
1 cup salad oil

Whisk together the first 4 ingredients. Whisk in the parsley and minced onion. Whisk in oil until thoroughly incorporated. Stores almost indefinitely in refrigerator. Yields 3 cups.
Bill Hall, Cortner Mill Restaurant cookbook, 2009

POPPY SEED DRESSING

1/2 cup sugar
1 teaspoon dry mustard
1 teaspoon salt
1/3 cup vinegar
1 1/2 Tablespoons onion juice
1 cup oil
1 1/2 Tablespoons poppy seed

Mix sugar, mustard, salt, and vinegar together. Add onion juice and mix well. Gradually add oil, beating constantly. Add poppy seed last. Makes about 2 cups.
What to Cook for Company, 1953

POPPY SEED DRESSING

1/2 cup vegetable oil
1/2 cup sugar
1 teaspoon onion juice
1 teaspoon poppy seed

1/2 cup white vinegar
1 teaspoon salt
3 Tablespoons lemon juice

Mix all the ingredients together and serve. Makes 1 3/4 cups.

NOTE: Ideal as a stand-alone dressing, but is the perfect complement to fresh fruit.
Mary McMillon, The Nashville Cookbook, 1977

HONEY POPPY SEED DRESSING

1/2 cup honey
1/2 teaspoon salt

1/3 cup wine vinegar
1 cup salad oil

1 Tablespoon poppy seed

Mix honey, salt, and vinegar. Add oil gradually, beating constantly. Add poppy seed, pour into container. Cover and refrigerate. Shake vigorously before using. Makes 2 cups.

NOTE: Delicious served with fresh fruit or vegetable salads.
Kay Waters, The Nashville Cookbook, 19777

HOMEMADE MAYONNAISE

1 teaspoon salt
1/4 teaspoon paprika
dash of cayenne pepper
1 teaspoon prepared mustard

2 egg yolks
2 Tablespoons vinegar
2 cups salad oil
2 Tablespoons lemon juice

Mix the dry ingredients and prepared mustard; add the egg yolks and beat well. Beat vinegar into this egg yolk mixture. Add oil, very slowly at first, beating with a rotary beater, until 1/2 cup has been added. Add 1 Tablespoon of the lemon juice and beat well. Continue to add remaining oil and lemon juice until all has been used. Makes 2 cups.
What to Cook for Company, 1953

MAYONNAISE VARIATIONS

Homemade Mayonnaise (above) combined with:
- Capers, shallot, parsley, water cress
- Chili sauce, pimento, green peppers
- Chutney
- Olives, pickles
- Onion, chili sauce, tarragon vinegar
- Pimientos, chives, chili sauce, tarragon vinegar
- Roquefort or bleu cheese, Worcestershire sauce
- Tomato catsup and green peppers
- Whipped cream

What to Cook for Company, 1953

PLAIN MAYONNAISE

1 cup oil
1 egg yolk
1 teaspoon lemon juice or good vinegar

salt, red pepper, dry mustard, marjoram, to taste

Beat egg yolk with rotary eggbeater. Add the oil drop by drop beating constantly. When the mayonnaise becomes very thick, add lemon juice or vinegar a drop at a time and continue beating. Season and blend without beating.

NOTE: 1 egg yolk has to be used for making mayonnaise no matter what smaller quantity is prepared.
Cooked to Your Taste, 1945

MAYONNAISE DRESSING

2 hard-cooked yolks of egg
1 raw yolk of egg
1/2 teaspoon salt (scant)
1/2 Tablespoon vinegar (large)

juice of 1/2 lemon
1/2 cup olive oil
paprika

Mash and work smooth the hard-cooked yolks of egg; stir in with a Tablespoon the raw egg yolk and mustard; work smooth. Add the oil by the Tablespoon and when half of the oil has been used, add vinegar and lemon juice, working them in very slowly. Add salt and paprika and slowly work in the remaining oil. If a greater quantity of mayonnaise is desired, continue to add oil, lemon juice, and vinegar until the original quantity is almost doubled. Use only a Tablespoon in working this dressing.

NOTE: *Satsuma Tea Room* made its own mayonnaise and we made lots of it. This recipe is very close to being spot-on to the mayonnaise we made.
The Southern Cookbook, 1939

BASIL MAYONNAISE

1 cup mayonnaise
1/2 cup sour cream
3 Tbl. fresh basil leaf, finely chopped

2 Tablespoons lemon juice, strained
1 teaspoon lemon zest, grated

Blend all the ingredients and let stand for 30 minutes. Takes 5 minutes to mix.
Steve Gunning, Fruit of the Spirit, Mt. Bethel United Methodist Church, Marietta, GA

CELERY SEED DRESSING

1 cup sugar
1 cup vinegar
1/4 teaspoon salt
1/4 teaspoon dry mustard
1 teaspoon paprika
1 Tablespoon celery seed
2 Tablespoons chopped onion
2 cups oil

Mix sugar, vinegar, mustard and onions. Boil 5 minutes. Add oil, celery seed, and paprika. Chill.

NOTE: Good on fruit salad or vegetable salad.
Satsuma Tea Room, Fun for the Cook, 1968

HONEY FRUIT SALAD DRESSING

1 cup strained honey
1 1/2 Tablespoons flour
1 teaspoon salt
1 teaspoon dry mustard
1 teaspoon celery seed
1 1/4 teaspoons paprika
1/3 cup vinegar or lemon juice
1 cup oil

Put honey in double boiler (for less sweet dressing use 3/4 cup honey). Mix flour, salt, mustard, celery seed and paprika with vinegar until smooth. Add to honey and stir until thick and well cooked. Cool; then beat in oil gradually until well blended; keep refrigerated, will not sugar or separate. Drizzle over fruit you have selected and placed on crisp lettuce.

NOTE: Perfect dressing to enhance all fruits and melons, grapefruit sections, pineapple chunks, pear halves, peaches and maraschino cherries, Bing cherries, grapefruit, banana, orange, apricot, pear, tangerine, tomato wedge, cantaloupe, peaches. Get the idea- this dressing goes great with any fruit!
Farm Journal's Country Cook Book, 1959

BLENDER SALAD DRESSING

1 clove garlic, minced
4 spring onions, chopped (tops also)
1 cup white wine vinegar
3 cups salad oil
1 teaspoon salt
3/4 cup sugar
1 teaspoon dry mustard

Mix garlic and onion with wine vinegar. Cover and let stand for 1 hour. When time is up, place other ingredients in blender and add vinegar mixture. Blend at high speed until thickened and foamy. Serve on tossed salad. Keeps several days stored in refrigerator. Makes 4 1/2 cups.
Ruth Gebhardt, The Nashville Cookbook, 1977

AVOCADO SALAD DRESSING

1 avocado, ripe but firm	2 Tablespoons lemon juice
1/2 cup mayonnaise	1/2 cup orange juice
1 Tablespoon sugar	1/4 teaspoon salt

Peel the avocado, halve and discard pit. Press the avocado through sieve. Add the remaining ingredients. Beat with a rotary beater. Makes 1 1/2 cups.
Farm Journal's Country Cookbook, 1959

SAVORY DRESSING

1/3 cup bleu cheese, mashed	1 cup dairy sour cream
8 ounce package cream cheese	1 teaspoon Worcestershire sauce
1 clove garlic, minced or crushed (optional)	1 teaspoon salt
	2 teaspoons lemon juice

Blend in bleu cheese, cream cheese; stir in sour cream. Add the remaining ingredients and blend well. Chill. Store in covered jar in cold place. Makes about 2 cups.

NOTE: Serve this dressing with garden-fresh vegetables such as carrot sticks, celery, cauliflower flowerets, etc.
Farm Journal's Country Cookbook, 1959

CURRY DRESSING FOR ENDIVE

Mix 1/4 teaspoon salt, 1 teaspoon of curry powder, with 1 Tablespoon of vinegar and stir in 1/4 cup of olive oil.
The Savannah Cook Book, 1933

"He who eats another man's food, will have his own food eaten by others."
-Swahili Proverb

VEGETABLES

"It is hard to imagine a civilization without onions."
-Julia Child (1912-2004)

Meats, potatoes, and pastry constituted the major diet components of Southerners and for that matter, Americans in general. It has only really been since the mid 1900's that the importance of maintaining a diverse balance in one's diet with fruits and vegetables, and not just potatoes at every meal, undertook a much greater and significant importance to the Southern eating habits. The importance of this shift in thinking created the need to make vegetables and vegetable dishes more appetizing for continuous and regular consumption and to conserve the vegetables and fruits nutritive values for Southern diets. The days of just cooking vegetables with a piece of hog meat fat were fast coming to an end.

Garden-fresh vegetables are among the top joys of country cooking and eating. From the time the first delicate green asparagus stalks and strawberry-red rhubarb shoots announce Spring, until pumpkins become a sign of Halloween and also become thick, spicy pies for Thanksgiving, there is an ever-changing succession of delicious fresh vegetables from the garden to the table. An abundant harvest of fresh, year-round vegetables is to be had from the end of the last springtime frost to the beginning of the first autumn frost; from A to Z, asparagus to zucchini.

Bill Neal observes in his book, *Southern Cooking*, "Whatever the source, the variety of fresh vegetables on the Southern table is staggering. Any one meal may present fried okra, corn, butter beans, sweet potatoes, sliced tomatoes, cucumbers and onions, coleslaw, cantaloupe, etc. Such abundance often eclipses any meat served; by mid-summer all vegetable meals (with biscuits and corn bread) are common. By the time the pickled beets, green tomato relish, pepper relishes, bread-and-butter pickles are out, the meal becomes a celebration of endless combinations, textures, and flavors. This is of course the hallmark of Southern cooking." Of the seasons Neal writes, "Before the days of freon, so many foods signaled such a particular time of year that they were symbols of the seasons more reliable than any calendar. Even today asparagus heralds spring more surely than any number of robins; blackberries mean July with hot weather and chiggers. Persimmons avenge themselves on those who try to jump into fall. And when the months of cooler weather-the 'R" months- return, so does the oyster."

OKRA

Northerners do not always like the gelatinous qualities of okra, but in Charleston this is a popular summer dish. The following is a favorite method of preparing this vegetable.

1 quart tender okra	1 teaspoon salt	1 Tablespoon butter
1/2 Tbl. lemon juice	pepper to taste	

Wash the okra well in cold water. Put in a saucepan with one teaspoon of salt in the water and cook for 1/2 hour. Take from the pot, season with pepper or lemon juice. Add the butter and serve hot as you would string beans or green peas with the meat course.
200 Years of Charleston Cooking, 1930

*"You don't have to cook fancy or complicated masterpieces;
Just good food from fresh ingredients."*
-Julia Child (1912-2009)

TO COOK OKRA

Wash well and trim stem end, leaving enough of the pod to keep the juices in so that the mucilage does not come out. Cover with boiling water and boil gently until tender. When half done, add a little salt. When ready to serve, drain, pour into a hot dish and add melted butter sufficient to season. Lemon juice or vinegar can be added if desired.
The Southern Cook Book, 1939

OKRA

3 cups (3 to 4 inch) okra pods	3 medium tomatoes
3 Tablespoons margarine	1/2 teaspoon salt
2 medium onions sliced	pepper to taste

Choose tender pods, wash thoroughly, remove stems. Melt margarine in skillet, add sliced onions. Cut okra in 1/4 inch slices onto top of onion. Cover and cook on low heat for 8 to 10 minutes. Slide onion and okra to one side of skillet, add tomato slices on the other side. Cover and cook until the okra is tender. Gently fold vegetables together. Season and serve at once so as to preserve the green color of the okra. Serves 4 to 6.
Satsuma Tea Room, Easy on the Cook-Garden Vegetables, 1975

FRIED OKRA

Select small, tender pods. Boil until tender, drain, season with salt and pepper, roll in egg, then in crushed cracker crumbs. Fry in deep hot fat.
The Southern Cook Book, 1939

FRIED OKRA AND POTATOES

2 cups fresh okra	1/2 cup fat	dash of salt and pepper
1 cup diced raw potatoes	1/4 cup cornmeal	(to taste)

Combine okra and potatoes. Sprinkle with salt and pepper and cornmeal. Fry in hot fat until brown and tender.

NOTE: One of our waitresses at Satsuma said her mother and grandmother always cooked this meal. She passed the recipe onto us. We also really like it.
Satsuma Tea Room, More Fun for the Cook, 1974

GREENS

Enslaved people would collect and boil various kinds of leafy plants, such as collards, kale, the tops of beets and turnips, or wild weeds like dandelions. In some cases, these enslaved people boiled greens that were characteristic to the Native American diets such as a marsh marigold and milkweed. Enslaved people would also flavor the food by boiling a piece of pork fat or bacon with the vegetables. This is because the field hands received such poor cuts of meat, their rations of meat were more ideally used for the seasoning rather than the meal itself.

POT LIKKER

The William and Mary Quarterly 53.1 (1996), 96.) quantified, "Wasting nothing, slaves saved and enjoyed the 'potlikker', or the water that the vegetables and greens had been boiled in, to gain additional vitamins". Cornbread, then and now, was a popular accessory to greens and was often used to soak up, "sop up", the juice.

POT LIKKER

In 3 quarts of cold water, put a half pound piece of salt pork and place on fire to boil for 45 minutes. Wash young turnip greens in several waters and clean them well. Put them in pot with pork and let boil for another hour. Drain the water from the greens and meat; chop the greens rather fine and season well with salt and pepper. Place the greens on a hot dish and on the top place slices of pork; pour over the greens and meat about 1 1/2 cups of the water in which the greens were cooked ("pot likker"). Cornmeal dodgers are frequently served along with this dish and are arranged around the greens.

NOTE: "Pot Likker" was made famous to the country as a whole by the late Senator Huey P. Long during the Great Depression.
The Southern Cook Book, 1939

SOUTHERN TURNIP GREENS

about 3 pounds of turnip greens
1/4 pound of "boiling meat" or "hog jowl"
salt to taste
pod of dried red or cayenne pepper

3 large and peeled onions (both are optional, although I highly recommend their use)

This recipe will work with any other typical Southern greens, mixed or substituted Carefully wash and pick over the greens by removing tough portions and stems. Bring seasoning meat of choice to a boil in enough water to cover greens. Cook at a low boil until green are tender (about 45 to 50 minutes). It is very difficult to overcook the greens. They become more tender the more you cook them. Stir often. Season to taste. Drain and serve hot with slices of hard cooked eggs and corn bread/pone. I have many customers who also request vinegar to have as a condiment for their greens. This is really a personal taste and not part of the recipe.

NOTE: Mustard greens, kale, collards, and also pole beans may be prepared as above. There can also be a mixture of the different types of greens.
Faye House, The Nashville Cookbook, 1977

BAKED KALE WITH POTATOES

1 1/2 pounds kale
4 medium potatoes
2 to 3 cups vegetable stock, or water
grated cheese, if desired

1 bay leaf
1 Tablespoon chopped parsley
salt and black pepper, to taste

Blanch kale and chop coarsely; peel potatoes and cut into halves or quarters. Barely cover kale and potatoes with liquid, add parsley and bay leaf. Cover and simmer for 10 minutes. Remove bay leaf, season, stir well, cover, and simmer until vegetables are tender (10 to 15 minutes). Serve sprinkled with cheese.
Cooked to Your Taste, 1945

GREENS OMELET

2 cups cooked greens (about 2 pounds, any greens or variety of greens will work)
1 egg

3 to 4 Tbl. cream or evaporated milk
2 Tablespoons butter or bacon fat
salt, pepper, and mace to taste

Mix greens, egg, milk and seasoning into smooth batter. Cook like omelet in frying pan in hot fat. Serve immediately.
Cooked to Your Taste, 1945

A NEW YEAR'S DAY TRADITION

Certain vegetables and recipes have taken on an almost "ceremonial importance", with a combination of the heritage and tradition within individual families and within the South in general. A perfect example is the black-eyed pea which will traditionally be found served on New Year's Day, because as the legend has it, eating black-eyed peas on New Year's will bring good luck to all who consume the peas for the rest of the year. Needless to say, my meal of choice every New Year's Day is black eyed peas or Hopping John (black eyed peas and rice), collard or turnip greens, and of course hot, buttered cornbread. Tradition!

HOPPING JOHN

1 cup dried black-eyed peas
4 cups water
2 teaspoons salt

1 cup raw rice
4 slices of bacon, fried
with 1 medium onion chopped

Boil peas in salted water until tender (1 1/2 hours). Add rice, bacon grease, and onion. Put in double boiler or vehicle that won't allow rice to stick and cook rice until done, about 1 hour. Crumble bacon and mix with the rice.
Makes 8 servings.

NOTE: In her *The Savannah Cook Book*, 1933, Harriot Ross Colquitt recounts that "As children, it was our custom, when the word went around that we were having Hopping John for dinner, to gather in the dining-room, and as the dish was brought on, to hop around the table before sitting down to the feast."
Satsuma Tea Room, More Fun for the Cook, 1974

BLACK EYED PEAS

First Day: Cover about 2 pounds of ham shank (include the skin and bone) and 1/4 to 1/2 pound smoked hog jowl with cold water in a 4-quart pot and boil gently for 2 hours or until the meat comes off the bone easily. Chill overnight

Second Day: Skim off most of the hardened fat. Discard the fat, skin, and bones, reserving the liquid. Add dried, and washed black-eyed peas (removing the brown ones, pebbles, etc.) and soak them overnight. Use 2 pounds of peas to 4 quarts of water.

Third Day: For each 2 pounds of black-eyed peas add:
2 large onions, diced
1 large green pepper, diced
2 teaspoons dry mustard
1 teaspoon salt
1/2 teaspoon black pepper

Bring to a rapid boil, cover, and simmer 3 hours on low heat, stirring frequently. The secret of the taste lies in soaking the peas in the ham flavored cooking liquid.

NOTE: The recipe dates from the 19th century. This same cooking method and other alternatives of cooking black-eyed peas flourish into our present-day. The many, wide-ranging ways to cook the peas are as plentiful as the stars in the sky, and there is no wrong or right way to perform this task. I relate this recipe from the past at this point more to illustrate the ritual, the reverence that goes into the cooking of the black-eyed pea. The "white bean" (Great Northern beans) approaches a very close second to the black-eyed pea with the reverence paid to the preparing of that vegetable (basically prepared same way).

SWEET POTATOES AND YAMS

As with corn, the "accident" of sweet potatoes in our Southern food was the result of a merger of the African and Native American traditions. The sweet potato was indigenous to the Americas, but then it also bore quite a striking resemblance to the yam of West Africa.

"Samuel Stoney in *Black Genesis*, traces the root of the word yam to the African word, "unyamo, "which has dropped the first and last syllable. He also says that the Negros called the white, or Irish, potato "buckra yam," buckra in Gullah meaning white man." *The Savannah Cook Book, 1933*

It was this resemblance that enabled the enslaved people brought to the new lands to easily adapt the cooking and growing techniques of these cousins, the yam and the sweet potato.

Southern cooks also made a distinction between yams and sweet potatoes. The cooks in the South would often stipulate the yam whenever they could get it- a moist, luscious, orange-colored tuber, which is much more exotic-looking than the light-yellow sweet potato with its dry, mealy texture. All sweet potato/yam recipes are applicable to both types of potatoes, but more liquid is usually required in cooking the dry, yellow kind.

Sweet potatoes are hearty vegetables that grow well in what might be thought less than productive and less than ideal soil. This made the sweet potato a perfect crop for the enslaved people and the lower-class whites to garden. The earth that had the best terrain, that had the most fertile ground, and also had the least amount of rock, was set aside by the plantation owner to grow the cash crops, which meant that the land that was set aside for the gardening of others was quite discouraging.

The sweet potato however was originally favored and flavored as a just a simple, more wholesome vegetable. Sweet potatoes were an appetizing starch that could be easily and quickly cooked. Enslaved people could roast the potatoes in hot ashes while they were wrapped in leaves, similar to what they would do while cooking cornbread or ash cake or they would roast them over a fire along with their other foods.

Today we seem to enjoy our sweet potatoes with lots of extra sweetness. We drizzle our cooked sweet potatoes with loads of butter, we often use copious amounts of sugar (mine and my wife's sugar preference is light brown), we also use cinnamon or similar spices when preparing our sweet potatoes to eat after baking. My wife cannot eat a sweet potato unless she has doused the potato with cinnamon, but of course she had previously spread on all the butter and sugar prior to using the cinnamon. Many people incorporate marshmallows into their cooked sweet potato preparations, but I think if they go that far, they should just go ahead and turn the sweet potatoes into a sweet potato pie. Yum! Sweet potato pie; there is none better.

In the past if you had asked for potatoes in the South, you were more likely than not to get sweet potatoes. If you wanted the white tuber of the North, you had to ask for Irish potatoes. The large, yellow skinned yam is more often baked in its own skin, then eaten hot with butter. The name "yam" is supposed to be a contraction of the Gullah word "nyam," which means to eat.

SUGARED YAMS

2 cups water
2 cups sugar
2 Tablespoons butter
dash of nutmeg
8 uncooked yams

Bring the sugar and water to a boil and add the butter and nutmeg. Peel and slice the yams, drop into boiling syrup, cover and cook slowly until the yams are done and transparent.
The Southern Cookbook, 1939

SWEET POTATO CROQUETTES

2 cups mashed sweet potatoes
2 Tablespoons butter
1 Tablespoon salt
2 Tbl. brown sugar
1/4 tsp. white pepper
egg
bread crumbs

Bake sweet potatoes until they are tender; then scoop out the centers and put them through a potato ricer. (Boiled sweet potatoes, mashed, may be used, although the flavor is not so delicate as with the baked ones.) Add the butter, salt, sugar, and pepper to the mashed sweet potatoes and beat these ingredients in well. Form the potatoes into small cylinders, dip in egg and then in the crumbs and fry in deep fat until golden brown.

NOTE: This amount will make 12 cylinders. This is supposed to be 6 servings, but we predict that most people will claim more than 1 serving.
William Deas, 200 Years of Charleston Cooking, 1930

YAM PUFF

4 large yams or sweet potatoes
1/4 cup butter
2 well-beaten eggs
2 teaspoons baking powder
1/3 cup sugar
1 teaspoon salt

Peel potatoes and boil until soft. Mash and add the remaining ingredients. Beat well and put in buttered casserole. Dot with butter and bake until brown, about 1/2 hour or more.
The Southern Cook Book, 1939

CANDIED SWEET POTATOES

This is by far the most popular way of serving this plentiful winter vegetable. Most of the receipts (recipe) direct you to bake it in a pan with sugar, water, and some particular flavoring, such as lemon or cinnamon and occasionally it is embellished with marshmallows. But the following receipt is much simpler and far, far nicer since all the potatoes get thoroughly candied in the process and never dry out in the baking. Make a syrup of 1 pint of water, 1 pound of sugar, butter the size of an egg and a little nutmeg. Peel 8 to 10 raw potatoes, slice and drop into this syrup. Cover and boil until well done. The potatoes will be clear and thoroughly candied and altogether heavenly.
The Savannah Cook Book, 1933

CANDIED YAMS

Parboil sweet potatoes or yams, and pare and cut in halves, lengthwise in a casserole, sprinkling each layer as it is set in place with salt, paprika, brown sugar. Dot with bits of butter and add a few dashes of cinnamon. Pour in about 1/2 cup of boiling water, cover and bake until tender. When about half baked. Lift the potatoes off the bottom of the dish placing them on top of the dish. Add more water if necessary.
The Southern Cookbook, 1939

MORE CANDIED SWEET POTATOES

The other method and the usual one, if you prefer, is like this. Boil several large sweet potatoes. Peel and cut in slices. Fill the bottom of a baking pan with a layer of potatoes and sprinkle with a Tablespoon of sugar and a small lump of butter. Add another layer of potatoes, another spoon of sugar, another lump of butter and so on to the top. Put in a few slices of lemon, cover well with cold water and bake until the potatoes are candied.
The Savannah Cook Book, 1933

SWEET POTATOES IN HONEY

Peel six sweet potatoes. Cut them in ¼-inch slices lengthwise. Boil them 15 minutes. Drain and remove to warm casserole. Add a small jar of honey, the juice of an orange, salt. Finish by baking in the oven.

NOTE: So easy to make and so delicious.
The Southern Cookbook, 1939

GEORGIAN STYLE SWEET POTATOES

3 cups mashed sweet potato	1 Tablespoon butter
2 Tablespoons molasses	

Mash the sweet potatoes and place in a buttered casserole. Boil together the molasses and butter for 7 minutes. pour over the sweet potatoes and bake in a moderate oven until delicately brown.
The Southern Cook Book, 1939

SWEET POTATOES WITH APPLE

6 large apples (tart apples are best)
5 medium-sized sweet potatoes
1/2 cup butter

1 cup sugar
1 cup hot water

Boil the potatoes until tender, peel and slice in thick pieces. Peel and core the apples and slice like the potatoes. Place a layer of potatoes in the bottom of a baking dish, dot with butter and sprinkle with sugar, then add a layer of apples. Continue alternating potatoes, apples, and butter and sugar until all the ingredients are used up. Then pour the cup of hot water over all. Bake in a moderately hot oven (375 F) about 1/2 hour.

NOTE: This dish may be varied by adding cinnamon or by using brown sugar *Mrs. Cornelius Youmans Reamer, 200 Years of Charleston Cooking, 1930.*

CREAMED SWEET POTATOES

2 cups cooked and mashed potatoes
1/2 teaspoon cinnamon
1/2 cup sugar

1/2 cup seeded raisins
1 cup milk
butter, the size of an egg

Beat all together until light and fluffy and cook in buttered baking dish. Remove and sprinkle marshmallows on top, return to oven and brown. Personally, I think this last item should be honored in the breach rather than in observance, but if you do like the marshmallow touch, you might even go one step further by stuffing the mixture in hollowed out orange skins, decorating these individual dishes with a few marshmallows and running them in the oven before serving.

NOTE: It tastes fine, but the recipe somewhat raises it out of the vegetable class; and then what have you? Even finer!
The Savannah Cook Book, 1933

STUFFED SWEET POTATOES

6 sweet potatoes
2 Tablespoons butter

table cream to soften
1/2 teaspoon salt

Bake the potatoes and then scoop out the centers and add the salt, butter, and cream to soften. Refill the skins and bake in a hot oven for about 5 minutes.
The Southern Cookbook, 1939

SCALLOPED SWEET POTATOES

Peel and dice six sweet potatoes. Drop them in boiling water and allow them to parboil about 15 minutes Drain the potatoes, dust with salt, add one Tablespoonful butter and 1/3-pint cream and finish baking them in a moderate oven until brown.
The Southern Cookbook, 1939

SCALLOPED SWEET POTATOES AND APPLES

4 cups cooked sliced sweet potatoes
3 cups peeled and sliced tart apples
1 1/2 cups water (preferably the water the potatoes were cooked in)
1/2 cup brown sugar
1/4 cup butter or margarine
1 teaspoon salt
2 Tablespoons flour

Heat oven to 350 F. Grease a 2-quart shallow baking dish. Place layer of potatoes in the baking dish and cover with sliced apples. Bring water to a boil along with sugar, butter, salt, and flour. Pour over the potato-apple mixture. Bake about 30 minutes or until apples are tender and transparent. Serves 6-8.
Callie Lillie Owen, The Nashville Cookbook, 1977

SWEET POTATOES WITH MADEIRA SAUCE

4 medium sweet potatoes   1 cup Madeira Sauce   1 Tablespoon honey

Cook, peel, and rice potatoes. Mix with sauce and honey and beat until light. Pile lightly in shallow baking dish and broil under medium heat for about 10 minutes.

MADEIRA SAUCE

2 cups vegetable stock
1/2 pound fresh mushrooms or 1 cup canned
4 Tablespoons dry red wine
3 to 4 Tablespoons butter
salt
chopped parsley

Chop mushrooms fine and pan in hot butter for 3 minutes. Stir frequently. Add vegetable stock and parsley, cover and simmer for 15 minutes or until liquid is reduced to 1 cup. Season. Add wine and simmer uncovered for 2 minutes.

NOTE: Sauce may be served hot or chilled.
Cooked to Your Taste, 1945

FRIED SWEET POTATOES

An old-fashioned breakfast dish, when breakfast was something to be reckoned with, was fried sweet potatoes. Peel and slice the raw potatoes, sprinkle with salt and fry in hot fat. Cold, boiled sweet potatoes or left over candied potatoes may also be fried in this fashion. These also make a very fine luncheon dish.
The Savannah Cook Book, 1933

SWEET POTATO SNOWBALLS

Blend 2 cups of mashed, cooked, sweet potatoes with 1/2 cup of brown sugar, 1 Tablespoon of butter and 1/2 teaspoon of ground spice. Take 10 marshmallows and roll each separately into this mixture, forming balls. Then roll these balls in shredded coconut; place in oven and cook long enough for the marshmallows to heat but not melt.
The Savannah Cook Book, 1933

SWEET POTATOES WITH CUMBERLAND SAUCE

4 medium sweet potatoes
8 cloves
6 marshmallows
1 cup Cumberland Sauce

Boil, peel, and cut potatoes in halves lengthwise. Scoop out the insides. Mix the potatoes with Cumberland Sauce and fill up the skins. Place in a shallow baking dish, stick clove in center of each stuffed shell, and dot with bits of marshmallow. Boil under medium broiler until marshmallow melts.

CUMBERLAND SAUCE

1/2 cup currant jelly
1/2 cup cranberry sauce
3-4 Tablespoons red wine
4-5 shallots, or young green onion
juice and peel of 1/4 lemon
juice and peel of ¼ orange
1/4 teaspoon dry mustard
salt, red pepper, and nutmeg to taste

Mix all the dry ingredients and stir in the wine. Add jellies and blend well, and add seasonings. Chop onions and peelings and add to sauce. Stir well. Chill for at least 2 hours and serve or use.
Cooked to Your Taste, 1945

SWEET POTATO PUFFS

6 medium sweet potatoes, peeled
1 teaspoon salt
1 egg, slightly beaten
2 Tablespoons salt

Cover potatoes with boiling water. Add salt; cook until tender, 25-30 minutes. Drain. Add butter; mash. Chill mixture. Stir in egg. Drop by spoonful onto lightly greased baking sheet. Bake in the oven at 375 F for 15 minutes. Puffs may be prepared for oven ahead of time. 6 servings.
Easy-on-the-Cookbook, 1960

SWEET POTATO CASSEROLE

8 medium sweet potatoes
3/4 cup milk
1 teaspoon vanilla
3 Tablespoons sugar
1/4 cup butter
1/4 teaspoon cinnamon
2 dashes nutmeg
2 Tablespoons orange juice
marshmallows

Bake the sweet potatoes at 350 F for 1 hour. Peel the hot potatoes and put through a ricer until completely mashed and the strings and eyes are removed. Scald the milk and add vanilla, sugar, and butter. To the potatoes, stir in cinnamon, nutmeg, and orange juice. Stir the milk mixture into the potatoes. Pour half of the potato mixture into a deep casserole dish. Add a layer of marshmallows. Pour the remaining potatoes on top of the marshmallows. Bake at 350 F for 60 minutes Add a top layer of marshmallows and brown. Serves 10.
Claudia Hazelwood, Cortner Mill Restaurant cookbook, 2009

PINEAPPLE MARSHMALLOW SWEET POTATOES

2 cups mashed sweet potatoes
1 cup milk
1/2 cup pineapple juice
1 cup diced pineapple
2 Tablespoons butter
1/2 teaspoon cinnamon
marshmallows

Thoroughly mix all the ingredients and beat until light and fluffy. Use more milk or fruit juice if needed. Place in a buttered casserole and bake until heated through. Remove from oven and cover top with marshmallows. Return to the oven to brown.

NOTE: I'll have this with my roast....and again for my dessert.
The Southern Cookbook, 1939

SWEET POTATOES MARGHERITA

Slice five boiled sweet potatoes and arrange in layers in a buttered baking dish, alternating with brown sugar, dots of butter, and slices of orange with the peel left on. Add enough water to make thick syrup but be careful not to add too much water for the syrup should be quite rich. Bake in a moderate oven (350 F) for one hour, baking occasionally with the syrup in the dish. Although this dish can be served with anything, it is especially nice to serve alongside duck or game.

NOTE: Slices of lemon may be mixed with the orange or only lemon may be used, if preferred.
Leize Dawson, Villa Margherita, 200 Years of Charleston Cooking, 1930

SWEET POTATO MERINGUE

6 potatoes
2 eggs
1 Tablespoon sugar
1/4 cup milk
salt to taste

Boil potatoes until tender, peel and mash. Add sugar, milk, yolks of eggs and salt. Beat hard until mixture is light and creamy. Put in dish and bake 1/2 hour. Take out and spread the well-beaten whites on top. Return to the oven to brown.
The Savannah Cook Book, 1933

SWEET POTATOES AND PINEAPPLE

3 cups cooked mashed sweet potato
3 Tablespoons brown sugar
2 1/2 pound can crushed pineapple
2 Tablespoons margarine, melted
1 egg, beaten
pinch of salt
pinch of cinnamon

Beat sweet potatoes and pineapple together with seasoning. Fold in beaten egg. Bake at 350 for 25-30 minutes. Serves 8.
Satsuma Tea Room, More Fun for the Cook, 1974

CORN

The most important foodstuff for the white European settlers and the most meaningful lesson taught by the Native Americans, was how to grow, prepare, and use corn, or as the Natives called it, maize. Corn proved to be the basic staple for these early Americans, and it established a deep-rooted and a markedly staunch grip on the South and its culture. The capability to grow corn, in my estimation, was the greatest lesson that the Native Americans ever imparted to the Europeans. Corn, and its byproducts, has occupied every Southern table in some form or fashion since its early introduction into the culture of the South. Corn could be eaten fresh or dried and dried corn could be stored for months. The dried kernels were often ground into a flour or meal. In this form, it was boiled for puddings or made into bread.

-"History of Southern Food/Best American Food" americanfood.net/history-of-southern-food/

Much like pork, corn was widely eaten by both the free and the enslaved people, but the enslaved were largely the most dependent on corn. Corn was the constant, everyday food provision for these enslaved Southerners. Cornbread, a resulting offshoot of cooking with corn, is often associated to the crueltiesof forced slavery. The enslaved were given only limited rations of food and limited time to eat and prepare their meals and thus they became heavily dependent on cornbread. Cornbread and all its different varieties were just the thing for those working in the fields because it didn't require utensils, could be easily carried, and could keep a long time.

Betty Fussell provides an account that highlights the significance of the combination of hog meat and hominy in the eighteenth century: "A favorite Southern dish was hog and hominy, a colonized version of the common Indian dish described by William Biggs when he was captured by the Kickapoos in 1788 and was adopted by the tribe. Biggs was given an Indian bride who made a wedding dish of 'hominy, beat in a mortar, as white as snow, handsome as I ever saw, and very well cooked. She fried some dried meat, pounded in a mortar, in oil, and sprinkled it with sugar.' Gentrified, the dish became New Orleans' grillades and grits (pounded smothered steak, fried with onion and tomato and served with grits on the side) and Charleston's grits and liver pudding (calf's liver with grits on the side)."

-Betty Fussell, The Story of Corn

Joe Gray Taylor imparts, "Corn was the staff of life on the Southern frontier; most Southerners depended on corn as a major part, if not the most important part, of their nourishment until World War II. It has been suggested that if the American pioneer had to eat wheat instead of corn it would have taken another hundred years for settlement to reach the Rocky Mountains. 'Corn will produce four times as much as wheat per acre and requires only one tenth the seed...and only one-third the time from planting until it can be used as food. Wheat planted in autumn cannot be harvested for nine months, whereas a woman can take a hoe in April and, with a quart of seed, plant a patch around a cabin and in six weeks she and her children can begin to eat roasting ears; and when it gets too hard for that she can parch it.'"

-Joe Gray Taylor, Eating, Drinking, and Visiting in the South: An Informal History

GRITS AND HOMINY

Historian Sam Bowers Hilliard writes, "In addition to the use of corn as ground meal, Southerners converted it into hominy and grits. Both were made from corn, but to make hominy the grains went through a soaking process which removed the husk (not the shuck) from the grain. Hominy consisted of whole-grain corn boiled and eaten as a vegetable."

-Sam Bowers Hilliard, Hog Meat and Hoe Cake

Hominy, a familiar food to all regions of the South, was a natural product of the abundant corn harvests. It was standard fare during the Civil War and Reconstruction period. Hominy was the product of corn made by soaking dry corn kernels in lye water to remove the husks. Hominy and grits are still enjoyed to this day all over the South. With the growing renaissance of Southern cuisine developing exponentially in the United States today, grits have now become synonymous with all things Southern. I have discovered that restaurants all over the country will invariably offer some variation of a grits dish on their menu; shrimp and grits being very popular.

Canned hominy and quick cooking grits make the preparation of these two foodstuffs much less laborious than was the practice of making *lye hominy* by the settlers in earlier times; when the using of spent wood ashes was their source of the lye. An example of one old recipe for lye hominy is below:

LYE HOMINY

Put one peck of old, dry, ripe, hulled corn into a pot filled with water, and with 1 quart of wood ashes in a bag and let this all soak awhile. Boil this mixture until the hulls, or skins, come off. Drain out the corn; wash it well in cold water to get off the taste of lye; boil it again in clear water with a little salt until soft. Wash some of it and serve hot or fry it a little brown and serve. It may be served with milk or cream. (Many individuals mash hominy with a fork and fry in a little butter and bacon drippings until very soft.)

HOMINY OR GRITS

1 cup hominy or 1 cup grits
4 cups boiling water
1 teaspoon salt
1 Tablespoon butter

Pour the hominy or grits into the hot water and stir until it comes to a boiling point. Then lower the flame and let simmer slowly for 1 hour, stirring frequently. When ready to serve, put the butter into the hominy or grits and beat well for a few minutes.
The Southern Cookbook, 1939

HOMINY SOUTH COAST

1 large can of hominy
1 teaspoon salt
3 Tablespoons butter
1 onion minced
1/2 cup chopped green pepper
3 Tablespoons flour
1/2 teaspoon dry mustard
dash cayenne pepper
1 1/2 cups milk
1 cup Cheddar cheese
1 cup chopped ripe olives
1/2 cup buttered bread crumbs

Melt butter and add onion and green pepper. Blend in flour and seasonings, add milk and cook to boiling. Add cheese and stir until melted. Remove from heat and add olives and hominy. Top with crumbs. Baked in a greased casserole at 350 for 30 minutes.
Betty Caldwell, The Nashville Cookbook, 1977

FRIED HOMINY

If you have any hominy left over, spread it out about 1 inch thick or so on a platter to get cold. Slice this cold mixture in any shape desired. Roll them in eggs and breadcrumbs and fry as you would croquettes. This dish is a very happy accompaniment to fowl or game, and as a simple addition to breakfast or supper.
The Savannah Cook Book, 1933

BAKED HOMINY OR GRITS

1 cup cold boiled hominy
or 1 cup cooked grits, cooled
1/2 cup milk
1 egg

1 Tablespoon butter
1/2 teaspoon salt
1 pinch of pepper

Heat the milk and butter, add the hominy or grits and mix until smooth. Then add the beaten egg, seasoning and pour into a buttered baking dish and bake slowly in a moderate oven (350 F) until firm and brown.

NOTE: A tremendously popular modern-day variation of this recipe is *Baked Cheese Grits*.
The Southern Cookbook, 1939

The following recipe is a "modernized" recipe for cheese-grits which combines a quick-cooking variety of grits with eggs and cheese.

BAKED GRITS AND CHEESE

2 1/2 cups cooked grits
(3/4 cup uncooked)
1/2 stick butter or margarine
2 eggs, lightly beaten

1/2 cup grated sharp Cheddar cheese
1/2 Tablespoon dry mustard
2 teaspoons onion juice

Cook grits. Add all ingredients to hot grits. Pour into greased casserole. Bake in 350 degree oven for 50 minutes.

NOTE: A young nephew of mine, who said he could not tolerate grits, ate three servings of this not knowing what it was. Delicious for a luncheon dish. Serves 4-6.
Satsuma Tea Room, Fun for the Cook, 1968

"Some folks say preachers won't steal,
but I caught two in my corn field.
One had a bushel, one had a peck,
One had a roastin' ear hung around his neck."

FRIED CORN

6 ears of tender corn
(Hickory Cane is the best)
3 Tablespoons butter

3 Tablespoons bacon drippings
1/2 teaspoon salt
pepper

Cut corn kernels and scrape the "milk" from the cob. Melt fats in heavy skillet and add corn with seasonings. Stir as it cooks to mix everything well. Cook on low heat until thick and tender (15 to 20 minutes). Serves 4 to 6.

NOTE: Corn is the "king" of Southern vegetables and enjoyed since the days of the American Indians and the Southern pioneers. With the recent development of many super-sweet corn varieties, some may question the use of Hickory Cane.
Satsuma Tea Room, Easy on the Cook-Garden Vegetables, 1975

TENNESSEE FRIED CORN

2 cups (6-8 ears) fresh corn

5 Tablespoons butter and bacon drippings, mixed
1 teaspoon sugar

salt and pepper to taste
1/2 to 3/4 cup water for each cup corn

Select corn with full round, milky kernels. Remove shucks and silks. Cut tips of kernels from ears of corn; scrape with edge of knife to remove the entire milky portion remaining on the cob. Heat fat in the skillet. Add corn, seasonings, and water, stirring constantly for about two minutes to heat through. Lower heat and cook, stirring frequently, until corn is thickened and color of corn almost transparent (about 15-20 minutes). Serves 4-6.

NOTE: Cream style fresh roastin' ears, not really fried but so called by most Middle Tennesseans.
Callie Lillie Owen, The Nashville Cookbook, 1977

CORN PUDDING

3 Tablespoons corn meal
1 Tablespoon salt
1/2 teaspoon paprika

1/2 cup cold milk
2 cups hot milk
1 Tablespoon butter

2 cups fresh corn pulp
2 eggs

Stir corn meal with salt, paprika and cold milk. Then stir into hot milk. Cook and stir over boiling water until the mixture thickens. Remove from fire and stir in the other ingredients. Turn into a buttered baking dish suitable to send to the table. Set in a pan of boiling water and cook slowly until the center is firm. Serve hot with the meat course. A Tablespoon of chopped green or red pepper may be added if desired.
The Southern Cookbook, 1939

CORN PUDDING

2 cups corn kernels with milk (6 or 7 ears)
3 Tablespoons melted margarine
2 Tablespoons sugar
2 Tablespoons flour
1 teaspoon salt
2 eggs
1 cup milk
pepper to taste

Beat eggs; add milk, sugar, pepper, and salt. Add flour to the cut and scraped corn. Mix well and combine with milk mixture. Pour into a buttered casserole (1 ½ quarts). Place casserole in a pan of hot water in 325 F oven. Bake 1 1/4 hours or until firm when dish is shaken. Serve immediately. Serves 5 to 6.
Satsuma Tea Room, Easy on the Cook-Garden Vegetables, 1975

SOUTHERN CORN CUSTARD

2 cups canned corn
3 eggs
2 Tablespoons melted butter
2 cups milk
1/2 teaspoon sugar
salt and pepper to taste
cracker crumbs

Beat the eggs well, add to the corn. Melt the butter and with the milk add to the corn and eggs. Stir well. Add the seasoning and sugar. Pour into a well-buttered casserole dish; sprinkle top with cracker crumbs, dot with butter and bake in a very slow oven (250 F) about 40 minutes or until custard is set.
The Southern Cookbook, 1939

SOUTHERN CORN PUDDING

#2 can cream style corn
3 cups milk
6 eggs
2 Tablespoons sugar
2 Tablespoons corn starch
1/4 teaspoon salt

Mix all ingredients, beating eggs before adding. Mix cornstarch with enough cold water to make smooth. Add to corn. Bake at 300 for 30 minutes. Serves 6-8.
Satsuma Tea Room, More Fun for the Cook, 1974

CORN PIE

1 cup drained corn
2 egg yolks
2 Tablespoons butter
salt and pepper
1 cup strained tomatoes
1 pound veal

Mix the corn (fresh corn may be used) with the other ingredients except the meat. The veal should be cooked and well-seasoned. Put half of the corn mixture into a well buttered baking dish, add the veal cut into pieces of serving size, and cover with the remainder of the corn and tomatoes. Bake in a moderate oven (350 F) for about 1/2 hour. This serves 4.

NOTE: Cooked chicken, slices of ham or other meat or shrimp may be substituted for the veal in making this dish.
Southern Cook Book Recipe shared through 200 Years of Charleston Cooking, 1930

GREEN CORN PIE WITH SHRIMP

2 cups corn
2 eggs, beaten slightly
1 Tablespoon butter, melted

1/2 cup milk
1 cup peeled raw shrimp
salt and pepper to taste

Grate enough corn to make two cups, or if canned corn is used, have it well drained. Add the eggs, melted butter, milk, shrimp and seasonings. Turn into a casserole and bake in a slow oven (300 F) for about 1/2 hour. This recipe may be varied by substituting tomato juice for the milk. Serves 6.

NOTE: As any good cookbook will tell you, shrimp may be peeled either before cooking or after cooking, but this job is more pleasant to handle after they have been cooked 3 to 5 minutes. Just long enough to make them turn pink. This recipe is also just as delicious made without shrimp.
Miss Ethel Norvell, 200 Years of Charleston Cooking, 1930

CORN SOUFFLE

4 eggs, separated

#2 can cream style corn

Beat egg yolks well. Add corn. Beat egg whites stiff and fold into corn mixture. Bake about 45 minutes in 350 oven. Serves 4-6.

NOTE: So easy and so good! We use this recipe at home all the time.
Satsuma Tea Room, Fun for the Cook, 1968

DEVILED CORN

3 cups kernel corn
cooked fresh or canned
4 medium tomatoes
4 to 5 Tablespoons butter

3 Tablespoons grated cheese
1 teaspoon grated mustard
salt and black pepper to taste

Cut tomatoes in half, dot with a little butter, season and put under medium broiler for 10 minutes. Mix corn with cheese, mustard, seasoning and remaining butter. Heat thoroughly. Turn out on platter, surround with broiled tomatoes and serve immediately.
Cooked to Your Taste, 1945

CORN CREOLE

1 cup canned corn
1 cup well-seasoned tomato sauce

1 red or green pepper, cut up

Stew all together a few minutes and serve on toast.

NOTE: A very simple and savory luncheon dish.
The Savannah Cook Book, 1933

OKRA, CORN, AND GREEN PEPPERS

4 slices salt pork
2 cups sliced okra
3 cups corn
2 sliced green peppers

2 Tablespoons flour
2/3 cup milk
salt

Fry until brown the slices of "white pork." Add the okra, corn, and green peppers. Then dredge in flour and stir thoroughly mixed. Add the milk and let the mixture come to the boiling point. Season with salt and cook until the peppers are tender. Serve hot.

NOTE: This dish may appear as a vegetable or served on toast as an excellent luncheon dish. Sufficient for eight servings.
A recipe offered by Mrs. H.A. Woodward, Augusta, Georgia as shared by
200 Years of Charleston Cooking, 1930

NOTES

RICE

"In most of the South, and particularly along the coast where rice plantations once thrived, rice and hominy are served daily in many different guises. Boiled hominy is an invariable breakfast and supper dish and boiled rice is served as regularly for dinner as Irish (white) potatoes are in the North.

The only exception to this rule is that rice is never served with fish (according to traditional stories). Be that as it may, boiled hominy and butter for breakfast as an accompaniment to shrimp, sausages, or bacon, and a plate piled high with white fluffy rice for dinner is a regular thing in the South; like wine is with your meals in France.

If you want the perfect accompaniment for game, you can't go wrong with fried hominy. Both rice and hominy form the foundation for many breads and batters. Rice is the backbone of meat and vegetable pilaus whose name is legion."

-Harriett Ross Colquitt, "The Savannah Cook Book", 1933

"The Oxford Dictionary says that a pilau is an oriental dish of rice with meat and spices. Yet few foods seem to be so at home in South Carolina as pilaus from India in the days when Charleston was a great seaport, before the Revolutionary War. Southern cooks shifted the emphasis from the second to first syllable and shifted ingredients from oil to tomatoes. In Charleston, they pronounce it pelos and they cook it so that the dish comes out dry and greaseless. In the North these recipes will be a godsend to those who have leftovers. But in the South, you never have such a thing. A pilau is a dish of amazing variations. It can be as rich or as parsimonious as you will. Rice is its main ingredient, which is only fitting in a country where so much rice is grown.

It was by a romantic accident that rice was first successfully grown in South Carolina. In 1694 a vessel set out from Madagascar, which was as remote in the thought of Americans as Mars might seem to us today. It was bound for Liverpool, but was blown so far off her course that she put into Charleston harbor for repairs. Landgrave Judge Thomas Smith boarded the ship. It was not known whether it was for duty or pleasure, and the captain of the vessel presented him with a small package of rough rice for growing seeds. The Landgrave, Thomas Smith, planted the seed in the proper marshy soil and there sprang up a crop so large, that he was able to supply the whole colony. From an accident of a storm-tossed ship, grew the enormous rice wealth of South Carolina."

"200 Years of Charleston Cooking", 1930

During my research into old Low Country recipes, I continuously encountered recipes called pilaus. These were not one-off recipes. The recipes were not limited to certain ingredients (although rice and spice were always included). The recipes of pilaus that I found seemed to be a foundation of foods and cooking realized throughout the entire region. For me there was one problem. I had never heard of pilau. I had no clue what it was. How could I write about cuisine I knew nothing about?

Today, we generally call variations of this rice dish pilaf. The Spanish make a very rice dish known as paella. Pela, Pilav, Pallao, Pulao, Pulaav, Palaw, Palavu, Plov, Palov, Polo, Polu, Kurysh, Fulao, Pulab, Fulav, etc. are names used the world over to describe the same category of dish, but always with variations dictated by their particular environment.

As exotic and extensive as I think these names above are, there is just something fabled about the word pilau used in the Carolina Low Country. But let's not forget, in my assessment, the most colorful, exceptional, and unusual rice and spice dish of all, is Jambalaya. Again, my assessment. My opinion.

BOILED RICE: TO STIR OR NOT TO STIR

"There are many cooks of many minds when it comes to boiling rice. One will tell you never to stir it after it begins to boil or the rice will become sticky. Another will warn you never to stop stirring rice or it will burn. And both of these cooks, if they be real cooks, can turn out the most delectable rice white and fluffy, 'with every grain standing apart' which is the rather alarming way we describe perfectly cooked rice.

But the real trouble is usually found at the bottom. The rice has not been properly washed. This is the most important part of the process. Wash it several times very carefully with cold water, and after you think you have finished, wash it again for luck. Put 3 cups of water, well salted, in a boiler (an iron pot is always best if you have one) and let it come to a boil.

Then sprinkle the rice in and let it cook briskly for 15 to 20 minutes, stirring occasionally with a fork. Pour off the water (Servants often saved this sticky rice-water for starch.), or put it in a colander and set it on the back of the stove to steam until dry.

Real rice-lovers literally scrape the pot to get the 'rice-cake' at the bottom. If you haven't been raised on a rice plantation, you won't miss that delectable bit.

Cold rice can be used, as can cold hominy, in breads, battercakes, and waffles; or for rice puffs, pilaus, gumbos, croquettes, etc."
-Harriett Ross Colquitt, The Savannah Cook Book, 1933

BAKED RICE (or Rice Puff)

Mix 2 cups cold, boiled rice, 1 pint of milk, 2 slightly beaten eggs, 3 Tablespoons of melted butter, and 1/2 teaspoon salt. Pour into baking dish and cook until firm and golden brown.
The Savannah Cook Book, 1933

JAMBALAYA

It would seem at first glance that the cooking of New Orleans and that of Charleston should be very much alike. I am puzzled to know why the two are so different. Both were settled by the French. Both had Negro cooks and both drew from their own neighborhood shellfish and game. I think the differences may lie in the fact that New Orleans cooking was so heavily influenced by Spain, which had left South Carolina untouched. Occasionally, however, one finds a New Orleans dish that came to South Carolina and was adapted, adopted there. The best one of these dishes was Jambalaya.

1 to 1 1/2 cups cold chicken, veal, or mutton	1 green pepper
1 cup boiled rice	1 large stalk celery
1 1/2 cups stewed tomatoes	salt and pepper
1 large onion	buttered crumbs

Mix the first three ingredients together and let cook for about 10 minutes on top of the stove. Then add the onion, green pepper, and celery (each vegetable having been chopped). Turn the mixture into a baking dish and cover with buttered crumbs. Bake in a moderately hot oven (375 F) for 1 hour. Serve very hot. Serves 4 and is an excellent way of making a small amount of leftover meat or chicken do double duty.
200 Years of Charleston Cooking, 1930

PILAUS

"Many of the old cooks call pilau "perlew," and we are apt to smile indulgently and explain with raised eyebrows that they mean "pilau," but we would not be so patronizing about it if we realized their authority. In looking over an old South Carolina cook book which specialized on rice dishes, I found this word spelled "purlow," so perhaps our admiring imitators are not so far afield after all."
-Harriett Ross Colquitt, The Savannah Cook Book, 1933

CHICKEN PILAU

6 Tablespoons butter
6 stalks celery, cut up
1 onion, chopped
2 tomatoes, sliced

2 cups rice
1 chicken (2 1/2 pounds), cut as for frying
chicken broth
salt and pepper

Brown onion and celery and tomatoes separately in butter. Put the raw rice into a saucepan, cover with the browned celery, onions, and tomatoes and the raw chicken. Pour over this enough chicken broth to cover (chicken bouillon cubes or canned soup may be used). Cover with a tightly fitting lid and cook slowly for 1/2 hour. If a larger chicken is used, it should be boiled first until half tender and the broth could then be used on the rice. Serves 6.
Essie Woodward Messervy, 200 years of Charleston Cooking, 1930

TOMATO OKRA PILAU

3 slices bacon
1 small onion
2 cups stewed tomatoes

2 cups thinly sliced okra
2 quarts water
1 teaspoon salt

2 cups rice

Cook chopped bacon until brown. Remove from pan and fry onion in bacon fat until yellow. Add tomatoes and okra and let them cook, stirring all the while. Cook rice in water for 12 minutes, drain, and mix with tomato mixture. Put in double boiler, steam for 15-20 minutes. Crumble bacon and add it at the end. Makes 8 servings.
Satsuma Tea Room, More Fun for the Cook, 1974

TOMATO PILAU

5 small slices salt pork, diced
1 small onion chopped
2 can tomatoes
2 cups cooked rice

1/2 cup water
salt to taste
3 Tablespoons butter

Fry the diced salt pork in a saucepan with the onion until brown. Add the tomatoes and cook over a slow fire for 10 minutes, then add the water and salt to taste. Stir in the rice and let the pilau cook slowly until all the liquid is absorbed. Just before serving, stir in the butter.
William Deas, 200 Years of Charleston Cooking, 1930

EGG PILAU

From Columbia, SC comes Mrs. Salley's egg pilau, a truly wonderful concoction for Sunday night supper.

2 cups rice	4 cups chicken stock	6 eggs
2 teaspoons salt	1/2 cup butter	pepper to taste

Cook the rice with the salt in the chicken stock, keeping the kettle tightly covered during the cooking process. The rice will absorb all the stock and should be done in about 20 minutes. As soon as it is done stir in the eggs (they may be broken in another dish and all added at once) and beat for a minute or two, adding the butter at this time. The heat of the rice will cook the eggs and melt the butter without returning the pan to the fire. Season to taste with black pepper and serve at once.

NOTE: This will serve 8 and furnishes a creamy rice dish which suggests scrambled eggs and has a decided chicken flavor.
Mrs. I.E. Salley, 200 Years of Charleston Cooking, 1930

CAROLINA PILAU

NOTE: The original recipe reads: "Boil 1 1/2 pounds of bacon; when nearly done add 1 quart rice; then put in 2 young fowls and season with salt and pepper."

3/4 pound bacon	1 broiler chicken
2 cups rice	salt and pepper
4 cups water	

Boiling the bacon gives, of course, a limp product and a product that is a little too greasy for our taste. Instead, we cut the bacon in diced form and fried it. Then the bacon was removed from the fat, part of the drippings turned off and rice added and browned slightly. Boiling water was then added, and as soon as the rice was boiling, chicken (cut as for fricassee) was added. The water was liberally salted. The pot covered and the fire lowered so that the rice continued to boil, but not too vigorously. At the end of 25 minutes the rice and chicken were both tender and the water had all been absorbed. A seasoning of salt and pepper was added. All pilaus should be highly seasoned. The bacon is now, again stirred in.
200 Years of Charleston Cooking, 1930

JAMBALAYA

This dish is in reality quite our old friend, a pilau with a more intriguing name. This was one of the receipts taught in Mrs. Habersham's famous cooking school and is a very convenient Monday dish, since any old hangover from Sunday's dinner seems to be a welcome addition to the brew. It is with pride that I give it a place here. Put 1 spoon butter in frying-pan and add 1 large cup cooked rice, 1 cup tomato juice or milk, 1 teaspoon chopped onion and parsley, and 1 cup of any vegetable, fish or meat. Stir together until hot.

NOTE: This is a life saver the day after a party.
Harriet Ross Colquitt, The Savannah Cook Book, 1933

JAMBALAYA (A Creole Dish)

1 1/2 cups cold chicken, veal, or mutton	1/2 green pepper	salt and pepper
1 cup boiled rice	1 large onion	buttered crumbs
2 large stalks celery	1 1/2 cups stewed tomatoes	

Mix together the chicken, rice, and tomatoes and allow them to cook for ten minutes. Then chop and add the onion, green pepper, and celery. Turn the mixture into a baking dish and cover with buttered crumbs. Bake for one hour in moderate oven (350). Serve very hot.

NOTE: This is an excellent way of utilizing left-over meat or chicken.
The Southern Cook Book, 1939

FRIED RICE

1/2 cup chopped onion
1 cup rice, uncooked
2 Tablespoons butter

2 1/2 cups canned consommé
1/2 teaspoon salt

Chop onions; add rice and sauté in butter until rice is done. Add consommé and salt. Cover and cook over low heat until done. 20-25 minutes.

NOTE: Frozen chopped onions are wonderful for a dish like this. Serves 4
Satsuma Tea Room, Fun for the Cook, 1968

WILD RICE AND MUSHROOMS

1 cup wild rice
3 cups boiling water

1 pound fresh mushrooms
2 Tablespoons butter

2 Tablespoons flour
1 cup milk
salt to taste

Cover the rice with boiling water and continue to boil fast for 15 minutes or until water is well absorbed; then let steam until the rice is dry and fluffy. Peel the mushrooms, sauté in the butter until well browned. Remove the mushrooms from the skillet and add the flour to the batter, rubbing to a smooth paste. Then add the milk and cook until thick. Add the mushrooms to this and heat. Pour the mushrooms over the rice and serve.
The Southern Cookbook, 1939

DINAH'S RICE CROQUETTES

2 1/2 cups cooked rice
1 cup grated American cheese
1/2 cup butter or other shortening
1/2 cup chopped pimiento
1 Tablespoon chopped onion

1/8 teaspoon salt and paprika
1 teaspoon baking powder
1 egg, beaten well
1/2 cup buttered bread crumbs

Milk all well and mold into balls and fry in hot fat until brown.
The Southern Cookbook, 1939

MULATTO RICE

Fry squares of breakfast bacon and remove from the pan. Then brown some minced onion (one small one) in this grease. Now add 1 pint can of tomatoes. When thoroughly hot, add 1 pint of rice to this mixture and cook very slowly until the rice is done. Or if you are in a hurry to eat, cold rice may be substituted, and all the ingredients are warmed thoroughly together.

NOTE: This is a very chic name given to rice that is cloudy and dull.
The Savannah Cook Book, 1933

MULATTO RICE

1/2 pound bacon	1 cup tomatoes
1 small onion	2 cups cooked rice

Cut the bacon in small pieces and fry. Remove from the skillet and brown minced onion in the bacon fat. Add the tomatoes and cooked rice. Blend well and serve while hot.
The Southern Cookbook, 1939

CURRIED RICE

2 cups cooked rice	2 cups tomatoes	1 1/2 tsp. curry powder
1 diced green pepper	2 cups water	
1 diced onion	4 Tablespoons butter	

Mix all the ingredients. Put in a well-greased casserole and bake in a slow oven until the onions and peppers are well cooked.
The Southern Cookbook, 1939

PAELLA (Valencian Rice)

3 Tablespoons olive oil	3 cans whole tomatoes
3 cloves garlic, chopped fine	3/4 teaspoon salt
2 onions, chopped fine	cayenne
1 1/4 cups uncooked rice	3 threads of saffron
3 1/2 cups boiling water	2 Tablespoons boiling water
3 pimientos, chopped	

Heat oil and brown garlic and onion in it. Add the rice, which has been washed and dried, and cook until brown. Add 3 ½ cups boiling water, pimientos, tomatoes, salt and pepper. Soak saffron for a few minutes in 2 Tablespoons of boiling water to get color out and add to mixture. Cover and cook until tender (about 15 to 20 minutes). Add chopped seafood, chicken, veal, or beef to rice before serving.

NOTE: In Spain, they add small sea fish to this dish. Absolutely delicious.
Holiday Hostess Cookbook, 1958

WILD RICE WITH MUSHROOMS

Wild rice is not a native Southern dish, but it has been made a specialty in the Colonial Kitchens, with the "receipt" given here along with creamed mushrooms and apple chutney. We cook it as we do native rice, though the directions on the boxes in which it is retailed will tell you to season it more highly. It has a delicious flavor which we think too much seasoning destroys.

Cover 1 cup of wild rice with about 3 cups of water and add a little salt. Let it boil hard for about 20 minutes, and when water is absorbed, remove it to the back of the stove and let steam until dry.

Peel 1 pound of mushrooms and boil the stems and skins to make a stock, which can be strained and used in creamed mushrooms or put aside for soup. Put 2 Tablespoons of butter in the frying-pan and broil the mushrooms until golden brown. Remove and add to the butter; 2 Tablespoons of flour, rubbing it to a paste. Then add 1 cup of milk (or cream if you are so elegant) and a little mushroom stock. Cook until thick Add the mushrooms to this, heat thoroughly and serve on a platter with a border of wild rice.

The Savannah Cook Book, 1933

SPANISH RICE

1 cup rice	2 cloves garlic
4 Tablespoons fat	1 red or green pepper, chopped
5 onions, chopped	or 1 canned pimiento
2 cups strained, canned tomatoes or	1 teaspoon paprika
3 ripe tomatoes	2 teaspoons salt

Wash rice thoroughly, place in frying pan with bacon or poultry fat, add onion and the garlic minced fine. Let fry 10 minutes; add rest of the ingredients and 1 cup water. Cook slowly, about 1 hour and as water evaporates, add more water to keep it from burning until the rice is tender.

NOTE: Spanish rice was one of our customer favorites at *Satsuma* and we made it often. I never knew how Southern it was, until I began my book research and learned about pilaus.

The Settlement Cook Book, 1940

RED RICE

1/2 pound bacon	salt and pepper to taste
1 small can tomatoes	4 cups chicken broth
1 pound rice	

Have the bacon sliced and cut into small pieces. Fry it until crisp and remove the bits of bacon. Leave about 4 Tablespoons of the drippings and in the drippings, brown the rice stirring constantly to assure that the rice doesn't burn. Then add the tomatoes, a teaspoon of salt, and the chicken stock. Cover closely and cook for 1/2 hour or until rice is tender. Add back the bacon bits and season to taste with salt and pepper.

Sally Washington's Recipe recounted in "200 Years of Charleston Cooking", 1930

ORANGE RICE

1/4 cup butter	2 cups chicken broth	grated rind of 1 orange
1 cup rice	1/2 cup dry white wine	salt and pepper
1/2 teaspoon salt	juice of 1 orange	chopped parsley

Place butter, rice, salt, broth, and wine in a casserole. Cover and bake at 350 F until light and feathery, about 45 minutes. Add the juice and rind; return to oven for 10 minutes. Correct the seasonings to your taste. Toss with a fork and sprinkle with chopped parsley or slivered almonds.
Helen Corbitt, The Nashville Cookbook, 1977

WILD RICE

1/4 cup butter	1 Tablespoon chopped green pepper (optional)
1 cup wild rice	
1/2 cup slivered almonds	1/2 pound sliced fresh mushrooms
1 Tbl. chopped chives or green onions	3 cups chicken broth

Heat oven to 350 F. Put all the ingredients, except chicken broth, in heavy frying pan and cook while stirring until rice turns yellow. Add broth. Put in baking dish; cover tightly and bake for about 1 hour. May be mixed ahead several hours before cooking. Serves 8 to 10.
Katherine Simpson, The Nashville Cookbook, 1977

RICE CROQUETTES

1 large cup boiled rice	1/2 cup milk	nutmeg, salt
1 Tablespoon butter	1 egg	

Boil milk, add rice and season. When it boils up, add the well-beaten egg, stir well, and let cool. Roll into shapes and then bread crumbs and then egg and then bread crumbs again. Fry in deep fat.

NOTE: Delicious with currant jelly.
The Savannah Cook Book, 1933

RICE AND PINEAPPLE

1 large-sized can sliced pineapple	1 cup brown sugar
4 cups cooked rice	

Put 1/2 inch layer of cooked rice in the bottom of the casserole, then dot with butter and place pineapple over the top. Sprinkle with some of the brown sugar. Repeat this until all the rice is used, making sure the top layer is pineapple. Pour the juice from the can over this and bake in a moderate oven (350 F) for 30 minutes.
The Southern Cookbook, 1939

MEXICAN RICE

Cook a cup of white rice in 1 pint of strong vegetable stock. Add 1 Tablespoon of chopped green peppers, 1 peeled tomato, 1 finely chopped onion, 1 Tablespoon of butter, 1/2 teaspoon salt and 1/2 teaspoon of paprika. Bake in a covered dish for 2 hours.
The Savannah Cook Book, 1933

CURRIED RICE

1 cup rice (cooked soft)	1 cup tomatoes	1 1/2 tsp. curry powder
1 green pepper, cut up	4 cups water	
1 large onion, sliced	2 Tablespoons butter	

Mix all the ingredients and bake in a moderate oven.
The Savannah Cook Book, 1933

IRISH POTATO PIE

Use any kind of cooked meat, cut into diced pieces. Line a deep dish with cooked, mashed, and salted potatoes, then put in meat and small bits of butter and 1 cup gravy if you have it. Cover with potatoes and bake 15 minutes.

NOTE: This dish is one of the life savers when there is "nothing in the house."
The Savannah Cook Book, 1933

SCALLOPED POTATOES

Slice about 6 raw potatoes with a slaw cutter. Cover the bottom of a baking dish with bread crumbs, bits of butter and a little parsley. Put over this a layer of potatoes, salt and pepper. Alternate potatoes and bread crumbs until dish is full. Pour a cup of milk over it and bake in a moderate oven (350 F) for 1 hour.
The Southern Cookbook, 1939

POTATO CROQUETTES

4 cups cooked Irish potatoes	1 egg
2 Tablespoons butter	salt to taste

Mash the potatoes while hot, and mix with egg, butter and salt and put aside to cool. When firm, roll into croquettes and fry in deep fat. Do not roll in bread crumbs.
The Savannah Cook Book, 1933

HALF BAKED POTATOES

4 medium potatoes	1 Tablespoon shortening

Scrub potatoes. Cut in half. Place cut side down in heavy skillet with fat. Cover tightly. Cook slowly for 30 minutes, until center is tender. May be served cut side up with butter, salt and pepper or sour cream.
Satsuma Tea Room, More Fun for the Cook, 1974

HASHED POTATOES-IRISH

Fry a dessert spoon of chopped onion in a little butter. Sift in a dessert spoon of flour, another spoon of butter, salt and pepper, and 1 cup of milk. Let boil until it coats the spoon. To this add a cup of cooked diced potatoes. Heat well and serve.
The Savannah Cook Book, 1939

PIEDMONT POTATO CROQUETTES

2 cups hot, riced potatoes	1 cup sifted flour
2 Tablespoons butter	1/2 cup finely chopped blanched almonds
1 whole egg	1/2 teaspoon salt
3 egg yolks	1 pinch paprika

Mix the potatoes, butter, egg yolks, salt and pepper and beat thoroughly. Shape into balls using 1 Tablespoon of the mixture for each ball. Roll in the flour and dip in the beaten egg and then roll in the almonds. Fry in deep hot fat (390 F) until golden brown, which generally requires about 1 minute.
The Southern Cookbook, 1939

BAKED STUFFED POTATOES

Bake large potatoes; cut into halves length wise and scoop out the center. Mix this with 1 teaspoon salt, 2 Tablespoons butter, enough cream or milk to soften, and 1 egg. Beat well. Return to the potato shells and brown on top. Sprinkle with paprika before serving
The Southern Cookbook, 1939

BAKED TOMATOES

Select nice firm tomatoes. Cut in half crosswise. Sprinkle cut side with salt, pepper, and a little sugar. Dot with butter and bake at 375 F until tender (about 30 minutes).
Satsuma Tea Room, Easy on the Cook-Garden Vegetables, 1975

STEWED TOMATOES

2 1/2 cups canned tomatoes	1 Tablespoon butter
3/4 teaspoon salt	2 biscuits
2 Tablespoon sugar	

Put tomatoes into a saucepan and cook over low heat for 10 minutes. Stir occasionally to prevent scorching. Add salt, sugar, and butter and mix well. Drop the biscuits into tomatoes to thicken and cook another 5 minutes. You can substitute 1/2 cup bread crumbs, if you didn't make biscuits for breakfast.

NOTE: This was a good dish to serve either in winter or summer. When the tomatoes were fresh, they were used although the cooking time needs to be increased. This was a very popular vegetable served for lunch at *Satsuma*. They used day-old sliced loaf bread instead of crumbs, or biscuits. They even lightly toasted the slices to maintain the bread's integrity.
David Boswell Hazelwood, Miss Lizzie's Heirlooms, 2009

STEWED TOMATOES

#2 1/2 can tomatoes
1 Tablespoon sugar
1/4 teaspoon salt
1 small onion
2 Tablespoons margarine
1/2 cup bread crumbs or croutons

Chop and cook onion in margarine until tender. Add tomatoes and seasonings to the saucepan. Heat all to boiling. Simmer 8 to 10 minutes. Add bread crumbs or croutons and serve. Serves 5 to 7.
Satsuma Tea Room, Easy on the Cook-Garden Vegetables, 1975

FRIED GREEN TOMATOES WITH BASIL MAYONNAISE

1 cup self-rising flour
1/4 teaspoon cayenne pepper
1 can evaporated milk
1 dash Tabasco sauce
3 green tomatoes, sliced 1/4 inch thick
3/4 cup canola oil
1/4 cup peanut oil
1/4 cup basil mayonnaise
salt and pepper to taste

Mix the flour with cayenne pepper, salt and pepper. Place in a sealable plastic freezer bag. Mix evaporated milk with Tabasco sauce. Place in another sealable plastic freezer bag. Place 4 slices of tomatoes into bag with evaporated milk. Seal and shake to coat. Transfer coated tomatoes to bag with the flour mixture and seal and shake. Repeat the process until all the tomatoes have been coated with the flour mixture. Set on wire rack to rest 10 minutes. Heat oils to medium in large heavy skillet. Place tomato slices, four or five at a time into oil and lightly brown each side for about 4-5 minutes. As tomatoes are done, place them on paper towels into warm oven. When all the tomatoes are done, arrange on a platter with basil mayonnaise served on the side.

BASIL MAYONNAISE

1 cup mayonnaise
1/2 cup sour cream
3 Tablespoon fresh basil leaf, finely chopped
2 Tablespoon lemon juice, strained
1 teaspoon lemon zest, grated

Blend all the ingredients and let stand for 30 minutes. (Takes 5 minutes to mix)
Steve Gunning, Fruit of the Spirit, Mt. Bethel United Methodist Church, Marietta, GA

FRENCH FRIED TOMATOES

4 very firm tomatoes
salt and pepper, to taste
drop batter
fat for deep frying

Slice the tomatoes. Dip in batter until well coated. Drop into hot deep fat until golden brown. Drain on paper, sprinkle with salt and pepper, and serve.
Cooked to Your Taste, 1945

KALE WITH TOMATOES

2 pounds kale
4 large tomatoes or 2 cups canned
8 black olives
1 cup vegetable stock or water

1 Tablespoon butter or bacon drippings
1 teaspoon sugar
salt and marjoram to taste

Blanch kale and chop coarsely. Cut up tomatoes. Pit and chop olives. Pan (sautee) tomatoes in hot fat for 3 minutes, add kale, olives and enough liquid to prevent scorching. Cover and simmer for 10 minutes. Add sugar and seasoning. Stir well, cover, and simmer until kale is tender (10 to 15 minutes).
Cooked to Your Taste, 1945

TOMATOES AND BELL PEPPERS

Chop 1 bell pepper and 1 piece of celery in small pieces and cook a few minutes in 3 Tablespoons of melted butter. Add 1 quart of tomatoes, 2 cups of bread crumbs, 1 Tablespoon sugar, salt and pepper, and put in a deep pan. Sprinkle with bread crumbs and bake about 1/2 hour.
The Savannah Cook Book, 1933

OKRA AND TOMATOES

Take an equal quantity of young sliced okra and skinned tomatoes. Put them together in a pan, without water, adding a lump of butter, a finely chopped onion, some salt and pepper. Stew over a slow fire for 1 hour.
The Southern Cookbook, 1939

BROILED TOMATOES

4 large ripe tomatoes (not soft)
8 teaspoons bacon fat or butter
chopped parsley

1 teaspoon dry mustard
salt, pepper, and sugar

Wash the tomatoes. Cut off stem ends. Cut in half. Place in baking pan sliced end up. Mix seasonings and put seasoning on each tomato. Dot with butter or bacon fat. Bake at 375 for 20-30 minutes. Serves 8.

NOTE: For those on a diet, omit bacon fat and use sugar substitute. This recipe is a very good way to use store bought tomatoes in the winter.
Satsuma Tea Room, More Fun for the Cook, 1974

PARSNIPS AND SALT PORK

2 pounds salt pork
6 parsnips

Cut salt pork into small pieces. Partly cover with water and cook until almost done. Add parsnips, cut into one-inch pieces. Cook until salt pork and parsnips are tender.
The Southern Cookbook, 1939

FRESH LIMA BEANS

1 quart lima beans
1 Tablespoon butter
1/2 teaspoon salt
2 Tablespoons milk
2 Tablespoons cream

Wash and pick over the beans. Cover with boiling water, adding salt and butter. Let simmer eighteen minutes; raise the heat and boil quickly until the water has evaporated. Add the cream and the milk and bring to a boil. Serve hot.
The Southern Cookbook, 1939

HOME-BAKED BEANS

1 pint navy beans
1/4 pound fat salt pork
1 teaspoon mustard
1/2 teaspoon salt
1 Tablespoon molasses
1/2 cup boiling water
1 1/2 Tablespoons sugar

Cover beans with cold water and soak for at least 12 hours, then change water and cook at slightly below boiling point until the skins burst. To test beans, take a few and expose to cold air, if shells burst, they are done. Then drain and add pork, cut it in small strips and stick it in the beans with tip exposed. Mix mustard, sugar, salt, pepper, and water enough to cover beans. Bake in a pot slowly for six to seven hours removing lid for last hour to brown and crisp.

NOTE: Everyone has or knows of a "great!" baked bean recipe. The main focus for these different baked bean recipes is basically the same, but the difference lies in how the variations are tweaked; adjusted and fine-tuned.
The Southern Cookbook, 1939

BOSTON BAKED BEANS

1 quart pea beans
3/4 pound salt pork
4 Tablespoons molasses
or up to 1 cup according to taste
3 Tablespoons brown sugar
1 Tablespoon salt
1/2 teaspoon dry mustard
boiling water

Cover the beans with cold water and soak overnight. Drain and cover with fresh water and simmer until skins burst. Drain. Pour boiling water over the pork and scrape rind, remove 1/4 inch slice; score remaining pork in 1/2 inch strips. Put the 1/4 inch slice of pork in bottom of bean pot, cover with the beans and bury pork strips in them. Cover with the pork rind. Mix salt, mustard, sugar, and molasses, and add enough boiling water to cover mixture. Stir all this until well mixed and pour over the beans. Add enough boiling water to cover beans. Cover pot and bake in a slow oven for 6 to 8 hours, adding more water to cover beans until the last hour. Bake uncovered the last hour and raise pork to the surface to crisp.
Cooked to Your Taste, 1945

BEST-EVER BAKED BEANS

2 pounds navy beans
1 teaspoon baking soda
1 large onion, quartered
1/2 pound salt pork, sliced or cut in chunks
1/2 cup molasses
1/2 cup firmly packed brown sugar
1 Tablespoon mild vinegar
1 Tablespoon salt
2 teaspoons dry mustard
11 or 12 ounce bottle chili sauce

Cover beans with warm water; soak several hours or overnight. Drain; add fresh water to cover and baking soda. Bring to a boil and cook for 10 minutes; drain. Add fresh boiling water to cover and cook gently until the skins on the beans will crack when blown upon. Drain liquor and save. Pour beans into a bean pot; bury onion in beans. Parboil salt pork about 5 minutes; drain and brown slightly. Bury some of the pork in the beans and arrange some on top. Blend the remaining ingredients; pour half over beans; add enough of saved liquor to cover beans. Bake at 250 for 3 to 4 hours, adding remaining sauce mixture at intervals and more of the liquor, or water, as needed. Makes 10-12 servings.

NOTE: Understand that this recipe is from mid 20TH century. Much has changed to the existence of baked beans that has made the cooking and serving of the beans just plain easier to deal with and in many ways, there are certain canned baked beans that are just as good tasting as "made from scratch" beans. I personally have been guilty on many occasions of using the canned beans and "doctoring" them with many of the ingredients used above. I offer this recipe to show what goes into the cooking of very good baked beans, the best ever.
Easy-on-the-Cookbook, 1960

LIMA BEANS IN SOUR CREAM (One of my favorites)

2- 10 oz. packages frozen lima beans
1 1/2 teaspoon salt
1/2 cup boiling water
2 Tablespoons chopped onion
2 Tablespoons chopped pimiento
2 Tablespoons butter
1 cup sour cream
1/8 teaspoon white pepper

Cook beans in salted boiling water, covered, until tender. Drain. Sauté onion and pimiento in butter. Add sour cream and pepper. Combine with beans. Heat thoroughly. Serves 6-8
Satsuma Tea Room, More Fun for the Cook, 1974

CREOLE LIMA BEANS

4 slices bacon, diced
1/4 cup grated onion
2 Tablespoons flour
1/2 teaspoon salt
1/4 teaspoon pepper
1/2 teaspoon paprika
2 1/2 cups tomatoes
2 cups lima beans, drained
1 bay leaf

Fry bacon until crisp; add onion and cook until lightly browned. Blend in flour and seasonings. Add tomatoes, slowly; cook until thickened. Add lima beans and bay leaf; simmer about 20 minutes. Remove bay leaf. Serves 6.
Easy-on-the-Cookbook, 1960

LIMA BEAN CASSEROLE

2 1/2 cups lima beans
3 medium fresh tomatoes or 1 cup canned
1 clove garlic
1 Tablespoon butter or bacon drippings
vegetable stock or water

Cut up tomatoes and mix with beans, garlic, and fat. Barely cover with liquid and simmer, pot covered, until beans are tender. Remove garlic, season and serve.
Cooked to Your Taste, 1945

SOUR CREAM SUCCOTASH

1 to 1 1/2 cups cooked fresh lima beans or
2 cups quick frozen baby limas, cooked
2 cups kernel corn
1 cup sour cream
1 Tablespoon butter
salt and black pepper or sage to taste

Heat corn and lima beans with butter in top of double boiler. When thoroughly hot, stir in sour cream and seasoning. Heat thoroughly and serve.
Cooked to Your Taste, 1945

OLD-FASHIONED STRING BEANS AND BACON

1 can string beans and liquid
or an equal amount of fresh beans
2 medium potatoes (1/2 inch diced pieces)
1/4 lb. bacon, well browned, ½ in. pieces
1/4 teaspoon salt
1 cup water
1 small onion (left whole)
pepper

Put all the ingredients into a kettle and boil until the potatoes are soft (about 15 minutes).
The Southern Cookbook, 1939

SWEET-SOUR GREEN BEANS

4 strips bacon
1 onion, thinly sliced
2 Tablespoons sugar
5 Tablespoons vinegar
3 to 4 cups cooked or canned green beans, partially drained

Fry bacon and keep drippings; remove from pan. Add onion, sugar, vinegar, beans and remaining bean stock to drippings. Simmer for 20 to 25 minutes; crumble bacon on top.
Satsuma Tea Room, More Fun for the Cook, 1974

GREEN BEANS BLEU

2 Tablespoons margarine
1 can mushroom soup
2/3 cup mushrooms, fresh or canned
5 ounces bleu cheese spread
3 packages cooked French green beans

Sauté mushrooms in margarine. Add the milk and heat. Add cheese spread stirring until melted. Add mushroom soup, 1 cup cracker crumbs and beans. Pour into 3 quart baking dish. Sprinkle remaining crumbs on top. Bake at 400 half an hour. Serves 10.
Satsuma Tea Room, More Fun for the Cook, 1974

GREEN BEAN DELUXE (Before green bean casserole had been heard of)

18 ounces frozen French-style green beans
10 1/2 ounces cream of mushroom soup
slivered almonds (optional)
juice of 1 lemon (optional)

1/4 to 3/4 cup milk
(or bean stock optional)
3 ½ ounces French fried onions
(optional 1/2 to 1 cup buttered bread crumbs)

Cook beans partially; drain. Combine with soup, almonds, lemon juice or milk in 1 1/2 quart casserole. Bake at 350 for 15 minutes. Sprinkle with onions or crumbs; bake for 5 to 10 minutes longer. Serves 6-8.

NOTE: 1 or 2- 16 ounce cans of beans may be used.
Satsuma Tea Room, More Fun for the Cook, 1974

FRIED GREEN BEANS

3 pounds fresh pole beans
bacon drippings or ham seasoning

1/2 to 1 cup water
salt and pepper to taste

Wash and snap the beans. Add the drippings of about 3 strips of bacon or ham fat to large skillet. Add beans and stir-fry for about 10 minutes. Add water, salt, and pepper to taste. Cover and cook for about 20 minutes. Though cooked only for a short while, the beans have a flavor considered typical of Southern cooked green beans. Serves 6.
Gloria Watson, The Nashville Cookbook, 1977

FRENCH FRIED ASPARAGUS

20 asparagus, 3 to 4 inches long
flour
salt and red pepper, to taste

French pancake (crepes) batter
fat for deep frying

Partially cook asparagus (3 to 5 minutes); the tips must be firm enough so they can be handled without difficulty. Drain and cool. Dredge in well-seasoned flour. Tie 3 to 4 tips into individual bundles and dip into batter until well covered. Fry in hot deep fat until crisp and golden brown. Drain on paper and serve.
Cooked to Your Taste, 1945

CREAMED ASPARAGUS AU GRATIN

1 bunch fresh cooked asparagus or #2 can
1 cup medium white sauce
3 Tbl. cottage cheese or grated cheese

1 Tablespoon bread or cracker crumbs
1 Tbl. butter or vegetable shortening
salt, nutmeg, and red pepper to taste

Cut cooked fresh or drained canned asparagus into 3 inch lengths. Place in a greased baking dish and cover with white sauce seasoned with nutmeg, salt and a dash of red pepper. Sprinkle with bread crumbs and cheese, dot with butter or shortening, cover, and bake in a moderate oven for about 20 minutes.
Cooked to Your Taste, 1945

ASPARAGUS

Asparagus boiled, served with butter sauce and Parmesan cheese grated over all, makes an unusually nice supper dish. We would suggest serving it with sliced Virginia ham and rice croquettes.
Mrs. Rhett, 200 Years of Charleston Cooking, 1930

ASPARAGUS AND EGG CASSEROLE

1 1/4 pound can asparagus	1/2 cup milk
2 Tablespoons butter	2 hard-boiled eggs-sliced
2 Tablespoons flour	1/2 cup grated cheese
1 teaspoon salt	Cheddar or Parmesan
1/4 teaspoon pepper	

Drain asparagus, saving 1 cup juice. Melt butter, add flour, salt and pepper. Add milk and asparagus liquid, stir until smooth. Add asparagus and eggs. Put in a baking dish and top with grated cheese. Bake about 30 minutes at 350. Serves 4.

NOTE: This dish is an old standby at *Satsuma*. This dish is also an excellent meat substitute.
Satsuma Tea Room, Fun for the Cook, 1968

ASPARAGUS SOUFFLE

1 can asparagus, dark green preferred	2 cups milk
2 cups breadcrumbs	1 Tablespoon butter
3 eggs	salt and pepper

Beat the eggs with the salt and pepper until light. Add asparagus (cut up), bread crumbs and milk. Pour into buttered dish and bake in a pan of hot water twenty minutes.
The Savannah Cook Book, 1933

CHEESE SOUFFLE

2 Tablespoons butter	1 teaspoon prepared mustard
1/4 cup flour	2 drops Worcestershire sauce
1 7/8 cups milk	1 cup grated American cheese
1 teaspoon salt	6 eggs, separated

Make cream sauce of butter, milk, flour, and seasoning. Remove from stove. Cool slightly. Add cheese. Beat egg yolks light and add to the cheese mixture while stirring constantly. Beat egg whites stiff. Fold into cheese mixture. Fill well buttered baking dish 3/4 full. Bake at 300 in pan of hot water until a knife comes out clean, about 45 minutes.
Serve at once. Serves 4.
Satsuma Tea Room, Fun for the Cook, 1968

SPINACH SOUFFLE

3/4 cup cooked spinach chopped fine
2 Tablespoons butter
2 Tablespoons flour
1/2 cup milk
1/2 cup grated cheese

3 egg yolks, beaten
1/2 teaspoon salt
pepper to taste
3 egg whites, beaten

Make cream sauce with butter, flour, and milk. Add cheese, egg yolk, and seasoning, then spinach. Fold in beaten egg whites. Pour into buttered pan. Set pan in hot water. Bake at 350 for 30-40 minutes. Serves 5-6.
Satsuma Tea Room, Fun for the Cook, 1968

SPINACH WITH EGG SAUCE

1 pound spinach
or 10 ounces frozen (chopped)

1/4 cup water
½ teaspoon salt

Drop washed spinach into boiling water. Cook 6 to 10 minutes. Drain. Serve at once with egg sauce. Serves 4.

EGG SAUCE

1 hard cooked egg (chopped)
1/4 teaspoon salt
2 slices of bacon (cooked and crumbled)

2 Tablespoons mayonnaise
1/2 teaspoon grated onion

Mix ingredients thoroughly. Serve on hot spinach. Serves 4.
Satsuma Tea Room, Easy on the Cook-Garden Vegetables, 1975

SPINACH CASSEROLE

1 package frozen chopped spinach,
cooked and drained
1 small package egg noodles,
cooked and drained
1 can Cheddar cheese soup

1/2 cup extra sharp cheese grated
1 small can evaporated milk
grated onion
salt and pepper to taste
1/4 stick butter or margarine

Mix all ingredients except some of the grated cheese. Pour into a casserole dish, sprinkling remaining cheese on top. Bake at 350 until bubbly, about 20 minutes. May be made the day ahead. Serves 6.
Satsuma Tea Room, More Fun for the Cook, 1974

FRIED SQUASH CAKES

Slice the squash very thin, being certain to slice it across. Place the slices in salt water, wipe them dry, sprinkle with salt and pepper, and then dip in flour, in beaten egg, and then in cracker crumbs. Repeat the process twice and then drop into pot of deep hot fat for frying. When the squash has been cooked through, drain on crumpled brown paper and serve.
The Southern Cookbook, 1939

ANNIE LAURIE ATKINSON'S SQUASH CASSEROLE

2 cups cooked mashed yellow squash (drain extra liquid)
1 small onion, chopped
1 cup milk
2 eggs, well beaten
1/2 stick margarine or butter
dash of oregano (leaves)
2 Tablespoons mayonnaise (She always used Dukes.)
salt and pepper to taste
1 cup saltine cracker crumbs
1/2 cup grated sharp Cheddar cheese
1/2 cup sliced almonds, toasted

Sauté chopped onion in large pan. Add the cooked and drained mashed squash. In separate bowl, mix together milk, eggs, mayo, and seasonings. Stir in melted margarine/butter. Pour into pan of squash and onion mixture and cook on low heat until slightly thickened. In shallow baking dish, arrange layer of saltine cracker crumbs. Add squash mixture. Top with almonds and cheese. Bake at 350 for 45 minutes.

NOTE: Annie Laurie was a relative of my wife (David S), who resided in the Carolina low country on the border of North and South Carolina. She lived to a ripe old age of 103 and this recipe is one of those recipes that is passed down from generation to generation to where it ends up becoming family lore. An example of this fact is in the using of Dukes mayonnaise as the recipe's mayonnaise. Any mayonnaise will work but Duke's was so special to Annie Laurie and her recipe that it was her belief that no other mayonnaise would be successful; tradition? custom?
Annie Laurie Atkinson as shared by Lisa Beth Atkinson

STUFFED SQUASH

Clean 6 scalloped squash. Boil in cold water until tender but not too soft. Drain and scoop out about half the insides, leaving enough pulp to keep the shape of the squash; drain as much liquid as possible from the scooped-out portion. Press through a sieve and add 1 Tablespoon butter, 1 Tablespoon heavy cream, salt and pepper and let simmer four minutes. Fill shells with mixture and place in baking pan. Sprinkle with sifted bread crumbs, chopped parsley and melted butter. Pour half a cup of warm water into bottom of pan and bake in hot oven (400 F) until squash are well browned on top. Lift from pan with spatula. Serve at once.
The Southern Cookbook, 1939

BAKED STUFFED SQUASH

6 yellow crook necked squash
1/2 cup Cheddar cheese
salt and pepper to taste
Tabasco sauce to taste
1 small onion chopped
1 1/2 Tablespoons butter
1 cup bread or cracker crumb

Cook squash in salted water until tender. Scoop out center of squash, just leaving the shell. Mash the squash, add grated Cheddar cheese, onion, butter, and seasoning plus 1 cup bread or cracker crumbs. Stuff in the shells and sprinkle with cracker crumbs and paprika. Place dish in a pan with a little water. Bake 1/2 hour at 325. Serves 6.
Satsuma Tea Room, More Fun for the Cook, 1974

BAKED STUFFED SUMMER SQUASH

4 medium squash, yellow or zucchini	1 teaspoon salt
1 cup bread crumbs, toasted	1 teaspoon dried oregano
1 cup Parmesan cheese	1/2 cup butter, melted
1/2 clove garlic, minced	

Cook squash in salted, boiling water 6-8 minutes. Drain and let cool. Cut the squash in half and scoop out the pulp. Combine the pulp with remaining ingredients. Stuff squash cavities with the pulp and drizzle butter over them. Bake in a 350 oven 20-25 minutes. Serves 4.

NOTE: Sometimes I feel one squash plant in the garden will feed the whole neighborhood, so I'm always looking for new ways to use yellow squash. They work in breads, cakes, pies casseroles, soups, salads, pickled, and fried. I haven't found a squash ice cream recipe yet.
David Hazelwood, Cortner Mill Restaurant cookbook, 2009

ZUCCHINI WITH PARMESAN CHEESE

4 small zucchini squash	1/2 cup milk	1/4 cup Parmesan cheese
3/4 cup water	1/4 cup butter	salt and pepper to taste

Peel zucchini and slice. Cook in water until tender. Drain, add milk, butter and seasonings. Put in baking dish and top with Parmesan cheese. Bake 20 minutes in 350 degree oven. Serves 4.
Satsuma Tea Room, Fun for the Cook, 1968

SQUASH IN CREAM

2 pounds summer squash	flour
1/2 cup cream, sweet or sour	salt and paprika to taste
4 Tablespoons tomato juice	chopped parsley or dill
4 Tablespoons oil or butter	

Slice or cube squash; dredge in flour and pan in hot fat until slightly brown; season. Mix cream, tomato juice, and parsley or dill. Place squash in well-greased baking dish and cover with tomato-cream mixture. Bake in a moderate oven for 10 to 15 minutes.
Cooked to Your Taste, 1945

SQUASH SOUFFLE

2 pounds summer squash	1/2 teaspoon salt	3 eggs separated
1 medium onion chopped	1 cup grated cheese	1/2 cup croutons
2 Tablespoons margarine	1/4 cup half and half	

Heat oven to 350 F. Grease 2-quart baking dish. Cook squash with croutons and milk. Mix well, add beaten egg yolks and then cheese. Beat the egg whites until stiff and gently fold into squash. Put all into casserole and place casserole in pan of hot water and cook 30 to 40 minutes or until firm. Serves 6 to 8.
Satsuma Tea Room, Easy on the Cook-Garden Vegetables, 1975

SUMMER SQUASH SOUFFLE

2 1/2 to 3 cups cooked squash
1 teaspoon minced onion
1 Tablespoon sugar
1 cup thick white sauce
2 eggs beaten
salt and pepper to taste

Blend all together. Pour into buttered baking dish. Bake 30 minutes at 350 degrees until set.

NOTE: Really good with the canned French fried onions added on top the last 5 minutes.
Satsuma Tea Room, More Fun for the Cook, 1974

BAKED ACORN SQUASH

2 acorn squash
4 Tablespoons butter, melted
4 Tablespoons brown sugar
2 teaspoons grated orange rind
1 cup orange sections

Heat oven to 350 F. Cut squash in half and remove seeds and pulp, holding the seeds. Place cut side down in a shallow baking pan. Add water to a depth of 1/4 inch. Bake for about 40 minutes. Carefully turn the halves and fill the centers with a mixture of sugar, butter and orange rind. Top with orange sections and bake about 20 minutes longer, until tender. Serves 4.
Mildred R. Wright, The Nashville Cookbook, 1977

OPHIR PLANTATION'S COOKED PUMPKIN

Ophir is one of the plantations of South Carolina which was settled before the American Revolution. This house, standing among its large, live oaks, is a beautiful example of colonial architecture. The plantation was a place of joyous activity before the Civil War, but it descended as so many other Southern plantations, into silence.

From Miss Virginia Porcher, whose family always owned Ophir, comes the Ophir way of cooking pumpkin:

"This method is similar to the one used for baking Hubbard squash in many northern homes. Cut slices of pumpkin and place them in a baking pan with a very little water in the bottom. Bake them in the oven, which should be moderately hot, until soft. With a spoon, remove the soft pumpkin from the rind and mix with butter, salt and sugar to taste. Put into a baking dish and allow to brown nicely in a hot oven."
Miss Virginia Porcher, St. James, Berkeley, 200 Years of Charleston Cooking, 1930

ACORN SQUASH

Cut three squash in half, remove seeds and place cut side down in baking dish with 1/4 inch of water. Bake 40 minutes at 350 F. Carefully turn squash over; butter, sprinkle with brown sugar and 1/2 teaspoon orange rind. Bake 20 minutes.
Satsuma Tea Room, Easy on the Cook-Garden Vegetables, 1975

ACORN SQUASH WITH APPLE

Cut acorn squash in half lengthwise. Remove all the seeds. Bake cut side down in 350 oven for 30 minutes with a little water in the pan.

Chop tart apples. Season each 1/2 squash with butter, salt, and brown sugar. Put the apples in the squash with some sugar and butter on them. Bake until the apples are done, about 30 minutes or more. This vegetable dish is a favorite of ours. Serving size is 1/2 acorn squash per person.
Satsuma Tea Room, More Fun for the Cook, 1974

EGGPLANT

Pare eggplant and cut into slices. Sprinkle with salt, cover and let stand to draw out juice (moisture). Dip in beaten eggs, then in bread crumbs. Fry in deep fat.
The Southern Cookbook, 1939

STUFFED EGGPLANT

Select 2 medium sized eggplants and, after washing, dry and cut into halves lengthwise. Scoop out the meat, leaving the rind thick enough to keep shape. Chop the meat fine and mix with bread crumbs (about an equal quantity), 2 Tablespoons of melted butter, salt and pepper (a little chopped onion and bell pepper give additional flavor if desired). Moisten with brown stock, fill the shells with the prepared meat. Place a strip of bacon on top of each shell, place in a buttered pan and bake for 35-40 minutes.
The Savannah Cook Book, 1933

EGGPLANT SOUFFLE (One of my favorites)

1 eggplant	1 cup cream
4 eggs	1/4 cup melted butter or margarine
salt and pepper to taste	

Peel eggplant and cut in small chunks. Cook in water until tender. Drain well. Beat eggs. Add other ingredients and then beat into eggplant. Bake in a 350 degree oven about 30 minutes or until soufflé puffs up. Serve at once. Serves 8-10.
Satsuma Tea Room, More Fun for the Cook, 1974

BROILED EGGPLANT

1 eggplant	salt
soft butter	paprika

Peel eggplant, cut crosswise into 1/2 inch slices. Spread with butter and seasoning. Place on baking sheet and cook in 400 degree oven until tender, about 12 minutes. Turn-over and brown on other side. This meal is good plain or with tomato sauce and grated cheese.

NOTE: This is so simple to prepare but oh so very good!
Satsuma Tea Room, Fun for the Cook, 1968

BAKED EGGPLANT

Cook two eggplants in boiling water, drain and then cool and peel. Put through colander and add 1 cup of bread crumbs, 2 eggs, a little bell pepper, 2 teaspoons of chopped onion, 2 Tablespoons of butter, and salt to taste. Put in deep dish, cover with bread crumbs and brown.
The Savannah Cook Book, 1933

STUFFED EGGPLANT

1 large eggplant	2/3 cup cracker crumbs
3 Tablespoons butter or margarine	salt and pepper to taste
1 cup cooked ground meat	1/2 cup cracker crumbs
1 cup tomato puree	

Cut a slice from the side of eggplant. Remove center, leaving a thin shell. Dice the pulp and cook in butter or margarine over low heat, until tender. Add meat, tomato puree and 2/3 cup cracker crumbs. Fill eggplant shell. Sprinkle with 1/2 cup cracker crumbs. Bake in a hot oven, 400 degrees, for 30 minutes.
Holiday Hostess Cookbook, 1958

EGGPLANT, TOMATO, AND CHEESE BAKE

Summer in Tennessee means plenty of fresh delicious produce. Why not use some fresh-from-the-garden vegetables for this easy baked dish.

1 large eggplant, sliced	1/4 teaspoon black pepper
1 medium onion, thinly sliced	2 teaspoons extra virgin olive oil or canola oil
2 zucchini, cut in bite sized pieces	
3 cups mushrooms, sliced	3/4 cup low fat ricotta cheese
29 ounces, canned, diced tomatoes	1 cup part-skim mozzarella cheese
8 ounces canned tomato sauce	1 cup breadcrumbs (either panko or whole wheat)
3 Tablespoons fresh basil, chopped	
2 Tablespoons water	

Preheat oven to 375. Arrange eggplant, onion, and zucchini on a baking sheet, sprayed with cooking spray. Spray the tops of the vegetables as well. Cover with foil. Bake for 10 minutes covered then 10 minutes uncovered.

In a small saucepan, heat the oil over medium heat. Add mushrooms, garlic, water and pepper. Cook until mushrooms soften. Add tomatoes, tomato sauce and basil. Reduce heat and simmer for 10 minutes. Spread half the tomato mixture on the bottom of a baking dish coated with cooking spray. Add half of the eggplant, zucchini and onion. Layer all the ricotta and half the mozzarella. Repeat layers with another 1/2 of the tomato-mushroom mixture and the remaining eggplant, onion and zucchini. Add the remaining tomato mixture and sprinkle the remaining mozzarella. Top with breadcrumbs. Bake for 30 to 45 minutes, until the cheese begins to brown. Serves 8.
HEART.org

EGGPLANT SOUFFLE

1 eggplant	3 Tablespoons cream	1 teaspoon salt
3 slices toasted bread	1 onion, chopped	pepper to taste
2 eggs beaten	1 Tablespoon margarine	

Peel and cube the eggplant, cook in salted water until tender. Pour 1/4 cup milk over toast to soften and mix with the mashed eggplant, add beaten eggs and seasonings. Place into buttered casserole. Pour cream on top. Bake at 350 F for 25 minutes. Serves 5 to 6.
Satsuma Tea Room, Easy on the Cook-Garden Vegetables, 1975

FRENCH FRIED BRUSSELS SPROUTS

1 pound Brussels sprouts	fat for deep frying
salt and nutmeg to taste	tartar sauce or Spanish mayonnaise
French pancake (crepe) batter	

Cook the sprouts; drain if necessary and season. Dip into batter until well covered, fry in deep fat until crisp and golden brown, drain on paper. Serve with sauce in a separate dish.
Cooked to Your Taste, 1945

RICH TASTY BRUSSELS SPROUTS

1 quart Brussels sprouts	1 cup milk	1/4 teaspoon salt
2 cups boiling water	2 Tablespoons margarine	1/3 cup bread crumbs
1/2 teaspoon salt	3 ounces sharp cheese, grated	3 slices bacon
2 Tablespoons flour		

Trim damaged leaves from the sprouts. Cut an x in the stem ends. Drop in boiling water with salt, uncovered until tender (10 to 12 minutes). Drain and serve with sauce.

CHEESE SAUCE
Melt the margarine in top of a double boiler, blend in the flour and add milk, stirring until thickened. Add cheese, stirring until melted. Drain sprouts and place in a hot dish. Pour the sauce over the sprouts. Sprinkle with crumbs, browned in margarine. Top with the crumbled crisp bacon. Serves 5 to 6.
Satsuma Tea Room, Easy on the Cook-Garden Vegetables, 1975

BROCCOLI

When a few years ago eager hostesses in New York began to serve broccoli, they felt they had made an exciting new discovery. Yet old books about Charleston show that broccoli was eaten there 100 years ago (Today about 200 years ago). But it was forgotten in Charleston for generations and was really brought to New York from Italy. Now South Carolina is astonished to find that broccoli can be grown easily and profitably in the flats around Charleston. It is not so expensive as in New York and therefore it is often served without any stalk. The crinkly tops are cut off and served with butter; all the stalk part being thrown away. This makes a rather more delicate way of serving broccoli.
As served at the Villa Margherita, 200 Years of Charleston Cooking, 1930

BROCCOLI

Trim off leaves and cut off tough parts of stem. Have ready 2 quarts of boiling, salted water. Put in the broccoli with a pinch of soda and cook hard for 10 to 15 minutes. Remove from water and serve immediately with drawn butter sauce. If a large quantity of broccoli is to be cooked, it is a good idea to tie several heads together. Great care should be taken in removing from pot so as not to break the stalks.

NOTE: Hollandaise is a popular sauce with this vegetable, but the flavor is so delicate that many prefer the drawn butter. Cold broccoli with French dressing is a delicious salad.
The Savannah Cook Book, 1933

RICE AND BROCCOLI CASSEROLE

1 cup cooked rice	1 can cream of chicken soup
1/4 to 1/2 chopped onion	1 can cream of mushroom soup
1/2 cup chopped celery	1 small jar of Cheese Whiz
1/4 cup butter	grated Parmesan and paprika
1 or 2 packages chopped broccoli, cooked	

Sauté onion and celery in butter. Combine this with broccoli, the soups, rice, and Cheese Whiz. Sprinkle with the Parmesan. Bake at 350 to 375 for 10 to 20 minutes or until bubbly and lightly browned. Serves 8-10.

NOTE: This recipe is "just plain good!" and one of the most successful, popular, and best-ever dishes from our grocery store frozen food vegetables.
Satsuma Tea Room, More Fun for the Cook, 1974

BROCCOLI WITH CHEESE SAUCE

1 large bunch broccoli	1/2 cup sour cream
1 teaspoon salt	1/4 cup milk
1 cup Velveeta cheese	

Cook broccoli in salted water until tender, but never until it is yellow. Drain well. Cut the cheese while the broccoli is cooking and put into a double boiler to soften. Add sour cream and milk; beat with hand beater until smooth. Make sure the broccoli is well drained. Serve with the sauce on the broccoli. Serves 4.
Satsuma Tea Room, Fun for the Cook, 1968

CANDIED CARROTS

6 medium sized carrots	1 cup brown sugar
1/2 cup water	2 Tablespoons butter

Boil carrots, scrape and cut them in strips as you would potatoes for French frying. Mix the other ingredients in a baking dish and warm to make a syrup. Place the carrots in this syrup so that the syrup covers them entirely and bake until candied.
The Southern Cookbook, 1939

CARROT PUDDING

2 Tablespoons butter	1/4 teaspoon salt
1 cup sugar	1 cup flour, sifted
2 eggs	grated rind of 1 orange
1 1/2 cups grated raw carrots	grated rind of 1 lemon
1/4 teaspoon ground cloves	1 teaspoon baking soda
1/2 teaspoon cinnamon	1 cup raw potatoes
1/4 teaspoon nutmeg	1/4 pound thinly sliced citron

Cream the butter and sugar; add eggs and beat well. Add carrots, spices and salt, and sifted flour, orange and lemon rinds to the mixture. Add the soda to the grated raw potatoes and stir until it is dissolved; add the potatoes to the carrot and flour mixture. Add the citron, mixing it well through the batter. Butter a mold and place a sheet of greased paper on the bottom; pour in the pudding. Cover the mold and place it in a pot of boiling water to steam for 2 hours. The pudding may be served with cream or your favorite sauce.
The Southern Cookbook, 1939

GLAZED CARROTS

1 pound carrots	1/2 teaspoon salt
1/3 cup brown sugar	3 Tablespoons margarine

Steam carrots in salt water until tender, place in Pyrex plate, add sugar and margarine. Bake for 10 minutes in 375 F oven.
Satsuma Tea Room, Easy on the Cook-Garden Vegetables, 1975

CARROT SOUFFLE

3 medium carrots	3 Tablespoons butter	1/2 teaspoon salt
3 Tablespoons flour	1 cup milk	4 eggs, separated

Peel carrots. Cook in boiling salted water until tender. Drain and mash the carrots. Melt butter in double boiler. Stir in flour and milk stirring constantly until slightly thickened. Add salt. Let mixture cool slightly. Beat egg yolks light and add to mixture. Add carrot pulp and blend. Beat egg whites stiff. Fold into mixture. Bake at 375 for 30-40 minutes. Serves 4.
Satsuma Tea Room, Fun for the Cook, 1968

PICKLED CARROTS

1 bunch of carrots cut crosswise

Steam the carrots until tender (about 40 minutes). Serve with the sweet-sour sauce, located on following page in the Sweet-Sour Beets recipe, using 1/2 cup carrot liquid instead of 1/2 cup liquid from the beets.
Satsuma Tea Room, Easy on the Cook-Garden Vegetables, 1975

SWEET-SOUR BEETS

2 cups cooked cubed beets	1/2 cup liquid from the beets	1/2 teaspoon salt
2 Tablespoons margarine	1/4 cup vinegar	few grains of pepper
2 Tablespoons flour	1/4 cup sour cream	

6 or 8 beets (or a 16 ounce can) cooked without peeling until tender (about 40 minutes). Cool, peel and cube. Make sauce of the seven ingredients and serve over the beets.
Satsuma Tea Room, Easy on the Cook-Garden Vegetables, 1975

BEETS IN MADEIRA SAUCE

3 cups sliced beets cooked fresh or canned

1 cup Madeira sauce
sprigs of parsley

Drain beets if necessary. Mix with Madeira sauce in top of double boiler and heat thoroughly over boiling water. Serve garnished with sprigs of parsley.

MADEIRA SAUCE

2 cups vegetable stock
1/2 lb. fresh mushrooms or 1 cup canned
4 Tablespoons dry red wine

3 to 4 Tablespoons butter
salt
chopped parsley

Chop mushrooms fine and pan in hot butter for 3 minutes. Stir frequently. Add vegetable stock and parsley, cover and simmer for 15 minutes or until liquid is reduced to 1 cup. Season. Add wine and simmer, uncovered for 2 minutes.

NOTE: Sauce may be served hot or chilled.
Cooked to Your Taste, 1945

HARVARD BEETS

1/3 cup sugar
1/3 teaspoon salt or to taste
2 Tablespoons cornstarch
1/2 cup mild vinegar

2 cups sliced beets or
10-12 small beets, cooked, peeled, sliced
1-2 teaspoons margarine

Mix sugar, salt, and cornstarch; add vinegar. Boil for 5 minutes. Pour over hot beets; cover. Cook over low heat for 30 minutes. Add butter just before serving.

NOTE: 1/4 cup vinegar and 1/4 cup water or beet liquid may be substituted for 1/2 cup vinegar. Serves 6.
Satsuma Tea Room, More Fun for the Cook, 1974

SPICY BEETS WITH APPLES

3 cups sliced beets, cooked fresh or canned
2 medium apples
2 small onions
1/2 cup vegetable stock or water
1 Tablespoon vegetable shortening or oil
1/2 teaspoon caraway seeds
1/2 teaspoon lemon juice
salt, nutmeg, basil, black pepper to taste
2 Tablespoons, light sour cream, if desired

Chop the onions fine and pan in hot fat until tender but not brown. Core but do not peel the apples, shred in a glass or non-metallic shredder, add to the onion together with the caraway seeds and salt. Pan for 2 minutes. Add sliced beets and enough liquid to prevent scorching, cover and simmer over a low flame for 10 minutes. Season with lemon juice and spices to taste. Mix well with the sour cream, let come to a quick boil and serve.
Cooked to Your Taste, 1945

ORANGE BEETS

1/4 cup fresh orange juice
2 teaspoons grated orange peel
2 teaspoons fresh lemon juice
2 Tablespoons butter
1/8 teaspoon salt
3 cups fresh beets (coarsely shredded)
1 teaspoon cornstarch
1 teaspoon water

Combine the orange juice, orange peel, lemon juice, butter, and salt in a one-quart saucepan. Bring to a boiling point. Add the beets that have been peeled and grated (about 4 large beets). Cover the saucepan and cook for 4 or 5 minutes, until beets are tender. Mix the cornstarch with the water and add to the beets. Cook, stirring lightly, for about 30 seconds just until thickened and smooth. Serves 6-8.

NOTE: This is a great recipe for fresh beets. The crispy goodness is there when served hot or refrigerated and served cold.
Ann Rowland, The Nashville Cookbook, 1977

BEETS IN ORANGE SAUCE

1 cup orange juice
1/3 cup seedless raisins
3/4 teaspoon salt
1/4 cup sugar
2 Tablespoons cornstarch
2 Tbl. beet liquid, drained from the can
1 Tablespoon lemon juice
1 Tablespoon butter
1 pound can (2 cups) sliced or diced red beets, drained

Combine orange juice with raisins, heat to boiling. Mix salt, sugar, and cornstarch. Add beet liquid; stir to a smooth paste. Add to the orange juice; cook stirring constantly, until thick and clear. Add lemon juice, butter and drained beets. Heat. Serves 4 to 5.
Easy-on-the-Cookbook, 1960

CAULIFLOWER AND MUSHROOM SOUFFLE

1 medium head cauliflower	3 Tablespoons bread or cracker crumbs
1/2 pound mushrooms	3 Tbl. vegetable shortening or butter
2 eggs	salt, nutmeg, paprika and white pepper to taste
1 medium white sauce	
4 Tablespoons grated cheese	chopped parsley

Cook cauliflower until tender and drain. Chop mushrooms. Break cauliflower into flowerets and mix with white sauce, mushrooms, parsley, and cheese; season to taste. Separate eggs; beat yolks until light and creamy and beat whites until stiff, but not dry. Add the egg yolks to the cauliflower, blend well and cut and fold in the egg whites. Turn into well-greased baking dish, sprinkle with bread or cracker crumbs, dot with fat, cover and bake in a moderate oven for about 25 minutes. Serve immediately.
Cooked to Your Taste, 1945

SCALLOPED CAULIFLOWER

1 head cauliflower	1 egg
1 cup bread crumbs	salt and pepper to taste
2 Tablespoons melted butter	
1 cup milk (about)	

Boil the cauliflower in salted water until tender. Break into flowerets and place them, stems down in a buttered baking dish. Beat the bread crumbs to a soft paste with the melted butter and milk. The amount of milk required will depend on the dryness of the crumbs. Season to taste and whip in the egg. Season the cauliflower with salt and pepper and a little butter if desired and pour the mixture over it. Bake for 10 minutes covered in a quick oven (425 F). Then uncover and bake until brown.
200 Years of Charleston Cooking, 1930

CAULIFLOWER-ITALIAN STYLE

1 large head cauliflower	4 Tablespoon tomato paste
1 hard-cooked egg	salt and marjoram, to taste
4 Tbl. butter or vegetable shortening	grated cheese

Cook cauliflower; drain if necessary and leave whole. Blend the butter or vegetable shortening with tomato paste and seasoning. Place cauliflower in a well-greased baking dish, cover with tomato sauce, and bake covered in a moderate oven for 15 minutes. Uncover and bake for 15 minutes. Garnish with egg slices, sprinkle with cheese and serve.
Cooked to Your Taste, 1945

MACARONI CROQUETTES

Boil 1 cup macaroni in salted water until tender. Drain and stir macaroni into cream sauce of 2 Tablespoons butter, 1 Tablespoon flour and 1 cup milk. Add 1/2 teaspoon salt, 1/2 cup grated cheese. Let cool. Mold into shapes, roll in eggs and bread crumbs. Fry in deep fat.
The Savannah Cook Book, 1933

CAULIFLOWER

Select compact, curd-like flowers. Soak in cold salt water for 1/2 hour. Drain, place into boiling water with 1 teaspoon salt. Cook rapidly for 8 to 10 minutes or until tender. Serve at once with a favorite sauce. Sprinkle with paprika.

NOTE: Broccoli, Brussels sprouts, cabbage, and asparagus may be cooked as above. Serve with butter or one of the sauces.
Satsuma Tea Room, Easy on the Cook-Garden Vegetables, 1975

GREEN PEAS-FRENCH STYLE

24 ounces frozen green peas	2 bunches small green onions	1/2 pound butter
1 small head lettuce in pieces	2 Tablespoons sugar	1/2 cup water
		salt and pepper

Put all ingredients into a saucepan with a heavy lid. Cook covered for 15 minutes. Remove lettuce before serving. Serves 6-8.

NOTE: When my aunt ate this dish in France, she recounted that part of the lettuce was left in the dish.
Satsuma Tea Room, Fun for the Cook, 1968

CREAMED GREEN PEAS

Cook 2 cups of shelled green peas quickly in boiling water until tender. Add 1 teaspoon salt, level. Drain off water and add 1/2 cup cream. Slowly bring this to a boil and serve.
The Southern Cookbook, 1939

CREAMED CABBAGE

Shred a small head of white cabbage and plunge a handful at a time into salted boiling water. As soon as it boils up once, drain and serve with a white sauce made of one Tablespoon of butter, 1 Tablespoon of flour and a cup of milk.

NOTE: This is a fine and inexpensive dish to serve in a hurry.
The Savannah Cook Book, 1933

CREAMED KALE AND ONIONS

1 1/2 pounds kale, cleaned	3 Tablespoons flour
12 small white onions peeled (2 lbs.)	1 1/2 cups vegetable liquid or milk
1/4 cup shortening	seasonings

Cook kale in boiling salted water- enough to come half-way up – until tender, about 15 minutes. Cook onions in boiling salted water until tender, about 15 minutes. Drain and save vegetable liquid. Combine vegetables. Make white sauce of shortening, flour, milk and seasonings (salt, pepper, etc.). Pour over kale and onions. Serve hot. Makes 6 servings.
Farm Journal's Country Cookbook, 1959

VEGETARIAN STROGANOFF

1 large onion, chopped coarse
4 Tablespoons butter
2 cloves garlic, minced
2 Tablespoons dry vermouth
5 cups fresh mushrooms, sliced
1 zucchini, parboiled and sliced

12 ounces sour cream
5 Tablespoons flour
2 cups water
1 cube vegetable bouillon
1/2 teaspoon black pepper

In a large skillet sauté the onion, butter and garlic until the onion is tender. Add the vermouth, zucchini and mushrooms and cook until zucchini is tender. Remove from skillet. Add remaining ingredients to skillet and cook until thick and bubbly, about 5 minutes. Add vegetable mixture to sauce and simmer 5 minutes. Serve over rice or egg noodles.
Jim Long, Cortner Mill Restaurant cookbook, 2009

STEWED CUCUMBERS

It is very seldom that one thinks of serving cucumbers any way except sliced raw. They seem like another vegetable entirely stewed, and a very good one too.

2 large cucumbers
1 medium-sized onion

1/2 cup vinegar
salt and pepper to taste

2 Tablespoons butter

Cut the peeled cucumbers in ¼-inch slices, chop the onion, add a little salt and simmer them for 20 minutes or until very tender. Drain, add the vinegar, salt and pepper to taste, and the butter. Cook for 3 minutes longer and serve with the sauce from the pan. The sauce may be thickened by adding a little flour; but while this is good, we felt that it was better without the flour.
200 Years of Charleston Cooking, 1930

STUFFED CUCUMBERS

2 large cucumbers
2 tomatoes
1/2 pound mushrooms
1/2 cup cooked rice or
6 Tablespoons oatmeal

2 Tablespoons chopped nuts
5 Tablespoons vegetable shortening
3 Tablespoons grated cheese
salt
chopped parsley

Pare cucumbers, cut lengthwise into halves and hollow out centers. Remove the seeds and chop remaining pulp. Cut mushrooms and pan in 3 Tablespoons hot fat for 5 minutes; add cucumber pulp, parsley and rice (or oatmeal and nuts), and pan for another 5 minutes; season. Stuff cucumber shells. Slice tomatoes, place over stuffed cucumbers and dot with remaining fat. Place in well-greased baking dish; bake uncovered in a moderate oven for 15 minutes or until well-browned. Sprinkle with cheese and serve.
Cooked to Your Taste, 1945

MUSHROOMS IN CREAM

1 1/2 pounds mushrooms
1 cup cream or top milk
2 Tablespoons oil or butter

1 teaspoon flour
salt and red pepper to taste
chopped parsley or dill or chives

Slice mushrooms and pan in hot fat for about 5 minutes; season. Mix cream with flour and stir into mushrooms; let come to a quick boil. Place under medium broiler for 10 minutes. Serve sprinkled with parsley or dill or chives.
Cooked to Your Taste, 1945

MUSHROOMS IN BATTER

1 1/2 pounds very large mushrooms
2 firm tomatoes
1 small lemon
pinch of cayenne

salt
French pancake +(crepes) batter
fat for deep frying

Peel and cut mushrooms in halves, leaving the stems on. Dip in batter and fry in hot deep fat until golden brown. Drain on paper. Serve garnished with slices of tomato and lemon.
Cooked to Your Taste, 1945

BRUSSELS SPROUTS IN SOUR CREAM

1 1/2 pounds Brussels sprouts
1 medium onion
1 cup vegetable stock, or water
chopped chives or parsley
1/2 cup sour cream
or evaporated milk soured with lemon juice
3 Tablespoons vegetable shortening or butter
salt, white pepper and marjoram to taste

Blanch sprouts or let stand in cold salted water for 10 minutes. Chop the onion and pan in hot fat until tender. Add sprouts and cook over a low flame for 10 minutes, stirring frequently. Add vegetable stock, cover and simmer until tender. Season to taste, add the sour cream or soured evaporated milk and let come to a quick boil. Garnish with chives or parsley and serve.
Cooked to Your Taste, 1945

JERUSALEM ARTICHOKES

Scrape or peel artichokes. Let your conscience be your guide, but I think they are better scraped. Throw them into cold water to keep them from turning dark. Cook in salted, boiling water until tender and serve with drawn butter.

NOTE: A delicate and most delicious vegetable.
The Savanah Cook Book, 1933

ARTICHOKES

Trim the outer leaves from the artichoke and boil the artichoke in salt water for 3/4 hour. Serve with Hollandaise sauce or melted butter.
The Southern Cookbook, 1939

CANDIED BEANS WITH NUTS AND APPLES

1 1/2 cups dried beans, any kind	1 Tablespoon brown sugar or honey
2 canned pimientos	1 Tablespoon butter or bacon drippings
2 medium apples	salt and nutmeg to taste
2 Tablespoons chopped nutmeats	

Cook beans and drain; chop pimientos; core and slice or dice unpeeled apples. Mix beans with pimientos and apples and season. Put into a well-greased baking dish, sprinkle with sugar and nutmeats. Dot with fat. Bake uncovered in a hot oven for 10 minutes.
Cooked to Your Taste, 1945

SHOESTRING ONIONS

Take a large, white, Bermuda onion and slice into pieces about 1-inch thick. Soak these pieces for several hours in iced water and, when ready to cook, drain well, salt, and roll in flour. Fry in deep fat until golden brown.
NOTE: This is a delicious and delicate dish for luncheon or supper.
The Savannah Cook Book, 1933

ONIONS BAKED IN WINE

2 to 3 large Bermuda onions	vermouth or sherry, to taste
1/2 cup cream or evaporated milk	salt and cinnamon, to taste
1 teaspoon brown sugar	

Cut onions in thick slices and arrange in in greased baking dish. Mix the cream with the sugar and wine to taste, pour over the onions and sprinkle with salt and cinnamon. Bake uncovered in slow oven for about 35 minutes, basting several times. Serve with the liquid.
Cooked to Your Taste, 1945

CREOLE STUFFED PEPPERS

4 ears of corn	6 green olives
6 green peppers	1 small onion
4 tomatoes	1 Tablespoon butter

Cut off the tops and remove the centers from the peppers. Put in hot water and cook slowly for 1/2 hour. Brown the onion in the butter, add the tomatoes and corn cut from the cob and let cook about 15 minutes. Just before removing from the fire, add the chopped olives and salt. Stuff the peppers with the mixture and cover with bread crumbs, dot with butter, bake in oven until the crumbs are well browned.
The Southern Cookbook, 1939

APPLE CHARLOTTE (As a vegetable)

Line a buttered baking dish, bottom and sides, with very thin slices of bread, buttered and sprinkled with nutmeg. Fill the center with stewed apples, stopping when half full to put a layer of bits of butter and a few gratings of nutmeg. Then continue filling with apples until the dish is full and bake in a moderate oven (350 F) for about 25 minutes.

Put a meringue on top and cook in a slow oven (300 F) for 12 minutes to brown the meringue. Or instead of meringue, try marshmallows and brown them in the oven. Do not let the marshmallows touch the edge of the baking dish as they are hard to clean off.

The apples may either be sliced or quartered for stewing and cooked in a syrup made of one cup of water to one cup of sugar. A little lemon juice added to the syrup improves the flavor of the apples.

NOTE: This dish is intended as a luncheon or supper dish to be eaten with the meal, not as a dessert.
200 Years of Charleston Cooking, 1930

BAKED DESSERT APPLES (or at any time apples)

NOTE: Some think these apples are better than apple dumplings and are so easy to prepare.

6 large cooking apples	1/2 teaspoon cinnamon	1 egg, slightly beaten
1/3 cup flour	1/3 cup margarine, softened	3/4 cup orange juice
2/3 cup sugar		

Heat oven to 350 F. Butter a baking dish. Core and pare apples. Combine flour, sugar, and cinnamon. Cut in margarine until the mixture resembles coarse cornmeal. Completely dip apples in beaten egg, and then roll in flour mixture. Put apples in baking dish. Fill centers with remaining flour mixture. Pour orange juice into dish. Bake uncovered about 1 hour or until apples are tender. Serve warm with the sauce left in the dish. May be topped with whipped cream. (Why not!)
Ethel Friedman, The Nashville Cookbook, 1977

MACARONI PIE

1/2 pound macaroni	1 teaspoon mustard
1 Tablespoon butter	1 teaspoon each of black and red pepper
1 egg, well-beaten	2 cups grated cheese
1 teaspoon salt	1/2 cup milk

Boil the macaroni in salted water until tender. Drain; stir in the butter and egg. Mix the mustard with a Tablespoon of hot water and add it to the other seasonings. Add the cheese and milk, mix well and turn into a buttered baking dish. Bake in a moderate oven (350 F) until the cheese is melted and the dish brown on top. About 1/2 hour.
Martha Laurens Patterson, 200 Years of Charleston Cooking, 1930

FRUITS

*"A dessert (or meal) without cheese (or fruit)
is like a beautiful woman with only one eye."
-Brillat-Savarin (1755-1826)*

Finding an abundant number of colorful fruits and melons from the farmer's market and local orchards or obtained growing wild from the forests and fields brings an excellent diversity to all the food and drink found on the Southern table. Fruit is wonderful as a complement to any entrée, vegetable, or salad. Dried, canned, or fresh fruit desserts are also time-honored and a delicious welcome at any table.

CHEESE PAIRED WITH FRUIT

CHEDDAR	Best with tart Jonathan apples
SWISS	Best with tangy greening apples and green Finger grapes
BLEU	Best with sweet, Anjou pears or spicy, cinnamon colored Bosc pears
BRICK	Best with sweet-sour Tokay grapes
GOUDA	Best with Golden Delicious apples
BRIE	Best with deep purple Ribier grapes
PROVOLONE	Best with Bartlett pears

Easy-on-the-Cook Book, 1960

POACHED PEARS

6 Bartlett pears
1 cup white and 1 cup brown sugar

3 cups water
brandy or orange cordial to taste

Peel pears and simmer in syrup until tender, but still whole. Remove the pears and reduce the syrup until thick. Add brandy or orange cordial to the syrup and spoon over pears placed in a serving dish. Chill and serve with very cold sweet cream, partially frozen, or with sour cream.

NOTE: I can remember, as a child, when the pear trees in the orchard began to produce ripe fruit ready for harvesting, my brothers and sister and I took bushel baskets and filled them up with ripe pears to be made available for cooking this vegetable and/or dessert in our restaurant, *Satsuma*. Like the early Southern settlers, we too found our food, at least our pears, from what was available from the land; and in the case of the pears, our orchard trees.
The Nashville Cookbook, 1977

*"Watermelon red, peaches sweet,
Trout line callin' f'om de river's feet.
Mockin' bird singin' 'e song so neat,
I's livin' easy! I's livin' high!"*

WATERMELON

"It is said that the Louisiana sun is needed to bring any melon seed to absolute perfection. Melons are among our most common articles of food and are within the reaches of all classes, rich and poor, black and white. Watermelon is preeminent among most all melons. The watermelon is as great a favorite for luncheon and dinner and supper desserts as is the Muskmelon for the Louisiana breakfast. Indeed, at all hours during the summer, except in early forenoon, a watermelon is considered most refreshing and welcome.

The Creoles, as a rule, cut the melon in great round slices, so that each person may have a piece of the "heart" of the fruit. A lengthwise slice is also acceptable, but it all comes down to individual taste preference. The practice of "scooping the melon out with a spoon," and thus serving it, is not favored at all by the Creoles."
The Picayune Creole Cook Book, 1922

PEACHES

Many of the peaches found in the markets today are picked green and shipped a great distance. They are beautiful to look at, but the texture is often woody and the peach has little juice. For the best peach, buy local and in season. These peaches may not be perfect or even good-looking but they will have a rich juicy peach flavor if they have been tree ripened.

STEWED PEACHES

10 medium-sized peaches
1/2 pound granulated sugar

1 pint of cold water

Peel the peaches and cut them in quarters, carefully removing the stones. Put the peaches into a saucepan with a pint of cold water and ½-pound granulated sugar. Set on the stove and when they begin to boil, skim well. Then let them cook for 6 minutes longer; stirring slowly avoiding not to mash the peaches. Remove from the fire and pour the peaches into a dessert dish to cool. Serve cold; either plain or with cream.

NOTE: The peaches may also be boiled whole.
The Picayune Creole Cook Book, 1922

PEACHES DELIGHTFUL

2/3 cup sugar
1 cup water
3 slices lemon
6 fresh peaches, peeled, halved and pitted
1/2 teaspoon vanilla

dash of salt
1 pint fresh raspberries washed, drained
or 1 pound frozen raspberries, thawed
shredded coconut
toasted slivered almonds

Cook sugar, water, and lemon slices until sugar is completely dissolved. Add peaches; simmer until just tender. Stir in vanilla and salt. Chill. Lift 2 peach halves onto individual dessert plates. Spoon raspberries into peach cavities. Sprinkle with coconut and almonds.
Easy-on-the-Cook Book, 1960

DELMONICO PEACHES

3 medium-sized apples	4 double almond macaroons
#2 can peaches	-page 485
2 ounces blanched almonds	1 Tablespoon butter

Pare the apples and cut them in quarters. Cook the apples in the juice from the can of peaches until soft. Then add the peaches and continue cooking until both fruits are soft enough to mash. Mash them well with the potato masher. Chop the almonds very fine and roll or grind the macaroons. Butter a baking dish and put in a layer of the mashed peach and apple. Sprinkle with a mixture of almond and macaroon crumbs, dot with bits of butter and put in another layer of peach and apple. Continue until the ingredients are used having the almond and macaroon mixture on top. Bake in a moderate oven (350 F) until the top is brown, about 40 minutes. This will make eight servings.

NOTE: This peach and apple combination may be served with the meat course or topped with whipped cream. May be eaten hot or cold for dessert. This dish is delicious with any meat course, especially good with turkey, duck, or quail.
Eunice Hunter Clark, 200 Years of Charleston Cooking, 1930

BROILED PEACH HALVES

Halve peaches and peel them. Arrange them on a greased baking sheet and sprinkle lightly with brown sugar or maple sugar. Dot liberally with butter and broil until sizzling on top and soft through, but not mushy. Serve with whipped cream flavored with vanilla and sugar.

BROILED PEACHES FLAMED WITH BOURBON A variation to the above recipe, is to omit whipped cream and arrange the peaches in a hot serving dish. Pour slightly heated Bourbon over them (allowing 1 ounce to a serving) and ignite. Carry blazing dish to table.
The James Beard Cookbook, 1959

POACHED PEACHES

4 peaches	1- inch vanilla bean or	1 cup of water
1 cup sugar	1 teaspoon vanilla extract	

Peel and halve the peaches. Combine the sugar and water and add the vanilla bean and extract. Bring this to a boil and cook for 5 minutes. Add the peach halves and poach gently, spooning the hot liquid over them and turning them once during the cooking. When they are tender, but not mushy, take the pan from the stove and let peaches cool in the syrup. Serve plain or with custard sauce or whipped cream.

POACHED PEACHES WITH LIQUEUR variations: After the peaches are cooked, flavor them with cognac, Bourbon, or Kirsch, allowing 1 ounce of liqueur per serving. Orange flavored variation: Omit the vanilla bean and add good-sized strips of orange peel to the syrup. Flavor the peaches with Grand Marnier or Cointreau. Serve plain or with a custard sauce flavored with Grand Marnier or Cointreau.
The James Beard Cookbook, 1959

PEACH/PEAR MELBA

Serve poached peach halves or poached pear halves topped with vanilla ice cream and crushed raspberries along with raspberry syrup.
The James Beard Cookbook, 1959

FRIED PEACHES

6 peaches
2 Tablespoons butter
¼ cup brown sugar

Peel and split peaches. Melt the butter in an iron skillet and drop in the peaches. Fill the hollows with the brown sugar and let simmer until well cooked. Serve with either whipped cream, ice cream, or meats.
The Southern Cookbook, 1939

DRIED APPLES

firm, mature, high quality apples
white vinegar
1 cup lemon juice
4 cups water

Wash apples with vinegar and rinse well with water. Peel and core apples. Cut into uniform ¼-inch slices or rings. Dip apples in lemon juice and water solution for 8 minutes to prevent turning brown. Place a newspaper on top of a wire or screen rack. Spread the apples evenly without overlapping on the paper. Choose sunny, low humidity days for drying. Place apples in a sunny location such as a southern window, lawn table, or car window. Apples are properly dried when they are pliable. Store in canning jars or plastic containers. Rehydrate by boiling for 10 minutes or let stand in room temperature water for 30 minutes. Drain and use in apple recipes.

NOTE: Miss Lizzie dried her apples in July near the windows of her enclosed back porch. The drying was aided by lack of air conditioning. I got my first lesson in paring apples the summer I was 8, as she and I prepared apples for drying. I tried my hand at paring but was never able to cut the peeling into one continuous spiral like she did.
David Boswell Hazelwood, Miss Lizzie's Heirlooms, 2009

BAKED APPLES

6 fine apples
6 spoons of sugar
1 cup water

Cut the blossom end of the apple flat and wash, do not peel. Set them in a baking pan, heap a spoon of sugar over each in the little place scooped out at the blossom end and pour a cup ';lkmjnof water in the bottom of the pan. Set in the oven, and bake till very tender, basting them often to keep them soft. Place in a dish, pour over the syrup and serve either hot or cold. They are much nicer served cold with a glass of milk. They are then used as a dessert.

NOTE: A scoop of fresh-churned vanilla ice cream awaits these apples.
The Picayune Creole Cook Book, 1922

BAKED APPLES

8 Granny Smith apples	2 teaspoons cinnamon
2/3 cup brown sugar	1 teaspoon ground cloves
3 Tablespoons butter, melted	1/4 cup water

Core and halve apples and place on a 9 x 13 baking dish and sprinkle with brown sugar, cinnamon, and cloves. Pour melted butter over fruit. Cover and seal with foil and bake for 30 to 40 minutes in a (350 F.) oven. Serve hot.
Cortner Mill Restaurant cookbook, 2009

FRIED APPLES

3 fine apples	white powdered sugar	boiling lard

Peel and core the apples and cut into round slices. Fry them to a delicate golden brown in a pan of boiling lard. (or a similar fat i.e., Crisco) Place them in a heated colander in which you have fitted a piece of brown paper. Drain in the mouth of the oven. Place in a dish and sprinkle with sugar. Serve hot as a side dish to roast meat, roast pork, etc.
The Picayune Creole Cook Book, 1922

SOUTHERN FRIED APPLES

10 tart young apples, unpeeled	4 Tablespoons butter
3/4 to 1 cup sugar	1/2 cup water, or as needed

Core and slice apples; add to sugar, butter, and water in heavy skillet or saucepan. Stir until hot. Cover and cook until tender, stirring frequently. Remove cover near end of cooking; add a bit more water if needed, or allow excess liquid to evaporate. Apples should be quite moist but firm enough to hold shape when served. Adjust the sugar used to taste and serve warm.

NOTE: This is a long-time favorite way to prepare young apples from the orchard. This dish combines stir-frying and steaming and is sweetened to taste. Many cooks like to add bacon drippings as part of the fat. Serves 4-6.
Katherine Nichols, The Nashville Cookbook, 1977

GLAZED BAKED APPLES

8 apples	1 pint heavy cream
1 cup sugar	1 cup boiling water

Wash apples thoroughly, remove cores and skins from top of each apple, place in saucepan with one apple touching the other, with the peeled side up. Add water and cook slowly, testing occasionally with a toothpick, until they are soft. When done place in a baking dish, sprinkle with sugar and put in hot oven (425 degrees F), basting with the water in which they were originally cooked until tops are crisp, rich brown. Serve cold with heavy cream.
The Southern Cookbook, 1939

APPLE CARAMEL

6 Roman (Rome) Beauty apples
or any good cooking apple
3/4 cup sugar

3/4 cup butter
1 teaspoon vanilla
cream

Pare, core, and cut each apple into 8 wedges. Spread sugar evenly in a very large skillet. Heat until sugar melts and turns a light brown color. Stir occasionally. Add butter; mix well. Add apples in a single layer. Cover; cook over medium heat 10 minutes. Turn; cook 10 more minutes. Add vanilla. Serve warm with cream. Serves 8.
Easy-on-the-Cook Book, 1960

BUTTERSCOTCH BAKED APPLES

6 baking apples
1/3 cup light cream

1/3 cup dark corn syrup
1/3 cup chopped nuts

Wash and core apples; place in a greased, shallow baking dish. Combine cream, corn syrup and nuts; use to fill centers of apples. Bake until tender in moderate oven (350 F). Serve with Butterscotch Sauce.

BUTTERSCOTCH SAUCE

Combine 1 cup light cream, 1/3 cup dark corn syrup, 2 Tablespoons butter or margarine and 1 teaspoon vanilla. Cook over low heat until thickened (20 to 30 minutes), stirring occasionally. Serve warm. Makes 6 servings.

NOTE: Buttery, sweet sauce and apples. What more could one hope for?
Farm Journal's Country Cook Book, 1959

APPLE SAUCE

2 1/2 pounds cooking apples
1/2 cup sugar

1 Tablespoon lemon juice
1 cup water

Wash, quarter, and core cooking apples. Add water to barely cover, cook until nearly soft, add sugar, nutmeg, and cinnamon; cook a few minutes longer. Press through strainer. Cool and serve.
The Settlement Cook Book, 1940

CONGEALED APPLESAUCE

3 ounces flavored gelatin
1 cup boiling water

2 cups applesauce

Dissolve gelatin in boiling water. Cool until slightly thickened. Add the cold applesauce. Pour into a relish dish or mold and chill. Serve as a salad or to accompany a meat dish. Serves 6.

NOTE: Substitute sugar free gelatin and unsweetened applesauce for sugar free diets.
The Nashville Cookbook, 1977

CARAMEL CANDY APPLES

12 medium-size red apples
12 wooden skewers or orange sticks
1 pound light-colored caramels
1/4 cup light cream

Wash and dry apples; stick skewers into the stem end. Put caramel and cream in top of double boiler; cook over very hot water, stirring occasionally, until caramels melt. Plunge apples into syrup; twirl once or twice to coat evenly. Place in refrigerator on tray covered with wax paper or foil. (Takes two hours to harden.) Makes 12 caramel-coated apples.
Farm Journal's Country Cook Book, 1959

HONEYED APPLES

6 to 8 medium-size cooking apples
2/3 cup raisins
2/3 cup honey
2/3 cup sugar
3 teaspoons cinnamon
1/8 teaspoon red food color

Peel and core apples. Plump raisins in hot water. Blend together in saucepan the honey, sugar, cinnamon, and food color. Add apples and cook until tender, but not soft, turning often so that they cook evenly. Lift apples onto the platter. Spoon the raisins into the center of the apples; pour syrup over the apples. Serve with cream or ice cream. Makes 6 to 8 servings.

NOTE: This is a great recipe where the apples cook on top of the stove and they come off radiant and enticing.
Farm Journal's Country Cook Book, 1959

APPLES IN CRANBERRY SAUCE

1 cup sugar
1 cup water
2 apples
1 cup cranberries

Boil sugar and water 3 minutes. Pare apples, cut into balls using a potato ball cutter. Drop a few at a time into the boiling syrup. Remove with skimmer when tender, but not broken. Place 3 balls each in individual molds. Wash and drain cranberries, add to hot syrup with the apple trimmings. Let boil soft about 5 minutes. Put through strainer and then pour over apples. Serve as a garnish for meat.

NOTE: As I am writing this recipe, I'm not thinking about a garnish. I'm thinking of a dish served with whipped cream or vanilla ice cream and, I must admit, with my mouth watering.
The Settlement Cook Book, 1940

FRIED PINEAPPLE

Take canned pineapple or pears. Drain. Dip in flour. Fry quickly on all sides in butter until delicately browned. Perfect as a garnish for roast meats.
The Settlement Cook Book, 1940

FRIED BANANAS

4 bananas
boiling lard
white powdered sugar

Peel the bananas and cut them in two lengthwise. Then slice lengthwise about 1/4 of an inch in thickness. Have ready a pan of boiling lard (shortening.) Lay the bananas in it and fry brown, first on one side and then on the other, sifting with a little powdered sugar. When done skim the fruit from the pan and place neatly in a dish. Sprinkle with powdered sugar again and serve hot as an entrée.

NOTE: The banana stalls in the French Market are famous and, at every corner or so, here and there throughout the city, there are fruit stands where the banana is always to be found in a perfect state; very fresh and inviting. Don't forget serving bananas in their natural state as a fruit dessert.
The Picayune Creole Cook Book, 1922

BAKED BANANAS

6 bananas
2 Tablespoons melted butter
2 Tablespoons lemon juice
1/3 cup sugar

Remove skins from bananas, cut in halves lengthwise, and place in shallow pan. Mix the melted butter, sugar and lemon juice and pour over the bananas. Bake in a slow oven (250 degrees F.) for 30 minutes.
The Southern Cookbook, 1939

ORANGE GLAZED BANANAS

3 Tablespoons butter
1/3 cup brown sugar
1/2 cup orange juice
3 bananas, sliced thickly
1 Tablespoon lemon juice
1 teaspoon grated orange rind
1/4 teaspoon ginger

Melt butter in shallow pan. Add sugar, juices and rind, and ginger. Boil about 5 minutes before adding bananas. Toss lightly to barely heat through. Serve as an accompaniment to meat dishes. Serves 4-6.
The Nashville Cookbook, 1977

SAVANNAH STEWED PRUNES

1 pound prunes
1/2 cup sugar
2 slices of lemon

Place the washed prunes and lemon in a double boiler with a little water and sprinkle with sugar. Let steam slowly until thoroughly cooked. Serve with cream.
The Southern Cookbook, 1939

BAKED APRICOTS

2 #2 1/2 cans peeled apricots, drained
1 box light brown sugar
1 eight ounce box Ritz crackers
1/2 pound butter

In a greased baking dish put layer of apricots, cover with brown sugar, then a layer of Ritz crackers crumbs. Dot with butter. Repeat this until the apricots are used up. Bake in 300 degree oven for 1 hour.
Satsuma, More Fun for the Cook, 1974

BAKED ORANGES

4 thin-skinned seedless oranges
2 cups sugar
1 cup of the water oranges were boiled in

Wash the oranges, place in kettle and cover with boiling water. Cook until tender when tried with a fork. Remove from the water, cut in half and arrange in a baking dish. Cook together the sugar and orange water for 5 minutes, pour over the oranges and dot each orange with a piece of butter. Cover the baking dish and bake in a hot oven about one-half hour or until the oranges become transparent. Fantastic served alongside roast duck.
The Southern Cookbook, 1939

CANDIED ORANGE PEEL

Cut orange peelings into ¼-inch strips; cover with cold water for 6 hours. Drain and cover with cold water and bring to boiling. Drain again. Measure the peel, place in a saucepan, cover with water; add sugar to equal the measure of peel and simmer until clear. More water may be added if syrup becomes too thick. Drain when clear and coat pieces with coarse granulated sugar. Store in airtight containers.
The Nashville Cookbook, 1977

SPICED CANTALOUPE

Peel rind and cut cantaloupe into 1-inch pieces. Soak overnight in weak vinegar. To each seven pounds of fruit, add three pounds of sugar and eight sticks of cinnamon, one Tablespoon of whole cloves. Cook about an hour and half or until the fruit becomes transparent. Place in sterile jars and seal.

NOTE: Ideal to serve with fowl or meats.
The Southern Cookbook, 1939

BROILED GRAPEFRUIT

To each grapefruit half add:
    a piece of butter
    3 teaspoons sugar
    a touch of cinnamon

Cook at 350 for 15 minutes.
Satsuma, Fun for the Cook, 1968

STEWED KUMQUATS AND PRUNES

6 kumquats sliced thin
1 cup pitted prunes
1/2 cup sugar

1/2 cup prune juice
1/2 cup orange juice

Wash 1 cup prunes and soak them in cold water overnight. Cook slowly in the water they were soaked with until soft. Add 1/2 cup sugar and cook 5 minutes longer. Season with orange juice. Drain and pit the prunes (Today, already pitted prunes can be bought and used). Add kumquats to the prune juice. Let simmer a few minutes; add the remaining sugar. Cook slowly until kumquats are tender, then add back the prunes.
The Southern Cookbook, 1939

PAPAYA

Papaya is a Southern fruit, a variety of melon. It is eaten raw or flavored with lemon, lime or tart orange juice. Select the melon at a mature unripe stage. Boil or steam the papaya as you would a vegetable. Add a little lime juice which makes a delicious French sauce. This unripe fruit may be used like any other melon in pickles or preserves if you so desire. It also combines well with other fruits for marmalades and jellies. Papaya is very good as a flavor for sherbet. As a breakfast food, it needs no accompaniments. As a dessert, it is perfect.

BAKED PAPAYA

Cut mature but unripe papaya into halves lengthwise. Add a little sugar and orange, lime or lemon juice; or a little cinnamon in place of the juice. Bake 20 minutes and serve immediately on taking from the oven.
The Southern Cookbook, 1939

BAKED PAPAYA

4 cups ripened papaya pulp
1 cup shredded coconut
1 orange- pulp, juice and grated rind

1 cup sugar
4 eggs
4 cups milk

Make a custard of the egg, milk, sugar, and orange. Place papaya and coconut in a baking dish. Pour the custard over and bake in a moderate oven.
The Southern Cookbook, 1939

PAPAYA CANAPE

Toasted rounds of bread, buttered and sprinkled with cinnamon and sugar, may be topped with a round of papaya sprinkled with lemon juice or toasted rounds with papaya crossed with red pimiento strips.
The Southern Cookbook, 1939

CURRIED FRUIT CASSEROLE

2 1/2 can peach halves
2 ½ can apricots
2 1/2 can pears
1 large can pineapple chunks
2 can canned black cherries, pitted
1/3 cup butter
1 cup brown sugar
4 teaspoons curry powder

Mix brown sugar and curry powder together. Drain the fruit, mix the fruit, and then place in a baking dish. Dot with butter, sugar and curry powder mixture. Bake at 325 for 1 hour. Baste frequently. 10 Servings. Can be made day ahead and reheated
Satsuma, More Fun for the Cook, 1974

GINGERED FIGS

Wash one pound dried figs and remove stems. Add cold water to cover and juice and rind of 1/2 lemon, and 1 large piece of ginger root. Stew until the figs are puffed and soft. Remove the figs to a dish. Measure syrup and add 1/2 as much more sugar, simmer until thick and add 1 Tablespoon lemon juice. Serve with whipped cream.
The Settlement Cook Book, 1940

STEWED RHUBARB

1 pound rhubarb
1 cup sugar
a few Tablespoons water

Wash the rhubarb and cut it into 1-inch pieces. If the skin is too tough to cut, pull it off stripping it down the length of the stalk. Place in a saucepan over very low heat with a few Tablespoons of water (it will get watery as it cooks) and the sugar. Cook gently, covered, until just tender and juicy. This will take 20 to 25 minutes.

NOTE: For baked rhubarb, rhubarb pies, etc., a delightful variation is 1/2 rhubarb and 1/2 fresh strawberries. They are perfect together just like toast and jam.
The James Beard Cookbook, 1959

COLD SPICED FRUITS

16 ounces pear halves
16 ounces figs
3 cups sugar
1/3 cup vinegar
juice drained from fruit
1 Tablespoon whole cloves
2 Tablespoons stick cinnamon
1/2 Tablespoon pickling spice

Drain fruits and reserve juice. Mix together and bring to a boil the sugar, vinegar, and juice. Add spices. Pour over drained fruit and simmer gently for about 1 hour. Chill before serving. Serves 4-6.

NOTE: Other combinations of canned fruits may be used. Serve with meats and main dishes. Figs are especially good used in this recipe.
Virginia Kendall White, The Nashville Cookbook, 1977

APPLE PLUM COMPOTE

1 quart applesauce
6 bananas
1 can blue plums

1/2 cup brown sugar
1/4 cup butter

Put applesauce in casserole. Slice bananas and put on top. Cut plums into pieces. Place on top. Sprinkle brown sugar over this and melted butter. Bake at 350 for 20 minutes. Serves 5.
Satsuma, More Fun for the Cook, 1974

BAKED CRANBERRIES

Place 1 quart of cranberries in shallow pan with 1 cup water and 1 cup sugar. Cover, and bake in a slow oven at 300 F. for 45 minutes or without water in quick oven; until thick and clear.
The Settlement Cookbook, 1940

POACHED APPLES

4 medium apples
1/2 cup sugar

1 cup water
1/2 teaspoon cinnamon

Core whole fruit. Remove about 1/2 inch strip of peel from the bottom and top of the fruit. Remove 1/4 strip of peel around the center of the fruit. Combine sugar, water and cinnamon; bring to a boil in a rather narrow, deep saucepan. Place fruit bottom side down in the syrup. Cover and simmer gently until fruit is tender, about 10 to 20 minutes. Turn once during cooking. Remove cover during last few minutes of cooking. Serve the apples from the syrup or place in a baking dish, top with butter, sprinkle with brown sugar and cinnamon and place under broiler to lightly brown. Spoon syrup over each fruit and top with a bit of sour cream, if desired. A teaspoon of sherry may be added for each serving. Serves 4.

NOTE: A delectable fresh fruit to accompany a meal or replace a dessert.
Allow 1/8 cup sugar and 1/4 cup water for each whole fruit. If poaching apple rings is your desire, use equal amounts of sugar and water for 1/2 inch rings.
Mildred Ann Smith, The Nashville Cookbook, 1977

HOT FRUIT CASSEROLE

2 1/2 can peaches drained, cut into chunks
2 1/2 can pear
2 1/2 can pineapple

4 oranges (juice and grated rind)
2 Tablespoons flour
2/3 cup sugar
1 teaspoon salt

Place fruit in casserole. Pour grated orange rind and juice over the fruit. Sift sugar, flour, and salt over fruit. Dot butter on top. Cook 10 minutes. Cool, add 3/4 cup sherry. Bake until hot. Serves 10.
Satsuma, More Fun for the Cook, 1974

MEATS & MAIN DISHES

"Bless the Food before us, the Family beside us, and the Love between us."
-Amen

Dinner's success often depends on what you put on the meat serving plate. It sets the pace for the meal, because all the other dishes are planned to complement this main course; so, choose carefully and thoughtfully.

CHICKEN AND TURKEY

"It seems to be the overall impression among the public at large, that in the South, we as Southerners consume fried chicken for breakfast, lunch, and dinner or breakfast, dinner, and supper; all the time, at every meal. It's hard to say "fried chicken" without preceding it with "Southern". There are recipes aplenty, an infinite number, for this delicacy...but the good old-fashioned way, is when the fried chicken comes to the table on the meat platter practically stewing in its own juices, seems to me to be the best version of all".

Harriet Ross Colquitt, The Savannah Cook Book, 1933

As I typed the above paragraph, my mouth is so watering, because the statement is so true!

Frying chicken became a major practice and custom of Southerners commencing with the migration into the region of Scottish pioneers and settlers. It is believed that the Scots had a practice of deep-frying chicken in fat, unlike their neighbors to their south, the English, who baked or broiled their chicken. This method of cooking chicken has now acquired the status of being truly a Southern dish

Fried chicken's recognition as "Southern" has been aided generously by Madison Avenue advertising and the emergence of Kentucky Fried Chicken, Minnie Pearl's Fried Chicken, Popeye's, Bojangles, Cracker Barrel and many other eateries, etc., to the pulpit of fast food. Now, we have the latest robust emergence to the food scene; the "Nashville Hot Chicken" movement that has taken root in our pop culture. Fried chicken is among the most famous dishes recognized to us today for being indeed a truly Southern food and now fried chicken has also earned the distinction as being quite famous as a "soul food".

Every Southern family appears to have their own fried chicken recipe handed down from generation to generation. My own family, being in the restaurant business in Nashville since Satsuma opened in 1918, began from generations of incredible cooks long before the occasion of a restaurant opening. Our family was well-acknowledged for the wonderful food served in our restaurant, but one of our most famous dishes was our fried chicken; where time and again as many as 200 to 300, or more, chicken breasts were iron skillet, deep fried daily for use in the restaurant dining room as a menu item and also with our catering.

This classic Southern dish originated for us at Satsuma from an unwritten long-established recipe of our chief cook's family. Her name was Louella Johnson and she was more than an employee; she was family. In fact, all of the children and grandchildren in our family, myself included, called her their Mama Louella. Starting at very young ages, we sat on stools in her corner of the restaurant kitchen mesmerized, watching and listening as she went through the day cooking and humming and telling stories. We worshiped her and we were big fans of everything she did and said. As a member of our family, she took part in all of our important family events; births, christenings, graduations, weddings, funerals, etc. She started working at our restaurant in 1942, while her husband was fighting in World War II. She continued up to the close of business on the very Friday before she died on Saturday, so jovial and enthusiastic as she left work that Friday in 1990.

Louella Johnson

During the entire time of her employment, she only missed 3 days of work and only then to bury her husband. She was the glue that held our restaurant kitchen together and she never used a written recipe for ANYTHING. We often observed her cooking to see how she accomplished her food magic because we were realistic enough to know that one day, she would not be able to continue her cooking and we had to prepare for that eventual transition, when she would no longer be with us. Needless to say, as we watched her day-to-day cooking, we did write down some of her methods and techniques.

Louella was born at home in 1917 in rural Tennessee and had learned to cook, as most people did in her time, by watching her maternal elders. She was a truly fantastic cook and a cook of incredible ability and instinct. This capability was achieved because of the skills passed to Louella by previous generations of her own family, who had shared with her the time-honored methods of her family's cooking. This tale was repeated by almost every family in every region of the South. This was the South and food was at its core, its tradition and way of life.

The key element to the remarkable success of our fried chicken at the Satsuma was not how the chicken was seasoned and floured- although that was a very important central step in preparing our great fried chicken. The most crucial and fundamental factor in frying chicken was how the chicken was cooked. Massive cast iron skillets were used to fry our chicken. I might add, pure lard was used as frying fat. Cast iron is at the heart of much Southern cooking; glistening black by cooking immeasurable meals. The older the skillet, the more used the skillet, the more valuable it became. Caught within the permeable nature of the cast iron, a cook's iron skillet or iron kettle captured, "soaked up", the flavors of immeasurable past-cooked meals yielding flavors for soon to be cooked meals that could never be matched. Years of this constant "seasoning" only served to make each cast iron skillet an heirloom as valuable as silver or gold.

FRIED CHICKEN

8 chicken breasts, bone-in	4 cups flour
3 Tablespoons salt	2 teaspoons baking powder
2 quarts water	4 teaspoons salt
3 large eggs	2 Tablespoons black pepper
1/3 cup buttermilk	1 Tablespoon white pepper

Soak chicken overnight in a solution of 3 Tablespoons salt and 2 quarts water. Remove chicken from water and drain well. Combine eggs and buttermilk and beat until frothy. Combine flour, salt, and peppers. Place chicken breast in seasoned flour and toss until well coated. Remove chicken from seasoned flour and place in egg wash until well coated. Lift chicken out of wash and drain until no longer dripping. Place chicken back into flour, covering it well and pressing the flour into the chicken with a downward motion. Remove the chicken from the flour and shake off excess flour. Place chicken on a sheet pan as you repeat steps for each chicken breast. Heat deep fryer to 350. Place only enough chicken in the fryer basket so they are not touching each other. Lower basket into oil and begin cooking. After 2 minutes, shake basket gently to keep chicken from sticking. Continue cooking for about 18 more minutes or until chicken is golden brown. Remove from oil and let drain.

NOTE: This fried chicken goes into our box lunches we serve to groups at Parish Patch. We frequently hear, "This is the best fried chicken I've ever eaten." We agree.
Isabel Woodlee, Cortner Mill Restaurant cookbook, 2009

I can testify with absolute certainty to the above statement regarding the fried chicken made by the late Ms. Woodlee. I have had the honor of experiencing her wonderful fried chicken and I think it is only fitting that her recipe is the representative fried chicken recipe picked to be included among these pages. It is that good. –David S.

FRIED CHICKEN MARYLAND

Select carefully a young tender fryer. Singe and cut into halves or quarters. Wash carefully and dry, then dip into flour to which has been added salt and pepper. Place large piece of butter or chicken fat in an iron skillet and when hot, drop in pieces of chicken and brown quickly on all sides. Reduce heat, add one cup of water and let simmer slowly until done. Remove lid and let chicken fry down slowly. Serve with creamed gravy.
The Southern Cook Book, 1939

CREAMED GRAVY FOR FRIED CHICKEN

Take 2 Tablespoons of fat from the pan in which you fried the chicken from the recipe for "Fried Chicken Maryland" Add a Tablespoon flour and a cup of thin cream; bring to a boiling point stirring constantly.
The Southern Cook Book, 1939

CHICKEN MILK GRAVY

2 Tablespoons drippings from frying
2 Tablespoon flour
1 cup cream or whole milk
1/4 teaspoon salt
1/4 teaspoon black pepper

Pour off all but 2 Tablespoons of drippings from the skillet used to fry chicken. Scrape the crumbles of breading left from frying the chicken from the skillet and remove. Stir the flour into the drippings until dissolved and return to medium high heat. Add cream or milk, the salt and pepper and stir 3-4 minutes or until it reaches its desired thickness. Serve over mashed potatoes or biscuits. This recipe can also be used for sausage gravy at breakfast.

NOTE: I learned where food came from, instead of just the grocery store, as I looked out Grandmother Boswell's long kitchen window. She would catch a chicken from the hen house and carry it upside down to a chopping block, where she used a hatchet to chop off its head. Needless to say, my seeing the blood flying and the chicken flopping around the yard created a horrifying and lasting impression.
Kathleen Boswell Fendt, Miss Lizzie's Heirlooms, 2009

BATTER FOR CHICKEN

This recipe contributed by *Mary Leize Simmons* was taken from the late 1700s notebook of collected recipes by *Miss Elizabeth Harleston of Bossis Plantation*. The recipe proved to be most delicious, though at first glance it appeared to be not very enlightening. It reads: "One pint of milk, one pint of flour, two eggs, a little salt; beat up very light yeast powder." After experimenting with this batter for deep fat frying, we found that the following amounts would make enough batter to cover a medium sized chicken.

1 ½ cups flour
1 Tablespoon baking powder
½ teaspoon salt
1 egg, well-beaten
½ cup milk

Mix and sift the dry ingredients. Mix the egg and milk together and combine with the dry mixture. Dip each piece of chicken in the batter and fry in deep fat until brown.
Mary Leize Simmons, 200 Years of Charleston Cooking, 1930

CHICKEN HASH   *"A Southern Sunday Breakfast Dish – A Northern Luncheon Delicacy"*

2 Tablespoons butter
1 1/2 Tablespoons flour
1 cup chicken stock
2 cups chopped chicken

Make a white sauce with the flour and butter, using chicken stock in place of milk. When thick, stir in the chicken. Place in a buttered casserole and bake. Garnish with slices of toast.
The Southern Cookbook, 1939

OVEN-FRIED CHICKEN

2 to 3 pound broiler/fryer chicken, cut up	1/4 teaspoon pepper
1 cup flour	2 teaspoons paprika
2 teaspoons salt	1/2 cup butter

Dip chicken pieces in mixture of flour, salt, pepper, and paprika. Melt butter in shallow baking pan in a 400 F. oven. Remove baking pan from oven. As pieces of floured chicken are placed in the pan, turn to assure coating with butter. Arrange skin side down in a single layer. Bake in the 400 F. oven 30 minutes. Turn chicken. Bake another 30 minutes or until tender. If the chicken can't be served at once, reduce oven heat and brush the chicken with more melted butter. 4 servings.

SAUCE VARIATIONS

Follow the directions for Oven-Fried Chicken, but when the chicken is turned after it has baked 30 minutes, pour one of the three following sauces over the pieces. Continue baking as directed.

LEMON BARBECUE SAUCE: Mash 1 small clove garlic with 1/2 teaspoon salt in a bowl. Add 1/4 cup salad oil, 1/2 cup lemon juice, 2 Tablespoons finely chopped onion, 1/2 teaspoon freshly ground black pepper, and 1/2 teaspoon thyme.

SPICY BARBECUE SAUCE: Combine the following ingredients in a saucepan: 1/2 cup sliced onion, 1 teaspoon salt, 1 Tablespoon vinegar, 1 Tablespoon sugar, 1 Tablespoon Worcestershire sauce, 1/2 teaspoon chili powder, 1/4 teaspoon black pepper, 1/2 cup catsup, and 1/4 cup water. Simmer 15 minutes. Pour.

BUTTER HONEY SAUCE: Melt 1/4 cup butter in saucepan. Add 1/4 cup honey and 1/4 cup lemon juice.
Easy-on-the-Cook Book, 1960

CHICKEN AND DUMPLINGS

1 large stewing hen	4 Tablespoons lard
1 teaspoon salt	2 cups milk
3 1/2 cups flour	2 Tablespoons baking powder
1 1/2 teaspoons salt	1 teaspoon white pepper

Into a large pot, place the chicken with enough salted water to cover and cook over medium heat until chicken is tender. Remove chicken from the broth and set aside to cool. Reserve the broth. In a mixing bowl, combine flour with salt, baking powder and pepper. Stir in milk and knead as if it were bread dough. Roll dough to 1/4 inch thick and cut into 1-inch squares or strips. Return the saved broth to heat and add water if needed. Bring to a boil and drop dumplings into boiling broth. Cover and let boil 15 minutes. Cut chicken into bite-size pieces and return to broth. Let stand to blend the flavors before serving.

NOTE: This was the best way to cook old hens that had stopped laying or tough, retired roosters.
David Boswell Hazelwood, Miss Lizzie's Heirlooms, 2009

STEWED CHICKEN AND DUMPLINGS

1 chicken
1 cup flour
2 teaspoons baking powder
milk to make a thick batter

salt and pepper to taste
sprig of parsley
1 small diced onion

Clean and cut up the chicken, place in kettle and partly cover with water, add the chopped onion, salt and pepper and cook until tender. Mix the flour, baking powder, salt and minced parsley and milk to a thick batter. Drop batter from the end of a spoon into the slowly boiling chicken broth. Cover tightly and let cook for 20 minutes without raising the lid. Place the chicken on a platter and surround with the dumplings.
The Southern Cookbook, 1939

ROAST CHICKEN OR TURKEY

Dredge a four-pound seasoned chicken with flour and place on its back in dripping pan with butter or chicken fat the size of an egg. Place in a hot oven (400 F) and when the flour is browned reduce the heat to (350 F) moderately hot, then add 1/4 cup of fat dissolved in 1/2 cup boiling water and baste every quarter of an hour. Turn chicken often until breast meat is tender, then it is done. About 1 1/2 hours are required. When doing a turkey, more liquid will be required and roasting time will be longer according to the size.
The Southern Cookbook, 1939

MISS CECELIA'S POT PIE

1 young chicken
pie dough

1/4 cup butter
salt and pepper

1 cup milk
1/4 cup chicken stock

Dress and cut a young chicken weighing 1 1/2 pounds as you would for frying. Place pieces into a stew pan and barely cover with boiling water. Cook slowly until the meat is tender. De-bone. Make the dough, but use a little less shortening than called for in the recipe. Divide the dough into two parts. Roll out one piece very thin. Line the sides of a baking dish with part of this dough, put in a layer of chicken and dot with butter salt and pepper. Cut the rest of this piece of dough into strips, cover the chicken, alternating until all the chicken and dough are used. Add the milk and about 1/4 cup of the stock in which the chicken was cooked.

Roll out the second piece of dough and dot with butter. Fold and roll again, until the butter is blended into the dough. Roll this dough out thin and cover the top of the pie; press the edges together and make small slashes in the crust to allow the steam to escape. Bake the pie in a moderate hot oven (400 F) until contents are cooked and crust is well-browned.

NOTE: Chicken Pot Pie is usually served in the same dish in which it was baked.
The Southern Cookbook, 1939

OVEN BARBECUED CHICKEN BREASTS

4 large halves of chicken breasts
1/2 cup flour
salt and pepper as desired
1/4 cup each of cooking oil and margarine
1 cup catsup
1/2 cup sherry wine

2 Tablespoons lemon juice
1/3 cup diced onion
2 Tablespoons brown sugar
2 Tablespoons margarine
1 Tablespoon Worcestershire sauce

Dredge chicken breasts in flour to which salt and pepper is added. Heat oil and margarine in a skillet. Place chicken in the hot fat, turning to a light brown. Arrange pieces in a lightly greased baking dish. Blend and heat all ingredients for the sauce. Pour over the chicken; cover and bake at 325 F. for 1 1/2 hours or until chicken is tender. Serves 4.
The Nashville Cookbook, 1977

HOT CHICKEN SALAD IN CASSEROLE

2 cups chopped cooked chicken
2 cups chopped celery
1/2 cup chopped almonds
1/3 cup chopped green pepper
1/2 cup mayonnaise
3 cups crushed potato chips

2 Tablespoons chopped pimiento
2 Tablespoons chopped onion
1/2 teaspoon salt
2 Tablespoons lemon juice
1/3 cup grated Swiss cheese

Mix all the ingredients, except the cheese and potato chips. Put into buttered casserole. Put the cheese on top. Bake at 350 F until cheese is melted. Put potato chips on top and bake 5 minutes more. Serves 6-8

NOTE: As a kid growing up, being the oldest of 6 children, I (David S) remember vividly my mother cooking this dish. As I transcribed this recipe, my mouth began watering.l It was that good!
Satsuma Tea Room, Fun for the Cook, 1968

CHICKEN AND ALMONDS

5 Tablespoons butter
3/4 cup thinly sliced onions
3 cups cooked chicken

1 Tablespoon flour
1/4 teaspoon pepper
1 cup canned chicken broth

1/4 pound fresh mushrooms, sliced
1 cup blanched, toasted, slivered almonds

Melt 4 Tablespoons butter in skillet. Sauté onions 5 minutes, stirring frequently. Add chicken and sauté 5 minutes. Mix flour and pepper with broth. Add to mixture while stirring constantly. Cook over low heat for 20 minutes. Sauté mushrooms in butter for 5 minutes. Add mushrooms and almonds to mixture. Taste for seasoning. Serve in patty shells (a shell of puff pastry often used with a cooked meat) or on toast. Serves 6.
Satsuma, Fun for the Cook, 1968

CHICKEN TETRAZZINI

1/4 pound butter
3/4 cup flour
4 cups milk
1 pound Velveeta cheese
1 can beer, small size
1/4 cup sherry

4 cups chicken or turkey, diced
1 cup fresh mushrooms sautéed in butter for 5 minutes
6 cups cooked spaghetti noodles, washed and drained
Parmesan cheese

Make sauce of butter, flour, milk, Velveeta cheese. Mix other ingredients. Pour into buttered shallow casserole. Cover with Parmesan cheese. Sprinkle with paprika. Bake at 350 F until light brown. Serves 12.
Satsuma Tea Room, Fun for the Cook, 1968

CHICKEN ON EGG BREAD

2 Tablespoons celery, minced
2 Tablespoons onion, minced
3 Tablespoons flour
1 pint chicken stock

3/4 cup cream
3 Tablespoons butter
chicken, boiled or steamed

Melt butter. Add celery and onion. Cook until golden brown. Add the flour, then stock and cream. Cook until it is like a medium white sauce. Bake your favorite egg bread (page 303). When done, cut into squares. Cut open and add white and dark pieces of chicken cut in medium pieces. Over this pour the sauce.

NOTE: In early times, as now, Chicken on Egg Bread frequently appeared on Nashville tables. This recipe is typical and was said to be a restaurant special of Kleeman's, a celebrated Nashville eatery.
The Nashville Cookbook, 1977

CURRIED CHICKEN

2 Tablespoons chopped onions
2 Tablespoons chopped celery
1/2 cup butter
1/2 teaspoon salt
1 Tablespoon curry powder
1/2 cup flour

1 1/2 cups milk
1 1/2 cups chicken stock
1 cup cream
2 Tablespoons sherry
3 cups cooked chicken

Sauté onions and celery in butter until onions are yellow. Add salt and curry powder. Add flour and cook until bubbly. Add milk, cream, sherry, and chicken stock. Cook until thickened, stirring briskly. Add chicken. Serve on rice with any of the following accompaniments: chutney, chopped cooked bacon, finely diced hardboiled egg, finely chopped salted peanuts, fresh shredded coconut, chopped ham, chopped green pepper, shredded radishes, or very thin shredded onions.

NOTE: The garnishes are the most interesting part of the curry. Serves 8.
Satsuma Tea Room, Fun for the Cook, 1968

CHICKEN A LA TARTARE

1 broiling chicken	1 small onion	salt and pepper
1/4 pound melted butter	1/4 pound mushrooms	bread crumbs
4 sprigs parsley	1 clove garlic	

Clean the broiler chicken and split it in half. Place it in a fry pan in which the butter has been melted. Chop the parsley, onion, mushrooms and garlic and add to the butter with salt and pepper. Cover the frying pan and allow the broiler to simmer for 15 minutes; turning it occasionally, so that the flavor is absorbed. The chicken is then dipped in bread crumbs and broiled until well-browned. The chicken meat is delicately flavored with the mushrooms, onion, garlic, and parsley combination. Pre-cooking in the butter sauce also assures the tenderness of the meat.
The Southern Cookbook, 1939

BRANDIED CHICKEN

2 whole chicken breasts, boned	1 cup heavy cream
1/2 pound thick sliced boiled ham	1 jigger brandy
1 clove garlic	1 teaspoon curry powder
1/2 stick butter	salt and pepper as desired

Heat oven to 350 F. Grease a 1 ½-quart casserole. Sauté chicken, ham, and garlic in butter and place in prepared casserole. Add cream, brandy, curry, salt and pepper. Bake for 45 minutes or until tender. May be served with rice. Serves 4.
Lillie M. Alexander, The Nashville Cookbook, 1978

CHICKEN CHILI CON CARNE

1 young chicken	3 buttons garlic, chopped
2 Tablespoons salt	1 1/2 teaspoons chili powder
1 large can tomatoes	1 quart cooked Mexican (pinto) beans
3 large onions, chopped	

Cover the chicken with water and add the can of tomatoes, salt, two buttons of garlic, and two onions. Cook until the chicken is done and remove the chicken from the broth. Bone and cut the chicken into small pieces and put the meat back into the liquid. Heat and, while stirring, add the chili powder. If more seasoning is desired, add more powder. In a separate pan, melt 2 Tablespoons butter and gently brown the remaining onion and garlic button. Add this to the original mixture and cook for 1 hour. When nearly done, add 1 quart of cooked Mexican beans. Cook about 10 minutes longer while just simmering. Serve in a deep bowl with crackers.
The Southern Cookbook, 1939

CHICKEN FRICASSEE

1 chicken and 1 egg (and it doesn't make any difference in this case which comes first)
2 Tablespoons flour
1 cup milk
2 Tablespoons butter
salt, pepper

Boil the chicken until done and cut up for serving. Make a sauce of the butter, flour, milk, and one well-beaten egg seasoned with the salt and pepper. Add to this, 2 hard-boiled eggs, cut up, and pour all over the chicken. Let stew together a few minutes and serve.
The Savannah Cook Book, 1933

CHICKEN IN SOUR CREAM

Brown 1 large broiling chicken, quartered, in 3 Tablespoons margarine. In saucepan, cook a large chopped onion until done, but not brown. Add chicken, 1/2 cup dry wine, sprinkle with salt and pepper. Cover and simmer 1 hour. Last half hour, add 1/2 pound sliced mushrooms. Just before serving, add 1 cup sour cream. Heat but do not broil. This can be frozen but do not add sour cream until just before serving.
Satsuma Tea Room, More Fun for the Cook, 1974

CHICKEN BREASTS BAKED WITH SHERRY AND FRESH MUSHROOMS

6 large chicken breasts
3/4 teaspoon salt
paprika
pepper
1/2 cup melted butter
1 can chicken bouillon
1/3 cup sherry
1/3 pound fresh mushrooms

Season chicken with salt and pepper. Sprinkle with paprika. Spread out in baking pan. Cover with chicken bouillon and melted butter. Bake at 325 F, basting 3 or 4 times for 1 hour. Sauté sliced mushrooms. Add sherry to chicken and cook 1/2 hour longer. When ready to serve, add mushrooms and pour sauce over chicken.
Satsuma Tea Room, More Fun for the Cook, 1974

GINGER GLAZED CHICKEN

2 (1 1/2-2 pound) broiler/fryer chickens
8 ounces Italian style salad dressing
3/4 cup apricot or pineapple preserves
2 teaspoons ginger
dash white pepper

Cut chickens in half. Place in shallow pan and coat all sides with dressing. Let stand at room temperature 2 to 3 hours or overnight in refrigerator. Remove chicken from the pan and place skin side up on broiler rack. Combine marinade liquid with preserves, ginger, and pepper. Brush mixture over chicken. Broil 20 to 30 minutes, basting frequently with the remaining mixture. Turn, coat again and broil until chicken is done and golden brown in color. Serves 4.
Easy-on-the-Cook Book, 1960

CREAMED STUFFED EGGS

8 hard-boiled eggs	1/2 teaspoon onion juice	2 cups white sauce, made
1 cup cooked chicken	1/4 cup chopped pecans	with chicken broth

Cut eggs in half. Remove yolks. Mash. Grind chicken and pecans and add to the egg yolks with onion juice, salt and pepper and enough white sauce to moisten. Fill the egg whites with the mixture. Place in casserole, stuffed side up and pour remaining sauce over eggs. Bake 25 minutes at 350 F. Serve with mushroom sauce. Makes 8 servings.
Satsuma Tea Room, More Fun for the Cook, 1974

CHICKEN LOAF

4 cups cooked diced chicken	1 teaspoon salt
2 cups soft breadcrumbs	1/4 teaspoon pepper
1 cup cooked rice	1/4 cup melted butter or chicken fat
1/4 cup chopped pimiento	3 cups milk or chicken stock
4 eggs	

Mix the ingredients in the order named (left column to right). Pour into buttered baking dish. Put baking dish in pan of hot water and bake at 325 F for one hour. Serves 8-10.
Satsuma Tea Room, Fun for the Cook, 1968

CHICKEN SOUFFLE

5 slices of bread (trim crusts)	1/2 teaspoon dry mustard
2 cups diced chicken	1/2 teaspoon salt
2 cups grated Cheddar cheese	dash pepper
3 eggs	dash paprika
2 cups milk	

Butter bread and cut into ½-inch cubes. Arrange layers of bread, chicken and 1 1/2 cups of cheese in a greased casserole. Beat eggs with the milk and pour over the mixture. Place casserole in shallow pan of water, about 1 inch deep. Bake at 325 F for 45 minutes. Sprinkle with the remaining cheese and bake 10 minutes longer. Serves 8.
Satsuma Tea Room, Fun for the Cook, 1968

CHINESE CHICKEN

2 cans mushroom soup	2 cans chicken and rice soup
4 cups chicken, cut up	3 #2 cans Chinese noodles
2 cans water chestnuts, sliced	buttered crumbs
2- 5 1/2 ounce cans Pet milk	slivered almonds

Combine all ingredients except crumbs and almonds. Put in a baking dish. Cover with buttered crumbs and almonds. Bake 30 minutes at 350 F. Serves 15.
Satsuma Tea Room, More Fun for the Cook, 1974

DIXIE CHICKEN SHORTCAKE

1 large chicken, cooked	2 Tablespoons butter melted
2 cups chicken stock	salt and pepper
2 Tablespoons flour	1 pan cornbread
1 pound mushrooms, cleaned	

Remove the skin and bones from the cooked chicken. Cut meat into small pieces. Make a sauce, using 2 cups of the chicken stock and thickening it with the flour. Sauté the mushrooms in the butter. Add the chicken and mushrooms to the sauce. Cut the cornbread into 4-inch squares and split. Cover the lower halves with some of the chicken mixture. Lay on the top crusts and cover with more of the chicken mixture. Left over chicken and gravy may also be used in this manner.
The Southern Cookbook, 1939

BROILED CHICKEN

Best size chicken half for broiling is 1 1/2 pounds. Sprinkle with salt. Refrigerate several hours. Before broiling, rinse off salt and pat dry with paper towel. Cover both sides of the bird with melted margarine. Place in a shallow pan skin side down. Put under broiler. When brown on the bony side, turn and brown on top side. Move to a pan with a cover. Use 1/2 cup hot water to clean off broiling pan and pour this over chicken. Cover and cook at 350 F for 45 minutes.
Satsuma Tea Room, More Fun for the Cook, 1974

CHICKEN CAKES

1 cup cooked chicken meat, chopped	bread crumbs, rolled fine
2 eggs, slightly beaten	1 cup white sauce
1 Tablespoon cream	1/2 cup finely chopped celery
salt and pepper	

Add 1 egg, cream, salt and pepper to the chopped chicken. Make into small flat cakes, dip in the remaining egg mixed with a little milk if desired and roll in the bread crumbs. Fry on both sides until well browned. Add the celery to the white sauce and pour over the cakes when ready to serve. Serve on toast and garnish with parsley.
The Southern Cookbook, 1939

BREAST O' CHICKEN CASSEROLE

8 chicken breasts	1/3 cup chopped onion
10 ¾ ounces cream of mushroom soup	1/3 cup chopped green pepper
1 cup slivered almonds	3 Tablespoons cooking sherry (optional)

Brown chicken breasts in boiler. Remove from bone, leaving each in one piece. Preheat oven to 400 F. Prepare sauce of remaining ingredients. Cover the bottom of casserole with thin layer of sauce, layer breasts, etc., with top layer being sauce. Cover and bake 30 minutes.
Hazel Spitze, University of Illinois Home Economics Faculty Favorites, 1965

"Never Believed Anything Could Taste So Good"

EASY CHICKEN CASSEROLE

2 ½ pound spring chicken, cut into pieces	1 can mushroom soup
1 can onion soup	salt and pepper

Put chicken into casserole with a little salt and pepper. Mix the two soups and pour over chicken. Cover. Bake at 300 F for 2 hours. Fresh mushrooms cut up and sautéed and 1/4 cup sour cream may be added at the end. Serves 4.

NOTE: I recently discovered this recipe was perfect to address a problem that I had encountered from time to time. I like to buy rotisserie chicken from our neighborhood supermarket. It is good and simple and I can buy it on my way home. The difficulty was that the chicken lasted a full two nights with just two people eating it. My wife does not do leftovers and in her defense this chicken is not really that good the second night. While writing this book, I ran across our Satsuma recipe, applied it to the rotisserie chicken leftovers, and WOW! So easy and so good.
Satsuma Tea Room, More Fun for the Cook, 1974

RICE AND CHICKEN CASSEROLE

2 cups rice	1 1/2 Tablespoons butter	1 cooked chicken
2 cups milk	2 eggs	

Bone the chicken and cut into 1-inch pieces. Boil the rice in salted water until tender. Stir in the butter, the milk, and the eggs. Put a layer of this into a casserole, then the chicken, then the rice. Bake in a (350 F) moderate oven until well-browned.
The Southern Cookbook, 1939

CHICKEN CASSEROLE WITH ONIONS

2- 2 1/2 pound fryers, cut into pieces	3 cups thinly sliced onions
2 teaspoons salt	1/2 teaspoon paprika
3/4 teaspoon pepper	3/4 cup water
1/4 cup butter	1/2 cup sour cream

Wash and dry the chicken. Rub with salt and pepper. Put in pan to broil. Dot with butter. Cook under broiler until brown. Turn and cook on other side. Add onions under chicken when it is turned. Put chicken and onions into casserole when well browned. Add water. Cook about 1 hour in slow oven at 300 F. Add sour cream at end. Heat, but do not broil. Serve on hot biscuit, rice, or noodles. Serves 8.

NOTE: A favorite at our house.
Satsuma Tea Room, Fun for the Cook, 1969

SAUTEED QUAIL

2 quail, butterflied	2 Tablespoons butter
1 cup flour	2 Tablespoons red wine
1 Tablespoon paprika	2 Tablespoons rosemary

Combine flour and paprika and roll the quail in this combination. Melt the butter in the skillet and sauté the quail over a medium heat for 2 minutes on each side. Pour wine and rosemary into skillet and cook quail until golden brown on each side. Serves 1.
David Hazelwood, Cortner Mill Restaurant cookbook, 2009

ROASTED DUCK

Prepare and clean duck as you would a fowl; rub with salt and pepper. Take 2 Tablespoons of ground ginger and rub on both the inside and outside. Peel one onion and into this stick 4 cloves and place on duck. Place in a roaster and add 1 cup of water. Roast, basting often. Add water when necessary. Stuff duck with bread, apple, or mushroom stuffing. The gravy should be highly seasoned, and a tart jelly may be added at the last. Serve with baked oranges.
The Southern Cookbook, 1939

ROAST SQUAB WITH RICE PILAU

4 squabs	3/4 cup chopped celery	4 eggs
6 slices bacon	2 cups rice	salt and pepper
1 onion	4 cups chicken stock	mustard pickle juice

Dress the squabs as usual, cleaning them thoroughly. Stuff the birds made as follows:
Dice the bacon and fry until crisp. Remove the bacon and brown the chopped celery and onions in the bacon drippings. Boil the rice in the chicken stock until tender, then add the bacon, celery, and onion. Beat the eggs and add them to the rice. Season with salt and pepper. Stuff the squabs with this mixture and make mounds of the remaining filling on which to lay the squab. Bake in a hot oven for about 25 minutes, basting the squabs frequently with mustard pickle juice.
The Southern Cookbook, 1939

ROAST PARTRIDGE

Thoroughly clean four partridges (or squab, quail, or any other small bird) inside and outside. Pin over the breasts of the partridges a long thin strip of bacon. Rub outside and inside with salt and pepper and put in roasting pan with a cup of water for four partridges. Roast in a hot oven for 30 minutes, basting every 5 minutes. When the birds and gravy are a thick, rich brown, pour over with a cup of slightly sour cream. Let the cream bubble up in pan for a minute, baste once more, and serve with gravy poured over the partridges on toast. Garnish with baked oranges.
The Southern Cookbook, 1939

CORNISH GAME HEN

2 (16 ounce) Cornish game hens	2 teaspoons butter, melted
1/2 cup croutons	1 dash cinnamon
1/2 baked apple, mashed	dash ground cloves

Combine ingredients and stuff inside hen. Bake hen at 375 F for 1 hour 15 minutes, basting with glaze occasionally. Brush glaze on hen last 15 minutes of baking time. Serve on bed of rice and spoon remaining glaze over hen.

GLAZE

1/2 cup water	1 Tablespoon butter
1/2 cup sugar	1/2 teaspoon cinnamon

Mix all the ingredients in saucepan. Heat until mixture boils and cook 2 more minutes. Pour glaze over hen and serve.

NOTE: It is hard to choose an entrée for a group of guests. Some don't eat fish and others don't eat beef, so we usually end up serving chicken to be on safe side. Cornish Hen is a good way to serve chicken and still make it special.
Cortner Mill Restaurant cookbook, 2009

TURKEY HASH

Turkey hash is a dish reported to have been a favorite at the Hermitage, home of Rachel and President Andrew Jackson in Nashville. The following recipe was adapted from the Hermitage recipe files. It was served to President Franklin D. Roosevelt and also to Mrs. Lyndon Johnson as their breakfast meal of choice on their visits to the Hermitage:

Steam a large turkey with enough water for the turkey not to become dry. Put diced celery and onion in the water to give flavor. When the turkey is tender, remove and chill. Strain the liquid into another container and chill long enough for all the fat to rise to the top. Skim away the fat. Meanwhile, remove the turkey from the bones and cut the best parts into rather large pieces, being careful to remove all the skin, bones and gristle. Make a rather stiff sauce of butter, sifted flour, and turkey liquid. Flavor with salt, white pepper, and Worcestershire sauce as desired. Allow 2 cups of heavy sauce to 1 cup of large pieces of diced turkey. Keep hot in double boiler until ready to serve.
Commentary, The Nashville Cookbook, 1978

PORK

Perhaps no two foodstuffs have played a more important role in Southern cooking than hog meat and corn. Separate or in combination, they have meant the difference between life and death for individuals, families, even entire communities. In the American South, Egerton writes, "Pigs and corn. Hog meat and hominy. Pork and pone. Separately, the meat of the hog and the grain of the cornstalk have enriched the diet. No other edible substances have meant more to the populace in nearly four centuries of history than pork and corn."

-John Egerton, Southern Cooking: At Home, On the Road, In History

Of the hog, Bethany Ewald Bultman writes, "It wasn't until 1493, when Christopher Columbus deposited a Spanish hog in Cuba, handpicked by Queen Isabella, that pigs arrived in the new world. Twenty-seven years later Admiral Alonso Alveraz de Pinana may have lost some of his porkers around Mobile, but it was when Hernando de Soto and his six hundred armor-clad men traversed the Gulf Coast in the early 1540's that swine made landfall in our region. Pigs would appear in the Gulf South at a time when the consumption of pork was a Christian duty for every Spanish-speaking Catholic."

-Bethany Ewald Bultman, "An Ode to the Pig"

Reay Tannahill reveals in his *Food in History*, "that during the Spanish Inquisition (1478-1834) it became obligatory to have pork simmering in a cauldron of chorizo, dried pork sausages, hanging from the rafters as a sure proof that no Jew or Muslim dined in the Christian home. De Soto certainly performed his Christian duty when he deposited fifteen hogs in Florida. Within five years this herd had multiplied to more than seven hundred.

By the eighteenth century, pork was served at almost every meal on most Southern tables and wealthy planters prided themselves on their smoked meats and their skills in accomplishing this feat. By the nineteenth century, an approximation put the "per capita consumption of pork during that period at three times that of Europe."

Before refrigeration, most, almost all the meat in the Southerner's diet was cured in some form or fashion. It was not fresh, unless freshly killed or caught. This concept had been the practice for centuries all over the globe. Meat was dried out in salt or in some cases pickled in order to safely keep for long periods of time. Southerners much preferred the taste of salted and smoked pork to the taste of pickled beef. Thus, being superior in preservation capabilities and taste, pork took the South by storm.

On the plantations, enslaved people prepared and cooked most of the meat for the master's tables. It was their job to prepare the meat for the smokehouse. They faced the job of slaughtering and butchering animals, salting meat, hanging meat in the smokehouse to cure, carefully keeping a low burning fire under the meat for days, and then storing the smoked meat. Many of the advances in curing techniques known and used by us today, including using different woods to get different flavors, originated with African Americans.

"On most Southern farms the first cold snap harkened the end of summer vegetables and the annual hog slaughter. Livers, cracklin's, and chitterlings (small intestines), were eaten immediately. Globs of hog fat were boiled in a gigantic black pot to be rendered into lard. Scraps of meat were ground up for sausages. Ribs were slowly steamed. Sides of bacon, hog jowls, shoulders, and hams were cured in salt for weeks. They were then hung in the smokehouse along with a variety of sausages, ham hocks, and knuckles to be smoked over hickory, pecan wood, peanut shells, or corncobs. Some farmers cured their meat with red pepper to prevent infestations of fly larvae in the era before refrigeration." Every part of the hog was used.

John Egerton, Southern Food: At Home, On the Road, In History

The late great Southern chef Edna Lewis, herself an African American, is remembered for saying, "Ham held the same rating as the basic black dress of today. If you had a ham in the meat house, any situation could be faced."
-Chef Edna Lewis, The Taste of Country Cooking

Methods for cooking ham vary widely. Many families adhere to the same techniques which have been passed down through their generations. Revealed among these pages are only a very few of the recommended cooking and curing techniques for ham, but all should satisfy the most discriminating connoisseurs of ham and country ham. Follow directions well to ensure the perfect outcome.

COUNTRY HAM AND RED EYE GRAVY

4 slices raw country ham, 3/8 inch thick   4 teaspoons sugar
3/8 cup black coffee

Heat a few drops of lard, oil, bacon drippings, or rendered ham fat in a large skillet until the skillet is medium hot. Slit the edges of the ham slices in several places to prevent the slice from curling during frying. Place ham slices in skillet and cook on one side for 8 minutes over medium-high heat. Turn the slices and fry 8 minutes more. Pour coffee into skillet along with ham slices. Sprinkle with sugar and stir. Cover and simmer over very low heat for 5 to 10 minutes. Serve the ham and red-eye gravy together. Serves 4.

NOTE: I sure hope you have some biscuits close by when you eat this ham! While it wasn't common for the Boswells to have a hog, they would get one from a neighbor or church member when they had a hog killing. It meant cured hams, shoulders, bacon, and jowl were frequently hanging in storage for ready use.
David Boswell Hazelwood, Miss Lizzie's Heirlooms, 2009

TO BAKE SUGAR CURED HAM

Use 1/2 sugar cured ham, about 7 pounds. Cover completely with aluminum foil. Bake at 275 degrees about 2 ½ - 3 hours. Open aluminum foil. Score ham and pour over sweet pickle juice or pineapple juice. Put 3/4 cup brown sugar on the ham. Recover and bake another hour. Ham is much better baked at low temperature.

NOTE: There are countless uses for leftover ham. It is like money in the bank. Use the ham sliced cold for sandwiches or slice and fry for breakfast, or etc. Many numerous and good recipes exist today to guide and assist us in this effort.
Satsuma Tea Room, More Fun for the Cook 1974

FRYING COUNTRY HAM

Skin should be removed only over the area from which the slices will be taken before attempting to slice the ham. Cut the ham slices 1/4 to 3/8 inch thick. Do not trim any excess fat from the slices until after frying. Use a heavy skillet that will distribute the heat evenly. Place slices in a skillet with fat edges towards the center. Fat edges should be scored to prevent buckling. Do not cover. Fry slowly. Turn slices frequently. Do not fry fast. Do not over fry. Grease should not splatter. Cook until both sides of the ham are very light brown

TO COOK COUNTRY HAM

Soak the ham overnight in water. Scrub off the entire mold. Put in boiler or large pot with: 2 cups brown sugar; 6 whole onions; 2 cups vinegar.

Cook, simmer but do not boil, for about 20-25 minutes per pound until ham is tender and bone is loosened. Remove from heat and pull off skin and allow ham to cool slightly. You may either serve now or glaze.

To glaze ham, cover with as much tart jelly as you can spread on the ham under the broiler or in a hot oven. It will melt and run off. Continue the basting with jelly that runs off and you will have a beautiful glaze. Serve hot or cold. A cold ham slices to much better advantage than a hot one. Cut slices thin and perpendicular to the bone. One should get two servings per pound if sliced cold.
Satsuma Tea Room, More Fun for the Cook, 1974

COUNTRY HAM GLAZES

As in most things pertaining to Southern food, there is no right or wrong when it comes to country ham glazes. I have found 6 different glazes in family lore which I will share here:
- Use 1 cup brown sugar and 2 tablespoons of flour or 1/4 cup of fine bread crumbs.
- Coat with brown sugar and baste with juice of pickled peaches, fruit juice, or cider.
- Mix 1 cup drained, crushed pineapple with 1 cup of brown sugar and spread over the ham. Baste often with the pineapple juice while baking.
- Coat the ham with a thin layer of prepared mustard, then sprinkle generously with brown sugar.
- Baste ham while baking with strained honey. Maraschino cherry juice or chopped cherries may be added to the honey.
- Decorate top of ham with thin slices of unpeeled oranges, canned pineapple or other colorful fruits. Basted the ham while it is baking with a thick brown sugar syrup, honey, or fruit juices. To make brown sugar syrup, mix one cup sugar with 1/2 cup water and boil for 5 minutes.

MAKING RED-EYE GRAVY FOR FRIED COUNTRY HAM

Use the juices left in the skillet after frying as a base for the gravy. Heat these juices until they smoke. Add 3 ounces of water for every three ham slices. A good country ham will make red-eye gravy without adding coffee (a procedure followed by some cooks). Before the liquid boils, remove to a serving bowl or pour over the ham slices on a warmed deep serving platter. Serve immediately.

BAKED HAM

1 slice ham, 1-inch in thickness	1 teaspoon dry mustard
1/2 cup brown sugar	2 cups milk

Place the ham in a baking dish, rub the mustard over the top, sprinkle with brown sugar and cover with milk. Bake in a slow oven (300 F) for 1 hour
The Southern Cookbook, 1939

BAKING A COUNTRY HAM

Prepare the ham exactly as you did for boiling. Soak the ham about 12 hours if you prefer. Place ham, skin side up, on a rack in an open pan. Start ham covered or in aluminum foil in a hot oven (375 F) for 1 hour. Reduce heat to 200-225 F and cook until the center of the ham registers 160 F on a meat thermometer. This will take about 45 to 50 minutes per pound for whole hams. Hams continue to cook after removal from the oven. (For well-done meat, internal thermometer should reach 170 F) Remove skin and allow the ham to cool slightly. You may either serve now or glaze. After the ham is cool, cover generously with your favorite glaze. Place under broiler or in hot oven until glaze is melted. Serve hot or cold. Baked hams are much easier to slice when chilled. Cut slices thin and perpendicular to the bone. Cooked ham can also be prepared for serving by removing the bones, tying in a roll then chilling before slicing.
The Nashville Cookbook, 1977

BAKED HAM

"Fortunately, this is not as complicated as it sounds." –Harriet Ross Colquitt

Take any good ham, not necessarily a very expensive one, wash it well and put it in a large boiler, skin side up. Pour over it one can of black molasses and four quarts of weak tea, pouring the tea in the empty syrup can to see that no sweetness lingers behind- and let the ham soak in this sweet bath overnight.

Next morning put the ham in a steamer fat side up this time and pour over it two quarts of water and bake in covered steamer three or four hours. Take out, skin, and plaster with a paste made of tomato catsup and mustard. Return it to the oven in this new dress and let it cook about half an hour, basting it frequently with a bottle of beer! Then sprinkle with brown sugar, bake until a little browner, and serve while hot.

NOTE: Good? Well, you would be surprised! Recap of the strange ingredients include, besides the ham: 1 large can black molasses, 1 cup of tomato catsup, several Tablespoons of mustard, 4 quarts of weak tea, 1 bottle of beer and 1 cup brown sugar.
The Savannah Cook Book, 1933

COOKING A SMITHFIELD HAM (The ham that made Virginia ham famous)

Soak a 10-12-pound ham for 12 hours, then boil, cooking very slowly for 4-5 hours, until tender. Cool in its own essence. When cold remove the skin and make crisscross gashes in the top of the ham with a sharp knife. Sprinkle on top of the ham 2 Tablespoons of cracker dust, 2 Tablespoons of brown sugar, and sprinkle lightly with pepper. Stick the ham with whole cloves. A wineglass of sherry sprinkled over the top of the ham will greatly improve the flavor. Bake in a hot oven (450 F) for 20 minutes until brown. Garnish with watercress and parsley.
The Southern Cookbook, 1939

HAM BALLS WITH RAISIN SAUCE

1 1/2 pounds ground pork
1 pound ground cooked ham
2 cups cracker crumbs (saltines)
2 eggs, beaten
1/2 cup milk
1/2 teaspoon salt

Combine first 6 ingredients. Shape into small balls. Place in a greased baking dish and bake at 350 for 15 minutes. Pour raisin sauce over ham balls; cover and bake 30 minutes at 350. Uncover and bake 30 minutes, basting occasionally with pan drippings. It is best to keep the ham balls in a single layer while baking.

RAISIN SAUCE

1 cup firmly packed brown sugar
1/2 cup vinegar
1/2 cup water
1/4 cup raisins
1 teaspoon dry mustard

Combine all the ingredients in a small saucepan. Cook over medium heat until sugar dissolves, stirring constantly. After baking the ham balls for 15 minutes, they may be cooled and then put in zip-locked bags and frozen. Thaw overnight in a refrigerator and bake as directed.
http://cooks.com/f77se60q

NOTE: As a personal note, we served ham balls with raisin sauce at the *Satsuma Tea Room* and this is roughly the same recipe that we followed. I absolutely loved them and ate them by the dozen. They were that good and they are so easy to make.

TO GLAZE BAKED OR BOILED COUNTRY HAM

NOTE: After the ham is cooked, remove the skin and use your favorite glaze. Hams should not be so over-done that they will fall apart while carving. Use of a meat thermometer will help avoid over or under cooking the meat. Remove the ham skin with a sharp knife. If desired, the fat may be scored into 1 or 2-inch squares down to the meat surface. Cover with one of the glazes mentioned below. Stick long stemmed cloves into each square, or about every inch, through the surface of the ham. Bake in a moderately hot oven (350 to 400 F) for about 30 minutes or until browned and glazed.
The Nashville Cookbook, 1977

BAKED HAM STEAK

1-inch slice of ham, (about 1 1/2 pounds)
1 cup pineapple juice
1 teaspoon whole cloves
1/4 teaspoon dry mustard
1/2 cup sour cream

Broil ham steak about 10 minutes. Boil pineapple juice with cloves and mustard until reduced by half. Strain and cool. Whip sour cream and fold into this. Pour over the ham. Bake at 350 until the cream is partly cooked in the ham, 15 to 20 minutes.
Satsuma Tea Room, Fun for the Cook, 1968

BROILED HAM

1 slice ham   1 cup water
1 cup milk

Trim all skin from ham and soak in the water and milk for about 1 hour. Wipe well and place on broiler rack and put under slow flame. Broil slowly and when cooked and slightly browned, remove from the rack and place on hot platter.
The Southern Cookbook, 1939

BOILED HAM

Wash a 10-pound ham carefully, and scrub with a brush. Soak in cold water overnight. Next morning, put in a ham boiler, skin side down, cover well with cold water into which you can put 1 cup of black molasses, 1 cup vinegar, 1 onion, and 1 apple. Boil until well done and leave in water overnight. On the morning of the second day, remove the skin, cover with a thick paste made from dry mustard, 1 cup of brown sugar and a little Worcestershire sauce. Stick the ham full of cloves, put in the oven and bake.
The Savannah Cook Book, 1933

BOILING COUNTRY HAM

- Cut off the hock, clean the whole ham thoroughly with a brush and rough cloth.
- Trim off any dark, dry edges and discolored fat. Hams over 1 year old can be soaked 8 to 12 hours before cooking if you prefer.
- Fill large roaster about 1/2 full of water. Put ham in skin side up. Start ham at 450 F and reduce the heat to 300 F when the water boils.
- Cook 30 minutes per pound or until meat thermometer registers 160 F
- Allow to cool in juice 4 to 5 hours. Remove from the broth and skin ham.
- Use your favorite glaze.

The Nashville Cookbook, 1977

UPSIDE-DOWN HAM LOAF   "Something to Write Home About"

1/4 cup brown sugar	1 pound ground cured ham
8 pineapple spears, canned or	1 pound ground veal or lean beef
4 pineapple slices, canned	1 cup dry bread crumbs
whole cloves	1/2 teaspoon salt
2 eggs, slightly beaten	1/4 teaspoon pepper
1 can cream of mushroom soup	3 Tablespoons grated onion
1/2 cup water	parsley

Preheat oven to 350 F. Grease a 9 x 5 x 2 3/4-inch loaf pan and sprinkle with the brown sugar. Stick pineapple with cloves and arrange clove side down on the bottom of the pan. Mix together all the remaining ingredients. Place meat mixture on top of pineapple and bake for 1 hour. Drain off liquid and invert loaf on a hot platter. Garnish with parsley.
Geraldine Acker, University of Illinois Home Economics Faculty Favorites, 1965

SAUSAGE RICE CASSEROLE

3/4 pound sausage
1/2 cup chopped celery
1/3 cup chopped onion
1/2 cup uncooked rice
10 1/2 ounce can mushroom soup
1/2 cup milk

Fry sausage, but do not brown too much. In the sausage grease, cook celery and onions until yellow, not brown. Mix all the ingredients together. Bake for 1 hour at 325 F. Serves 6.

NOTE: This dish is surprisingly easy, good, cheap and can be prepared a day ahead.
Satsuma Tea Room, More Fun for the Cook, 1974

HAM AND DEVILED EGG CASSEROLE

1/4 cup onions, finely chopped
1/4 cup green peppers, finely chopped
2 Tablespoons margarine
1/3 cup milk
2/3 cup cheese, grated
10 1/2 ounce can mushroom soup
2/3 cup cooked rice
1 cup cooked ham, diced
6 eggs, hard cooked and deviled
1 cup buttered bread crumbs

Cook onions and peppers in margarine until golden brown. Stir in the milk and cheese. Mix rice, ham, and 3/4 of soup mixture. Pour into greased casserole. Top with egg halves. Pour over remaining soup mixture. Sprinkle with cheese and crumbs. Bake in a moderate oven at 350 F for 30 minutes. Serves 4.
Satsuma Tea Room, More Fun for the Cook, 1974

HAM AND PINEAPPLE

1-inch slice of center-cut cured ham
2 cups of milk
2 Tablespoons butter
1 can sliced pineapple

Soak the ham in milk for 4 hours. When ready to cook remove the ham from the milk and place in a hot pan with the butter. Cook slowly until brown and then turn ham over and brown on other side. Transfer ham to another pan and place in warm oven where it will stay hot but not cook. Put slices of pineapple in pan with ham juice and brown on both sides. Then place ham on platter with slices of browned pineapple on top and around the ham. Mix pineapple juice with the ham gravy and pour over the ham.
The Southern Cookbook, 1939

HAM SOUFFLE

1 cup ground ham
1/4 cup butter
1/4 cup flour
1 cup milk
3 eggs
1 teaspoon lemon juice
1/2 teaspoon salt

Make cream sauce of butter, flour, and milk, then add seasonings and ground ham. Add beaten egg yolks. Cool and fold in beaten egg whites. Pour into buttered casserole dish and bake at 400 for 20-25 minutes. Excellent with any kind of ham, especially country ham.
Satsuma Tea Room, More Fun for the Cook, 1974

SAUSAGES IN WINE

1 can consommé	1 carrot, chopped
1 cup Chablis wine	12 sausages
1 stalk celery, chopped	4 servings of mashed potatoes

Bring the consommé and wine to a boil. Add the chopped vegetables and sausages. Cook until vegetables are tender. Serve over mashed potatoes in flat soup bowls. Serves 4.
Al Banner, University of Illinois Home Economics Faculty Favorites, 1965

HAM LOAF

2 cups cooked ground ham	1 cup grated carrots, raw
1 cup bread or cracker crumbs	2 Tablespoons chili sauce
1 egg	1 cup milk

Mix all the ingredients. Bake in a greased loaf pan about 45 minutes at 350 F. This recipe is good for leftover ham.
Satsuma Tea Room, Fun for the Cook, 1968

BAKED SLICED HAM AND APPLES

2 large, thin slices raw ham	1/2 cup brown sugar
1 teaspoon dry mustard	1 Tablespoon butter
2 teaspoons vinegar	2 apples

Remove the bone from the ham. Mix together the mustard and vinegar. Spread the mixture thinly on the ham. Slice apples very thin and spread 2 layers on the ham. Sprinkle well with brown sugar. Roll ham the long way. Hold together with metal skewers or tie with string. Place in baking pan and dot with butter. Bake in moderate oven for 25 to 30 minutes. Baste several times while baking.
The Southern Cook Book, 1939

ITALIAN PORK CHOPS WITH HERBS

1 1/2 teaspoons crushed dried rosemary	4 large 1-inch-thick pork chops
1 1/2 teaspoons powdered sage	water
1/2 teaspoon garlic salt	1/2 cup dry white wine
1/4 teaspoon pepper	

Combine the herbs and seasonings. Rub this mixture on both sides of the chops. Put chops in skillet and cover with water. Cook in covered skillet for about 1 hour. When the water has evaporated, the chops will begin to brown. Turn several times until browned on both sides. Add wine. Bring to a boil and remove from heat. Put chops in heated serving dish and pour liquid over them. Serves 4.
Barbara Fisher, The University of Illinois Home Economics Faculty Favorites, 1965

ELEGANT LEMON PORK CHOP BAKE

NOTE: So easy, but a so elegant tasting way to prepare thin bone-in or boneless pork chops. The sauce is wonderful over rice. This dish will make both a great casual family dinner or an elegant company entrée.

6 pork chops, 4 ounces, 1/2 inch thick	1/4 cup packed brown sugar
1 lemon	1 teaspoon white wine vinegar
3/4 cup ketchup	

Preheat oven to 325 F. In a large skillet over medium heat, brown the pork chops on both sides. Remove the chops and place them in a shallow baking dish. Combine the ketchup, brown sugar, and vinegar. Pour mixture over chops, spreading to cover chops evenly. Cut 6 slices from the lemon and lay 1 slice on top of each chop. Squeeze the juice from the remaining portion of lemon over the chops.
Cover and bake for 30 minutes at 325 F. Uncover and bake for 10 minutes more.

NOTE: I am the oldest of six children. This dish was very popular, tasty, and inexpensive to cook in our household. The recipe was passed from my grandmother. My brother, Steve, has picked up the mantle and cooks this dish often. He has five grown children. I am sure he has passed along the knowledge to the next generation. Sounds Southern, doesn't it?
https://allrecipes.com/recipe/14725/elegant-lemon-pork-chop-bake/

STUFFED PORK CHOPS

Select as many rib pork chops as needed. Have the butcher cut them an inch in thickness and make a pocket in each one. Fill with the following bread filling:

2 cups bread crumbs	season to taste
1 Tablespoon chopped onion	hot water to moisten
1 cup chopped apples	

Place in a baking dish, add a little water to keep from sticking and bake in a slow oven until the pork is very well cooked.
The Southern Cookbook, 1939

HUNGARIAN PORK CHOPS

6 pork chops, ½-inch thick	1 cup water
salt and pepper	1/2 cup sour cream
1 medium onion chopped	2 teaspoons paprika
3 Tablespoons butter	

Sprinkle chops with salt and pepper. Sauté onion in butter until soft and golden. Remove from skillet. Add pork chops and brown on all sides. Add water and onions, lower heat and cook slowly over very low heat about 45 minutes. Add more water if necessary. Add sour cream and paprika. Blend well. A little sour cream is all that is needed to improve flavor. Serves 6.
Satsuma Tea Room, Fun for the Cook, 1968

HAWAIIAN SPARERIBS

2 pounds spareribs in small pieces
1/2 teaspoon salt
1/4 cup soy sauce
1/2 cup salad oil
2 Tablespoons flour
3/4 cup pineapple juice
1/2 teaspoon salt
2 Tablespoons sugar
1/4 cup vinegar
1 cup water
1 teaspoon corn starch
1/2 cup diced pineapple

Add salt and soy sauce to ribs. Heat oil in skillet. Brown ribs. Add flour and stir in oil, then add pineapple juice, salt, sugar, vinegar, water. Simmer until pork is tender (around 40 minutes). Make paste of corn starch and 1 Tablespoon cold water. Add to pork mixture. Add pineapple to pork and simmer several minutes. Serves 4.
Satsuma Tea Room, Fun for the Cook, 1968

JUST FOR FUN- CHITTERLINGS (Chit'lings)

Wash chitterlings thoroughly and cover with boiling salted water. Add 1 Tablespoon whole cloves and 1 red pepper cut in pieces. Cook until tender. Drain. Cut in pieces the size of oysters. Dip each piece in beaten egg and then in cracker crumbs. Fry in deep fat until brown. Chitterlings (the small intestines of swine) are obtainable in Southern butcher shops.
The Southern Cook Book, 1939

BARBECUE

Although not a lot is known about the origin and history of barbecue, Sylvia Lovergren offers an insight: "We do know the Spanish conquistadors reported seeing Taino-Arawak and Carib natives in Hispaniola roasting and drying and smoking meat on wooden frameworks over small beds of coals. They called the wooden framework a babracot which became barbacoa with the Spanish. This method of cooking over coals (not uncommon as a cooking process) and very low heat (dubious as a cooking practice) appeared to be a totally absurd way of cooking to many of the early Europeans. Not coincidentally perhaps, these people also invented the hammock which was a great way to loaf while waiting for the barbecue to get done.

The European settlers evidently took to this very odd method of cooking with great enthusiasm. By the end of the 1600's, barbecuing parties had become so popular that Virginia had to enact a law prohibiting the shooting of firearms during these festivities. As the meat cooked long and slow, guests danced and socialized, played outdoor games similar to horseshoes, and partied with betting and liquid refreshment. Barbecuing had become known just not as a cooking method, but a true social event. George Washington remarks in his diaries attending barbecues a number of times including a "Barbicue of my own giving at Accomack in 1773."

"Barbecue", "American Heritage", by Sylvia Lovergren, Volume 54, Issue 3

While pork was a leading food source for free-white Southerners, the enslaved people were even more reliant on pork for their meat supply. Pork along with corn was the basic provisions issued to enslaved people on many plantations. They typically received an average of three pounds of pork per week, but this allotment was considered to be the lesser cuts of the hog; such as feet, head, ribs, fatback, or internal organs.

To hide the poor flavor of these cuts, the enslaved people drew inspiration from traditional African cooking and used a powerful mixture of red pepper mixed with vinegar on their meat. West African cuisine relied heavily on the use of hot spices and the enslaved continued this tradition by growing various peppers in their gardens to add to their dishes. They were the driving force behind the art of barbecue and what is regarded today as being at the center of the barbecue mania: smoke and sauce.

Eventually Southerners adopted this hot pepper vinegar method of flavoring for all cuts of meat (the birth of hot sauce? pepper sauce? Tabasco?). This combination of ingredients still serves as the base for almost all types of barbecue sauces, particularly in North Carolina.

Practically each state in the South will go to war to defend the type of barbecue and barbecue sauce by which they are customarily known to prepare and consume; tomato base, mustard base, vinegar base, mayonnaise base, are different varieties of barbecue sauces that will be championed, defended, to the death by citizens of specific Southern regions.

If cornbread is the backbone of Southern cooking, then barbecue is the heart and soul. Pork has been the leading go-to-meat of choice in the South for a long time. According to estimates prior to the Civil War, Southerners ate around five pounds of pork for every one pound of beef they consumed.

As the historian Sam Hilliard states, "If the 'king' of the antebellum Southern economy was cotton, then the title of 'queen' must go the pig." While beef was uniquely linked more strongly with barbecue in Texas, the majority of the South adores that other ruler of the smokehouse, pork.

Bowers Hilliard, <u>Hog Meat and Hoe Cake</u>

Barbecue, or barbeque, can refer to a cooking method by itself, the meat prepared by this cooking method, the cooking apparatus to prepare barbecue itself, or to a type of social occasion featuring foods that were cooked by means of the method of preparing known as barbecue. Present day barbecuing methods include smoking, roasting, baking, braising or grilling. The original technique is barbecuing using smoke at very low temperatures for very long cooking times. Each Southern locale has its own variety of barbecue and sauces.
"Barbecue"-Wikipedia

Sociologist John Shelton Reed wrote, "I once suggested, half seriously, that if the South needs a new flag, as it surely does, we could do worse than to use a dancing pig with a knife and fork. You want to talk about heritage, not hate….That represents a heritage we all share and can take pride in. Barbecue both symbolizes and contributes to community.
"There's no denying that barbecue can be divisive. Drive down the road a hundred miles and the barbecue does change….like Byzantine icon painters, barbecue cooks differ in technique and skill, but they are working within the traditions that pretty much tell them what to produce. And those traditions reflect and reinforce the fierce localism that has always been a Southern characteristic, the sense of place that literary folk claim to find in Southern fiction, the devotion to states' rights and local autonomy that was an established characteristic of Southern politics long before it became a major headache for the Confederate States of America."
-*John Shelton Reed, Cornbread Nation 2: The United States of Barbecue*

BARBECUED RIBS

3 to 4 pounds pork ribs, cut into pieces
1 lemon
1 large onion
1 cup catsup
1/3 cup Worcestershire sauce

1 teaspoon chili powder
1 teaspoon salt
2 dashes hot pepper sauce
2 cups water

Place ribs in shallow roasting pan, meaty side up. On each piece, place a slice of unpeeled lemon and a thin slice of onion. Roast in a very hot oven, 450 degrees for 30 minutes. Combine the remaining ingredients; bring to a boil and pour over the ribs. Continue baking in a moderate oven, 325 F, about 2 hours, basting ribs with the sauce every 15 minutes.
Helen M. Young, The Nashville Cookbook, 1977

SPICY DRY RUB RIBS

3 lbs. pork ribs, country-style or baby back
4 teaspoons salt
2 teaspoons black pepper

2 teaspoons paprika
1/4 teaspoon cayenne pepper
2 teaspoons sugar

Combine all spices and store up to 3 months in a tightly closed container. Two hours before grilling, rub the ribs with all the spice mixture and allow to rest before grilling.
David Hazelwood, Cortner Mill Restaurant cookbook, 2009

BARBECUED RIBS

2 to 3 sides pork spareribs

BARBECUE SAUCE

1 cup chopped green onion	1 Tablespoon dry mustard
2 Tablespoons butter or margarine	2 Tablespoons Worcestershire sauce
2 teaspoons paprika	1/8 teaspoon Tabasco
1/2 teaspoon pepper	1/2 cup catsup
dash cayenne pepper	2 Tablespoons vinegar
2 Tablespoons brown sugar	

Cook green onion in butter until tender, about 5 minutes. Add remaining ingredients. Simmer about 10 minutes, stirring frequently. This is a thick sauce and keeps well in a covered jar in the refrigerator. Simmer spareribs in small amount of water in heavy covered pot for about 1 hour. Refrigerate until ready to grill. Cut ribs into serving portions, 2 or 3 rib pieces. Grill over glowing coals, brushing with barbecue sauce frequently until tender, about 15 minutes. For brushing on the barbecue sauce, use a long-handled brush or a "swab" made by tying a soft cloth on the end of a long-handled fork.

NOTE: If the spareribs are barbecued without the precooking, they will take about an hour. Simmering them first is preferred; they are much more moist and better flavored and even in 15 minutes they will get a zesty barbecue coating. Cooking time is approximate, varying with the heat of the charcoal and distance of meat from the heat. 4 servings.
Easy-on-the-Cookbook, 1960

BARBECUED CHICKEN

1 young broiling chicken	1/2 teaspoon Worcestershire sauce
5 Tablespoons melted butter	pinch of red pepper
2 Tablespoons vinegar	
1/2 teaspoon dry mustard	

Split the young chicken for broiling. Place them on a broiling rack, skin facing downward, and cook on moderate flame until well browned and almost tender. Turn and brown the other side. While the chicken pieces are baking, baste frequently with the above mixture.
The Southern Cookbook, 1939

BBQ CHICKEN

chicken (whatever pieces you like to eat/serve)	olive oil	your favorite BBQ sauce
	salt and pepper to taste	brown sugar

Preheat oven to 225. Arrange chicken in 9 x 13-inch baking dish and brush with olive oil. Sprinkle with salt and pepper to taste. Cover and bake at 225 for 4 hours. Remove from the oven and grill for 5 minutes per side, liberally applying favorite BBQ sauce. Sprinkle with brown sugar and serve warm.
Brandon Mosley, Fruit of the Spirit, Mt. Bethel United Methodist Church, Marietta, GA

BARBECUED CHICKEN

1 broiler-fryer cut up or quartered
1 cup salad oil
1/4 cup wine vinegar
2 Tablespoons lemon juice
1 teaspoon salt
1 cup prepared mustard
1/4 pound butter or margarine
2 teaspoons Worcestershire sauce
1/3 cup sugar
1/4 cup sherry
1/2 teaspoon salt

Combine oil, vinegar, lemon juice and salt. Marinate the chicken in this mixture for 3 to 4 hours. Place the chicken on the grill over low coals or under the broiler. Blend all the remaining ingredients into a sauce over a low heat. Baste the chicken frequently with this sauce. Yields 4 servings.
Dr. Queenie B. Mills, University of Illinois Home Economics Faculty Favorites, 1965

BARBECUED HAM

6 slices boiled ham
2 Tablespoons butter
1 Tablespoon vinegar
1/4 teaspoon dry mustard
salt and pepper to taste

Brown the ham slightly in butter. Mix the mustard, salt, pepper and vinegar together; pour this over the ham and butter. Cook for a minute or two. Serve very hot.

NOTE: This is an easy way of preparing ham so that it will seem different and appetizing, even when ham is featured several times in rather close succession.
Mrs. Cornelius Reamer, 200 Years of Charleston Cooking, 1930

BBQ BRISKET

MARINADE

1 Tablespoon garlic salt
1 Tablespoon celery salt
4 Tablespoons Worcestershire sauce
1/2 bottle Liquid Smoke
6 pounds beef brisket

Combine the ingredients for the marinade and brush both sides of brisket. Place in a container and seal. Turn about every hour. Let stand 8 hours. (you can fix ahead and refrigerate overnight.) When ready to cook, place brisket in a 9 x 13-inch pan in a 200-250 degree oven. Cover lightly with foil but do not seal edges. Bake 8 hours. Approximately 30 minutes before the 8 hours is up, make the sauce recipe below.

SAUCE

1/4 pound margarine or butter
1 large onion chopped
4 ounces ketchup
1/2 cup dark brown sugar
1/4 cup cider vinegar
8 ounces tomato sauce

Sauté onions in butter until tender and translucent. Add rest of ingredients and simmer for approximately 10-15 minutes, until all ingredients are well blended. Drain the marinade from the cooked brisket. Pour sauce over brisket and cook uncovered 1-1 1/2 hours. Serves 8-10
Judy Spell, Fruit of the Spirit, Mt Bethel United Methodist Church, Marietta, Georgia

BARBECUED LAMB

1 leg of lamb	1 teaspoon ground ginger
2 Tablespoons chili sauce	1 teaspoon dry mustard
2 onions sliced	1 Tablespoon vinegar
1 clove garlic	salt and pepper
1 Tablespoon Worcestershire sauce	2 Tablespoons olive oil

After wiping lamb well with a damp cloth, rub thoroughly with the spices, all of which have been mixed together. Dredge well with flour and brown quickly in a hot oven (400 F) about 25 minutes. Reduce heat and baste with the following sauce made by mixing the chili sauce, Worcestershire sauce, vinegar and olive oil together. Slice onion and place around the meat with the clove of garlic. Baste every 15 minutes, allowing about 30 minutes to the pound for roasting. One hour before being finished, add 1 cup of boiling water. Skim fat from pan and use for gravy.
The Southern Cookbook, 1939

BUILD AN OPEN PIT FOR BARBECUE

Dig a pit the size that is required for the amount of meat you have. A small hole is about 9 inches deep (equals roughly to grill space about 2 feet square). For large barbecues, dig a pit about 12-18 inches deep, 3-4 feet wide and as long as you wish. Tip: never get your pit so wide that you can't safely tend your fire and barbecue.

Never start to barbecue until your fire and coals have died down. Keep a fire of hickory wood going to aid and continue to feed coals into the pit. Tip: this fire should be close to the pit and is called the feeder fire.

Use heavy chicken wire frames to stretch across the pits. These wire frames should be only a few inches above the charcoal embers. If you are barbecuing large portions of meat, new brooms or mops are used to brush the sop onto the meat. Keep sopping throughout the entire process to keep it moist and well basted. Warm salted water is used to baste the meat until it gets hot enough to keep away insects and flies.

The same sop or mopping sauce can also be used for oven-cooked barbecue. Allow 12-18 hours to cook large pieces of meat over the open pit.

GOOD MOPPING SAUCE

1 quart apple cider vinegar	3 Tablespoons crushed hot red pepper
1 stick butter	salt and pepper to taste

Bring it all to a boil and sop. This makes a good mopping sauce recipe for larger amounts of meat, (20-30) pounds
The Nashville Cookbook, 1977

BEEF

"Spiced Round of Beef has been a traditional food during the Christmas season in Nashville since about 1865. This cherished delicacy has particular uniqueness to Middle Tennessee. The recipe for curing round of beef in this manner was developed by the German and Swiss pioneer ancestors out of the necessity of extending the time that the beef could be preserved. Strips of hog fat were rolled in spices and threaded through thick cuts of beef round. The rounds were then cured in brine in much the same way as corned beef; the delightfully spicy flavor and striking appearance of spice-coated circles of fat in each slice makes Spiced Round a specialty all its own.

Although old cookbooks include instructions for spicing a round, most Spiced Rounds are now made commercially. Exact recipes for processing are heavily guarded secrets. Although methods vary, the resulting product is much the same."

The Nashville Cookbook Commentary, 1977

COOKING SPICED ROUND

12 pounds Spiced Round
1 cup sugar or sorghum molasses

Remove Spiced Round from brine solution, or from packaging if it is commercially cured. Place it in cold water for 1 hour. Rinse in additional cold water. Place in a cloth sack or in the center of a 36-inch square of loosely woven material. Wrap firmly and sew in place in order to keep the meat very compact. (Wrapping tightly in heavy foil will achieve the same purpose.) Place wrapped round on a trivet in a large kettle or large stand. Cover with cold water; add sugar or sorghum and heat to boiling. Reduce heat and simmer 1 hour per 4 pounds of round. Allow to cool in the water in which it was cooked; chill before removing the wrappings. Trim darkened outside areas. Slice thinly across the grain so each slice will contain 2 to 3 circles of the spice-coated fat.

NOTE: This recipe was found on The Maxwell House Hotel Christmas Menu, 1879
The Nashville Cookbook, 1977

ROASTED PRIME RIB OF BEEF

5 pound prime rib loin	1 Tablespoon salt
1 1/2 Tablespoons garlic, minced	1 Tablespoon black pepper

Mix garlic, pepper, and salt. Rub this mixture on the rib loin. Place the loin in a large roasting pan and bake at 350 F for 10 minutes per pound for rare.
Jim Long, Cortner Mill Restaurant cookbook, 2009

RIBS OF BEEF A LA MISSION

Season short ribs with salt and pepper, also rub over slightly with a clove of garlic. Cover with boiling water, add 1 large sliced onion. Cook slowly two hours. Add 2 cups tomatoes, 1 teaspoon paprika, and cook gently 1 hour.
The Southern Cookbook, 1939

Boiled beef (but don't boil it!) is an old-fashioned term used for less tender cuts of beef that are covered with water, seasoned and simmered (not boiled) 2 to 4 hours until tender. When you truly boil, the meat will toughen. Boiled beef is many times served with catsup, mustard, or a meat sauce. The broth should be used and is perfect for soup or gravies.

Put the meat in a deep kettle. Cover with water. For each 1 pound of meat add 1/2 teaspoon salt and you may wish to add 1/2 teaspoon pepper, or a sliced onion, or a bay leaf and other herbs.

Vegetables may be cooked in water around meat during the last 1/2 hour. Sauerkraut is often cooked with boiled beef, but if canned kraut is used, add this mixture 30 minutes before the beef is done. Boiling beef can be done in a pressure cooker or in a crock pot.

DRIED BEEF A LA MARYLAND

1/2 pound chipped smoked beef	1 Tablespoon butter
1/2 cup thin cream	1 scant Tablespoon flour
1 cup milk	pepper

Soak chipped beef in boiling water for 5 minutes. Drain and dry with a towel. Make a sauce by melting butter in top of double boiler, stir in flour and blend well, then gradually add milk and cream, cook for a few minutes, then add seasonings and beef. Cook 10 minutes and serve on crisp toast.

NOTE: Everyone of a certain age or older has had this dish in some form of fashion many times in their lives. My mom made it often.
The Southern Cookbook, 1939

MEAT LOAF

1 small onion chopped	1 1/2 teaspoons salt	1 egg
1/2 pound ground beef	1/8 teaspoon pepper	1 1/4 cups milk
	1 1/2 cups bread crumbs	

Mix beef, seasonings, onion, bread crumbs, and egg. Add milk and mix well. Form into a loaf pan and bake one hour at 350 F. During the last 20 minutes of baking, pour 1 cup canned tomatoes on top and continue baking. Serves 6.

NOTE: A variation to this recipe, and one that is quite good, is instead of 1 1/2 pounds ground beef, use 1 pound beef and 1 pound country sausage. Uncooked oatmeal can also be used in combination with the breadcrumbs or as a stand-alone ingredient.
Satsuma Tea Room, Fun for the Cook, 1968

POT ROAST

4 pound rump roast   1/2 package Lipton onion soup

Shake onion soup together. Use to rub all over the beef. Wrap completely in aluminum foil and roast 300 F for 2 1/2 hours.
NOTE: The same idea can be used with a thick cut of round steak.
Satsuma Tea Room, Fun for the Cook, 1968

POT ROAST IN PAPER BAG

5 pound chuck roast, not boned
1 Tablespoon flour
10 ½ ounces mushroom soup
1/4 cup grated onion

Place all in a paper bag designed for that purpose. Place on pan, punch holes in bag. Cook 2 1/2 hours at 325. Oven can be set at a still lower temperature and cooked for a longer time.

NOTE: Roast will be brown and have a lovely gravy with no pots to wash! Special bags are made for this method of cooking.
Satsuma Tea Room, More Fun for the Cook, 1974

VEAL PAPRIKA

2 pounds veal
1/3 cup flour
1 1/4 teaspoons salt
1/8 teaspoon pepper
5 Tablespoons fat
2 chopped onions
1 teaspoon paprika
1 3/4 cups water
1/2 cup sour cream

Cut veal into 2-inch squares. Mix flour, salt, and pepper; dredge meat in mixture. Heat fat in skillet. Add chopped onions. Cook 2 minutes. Remove onions, add veal. Brown well on both sides. Add onions, water, and paprika. Bring to a boil. Cover and simmer until tender, about 45 minutes. Stir in sour cream. Heat and serve on rice or noodles. Serves 6.
Satsuma Tea Room, Fun for the Cook, 1968

VEAL RACK WITH CHAMPAGNE CHERRIES

2 pound veal rack
salt
pepper

Have your butcher saw down the backbone to divide your rack in half. Sprinkle all sides of racks liberally with salt and pepper. Grill racks over medium high heat for 7 minutes on each side for medium rare. Remove from grill and separate into individual chops by cutting between the ribs. Arrange ribs on plate over a bed of rice and drizzle with Champagne Cherry Sauce. Serves 2.

CHAMPAGNE CHERRY SAUCE

3 Tablespoons dried cherries
3 Tablespoons Champagne
1/2 cup honey
3 Tablespoons Dijon mustard
1 teaspoon dry mustard
1/4 teaspoon cayenne pepper
2 Tablespoons butter, melted

Put cherries into a bowl with the Champagne. Cover the bowl and microwave on high for 45 seconds. Remove and let stand for 5 minutes. Combine remaining ingredients and add to cherries. Left over sauce can be stored in refrigerator 6-8 weeks.
Jim Long, Cortner Mill Restaurant cookbook, 2009

VEAL WITH CURRY POWDER

2 pounds ground veal
1 Tablespoon butter
2 medium sized onions

1 teaspoon curry powder
1 Tablespoon flour

Stew veal and strew over it the onions. Rub together the butter, curry powder and flour and add to this a cup of broth in which the meat was cooked. Stew for 5 minutes and when the meat is done, take up and serve with hot curry gravy.

NOTE: Chicken and turtle are also excellent cooked this way.
The Savannah Cook Book, 1933

CORNED BEEF

What is corned beef? What is this piece of meat with a such a unique flavor and a pinkish color with a touch of grey? Corned beef is a cut of meat, generally a brisket, that has been cured with salt and brine for about 10 days. The salt used comprised large grains of rock salt or "corns", hence "corned beef".

The brine is comparable to that of a pickling brine and consists of spices such as peppercorns, bay leaves, cinnamon, ginger, coriander, cloves, nutmeg, mustard seed. Throw in some fresh garlic too for good measure and flavor. After the ten days, remove the meat from the salt and brine and wash thoroughly in cold water.

BEEF BRISKET, FRESH AND CORNED

Beef brisket is one of the old-fashioned boiling pieces which is too often overlooked by the new cook and with the popularity and ease of today's outdoor grilling and smoking, it has become almost totally synonymous with BBQ. Better grades of brisket are well streaked with layers of fat. The whole brisket is a large wedge-shaped piece varying in thickness from 2 inches at one end to 4 or 5 inches at the other end. In the meat case, brisket is usually displayed cut into pieces weighing 2 to 4 pounds and is usually boneless.

Corned beef brisket is a reddish gray piece of meat resulting from the mild cure (seasoning), which gives this meat a distinctive flavor. Corned beef is usually cut into 3 to 6 pound boneless pieces.
Martha Logan's Meat Cook Book, 1952

CORNED BEEF BRISKET

This is a fine flavored piece of meat, if well cooked. There is a great deal of difference in the quality of corned beef due to the quality of the meat and the method of curing. Good quality corned beef brisket will have about 1/4 as much fat as lean. Cover the corn beef with water and simmer until tender (3 pounds meat takes about 3 hours). Do not boil. This meat can be served with horseradish or mustard and can also be served hot or cold.
Martha Logan's Meat Cook Book, 1952

CORNED BEEF AND CABBAGE

NOTE: Plan for leftovers when you cook corned beef, so you can have some for sliced cold for sandwiches or chopped up for corned beef hash.

4 pounds corned beef   1 head cabbage

Cover the corned beef with water in a kettle and simmer slowly about 4 hours or until tender. Do not boil. Cut the cabbage into 8 wedges. About 15 minutes before the corned beef is done, add the cabbage. Cook uncovered 10 to 15 minutes more. Yields 8 servings.
Martha Logan's Meat Cook Book, 1952

SPECIAL GLAZED CORNED BEEF BRISKET

Remove the hot "boiled" brisket from the broth. Cut the fat covering of the brisket into diagonal strips, then into diamond strips. Spread lightly with prepared mustard. Sprinkle lightly with sifted brown sugar. Stick a whole clove into the center of each diamond. Place the brisket in a shallow pan and bake in a hot oven (400 F) about 20 minutes to melt the sugar and glaze the surface of the brisket.
Martha Logan's Meat Cook Book, 1952

HAMBURGER-BACON ROAST

3 pounds ground beef or pork	3 hard cooked eggs
2 large potatoes, cooked and mashed	chopped parsley
1 onion, chopped fine	salt and pepper
2 slices bread, diced	1/4 pound sliced bacon

Combine the meat, potatoes, onion, bread and seasonings. Divide into 2 parts; place 1/2 into baking pan, cover with the whole hard cooked eggs and then the remaining half of the meat. Cover meat with the slices of bacon and bake in a moderately hot oven (400 F) for 1 1/2 hours.
The Southern Cookbook, 1939

CHEESE HAMBURGER BAKE

2 Tablespoons margarine	8 ounces noodles
1 1/2 pounds hamburger	(Cook 8 minutes and drain.)
1 teaspoon salt	1 cup cottage cheese
1/4 teaspoon garlic salt	1 cup sour cream
8 ounces tomato sauce	6 green peppers, chopped fine

Mix all together and add noodles

Cook hamburger in skillet until slightly brown then add 8-ounce can tomato sauce. Put meat mixture into casserole and layer with noodle mixture until all is used. Then add 3/4 cup grated Cheddar cheese on top. Bake at 350 F for 30 minutes. Serves 8.
Satsuma Tea Room, More Fun for the Cook, 1974

BROILED HAMBURGER STEAK

1 pound chopped beef	1 Tablespoon cold water
2 teaspoons chopped onion	1 Tablespoon chopped fat
salt and pepper to taste	

Mix all together and shape into small round cakes. Place a piece of butter on top of each cake and broil fast on both sides. 1 pound of beef will make 4 cakes.
The Southern Cookbook, 1939

BEEF AND NOODLES (Really easy)

1 pound ground beef	1 cup tomato sauce	pepper
1 onion, chopped	1 cup water	1 cup grated cheese
2 Tablespoons butter	1 teaspoon brown sugar	
2 cups noodles	salt	

Sauté onions in butter, add meat. Brown. Add tomato sauce, water, noodles, and seasoning. Cook until noodles are tender- about 15 minutes. Add cheese, place in a casserole dish. Cook about 15 minutes at 350 F. Serves 6.
Satsuma Tea Room, Fun for the Cook, 1968

"Let No Man Ever Sneer at Hash Again"

HASH

Hash begins with ground, chopped, or finely cut leftover meat, finely cubed potatoes and seasoning. Cook this mixture slowly in a Tablespoon or two of meat drippings in a heavy skillet. Turn with a pancake turner to brown well (almost crisp).

NOTE: One of the beauties of a good hash is the almost infinite variations that can be cooked from a good core hash; hash with eggs, baked hash au gratin, baked barbecue hash, baked red flannel hash (beets), etc.
Martha Logan's Meat Cook Book, 1952

A GOOD HASH

In the South, where some people are still guilty of eating a comfortable breakfast, this economical receipt is very popular.

1 small cup water	1 teaspoon chopped parsley
1/2 teaspoon lemon juice	1 teaspoon flour
1 Tablespoon butter	1 cup of any kind of cold meat, chopped
1/2 teaspoon chopped onion	fine

Make a sauce by stewing together the water, onion, lemon juice and parsley, thickened with the flour and butter which have been rubbed together. Just before serving, add the meat and heat well, but do not cook.
The Savannah Cook Book, 1933

CORNED BEEF HASH

2 Tablespoons butter
3 cups cubed boiled potatoes
3/4 cup cream

3 teaspoons finely-chopped parsley
2 cups cooked corned beef

Melt the butter in a double boiler, add the potatoes, mix, then pour in the cream, and now add the chopped corned beef and the chopped parsley. Stir well but do not mash the potatoes. Place in a pan or individual molds, butter the top and bake until well browned. If desired, the top may be indented for raw egg per portion which is dusted with paprika and baked until egg is set. Garnish with a sprig of parsley.

NOTE: This was a dish that my mother made a lot when we were growing up. She used an electric frying skillet to cook hers; not like this recipe. There is no wrong or right way to prepare this or many other dishes. It was easy and very economical and man did it taste good. The advent of corned beef in a can simplified cooking a great deal and for cooking hash I would recommend using the canned variety. -David S.
The Southern Cookbook, 1939

CASSEROLE OF BEEF

5 pounds beef round
4 Tablespoons Worcestershire sauce
1 Tablespoon white vinegar
3 small white onions
2 slices bacon
a little nutmeg

1 teaspoon celery seed
6 cloves
1/2 cup flour
pinch mustard
salt and pepper

Sear the beef on both sides to keep the juices in. Brown the flour and sprinkle over the beef. Season with salt, pepper, and put in iron pot with vinegar, onions (cut up), Worcestershire sauce, cloves, celery seed, nutmeg and mustard. Lay bacon across the top, and cover 2/3 with cold water. Put in oven and cook slowly for 4 hours.

NOTE: Potatoes placed around this and allowed to cook slowly with the meat have a delicious flavor.
The Savannah Cook Book, 1933

BEEF A LA STROGANOFF

2 pounds round steak 1/4 inch thick. Rub with garlic on both sides. Pound steak into a mixture of 2 teaspoons flour, 3 teaspoons salt, and 1/4 teaspoon pepper. Cut into strips. Brown 2 sliced medium onions in frying pan. Remove onions, then brown meat in same fat. Return onions. Cover tightly and simmer very slowly with a little water until meat is tender. Add 1 cup water, 1 chicken bouillon cube, and 1 pound fresh mushrooms. Cover tightly and simmer 10 minutes until tender. Let all cool. Just before serving, stir in 1 cup sour cream at room temperature. Season to taste with salt, pepper, and about a teaspoon of sugar. Reheat carefully and serve on rice or fried noodles.
Satsuma Tea Room, Fun for the Cook, 1968

BEEF STROGANOFF

1/2 pound round or boneless chuck	1 1/2 teaspoons salt
2 medium onions, sliced	1/8 teaspoon pepper
1/4 cup shortening	1/4 teaspoon Worcestershire
2 Tablespoons flour	4 ounce can mushrooms drained
3/4 pound tomatoes (3 medium)	1/2 cup sour cream
or 1 cup canned tomatoes	2 1/2 cups cooked rice or cooked noodles

Cut meat into 2-inch strips, 1/4 inch thick. Sauté onions in shortening 10 minutes. Remove onions to a bowl. Add the meat to the shortening; brown slowly and thoroughly. Sprinkle with flour and blend. Add tomatoes and seasonings. Cover and simmer 1 hour, stirring occasionally. Add mushrooms, onions and cream. Simmer for 30 minutes or until meat is tender. Serve over rice or noodles. Yield 3 servings.
Elsie Crouthamel, University of Illinois, Home Economics Faculty Favorites, 1965

HAMBURGER STROGANOFF

1 onion chopped	1/8 teaspoon powdered ginger
¼ pound margarine	1 teaspoon salt
½ pound fresh mushrooms, sliced thin	1/8 teaspoon black pepper
1 pound ground beef, browned	1 cup sour cream

Cook onion in margarine until soft. Add mushrooms, cook 5 minutes. Add meat. Stir in seasoning. Add sour cream, cook only until hot. Makes 4 servings.
Satsuma Tea Room, More Fun for the Cook, 1974

SOUR CREAM PORCUPINES

1 1/2 pounds lean ground beef	1/2 cup water
1/3 cup precooked rice, uncooked	1 beef bouillon cube
1 teaspoon paprika	1 teaspoon Worcestershire sauce
1 teaspoon salt	1 can cream of mushroom soup
1/4 cup chopped onion	1/2 cup dairy sour cream
2 Tablespoons shortening	Chinese noodles

Combine ground beef with rice, paprika, salt and onion. Shape into 16-20 balls. Brown in hot shortening. Arrange balls in 1 ½-quart casserole. Drain fat from skillet. Combine in skillet the water, bouillon cube, Worcestershire sauce and soup. Stir until well blended. Add sour cream and pour mixture over meat balls. Cover and refrigerate 3 to 4 hours. Preheat oven to 350 F and bake uncovered at 350 F about 45 minutes. Serve hot over crispy Chinese noodles. Serves 6.
Trudy Gobbel, University of Illinois Home Economics Faculty Favorites, 1965

BEEF WITH MUSHROOM GRAVY AND WINE

2 pounds cubed beef	1/2 cup red wine
1 can cream of mushroom soup	1/2 teaspoon salt

Cut lean beef into cubes. Mix other ingredients; pour over cubed beef, put into casserole. Bake at 325 F for 3 hours. Serve over hot steamed rice. Serves 8.

NOTE: An easy way to cook rice, if you are cooking regular long grain rice and are not using a rice cooker, is to put 1 cup rice to 3 cups water, 1 teaspoon salt in a casserole with a tight lid. Bake in the oven at 400 F. With warm water the rice will cook in 40 minutes, shorter time when boiling water is used. So easy to cook and such an excellent way.
Satsuma Tea Room, More Fun for the Cook, 1974

OLD DOMINION VEAL FRICASSEE

Cut into pieces 2 pounds veal loin. Cook slowly in boiling water to cover, add 1 onion, 2 stalks of celery, 6 slices carrot. Remove the meat. Season with salt and pepper, dredge with flour and brown in butter. Serve with brown sauce.
The Southern Cookbook, 1939

SWEDISH MEAT BALLS

1 1/2 pound beef round, ground	1 1/2 teaspoons salt
1 pound pork, ground	1/4 teaspoon pepper
2 eggs, beaten	1 pint milk
1 medium onion, chopped fine	1 cup bread crumbs
1 teaspoon ginger	1/2 cup fat
1/2 teaspoon nutmeg	

Grind the meat together 3 or 4 times. Mix all the ingredients except the fat. Form the meat into balls size of a walnut. Melt fat in skillet. Add meat balls and fry until brown. Add 2 cups of water and cook in 350 F oven about 30 minutes. Thicken with 2 Tablespoons of flour and 1/2 cup cold water. Cook a few minutes longer. Serves 10-12.
Satsuma Tea Room, Fun for the Cook, 1968

LAZY DAY STEW

2 pounds raw beef cubes (arrange single layer in roaster, do not brown meat).	sliced carrots	1 teaspoon sugar
	potatoes	salt and pepper to taste
	onions	1/2 cup water
	#2 can tomatoes	2 teaspoons tapioca

Put in pan with tight fitting cover or seal with aluminum foil. Put in a 325 F oven for 2 to 3 hours or in 200 F oven for 8 hours. This is a complete dinner. Serves 8.

NOTE: This is one of our favorite dishes at home.
Satsuma Tea Room, More Fun for the Cook, 1974

LAMB

GINGER LEG OF LAMB

5-6 pound boned leg of lamb, butterflied
1/4 cup slivered ginger root
1/3 cup olive oil
1/3 cup lemon juice 1 small onion, diced
2 Tablespoons honey

1 clove garlic
1 teaspoon coriander
1/2 teaspoon ground cumin
1 1/2 teaspoons salt
pinch of cayenne

Place lamb in shallow casserole or pan. Mix rest of ingredients and put into blender. Pour over lamb, cover, and let stand overnight. During the day, turn occasionally. Remove and place on broiler pan, and broil 4 inches down from heat for 20 minutes. Baste once. Turn, broil 20 minutes, baste frequently. Turn off heat and let lamb remain in oven 15 minutes. Carve in thin slices and serve with the juices from the cooking.

NOTE: The recipe credit goes to Helen Corbitt, noted cookbook author and lecturer, from Helen Corbitt Cooking School, Nashville, September 1976
The Nashville Cookbook, 1977

SWEET 'N' SOUR LAMB CHOPS

4 shoulder lamb chops, about 1 inch thick
1/4 cup vinegar
1/4 cup firmly packed brown sugar
1 teaspoon salt

1/8 teaspoon pepper
1/4 teaspoon ginger
1 medium orange, sliced
1 medium lemon, cut in wedges

Brown the shoulder lamb chops on both sides over low heat. Combine vinegar, brown sugar, salt, pepper and ginger; mix well. Pour the sugar mixture over chops. Add orange slices and lemon wedges. Cover and continue cooking about 30 minutes or until chops are tender. 4 servings.
Easy-on-the-Cook Book, 1960

LEG OF LAMB NEAPOLITAN

1 leg of lamb, about 6 pounds
2 teaspoons salt
1 teaspoon oregano

3 medium-sized onions, chopped
1 medium sized green pepper, chopped

1 clove garlic, crushed
28 ounce can tomatoes

Sprinkle lamb with salt and oregano; place on rack in shallow roasting pan. Roast in oven at 325 F for 1 1/2 hours; drain off drippings. Mix together the onions, green pepper, garlic, and tomatoes. Baste lamb with some of the tomato mixture, and roast, basting occasionally, 1 hour or a little longer. You may need to add water to the sauce during the latter part of the cooking time. Let the roast stand in a warm place for about 15 minutes before slicing. Serve roast with sauce.
Ruth Fay Kilgore, The Nashville Cookbook, 1977

ROAST LEG OF LAMB

6 pound leg of lamb
2 Tablespoons olive oil
2 teaspoons salt
1 head of garlic

2 Tablespoons dried thyme leaves
2 Tablespoons dried tarragon leaves
2 Tablespoons crumbled sage
2 Tablespoons black pepper, coarse

Trim fat from the outside of lamb leg. Brush with oil and sprinkle with salt. Mix the dried seasonings in bowl and pat all over lamb. Put garlic cloves in layer in roasting pan with 2 cups water. Put lamb on rack in pan and roast at 425 F for 30 minutes and reduce heat to 375 F. Roast 45 minutes longer for rare, 60 minutes for medium. If using a meat thermometer, 120 degrees for rare, 140 degrees for medium. Let roast stand 30 minutes before carving.

NOTE: Leg of lamb is so popular on our Easter buffet, but people ask for it all year long. Many don't think they like lamb because their first experience was often with the stronger flavored mutton, but the sweetness of young lamb will surely win them over every time.
Cortner Mill Restaurant cookbook, 2009

NOTES

GAME

"Game should never be fried. Smaller game should be roasted or broiled, and the larger ducks, venison, squirrels, rabbits, and raccoons are best made into stews or 'salmis'."
The Picayune Cook Book, 1922

While looking through my stash of very old cookbooks, I have discovered many recipes for the preparation and cooking of wild game and fish. I realize these recipes are very interesting and historical as they offer even more of a window into the early Southern personae and existence. But, if the main purpose of my overall narrative is to offer recipes that can be used in our present, daily life, as they were used in our traditional past, then with the advent of the modern-day super market and butcher shops and the ready access to domesticated, ready-for-cooking meats then these old recipes are not so relevant. No longer is it crucial that our mere survival depends on taking your gun into the woods and killing the evening meal. But, the historic value of this treasure trove of wild game recipes necessitates some reference, so I have included just a few below.

ROAST WILD GOOSE

1 young wild goose, 6 to 8 lbs. dressed
juice of 1 lemon
seasonings (salt, pepper, etc.)

4 to 6 slices bacon
melted fat or drippings

Rub the cleaned goose inside and out with lemon juice and seasonings. Spoon stuffing lightly into cavity. Close opening with skewers and truss the bird. Cover the breast with bacon slices and a cheesecloth soaked in melted fat. Place breast side up in a roasting pan. Roast in a slow oven (325 F), allowing 20 to 25 minutes per pound, until tender. Baste frequently with fat or pan drippings. Makes about 6 servings.

NOTE: If the age of the goose is uncertain, pour 1 cup water into the pan and cover during the last hour of cooking. Remove the cheesecloth, skewers, and string before serving.

STUFFING

1/4 cup butter or margarine
1/4 cup chopped onion
1 cup chopped tart apple
1 cup dried apricots

3 cups soft bread crumbs (day-old bread)
1/2 teaspoon salt
1/4 teaspoon pepper

For stuffing, melt butter in heavy skillet or saucepan. Sauté onion until soft and clear; mix in the apple, apricots, crumbs, salt and pepper.
Farm Journal's Country Cook Book, 1959

VENISON

Soak a saddle of venison in cold water. Peel off the thick skin and lard it with white meat (pork fat) or bacon (that is, cut slits in the venison with a sharp knife and insert slices of bacon). Put a little water in the pan and plenty of Worcestershire sauce and cook like any other roast, basting frequently.
The Savannah Cook Book, 1933

VENISON STEAKS

The steaks should be fried with very little lard, or butter, turning frequently. "They should be treated as a child, and never left alone a moment," says the old cook who gave me the venison receipt. When they are fried to a turn, they should be covered and allowed to simmer until tender. The back strap is best to use for steaks. Slice with the grain of the meat in pieces of about 1 inch thick. Broil in butter with pepper and salt to taste. Just before removing the steaks from the heat, add sherry wine to the dish for added flavor.
The Savannah Cook Book, 1933

VENISON STEAKS

3 Tablespoons flour
1 1/2 teaspoons salt
1/4 teaspoon marjoram
6 venison steaks, cut from the round
fat for frying

1 small onion, peeled
4 medium carrots, scraped
1/2 cup diced celery and celery tops
1 1/2 cups beef broth

Mix the flour, salt, marjoram; rub over the meat. Brown steaks in hot fat in pressure pan. Add vegetables and broth; cover and set pressure cooker control to 10. Cook 20 to 30 minutes after control set. Cool normally 5 minutes, then place pan under cold water to reduce pressure quickly. Thicken liquid for gravy by rubbing vegetables through sieve, food mill or blender. Makes 6 servings.

NOTE: The pressure cooker is used here because of the efficiency it was known for in tenderizing game. This recipe was written in 1959. The crock pot and its different innovations was at that time not close to being invented. It is now a reality today and functions masterfully with game.
Farm Journal's Country Cook Book, 1959

HOW TO ROAST VENISON

The best eating venison is stripped of all fat (which isn't edible). For roasts, keep the meat from drying out by larding with salt pork or bacon before cooking. Ripen meat by hanging at least 4 days to 2 weeks. If the deer is full grown the meat should be marinated.

TO MARINATE

Chop 1 onion, 1 carrot and a celery stalk. Make bouquet of cheese cloth containing parsley, thyme, bay leaf and a few cloves. Cook 1 to 2 minutes in hot fat or oil, then add 1 cup vinegar. Bring to boil, and simmer about 20 minutes. Strain; then cool. Pour over venison. Let stand 12 to 24 hours in glass, earthenware, or a china container, not metal.

Marinating tenderizes meat and takes away some of the gaminess. After marinating the meat 24 hours, lard well with salt pork and a few pieces of garlic. Roast on a rack in shallow pan in moderate oven (350 F) allowing 30 minutes per pound, basting frequently with drippings. Serve with red currant jelly.
Farm Journal's Country Cook Book, 1959

WILD TURKEY

The wild turkey abounds in the state of Louisiana, as it is also teeming in numbers throughout the South. After preparation, it is roasted in the same manner as the domestic turkey. It is always served with cranberry sauce.
The Picayune Cook Book, 1922

SMOTHERED PHEASANT

12 pheasant halves	2 cans (10 1/2 ounces) celery soup
salt and pepper	1 can (10 ounces) onion soup
fat for browning pheasants	water to equal 3 soup cans
21 1/2 ounces mushroom soup	

In a Dutch oven or heavy skillet, brown pheasant halves in mixture of cooking oil and butter until both sides are golden. Arrange the halves, with meat side down, in a roaster. Salt and pepper as desired and pour soups and water, which have been mixed over the halves. Cover and bake at 350 F. for about 1 hour. Reduce heat to 300 F and cook 1/2 hour longer or until tender. Serve with wild rice. Serves 12.
Louise Reynolds, The Nashville Cookbook, 1977

RABBITS

Rabbits are cooked like chicken: stewed, fricasseed, or baked. My wife and I ate it at one of Nashville's most trendy new restaurants. I mean, it was so popular, it took 3 months to get a reservation. Featured prominently on the menu was braised rabbit. What goes around, comes around! -David S.
The Settlement Cookbook, 1940

FRIED RABBIT

1 young rabbit	4 cups flour
3 Tablespoons salt	2 teaspoons baking powder
2 quarts water	4 teaspoons salt
3 large eggs	2 Tablespoons black pepper
1/3 cup buttermilk	1 Tablespoon white pepper

Dress rabbit and soak overnight in a solution of 3 Tablespoons salt and 2 quarts water. Remove rabbit from water and drain well. Cut rabbit into 5 pieces, 2 legs 2 thighs and the back. Combine the eggs and buttermilk and beat until frothy. Combine the flour, salt and peppers. Place the rabbit pieces in the seasoned flour and toss until well coated. Remove rabbit pieces from seasoned flour and place in egg wash until well coated. Lift the rabbit out of the egg wash and drain until no longer dripping. Place rabbit back in the flour, covering it well. Remove the rabbit from the flour shaking off excess flour. Place the rabbit on a sheet pan and repeat these steps for each piece of rabbit. Place lard in a large skillet over medium to high heat, or about 350 F. When lard is hot, place rabbit in skillet without pieces touching each other and cook for 10-12 minutes per side or until golden brown. Do not cover the skillet.
David Boswell Hazelwood, Miss Lizzie's Heirlooms, 2009

ONION-STUFFED RABBIT

1 rabbit (about 2 pounds)
1 1/2 teaspoons salt
1/8 teaspoon pepper

1 1/2 cups onion slices
3 bacon slices

Rub salt and pepper inside rabbit. Stuff with onion slices. Truss. Lay strips of bacon over the rabbit. Wrap in aluminum foil; place in a shallow baking pan. Bake in moderate oven (350 F.) for 1 1/2 hours. Serves 4.

NOTE: Excellent way to cook squirrels, too.
Farm Journal's Country Cook Book, 1959

POSSUM HUNT

"A cold night in January is usually selected for the popular alfresco evening's entertainment of a possum hunt. The crowd collects at some country house or a convenient cross-roads and then makes into the woods with trained hounds and the crowd following through hill and dale; through underbrush and swamps until the dogs have treed their game. One knows this when the dogs stand under a tree yelping like nothing human, or at least until the crowd gathers and tries to coax Br 'Possum down.

In the old days when only lanterns were available for such sport, the correct thing to do was to shake the possum out of the tree, but nine times out of ten the dogs got away with the prize. Large flashlights are now taken along and turned onto the tree and the poor old possum hasn't a chance.

First you see a piece of Spanish moss which you mistake for the prize or it might be a bunch of mistletoe that deceives you, but suddenly two bright eyes burn from a silent mass and then you know you have Mr. Possum within reach. A designated someone climbs up and quietly takes him.

A rabbit may run but a possum will never move, but when you catch his gleaming eye with the light, it is all up with him. In short order the possum is dropped safely into a crocus sack and headed for home."

-Harriet Ross Colquitt, The Savannah Cook Book, 1933

POSSUM AND 'TATERS

While it is generally conceded that the fun lies more in the chase of the elusive coon than in the eating, there are those who hold that possum and 'taters is a most delectable diet, so here is the prescription for cooking your game before you bagged it.

Before you go to bed that night scald the possum with lye and scrape off the hair. (Or have it done, which would be altogether more pleasant all around.) Dress whole, leaving on head and tail. Rub well with salt and put in cool place overnight. When ready to cook, put in a deep pan with 1 quart of water. Place 2 or 4 slices of breakfast bacon reverently across the possum's breast and then put in the oven. When half done, remove from the oven and stuff with bread crumbs, a little onion, salt and pepper and possum juice taken from the pan in which he had been reposing. Return him to the pan and place around him some small peeled sweet potatoes. Bake until all is light brown, basting frequently with gravy.
The Savannah Cook Book, 1933

COLD WILD DUCK   Tastes so good!

wild duck leftovers   1/2 tumbler of currant jelly
1 Tablespoon butter

Cut the cold wild duck nicely into thick slices and serve with a sauce made as follows: take 1 Tablespoon butter, 1/2 tumbler of currant jelly, and 1 Tablespoon of lemon juice. Warm the butter in the saucepan; add the lemon juice and jelly, thoroughly blended. Mix well and serve with the slices of cold duck.

NOTE: Many think cold duck is delicious with currant jelly alone and buttered toast.
The Picayune Cook Book, 1922

OLD TERMS EXPLAINED

TERMS

Prescriptions and receipts are often used to describe recipes.
Wine and liquor "flavoring" were used to describe alcohols during Prohibition.

MEASUREMENTS

Old Southern cooks seldom had written recipes or measurements. Dishes were made and passed along with approximations. Cooks said, " Take a handful of flour and add a glass of milk."

Glass- Sometimes it was just a glass of milk. If more specifics were asked for, they said, "you know, a large one" or "just a small one."
Handful- A good handful could only be specified by looking at the cook's hands.
Size of an egg- Most can be guessed correctly, but it doesn't allow for small, large , or jumbo.
Lump- Go with the size of an egg, but be prepared to take your lumps.
Mere idea of…-A dash or pinch should be close enough.
Gill- This has nothing to do with fish. One gill equals a half cup.
One pound sugar- Equals two cups. One ounce equals two Tablespoons.
One pound flour- Equals 3 ½ cups all-purpose or 4 ½ cups bread flour.
Breaking Tablespoon- Equals 1 ½ Tablespoons.
Soup plate- Size between 9" lunch plate and 12" dinner plate with deeper well and wider lip.

PROCEDURES

Slow oven- 275-300°   Quick oven- 450-475°
Moderate oven- 350-375°   Very quick oven- 500-525°
Hot oven- 400-425°
Pan- Sauté
Remove from the fire- Remove from stove burner
Over flame- On stove burner
Cook slowly over fire- Simmer on stove burn
Larding- Covering meat with pieces of pork fat or bacon

OLD TERMS EXPLAINED

INGREDIENTS

Sweet milk- Use 3 ½% butterfat whole milk
Sour milk- Use buttermilk
Top milk- Cream that has risen to the top of unhomogenized milk. Use half and half.
Clabber- Use sour cream
Table cream- Use 20% butterfat coffee cream
Indian meal- Use yellow cornmeal
Soda- Use baking soda, not soda pop
White gum Arabic- Still available, helps cakes rise
Pastry flour- Also called cake flour, very fine-textured from soft wheat
Bread flour- 99.8% hard wheat, 0.2% barley flour
Baking flour- Use bread flour
All-purpose flour- Blend of soft and hard wheat
Yeast cake
- Equals ¼ ounce active dry yeast or about 1 scant Tablespoon

UTENSILS AND SUPPLIES

Salt spoon- Measures ¼ teaspoon. Used by head of household before shakers to serve table salt.
Ice box- A cabinet with a box for a block of ice on top from storing food. Replaced by refrigerators.
Frigidaire- A brand of refrigerators. See Kleenex and Coke.
Wheel egg beater- A hand turned egg beater.
Stove pipe pan- Angel food cake tube pan. The one with a "horn".
Ice cube trays- Metal trays with removeable sections.
Large stand or lard stand- Five gallon thin metal container for storing lard
Gem pan- Muffin pan than makes mini-muffins.

NOTES

CHEESE

FOOL PROOF CHEESE SOUFFLE

4 slices of bread 2 or 3 days old
1/4 pound grated sharp Cheddar cheese
2 teaspoons minced onions
1/2 teaspoon salt

1/8 teaspoon dry mustard
2 eggs beaten
1 1/2 cups milk

Remove the crusts from the bread and cut pieces into small squares. Arrange bread and then cheese into 3 layers in greased shallow baking dish. Put onions and seasonings between layers. Have the bread on top and bottom layers. Mix eggs and milk and pour over the bread. Let stand 45 minutes or longer. Place baking dish in pan of hot water. Bake at 350 F about 40 minutes. Serve from baking dish. Serves 4.

NOTE: We often serve this at home for buffet dinners with a platter of cold baked ham.
Satsuma Tea Room, Fun for the Cook, 1968

CHEESE MOLDS, INDIVIDUAL

1 cup bread crumbs
1 cup milk
(cook together until smooth)

Add 6 Tablespoons grated cheese
2 Tablespoons melted butter
1/2 teaspoon mustard

Put on the stove and heat for a moment, stirring constantly. Remove from heat and add:

2 egg yolks slightly beaten
2 egg whites beaten stiff

1/2 teaspoon salt
dash Tabasco

Fill molds and bake for 15 minutes at 350 F. Serve very hot.
Satsuma Tea Room, More Fun for the Cook, 1974

WELSH RAREBIT

3 Tablespoons butter
1 pound American cheese, dry
1 teaspoon Worcestershire sauce
1/2 cup milk

2 eggs
1/2 teaspoon salt
1/4 teaspoon mustard

Melt the butter, add the cheese which has been cut up in small pieces, and cook in double boiler over hot water, stirring continuously until cheese is melted. Add the salt, mustard, Worcestershire and then pour in the milk gradually, stirring constantly. Then add the slightly beaten eggs and stir until it becomes thick. Serve instantly on crisp toast.

NOTE: Beer may be substituted for milk.
The Southern Cookbook, 1939

CHEESE PIE

1 cup grated cheese
1 cup bread crumbs
1 cup milk

1/2 teaspoon salt
2 eggs, slightly beaten

Mix well and pour in greased pie pan to bake. Bake 20 minutes at 350. Can be prepared ahead and baked later.

NOTE: Excellent to serve with cold meat.
Satsuma Tea Room, More Fun for the Cook, 1974

NOTES

SEAFOOD

For a pioneer settler in the South, or for that matter, anywhere in this vast country, fish and wild game were free for the taking from streams, fields, and woods. Men grew up knowing how to attain their spoils and how to dress and prepare them for cooking. Their mothers and sisters were equally skilled at handling the prized quarry in the kitchen. Even today, these inherited fishing and hunting skills and techniques of food gathering that were of such great importance to the mere survival of life in pioneer days, are regarded by many people as favorite sports. Tradition!

No longer do you have to live near coasts or close to rivers and lakes, as in days of old, to take advantage of the plentiful resources of the oceans or other bodies of water. Modern cooling, freezing and canning methods have made a wide variety of fish available even to remote inland cities and towns.

It is fun to witness all the different types of fish in our markets and then discover delicious ways to cook and serve them. You will find it will pay off, not only by means of delightful meals, but in healthy, more varied choices for those meals.

"Did you eber see where de boatman live?
His house in de holler wid a roof like a sieve!
Boatman say he got one wish
Ef it gets much wetter he's gonter be a fish."

FRIED FISH

In all the stories about the sizzling cooking sound, the inviting smell, and the delicious taste of frying fish, one has to understand that these don't have to be restricted to fiction. These senses can be had in the home dining room by following this very simple method of frying fish.

Roll the fish in corn meal, fry it in deep bacon fat, cooking fat, or butter. Dry (drain) it thoroughly before serving. That is all there is to it!!!
200 Years of Charleston Cooking, 1930

FRIED CATFISH

2 (4 ounce) catfish filets
2 cups corn meal, self-rising

Pat filets dry. Drop filets into corn meal until covered really well. Shake off the excess cornmeal. Cook in deep fat, 350 degrees for 5-7 minutes until golden brown. Serves one.

NOTE: Is it really this simple? I wish there was some exotic ingredient or special technique that makes our catfish the best you will ever eat, but this is it! Isabel should know her catfish. Before coming to manage Cortner Mill from 1992-2004, she owned and operated *The Classy Catfish* in Shelbyville, Tennessee.
Isabel Woodlee, Cortner Mill Restaurant cookbook, 2009

FRIED FISH

Catfish	cornmeal
Crappie	salt and pepper
Bass	bacon drippings or oil

Clean fish. Leave whole if small, fileted if large. Dip the fish in cornmeal. Fry over medium heat until brown. Use about 1/2 inch hot fat in the skillet. Make sure that before putting the fish into the skillet the grease is hot!
The Nashville Cookbook, 1977

GARNISHES FOR FRIED FISH

- Lemon, lime, or orange slices sprinkled with minced pimiento, parsley or green pepper.
- Grapefruit sections dusted with paprika.
- Thick tomato slices topped with pickle relish or with thin lemon slices topped with slice of stuffed olives.
- Canned pineapple slices, drained, topped with little haystacks of coleslaw.
- Celery sticks or fans or cheese stuffed.
- Cucumber slices fluted and sprinkled with tarragon vinegar.
- Pickled beet slices dotted with horseradish sauce.

BAKED TROUT

8 ounces trout, boned	2 Tablespoons lemon pepper
4 lemon slices	1 cup water
1 Tablespoon butter	

Open trout and spread with 1 teaspoon melted butter and 1/2 teaspoon lemon pepper. Place two lemon slices inside trout. Close trout and spread remaining butter on top and sprinkle with remaining lemon pepper. Place 2 lemon slices on top of trout and place trout in baking pan with water. Cover pan and bake in 350 degree oven for 15 minutes. Uncover and bake 10 minutes more.

NOTE: When tomatoes are fresh from the garden, I like to substitute tomato slices for the lemon slices. -David H.
Cortner Mill Restaurant cookbook, 2009

TROUT AMANDINE

1 trout filet (7 ounces)	almonds, sliced
flour	2 Tablespoons butter, melted
lemon pepper	

Lightly dust trout with flour and place skin side down into greased baking pan. Sprinkle with lemon pepper and top with almonds. Drizzle with butter and bake at 425 F for about 15 minutes until fish lightly flakes.
Bill Hall, The Cortner Mill Restaurant Cookbook, 2009

FISH CAKES

2 cups boiled fish, flaked	1 Tablespoon butter	salt and pepper to taste
2 cups mashed potatoes	1 egg, beaten	

Any fresh fish that is suitable for boiling may be used for this recipe, but codfish is preferred. Mix all the ingredients together, shape into round flat cakes and dredge in flour. Then fry in butter on both sides and serve with tomato sauce. Recipe on page 262..
The Southern Cookbook, 1933

SAVORY BAKED FISH

2 pounds cod fillets, fresh or frozen	1/4 cup flour
3 Tablespoons butter, melted	1/2 teaspoon salt
1/2 teaspoon salt	dash pepper
dash of pepper	1/4 teaspoon oregano
1 small onion, chopped	1 cup canned whole tomatoes
1/4 cup chopped celery	1 cup buttermilk
1/4 cup butter	

Thaw the frozen fillets. Cut cool into serving size pieces. Dip in melted butter. Season with 1/2 teaspoon salt and pepper. Arrange in shallow baking pan. Cook onion and celery in butter until tender, about 10 minutes. Stir in flour and seasonings. Gradually add tomatoes and buttermilk. Simmer 10 minutes, stirring constantly. Pour sauce over cod. Bake in 350 F oven 45 minutes or until fish flakes easily when tested with a fork. 6 servings.

NOTE: Variations can be used of halibut, perch, or whitefish instead of cod.
Easy-on-the-Cook Book, 1960

POACHED FISH

2 pounds fish steaks or filets	1 teaspoon salt
2 cups water	3 peppercorns
1/4 cup lemon juice	2 bay leaves
1 small onion, thinly sliced	

Remove the skin and bones from the fish. Cut the fish into serving portions. Mix water and other ingredients in an oiled skillet and bring to a boil. Reduce to a simmer. Place fish in single layer into hot liquid. Cover and simmer 8-10 minutes or until fish flakes, when tested with a fork. Drain and place on a hot platter. Serve with Hollandaise Sauce, lemon juice, or lemon sauce. Sprinkle with Paprika and garnish with parsley sprigs if desired. Serves 6.

NOTE: This dish is a good choice for a low-calorie meal when served with lemon juice. When calories are no concern, fantastic with Hollandaise.
Cookbook Committee, The Nashville Cookbook, 1977

BAKED SHAD

1 large shad
2 cups fine bread crumbs
1 onion, chopped fine
salt and pepper

1/4 cup butter, melted
1 Tablespoon parsley, chopped

Select a large shad and have the head removed and cleaned without slitting it (it must not be cut open since it is to be stuffed). For the stuffing, mix the chopped onion and parsley with the bread crumbs. Season to taste with salt and pepper and moisten with the melted butter. The dressing should be rather dry, but a few drops of water may be needed to moisten it.
Stuff the fish, put it into a baking pan, season with salt and pepper and sprinkle bread crumbs over it. Dot the fish with lumps of butter, turn some water into the pan, sprinkle a teaspoon or two of flour over it, put the pan into a moderately hot oven (375 F) and bake it for 1 1/2 hours. While baking, it must be basted occasionally with the pan gravy to prevent the fish becoming too dry.
Recipe found in "Carolina Housewife" recounted in 200 Years of Charleston Cooking, 1930

PLANKED SHAD

3 to 4 pound shad
1/2 cup melted butter

salt and pepper
parsley and lemon

Clean and bone fish. Broil for 10 minutes and then place on a buttered plank, skin side down, season well and pour melted butter over and bake in a hot oven (400 F) for 15 minutes. Remove from oven and place mounds of mashed potatoes pressed through a pastry bag around the fish. Return to the oven until potatoes are brown and fish well done. Garnish with parsley and lemon slices.
The Southern Cookbook, 1939

BAKED FLOUNDER WITH BACON

4 slices bacon
2 pounds flounder fillets
4 thin slices lemon
1/2 cup condensed tomato soup
1/2 cup water

2 bay leaves
salt and pepper
1 large onion, sliced
paprika

Place the fish on top of two slices of bacon in a greased baking dish. Cover with remaining bacon and lemon slices. Combine tomato soup and water. Add bay leaves, salt, pepper, and sliced onion. Pour over fish. Bake in a moderate oven at 350 for 30 minutes. Place on a heated serving platter. Strain sauce and place and around fish. Makes 4-6 servings.

NOTE: Spicy, colorful with tomatoes with a hint of bacon in the flavor.
Farm Journal's Country Cookbook, 1959

FILLETS OF FLOUNDER

5 flounder filets
3 Tablespoons butter
1 cup milk
bread crumbs, sifted

1 egg
1 cup tomato sauce
salt and pepper

Combine the egg, milk, and salt and pepper and soak the filets in this mixture 15 minutes. Dip each filet in the bread crumbs. Allow frying pan with the butter to become hot before placing the fillets in pan. Fry on both sides until browned, then pour tomato sauce over all.
The Southern Cookbook, 1939

FISH FILETS, GOURMET

1 pound fish
1 Tablespoon butter

1/4 cup sour cream
1/4 cup mayonnaise

juice of 1/2 lemon

Place fish filets in buttered baking dish, put in oven and bake 10 minutes in a 350 degree oven. Mix sour cream, mayonnaise, and lemon juice. Spread over the fish. Bake 10-15 minutes longer. Serves 4
Satsuma Tea Room, More Fun for the Cook, 1974

SALMON WITH SHERRY BASIL SAUCE

2 (7 ounce) salmon filets

Grill salmon filets over hot fire for 3-4 minutes per side. Pour 2 Tablespoons of Sherry Basil Sauce onto each plate and place the salmon on top. Lightly brush top of salmon with sauce. Garnish with a fresh basil leaf. Serves 2.

SHERRY BASIL SAUCE

2 Tablespoons butter
2 Tablespoons onion, finely diced
1/2 cup chicken broth
1/2 cup dry sherry

1 Tablespoon fresh basil, diced fine
1/2 teaspoon salt
1/4 teaspoon black pepper
1/2 teaspoon cornstarch

Sauté onions in butter until clear. Add all other ingredients, except cornstarch and bring to a boil for 2 minutes. Pour off a small portion into cup and mix with cornstarch until smooth. Return the mixture to pan and cook over medium heat until thickened. Sauce can be stored and reheated.
David Hazelwood, Cortner Mill Restaurant cookbook, 2009

ROYAL POINCIANNA POMPANO WITH SHRIMP STUFFING

2 cups cooked shrimp
2 eggs
1 cup rich cream
1 boned pompano

1/2 cup chopped mushrooms
1/4 cup sherry wine
pepper, salt, paprika

Clean the shrimp and put through the grinder to chop. Beat the egg and half the cream together. Mix the shrimp, mushrooms, and seasoning together and stir in the cream and egg. Stir to a smooth paste. Put the mixture on 1/2 of the pompano. Position the two halves of the fish together and put in a baking dish. Pour remaining cream over fish and bake in moderate oven (350) for 45 minutes. Serve garnished with sliced cucumbers, which have been marinated in French dressing
The Southern Cookbook, 1939

STUFFED CRABS AND MUSHROOMS

2 Tablespoons butter
1 Tablespoon flour
1/2 cup cream
1 cup mushrooms
1 pound cooked crabmeat

juice of 1/2 lemon
1 teaspoon capers
1 teaspoon chopped parsley
2 egg whites, beaten stiff

Melt the butter and add the mushrooms, sliced or chopped. Cook until they are tender. Remove the mushrooms or put them to one side of the pan and add the flour. When that is well-blended, add the cream. When this cream sauce is thick, remove from the fire and add the other ingredients in the order given. Put the mixture back into the crab shells or, if the shells are not available. Bake in a buttered casserole in a moderate oven (350 F) for about 20 minutes. (This dish is delicious made from canned crabmeat!) Makes 8 servings.
William Deas, 200 Years of Charleston Cooking, 1930

DEVILED CRABS

Meat from 1 dozen crabs (12 crabs afford about 2 pounds of crabmeat)
1 Tablespoon butter
2 Tablespoons flour

2 cups milk
pepper and salt
1 teaspoon dry mustard
1 Tablespoon Worcestershire sauce

Make a sauce of melted butter, flour, milk, and season with salt, pepper, mustard, and Worcestershire. Scrub the crabs' backs (some of the Negros call them the "bark") and stuff with the mixture, sprinkling bread crumbs and a little butter on top. Bake until a light brown. Meat from 1 dozen crabs fills 9 backs.

NOTE: The same mixture with a little more milk or 1/2 cup of cream can be served as creamed crab, while a double dose of milk and a dash of wine or lemon will convert this mixture into a crab soup.
The Savannah Cook Book, 1933

DEVILED CRAB

One dozen fresh crabs are required for this recipe, but it may also be made using canned crabmeat and baked in a casserole instead of in crab shells.

2 cups crabmeat	1 Tablespoon melted butter
1/4 teaspoon mustard	1 egg separated
1/4 teaspoon nutmeg	salt and pepper
1/4 teaspoon mace	1/2 cup wine or sherry
2 cloves	cracker crumbs

Add the seasonings to the crabmeat, stir in the melted butter and the beaten egg yolk. Add the cooking sherry and season to taste with salt and pepper. Fold in the stiffly beaten egg white. Fill the crab-backs or put into a buttered baking dish, sprinkle with cracker crumbs and bake in a moderate oven (350 F) for 1/2 hour.

NOTE: As an aside, today one may purchase "crab backs" made of aluminum. Deviled crab was on the menu at *Satsuma* often and we made great use of these new shells.
Mrs. E.H. Sparkman, 200 Years of Charleston Cooking, 1930

CRAB SOUFFLE

1 pound crabmeat (about 6 fresh crabs)	1/2 teaspoon salt	2 eggs
	1 cup milk	cayenne, nutmeg
1/4 pound butter	1 Tablespoon flour	2 Tablespoons sherry

Make cream sauce of butter, flour and milk. Season and thicken by adding the slightly beaten egg yolks, and letting the mixture cook, stirring constantly, for a few minutes. Then remove and when cool add the well-beaten whites of eggs. Put into a baking dish, sprinkle with bread crumbs and bake in a slow oven 20 minutes.
The Savannah Cook Book, 1933

CRAB CROQUETTES

2 cups crab meat	1 cup white sauce (recipe on page 257)
1 teaspoon onion juice	cracker crumbs
salt and pepper	1 egg, beaten
chopped parsley	

Chop the crabmeat fine and add the seasonings. When well mixed, add to the white sauce. Mold into croquettes and then roll in cracker crumbs. Dip in the slightly beaten egg and then roll in the crumbs again. Fry in deep hot fat until golden brown.
The Southern Cookbook, 1939

CRAB CROQUETTES

1 cup milk	1 Tablespoon butter
little onion, pepper, salt	1 Tablespoon flour
yolks of 2 hard-boiled eggs	meat from 1 dozen crabs

Scald the milk with the onion, add pepper and salt and the mashed egg yolks. Thicken with butter and flour rubbed together and cook until it makes a thick sauce. Add crabs to this mixture and let cool. Then mold into shape, roll in egg and bread crumbs, and fry in deep fat.
The Savannah Cookbook, 1933

FISH SOUFFLE

1 pound coarse fish	6 egg whites
(rock fish, haddock, or cod)	salt and pepper

Whip the egg whites stiffly and add the flaked fish. Beat together until stiff again and season to taste with salt and pepper. Turn into a buttered casserole and bake in a moderate oven (325 F) for about 45 minutes. Serve at once with what is called, in the South, brown butter, in the North, lemon butter. This makes 8 servings.
William Deas, Butler and Cook for Mrs. Goodwyn Rhett, 200 years of Charleston Cooking, 1930

OYSTER CASSEROLE

Crisp 7 or 8 slices of salt rising bread in oven and crumble. Put layer of these crumbs on bottom of baking dish. Add 1 pint of drained oysters, 1 can water chestnuts, sliced, 1 can undiluted celery soup, 1 can undiluted mushroom soup. Put rest of crumbs on top. Dot with butter. Cook 25 minutes at 350. This dish may be made a day ahead. Serves 4-6.
Satsuma Tea Room, More Fun for the Cook, 1974

SEAFOOD CASSEROLE

6 ounces frozen crabmeat	1 can water chestnuts, sliced
2 cups cooked shrimp (frozen or canned)	salt to taste
2 cups diced celery	1 1/2 cups mayonnaise
1 medium onion, chopped	1/2 cup toasted bread crumbs
4 hard-boiled eggs diced	1/2 cup slivered almonds
1 cup mushrooms, pieces and stems	

Thaw and drain crabmeat. Mix all the ingredients except bread crumbs and almonds. Turn into a large buttered baking dish. Top with bread crumbs and almonds. Bake at 350 degrees for about 30 minutes. Just heat through; do not brown. (Long cooking will cause the mayonnaise to separate). Can be made several hours ahead and kept refrigerated before baking. Serves 6-8
Helen M. Young, The Nashville Cookbook, 1977

SHRIMP CURRY CASSEROLE

6 Tablespoons butter
2 large onions, chopped
1 cooking apple, chopped
3 Tablespoons curry powder
2 Tablespoons flour
1 1/2 cups chicken broth
1 cup cream
1/2 cup milk

2 cups shrimp, cut into 1-inch pieces
2 cups cooked rice
2 cups coarsely chopped hard cooked eggs (about 6)
4 slices cooked bacon, chopped
2 Tablespoons chives or parsley chopped
chutney (optional)

Preheat oven to 350. Melt butter in a 12-inch skillet. Lightly fry the onion and apple over moderate heat until golden but not brown. Mix curry powder and flour, blend into fat mixture to make a smooth paste. Gradually add chicken broth, cream and milk. Mix well and continue to stir until sauce thickens. Butter a two-quart casserole. Cover the bottom with 1 cup shrimp. Add some of the curry sauce, cover this with 1 cup of rice and then add more sauce. Add 1 cup of the egg and more sauce. Repeat shrimp, sauce, rice, sauce, eggs sauce. Sprinkle the top generously with bacon. Place in the oven until well heated, about 30 minutes. Garnish with chives or parsley. Serve with chutney if desired. 10-12 servings.
Dr. Mary Mather, University of Illinois Home Economics Faculty Favorites, 1965

CRAB SOUFFLE

1 1/3 cups Velveeta cheese
1 1/2 cups thick cream sauce
(4 Tbl butter, 4 Tbl flour, 1 cup milk)

1 pound crabmeat
4 eggs, separated

Melt cheese in cream sauce. Add crabmeat and egg yolks. When cool, fold in stiffly beaten egg whites. Pour in buttered baking dish. Set dish in pan of hot water. Bake at 325 degrees about an hour. Serves 6.
Satsuma Tea Room, Fun for the Cook, 1968

CRABMEAT LORENZO

4 slices of bread
1 teaspoon chopped onion
2 Tablespoons butter
1 cup crabmeat (fresh or canned)
1 Tablespoon flour
1/2 cup cream

1/2 teaspoon paprika
1/4 teaspoon mustard
1/4 teaspoon salt
4 Tablespoons Parmesan cheese
2 Tablespoons cream

Cook onions in butter. Add flour, cream, crabmeat, and seasonings. Cook, stirring constantly. Brown bread on one side. Put crabmeat on unbrowned side. Place on cookie sheet. Make a cheese paste of the cream and Parmesan cheese. Put a heaping Tablespoon on top of each piece of toast. Broil in hot oven 450 F for 3-4 minutes until cheese melts. Serve at once. Serves 4.

NOTE This dish has to be made at the last minute to be good.
Satsuma Tea Room, Fun for the Cook, 1968

HERB CRUSTED SALMON WITH SUN DRIED TOMATO SAUCE

4 teaspoons olive oil	1 teaspoon black pepper
2 Tablespoons shallots, minced	1 Tablespoon fresh basil, minced
1 Tablespoon lemon juice, strained	1 Tablespoon fresh thyme, minced
1/2 cup dry white wine	2 teaspoons fresh rosemary, minced
6 sun dried tomatoes, minced fine	1/2 cup dry bread crumbs
1/2 teaspoon coarse salt	2 (12 ounce) salmon fillets, skinless

In a non-stick skillet heat 2 teaspoons oil over medium heat. Add shallots and sauté, stirring constantly, until lightly golden, about 1 minute. Add lemon juice, wine, and sun-dried tomatoes. Turn heat to medium high and cook until sauce is reduced to 1/2 cup, about 2 minutes. Season with salt and pepper to taste and set aside. Sauce can be made up to 1 hour before cooking the dish. Adjust the oven rack to center of oven and heat to 400 degrees. Lightly grease a 9x13 casserole dish with cooking spray and set aside. On a piece of wax paper, combine basil, thyme, rosemary and bread crumbs. Dredge each fillet in this bread crumb mixture, coating well. Transfer fillets to prepared dish and place fillets 2 inches apart. Drizzle with remaining 2 teaspoons of oil. Bake until salmon is opaque and barely flakes when tested in the center with a knife, about 8-10 minutes. Reheat sauce over low heat just before removing fish from oven. Transfer fish to serving platter and slice each fillet in half crosswise. Spoon sauce over fillets and serve hot. Serves 4.
Anne Casale, Cortner Mill Restaurant cookbook, 2009

BROILED SPANISH MACKEREL (Baltimore style)

Wash the mackerel and split in half and remove bones. Season the fish with pepper and salt and place in a well-greased broiler in a broiling oven, (550 degrees F). Broil on both sides until tender. Place on a hot platter and sprinkle with cayenne and serve with a sauce made of three Tablespoons melted butter and juice of 1/2 lemon.
The Southern Cookbook, 1939

Both boiled and fried shrimp are delicious breakfast and supper dishes; served with hot hominy and plenty of butter.

SHRIMP

Shrimp is the name for this temperamental receipt found in an old cookbook. You will have to be a good cook or a good Southerner or both to be able to translate it. This receipt is as good as it is native:
"A soup plate of shrimp (cut not chopped). Dust a mere idea of nutmeg and a little black pepper, a breaking Tablespoon of butter and 1/2 pint of cream, a good handful of bread crumbs. Put in the peppers and sprinkle over with bread crumbs and bake."

P.S.: I forgot to say a wineglass of sherry (*H.R. Colquitt*).
The Savannah Cook Book, 1933

BOILED SHRIMP

Boil shrimp or prawns 15-20 minutes in strong, salted water. Pick (peel) and serve hot or cold.
The Savannah Cook Book, 1933

TO BOIL SHRIMP

1 pound fresh shrimp	2 Tablespoons salt
1 1/2 quarts fresh water	1 Tablespoon caraway seed

Wash shrimp, bring water to a boil, add salt and caraway seed, add shrimp, let boil 12-15 minutes or until just tender. Do not overcook in that they will become tough and chewy. Let the shrimp stand in the liquid until cool. Drain and keep in a cool place and when ready to serve, remove the shell and black line at the top and on the back.

NOTE: Serve hot with suggested Cream Sauce, Creole Sauce or Chili Sauce.
Or, serve cold as a salad with celery with suggested French dressing or Mayonnaise. Serve cold in shrimp cocktail with a good cocktail sauce.
The Settlement Cookbook, 1940

FRIED SHRIMP

1 pound large shrimp in shell	1 cup cracker meal or flour
1 egg slightly beaten	salt and pepper
vegetable oil or fat	

Wash, rinse and drain shrimps. Split along back, remove shell, leaving on first tail joint and tail. Take out the black line at top and on back. Place in refrigerator for about 2 hours. Beat the egg and add the seasoning, roll in flour or cracker meal and fry a few at a time in deep, hot fat until light brown. Splitting allows shrimp to curl while frying. Serve hot with catsup or Chili Sauce.
The Settlement Cookbook, 1940

FRIED SHRIMP

Pick the raw shrimp or prawn, sprinkle lightly with salt, roll in batter made of egg and bread crumbs and fry in deep fat.
The Savannah Cook Book, 1933

FRIED SHRIMP IN TOMATOES

Fry fresh uncooked shrimp in hot butter. Pour over them 1 cup of hot tomato sauce, boil 1 minute and serve.
The Savannah Cook Book, 1933

SHRIMP WITH HOMINY

NOTE: This is a delicious breakfast dish served in every house in Charleston during the shrimp season.

1 pound raw shrimp	salt and black pepper
1/2 cup butter	2 cups cooked hominy

Shell (and de-vein) the shrimp and put them in a saucepan in which butter has been melted. Add the seasonings and stir until the shrimp are hot. They may then be covered, stirred occasionally and allowed to cook for 10 minutes. Serve with the hot hominy. This will make 4 servings.

NOTE: A charming old gentleman, 78 years old, claims that as far back as he could remember he has eaten shrimp and hominy for breakfast every morning during the shrimp season and shrimp salad for supper every Sunday night and he has never tired of it.
William Deas, Butler and Cook for Mrs. Goodwyn Rhett, 200 years of Charleston Cooking, 1930

GARLIC SHRIMP AND GRITS

1 pound medium shrimp, cooked, peeled	1 cup extra sharp Cheddar cheese, shredded
3 cups water	2 cloves garlic, minced
1 cup whipping cream	fresh chives, chopped
1/4 cup butter or margarine	freshly ground pepper
1 teaspoon salt	
1 cup quick cooking grits, uncooked	

In a large saucepan over medium-high heat, bring water, cream, butter, and salt to a boil. Reduce heat to medium and whisk in grits. Cook, whisking constantly, 7-8 minutes or until mixture is smooth. Stir in shrimp, cheese and garlic and cook 2 minutes more or until heated through. Garnish with chopped fresh chives and freshly ground pepper.
Sandra Rascle, Fruit of the Spirit, Mt. Bethel United Methodist Church, Marietta, GA

SHRIMP SCAMPI

1/4 cup olive oil	dash of black pepper
1/2 teaspoon minced garlic	1/4 teaspoon minced parsley
2 pounds raw shrimp, peeled, deveined	6 Tablespoons dry white wine
1/4 cup green onion, minced	2 Tablespoons dry sherry
1/2 teaspoon salt	4 Tablespoons lemon juice

Heat oil over medium-high heat in large frying pan. Add garlic and sauté for 30 seconds. Add shrimp, green onion, salt, pepper and parsley. Sauté 4-5 minutes, stirring occasionally. When shrimp is pinkish white and the translucent look is gone, add wine, sherry, and lemon juice. Heat for another minute or two.
Diane Swearingin, Fruit of the Spirit, Mt. Bethel United Methodist Church, Marietta, GA

BAKED SHRIMP

Cut up 1 cup of boiled shrimp. Pour over this a sauce made of 2 Tablespoons butter, 1 Tablespoon of Worcestershire sauce and a little Tabasco. Put in individual dishes or shells. Sprinkle with bread crumbs and bake to a light brown.

NOTE: Makes a very good entrée.
The Savannah Cook Book, 1933

BAKED SHRIMP AND TOMATOES

2 pounds shrimp	2 cups stewed tomatoes
1 rule: don't over-work baking powder	2 Tablespoons butter
biscuit dough	pepper, mace or nutmeg, and salt

Boil the shrimp for a few minutes until they are pink and remove the shells. Butter a deep dish well and put in it a layer of baking powder biscuit dough, page 305.(Pounded biscuit is used for the real, original Southern dish, but few of us have the time to make beaten biscuits now, alas!)
On the dough put a layer of shrimp with small pieces of butter, pepper, salt, and mace or nutmeg sprinkled over them. Then add a layer of stewed tomatoes with more of the butter, pepper and salt and cover with a very thin layer of biscuit dough. Add another layer of shrimp and continue until all the ingredients are used, making the top layer of biscuit dough. Bake in a hot oven (425 F) for about 45 minutes and serve piping hot. Serves 8.
Carolina Housewife recipe recounted in the book, 200 Years of Charleston Cooking, 1930

SHRIMP AND CRABMEAT AU GRATIN

1/4 cup butter	2 teaspoons sugar
1 pound crabmeat	1 cup grated Cheddar cheese
1 pound shrimp, cooked	3 cups medium cream sauce
1/4 cup sherry	1/2 cup buttered bread crumbs
salt and pepper to taste	1/2 cup slivered almonds

Heat butter in a heavy skillet. Sauté the crabmeat and shrimp until heated through. Add sherry, seasonings, and cheese. Combine with cream sauce and turn into a large baking dish. Top with bread crumbs and almonds. Bake at 350 degrees for about 30 minutes, until heated through and lightly browned.

TO MAKE CREAM SAUCE

6 Tablespoons butter	1 cup milk
6 Tablespoons flour	2 cups light cream

Combine butter and flour in a saucepan over medium heat. Add milk and stir; add cream and cook, while stirring, until thickened. Use as directed above for this recipe. Serves 6-8
Judy Johnson, The Nashville Cookbook, 1977

SHRIMP CALIENTE

1 pound fresh shrimp	1/4 teaspoon paprika
2 large ripe tomatoes	1/2 teaspoon salt
1 stalk celery	mayonnaise

Drop shrimp into boiling saltwater and cook for 1/4 hour. When cool, remove the shells and set aside to chill. Peel blanched tomatoes and chop them fine, then add finely chopped celery and combine with shrimp and tomatoes. Season liberally with paprika and salt and add sufficient mayonnaise to moisten. Mix well, serve cold. This recipe may also be used for canned shrimp if desired.
The Southern Cookbook, 1939

SHRIMP PILAU

4 slices of bacon	1 cup rice (uncooked)
1 small onion	1 1/2 cups peeled cooked shrimp
2 1/2 cups tomatoes	salt to taste

Cut the bacon into inch pieces and fry until crisp. Remove from the pan and brown the onion, chopped fine, in the bacon fat. Add the tomatoes and cook for a few minutes. Add rice and steam in upper part of double boiler until rice is cooked (about 45 minutes). Add shrimp and bacon and turn all into a baking dish. Bake in moderate oven for about 15 minutes. This all should be rather solid in texture. The rice, while perfectly cooked, will not be as soft as when cooked by our usual method of boiling in quantities of water. Serves 6.
200 years of Charleston Cooking, 1930

CREOLE SHRIMP

1 large onion, chopped	1 teaspoon salt
1 clove garlic, chopped	1/4 teaspoon pepper
1 cup diced celery	few drops of Tabasco sauce
2 Tablespoons oil	2 pounds fresh, peeled, cooked shrimp
# 2 1/2 can tomatoes	

Cook onion, celery, and garlic in oil until light yellow. Add tomatoes and seasoning. Simmer for 40 minutes. Add shrimp. Cook for 10 minutes longer. Serve on steamed, hot rice. If you have time, longer and slower cooking of sauce is desirable. Serves 8.
Satsuma Tea Room, Fun for the Cook, 1968

SHRIMP OR PRAWN PIE

2 quarts shrimp	mace, salt, pepper	1 quart rice
1 pint milk	1 teaspoon butter	1 egg

Boil the rice in salted water until grainy. While hot, add the butter, milk, and seasoning. Put alternate layers of rice and shrimp in a deep dish, ending up with rice on top. Pour well-beaten egg over the top and bake in moderate oven.
The Savannah Cook Book, 1933

SPICY SHRIMP

5 pounds shrimp, (do not shell)
1 stick margarine
2 Tablespoons lemon juice
3 Tablespoons pepper
2 packages Good Seasons Italian Dressing
(prepared per package directions)

Wash shrimp. In a 9 x 13-inch pan, cook shrimp and all other ingredients at 350 degrees for 1 hour. Serve in sauce with corn on the cob and French bread. DELICIOUS!
Tina Hardee, Fruit of the Spirit, Mt. Bethel United Methodist Church, Marietta, GA

PEPPERS STUFFED WITH SHRIMP OR CRABS

1 cup shrimp meat (or crabmeat)
1 cup milk
2 Tablespoons butter
2 Tablespoons flour
1 teaspoon mustard
salt and pepper

Make white sauce of butter, flour, and milk and seasoned with salt, pepper, and mustard. Stir into this the shrimp and then stuff the peppers that have been hollowed. Cover the tops of the stuffed peppers with bread crumbs and a small piece of butter. Bake about 15 minutes. It will improve peppers to parboil them for a few minutes with a pinch of soda.
The Savannah Cook Book, 1933

SHRIMP CURRY

2 quarts shrimp, boiled and picked
1 quart milk
1 Tablespoon butter
salt and pepper
teaspoon curry

Cream together butter and flour, add boiling milk and cook 5 minutes. Rub curry powder smooth in a little water and add this to the sauce and then stir in the shrimp. A cup of cream added just before serving is a delicious touch.
The Savannah Cook Book, 1933

SHRIMP FONDUE

5 slices white bread, buttered
1 cup shrimp
salt
3 eggs, slightly beaten
2 cups American cheese grated
2 cups milk
pepper

Cut buttered bread into ½-inch cubes. Arrange layer in bottom of buttered casserole. Add layer of shrimp, then layer of cheese. Sprinkle each layer with salt and pepper. Repeat until all the ingredients are used. Combine the eggs and milk. Pour over the contents of the casserole. Set casserole into hot water and bake in a 350 degree oven for 50-60 minutes, until a knife inserted comes out clean. Serves 6.

NOTE: This recipe comes from Nags Head, North Carolina, where we enjoyed it very much.
Satsuma Tea Room, Fun for the Cook, 1968

SHRIMP STEWED WITH RED BELL PEPPERS

12 sweet red peppers or 1 can pimientos   2 quarts shrimp, boiled or cut up

Put a little water in the peppers and stew in water. When soft, mash and add the shrimp, a little salt, 2 Tablespoons of butter and cook slowly about 15 minutes.
The Savannah Cook Book, 1933

SHRIMP PATTIES

1 cup cooked, shelled shrimp
2 slices bread, cut 1-inch thick
1 Tablespoon butter
1/4 teaspoon mace
1/4 teaspoon black pepper
salt to taste

The shrimp should be pounded in a mortar according to the original directions. But we found running them through a meat grinder (or food processor) gave satisfactory results with much less work. Cut the crusts off the bread, which should be rather stale. Turn water over it, squeeze dry, and crumble into the shrimp. Add the butter and seasonings and mix well. Shape into little cakes and bake in a buttered pan in a moderate oven until brown or sauté in butter turning to brown both sides.

NOTE: These shrimp patties would be delicious entree to serve at a luncheon. Serve with a sauce that is bland so that it will not mask the delicate shrimp flavor. The patties would be excellent as a course for a formal dinner.
200 Years of Charleston Cooking, 1930

SHRIMP AND RICE CROQUETTES

1 cup rice
2 eggs
1 Tablespoon butter
2 quarts shrimp

After cooking the rice, add butter while still hot. Beat the eggs slightly and add lastly the shrimp, finely minced. Season with salt and pepper to taste, roll into shapes, dip in bread or cracker crumbs and egg. Fry in deep fat.
The Southern Cookbook, 1939

ANOTHER RECEIPT FOR SHRIMP CROQUETTES (Very, very old)

2 quarts shrimp
1 Tablespoon butter
1/2 wineglass vinegar
a little grated nutmeg
1 Tablespoon Worcestershire sauce

Run shrimp though a grinder (food processor), mix with butter, vinegar, Worcestershire and nutmeg. Form into little cakes and fry in deep fat.
The Savannah Cook Book, 1933

SHRIMP PASTE

Run a quart of boiled and picked shrimp through the meat grinder (food processor). Put into a saucepan with salt, pepper, mace and two heaping Tablespoons of butter. Heat thoroughly and place in molds, pressing down very hard with a spoon, and then pour melted butter over the mold top. Place in refrigerator and, when it is cold, slice and serve. This makes an excellent hors d'oeuvre or an addition to a tomato salad.
The Southern Cookbook, 1939

BARBECUE SHRIMP

2 bay leaves
1 1/2 Tablespoon dried rosemary
1/4 teaspoon dried basil
1/2 teaspoon dried oregano
1/2 teaspoon sea salt
1/2 teaspoon cayenne pepper
1 teaspoon paprika

1 Tablespoon whole peppercorns
1 stick unsalted butter
1/2 cup vegetable oil
2 cloves garlic, minced
1/2 lemon thinly sliced
1 pound shrimp (head on), rinsed, dried

Put bay leaves, rosemary, basil, oregano, salt, cayenne, paprika and peppercorns into mortar and pound into a fine mix. Heat butter and oil in a black iron skillet. When butter is completely melted, add all the ingredients except shrimp. Gently cook for about 10 minutes, stirring often so that spices do not settle and burn. Remove from heat and let stand for at least 1/2 hour or up to 2 days. When ready to cook, heat oven to 450. Add shrimp in one layer to the mix and place on medium stove top. Cook for 5 minutes then place in preheated oven for another 10 minutes. Remove from oven and serve in bowls with Cajun rice and plenty of French bread.
Steve Gunning, Fruit of the Spirit, Mt. Bethel United Methodist Church, Marietta, GA

TO OPEN OYSTERS

Pry shells open with oyster knife or narrow strong blade. Oyster liquid, when used in cooking, should be strained. To serve oysters hot, steaming is the easiest way.
The Settlement Cookbook, 1940

TO CLEAN OYSTERS

Take up oysters separately in the fingers and remove all bits of shell and seaweed. Pour cold water over them to cleanse and drain them in a strainer.
The Settlement Cookbook, 1940

TO SERVE RAW OYSTERS OR CLAMS

Arrange oysters or small clams on the shell, on finely chopped ice, on a plate. Serve with a thick slice of lemon and a teaspoon of horseradish.
The Settlement Cookbook, 1940

OYSTER STEW

1 pint oysters and liquid	3 cups milk scalded	pepper to taste
1/2 cup melted butter	1/2 teaspoon salt	
1 cup light cream, heated	1/2 teaspoon paprika	

Heat oysters in liquid and butter until edges curl. Add heated cream and milk. Bring almost to a boil; add seasonings. Serve at once. Stew may be thickened slightly with 1-2 Tablespoons flour mixed with butter before the liquid is added if desired.
The Settlement Cookbook, 1940

BROWNED OYSTERS

1 quart oysters	1 1/2 Tablespoons flour	salt and pepper
4 Tablespoons butter	juice of one lemon	Worcestershire sauce

Remove the oysters from their juice and drain. Dredge them in flour and brown them in two Tablespoons of the butter. Remove them from the pan and strain the juice through a colander or sieve. Make a brown sauce (roux) of the remaining butter and flour, add the juice from the cooked oysters. Add the lemon juice and a dash of Worcestershire sauce, pour over the oysters and serve.
The Southern Cook Book, 1939

BROILED OYSTERS

1 pint selected oysters	2/3 cup seasoned cracker crumbs
1/4 cup melted butter	

Clean oysters and dry between towels. Lift with fork by the tough muscles and dip in butter, then in cracker crumbs which have been seasoned with salt and pepper. Place in a buttered dripping pan and cook under broiler until the juices flow, turning while broiling. Ideal to serve with Maître d' Hotel butter.
The Settlement Cookbook, 1940

FRIED OYSTERS

24 large oysters	1 egg
1 teaspoon salt	1/8 teaspoon pepper
1/2 cup bread crumbs	

Clean and drain select oysters. Roll in bread crumbs, seasoned with salt and pepper. Let stand 15 minutes or more, then dip in beaten egg, roll in crumbs again, let stand again 15 minutes or more in a cool place. Fry for 1 minute or until golden brown in deep, hot fat. Drain on paper, serve on hot platter with parsley, pickle or lemon.
The Settlement Cookbook, 1940

STEAMED OYSTERS OR CLAMS

Take 2 dozen oysters or clams. Scrub shells to remove all sand, lay flat in kettle, add 1/2 cup boiling water to 2 dozen medium shells. Cover and steam until shells partially open (5 to 10 minutes). Serve with melted butter.
The Settlement Cookbook, 1940

ESCALLOPED OYSTERS-OLD FASHIONED

1 pint oysters, drained	2 Tablespoons cream
1 1/2 cups bread crumbs (coarse)	1 teaspoon Worcestershire sauce
1/2 cup dried breadcrumbs	1/2 teaspoon salt
1/2 cup melted margarine	1/4 teaspoon pepper
1/4 cup oyster liquid	

Mix cracker and breadcrumbs in melted margarine and seasonings. Mix cream, oyster liquid, and Worcestershire sauce. Put 1/3 of crumbs in flat baking dish. Put layer of oysters, pour 1/2 liquid over, then 1/3 crumbs, layer of oysters, liquid and remaining crumbs on top. Bake at 400 for 20-30 minutes. Makes 4 servings.
Satsuma Tea Room, More Fun for the Cook, 1974

SCALLOPED OYSTERS

1 pint oysters	1 cup cracker crumbs
2 Tablespoons oyster liquor	1/2 cup melted butter
2 Tablespoons milk or cream	salt
1/2 cup dry bread crumbs	pepper

Mix the bread and cracker crumbs and stir in butter and put 1/3 of this mixture in the bottom of buttered, shallow baking dish. Cover with 1/2 of the oysters, sprinkle with salt and pepper; add 1/2 each of oyster liquor or cream. Repeat, cover top with remaining crumbs. Bake 30 minutes in hot oven.
The Settlement Cookbook, 1940

OYSTER PIE

2 crust 9-inch pastry shell	1/3 cup flour
1 1/2 pints oysters	1 Tablespoon minced parsley
milk plus cream	1 teaspoon salt
1/3 cup butter or margarine	pepper to taste

Prick pastry well with fork, top and bottom. Bake at 450 degrees until lightly browned, 8 to 10 minutes. Drain oysters; reserve liquor. Add enough milk and some cream to the liquor to make 3 1/2 cups liquid. Melt butter or margarine in a saucepan. Stir in the flour. Add the liquid slowly; boil 2 or 3 minutes, stirring constantly. Add the parsley, salt, pepper, and oysters. Heat again just to the boiling point. Have your cooked pie shell ready and just before serving add the hot oyster filling. Place the cooked pastry on top. Garnish with festive splashes of paprika, pimiento, and green pepper. Makes 6 servings.
Farm Journal's Country Cookbook, 1959

OYSTER PIE

Make a thick white sauce of 2 Tablespoons of butter, 2 heaping Tablespoons of flour and 1 cup of milk. Season with celery, onion, and some allspice. Put into this sauce, 1 pint of well-drained oysters, salt to taste. Cover with a rich pie crust and bake.
The Savannah Cook Book, 1933

OYSTERS ROCKEFELLER

2 dozen large oysters in the shell	1 Tablespoon each of parsley and green
1/2 cup butter	onion tops, chopped
1 strip bacon	juice of 1 lemon
1/4 cup cooked spinach chopped	salt, pepper, cayenne

Wash oysters and clean them thoroughly. Open and leave oyster on the bottom of the shell. Mix the parsley, onion tops, and seasoning well with the butter. Put some of this mixture on top of each oyster. Then add bits of bacon, then a little cooked spinach. Place in oven for about 5 minutes until oysters swell. Set shells when cooking in a heavy pie plate filled with rock salt to preserve heat but also to keep heat evenly dispersed to hinder oysters from cooking unevenly and serve at once.
The Settlement Cookbook, 1940

CREAMED OYSTERS

	1 pint cream
1 quart oysters	small piece of onion
1 Tablespoon flour	mace, salt, pepper

Let cream, onion, and a little mace come to a boil. Mix flour with a little cold milk and stir into cream mixture. Let oysters come to a boil in their own juice, drain off the liquor. Remove onion from cream mixture, stir in oysters, season with salt and pepper and serve.
The Savannah Cook Book, 1933

OYSTERS ON TOAST

Clean oysters and drain from their liquor. Put into a stew pan and cook until oysters are plump and edges begin to curl. Shake the pan or stir the oysters with a fork as they cook to prevent sticking. Season with salt, pepper, and a few Tablespoons of butter and pour onto buttered toast. Garnish with parsley or toast points.
The Settlement Cookbook, 1940

OYSTERS IN BLANKETS

12 firm oysters	chopped parsley
red pepper	12 slices bacon, thin slices

Drain well and wipe oysters dry and dry. Lay each oyster on a thin slice of bacon. Add a little red pepper, sprinkle with chopped parsley, then fold bacon around oysters and fasten with a wooden toothpick. Brown slowly in a frying pan. Serve hot along with cocktails.
The Settlement Cookbook, 1940

OYSTERS LOUISIANE

1 dozen oysters	3 Tablespoons flour
3 Tablespoons butter	pinch of cayenne
2 Tablespoons red pepper, chopped	1/2 cup Parmesan cheese
2 teaspoons chopped onions	salt and pepper to taste

Parboil (partly cook by boiling) the oysters. Remove from the pan, reserve the oyster liquor, and add enough water to make 1 1/2 cups. Melt the butter and fry the onion and red pepper in it. Add the flour to the onion and pepper and blend; then gradually pour on the liquor and stir constantly. Bring to the boiling point and season. Arrange the oysters in a casserole. Pour the liquid over them, add the grated cheese and bake in the oven until thoroughly heated.
The Southern Cook Book, 1939

OYSTER RAREBIT

1 cup oysters	1/4 teaspoon salt
2 Tablespoons butter	few grains of cayenne pepper
1/2 pound soft, mild cheese, cut	2 eggs

Clean, parboil, and drain oysters, reserving liquor; then remove and discard the tough oyster muscle. Melt butter, add cheese and seasonings; as the cheese melts add gradually the oyster liquor and eggs slightly beaten; when smooth add oysters. Serve at once.
The Settlement Cookbook, 1940

CHESAPEAKE OYSTER LOAF

1 loaf French bread	pepper
2 dozen oysters	salt
½ cup cream	2 drops Tabasco sauce
1 Tablespoon chopped celery	

Cut off the top crust of a loaf of French bread and scoop out the inside. Butter 1/3 of the portion you have scooped out and toast in the oven. Fry 2 dozen oysters in butter, add 1/2 cup cream, a Tablespoon of chopped celery, pepper, salt, and two drops of Tabasco sauce and toasted bread. Fill the hollowed-out loaf with this mixture, cover with the top crust and bake 20 minutes, basting frequently with the liquor from your oysters. Slice and serve hot.
The Southern Cookbook, 1939

TO BOIL HARD SHELL CRABS

Drop crabs, one at a time, into boiling water (2 Tablespoons salt to 1 quart water). Boil 20 to 25 minutes. Drain and wash carefully, remove claws, pull off hard-shells and remove spongy part. Serve remaining soft shell with the claws. Crack the claws with a nut cracker and remove the meat.
The Settlement Cookbook, 1940

FRIED SOFT SHELL CRABS

Prepare crabs by removing the sand bags. Raise the apron of shell and cut from the crab and remove spongy substance surrounding the apron. Wash and wipe the crab, season with salt and pepper; dip in crumbs, egg, and crumbs again; fry in deep hot fat about 3 to 5 minutes. Serve immediately with tartar sauce.
The Settlement Cookbook, 1940

CREAMED CRABMEAT

2 Tablespoons butter	1 pint crabmeat
1/2 cup bread crumbs	2 egg yolks, beaten
1 cup cream	salt and cayenne pepper
1/2 teaspoon dry mustard	Tabasco sauce

Mix and heat the first four ingredients; then add the rest. Ideal served on toast.
The Settlement Cookbook, 1940

DEVILED CRABS

Follow the recipe right above. Put in serving crab shells or ramekins. Dot with butter, brown in oven.
The Settlement Cookbook, 1940

DEVILED CRAB NORFOLK

Make a white sauce by mixing one Tablespoon melted butter and 1 Tablespoon flour; add 1/2 cup cream or milk and let come to a boil, stirring constantly. Add salt and pepper. Then add 1 pint of crabmeat, picked of shell, two chopped hard-boiled eggs, sprig of parsley, dash of Worcestershire sauce and place into serving crab shells. Brush with melted butter and cracker crumbs and bake in a slow oven until well browned. Serve with tartar sauce.

NOTE: At *Satsuma*, this was one of our more popular seafood dishes with two crab shells per serving. It was brought back on a regular basis by popular demand. Fantastic flavor.
The Southern Cookbook, 1939

FRESH CRABMEAT AND GREEN PEPPERS

1 pint crabmeat	1 cup White Sauce
2 green peppers, diced	

Heat the crab meat in White Sauce. When hot, add peppers.
The Settlement Cookbook, 1940

CRAB STEW

Make a roux of 2 large Tablespoons of butter and 2 scant Tablespoons of flour. When smooth, add 1 pint of milk and season with salt. When this comes to a boil, stir in 1 lemon chopped fine (skin and all), plenty of pepper and paprika and cook well. Just before removing from the fire, add the meat of 1 dozen crabs. Heat well but do not boil. Add 1 Tablespoon of Worcestershire sauce, 1 Tablespoon of wine and serve.
The Savannah Cook Book, 1933

CRABMEAT IN CASSEROLE

1 Tablespoon butter	2 teaspoons lemon juice
1 Tablespoon flour	1/2 teaspoon salt
1/2 cup milk	2 Tablespoons butter
3 teaspoons grated onions	1 pound fresh or canned crabmeat
1/2 cup cubed fresh bread	1 1/2 teaspoons Worcestershire sauce
1/2 cup mayonnaise	

Blend butter, flour, and milk into pan. Add onion, Worcestershire sauce and bread cubes. Cool. Fold in mayonnaise, lemon juice, salt and pepper. Brown crabmeat in butter and combine with sauce. Turn into buttered casserole. Brown in hot oven at 450 for 10-15 minutes. Serves 6.
Satsuma Tea Room, Fun for the Cook, 1968

TO BOIL LOBSTER

Put live lobsters, head first, one at a time, into a large kettle of boiling salted water to cover, 2 Tablespoons of salt to 1 quart of water, and let boil steadily 20 to 30 minutes according to lobster size. Drain and cool quickly. Lobster should not be eaten until cold.
The Settlement Cookbook, 1940

TO OPEN BOILED LOBSTER

Take off the claws. Separate the large claws at the joints, and crack or cut each claw shell to remove lobster meat. Separate the lobster tail from the body, draw out tail meat open through center of meat, take out intestinal vein. Hold body shell firmly, draw out the body, remove the stomach and liver (green). Pick out meat from the body bones. The stomach, liver and intestinal vein are not to be eaten. To split lobster in half, cross large claws and hold with left hand. With the right hand, draw a sharp pointed knife quickly through the body lengthwise from head to tail. Crack the claws slightly.
The Settlement Cookbook, 1940

STEWED LOBSTER

Cut boiled lobster meat fine; put into a stew pan with a little milk or cream. Heat; add one Tablespoon of butter, a little pepper, and serve plain or on toasted crackers. Cook lobster just long enough to heat it as longer cooking renders lobster tough.
The Settlement Cookbook, 1940

BROILED LIVE LOBSTER

Split the lobster and glaze with olive oil. Broil on hot fire with the meat side to the fire. When well broiled, season with salt, cayenne and plenty of melted butter or place in spider, season, place in oven and baste.
The Settlement Cookbook, 1940

LOBSTER A LA NEWBURG

2 cups boiled lobster meat	2 egg yolks
2 Tablespoons butter	1/4 teaspoon salt
1 cup Madeira or sherry wine	dash cayenne
1 cup cream	

Melt the butter in a saucepan and add the lobster, which has been cut into small pieces; cover and let simmer slowly for 5 minutes, then add the wine and cook 3 minutes. Beat the egg yolks and to them add the cream. Beat together and add to the lobster. Shake pan until the mixture is thickened. If the mixture is stirred, it will break up the lobster. This dish curdles quickly and should be made just in time to serve immediately, but it is worth it.
The Southern Cookbook, 1939

LOBSTER THERMIDOR

4 cups lobster meat, in small pieces	1 Tablespoon flour
1 pound fresh mushrooms or 1 large can	2 Tablespoons butter
1 cup Sauterne	bread crumbs
1 pint rich cream	Parmesan cheese
2 egg yolks	paprika

Sauté mushrooms in the butter. Cover tightly while cooking. Season with the wine and add the rich cream to which the beaten egg yolks have been added. Thicken with flour. When smooth, add the lobster. Place in buttered ramekins or lobster shell which has been cut lengthwise. Dot with butter, sprinkle with paprika and bread crumbs mixed with the Parmesan cheese. Place in the oven and bake until a delicate brown.
The Southern Cookbook, 1939

CREAMED LOBSTER

Cut two cups boiled lobster meat fine. Add 1 1/2 cups White Sauce. Heat through about 5 minutes. Season and serve on toast.
The Settlement Cookbook, 1940

FROG LEGS A LA NEWBURG

Boil the frog legs in saltwater and drain. Separately heat 2 Tablespoons butter, add 1/2 cup soup stock, 1/2 cup Madeira wine, salt, and cayenne pepper to taste. Boil for 3 minutes. Add 1/2 pint cream and 3 yolks slightly beaten. Cook 2 minutes, stirring constantly and pour over the frog legs.
The Settlement Cookbook, 1940

FRIED FROG LEGS

1 egg	1 teaspoon
1 cup milk	1 teaspoon garlic powder
1 teaspoon baking powder	1 teaspoon black pepper
1 1/2 teaspoons salt	4 heaping teaspoons paprika
2 cups flour	

Combine flour, baking powder, paprika, black pepper, and salt. Beat egg and stir in milk. Dip frog legs in egg-milk bath, then roll them in flour mixture two more times. Deep fry until golden brown.

NOTE: Cortner Mill Restaurant is located on the banks of the Duck River in Normandy, Tennessee. In those surroundings, it is fitting that it has frog legs on its menu. Their reputation for frog legs has spread around the world with people from many countries making inquiries on how Cortner Mill cooks their frog legs.
Isabel Woodlee, Cortner Mill Restaurant cookbook, 2009

CALVERT MANOR FROGS' LEGS

8 frog legs	salt and pepper
boiling saltwater	1 egg, beaten
1/2 cup lemon juice	cracker crumbs

Only the hind legs of the frogs are eaten. Skin the legs and scald them in boiling salt water and lemon juice for about two minutes. Dry after scalding. Season with salt and pepper; dip in beaten egg and then in cracker crumbs. Fry for three minutes in deep fat and serve two legs per person.

NOTE: A dish for the epicure!
The Southern Cookbook, 1939

FROG LEGS SAUTEED

1 pound fresh frog legs (4 sets)	1 cup flour
salt and pepper	1 cup light cream

Season the frog legs with salt and pepper. Marinate the frog legs in cream for an hour or more. Remove the frog legs from the cream and coat with flour. Sauté them in hot cooking oil in heavy frying pan until done or golden brown. Serve hot. Serves 2.

NOTE: Sautéed frog legs may be gently simmered, covered in light cream sauce for about 30 minutes for smothered legs and gravy.
Ann Rowland, The Nashville Cookbook, 1977

TO BOIL CRAWFISH

Put live crawfish in boiling water with caraway seed. (2 quarts water, 1 Tablespoon salt, and 1 Tablespoon caraway). Boil 5 minutes, let stand until cool. Drain, chill, and serve.
The Settlement Cookbook, 1940

CLAMS A LA ST. LOUIS

30 clams	1/2 teaspoon mustard	parsley and truffles
12 fresh mushrooms	1 onion	salt and pepper
4 egg yolks	2 Tablespoons butter	
1/2 teaspoon red pepper	1 Tablespoon flour	

Fry the finely chopped onion in the butter, adding flour, stirring well. Then add the clams, chopped. Season with salt, red and white pepper and the mustard. Cook for 30 minutes, remove from fire, add egg yolks, slightly beaten, with 2 Tablespoons cold water. Reheat for just a moment. Serve.
The Settlement Cookbook, 1940

Scallops are a shellfish of which the muscle is the only edible part. They are used like oysters while cooking. For parboiling, clean, wash, and drain; then drop in boiling salted water and just simmer a few minutes until tender.

FRIED SCALLOPS

Pick over and wash quickly 1 quart of scallops. Parboil for 3 minutes. Drain and dry between towels. Prepare the same way as *Fried Oysters* recipe on page 246. Serve with Tartar Sauce.
The Settlement Cookbook, 1940

SCALLOPED SCALLOPS

Pick over and wash 1 pint of scallops. Parboil and then follow the *Scalloped Oysters* recipe on page 247 using scallops instead of oysters. Bake 1/2 hour or until crumbs are brown.
The Settlement Cookbook, 1940

TUNA AND NOODLES IN CASSEROLE

1 package of noodles	1 green pepper, cut fine	2 Tablespoons sherry, if
1/2 clove garlic, chopped	1 can mushroom soup	desired
6 ½ ounces tuna	1/8 teaspoon pepper	1 cup grated cheese
1/2 teaspoon salt		

Cook noodles in salted water. Drain, rinse, and drain again. Mix all other ingredients and save 1/4 cup of cheese to sprinkle on top. Add cooked noodles and put them into a greased casserole. Cook at 350 for 45 minutes. If you have been away all day and have to get dinner in a hurry, this recipe is a gem and reasonable in price also.
Satsuma Tea Room, Fun for the Cook, 1968

LOW COUNTRY BOIL

3-4 Tablespoons salt
3-4 pounds golf ball size new red potatoes
6-10 ears white corn (Silver Queen if possible), shucked and halved
2 bottles beer
1/2 jar Crab Boil liquid concentrate
1 bag Crab Boil seasonings
1-2 smoked sausage, 1-2 inch pieces
1-2 Andouille sausage, 1-2 inch pieces
3-5 pounds frozen king or snow crab, or fresh blue crabs if available
1-2 pound bag raw, peeled shrimp thawed, roughly 31-35 count
1-2 pound bag raw, peeled shrimp thawed 14-16 count

Fill large pot with water to about 60% level. Add salt and bring to a boil. Add potatoes and cook 20 minutes. Add corn, cook additional 10-12 minutes. Add beer and crab boil. Add sausage and cook 3-4 minutes. Add crabs and shrimp and cook 4-5 minutes. Remove the ingredients and drain. Take to the table. Hearty, but messy!

NOTE: The shrimp will be different sizes for diversity.
Jack Horn, Fruit of the Spirit, Mt. Bethel United Methodist Church, Marietta, GA

NOTES

SAUCES

"Hunger is the best sauce in the world."
-Cervantes

Sauces have been called "The Sonnet of the Table". The simplest dish can be greatly improved and made mouth-wateringly delicious by the addition of a smooth, creamy, well-blended sauce that elevates a dish from the ordinary. It takes patience to make a good sauce. Cooking a sauce cannot be hurried. Sauces are a true test for a cook's talent.

There are several types of sauces, each with its own variations. A "foundation sauce" or a medium white sauce is made from milk thickened with a roux (equal parts of fat and flour). Cream sauce substitutes cream for milk in the same recipe. Brown sauce has browned flour in place of white flour.

The smooth consistency of a sauce starts with the proper blending of the fat, flour, and the seasonings, and then the blending with the liquid to make a smooth sauce. The hot or cold liquid is added slowly to the roux and cooked with constant stirring until the sauce is smooth and thickened.

COOKING PLAIN SAUCES

Allow the sauce to cook at least 10 minutes from the time the liquid is added. When a sauce is cooked less than that time, the flour will not have had time to cook completely. The butter will then separate, which will give an oily appearance to the sauce.

Sauces that have a high proportion of butter and eggs, such as Hollandaise and Mousseline sauces, require careful method in their making so they don't separate; so, follow the directions for the cooking of the sauce carefully. Sauces of the Hollandaise type should be cooked in a double boiler and over low heat. These types of sauces don't keep well on standing and should be served at once.

SEASONING

A plain sauce may be spoiled by over-seasoning or by too spicy a seasoning. The sauce should be seasoned just enough to bring out the natural flavor. No matter what the flavoring, whether the sauce is plain or rich, the rule for seasoning and flavoring should be the same; the ingredients used for this purpose should be so proportioned that no one flavor predominates over the other.

Only a small amount of sauce is needed with most foods; it is the accompaniment to the food, not the food itself. The right sauce compliments the food and becomes an integral part of the dish.

A simple, but well-made and imaginative, sauce is much preferred to an elaborate and badly made sauce. Essentially there are only a few basic sauces with countless variations based on their seasonings or one or another changed ingredient.

First and foremost, of these sauces is the *White Sauce*. It is used for creaming vegetables and, with slight additions or changes, can be used with fried, baked, and au gratin dishes. The thin white sauce is used in making creamed soups; the medium white sauce creams vegetables, scalloped dishes, and gravies, while the thick white sauce is best used for puddings and soufflés.

WHITE SAUCE

2 Tablespoons butter	1 1/2 cups milk
2 Tablespoons flour	1/2 teaspoon salt

Melt the butter, without browning. Add the flour and salt and cook until it is well blended. Add the milk slowly, stirring all the while to keep from scorching, and, when it reaches the boiling point, remove from fire and beat well or until creamy.
The Southern Cookbook, 1939

WHITE SAUCE

1 cup liquid, milk or vegetable stock	1 Tablespoon butter
1 Tablespoon sifted flour	1/4 teaspoon salt

Melt the fat. Add the flour and salt, stirring constantly until the mixture begins to brown. Keep the flame low. Remove from the flame and add cold milk gradually. Stir constantly to keep mixture smooth. Place over a low flame and let come to a boil, stirring constantly. Cook for 2 minutes.

NOTE: This recipe is for the, so-called, *thin sauce*. A white sauce of *medium thickness* will result from 2 Tablespoons of fat and 2 Tablespoons of flour. A *thick sauce* can be made with 3 Tablespoons each of fat and flour. In all cases, only 1 cup of liquid is used.
Cooked to Your Taste, 1945

WHITE SAUCE

2 Tablespoons margarine	1/2 teaspoon salt
2 Tablespoons flour	1 cup milk

Melt the margarine in a saucepan on medium heat. Add flour and salt, blending until smooth. Gradually add milk stirring until thickened. White sauce is easier to keep warm, if made in a double boiler.
Satsuma Tea Room, Easy on the Cook-Garden Vegetables, 1978

WHITE ROUX

1 Tablespoon butter
1 Tablespoon flour

The white roux is made exactly like Brown Roux, only that the butter and flour are put in simultaneously into the saucepan and not allowed to brown. The sauce is then moistened with a little broth or boiling water and allowed to boil a few minutes till thick. The white roux is the foundation of all white sauces or those containing milk and cream. This sauce is used in nearly all purees.
The Picayune Creole Cookbook, 1922

BROWN ROUX

The Creoles are famous for their splendid sauces, and the perfect creation of a good sauce is considered an indispensable part of the culinary art and domestic food cost savings. The first thing to learn in making sauces of every kind is how to make a good "*Roux*", or the foundation mixture of flour and butter, or flour and lard. We have the "*Brown Roux*" and the "*White Roux*" and the "*Glace*" as foundations for all sauces. *Glace* is the foundation of all sauces for roasts, filets, etc. In making a *Brown Roux*, this reliable rule must be the guide: Never under any circumstance use burnt or over-browned flour.

We mention a *Brown Roux* at this moment because many gumbo recipes in this cookbook are tomato-based. If you were to talk to a New Orleans native about gumbo, a tomato-based gumbo is blasphemy. It is a fake. A true New Orleans gumbo is brown, and it begins with a "Brown Roux".

BROWN ROUX

1 Tablespoon butter   1 Tablespoon flour

In making the roux, which is the foundation of a fancy sauce, melt the Tablespoon butter slowly and add flour gradually, sprinkling it in and stirring constantly till every portion is a nice delicate brown. Never make it too brown because it must continue browning as other ingredients are added in the order the recipe calls for. The secret of good cooking lies in following completely the gradual introduction of ingredients as stated.

In making a roux for cooking gravies or smothering meats, use 1 Tablespoon lard and 2 Tablespoons flour. The Creoles hold that butter should be used in its proper place and lard in its own. Butter might sometimes have a way of overpowering the taste of the roux and when used properly the taste of lard is undetectable.

NOTE: Again, if there is the slightest indication of burnt order or over-browning, throw the roux away and wash the utensil before proceeding to make another. Remember that even a slightly burnt sauce will spoil the most savory dish!
The Picayune Creole Cookbook, 1922

BROWN SAUCE

2 Tablespoons butter or fat   1/8 teaspoon pepper
2 Tablespoons flour   1 cup water
1/2 teaspoon salt   or meat, fish vegetable stock

Brown the butter or fat and, if desired, add a small onion-chopped and, when brown, add the flour. Let this brown, add 2/3 cup of the liquid, and gradually the rest of the seasoning. Let cook 5 minutes and serve over hot meat, vegetables, dumplings, etc.
The Settlement Cookbook, 1940

Another group of sauces depends on eggs and butter, either alone or together. One of the best-known representatives of this sauce group is the *Hollandaise* and its two variants, *Sauce Bearnaise* and *Sauce Mousseline.*

HOLLANDAISE SAUCE

2 eggs	chopped parsley and scallions
4 Tablespoons butter	salt and pepper to taste
juice of 1/2 lemon	

Put all ingredients in double boiler and stir over boiling water until thick and creamy.

SAUCE BERNAISE

Add chopped parsley, chervil, almonds and 1 Tablespoon white wine or apple juice to 1 cup of Hollandaise and blend well.

SAUCE MOUSSELINE

Add 2 Tablespoons of stiffly whipped cream to 1 cup Hollandaise and blend well.
Cooked to Your Taste, 1945

HOLLANDAISE SAUCE

1/4 cup margarine	2 egg yolks	1/4 teaspoon salt
1/4 cup cream	1 Tablespoon lemon juice	cayenne to taste

Melt margarine in top of double boiler, add cream and beaten egg yolks. Stirring constantly add the lemon juice and seasonings. Cook over boiling water until thickened and smooth.

NOTE: Serve hot over cauliflower, broccoli, asparagus or beets.
Satsuma Tea Room, Easy on the Cook-Garden Vegetables, 1975

HOLLANDAISE SAUCE

3 egg yolks, beaten slightly	1/2 cup (1 stick) butter
1/4 teaspoon salt	1 Tablespoon lemon juice
dash cayenne pepper	

Blend egg yolks and seasonings in top of stainless steel or enamel double boiler. Add 1/2 of the butter, and lemon juice. Set over hot water over low heat. Stir or whisk constantly until butter is melted; add remaining butter, whisking all the while until butter is melted and mixture is thickened. Do not let pan come in contact with boiling water or mixture may curdle. Remove from heat and stir until sauce is slightly cooled. Serve over crisp cooked vegetables. Make 3/4 to 1 cup.

NOTE: Should this sauce separate, it may be brought together again, if a small amount of hot thin cream sauce is added.
Nell Pinkerton, The Nashville Cookbook, 1977

MOCK HOLLANDAISE SAUCE

1/2 cup butter
4 egg yolks
3 Tablespoons fresh lemon juice
1/4 teaspoon salt
1 dash white pepper

Heat the butter until bubbly. Put all the other ingredients in blender. Pulse blender on and off, then turn blender on high speed. Slowly add the butter in thin but steady stream. Blend until thick and fluffy, about 30 seconds. Heat in double boiler over warm, not hot, water until ready to serve. Makes 1 cup of sauce.
Claudia Hazelwood, Cortner Mill Restaurant cookbook, 2009

MORNAY SAUCE

2 Tablespoons butter or margarine
2 Tablespoons flour
1/2 teaspoon salt
1/2 teaspoon prepared mustard
dash of cayenne
1 cup milk
1/2 teaspoon Worcestershire sauce
1/2 cup shredded sharp process cheese
1 Tablespoon lemon juice

Melt the butter; stir in flour, salt, mustard and cayenne. When well blended, add milk slowly, stirring constantly over low heat until mixture thickens and bubbles. Add Worcestershire sauce, cheese, and lemon juice; heat to melt cheese. Makes 1 1/2 cups.
Farm Journal's Country Cook Book, 1959

MAITRE D'HOTEL SAUCE

1/4 cup butter
1/2 teaspoon salt
1/8 teaspoon pepper
1/2 teaspoon finely chopped parsley
3/4 Tablespoon lemon juice

Put butter in bowl and, with small wooden spoon or spatula, work until creamy. Add salt, pepper, and parsley, then lemon juice, very slowly.

NOTE: Serve over hot broiled fish, steak, or sweetbreads.
The Settlement Cookbook, 1940

CREAM SAUCE

1 Tablespoon butter
1 Tablespoon flour
2 gills of fresh milk or cream
salt and pepper to taste

Melt butter in saucepan and add flour gradually; letting it blend without browning in the least. Add boiling milk or cream and stir continuously. Add salt and white pepper to taste and serve immediately.
The Picayune Creole Cookbook, 1922

CUMBERLAND SAUCE

1/2 cup currant jelly
1/2 cup cranberry sauce
3-4 Tablespoons red wine
4-5 shallots, or young green onion

juice and peel of 1/4 lemon
juice and peel of 1/4 orange
1/4 teaspoon dry mustard
salt, red pepper, and nutmeg to taste

Mix all the dry ingredients and stir in the wine. Add jellies, blend well, and add seasonings. Chop onions and peelings and add to sauce. Stir well. Chill for at least 2 hours and serve on use.
Cooked to Your Taste, 1945

BUTTER SAUCE

4 Tablespoons butter
4 Tablespoons, sifted all-purpose flour
2 cups milk or vegetable stock

salt, nutmeg, basil, and white pepper, to taste

Melt butter. Add flour and stir until slightly brown. Salt milk and add gradually, while stirring constantly. Let come to a boil, cover and cook for 2 minutes. Season.

NOTE: A thicker Butter Sauce can be made by using 1/2 cup light cream and 1/2 cup milk, or 1 cup milk or 1 cup vegetable stock instead of 2 cups liquid.

GREEN PEPPER SAUCE: Add 2 finely chopped peppers to Butter Sauce. Bring to quick boil.

HORSERADISH SAUCE: Add 3 to 4 Tablespoons of grated horseradish and 1 small cored and grated apple to Butter Sauce and mix well.
Cooked to Your Taste, 1945

LEMON BUTTER

1/4 cup margarine
1 Tablespoon lemon juice

1/8 teaspoon grated lemon rind

Use room temperature margarine. Add lemon rind and juice. Mix well and serve on broccoli, asparagus, or beets.
Satsuma Tea Room, Easy on the Cook- Garden Vegetables, 1975

BLUE DEVIL BUTTER

6 Tablespoons softened
butter or margarine
3 Tablespoons bleu cheese
1 Tablespoon anchovy paste

1/2 teaspoon dry mustard
1 teaspoon white vinegar
1 teaspoon lemon juice

Combine butter bleu cheese and anchovy paste. Dissolve mustard in vinegar and lemon juice. Blend into butter mixture. Serve with Baked Trout. Makes 1/2 cup.
Farm Journal's Country Cookbook, 1959

SAUCE REMOULADE

3 hard-boiled eggs
1 raw egg yolk
1 Tablespoon tarragon vinegar
3 Tablespoons olive oil
1/2 clove garlic, minced very fine
1/2 teaspoon prepared mustard
salt and cayenne to taste

A Remoulade is a cold sauce and is always served with cold meats. Boil the eggs till hard. Remove the shells and set aside the white, which you will later crumble fine for a garnish. Put the yolks into a bowl, mash very fine, till perfectly smooth. Add the mustard and mix well, and the seasonings of vinegar and then add salt and cayenne to taste. Then add the olive oil, drop by drop working it into the egg all the time, and then add the yolk of the raw egg and work in thoroughly, till light. Then add the juice of 1/2 lemon. Mix well while increasing the quantities of oil and vinegar only very slightly, according to taste. If this sauce is not thoroughly mixed, it will curdle. This sauce is now ready to serve with cold meats, fish, or salads.
The Picayune Creole Cookbook, 1922

TOMATO SAUCE

4 to 5 ripe tomatoes or
1 1/2 cups canned tomatoes
1 small onion
3 Tablespoons oil or butter
1 teaspoon sugar
salt

Chop the onion and pan in hot fat until tender. Cut up tomatoes and add to the onions and season with sugar and salt. Cover and simmer until done.

NOTE: A few Tablespoons of vegetable stock or water may be added if a thinner sauce is desired.
Cooked to Your Taste, 1945

TOMATO SAUCE

3 Tablespoons butter
3 Tablespoons flour
1 cup canned tomatoes
1 Tablespoon sugar
1/4 teaspoon cloves
1/2 teaspoon allspice
salt and pepper to taste

Make this sauce the same as you would a white sauce, but use the tomatoes in place of the milk. The tomatoes may be strained if desired.

NOTE: This is a very good sauce for veal cutlets, fish, rice, or baked macaroni.
The Southern Cookbook, 1939

SWEET-SOUR SAUCE

3/4 cup water	1/4 teaspoon salt
2 Tablespoons vinegar	1 Tablespoon cornstarch
1 Tablespoon soy sauce	2 Tablespoons water
1/4 cup sugar	

Combine water, vinegar, soy sauce, and salt. Heat to boiling. Add cornstarch to water to make paste. Stir slowly into boiling mixture. Cook over low heat 2 to 3 minutes, until sauce is clear and thickened. If a sauce of a darker color is desired, replace 1 Tablespoon of water with 1 Tablespoon soy sauce.
What to Cook for Company, 1953

LOUIS SAUCE

1 cup mayonnaise	1 teaspoon Worcestershire sauce
1/4 cup ketchup	salt
1 teaspoon prepared horseradish	pepper

Mix all the ingredients. Serve on broiled or fried fish, in fish salads, or on seafood cocktails. Makes 1 1/2 cups.
Farm Journal's Country Cookbook, 1959

BARBECUE SAUCE

1/4 pound butter	2 Tablespoons chili sauce
1 cup vinegar	4 slices lemon
1 sour pickle, finely chopped	1 teaspoon brown sugar
2 Tablespoons chopped onion	1 green pepper, finely chopped
2 Tablespoons Worcestershire sauce	

Combine all the ingredients and mix thoroughly. Place in a saucepan on a slow fire and cook until butter melts, stirring constantly. Place in top of double boiler and keep warm until ready to use on barbecued meats or as a sauce for barbecue sandwiches.
The Southern Cookbook, 1939

BARBECUE SAUCE

1 cup catsup	1/4 cup Worcestershire sauce
1/2 cup dark corn syrup	1/4 cup mustard
1/4 cup vinegar	2 teaspoons salt
1/4 cup chopped onion	1/4 teaspoon hot sauce

Combine all the ingredients in a sauce pan and bring to a boil while stirring. Simmer 5 minutes. Makes 3 cups sauce, enough for 2-3 pounds of ribs.
Margaret Thomas, The Nashville Cookbook, 1977

WINE BARBECUE SAUCE

1/4 cup salad oil	1/2 teaspoon celery salt
1/2 cup white table wine or dry vermouth	1/2 tsp. black pepper, coarsely ground
1 clove garlic, peeled and crushed	1/4 teaspoon each dried thyme,
1 onion, grated	marjoram, and rosemary or
1/2 teaspoon salt	1 teaspoon fresh herbs

Mix and let stand for several hours before using. Makes about 1 cup.

NOTE: Great on Rock Cornish hens or chicken.
Helen L. Harper, The Nashville Cookbook, 1977

DILL SAUCE

2 1/2 cups mayonnaise	4 teaspoons vinegar
1 cup sour cream	1 Tablespoon black pepper
3 Tablespoons Parmesan cheese	2 teaspoons lemon juice
1 Tablespoon dill weed	2 teaspoons Worcestershire sauce
3 Tablespoons onion, chopped	2 cloves garlic, minced

Combine all ingredients and allow flavors to blend several hours before serving.
Bill Hall, Cortner Mill Restaurant cookbook, 2009

HORSERADISH SAUCE

2 Tablespoons finely chopped onion	1 cup cream, milk or soup stock
2 heaping Tablespoons butter	1/2 cup freshly grated horseradish
2 egg yolks	

Melt butter and cook onion until done, add the cream or milk and cook for several minutes. Strain through a fine sieve and pour onto the well beaten egg yolks, place in a double boiler and cook until thick, stirring constantly. Add the horseradish and serve with meats and fish.
The Southern Cookbook, 1939

CREAMY HORSERADISH SAUCE

1/2 cup heavy cream	1/2 teaspoon seasoned salt
1/4 cup sour cream	1 Tablespoon powdered horseradish

Combine heavy cream and sour cream; whip until stiff. Stir in the seasoned salt and powdered horseradish. Let stand 30 minutes to 1 hour in refrigerator for flavors to blend. Makes about 1 1/2 cups.

NOTE: Serve with roast beef, boiled beef, or corn beef.
Ann Eaden, The Nashville Cookbook, 1977

FINES HERBES SAUCE

1 cup buttermilk or light sour cream	1 teaspoon of chopped tarragon
1 teaspoon of chopped chervil or parsley	1 teaspoon of chopped water cress
1 teaspoon of chopped chives	salt and dry mustard

Mix all the ingredients and season to taste. Chill for about 30 minutes before serving.

NOTE: If powdered herbs are used instead of fresh, use about 1/2 the quantity and chill about 1 hour before serving.
Cooked to Your Taste, 1945

COLD GARLIC SAUCE

This sauce is total simplicity to prepare. Just rub a bowl with a cut clove of garlic, add a cup of cream or light sour cream to the garlic in the bowl, cover, and chill for 20 minutes. Remove the garlic, sprinkle with chopped parsley or chives, and use.
Cooked to Your Taste, 1945

HOT GARLIC SAUCE

Rub a saucepan with a cut clove of garlic and a little salt. Melt 2 Tablespoons of butter in the saucepan. Add 1 Tablespoon sifted flour and brown slightly, stirring constantly. Gradually add 1/2 cup each of light sour cream and vegetable stock or water, stirring constantly and let come to a quick boil. Season to taste with salt, nutmeg, chervil (French herb, parsley) and savory. Serve.
Cooked to Your Taste, 1945

ONION SAUCE

3 onions, sliced	3 Tablespoons flour
2 Tablespoons butter or margarine	2 cups meat or vegetable broth

Lightly brown the onions in butter and then cover and simmer 5 minutes. Stir in the flour. Slowly add the broth. (If you have no broth on hand, dissolve 2 bouillon cubes in 2 cups boiling water.)
Cook, stirring constantly, until thickened. If deeper brown is desired, add 1 teaspoon bottled gravy flavor to color. Serve warm over hot fritters. Makes about 2 cups.

NOTE: Serve with meat and vegetable fritters.
Farm Journal's Country Cookbook, 1959

ONION SAUCE

1/2 pound onions	1 Tablespoon sifted flour
1 green pepper	1 Tablespoon lemon juice
2 cups vegetable stock or water	1 teaspoon sugar
3 Tablespoons butter or oil	salt, paprika, basil to taste

Chop onions and green pepper very fine; keeping the two separate. Pan onions in hot fat until tender. Add flour and sugar and mix well. Add cold liquid gradually, stirring constantly. Let come to a boil, cover and simmer 5 minutes. Add pepper and simmer another 10 minutes.

NOTE: One Tablespoon sugar browned in 1 Tablespoon liquid can be added to sauce just before serving, if brown sauce is desired.
Cooked to Your Taste, 1945

MUSTARD SAUCE

Mix 1 cup of light sour cream with 1/4 teaspoon dry mustard and chopped chives or parsley and, if too thick, thin with a little cold vegetable stock. Blend well, chill and serve.
Cooked to Your Taste, 1945

MUSTARD SAUCE

1 cup wine vinegar	2 eggs, beaten
1 cup dry mustard	1/2 teaspoon salt
1 cup sugar	

Combine vinegar and mustard; let stand several hours. Mix sugar, eggs, and salt and add to vinegar mixture. Place in top of double boiler and cook while stirring, over hot water, until thick. Cool. Serve with ham or other meats. Mayonnaise may be added to the sauce before serving if desired. Makes 1 1/2 cups.
Rubye Bell, The Nashville Cookbook, 1977

MUSHROOM SAUCE

½ pound fresh mushrooms or	3 Tablespoons, butter
1 cup canned	1 teaspoon flour
1 cup vegetable stock, mushroom liquid,	salt and red pepper to taste
or half milk/half stock	chopped parsley
1/2 cup cream	

Slice mushrooms fine and pan in hot butter together with parsley until tender (about 8 minutes). Add liquid, cover, and simmer for 5 minutes. Stir flour and seasoning into cream; add to sauce, and let come to a quick boil, stirring constantly.
Cooked to Your Taste, 1945

MUSHROOM SAUCE

2 mushrooms, sliced	1 cube chicken bouillon
3 cups water	2 teaspoons butter
3 Tablespoons flour	

Sauté mushrooms in butter. Bring water to a boil and add chicken bouillon cube. Add mushrooms to water. Make paste with flour and a little water and add to mushrooms. Cook until thickened.
Cortner Mill Restaurant cookbook, 2009

MUSHROOM SAUCE

1 medium sized can mushrooms	3 Tablespoons flour
4 Tablespoons butter	1 cup rich milk or thin cream

Sauté mushrooms in butter, add flour slowly and brown slightly, add the thin cream and cook until it thickens. Pour over either steak or chicken.
The Southern Cookbook, 1939

ASPARAGUS-MUSHROOM SAUCE

12 to 15 stalks fresh or frozen asparagus	10 ½ ounces condensed cream of
3/4 cup boiling water	mushroom soup

Perfect as a stand-alone sauce or for that really special breakfast omelet. Cook asparagus covered in boiling water until tender, about 15 minutes. Place about 3 cooked stalks on one omelet half and then fold the omelet over. Heat the undiluted soup, stir until smooth. Pour over the omelet and remaining asparagus. Makes 1 1/3 cups.
Farm Journal's Country Cook Book, 1959

CHEESE SAUCE

2 Tablespoons butter	1/8 teaspoon pepper	1/2 cup Cheddar cheese
2 Tablespoons flour	1/4 teaspoon dry mustard	
1/4 teaspoon salt	1 cup milk	

Melt margarine or butter; add the flour and seasonings. Add milk while stirring over low heat. Cook until thickened. Add cheese and stir until melted. Makes 1 cup.

NOTE: This sauce is perfect as a base for many dishes, Season as desired. Don't like broccoli? Your tune will change completely with broccoli and cheese sauce.
Nancye Shannon, The Nashville Cookbook, 1977

CHEESE SAUCE

Prepare a white sauce in a double boiler and add 1/2 cup grated Cheddar cheese. Stir until cheese melts. Cover until time to serve.
Satsuma Tea Room, Easy on the Cook-Garden Vegetables, 1975

CHEESE SAUCE

2 cups buttermilk	2 egg yolks	lemon juice
1 cup grated cheese	1/8 tsp. dry mustard	salt

Blend milk with egg yolks, beating constantly until mixture begins to thicken. Add grated cheese and blend. Season and use.
Cooked to Your Taste, 1945

TOMATO-CHEESE SAUCE

10 1/2 ounce can condensed tomato soup   1/4 teaspoon prepared mustard
1 cup grated or shredded cheese

Heat all ingredients together until cheese melts. Very nice on oven-fried or baked fish.
Makes about 1 ½ cups
Farm Journal's Country Cookbook, 1959

EGG SAUCE

3 egg yolks	2 Tablespoons flour
2 chopped hard boiled eggs	2 Tablespoons butter
1 bay leaf, minced fine	1 to 2 teaspoons grated nutmeg
1 onion	1 pint veal or chicken broth
6 peppers	

Chop onion and put into saucepan with butter and bay leaf. Stir in flour to thicken. Moisten with broth. Mix well and add the nutmeg. Salt and pepper to taste. Beat yolks of eggs separately with juice of half a lemon. Pour gradually into sauce, but do not let boil after this is added. Press through a sieve and, when ready to serve, sprinkle with 2 chopped hard boiled eggs and a teaspoon of minced parsley.
The Picayune Creole Cookbook, 1922

HARD-EGG SAUCE

Make a white sauce and add 2 to 3 hard-boiled eggs, chopped, but not too fine, and a little finely minced parsley as a garnish. This sauce is served with fish, chicken or other fowl.
The Picayune Creole Cookbook, 1922

TO MAKE EGG SAUCE

Combine 1/2 cup mayonnaise or salad dressing, 1 chopped hard-cooked egg, 2 Tablespoons ketchup, 2 teaspoons grated onion, 1/2 teaspoon salt and a dash of black pepper (freshly ground the best)
Farm Journal's Country Cookbook, 1959

TEXAS SPECIAL SAUCE

3/4 cup ketchup
1/2 cup oil
1/2 cup vinegar
2 Tablespoons garlic vinegar
1 Tablespoon tarragon vinegar
1/2 cup water
1 Tablespoon Worcestershire sauce
1 small onion minced

2 teaspoons brown sugar
1/2 teaspoon salt
1/2 teaspoon each of celery salt, garlic salt, mustard seed, celery seed, and ground clove
1 teaspoon each of chili powder and oregano
1 small crushed bay leaf

Place all the liquids in a heavy saucepan; set over medium heat and stir well. Mix dry ingredients in mixing bowl, add the liquid and stir well until blended. Reduce heat and simmer gently 25 minutes, stirring occasionally to prevent sticking. Remove from heat. Perfect sauce to marinate or baste meats while broiling or grilling. Makes 2 1/2 cups.
Farm Journal's Country Cookbook, 1959

CHILI SAUCE

15 ripe tomatoes, medium size
6 onions, medium size
3 or 4 green hot peppers
1 pint vinegar
2 1/4 cups sugar

4 teaspoons salt
6 teaspoons cinnamon
1 teaspoon prepared mustard
1 teaspoon black pepper
1/4 teaspoon cayenne

Chop tomatoes, onions, and peppers into small pieces. Add remaining ingredients; cook on medium heat 1 1/2 hours or until desired consistency, stirring frequently. Seal in hot sterilized pint jars while hot. Makes 6 pints.
Martha Bell White, The Nashville Cookbook, 1977

TABASCO A LA CREOLE

3 dozen large red peppers
1 clove of garlic

1/4 pint of hot spiced vinegar

This is one of the most famous of our Creole sauces. It is made from the celebrated Louisiana Tabasco peppers of unsurpassed flavor. These hot peppers are much sought after.

Take 3 dozen large red Tabasco peppers or chili peppers and 1 clove of garlic, chopped very fine, and scald them until tender. Then mash the peppers and garlic together and press them through a sieve. Dilute paste, thus formed, with spiced vinegar until it reaches the consistency of rich cream. Bottle and seal for use. The garlic may be omitted.
The Picayune Creole Cook Book, 1922

DEVIL'S SAUCE

1 onion	1 pickle, a finger long	salt and cayenne
2 cloves garlic	1 Tablespoon mustard	juice of a lemon
3 Tablespoons butter	2 gills consommé	

Brown the onion in butter and add the two cloves of garlic, minced very fine. When brown, add 1 pickle also minced very fine and then add a Tablespoon of prepared mustard. Then add two gills of consommé and the juice of a lemon. Allow this to cook slowly. Season with salt and hot pepper. Goes great with shell fish, chicken, etc.

NOTE: This is a hot sauce.
The Picayune Creole Cookbook, 1922

CREOLE SAUCE

1 1/2 cups Brown Sauce	3 Tablespoons canned tomatoes
2 Tablespoons butter	1/2 teaspoon salt
2 Tablespoons onion, chopped	1/2 teaspoon paprika
2 Tablespoons chopped green peppers	1 teaspoon catsup
1/4 cup mushrooms	dash Kitchen Bouquet

Follow the directions for Brown Sauce (page 258) increasing the proportions one-half. Heat the butter, add the onion, let fry lightly, then the peppers, tomato and mushrooms; add to the Brown Sauce, season with the rest of the ingredients, cook together 20 minutes. If desired, add 1/2 cup blanched, roasted almonds sliced. Serve this sauce hot over thick broiled steak or sweetbreads.
The Settlement Cookbook, 1940

CREOLE RED PEPPER CATSUP

4 dozen pepper pods	5 onions
2 quarts of the best French vinegar	1 garlic
3 Tablespoons grated horseradish	

Take 4 dozen pods ripe green peppers, 2 quarts vinegar, 1 quart water, 3 Tablespoons grated horseradish, 5 onions sliced and 1 garlic. Boil all together until the onions are soft. Then mash all together to a paste and then strain through a sieve until nothing remains, but the seeds and skins. When it becomes cold, bottle and cork tightly for use.
The Picayune Creole Cook Book, 1922

SPICED VINEGAR

1 pound of sugar
1 1/2 gallons of the best cider
1 ounce each of cloves, allspice. mace, celery and mustard seed

1 1/3 ounces (8 tsp) each of black pepper, turmeric, and white ginger

Mix all spices together with vinegar and bits of ginger and place in an earthen jar and cover closely. For smaller proportions take one quart of cider vinegar and put it into 1/3 ounce (2 tsp) each of dried mint, dried parsley, 1 grated garlic, 2 small onions, 2 cloves, 1 teaspoon pepper, 1 teaspoon grated nutmeg, salt to taste, and 1 Tablespoon sugar. Put all into a jar and let stand for 3 weeks, then strain and bottle.
The Picayune Creole Cook Book, 1922

SAUCE FOR GREEN BEANS

2 cups mayonnaise
1 small onion chopped fine
1 teaspoon mustard, prepared
salt and pepper

1/2 cup oil
1 teaspoon Worcestershire Sauce
dash Tabasco

Combine all ingredients and mix well. Serve on hot green beans.
Satsuma Tea Room, More Fun for the Cook, 1974

SAUCE FOR COOKED PINTO BEANS

10 o ounce can tomatoes and chilies
1/2 cup tomato catsup
1/2 cup vinegar

2 Tablespoons sugar
dash of cinnamon, allspice, and salt

Combine the ingredients and pour over cooked pinto beans. Beans may be turned into oiled baking dish and baked at 350 degrees for 30 minutes.

NOTE: This hot, piquant sauce is good for other legumes or meats. Makes about 2 1/2 cups.
Jane Kersten, The Nashville Cookbook, 1977

SAUCE FOR SPINACH

A little brown sugar, a very little dry mustard, cayenne pepper, salt, and one well-beaten egg. Mix well in a little boiling vinegar.
The Savannah Cook Book, 1933

TO MAKE CUCUMBER SAUCE

Combine:

1/2 cup mayonnaise or salad dressing	1 teaspoon vinegar
1/2 cup finely chopped fresh cucumber	1/4 teaspoon Worcestershire sauce
1/4 teaspoon salt	1 teaspoon grated onion

Farm Journal's Country Cook Book, 1959

SOUR CREAM CUCUMBER SAUCE

3/4 cup dairy sour cream	chopped parsley
1/4 teaspoon prepared mustard	1/2 cup chopped cucumber
1/2 teaspoon salt	juice of 1/2 lemon
1 teaspoon grated onion	

Combine all the ingredients; Chill. Makes about 3/4 cup.
Farm Journal's Country Cook Book, 1959

CREAM CHEESE-CHIVE SAUCE (for baked potatoes)

1/3 cup cream	1/2 teaspoon garlic salt
8 ounces cream cheese	4 to 6 hot baked potatoes
1 Tablespoon chopped chives	parsley
1 1/2 teaspoon lemon juice	

s

Add cream to cream cheese gradually, blending until smooth. Add chives, lemon juice and garlic salt. Mix well. Serve over baked potatoes. Garnish with parsley. Serves 4 to 6.
Easy-on-the-Cookbook, 1960

ORANGE SAUCE

peel from 1/2 large or 1 small orange	paprika to taste
2 Tablespoons butter, margarine or duck fat	1 1/3 cups stock
	1/4 cup sherry wine, if desired
2 Tablespoons cornstarch	2/3 cup orange juice
1/4 teaspoon salt	1 orange, sectioned

Cut orange peel into thin strips; cover with cold water; bring to simmering temperature and simmer 30 minutes or until tender; drain. Melt butter, margarine or duck fat in a saucepan; stir in cornstarch, salt and paprika. Add stock, sherry, and orange juice. Cook, stirring constantly until mixture thickens; reduce heat and cook 10 minutes. Just before serving add orange peel and sections. Serve hot. (For stock add 1 chicken bouillon cube to 1 1/3 cups boiling water, use the packaged chicken stock or use the stock in which the duck giblets are cooked.) Makes about 2 1/2 cups sauce.
Holiday Hostess, 1958

CAULIFLOWER SAUCE

For this sauce, first make *Cream Sauce* as the foundation and add it to the cauliflower florets which you have cut very fine and previously boiled until tender.
The Picayune Creole Cookbook, 1922

ORANGE SAUCE (Ideal for pineapple, banana, or orange fritters)

3 Tablespoons sugar	1/8 teaspoon salt	grated rind of 1 orange
1 Tablespoon cornstarch	1 cup orange juice	

Combine in a pan the sugar, cornstarch, and salt. Gradually stir in the orange juice and rind.
Cook, stirring constantly, over low heat until thick and clear. Serve over hot fritters. Makes about 1 1/4 cups.

NOTE: First choice for use over pineapple, banana, and orange fritters.
Farm Journal's Country Cookbook, 1959

COCKTAIL SAUCE

3 cups tomato ketchup	1 1/2 teaspoons Worcestershire sauce
1/3 cup horseradish	1 teaspoon Tabasco sauce
1 medium lemon	1/2 teaspoon curry powder

Juice the lemon and combine with all the other ingredients. Stir until well blended and refrigerate overnight.

NOTE: I once thought I liked shrimp cocktails, but I discovered it was the cocktail sauce I really liked. Then after making my own sauce, it was the horseradish I was loving. Now I can't get enough horseradish. We buy it by the quart and add it to everything from pizza to JELL-O. Well not actually JELL-O, but I'm still experimenting.
David Hazelwood, Cortner Mill Restaurant cookbook, 2009

COCKTAIL SAUCE FOR SHRIMP

1 cup mayonnaise	1 teaspoon lemon juice
2 Tablespoons catsup	2 Tablespoons thick cream
2 Tablespoons chili sauce	
1 Tablespoon tarragon vinegar	

Combine the ingredients, whipping in the cream, and turn over chilled shrimp. Sufficient for 8 cocktails. Allow 6 shrimp for each cocktail unless a very heavy dinner is following. If that is the case, then 3 or 4 will be enough.
200 years of Charleston Cooking, 1930

COCKTAIL SAUCE

A most delectable cocktail sauce for shrimp is made by adding to 1 cup of mayonnaise to about 1/2 cup chili sauce. Have this thoroughly chilled and, just before serving, thin it out with a little cream.

NOTE: Totally marvelous!
The Savannah Cook Book, 1933

RAISIN SAUCE FOR HAM

1 cup raisins	1 teaspoon cornstarch	1 Tablespoon vinegar
1 cup water	1/4 teaspoon salt	1/4 teaspoon
5 cloves	pinch of pepper	Worcestershire sauce
3/4 cup brown sugar	1 Tablespoon butter	

Cover raisins with water, add cloves and simmer 10 minutes. Then add sugar, cornstarch, salt and pepper which have already been mixed together. Stir until slightly thickened and then add the remaining ingredients.
The Southern Cookbook, 1939

RAISIN SAUCE

3/4 cup sugar	2 Tablespoons butter	1/2 teaspoon salt
1 Tablespoon corn starch	2 Tablespoons vinegar	1/4 teaspoon cloves
1/2 cup orange juice	1/2 teaspoon	1 cup currant jelly
3/4 cup raisins	Worcestershire sauce	

Combine sugar, corn starch and orange juice. Bring to a boil; add all other ingredients. Heat to simmering and cook for about 10 minutes. Serve hot with ham or ham balls. Makes 3 cups.
Roaena Goodman, The Nashville Cookbook, 1977

LOUISIANA POULTRY SAUCE (Sauce Poulette)

1 1/2 cups chicken broth or stock	2 teaspoons flour
1 medium onion sliced	1 Tablespoon butter
2 Tablespoons chopped celery	2 teaspoons tarragon vinegar
Salt and pepper to taste	2 teaspoons chopped parsley
2 egg yolks	

Place soup stock into saucepan with onion, celery, salt, and pepper and boil 4 minutes. Mix egg yolks with flour and, when well mixed, add a teaspoon of cold stock, pour contents of saucepan over egg mixture very slowly, place back on heat and let thicken, stirring fast and evenly, so that sauce will not curdle. Add butter, vinegar, and parsley and stir until butter melts. Strain into a gravy dish.
The Southern Cookbook, 1939

TARTAR SAUCE

1 cup mayonnaise dressing
1 Tablespoon chopped capers
1 Tablespoon tarragon vinegar
1 Tablespoon chopped olives
1 Tablespoon cucumber pickles

Add all the ingredients together.

NOTE: Serve cold with fish or cold meat dishes. Add minced chives or onions if desired.
The Settlement Cookbook, 1940

TARTAR SAUCE

2 hard-cooked eggs
6 to 8 capers
3 Tablespoons oil
2 Tablespoons prepared mustard
1 Tablespoon lemon juice
salt, nutmeg and black pepper to taste

Chop the eggs very fine and mix with oil, blending well until a smooth paste is formed. Add the mustard and blend again. Chop the capers. Add lemon juice, seasonings, and capers to egg paste. Set in bowl of ice and blend well. Chill for 20 minutes.
Cooked to Your Taste, 1945

SHRIMP SAUCE (To be served with fish)

1 1/2 cups chopped cooked shrimp
3 Tablespoons lemon juice
salt and pepper to taste
1 1/2 cups white sauce
2 hard cooked eggs

Soak shrimp in lemon juice one-half hour and add them to white sauce; when ready to serve add the finely chopped hard cooked eggs and a little minced parsley. Pour this mixture over the fish.
The Southern Cookbook, 1939

SHRIMP CREOLE SAUCE

2 Tablespoons butter or margarine
1/4 cup chopped onion
1/4 chopped green pepper
10 1/2 ounces condensed tomato soup
1/4 teaspoon salt
dash of pepper
1 teaspoon sugar
5 ounce can of shrimp, drained

Melt butter in a saucepan, add onion and pepper. Cook until green pepper is soft. Stir in undiluted soup, salt, pepper, and sugar. Simmer until thick, about 45 minutes. Just before serving, add the cleaned shrimp and then heat. Makes about 1 1/2 cups.

NOTE: This sauce is often used with or on omelets or as a stand-alone sauce. It's a pretty good idea to prepare this sauce before starting an omelet.
Farm Journal's Country Cook Book, 1959

SEAFOOD SAUCE

1/2 cup chili sauce (page 269)	1/4 teaspoon salt
1/3 cup ketchup	2 Tablespoons lemon juice
1 cup prepared horseradish	1/8 teaspoon pepper
1 1/2 teaspoons Worcestershire sauce	1/4 cup minced celery

Combine all ingredients. Place in jar, cover and chill before serving. If a milder sauce is preferred, substitute 1/4 cup pureed tomato sauce for half the chili sauce. Makes 1 1/2 cups.
Farm Journal's Country Cook Book, 1959

SAUCE FOR FISH

A wonderful sauce for fish is made by mixing together 1 Tablespoon of Worcestershire sauce, 1 Tablespoon tarragon vinegar, 1 Tablespoon lemon juice, 2 Tablespoons butter, and salt and pepper to taste.
The Savannah Cook Book, 1933

TOMATO SAUCE FOR BAKED FISH

1/4 cup cooking oil	#2 can tomatoes	cayenne pepper, cloves and thyme
2 large onions, sliced	1/2 cup sherry	
2 Tablespoons flour		

Heat the oil in a saucepan and add the onions. Cook until tender and golden brown. Then stir in the flour and add the tomatoes through a sieve. Bring to a boiling point stirring constantly, and then add the cooking sherry. Season to taste with the cayenne pepper, a few cloves and a little thyme if desired. Let season about three minutes and pour over the baked fish.
200 Years of Charleston Cooking, 1930

SHRIMP SAUCE FOR FISH

Grind up 1 dozen shrimp and mix with 1 cup drawn butter, 1 spoon of vinegar, and salt and pepper to taste. Boil up once and then serve.
The Savannah Cook Book, 1933

CRANBERRY SAUCE

1 quart cranberries	2 cups sugar	2 cups water

Boil water and sugar to a syrup about 10 minutes, add cranberries, washed and picked over. Cover at first and cook until cranberries are clear. Serve cold alongside meat and poultry.
The Settlement Cookbook, 1940

BLACKENING SPICE MIX

1/3 cup plus 1 Tablespoon salt
1/3 cup plus 1 Tablespoon paprika,
1/3 cup cayenne pepper
1/4 cup black pepper

1/4 cup garlic powder
3 Tablespoons granulated onion (optional)
2 Tablespoons thyme

Combine all ingredients and mix thoroughly. Store in tightly covered container. Mix keeps indefinitely. Heat the skillet over high heat. Add clarified butter and when it is ready to smoke, add the item to be cooked which has been coated with the blackening spices.

NOTE: My interpretation of blackening is that the spices are cooked to between browned and burnt, rather than burning the meat cooked. An iron skillet should be used. I normally blacken swordfish, salmon, grouper, snapper or drum; but we have also blackened steaks at the customer's request.
Bill Hall, Cortner Mill Restaurant cookbook, 2009

MINT SAUCE

1/4 chopped mint leaves
1/2 cup cider vinegar

1 Tbl. powdered confectioners' sugar
or 1/2 cup strained honey

Add sugar to vinegar; when dissolved pour over the mint and let stand 30 minutes over slow fire to infuse flavors. If the vinegar is strong, you can dilute with water. Serve hot over hot lamb or boil sugar and vinegar, throw in the mint leaves and let boil up once. A few drops of mint extract may be added to vinegar and sugar instead of boiling. Set aside and serve cold with lamb. Delicious!
The Settlement Cookbook, 1940

SAUCE FOR MUTTON OR LAMB   (Sauce Béarnaise)

Warm together 1 Tablespoon Worcestershire sauce, 2 Tablespoons wine, 1 teaspoon butter, 1 teaspoon mustard, salt and pepper to taste, and a little gravy in which the meat has been cooked.
The Savannah Cook Book, 1933

FROZEN MINT ICE FOR ROAST LAMB

5 sprays of fresh mint
1/2 cup lemon juice
1/2 cup confectioners' sugar

4 cups water
1/4 teaspoon peppermint extract
green vegetable coloring

Wash and pick the mint from the stems and soak these in lemon juice for ½ hour, strain. Dissolve 1/2 cup sugar in 4 cups water and add this to the strained lemon/mint juice. Just before freezing add the peppermint extract and coloring. Freeze as a water ice.
The Southern Cookbook, 1939

STEAK RUB

1 teaspoon black pepper
1 Tablespoon dry ground mustard
1 Tablespoon garlic powder
1 Tablespoon onion powder
3/4 teaspoon lemon pepper
3/4 teaspoon ground rosemary
1/2 teaspoon salt

Blend all ingredients thoroughly and store in a tightly closed container for up to 3 months. Sprinkle liberally on steaks, approximately 1/2 Tablespoon per side of a 10-ounce T-bone, before grilling.

NOTE: I've never understood why cooks season every other cut of meat or fish, but when it comes to beef steaks, it's just thrown onto the grill and onto the plate. I love the natural flavors of beef, but I like them even more when they are enhanced with just the right seasoning. Use this rub or come up with a combination of your own.
David Hazelwood, Cortner Mill Restaurant cookbook, 2009

STEAK MARINADE

2 cups Worcestershire sauce
2 Tablespoons garlic, minced
1 teaspoon rosemary leaves
1 Tablespoon red wine vinegar

Combine all the ingredients. Can be stored in refrigerator for several weeks. One hour before grilling steaks, place steaks in shallow pan and pour marinade over steaks. After 30 minutes, turn steaks over in the marinade. Grill steaks to the desired degree. Dispose of the used marinade.
David Hazelwood, Cortner Mill Restaurant cookbook, 2009

STEAK SAUCE SUPREME

1/4 cup vinegar
1/4 cup oil
2 Tablespoons minced onion
1/2 teaspoon salt
1/2 teaspoon dry mustard
dash each of mace, nutmeg, cloves
1/2 clove of garlic, crushed

Mix together all the ingredients. Marinate sirloins or T-bones 1 or 2 hours before broiling or grilling. Spoon the sauce on meat as it broils.
Farm Journal's Country Cook Book, 1959

HOT DRESSING FOR GAME

Rub together a heaping Tablespoon butter, 1 Tablespoon flour, and 1/2 pint broth (or canned bouillon), 1 teaspoon mushrooms, a little Worcestershire sauce, 2 teaspoons of lemon juice, and 2 Tablespoons cream. Put into a double boiler and stir in lightly beaten yolks of 2 eggs. Stew all together, but do not boil.
The Savannah Cook Book, 1933

APPLE BALL SAUCE FOR GOOSE OR SUCKLING

1 cup sugar
1 cup water
4 cloves
grated rind of 1/2 lemon
1 1/2 cups apple balls

Make a syrup of the sugar and water, adding the lemon peel and cloves. Cook for several minutes, remove the lemon rind and cloves and drop in the apples, which have been cut into balls with a potato cutter. Cook until apples are done.

NOTE: Serve with poultry, roasts, or goose too!
The Southern Cookbook, 1939

SAUCE FOR GAME

1 stick broken cinnamon, a little lemon peel, 1 1/2 glasses port, 1 Tablespoon brown sugar, a few cloves and 1/2 glass currant jelly. Put spices, lemon, sugar and wine into a sauce pan to heat, not boil. Strain this over jelly and let boil up once before serving.
The Savannah Cook Book, 1933

GEORGE ATHERTON'S BARBEQUE SAUCE

16 ounces vinegar
1 ½ Tablespoons lemon juice
3 ½ Tablespoons Worcestershire sauce
1 ¼ teaspoons Frank's Hot Sauce
8 ounces ketchup
1 ½ Tablespoons light brown sugar
5 Tablespoons butter
1 teaspoon salt
½ teaspoon black pepper
2 ounces beer

Combine all ingredients, except beer in stock pot and bring to a boil. Lower to simmer. Add beer. Simmer 3 to 4 hours until ready to use. Salt and pepper 14 chicken thighs liberally. Cook chickens over slow grill for about 2 to 2 ½ hours. Turn chickens and dip into sauce every half hour. At end of cooking allow sauce on chickens to dry.

NOTE: George was Buford, Kentucky's grill master. In the 1960s he started barbequing rabbits for the church's annual Thanksgiving Rabbit Supper. It was the culmination of a contest among local hunters to see who could contribute the most rabbits to the meal. As expected, the local rabbit population soon dwindled and George had to supplement them with chicken. Everyone was glad he did, especially the rabbits. -David H.
From George Atherton by way of Joey Hazelwood

OVER-THE-COALS COOKERY

"The only time to eat diet food is while you are waiting for the steak to cook."
-Julia Child (1912-2004)

Outdoor eating and cooking have become a desired pass time of the American family and now it is even more so with outdoor grills becoming so advanced, affordable, and readily available. Old-time picnics are giving way to meals served on the porch, deck, or just wherever you find the nearest breeze. Food seems to have a way of disappearing faster because it just tastes extra-good combined with fresh air.

More and more American backyards are providing proof that the family has succumbed to the gentle nudge to cook meals out-of-doors. The flavors of the foods that go together with the cooking and eating out in the fresh air are hard to match. Different types of dishes lend themselves to cooking over the coals. Below, we have provided some special and super delicious recipes for the grill to add to your traditional family favorites. There are or course many, countless more recipes. This is the South remember?

Our own backyard gardens, our weekend neighborhood farmers' markets, the summer fresh produce from our supermarkets or roadside stands, offer so many choices of fresh vegetables to be grilled for the most delicious and delectable dishes that you can imagine. Books could be written, and have been, just on this one topic. Besides the advent of spring and summer flowers, warmer weather, and daylight savings time; there is the belief that the garden will shortly come to life and soon fresh vegetables will be available to be picked, cooked, and grilled. The Easter Bunny equals garden vegetables and the ensuing fabulous tastes for the coming season.

OLD-FASHIONED HAMBURGERS

1 pound ground beef
2 Tablespoons chopped onion
1 teaspoon salt
1 teaspoon Worcestershire sauce
1 Tablespoon prepared mustard
4 sandwich buns

Mix together the ground beef, onion salt, Worcestershire sauce and mustard. Form into 4 hamburger patties about 1/2 to 3/4 inch thick. Grill over hot coals until done the way you like it. Serve on warm, split and toasted buns.
Easy-on-the-Cookbook, 1960

BARBECUE SAUCE

1/2 cup catsup
2 Tablespoons chopped onion
1 tablespoon Worcestershire sauce
1 Tablespoon brown sugar
1 teaspoon dry mustard
4 drops Tabasco

Combine catsup and the remaining ingredients. 8 servings.
Easy-on-the-Cookbook, 1960

BEEF SHISH KABOBS WITH VARIATIONS

Beef sirloin steak cut about 1/2 inch thick. Allow 1/3 to 1/2 pound per person counting bone and fat weight or about 1/4 pound per person trimmed. Cut meat into large cubes.

Mushrooms not required, but they are a wonderful flavor addition. Allow one or two per person. (One pound of mushrooms is enough for 8 to 10 people).

Onions, one medium size, whole onion per person. Par boil about 15 minutes in boiling water (add 1 teaspoon salt per quart of water). Drain well. Or cut large Spanish onions into 1/2 inch slices to be grilled raw.

Tomatoes, medium to small, 1 per person. Wash and remove stem ends. Grill these whole; or if the tomatoes are large, cut into halves or quarters.

Skewers rubbed with paper towels dipped in oil for easier handling. Spear cubes of steak, mushrooms and onions onto skewers and take turns at the seasonings. Brush beef with *Garlic Dressing* or season with salt and pepper; brush mushrooms and onions with melted butter or margarine.

Hold kabobs over fire, turning until cooked just the way you like it. Place tomato chunks onto the end of the skewer for the last 5 to 10 minutes of cooking time. Rest point of skewer on plate and push off grilled food with a fork.

CHARCOAL GRILLED STEAK

1 porterhouse steak, 1 1/2 inches thick	salt pepper	garlic salt (optional) butter

Slash the fat edge of the steak at 2 inch intervals. Top off the hot ash from the coals to increase the heat. Place steak on the grill over the hot coals. Grill 8 to 10 minutes on first side; season. Turn. Grill 6 to 8 minutes on second side for medium rare. Season. Top with butter just before serving. Allow 3/4 pound of uncooked beef per serving.
Easy-on-the-Cookbook, 1960

SIN FILLET

6-8 ounce filet mignon steak	1 Tablespoon salt
1/2 cup sweet onion, sliced	1 ounce Boursin cheese

Grill the steak to your desired degree of doneness. While the steak is grilling, sauté the onions in butter until caramelized. Place the cheese on top of the steak, then the onions, and then serve to the wonderful fanfare.

NOTE: The sin is in the Bour-sin, not in any culinary transgression.
David Hazelwood, Cortner Mill Restaurant cookbook, 2009

GARLIC DRESSING FOR BEEF

Chop fine 4 cloves of garlic. Add Tablespoon of salt. Continue chopping until garlic and salt are a pulpy mess. Add 2 Tablespoons lemon juice, 2 teaspoons Worcestershire sauce and 1/4 cup oil. Blend well. Brush over skewered steak cubes just before grilling/broiling.
Farm Journal's Country Cookbook, 1959

FLANK STEAK PINWHEELS

2 1/2 pounds flank steak   salt & pepper

Diagonally score flank steaks on both sides, forming a diamond shape pattern in the meat. Brush barbecue sauce on top of steaks. Starting from the side, roll each steak jelly-roll fashion, fastening at 1-inch intervals with metal skewers. Slice between the skewers. Grill the resulting "pinwheels" 4 to 5 inches from the glowing coals. Grill on one side about 10 minutes; turn and season with salt and pepper. Brush barbecue sauce on top of pinwheels. Grill second side 5 to 6 minutes for rare, about 10 minutes for medium and 15 minutes for well done.
Easy-on-the-Cook Book, 1960

PORK CHOPS WITH CHERRY BARBECUE

4 boneless pork loin chops, 1-inch thick   1/4 cup fresh squeezed orange juice
2 Tablespoons brown sugar   2 teaspoons chili powder
2 Tablespoons extra-virgin olive oil   1 teaspoon cumin

In a small bowl combine all the ingredients for the marinade and stir together. Place the chops in a re-sealable freezer bag and pour in the marinade, making sure to coat the meat on all sides. Keep cold in a refrigerator for at least 4 hours and up to 24 hours. Remove the chops from the marinade and grill over medium heat for about 6 minutes per side. Remove from the grill and serve immediately with Cherry Barbecue Sauce. Serves 4

CHERRY BARBECUE SAUCE

1 medium onion   1/2 cup fresh squeezed orange juice
3 cloves garlic   1/2 cup ketchup
1 Tablespoon chili powder   1/4 cup light brown sugar
2 cups tomatoes, crushed and canned   1 cup frozen sweet cherries

In medium saucepan cook the onion over medium heat until it softens, about 8 minutes. Add the garlic and chili powder and cook 1 minute more. Add the tomatoes, orange juice, ketchup, sugar, and cherries and cook 5 minutes more, stirring frequently. Transfer the mixture to a blender and blend until smooth. Transfer to a plastic container and keep cold in refrigerator until ready to use or for up to one week.
Mario Batali, Mario Tailgates NASCAR Style, by way of Cortner Mill Restaurant cookbook, 2009

GRILLED SAUSAGE, TOMATOES AND PORTOBELLO MUSHROOMS (A pasta dish)

1 pound sweet mild Italian sausage	1 teaspoon garlic, minced
2 pounds tomatoes, halved	1/4 teaspoon pepper
1 large portobello mushroom	1/4 teaspoon thyme
1 Tablespoon vegetable oil	16 ounces pasta, cooked (rigatoni or corkscrew)
1/2 teaspoon salt	
2 Tablespoons olive oil	

Grill sausage until done, approximately 15-20 minutes. Prick with fork. Grill tomatoes and mushrooms, 8-10 minutes, brushing with vegetable oil and salt. Chop and slice tomatoes, sausage and mushrooms. Toss with olive oil, garlic, salt, pepper and thyme. Toss with pasta and serve.
Helen Vento, Fruit of the Spirit, Mt Bethel United Methodist Church, Marietta, GA

PORK CHOP WITH BALSAMIC SAGE

10 ounce pork loin chop	salt
1 teaspoon ground sage	black pepper
balsamic vinegar	

Sprinkle each side of the chop with balsamic vinegar. Sprinkle and press remaining seasoning onto each side of chop. Grill and serve
David Hazelwood, The Cortner Mill Restaurant Cookbook, 2009

HONEYED HAM SLICES

6 slices pre-cooked lean ham, about ½-inch thick   3/4 cup Honey Glaze

When coals are white with ashes, place heavy duty metal foil on top of grill. Lay the ham slices on the foil; broil on one side about 20 minutes.
Turn ham; grill about 10 minutes. Brush generously with glaze and cook until ham looks shiny. Makes 6 to 8 servings.

HONEY GLAZE

Combine 1/2 cup honey, 1/2 cup brown sugar, 2 Tablespoons flour and enough pineapple juice (about 2 Tablespoons), orange juice, or apricot nectar to make smooth paste. Makes about 1 cup.

MUSTARD GLAZE

Combine 1/2 cup brown sugar, 2 Tablespoons flour and 1 teaspoon dry mustard. Rub into both sides of ham slices before grilling.
Farm Journal's Country Cookbook, 1959

GRILLED ITALIAN CHICKEN BREASTS

4 whole, skinless chicken breasts	1 teaspoon garlic salt
1 gallon-size Ziploc bag	1 teaspoon extra virgin olive oil
1/2 cup lite (not fat free) Italian salad dressing	pinch of lemon pepper seasoning
	pinch of oregano
2 teaspoons A-1 Steak Sauce	pinch of salt and pepper

Place the chicken in a plastic bag. Mix all the other ingredients, then pour into bag over chicken. Let stand in refrigerator overnight, turning occasionally. Light coals and wait until they are glowing red and covered with white ash. Place chicken on grill grate, that has been brushed with oil. Flip chicken once (usually about 10 minutes) halfway through cooking time. Remove from the grill, when the chicken is no longer pink inside. This chicken is very juicy and moist! Great for low cholesterol diets. Can be made ahead.
Shelley Prevost, Fruit of the Spirit, Mt Bethel United Methodist Church, Marietta, GA

CHARCOAL-BROILED CHICKEN

4 broilers (not over 2 1/2 pounds each)   Golden Ember Sauce

Split chickens in half lengthwise. Brush generously on both sides with Golden Ember Sauce. Let the flavors penetrate for several hours or overnight. Store in refrigerator.

Place on grill, hollow side down, over coals white with ash (intense heat must have subsided). Cook for 20-25 minutes; brush with sauce and turn. Cook 20 or more minutes until chicken is tender. To check for doneness, grasp end of leg. If leg joint moves easily, meat is done. If your cooking fire is too hot, the chicken will have a charred coating before the chicken is done, so beware. Each half of chicken should serve 1 adult or two children.

GOLDEN EMBER SAUCE

Combine 3/4 cup oil, 1/4 cup melted butter or margarine, 1/4 cup lemon juice, 1 Tablespoon prepared mustard, 2 Tablespoons brown sugar, 1 Tablespoon salt, 1 teaspoon paprika, 1/4 teaspoon pepper, 2 teaspoon grated onion, 2 cloves garlic cut in half, 1/2 teaspoon Worcestershire sauce, 1/4 teaspoon Tabasco sauce and 1/4 cup ketchup. Mix in a jar or bottle by shaking thoroughly. Let stand several hours before using.

Shake well before brushing on chicken.

NOTE: Another method of cooking is to brush with sauce often and turn chicken every 10 minutes.
Farm Journal's Country Cookbook, 1959

DILLY BARBECUED CHICKEN

1/2 cup butter	2 teaspoons dill weed
2 teaspoons salt	2- 1 1/2 to 2 1/2 pound broiler/fryer
1 teaspoon paprika	chickens (cut into halves or quarters)

To make sauce, melt butter in saucepan. Add salt, paprika and dill weed; blend well. To prepare chicken for grilling, break joints between drumstick and thigh, where the thigh joins the body and where the wing is attached to the breast. Pull leg and wing close to the body and use skewers to hold in place. Brush chicken generously with sauce before and during cooking. Grill over hot coals 50-60 minutes or until well done, turning frequently. To test for doneness, cut slash in thigh next to bone. There should be no trace of pink. Makes 4 servings.
Easy-on-the-Cookbook, 1960

BEST GRILLED SALMON

salmon filets for 4	1 good-sized fresh ginger root
1/3 cup soy sauce	peeled, grated, or shredded

Peel most of the brown outer skin off the ginger root (don't have to be neat here) and then grate or shred finely until you have 1/3 cup of grated ginger (keep as much juice as you can as this has lots of flavor). Put the ginger in a large Zip-Loc bag. Rinse the fillets and pat dry. Put them in the bag and rub the ginger into the fish. Add the soy sauce. Let this sit until the grill gets hot.

Take out the filets and grill first with skin up. When ready (about 5-7 minutes, depending on how hot the grill is and how thick the filets are, etc.) turn and pour some of the soy and ginger over the tops and continue grilling until cooked to your taste.

NOTE: The seared ginger adds to the taste and, depending on how hot the grill is, will add a ginger smoke flavor as well. Cooking over charcoal always adds to the flavor of anything grilled.
Jim Williams, Fruit of the Spirit, Mt Bethel United Methodist Church, Marietta, GA

SKEWERED FISH STEAKS

1 pound fish steaks, fresh or frozen,	2 green or red peppers, cut into 8 pieces 1
cut into ½-inch squares	½-inch squares
1/4 cup French dressing	1 can (2 cups) onions

Marinate fish squares with French dressing in refrigerator at least 1 hour. Alternate fish with vegetables on 4 skewers. Grill over hot coals about 20 minutes; baste with French dressing once or twice. For indoor cooking, cook on a rotisserie or broil skewered fish. 4 servings.
Easy-on-the-Cookbook, 1960

FOIL FISH FRY

Shape a large shallow pan from heavy-duty aluminum foil by turning up the edges and overlapping the corners. Place on the grill over a medium hot fire. Add butter, margarine or some other fat to the pan. Remove fish and roll in seasoned flour (equal parts cornmeal and flour give a crisp coating). Fry until golden brown, turning once or twice.
Farm Journal's Country Cookbook, 1959

LAMB KABOBS

1 1/2 pounds lamb shoulder	1/4 cup ketchup
2/3 cup oil	1 clove garlic cut in half
1/2 cup lemon juice	2 onions, sliced
2 teaspoons salt	1/2 pound mushrooms
1/4 teaspoon pepper	

Cut lamb into 1-inch cubes. Combine the remaining ingredients except the mushrooms; pour over the lamb. Let stand at minimum 1 hour or overnight in the refrigerator. Alternate lamb and mushrooms on metal skewers (about 6 skewers). Allow space between pieces for thorough cooking. Grill/broil 3 inches from source of heat, about 15 minutes. Turn to brown evenly.

Arrange tomato wedges, cooked small onions and green peppers on additional skewers. Cook these the last 5 to 10 minutes. Turn to brown. Makes 6 servings.
Farm Journal's Country Cookbook, 1959

GRILLED DUCK WITH MUSCADINE

1 duck breast	black pepper
salt	1/4 cup muscadine jam

Split breast into two halves and cut slits 1/2 inch apart in skin. Sprinkle with salt and pepper. Grill over high heat for 4 minutes per side. Cut each breast half on the bias into 1/4-inch slices. Plate each breast half on a bed of rice. Heat jam in a saucepan and pour over breasts. Serves 2.
David Hazelwood, Cortner Mill Restaurant cookbook, 2009

FRANKFURTERS IN HERB BUNS

1 pound frankfurters	3 green onions, finely chopped
1/2 cup butter	10 frankfurter buns, split
1/2 teaspoon rubbed sage	

Place franks (hot dogs) on open grill over hot coals. Turn while they cook to brown evenly. Blend butter, sage and green onions thoroughly and spread on buns and place split side down on the grill and toast lightly. Serve the hot franks in toasted buns. 10 servings.
Easy-on-the-Cookbook, 1960

FANCY FRANKFURTERS (Hot Dogs)

Split frankfurters lengthwise, but not quite split in two. Spoon ketchup into cavities and then add thin slices of cheese. Wrap slice of bacon around each frankfurter; fasten with toothpick. Slowly grill over embers, turning to cook bacon. When finished serve in long buns.
Farm Journal's Country Cookbook, 1959

SPECIAL FRANKS (Hot Dogs)

1 pound franks	3 large dill pickles cut into strips
2 Tablespoons prepared mustard	8 slices bacon

Slit franks length wise. Spread with the mustard and insert pickle. Wrap franks spiral fashion with bacon strip; fasten with toothpick. Grill/broil until bacon is crisp. Remove toothpicks before serving. Makes 6 servings.
Farm Journal's Country Cookbook, 1959

HOW TO GRILL VEGETABLES FOR AMAZING FLAVOR

- Make room on the grill for veggies. The caramelizing flames and the touch of smoke do wonders for vegetables.
- Lots of veggies do well on the grill, but some really stand out: asparagus, corn, eggplant, mushrooms, peppers (bell or hot), onions, even cabbage.
- Most vegetables cook better on the grill and less likely to stick if they are marinated first or brushed lightly with olive oil or cooking oil. For added flavor, sprinkle grilled vegetables with fresh herbs, a little salt, or pepper.
- Cut larger veggies, like eggplant, squash, zucchini and onions, into smaller pieces. With more surface area touching the grill, they will pick up yummier grilled flavor.
- Small vegetables like cherry tomatoes or sliced veggies work best threaded through kabobs. You can also wrap vegetables in heavy duty foil, though cooking in foil cuts back on that appealing smoky flavor.
- Keep a close eye on your vegetables. Grilling times vary from veggie to veggie, but they are generally more delicate than meats. Harder vegetables like potatoes will take a little longer to cook on the grill.
- Corn is perfect for grilling and it even comes in its own wrapper (husk).
- Corn's companion, the tomato, might not seem well-suited for grilling, but it grills very well. Grilling also brings out the best in mushrooms, especially portobellas.
- While you're tossing veggies on the grill, add some pizza dough for a super-quick dinner and the best homemade and healthy pizza going, grilled pizza.
- Most vegetables love the grill, but a few like cucumbers, celery, and most leafy greens don't do as well because of their high-water content; although, you can grill Romaine lettuce with excellent results!"
http://dish.allrecipes.com/grilling-101-grilled-vegetables/

BAKED POTATO SLICES

8 medium or large baking potatoes
1/2 cup soft butter or margarine
Salt or seasoned salt

Scrub and dry potatoes well. Cut into ¾-inch crosswise slices. Brush all surfaces with soft butter; sprinkle with salt (about 1 teaspoon for each potato).

Put potatoes back together and wrap each tightly in a square of heavy-duty foil. Grill/broil over coals about 1 hour or until soft. Unwrap and eat with fingers, delicious finger food, or forks. Makes 6 to 8 servings.
Farm Journal's Country Cookbook, 1959

BAKED POTATOES

Select medium-size baking potatoes. Wrap them in double layers of foil. Place directly on top of the coals. Turn the potatoes several times; pierce with a fork through the foil to tell when done. Serve hot with foil-roasted corn.
Easy-on-the-Cook Book, 1960

CORN ON THE COB

Remove the silk from the corn by turning back the husks. Dip corn in water. After doing this, replace the inner husks. Wrap corn in foil. Place the corn on the grill, turn often. Roast about 20 to 30 minutes. Serve with plenty of butter, salt and pepper.

If desired, corn can be husked before grilling. Spread the corn with butter, sprinkle with salt. Wrap the prepared corn in foil. Place over the hot coals about 10 to 15 minutes, turning several times.
Easy-on-the-Cook Book, 1960

GRILLED ROQUEFORT TOMATOES

3 large tomatoes
3 teaspoons Roquefort or bleu cheese

Cut tomatoes in half, crosswise and place each half in the center of a square of heavy aluminum foil. Spread 1/2 teaspoon cheese over the cut surfaces. Seal foil securely and grill over hot coals for about 5 minutes. 6 servings.
Easy-on-the-Cookbook, 1960

CHEESE TOMATOES

4 medium tomatoes, washed and cut in half
1/4 cup shredded cheese

Use shallow foil trays or make trays from aluminum foil. Place tomatoes, cut side up, in a tray; sprinkle with cheese. Heat on the grill 10 minutes. Makes 4 servings.
Easy-on-the-Cookbook, 1960

GRILLED FRENCH TOAST WITH BACON

2 eggs, slightly beaten
2/3 cup milk
1/2 teaspoon salt
dash pepper

12 slices bread
12 slices bacon, cut in half crosswise
maple syrup

Combine eggs, milk, salt and pepper in a shallow pie pan. Quickly dip each slice of bread into egg mixture, turning them to coat both sides. Place in a long-handled, broiler/toaster and top with 2 half slices of bacon, side by side. Brown both sides of bread over hot coals, toasting the side with bacon last. Serve hot with maple syrup. 6 servings.
Easy-on-the-Cook Book, 1960

SOME-MORES

Graham crackers
thin sweet chocolate

hot toasted marshmallow

Arrange a piece of the thin sweet chocolate on graham cracker, put hot toasted marshmallow on chocolate, then cover with another graham cracker. Press the two crackers together. The hot marshmallow melts the chocolate to form a delicious dessert sandwich.

NOTE: This is a long-time children's delight, but grown-ups love them also.
Farm Journal's Country Cookbook, 1959

ANGELS ON WINGS

12- 3/8 inch slices angel food cake
6- 7/8 ounce milk chocolate bars without nuts cut into 2-inch squares

12 marshmallows

Using a long-handled wire grill, fork or skewer, hold cake slices over coals until toasted on both sides. Toast marshmallows over the coals. For each serving, place a square of chocolate on each hot cake slice. Top with 2 hot marshmallows, then place another square of chocolate and another toasted cake slice on top. Press the cake slices together. 6 servings.
Easy-on-the-Cookbook, 1960

NOTES

BREADS, BISCUITS & STUFFINGS

"Here is bread, which strengthens man's heart, and therefore is called the staff of Life."
-Matthew Henry (1662-1714) "Commentaries" Psalm CIV

"The history of the world is the record of man in quest of his daily bread and butter."
Hendrick Van Loon (1882-1944)

Breads are festive. Even the simplest biscuit, freshly baked and served with butter and your favorite jam or jelly, is an adventure in pleasurable eating. Any meal is made more notable and unique by the addition of a wonderful biscuit, corn bread, hot roll, and hot bread or muffin. A meal at a Southern table is never complete without delicious bread; the staff of life.

Many characteristics of Southern cooking have changed and evolved, often radically, over the millennia by way of frequent exposure to outside influences, but baking continued definitely in the original manner of preparation and cooking from its English beginnings, being brought to the New World without a great deal of evolution across the passage of time.

Few aromas coming from the kitchen can equal that of bread baking in the oven. It suggests a welcoming home with an enjoyable meal to come. As our lifestyles turn into a condition of being constantly on the go, very few have the time to bake breads regularly. Thanks to modern innovations and access to fresh bread from many different sources, home baking just isn't required. Bread, which is a life-giving staple, isn't needed to be prepared. But, sometimes, it's fun for the cook and their loved ones to have some kind of home-baked breads, biscuits, or muffins,

In the South, during the Civil War, flour became very scarce and expensive because little wheat was raised there and levies on flour brought from the North were placed on it by the Confederate Commissary. Thus, corn bread became universal instead of biscuits, rolls, or waffles.

"Carry dat load on your head, De Lord will bless your good corn bread."

BUTTERMILK CORN BREAD

1 pint corn meal
3/4 pint buttermilk
1 teaspoon salt

3/4 teaspoon baking soda
1 egg
1 large, rounded spoon shortening

Sift meal, mix with salt, egg and milk in which baking soda has been dissolved. Add, hot melted shortening and bake in greased hot iron skillet in a hot oven.
The Savannah Cook Book, 1933

DABS

1 cup corn meal
1 teaspoon lard
1 egg
1 wine glass of milk
1 teaspoon salt

Scald meal with boiling water and, while hot, rub in lard. Beat egg and add to mixture, then stir in milk and salt. Drop from spoon onto buttered pan and bake.

NOTE: This recipe was found in a very old receipt book (note "very old" written in 1933, so today that translates to "REALLY very old") and is similar to fritters, only baked not fried .
The Savannah Cook Book, 1933

TENNESSEE CORN BREAD

1 1/2 cups cornmeal
1/2 cup flour
1 teaspoon salt
1 teaspoon baking powder
1/2 teaspoon baking soda
2 eggs, lightly beaten
1 cup buttermilk
3 Tablespoons fat or cooking oil

Heat oven to 400 degrees. Sift dry ingredients into a bowl. Add eggs and buttermilk; stir just enough to blend. Heat fat in a 9-inch skillet, allowing the skillet to be completely greased. Pour excess hot fat into the corn bread batter. Pour the batter into hot skillet (Key is to make sure skillet is hot.) and bake for 25 minutes or until brown. Makes 12 pie-shaped wedges or 6 cups crumbs for cornbread dressing.

NOTE: This recipe makes an excellent bread for serving with fresh vegetables; it is also fine for making cornbread dressing. This batter may be cooked in corn stick irons for crisp corn sticks in lieu of the skillet-cooked bread.
Moiselle Peay, The Nashville Cookbook, 1977

CORN STICKS

2 cups meal
1 egg
2 teaspoons baking powder
1 cup milk
1 Tablespoon lard
1/2 teaspoon salt

Beat all together and bake in tins the shape of bread sticks or ears of corn in a quick oven (500 F) for 10-12 minutes.

NOTE: I prefer using cast iron corn stick molds to cook my corn sticks. These molds need to be heated in the oven well ahead of cooking the sticks to ensure a really good crust. A little more salt might be needed for this recipe.
The Southern Cook Book, 1939

MISS LEE'S SOUTHERN CORN BREAD

1 cup white corn meal
1/4 cup wheat flour
1 teaspoon baking powder
1/2 teaspoon salt

1 beaten egg
1/2 cup milk
1 Tablespoon melted butter

Sift together the dry ingredients; combine the milk with the egg and add to the dry ingredients. Add the melted butter and pour batter into a well-greased pan. Bake in a hot oven (425 F) about 25 minutes
The Southern Cook Book, 1935

MEXICAN CORN BREAD

1 1/2 cups grated sharp Cheddar cheese
1 1/2 cups self-rising cornmeal
1 cup buttermilk
2 eggs
1 Tablespoon chopped bell pepper

1 cup cream style corn
2 Tablespoons finely chopped hot pepper
(or 1/2 teaspoon ground red pepper)
1/2 cup cooking oil (or bacon drippings)

Heat oven to 400 F. Mix all the ingredients together except the cheese and oil. Heat oil in 8-inch iron skillet. Pour the hot oil into the batter. Stir lightly and pour one half of the mixture into the hot skillet. Sprinkle half the grated cheese on the mixture in the skillet, then pour the remaining cornmeal over this. Sprinkle the remaining cheese on top. Bake for 40 minutes. Serve hot. Serves 8.

NOTE: This bread may be varied by stirring any of the following ingredients into the batter: 1 small onion, finely chopped; chopped pimiento; garlic to taste; or one Tablespoon sugar.
Jo Ellen Hunter, The Nashville Cookbook, 1977

SCALDED CORN BALLS

1 1/4 cups corn meal
2 cups boiling water
1 teaspoon salt

Add the salt to the meal and gradually stir meal into boiling water. Mix well. Let cool. Shape into walnut size balls. Fry in 1 inch fat until golden brown, then turn over. Drain on absorbent paper. Serve hot. Yield 18 to 20 balls.
Satsuma Tea Room, Easy on the Cook-Southern Breads, 1975

CORN FRITTERS

1 cup flour
1 teaspoon baking powder
1/2 teaspoon salt
1 egg
1/4 cup milk
1/2 Tablespoon butter
1 cup drained crushed corn

Mix the dry ingredients, gradually adding the milk and the well beaten egg; beat all thoroughly and then add the melted butter and corn. Drop by spoonful into hot deep fat and fry until well browned. Drain on brown paper.
The Southern Cook Book, 1939

CORN MEAL BATTER CAKES

2 eggs
3 cups cornmeal
buttermilk
baking soda
salt to taste

Beat eggs well, stir in corn meal and enough buttermilk to make a stiff batter using 1 teaspoon of baking soda to 1 pint milk. Beat hard and bake, browning on both sides.

NOTE: Ideal when eaten with cane syrup.
The Savannah Cook Book 1933

CORN BREAD FRITTERS

1 cup corn meal
1 cup flour
1 egg
enough milk to make stiff batter
2 teaspoons baking powder
1/2 teaspoon salt

Mix the meal, flour, salt, and baking powder. Beat in the egg and add milk to make a stiff batter. Drop from a spoon into deep boiling fat and fry until golden brown. Drain on brown paper before serving.

NOTE: These fritters are delicious with soup.
The Southern Cook Book, 1939

CORN MEAL MUFFINS

1 cup corn meal
2 cups white flour
4 teaspoons baking powder
1/2 teaspoon salt
2 Tablespoons melted butter
1/2 cup sugar
1 cup milk
2 eggs, beaten

Sift all the dry ingredients into a bowl; add the milk, mixing well. Stir in the beaten eggs, add the melted butter and beat mixture vigorously for 2 minutes. Bake about 20 minutes in a hot oven (400 F) in well buttered muffin pans.

NOTE: For best results and good crisp crust, heat the pans before turning in the mixture.
The Southern Cook Book, 1939

CORN LIGHT BREAD

In Nashville, as anywhere else in the South, one finds a multitude of diverse assortments of hot freshly baked breads and their recipes that are broadly sought after. Immeasurable bounties of infinite savors and types of breads, from the simple hush puppies to the professed gourmet varieties of breads, are obtainable. Corn meal breads, often from recipes dating to our beginnings, are tasty accompaniments to the wealth of vegetables and meats enjoyed in the area. One such specialty bread almost always on hand at barbeques is *corn light bread*. Most people now choose to make the quick version of this bread rather than the following recipe below which dates back about more than 175 years.

CORN LIGHT BREAD (19TH century version)

Let 1 quart of water boil. Slowly add 1 1/3 cups meal and cook to mush. Cool. Add 1 cup cold water and stir in 1 1/3 cups meal. (1/2 cup flour may also be added for a finer texture) Cover and set in warm place overnight. In the morning stir in 3/4 to 1 cup sugar or sorghum molasses or a mixture of both, 1 teaspoon of soda which has been dissolved in 1 cup buttermilk, 1 Tablespoon salt, 1 egg, and 2 1/2 cups meal. In a large bread pan put 1/2 cup lard. Heat in the oven as you would for making corn bread; add the melted lard to the batter mixture. Stir and pour the batter into the hot greased bread pan. Bake at 350 degrees for about 1 hour or until well done, brown and crisp on top. The loaf will crack on top. Cool before slicing.
Commentary, The Nashville Cookbook, 1977

CORN LIGHT BREAD

1 cup meal
1 cup flour
1/2 cup sugar
1/2 teaspoon salt
2 teaspoons baking powder

1 egg, beaten
1 1/4 cups buttermilk
1 Tablespoon melted shortening or cooking oil

Heat oven to 400. Heat and grease an iron skillet to give a crispy, crusty crust on this dense southern bread. (I like to use a loaf bread pan to cook my corn light bread to make my slicing easier, but the skillet works great. The end result is just round.) Mix all the dry ingredients. Add beaten egg to the buttermilk; add melted shortening. Combine all the ingredients and turn into the greased hot skillet or bread pan. Bake about 25 minutes or until done. Makes 1 loaf.

NOTE: Slices well, but cool before slicing. A perfect companion for barbeque and barbeques!
Mary Stanfill, The Nashville Cookbook, 1977

QUICK CORN LIGHT BREAD

3 cups self-rising corn meal
1 1/2 cups self-rising flour
1/2 teaspoon salt
1 cup sugar

2 Tablespoons cooking oil or melted shortening
3 cups buttermilk

Heat oven to 450 degrees. Generously grease and heat a 10-ounce iron skillet. In a mixing bowl combine meal, flour, salt and sugar. Add shortening and buttermilk. Mix lightly and pour into hot skillet. Cook for 10 minutes at 450; reduce heat to 375 and cook 50-60 minutes or until golden brown and firm. Turn out and cool completely before slicing. Serves 10-12.

NOTE: Corn light bread has been served traditionally at Middle Tennessee barbeques. In the "olden days" corn light bread was made up at night and allowed to set overnight to "sour." It was cooked early in the morning for the noon and evening meals. This quick version recipe can be kept wrapped and served several days after baking or frozen to have later.
Sandra C. Fleming, The Nashville Cookbook, 1977

SPOON CORN BREAD

2 cups water ground meal
1 teaspoon butter
1 slack Tablespoon sugar
1 teaspoon salt

1 Tablespoon lard
2 teaspoons baking powder
2 eggs
2 cups milk

Mix the lard, butter, sugar and salt with the meal. Scald with about a cup of boiling water and add milk, then the eggs, beaten lightly, and lastly the baking powder. Turn into a buttered pan or glass dish and cook for 45 minutes.

NOTE: Cold rice, hominy, or cream of wheat may be added.
The Savannah Cook Book, 1933

SOUTHERN SPOONBREAD

2 cups corn meal
1 1/2 cups sweet milk
2 cups boiling water
1 teaspoon salt

3 large Tablespoons butter (melted)
1 cup cooked rice
3 eggs

Sift the meal 3 times and dissolve in boiling water, mix until it is smooth and free from any lumps. Add the melted butter and salt. Thin with the milk. Separate the eggs; beat until light; add the yolks and then the whites. Before adding the egg whites, add the cooked rice. Pour into a buttered baking dish and bake in a moderate oven (350 F) about 30 minutes. Set casserole cooking dish.

NOTE: This dish should be served in the dish in which it is baked.
Satsuma Tea Room, Easy on the Cook-Southern Breads, 1975

SOUTHERN SPOON BREAD (One of my favorites and so unusual)

2 cups milk
1/2 cup corn meal
1 teaspoon salt
1/4 teaspoon baking powder

3 egg yolks
2 Tablespoons butter
3 egg whites

Scald milk, add corn meal, and cook until mixture is very thick. Add salt and baking powder. Beat egg yoks until light and add a small amount of corn-meal mixture and then combine both mixtures. Add butter and fold in egg whites beaten to soft peak stage. Turn into buttered 1 1/2-quart casserole dish and bake uncovered in a moderate oven (375) 25 to 30 minutes or until well puffed. Serve immediately in casserole. 6 servings.

NOTE: Light spoonbread has a moist texture like a soufflé. It is many times served with meat instead of potatoes in the South. It is also especially good with lots of butter, almost a mandatory way to eat spoon bread. Try creamed chicken or creamed dry beef over spoonbread for breakfast or lunch. You should be at the table when spoonbread makes an appearance, so it can be served while it is still light and fluffy.
What to Cook for Company, 1952

OLD VIRGINIA SPOON BREAD

1 cup white cornmeal
1 cup boiling water
1 Tablespoon butter
1 teaspoon salt

1 egg, well beaten
1 cup rich milk
1 1/2 teaspoons baking powder

Scald the cornmeal with the boiling water, then stir in the butter, salt and well-beaten egg. Add the baking powder and milk. Turn into a well-buttered pan and bake for 40 minutes in a moderately hot (375 F) oven. Serve hot with butter. This bread is especially delicious and not at all difficult to make. This recipe makes 8 large portions.

NOTE: Cold rice, hominy or cream of wheat may be added. I like my spoon bread with rice added. It has to be cold and soft boiled
Mrs. Frederick Gardner, 200 Years of Charleston Cooking, 1930

RICHMOND CORN CAKES

1 cup crushed canned corn
1/2 cup milk
2 teaspoons sugar
2 eggs, well beaten

3/4 cup flour
1 Tablespoon baking powder
pinch of salt

To the corn meal add milk, sugar, and eggs. Mix and then sift flour, baking powder and salt. Combine the mixtures, drop by teaspoons into buttered muffin pans. Bake in moderate oven (325-350 F).
The Southern Cook Book, 1935

HOE CAKE

The hoe cake and the corn dodger seem to be the humble forerunners of the more complicated Johnny Cake (the name seems to have first appeared in an old Confederate recipe book calling it Johnny Cake instead of the Journey Cake by which it should have been identified.) Originally hoe cakes, corn dodgers, and Johnny Cakes consisted of just simply mixing corn meal with water and salting them to taste and then "planking the dough" (spreading the dough on a wood plank or barrel top) and standing it upright in front of the fire until it was cooked and crusty.

Gradually flour and eggs found their way into these original simple mixtures and the recipes became more complex. The method of cooking also progressed from the open fire to the oven.

"200 Years of Charleston Cooking," written in 1930, says of the hoe cake in the instructions for their recipe: "mix the cornmeal, salt and sugar and add enough boiling milk or water to make a batter which will not spread when put on the griddle. Grease the griddle with salt pork and then drop mixture on the griddle with a large spoon. Each cake should be about 1/2 inch thick. Cook slowly and when browned, put a bit of butter on top of each cake and turn over. They cannot be cooked too long, provided they do not burn."

Sometimes the dough is put into one large cake and, as soon as browned underneath, it is turned over onto a freshly greased plate. The thin, crisp crust is peeled off with a knife, laid on a hot plate and spread with butter. When another browned crust is formed, the cake is turned again; the crust is removed and buttered; with the process continued until the cake is all browned. The crisp, buttered crusts are served piled together and cut into sections.

Today, when a hoe cake is made, it is made on the griddle, just as you would a griddle cake, and then served with butter. But the old Southern cooks always baked them on a hoe on hot coals in front of a wood fire, out in the open air, just before the cabin doors or in the cabins before the roaring hearth fire. Hence the name hoe cake. The hoe cake was made of flour with sufficient water to moisten it well. A teaspoon of butter or lard was added.

HOE CAKE

1 cup white-water ground cornmeal
1 teaspoon salt
2 Tablespoons bacon fat or lard
1 1/2 to 2 cups boiling water

Mix cornmeal, salt and fat in a bowl. Pour in boiling water enough to make a thick mush. Be sure the water is boiling. Mix thoroughly and shape dough into pone (flat oval shaped) cakes. Heat greased iron griddle and put pones onto the hot griddle. Bake in a hot oven preheated to 450 degrees. Rightly made, this is the very best of all Southern corn breads. Making good corn bread is an art.
Satsuma Tea Room, Fun for the Cook, 1968

HOMINY BREAD

2 eggs
2 cups boiled hominy
1 cup corn meal
1 Tablespoon melted lard
sweet milk
salt to taste

Beat eggs and mix all ingredients into a soft batter. Bake in a deep dish.
The Savannah Cook Book, 1933

OWENDAW CORN BREAD

Hominy gives this bread its distinctive flavor. Like all of the spoon breads, it should be eaten very hot and with much butter.

1 cup cooked hominy	2 eggs	1/2 cup cornmeal
2 Tablespoons butter	1 cup milk	1/2 teaspoon salt

While the hominy is hot, stir in the butter. Beat the eggs until light and add to the hominy, then add the milk and lastly the cornmeal and salt. This makes a very thin batter. Pour it into a deep, buttered pan and bake in a moderately hot oven (375 degrees F) for about 30 minutes. This will serve 6. When baked, it has the appearance of a baked batter pudding, and when rich and well mixed it has almost the delicacy of baked custard.
200 Years of Charleston Cooking, 1930

JOHNNY CAKE

In the olden days, Johnny Cake was baked on a clean, green board, before a hot coals fire. The board had to be oak wood. The cake was formed and placed on the board and the board was then inclined at an angle before the hot fire with a piece of wood or flat iron to hold it, since the cake was placed at such an angle that it could harden without slipping. When the bread became quite hard it was stood upright and baked to a nice, crisp brown on both sides, being turned as needed and often basted with butter.

The Johnny Cake was served for lunch or for tea, being sent to the table hot, split and buttered, or served with fresh sweet milk and buttermilk.

JOHNNY CAKE

5 heaping Tablespoons corn meal	2/3 pint clabber
2 Tablespoons flour	1 teaspoon salt
1 Tablespoon sugar	1/2 cup melted butter
2 eggs	1 teaspoon baking soda

Mix dry ingredients, add baking soda, eggs and butter, and bake. Corn bread in the shape of batter breads, muffins or batter cakes are popular breakfast or supper dishes, while they more usually appear at dinner in the guise of corn sticks or cornbread fritters. Makes fine accompaniments for soup. Water ground meal is a necessity for the best corn bread.
The Savannah Cook Book, 1933

JOHNNY CAKE

1 1/2 pints of Indian meal (corn meal)
3 eggs
1 pint sweet milk or buttermilk or water
2 Tablespoons melted butter
or 1 Tablespoon lard
1/2 teaspoon baking soda, optional

Beat the eggs until very light, add the corn meal, then beat once more. Add the melted butter and the milk or water. If buttermilk is used, you may use the soda, dissolving it in two Tablespoons of boiling water. Do not use the baking soda with the sweet milk. Make a dough or batter thick enough to be spread into round cakes, 1/2 inch thick and about 5 inches in diameter. Place them into buttered tins and bake in moderate oven for about 1/2 hour, frequently brushing across with melted butter while baking; about 4 to 5 times.
The Picayune Creole Cook Book, 1922

ASH CAKE

1 quart corn meal
1 Tablespoon lard
1 teaspoon salt

This is a genuine Southern African American made cake. The old African American Creoles of Louisiana excelled in making and baking this bread in such a way that no ashes clung to the clean white cake. An ash cake, as the name suggests, is always baked in the ashes on the open hearth, and only wood ashes must be used. There was a roaring fire which produced a sufficient quantity of hot ashes. A clean spot was swept on the hearth and a pile of hot ashes was drawn out and the pone of bread (shaped like corn dodgers was placed on top of these ashes. This bread was then covered with hot ashes and baked to a nice brown. The cake was then drawn out of the ashes, wiped clean with a cloth till every particle of ash had disappeared. This cake was then served hot with butter and molasses.

NOTE: Sometimes the bread was wrapped in fig leaves to bake more evenly, but the real, true ash cake was made as above.
The Picayune Cook Book, 1922

CORN DODGERS

1 quart corn meal
1 Tablespoon lard
1 teaspoon salt

Scald the meal with boiling water. Add the melted lard and the salt. Use sufficient boiling water to make a very stiff batter or soft dough. Then take a handful of the mixture and mold it with your hands into an oval mound, tossing the cake of dough lightly between your hands in a dexterous manner, leaving the impressions of your fingers across it. Bake the pones thus formed in a quick oven. They may be served at dinner and are absolutely delicious when properly made.
The Picayune Creole Cook Book, 1922

*"Case cookin's lak religion is some's 'lected an' some ain't,
An' rules don' no mo' mek a cook den sermons mek a saint."
-(Maria) Howard Weeden (1847-1905)*

FRIED CORN DODGERS

1 cup self-rising cornmeal   2/3 cup buttermilk

Heat fat (1 inch depth) in heavy skillet. Mix milk into meal. Shape with dessert spoon and place in hot fat. Turn once until brown. Drain and serve hot. It is best not to let this batter stand. If so, you may add more milk. Yields:10-12.
Satsuma Tea Room, Easy on the Cook-Southern Breads, 1975

CORN DODGERS

Sift one pint of Southern corn meal. Mix with enough cold water to form stiff dough and salt to taste. Form into long, round dodgers with the hand (about 4 or 5 inches long and one inch in diameter) and place onto hot griddle, which has been greased with a little lard. Put a small piece of butter onto each and bake in oven until rich brown. NOTE: Bread does not rise.
The Savannah Cook Book, 1933

CORN MEAL DODGER FOR POT LIKKER

1/2 teaspoon   cold water
2 Tablespoons melted butter   1/2 pint white corn meal

Add salt to corn meal and stir in the melted butter. Add sufficient cold water, so dough will hold shape. Shape dough into biscuit size pieces and drop into the boiling "pot likker". Cook 20 minutes in covered pot. Serve garnished with the greens from the "pot likker".
The Southern Cook Book, 1939

CRACKLINGS

"Cracklings are the bits of fat meat left after the lard has been rendered from the fat pork. These pieces are eaten throughout rural Louisiana. The fat pork is cut into small bits, about the size of a man's hand and then fried until every bit of grease has been extracted. This grease is then clarified and used as lard. The cracklings are saved and eaten from time to time within the next two weeks, simply being warmed again.

These cracklings, to use the country parlance 'go very well with corn bread' and are not only eaten with it "au naturel", but also into the rural bread of the country parishes, crackling bread or gratons. Crackling bread is very crisp, and if made properly, it is a very palatable bread requiring no butter or other accompaniment to make it toothsome."
–The Picayune Creole Cook Book, 1922

CRACKLING BREAD

1 cup cracklings (diced)   3/4 cups wheat flour   1/4 teaspoon salt
1 1/2 cups corn meal   1/2 teaspoon baking soda   1 cup sour milk

Cracklings are the little pieces of meat remaining after the lard has been rendered from the pork. Mix and sift together all the dry ingredients. Add milk, stir in the cracklings. Form into oblong cakes and place into greased baking pan. Bake in hot oven (400 F) 30 minutes.
The Southern Cook Book, 1939

CRACKLING CORN PONES

1 teaspoon salt	2 1/2 cups corn meal
1/2 teaspoon baking powder	1 teaspoon baking soda
1 cup finely chopped cracklings	1 1/2 cups thick sour buttermilk

Heat oven to 400 degrees. Heat iron skillet in the oven. Mix salt, baking powder, and cracklings with the meal. Add soda to the milk and stir into the meal mixture. Allow to stand 5 minutes. Mixture should be thick enough to shape with hands into "pones" using 1/2 cup mixture for each. Lightly grease the hot skillet, place the pones close together and bake for 25 minutes or until well-browned. Makes 8-10 pones

NOTE: This recipe may be made using 1 1/2 teaspoons baking powder and 1 cup milk and omitting the baking soda and sour milk.
Nelle Stewart, The Nashville Cookbook, 1977

CRACKLING CORN PONE

2 1/2 cups corn meal	1 cup finely cut cracklings
1 teaspoon salt	1 teaspoon baking soda
1/2 teaspoon baking powder	1 1/2 cups buttermilk

Mix first four ingredients. Add baking soda to buttermilk and mix with the meal mixture. Shape with a spoon or your hands. Place on a well-greased hot iron baker. Place pones close together. Bake 30 minutes or until brown in a 425 F oven. Yield: 8-10 pones.
Satsuma Tea Room, Easy on the Cook-Southern Breads, 1975

BATTER BREAD, MULATTO STYLE

1 egg	1 teaspoon salt	1 Tablespoon lard
1/2 cup cold hominy	1/2 pint corn meal	

Mix the cold hominy, beaten egg, corn meal and salt with enough boiling water to make a batter with the consistency of milk. Put the lard into a deep baking pan and heat until it smokes. Pour the cold batter into this hot lard; the melted lard will bubble up on the side of the pan, making a delicious crust. Bake in a moderate (350) oven about 40 minutes.
The Southern Cook Book, 1939

GRIST BREAD

1 cup cold hominy	1 egg	1 pint raw grist
1 Tablespoon butter	pinch of salt	(uncooked hominy)

Beat egg yolk with the cooked hominy, mash in the butter and salt, put into grist which has been washed and drained and free of water. Mix together and cook in deep buttered pan.

NOTE: This bread is grainy but is so very good.
The Savannah Cook Book, 1933

CREOLE RICE CAKE

4 slices bacon, chopped	3 cups rice, cooked
3 Tablespoons chopped onion	1 cup flour
3 Tablespoons green pepper	1 teaspoon baking powder
1 teaspoon salt	1 can tomato pulp
1/2 teaspoon pepper	

Fry the bacon crisp, leaving the bacon fat in the frying pan. Chop the bacon and add to the onion, pepper and the rest of the ingredients. Mix thoroughly. Fry in the bacon fat as pancakes.
The Southern Cook Book, 1939

RICE CORN BREAD

1 cup boiled rice	1 egg	1 cup corn meal
1 teaspoon butter	salt	1 teaspoon baking soda

Mash rice smooth and add butter, milk, well-beaten egg, and lastly baking soda. Bake in shallow tins and cut into squares.
The Savannah Cook Book, 1933

RICE BREAD

1 1/2 cups boiled rice	1 1/2 cups flour	1 teaspoon baking
1 egg	1 1/2 cups milk	powder
1 Tablespoon lard		

Mix all ingredients, bake in buttered biscuit tin and cut in squares.

NOTE: An easy and delightful breakfast dish.
The Savannah Cook Book, 1933

ASHLEY BREAD

NOTE: This is much like other spoon breads except that it has a characteristic rice flavor.

1 cup rice flour	1 egg
1/2 teaspoon salt	1 cup milk
1 1/2 teaspoons baking powder	1 1/2 Tablespoons melted butter

Mix and sift the dry ingredients. Beat the egg well and add the milk to it. Combine with the first mixture. Then stir in the melted butter and turn into a well-greased, shallow pan. Bake in a moderate oven (350 F) for 45 minutes.
Panchita Heyward Grimball's recipe from Wappaoolah Plantation, Cooper River recounted in 200 Years of Charleston Cooking, 1930

RICE GRIDDLE CAKES

| 1 1/2 cups boiled rice | 1 teaspoon baking soda | 1 egg |
| 1 pint flour | 1 pint sour milk | 1/2 teaspoon salt |

Mash rice well, add milk, flour, and egg. Stir in the flour just before frying.
The Savannah Cook Book, 1933

EGG BREAD (A bit different style from the usual!)

1 cup milk	3 eggs	2 cups buttermilk
1 cup water	1 teaspoon salt	2 Tbl. shortening
2 cups corn meal	1 teaspoon baking soda	1/4 cup meal

Heat oven to 400 degrees. Combine milk and water in saucepan. Bring to a boil and add meal, stirring constantly to make a mush. Beat eggs until very light; add salt. Stir baking soda into buttermilk. Combine mush, eggs, and buttermilk mixtures. Melt shortening in iron skillet. Pour shortening into entire mixture. Mix and stir in 1/4 cup meal. Pour batter into hot skillet (or iron muffin rings). Bake 25-30 minutes until firm and brown. Serves 12.

NOTE: This bread is very light and tender made from a recipe which is an old, generational one from a family in Franklin, Tennessee.
Jeanne G. Webb, The Nashville Cookbook, 1977

EGG BREAD-VIRGINIA STYLE

2 cups corn meal, sifted	salt
2 eggs	pinch of baking soda
1 heaping teaspoon butter	

Mix corn meal, salt, and baking soda. Pour in enough boiling water to make a soft batter. Beat in eggs and butter. Bake in oven about 1/2 hour. Cut into squares and serve hot.
The Savannah Cook Book, 1933

HUSH PUPPIES

This hush puppy legend account is from the Tallahassee area of North Florida. The story had been passed down in folklore, but this recounting was chronicled in the 1939 *The Southern Cook Book*. There are countless other stories pertaining to the derivation of the name. The hush puppy story which I grew up telling, and as I might add as believing as gospel truth, involved Confederate soldiers around a campfire during the Civil War. As with all things Southern, there are multiple accounts. One thing is certain; whichever of the many stories of the origin of the Hush Puppy you go with, dogs were involved.

"Years ago, enslaved people congregated on warm fall evenings for sugar cane grindings. Some of them fed the sugar cane into a one mule treadmill to grind while others poured the resulting juice into a large iron kettle where that juice was then boiled to sugar. After their work was completed, the workers would gather around an open fire where there was generally a suspended iron pot in which fish and corn pones were cooked in fat.

Enslaved people had a certain way of making these corn pones, which were unusually delicious and appetizing. While the food was sizzling in the pot, they would share "tall" tales and stories around the fire. On the outer edge of the circle of light, reflected by the fire, their hound dogs would sit, their ears alert for strange sounds and their noses upturned to catch a whiff of the savory odor of frying fish and pones. If the talking ceased for a moment, a low whine of dog's hunger would attract the attention of the men and subconsciously a hand would reach for some corn pone which had been placed on a slab of bark to cool. The donor would break off a piece of the pone and toss it to the hungry dog, and with the shorten mumble of, "Hush, puppy!" causing an immediate end to the dog's barking. The pones just tasted that good and had such a remarkable flavor that it would quiet a hungry animal." -*The Southern Cook Book, 1939*

HUSH PUPPIES

3 cups water-ground cornmeal
1 1/2 teaspoons salt
2 cups milk

1 egg (unbeaten)
1/4 cup finely chopped onion

Gradually add milk to the other 4 ingredients. Heat fat and drop from a teaspoon into the hot fat. Cook until golden brown. Drain. Yield: 24

NOTE: Used grease (fish, bacon, or chicken) can be used for cooking puppies. Tomato juice can be substituted for 1/2 of the milk.
Satsuma Tea Room, Easy on the Cook-Southern Breads, 1975

HUSH PUPPIES (self-rising)

2 cups self-rising corn meal
1/4 cup chopped onion
1 Tablespoon minced garlic

1 egg
1/2 cup milk
1/2 cup flour

Beat eggs well and stir in remaining ingredients. Use 1-inch scoop to place balls of dough into 360 F deep fat oil one at a time. Cook until golden brown.
Cortner Mill Restaurant cookbook, 2009

HUSH PUPPIES

NOTE: This recipe, using boiling water to "pre-cook" the cornmeal before frying, is preferred by many Southern cooks.

2 cups cornmeal
4 tablespoons flour
1 teaspoon baking powder
1/2 teaspoon salt

4 tablespoons chopped onion
(optional, but helps flavor)
1 egg, beaten lightly
2 cups boiling water

Combine all dry ingredients, onions and egg. Add boiling water, stirring vigorously to make smooth. Mixture will be thick. A little water or buttermilk may be added if necessary. Form into small balls or rolls and drop into deep fat. If this fat has been used previously to cook fish, then all the better. Fry until golden brown. Drain on absorbent paper. Really good served with fried fish. Makes about 2 dozen.
Ann C. Cox, The Nashville Cookbook, 1977

BISCUITS

"When someone asked a Northern visitor, after his first stay in the South, what impressed him the most, he promptly replied; 'The invariable advice given by every hostess as the biscuits were passed: 'Take two and butter them while they are hot,"

Another Northern visitor tells this one upon returning home after a sojourn in Dixie. Someone asked him how he liked the Southern biscuits. "Never tasted one," he replied. "Never tasted a biscuit?' echoed the friend "Why, I've been told they serve them with every meal." "And so, they do," said the weary traveler, "for breakfast, dinner and supper, but I was never allowed to eat one. Every time they were passed, I would take one and butter it according to directions. And invariably, just as I would get it to my mouth, my arm would be seized and someone would cry, 'Don't eat that. It's cold. The hot ones are just coming in.' So, I would relinquish my morsel, take another, butter it and put it down, and before I could eat it, more hot ones would appear, and the whole thing began over again."

–Harriet Ross Colquitt, story told in The Savannah Cook Book, 1933

BISCUITS

2 cups flour
1/2 teaspoon salt
4 level teaspoons baking powder

lard the size of an egg
milk
1 teaspoon butter

Sift baking powder and salt with flour. Mix in the lard and butter with tips of the fingers. Work lightly with water and a very little milk, until you reach right consistency, and then roll on board. The dough should be as soft as can be conveniently handled. Cut out with biscuit cutter, put into pan and bake in quick oven.
The Savannah Cook Book, 1933

BISCUITS

2 cups self-rising flour   1/4 cup shortening   3/4 cup milk

Heat oven to 450 degrees. Cut or rub shortening into flour until particles are as fine as coarse crumbs. Add milk and stir with a fork. Turn dough out on lightly floured board or pastry cloth and knead just until smooth. Roll dough about 1/2 inches thick and cut with a floured cutter. Place biscuits on a lightly greased baking sheet. Bake 10 to 12 minutes.
Alice Jarman, The Nashville Cookbook, 1977

OLD-FASHIONED SODA BISCUITS

2 cups not sifted flour
1 Tablespoon lard
1/2 pint sweet milk (or milk and water)

1/2 teaspoon baking soda
1/2 teaspoon salt
1 heaping teaspoon cream of tartar

Sift the cream of tartar with the flour. Mix in lard with hand, then stir in milk (in which the soda has been dissolved) working as little as possible. Roll out 1 inch thick and cut into shapes. The old-fashioned way of pricking each biscuit with a fork before cooking makes them look more like grandmother used to make, even if the taste is not affected.
The Savannah Cook Book, 1933

GOOD MORNING BISCUITS

1 Tablespoon butter
1 egg, well beaten
1 Tablespoon sugar
1 teaspoon lard
1 pint of milk

1 heaping teaspoon salt
1/2 yeast cake dissolved in
1/4 cup lukewarm water
6 cups flour

Pour milk, butter, salt, lard, and sugar into a double boiler and scald; let mixture cool until lukewarm; then dissolve yeast and stir into the mixture. When mixture has cooled, add 2 1/2 cups of flour and mix into a stiff batter. Then add 1 well-beaten egg to the batter and put in a warm place to rise. After about 5 hours knead as for biscuits using the balance of the flour, and when the dough can be handled easily roll out to 1/2 inch thickness. Cut with a biscuit cutter, butter the tops of the biscuits, placing one on top of the other to form a double biscuit and place into a pan far enough apart from others so they will not touch each other. Bake for about 1/4 of an hour in a hot (400 F) oven.
The Southern Cook Book, 1939

MAMMY'S BAKING POWDER BISCUITS

2 cups flour
4 teaspoons baking powder
1/4 teaspoon salt

2 Tablespoons shortening
1/2 cup milk

Sift dry ingredients together. Work in shortening with fingertips. Then add milk slowly, stirring the batter until it is smooth. Roll the dough on a floured board until it is 1/2 inch thick. Cut with a round cookie cutter and bake in a hot (450 degree) oven for 15 minutes.
The Southern Cook Book, 1939

LIZZIE'S BUTTERMILK BISCUITS

2 cups sifted flour
1 Tablespoon baking powder
1/4 teaspoon baking soda

1/2 teaspoon salt
1/3 cup lard
3/4 cup buttermilk

Sift dry ingredients into a bowl. Cut in the lard until they become like coarse crumbs. You can use lard, like we did, or substitute shortening. Make a well and add buttermilk all at once. Stir quickly with a fork just till dough follows fork around bowl. Turn onto a lightly floured surface. Dough should be soft. Knead gently 10 to 12 strokes. Roll or pat dough 1/2 inch thick. Dip biscuit cutter into flour and cut dough straight down, no twisting. Place onto ungreased baking sheet and bake at 450 F. for about 12 minutes. Makes 10 biscuits.

NOTE: We had to double the recipe for 5 Boswells. These amounts are approximate. I just never measured. They were second nature for me. It was my job to make two pans of biscuits every morning, right before my sister, Jeanette, and I went to do the milking.
Sarah Boswell Westerfield, Miss Lizzie's Heirlooms, 2009

SOUTHERN BISCUITS

2 cups flour	1 teaspoon salt
2 teaspoons baking powder	1/4 cup shortening
1/2 teaspoon baking soda	7/8 cup buttermilk

Mix dry ingredients and cut the shortening in until like crumbs. Add milk and stir into a ball. Turn out onto floured cloth; knead until smooth. Roll to 1/2 inch thickness. Cut and place on cookie sheet. Cook 10 to 12 minutes at 450 F. Yield 2 dozen.

NOTE: This dough can be kept overnight covered in refrigerator.
Satsuma Tea Room, Easy on the Cook-Southern Breads, 1975

BEATEN BISCUITS

3 cups sifted flour	1/3 cup lard (or Crisco)	3/4 teaspoon sugar
1/2 cup milk	1/2 teaspoon salt	

Sift sugar and salt into the flour, blend in the lard and make a very stiff dough, using more or less of the milk as needed as the dough must be stiff. Place on a floured board and roll until it blisters and is smooth. Roll to 1/2 inch in thickness, cut with biscuit cutter, poke holes with fork and bake in a moderate oven (350 degrees) for 30 minutes.

NOTE: The old cookbooks say "...make a very stiff dough and knead until perfectly smooth. Beat with an iron pestle until it 'blisters'. The old cook books say from 3 to 500 licks will do it, but a more modern biscuit machine would be less exhausting."
The Southern Cook Book, 1939

CREAM BISCUITS

2 eggs	flour enough to make a stiff dough
1 pint cream	
1/2 cake yeast	

Beat egg, add cream and yeast and stir in enough flour to make a stiff dough. Make into biscuits and let rise 5 hours. You'll feel like ascending yourself when you have sampled one of these delicacies.
The Savannah Cook Book, 1933

QUICK BISCUITS

2 cups flour	1/4 cup shortening
5 teaspoons baking powder	1 cup milk
1 teaspoon salt	

Mix and sift the dry ingredients; rub in the shortening and mix with the milk to soft, thick dough. Drop by spoonful onto a well-greased tin and bake in a quick oven (425 F) for about 15 minutes. These are best when made with butter and come out of the oven as thin crusty biscuits rather than the thicker variety. Makes 12 biscuits.
Mary Leize Simons, 200 Years of Charleston Cooking, 1930

ANGEL BISCUITS

1 cake yeast	3 teaspoons baking powder
2 Tablespoons warm water	1 teaspoon salt
2 Tablespoons sugar	1 cup shortening
5 cups flour	2 cups buttermilk
1 teaspoon soda	

Dissolve yeast in water. Sift together dry ingredients; put in shortening. Add yeast mixture with buttermilk to dry mixture. Knead enough to hold together. Roll about 1/2 inch thick and cut. Place on a greased baking sheet. Bake for 20 minutes or until golden brown. Dough can be stored in refrigerator until baking time or can be frozen well up to two weeks. Makes about 3 dozen.

NOTE: A quick recipe for yeasty biscuits; a party biscuit for a luncheon or to serve with slices of ham or with chicken salad.
Ruth DeFreise, The Nashville Cookbook, 1977

HIGH BISCUITS

2 eggs	1 Tablespoon lard
1 cake yeast	1 quart flour
milk	1/2 teaspoon salt
1 Tablespoon butter	

Melt the yeast in cold water. Mix the warm butter and lard with flour. Break in the eggs, unbeaten one at a time, stir and mix with enough milk to make a soft dough. Roll out onto a board and cut into biscuit shapes. Lay aside in pan to rise. In winter this will take 3-4 hours. In summer only 2-3 hours. Bake in a quick oven.

NOTE: This dough may be made as soft as batter and cooked in muffin rings for delicious muffins.
The Savannah Cook Book, 1933

RIZ BISCUITS

2 1/4 cups flour (if needed, use more)	1/2 teaspoon soda
1 Tablespoon sugar	3 Tablespoons fat
1 1/2 teaspoons salt	1 yeast cake in 1/2 cup warm water
1 teaspoon baking powder	3/4 cup buttermilk

Dissolve the yeast in warm water. Mix the dry ingredients. Cut in fat until mixture is mealy. Stir milk into yeast mixture and then add to flour mixture. Roll out 1/2 inch thick and cut. Brush tops with melted butter. Let rise 1 hour or more. Bake at 375 F. These biscuits can be baked a light brown and frozen until ready to use.

NOTE: This is an excellent roll that can be made in a hurry.
Satsuma Tea Room, Fun for the Cook, 1968

RAISIN BISCUITS

2 1/2 cups flour	1 Tablespoon sugar	4 teaspoons baking
2 eggs	3/4 cup milk	powder
1/3 cup butter	1 ½ cups seeded raisins	1/2 teaspoon salt

Sift flour, sugar, baking powder and salt. Beat the eggs and add to the milk. Mix the shortening into the flour, stir in the milk and egg. Add the raisins. Turn onto a well-floured board and knead until smooth, using more flour if necessary. Cut with small biscuit cutter and bake in hot oven (450 F) for 15 minutes. Serve hot.
The Southern Cook Book, 1935

CHEESE BISCUITS

1/2 cup flour	1/4 pound butter	3 Tablespoons ice water
1/4 pound grated cheese	salt to taste	

Mix quickly with as little handling as possible. Roll thin, cut with cookie cutter and bake in quick oven (500 degrees F) for 10 minutes.
The Southern Cook Book, 1939

SALLY LUNN

Early Southern settlers brought their favorite *Sally Lunn* bread recipes from England when they immigrated to America; recipes that were truly treasured among their collections. But, as in the case of most multi-generational family recipes, they were as different and as plentiful as the stars in the night sky.

SALLY LUNN

1 pint of milk	1 teaspoon salt
1 1/2 pints of flour	1/2 cup sugar
1/2 cup butter	1/4 cake of compressed yeast
4 eggs	

Warm the butter in a pint of milk till the milk reaches the boiling point. Do not let it boil. Simply scald. Then add the salt and a Tablespoonful of sugar. Let it cool. When tepid add the flour, well-sifted and beat thoroughly into the mixture. Lastly add the yeast, dissolved in a little hot milk or water. Beat it continuously for at least 5 minutes. Then, when the batter begins to break into blisters, cover it and set it to rise for the night. In the morning add the yolks of the eggs, beaten till very light and the whites beaten to a stiff froth. Mix carefully and dissolve a half teaspoon of baking soda if it seems in any way sour. Turn the whole into a shallow buttered dish and set to rise for 15 minutes longer. Bake about 20-25 minutes in a moderately quick oven, till it is a light brown. This cake, like all muffin batter, should not be cut with a knife, but torn apart with your hands. If it is cut, all muffin batter at once becomes heavy. The cake may be also made much more quickly by mixing in the morning, using the above ingredients, but adding only 3 teaspoons of baking powder, instead of the yeast. Beat quickly and thoroughly, and turn into a buttered tin, and set to bake at once. Send it to the table hot.
The Picayune Creole Cook Book, 1922

SALLY LUNN HOT BREAD

3 eggs	1 yeast cake	2 Tablespoons butter
4 cups of flour	1 cup milk	
2 Tablespoons sugar	1/2 teaspoon salt	

Place sugar, eggs, milk, salt, and butter in a double boiler and scald. Let cool and add yeast which has been dissolved in a 1/4 cup of warm water. When cold, add flour, put into a bowl and cover with a cloth and put away to rise. When twice its bulk, knead and put into pan to rise again. When light, roll out on floured board. Cut with a biscuit cutter, place in a greased pan, and bake in a hot oven (400 F) fifteen minutes.
The Southern Cook Book, 193

SWEET SALLY LUND

1 egg	1 cup cream	1 teaspoon baking flour
1 cup sugar	1 cup flour	1 teaspoon mace

Beat the egg, add the sugar and beat again. Sift the mace and baking powder with the flour and add alternately with the cream to the first mixture. Turn into a well-greased square tin and bake in a moderate oven (350 F) for about 1/2 hour. The cake (it is so sweet that it could fall into that category) is quite rich bread.
Mrs. Rhett, 200 Years of Charleston Cooking, 1930

SPOON ROLLS

	1/4 cup sugar
1 package dry yeast	1 egg
2 cups very warm water	4 cups self-rising flour
1 1/2 sticks margarine, melted	

Melt margarine. Mix with sugar and water in a large bowl. Then add beaten egg. Add dissolved yeast to mixture. Add flour. Stir well until mixed. Place in airtight bowl. Put in refrigerator (where it will keep about a week). To cook, drop by spoonful into greased muffin tins. Bake at 350 for about 20 minutes or until well browned. Makes 2 dozen.

NOTE: This dough keeps for days in the refrigerator. Stir down lightly before using. Product is better if the dough has been "seasoned", worked somewhat before use.
Satsuma Tea Room, More Fun for the Cook, 1974

POPPY ONION LOAF

4 Tablespoons butter	1 Tablespoon poppy seed
1 Tablespoon minced onion	2 packages refrigerator butter-flake rolls

Melt butter. Add onion and poppy seed. Separate each roll into 2 or 3 pieces. Dip each piece in the butter mixture. Coat the entire piece. Place each piece on edge in loaf pan in two rows. Bake at 350 degrees for 20-30 minutes. Serves 8.
Satsuma Tea Room, More Fun for the Cook, 1974

SOURDOUGH BREAD

1 cup starter	1/2 cup sugar
3 1/2 cups bread flour	1/2 cup vegetable oil
1/2 Tablespoon salt	2 cups warm water

Sift flours, salt, and sugar together in large bowl. Add oil, starter and water to dry ingredients. Mix well. Cover with plastic wrap and let rise overnight in an eighty degree temperature location free of drafts. Next day knead the dough for two minutes. Divide the dough in two equal portions and knead again. Put the dough into two loaf baking pans. Cover and let rise 4-5 hours. Should not double in bulk. Too much rising will cause bread to be flat. Bake approximately 20-25 minutes in a 325 degree oven. Makes two loaves.
Jeanette Hazelwood, Cortner Mill Restaurant cookbook, 2009

SOURDOUGH BREAD STARTER

6 Tablespoons sugar	1/2 cup warm water
1 1/2 Tablespoons potato flakes	1 teaspoon dry yeast or 1 cup starter

Mix ingredients in 1 quart non-metallic container. Cover loosely. Let starter set out all day in an eighty degree location free from drafts. Pour 1 cup of new starter into non-metallic container to make bread and store unused portion in refrigerator. Always use a wooden spoon or plastic spoon.
Jeanette Hazelwood, Cortner Mill Restaurant cookbook, 2009

NOTE: I want to thank my mom (David H) for sharing her starter and bread recipes. It has become one of Cortner Mill's signature items. We have to warn our guests not to eat so much bread or they will be too full for dessert. Of course, even with the recipe, our bread is never as good as what mom makes!
Jeanette Hazelwood, Cortner Mill Restaurant cookbook, 2009

PARKER HOUSE ROLLS

4 yeast cakes	1 1/2 teaspoons salt
1/2 cup lukewarm water	1/2 cup butter
2 1/2 cups lukewarm milk	9 to 10 cups sifted flour
6 Tablespoons sugar	

Dissolve yeast in lukewarm water. Put milk, sugar, salt and half of the butter into a saucepan and heat until lukewarm. Add the dissolved yeast, mix well and add gradually the sifted flour, blending thoroughly after each addition. Cover and put in warm place for 15 minutes. Turn onto floured board and pat to 1/2 inch thickness. Cut with a 2 inch biscuit cutter; brush with butter and fold over. Let rise on greased baking sheet in a warm place for 15 minutes. Then bake in hot oven (450 F) for 10 minutes. Makes 4 dozen rolls.
L.P. DeGouy, Chef's Cook Book, 1939

ICE BOX YEAST ROLLS

2 yeast cakes	1/2 cup sugar
1/4 cup lukewarm water	1 teaspoon salt
1 beaten egg	1 cup boiling water
2 Tablespoons shortening	4 cups sifted flour

Dissolve salt, sugar, and shortening in boiling water. Cool, add beaten egg. Mash yeast and add to the above mixture (which should be cooled). Add sifted flour. Let rise 1 hour. Work down and put in refrigerator. When ready to make into rolls, take out on floured board. Roll. Cut rolls, brush with melted butter and fold over in pocketbook shape. Let rise two hours and bake at 425. Keep dough in refrigerator and use as desired. Should last several weeks.
Satsuma Tea Room, More Fun for the Cook, 1974

YEAST ROLLS

4 cups milk	3 teaspoons salt
1 cup sugar	1 teaspoon baking soda
1 cup shortening	2 teaspoons baking powder
7 or 8 cups flour	2 packages yeast

Heat 1 cup milk with sugar and shortening until dissolved. In a 6 quart container put 3 cups milk, add the heated milk and 4 cups of flour with salt, soda, baking powder and yeast. Beat until smooth. Add enough more flour to make the consistency of cake batter. Let rise until double in bulk. Add more flour for soft dough. Take an amount needed for a meal and knead well. Roll to 1/2 inch; cut then fold. Place on greased cookie sheet. Let rise 1 hour. Bake at 425 F for 10 to 12 minutes. Store the remainder of the dough, tightly covered, in the refrigerator for 1 to 2 weeks. Yields 100 rolls.

NOTE: This dough can be used for cinnamon rolls or made into loaves.
Satsuma Tea Room, Easy on the Cook-Southern Breads, 1975

YEAST ROLLS

1 yeast cake	1 heaping teaspoon sugar
1 quart flour	1 large Tablespoon Snowdrift
1 teaspoon salt	(shortening)
1 cup lukewarm milk	3/4 cup warm water

Mix yeast cake with warm milk. Put 1 pint flour into a bowl and add Snowdrift (shortening) and salt, then milk and yeast. Mix thoroughly with warm water and sugar. Mix well and beat hard. Put aside in warm place to rise about 5 hours. When well risen, add another pint of flour. Knead about 5 minutes and then roll out. Put into pans and set aside about 1 1/2 hours before baking
The Savannah Cook Book, 1933

TWO HOUR ROLLS

3 cups sifted flour	1 teaspoon salt	1/2 cup milk
2 good Tablespoons lard	1 yeast cake	1/2 cup warm water

Mix dry ingredients and lard working as if to make pie crust. Dissolve yeast in warm water and add to milk. Finish making dough. Turn out onto floured board and knead well. Roll out and cut into shapes. Put in biscuit pans and let rise 2 hours. Cook 20 minutes.
The Savannah Cook Book, 1933

MOM'S LIGHT BREAD ROLLS

1/2 cup warm water	¼ cup sugar
¾ cup milk	1 teaspoon salt
2 packages dry yeast	1/3 cup shortening
2 eggs	4 ½ cups plain flour

Soak yeast in warm water for 5 minutes. Pour milk, sugar, and salt into bowl. Stir to dissolve. Add shortening, eggs, 1 cup flour, and softened yeast. Beat until smooth. Add remaining flour to make a soft dough. Turn onto a lightly floured board. Knead until dough becomes smooth and elastic. Place in lightly greased bowl. Grease top and cover with waxed paper. Rise in warm place until doubled in size, about 1 – 1 ½ hours. Turn onto lightly floured area and punch down. Form balls and place in greased muffin pan. Let rise until double in size, about 30 minutes. Longer won't hurt. Bake at 375 degrees for 12-15 minutes.
Sarah Elizabeth "Lizzie" Boswell, Miss Lizzie's Heirlooms, 2009

NOTE: Miss Lizzie gave her daughter, Jeanette, this recipe in 1946 for Jeanettes's home economics class recipe book.

QUICK FRENCH BREAD

2 cans refrigerator biscuits	sesame seeds
1 egg white, beaten	

Stand biscuits on edge on ungreased cookie sheet. Lightly press together and shape ends to form a long loaf. Brush with egg white. Sprinkle with sesame seeds. Bake at 350 for 20-30 minutes.
Satsuma Tea Room, More Fun for the Cook, 1974

OATMEAL YEAST BREAD

1 package dry yeast	1/3 cup shortening	3 1/4 - 3 1/2 cups flour
1/4 cup warm water	1/4 cup brown sugar	1 1/2 cups oatmeal
1 1/2 cups scalded milk	1 Tablespoon salt	

Pour scalded milk over shortening, sugar and salt. Cool to lukewarm. Stir in 1/2 cup flour, yeast, and oatmeal. Then stir in enough flour to make a soft dough. Turn out onto board and knead until smooth. Make dough into round ball. Grease and let rise in bowl until double in size. Push down and let stand 10 minutes. Shape into loaves and put into loaf pans. Brush with melted shortening. Cover and let rise about 45 minutes until nearly double in size. Bake at 375 for about 45 minutes until golden brown.

NOTE: We like to make our bread in small loaves as this makes more crust. This bread is excellent for toast for breakfast. Good with just butter or apricot preserves.
Satsuma Tea Room, More Fun for the Cook, 1974

BROWN BREAD

10 1/2 to 11 cups flour, half white and half rye or whole wheat

1 package dry yeast	1 Tablespoon salt	2/3 cup non-fat dry milk
1/4 cup lukewarm water	3 cups very warm water	1 or 2 eggs
1/3 cup sugar	2/3 stick margarine	

Dissolve yeast in 1/4 cup lukewarm water. Add sugar to dissolved yeast in large mixer bowl. In another bowl, add salt and margarine to the warm water. Add dry milk. When lukewarm, pour into mixer bowl with dissolved yeast and sugar. Add 4 cups white flour and 1 or 2 eggs. Beat 4 minutes at medium speed. Add additional flour to make a soft dough. Knead on floured surface until smooth and elastic, about 8 minutes. Place dough into greased bowl and turn to grease other side. Cover and let rise in warm place until double in size. Punch down and shape into loaves. Cover and let rise in greased pans until double in size. Bake at 375 F for 30-40 minutes. Cool on rack. The bread freezes well or may be kept in the refrigerator. This dough may also be used for rolls. All white flour may also be used. Makes 3 loaves.

NOTE: I remember growing up, mom making this brown bread but as rolls. This was pre-Sister Shubert and man were they good. No way could you eat 1, 5, or 10.
Ethel Friedman, The Nashville Cookbook, 1977

BAKED BROWN BREAD

1 cup All Bran	1/4 cup sugar	1 teaspoon soda
1 cup buttermilk	4 Tbl. dark molasses	1/4 teaspoon salt
1 cup flour	1/2 cup raisins	

Mix all ingredients together. Bake in a well-greased loaf pan at 325 degrees for 1 hour.

NOTE: Much easier than steamed brown bread and equally as good.
Satsuma Tea Room, Fun for the Cook, 1968

"If you are afraid of butter, use cream."
-Julia Child (1912-2004)

MUFFINS

Countless country cooks, not unlike Miss Lizzie, and I might add almost every other homemaker during certain eras in the South, followed this motto: "Use butter and cream with a free hand." It became the secret kitchen weapon, a quick and certain path towards cooking triumphs. It is the distinctive flavors of these two dairy products that produce this result. Inserting these ingredients into any dish provides that extraordinary touch, taste; just like adding a few drops of vanilla or almond extract, or slivers of lemon or orange rind. Flavor!

Exquisite events occur when those fluffy, tender morsels called muffins are served. It adds a delightful touch with every meal. Muffins are wonderful accompaniments to broaden the menu when the balance of the dinner is on the sparse side.

BASIC MUFFIN RECIPE

2 cups sifted flour
1 Tablespoon baking powder
1/2 teaspoon salt
3 Tablespoons sugar

1 egg, beaten
1 cup milk
3 Tablespoons oil or melted shortening

Sift together flour, baking powder, salt, and sugar. Combine egg, milk and oil in a bowl; pour this into the dry ingredients all at once. Stir until the dry ingredients are moist, but still lumpy, about 17-23 strokes. Spoon batter into greased muffin pans, filling pans only 2/3 full. Bake in a hot oven (425 F) 20 to 28 minutes, depending on the size of the muffins.
Farm Journal's Country Cookbook, 1959

PLAIN MUFFINS

1 3/4 cups flour
3/4 teaspoon salt
1 Tablespoon sugar
4 teaspoons baking powder

1 1/4 cups milk
1/4 cup melted fat
2 eggs

Mix dry ingredients. Beat eggs, add alternately with milk to dry ingredients. Mix enough to combine ingredients. Do not overmix. Bake in hot greased muffin tins at 425 F for 20-25 minutes.

NOTE: Fruits may be added. 3/4 cup chopped apricots or cranberries plus 1/4 cup sugar.
Satsuma Tea Room, Easy on the Cook-Southern Breads, 1975

BUTTERMILK MUFFINS

2 eggs
1 Tablespoon sugar
1 quart buttermilk
1 quart sifted flour

2 Tablespoons corn meal
1 teaspoon salt
1 teaspoon baking soda

Beat eggs, then add sugar, then milk, and finally the three times sifted (this is important) flour, meal, salt and baking soda. Beat hard one minute and bake in muffin tins.
The Savannah Cook Book, 1933

BUTTERMILK MUFFINS

1 quart buttermilk
2 eggs
1 Tablespoon sugar

4 cups sifted flour
2 Tablespoons corn meal
1 teaspoon salt

1 teaspoon baking soda

Cream the sugar and eggs, add milk and finally the flour, corn meal, salt and baking soda, which has been sifted 3 times. Beat hard 1 minute and bake in a hot (400) oven for 20 minutes in greased muffin tins.
The Southern Cook Book, 1939

FOUR WEEKS MUFFINS

1 cup boiling water
1 cup 100% bran
2/3 cup shortening
1 1/4 cups sugar
2 eggs, beaten

2 cups buttermilk
3 cups flour
1 teaspoon salt
2 1/2 teaspoons baking soda
2 cups Bran Buds

Pour water over 100% bran. Set aside. Mix shortening, sugar and eggs. Add buttermilk and beat well. Add sifted flour with salt and soda, then bran mixture and Bran Buds. Put into muffin tins and bake at 400 F for 12-15 minutes. This can be stored tightly covered in refrigerator for 4 weeks. Dip out each time you use. Do not stir. Nuts, dates, or raisins may be added.
Satsuma Tea Room, More Fun for the Cook, 1974

RICE MUFFINS

2 eggs, beaten
1 cup cooked rice
1 1/4 cups milk
4 Tablespoons melted fat

1 1/2 cups flour
1 Tablespoon sugar
1/2 teaspoon salt
3 teaspoons baking powder

To beaten eggs, add rice, milk and melted fat. Sift dry ingredients. Combine dry ingredients into eggs and milk. Put batter in hot greased muffin pan. Bake at 425 degrees for about 25 minutes.
Satsuma Tea Room, Fun for the Cook, 1968

BLUEBERRY MUFFINS

1 3/4 cups flour	3 teaspoons baking powder
3/4 teaspoon salt	2 eggs, beaten
1/3 cup sugar	1/4 cup melted fat
3/4 cup milk	1 cup blueberries, floured

Sift dry ingredients. Beat eggs, add milk and melted butter. Stir liquid into dry ingredients. Add blueberries. Stir as little as possible. Bake 20 minutes at 425 in greased muffin pans.
Satsuma Tea Room, Fun for the Cook, 1968

GINGER MUFFINS

2 1/2 cups flour	1 teaspoon ginger	1 cup molasses
2 teaspoons baking soda	1 teaspoon cinnamon	1 cup boiling water
1 teaspoon salt	1 cup shortening	2 well beaten eggs

Sift dry ingredients. Cream shortening and sugar. Add boiling water and molasses. Combine with dry ingredients. Alternating with beaten eggs. Bake at 375 degrees. This batter can be stored and used for several weeks.
Satsuma Tea Room, More Fun for the Cook, 1974

QUICK MUFFINS

2 cups flour	1/2 teaspoon salt	2 Tbl butter, melted
1 Tablespoon sugar	2 eggs, well-beaten	
3 tsp baking powder	1 cup milk	

Mix and sift the dry ingredients. Add the beaten eggs to the milk and add gradually to the dry ingredients. Then add the butter and turn into well-greased muffin tins. Bake for about 30 minutes in a hot oven (400 F) This recipe makes 12 muffins.
Mary Leize Simons, 200 Years of Charleston Cooking, 1933

CRANBERRY TEA MUFFINS

2 cups sifted all-purpose flour	2 Tablespoons butter
1 cup sugar	1 teaspoon grated orange rind
1 1/2 teaspoons baking powder	1/2 cup orange juice plus 1/4 cup water
1/4 teaspoon nutmeg	1 egg, beaten
1/2 teaspoon baking soda	1 cup raw cranberries, cut into halves
1/2 teaspoon salt	1 cup pecans, chopped

Preheat oven to 375 F. Grease the bottom of each muffin cup generously. Sift the flour, sugar, baking powder, nutmeg, baking soda and salt together. Cut in butter until mixture resembles corn meal. Make a well in the dry ingredients. Add orange rind, orange juice, and egg. Blend only until dry ingredients are dampened. Fold in cranberries and nuts. Fill muffin cups 2/3 full. Bake about 20 minutes or until the muffin springs back when lightly touched. Yields 12.
Frances M. LaFont, University of Illinois, Home Economics Faculty Favorites, 1965

CRANBERRY MUFFINS

1 cup cranberries, halved or chopped
1/4 cup sugar
2 cups sifted flour
1 Tablespoon baking powder
1/3 cup sugar

1/2 teaspoon salt
1/3 cup margarine
1 egg, slightly beaten
3/4 cup milk
1 teaspoon vanilla

Combine cranberries, 1/4 cup sugar. Sift together flour, 1/3 cup sugar, baking powder and salt. Cut in the margarine until mixture resembles coarse crumbs. Add combined egg, milk and vanilla. Stir just until the ingredients are blended. Fold in cranberry mixture. Fill muffin cups 2/3 full. Bake at 400 F for about 15 minutes.
Satsuma Tea Room, More Fun for the Cook, 1974

BACON MUFFINS

2 cups flour
4 teaspoons baking powder
1/2 teaspoon salt
2 Tablespoons sugar

2 eggs, beaten
1 cup milk
4 Tablespoons melted bacon fat
6 strips bacon, fried crisp and chopped

Mix and sift dry ingredients. Stir in melted fat and chopped bacon. Bake in greased muffin pan. Bake in 425 degree oven 20-25 minutes. Surprisingly good.
Satsuma Tea Room, Fun for the Cook, 1968

SPICED PUMPKIN MUFFINS

1 1/2 cups sifted all-purpose flour
2 teaspoons baking powder
3/4 teaspoon salt
1/2 cup sugar
1/2 teaspoon cinnamon
1/2 teaspoon nutmeg

1/4 cup shortening
1 egg, beaten
1/2 cup cooked or canned pumpkin
1/2 cup milk
1/2 cup seedless raisins
sugar

Preheat oven to 425 F. Sift flour, baking powder, salt, sugar and spices. Cut in shortening until the mixture resembles corn meal. Combine egg, pumpkin and milk and then add to the flour mixture. Mix until flour is well blended, about 15 strokes. Mix in the raisins. Fill well-greased muffin pans about 2/3 full. Sprinkle sugar on top of muffin batter before baking. Bake about 15 minutes or until muffins spring back when lightly touched. Yields 1 dozen medium-sized muffins.
Pearl Janssen, University of Illinois, Home Economics Faculty Favorites, 1965

FRITTER BATTER

2 cups sifted flour	2/3 cup milk
1 Tablespoon baking powder	2 Tablespoons melted butter
1 1/2 teaspoons salt	4 egg whites, stiffly beaten
2 Tablespoons sugar	1 to 2 cups chopped meat, fruit, or vegetables
4 egg yolks	

Sift flour, baking powder, salt and sugar together. Beat egg yolks well, add milk, and then stir in dry ingredients. Blend in butter. Carefully fold in egg whites and the meat, vegetables or fruit. Drop from Tablespoon into deep hot fat (363 F to 375 F) Fry 4 to 5 minutes or until crisp and brown. Makes 18 regular size fritters.

NOTE: For a sweeter dessert fritter, increase sugar in basic recipe from 1 to 3 Tablespoons.
Farm Journal's Country Cookbook, 1959

FRUIT FRITTER BATTER

1 cup flour	1/2 teaspoon salt	2/3 cup milk
1 teaspoon sugar	2 eggs, well beaten	

Mix the flour sugar and salt. Add the milk slowly and then gradually add the eggs.
The Southern Cook Book, 1939

APPLE, PEACH, APRICOT, OR PEAR FRITTERS

Cut fruit into pieces, dip in the fruit fritter batter above and fry in deep hot (375 F) fat or butter about 3 to 5 minutes or until a golden brown. Then remove with a skimmer and place on crumpled soft paper to drain. Sprinkle with powdered sugar and serve with a lemon sauce or other fruit juice sauce.
The Southern Cook Book, 1939

ORANGE FRITTERS

Peel oranges and separate sections. Remove the seeds, dip into the above batter and fry. Serve as above.
The Southern Cook Book, 1939

OKRA FRITTERS

Boil 1 quart of okra. Strain off water and mash. Season with salt and pepper. Beat in 2 eggs, 2 teaspoons baking powder and enough flour to make a stiff batter. Drop 1 Tablespoonful at a time in deep fat and fry.
The Savannah Cook Book, 1933

GOOD OLD SOUTHERN POPOVERS

3 eggs	1 1/2 cups flour
1 1/2 cups milk	1/2 teaspoon salt

Sift flour and salt into a bowl. Beat eggs and add the milk to them and stir gradually into the flour to make a smooth batter. Then beat thoroughly with hand held mixer (egg beater); put into hot greased muffin tins two thirds full of mixture. Bake in hot oven (450 degrees) for half hour, then in moderate oven (300 degrees) fifteen minutes until brown.
The Southern Cook Book, 1939

FRUIT PUFFS

First cousins to apple turnovers are the Southern fruit puffs. Make a rich puff pastry and cut it into squares. Place a spoonful of stewed fruit or preserves on each square and fold it over into a triangle, pressing the edges down well. Bake in a quick oven (425 F) until the pastry is browned.
Miss Mitchell, 200 Years of Charleston Cooking, 1930

CREAM MUFFINS (Popovers)

NOTE: The original recipe reads, "1 quart of flour, 1 quart sweet milk, 4 eggs and a small piece of butter, salt of course. Bake in a hot oven." The result is popovers.

Reducing the quantities, so that the revised recipe makes 12 popovers, the following amounts are needed.

1 cup flour	1 cup milk
1/4 teaspoon salt	1 teaspoon butter, melted
1 egg, well-beaten	salt

Mix and sift the flour and salt. Add the egg and milk and lastly the butter. Beat with a wheel egg beater for 2 minutes. Pour the batter into very hot iron gem (mini-muffin) pans which must be generously buttered. Bake in a quick oven (425 F) for about 30 minutes. This makes 12 popovers.
Bossis Plantation's recipe re-counted in 200 Years of Charleston Cooking, 1930

PUFF POPS

1 cup flour	1 egg, well-beaten
1/4 teaspoon salt	1 cup milk

Sift the flour and salt together. Mix the egg and milk together and add to dry ingredients. Beat for 2 minutes with a wheel egg beater and put into very hot iron gem pans which have been liberally greased. Bake in a quick oven (425 F) for about 1/2 hour. Yields 12.
Bossis Plantation's recipe re-counted in 200 Years of Charleston Cooking, 1930

CREAM PUFFS

1 cup boiling water	1 cup sifted flour
1/2 cup butter	3 eggs

Boil the water and butter together and, as soon as the butter is melted, add the flour all at once. Stir briskly until the mass will leave the sides of the pan. Remove from the fire and beat in the eggs, one at a time, beating thoroughly after each addition. Drop by spoonful onto a well-buttered baking sheet. The puffs should be far enough apart so that there is no danger of their touching and they should be slightly heaped in the center. Bake in a quick oven (425 F) until no moisture appears on the outside of the puffs. As long as any drop of moisture shows, there is danger that the puffs will collapse after being taken from the oven. This will make about a dozen puffs.

CREAM FILLING

For the filling, dissolve 6 Tablespoons of cornstarch in one cup of milk. Heat the mixture and add 1 egg beaten with 1/2 cup of sugar. Cook until thick, stirring constantly and add 1/2 teaspoon vanilla. When the puffs and filling have cooled, open the side of each puff with a sharp knife and fill it. Dust the tops of the cream puffs with confectioner's sugar.
Mrs. W.E. Turner, 200 Years of Charleston Cooking, 1930

UPSIDE DOWN ORANGE PUFFS

1/4 cup melted butter	2 teaspoons orange rind
1/3 cup orange juice	1 can refrigerator biscuits
1/2 cup sugar	

Combine all the ingredients except the biscuits. Place about 1 tablespoon orange juice mixture into 10 muffin rings. Punch hole in center of each biscuit. Place biscuit into each cup. Bake 15 minutes at 450 F. Let puffs remain in cups 5 minutes after removing them from the oven. Serve upside down.
Satsuma Tea Room, More Fun from the Cook, 1974

FOUR O'CLOCK TEA SCONES

2 cups pastry flour	3 Tablespoons butter
2 Tablespoons sugar	1 egg, beaten light
1 teaspoon salt	1/2 cup milk
4 teaspoons baking powder	sugar for dredging

Sift together the dry ingredients twice and work in the butter with a pastry mixer. Add a half cup of milk to the egg and gradually use in mixing the dough, using more milk if needed. Turn onto a floured board, knead slightly, pat and roll into a sheet, cut into rounds, set in buttered tin, brush over with melted butter and dredge with sugar. Bake in a hot oven (400 F) about 15 minutes. Serve with tea or cocoa.
The Southern Cook Book, 1935

EASY BREAKFAST ROLL

2 cans refrigerator biscuits
1/4 cup butter, melted
1 Tablespoon cinnamon
3/4 cup sugar
1/4 cup chopped nuts

Preheat oven to 375 F. Grease round cake pan. Dip each biscuit in melted butter. Then coat with a mixture of cinnamon and sugar. Pour the remaining butter over the top. Sprinkle with nuts. Bake for 25-30 minutes.
Satsuma Tea Room, More Fun for the Cook, 1974

HOT CROSS BUNS

2 packages yeast, compressed or dry
1/4 cup water (lukewarm for compressed yeast, warm for dry)
1 cup milk
1/2 cup sugar
2 teaspoons salt
1/4 cup shortening
5 cups (about) sifted flour
2 eggs
1 cup currants
1 teaspoon cinnamon
1 teaspoon grated lemon rind
1/4 teaspoon ground allspice
White Icing

Soften yeast in water. Scald milk. Add sugar, salt and shortening. Cool to lukewarm. Add flour to make a thick batter. Mix well. Add softened yeast, eggs, currants, cinnamon, lemon rind and allspice. Beat well. Add more flour to make a soft dough. Turn onto lightly floured board. Knead until satiny. Place in a greased bowl. Cover and let rise in a warm place until doubled (about 1 1/2 hours). When light, punch down. Let rest 10 minutes. Divide dough into pieces about 1 1/2 inches in diameter. Shape each piece into a ball. Place 1 inch apart on greased baking sheets. Let rise until doubles (about 45 minutes). Bake in moderate oven (350 F.) 20 to 25 minutes. Make cross of White Icing on each roll. Makes 3 1/2 dozen.

WHITE ICING

1 egg white
1 1/3 cups sifted confectioners' sugar
1/4 teaspoon vanilla extract

To the unbeaten egg white add sugar gradually, beating it in. Add vanilla extract. Drop from tip of spoon to form crosses on rolls.
Holiday Hostess, 1958

PEANUT TEA RING

1 package of 10 refrigerator biscuits
1/4 cup melted margarine
1 cup finely chopped peanuts
1/2 cup powdered sugar
1 Tablespoon water

Separate biscuits. Dip both sides in melted butter, then in peanuts, coating well. Arrange in overlapping circle (ring) on greased baking sheet. Bake at 425 F for 10 or 15 minutes until golden brown. Mix sugar and water. Drizzle over the hot tea ring at once. Serve at once. Serves 8.
Satsuma Tea Room, More Fun for the Cook, 1974

PECAN BISCUITS

maple syrup to cover bottom of pan
2 Tablespoons butter, melted
1/2 cup chopped walnuts or pecans
1 can refrigerator biscuits

Pour maple syrup and butter into pie plate. Scatter nuts over syrup. Arrange biscuits in pan. Bake according to package directions. Turn out onto plate. 10 servings.
Satsuma Tea Room, More Fun for the Cook, 1974

NUT BREAD

1/2 cup sugar
1 egg
1/2 teaspoon salt
1 cup milk
2 1/2 cups flour
4 teaspoons baking powder
1 cup nuts, chopped

Mix all the ingredients, put in a deep pan and let stand 20 minutes before baking. Bake in a moderate oven (350 F) for 40 minutes.
The Southern Cookbook, 1939

NUT BREAD

2 1/2 cups sifted flour
1/2 cup sugar
1/2 teaspoon salt
1 cup chopped pecans
3 teaspoons baking powder
1 cup milk
1 egg

Mix dry ingredients, then add milk and egg well beaten. Bake one hour in a slow oven.
The Savannah Cook Book, 1933

APPLESAUCE NUT BREAD

1 cup sugar
1 cup applesauce
1/3 cup salad oil
2 eggs
3 Tablespoons milk
2 cups sifted flour
1 teaspoon soda
1/2 teaspoon baking powder
1/2 teaspoon cinnamon
1/4 teaspoon salt
1/4 teaspoon nutmeg
3/4 cup chopped pecans

Heat oven to 350 F. Grease 8 1/2 x 4 1/2 x 2 1/2 inch loaf pan. Combine first 5 ingredients in large bowl. Sift dry ingredients together and add to the applesauce mixture. Stir in the pecans. Pour into prepared pan. Combine topping ingredients and sprinkle over the batter. Bake 1 1/4 hours or until done. After thirty minutes, cover loosely with foil. Makes 1 loaf

TOPPING

1/4 cup brown sugar
1/2 teaspoon cinnamon
1/4 cup chopped pecans

Jane Kersten, The Nashville Cookbook, 1977

APPLE NUT BREAD

1/2 cup butter or margarine	1 teaspoon baking powder
1 cup sugar	1 teaspoon baking soda
2 eggs, unbeaten	1/2 teaspoon salt
1 teaspoon vanilla	1 cup chopped nuts
1 1/2 tablespoons dairy sour cream	1 cup chopped unpeeled apples
2 cups sifted flour	

Cut butter into sugar; add eggs, one at a time, mixing well after each addition. Blend in vanilla and sour cream. Sift together dry ingredients; add nuts. Combine with first mixture. Stir in apples. Pour into greased 9 x 5 x 3-inch pan or 2 small loaf pans. Bake in a slow oven (325 F) about 1 hour. Makes 1 large or 2 small loaves.
Farm Journal's Country Cook Book, 1959

FRESH APPLE BREAD

2 cups sifted flour	1 egg
1 teaspoon baking powder	1/3 cup orange juice
1/2 teaspoon baking soda	3/4 cup raisins
1/2 teaspoon salt	1/4 cup chopped nuts
1/3 cup shortening	1 cup finely chopped apples
1 cup sugar	1 Tablespoon grated orange rind
1 cup sugar	

Sift together the flour, baking powder, baking soda, and salt. Cream the shortening; add sugar gradually. Add egg; beat thoroughly. Add the dry ingredients and orange juice alternately to creamed mixture; blend well after each addition. Add the remaining ingredients and mix well. Pour into 3 well-greased #2 sized tin cans. Bake in a moderate oven (350 F) for 45 minutes. Makes 3 loaves.

NOTE: Make open-face cheese sandwiches with this apple bread for a party. Garnish with slices of pimiento-stuffed olives.
Farm Journal's Country Cook Book, 1959

BANANA BREAD

2 cups flour	1/4 cup butter
1/2 teaspoon baking powder	3/4 cup sugar
1/2 teaspoon baking soda	1 egg
1/4 teaspoon salt	2/3 cup mashed bananas
1/2 cup broken nut meats	1/4 cup buttermilk

Sift the dry ingredients. Cream butter and sugar. Beat in egg and mashed bananas. Alternately add buttermilk and dry ingredients. Add nuts. Bake in loaf pan at 350 F for about 1 hour.
Satsuma Tea Room, Easy on the Cook-Southern Breads, 1975

BANANA BREAD

2 cups flour
1/2 teaspoon baking powder
1/2 teaspoon baking soda
1/4 teaspoon salt
1/2 cup broken nut meats

1/4 cup butter
3/4 cup sugar
1 egg
2/3 cup mashed bananas
1/4 cup buttermilk

Sift dry ingredients. Cream butter and sugar. Beat in egg and mashed bananas. Add nuts. Bake in loaf pan at 350 F for about 1 hour.
Satsuma Tea Room, Fun for the Cook, 1968

BANANA NUT BREAD

1/2 cup butter
1 cup sugar
2 eggs, well beaten
2 cups flour

1 teaspoon baking soda
1 teaspoon baking powder
3 ripe bananas, mashed
1 cup pecans, chopped

Cream butter, sugar, and eggs. Sift together flour, baking soda, and baking powder and add to the mixture. Stir in bananas and nuts. Pour into greased loaf pan and bake at 300 degrees for 1 hour and center test for completion.
Cortner Mill Restaurant cookbook, 2009

LEMON BREAD

1 cup sugar
1/4 cup shortening
2 eggs
grated rind of one lemon
1 1/2 cups sifted all-purpose flour

1 1/2 teaspoons baking powder
1/2 teaspoon salt
1/2 cup milk
1/2 cup nuts, chopped (optional)

Preheat oven to 350 F. Cream sugar and shortening together. Add eggs and lemon rind. Mix well. Sift dry ingredients together. Add dry ingredients to the creamed mixture alternately with the milk. Add nuts if desired. Pour batter into greased 5 x 9 x 2 3/4-inch loaf pan. Bake for 1 hour or until done. Remove from oven and allow to stand 5 minutes. Remove loaf from pan and brush with topping. Yield one loaf of bread.

TOPPING

1/4 cup sugar

juice of 1 lemon

Mix and use to glaze the loaf.
Bette Schaffner, Home Economics Faculty Favorites, University of Illinois, 1965

STRAWBERRY NUT BREAD

1 teaspoon cream of tartar	4 eggs
1/2 teaspoon baking soda	3 cups sifted flour
1 cup margarine	1 teaspoon salt
1 1/2 cups sugar	1 cup strawberry jam
1 teaspoon vanilla	1/2 cup sour cream
1 teaspoon lemon juice	1 cup chopped nuts

Cream the margarine. Add sugar, vanilla, and lemon juice. Beat until fluffy. Add eggs one at a time. Beat well after each addition. Sift together the dry ingredients. Combine jam and sour cream. Add jam mixture alternately with flour mixture to creamed mixture. Beat until well combined. Stir in nuts. Pour into well-greased loaf pans. Bake at 350 degrees for 50-55 minutes. Cool in the pans 10 minutes. Remove from pan and let cool on wire racks. Makes 2 loaves.

NOTE: A most delicious bread. Keeps very well. The bread will freeze and can be cut in thin slices.
Satsuma Tea Room, More Fun for the Cook, 1974

APRICOT NUT BREAD

1/2 cup diced dry apricots	3 teaspoons baking powder
1 egg	1/4 teaspoon baking soda
1 cup sugar	3/4 teaspoon salt
2 Tablespoons melted butter	1/2 cup orange juice
2 cups flour	1/4 cup water
1 cup sliced almonds	

Soak apricots 1/2 hour. Drain and grind. Beat egg until light. Stir in sugar and butter. Sift dry ingredients. Add alternately with orange juice and water. Add nuts and apricots. Mix well and bake at 350 about 1 to 1 1/2 hours.

NOTE: Very good with cream cheese filling and delicious with afternoon tea.
Satsuma Tea Room, Fun for the Cook, 1968

CRANBERRY BREAD

2 cups sifted flour	1/2 cup orange juice
1 cup sugar	2 Tablespoons hot water
1 1/2 teaspoons baking powder	2 Tablespoons melted shortening
1/2 teaspoon baking soda	1 cup cranberries, cut in half
1/2 teaspoon salt	1/2 cup chopped nuts
1 egg, beaten	grated rind of 1 orange

Sift dry ingredients together into a mixing bowl. Add egg, juice, water and shortening. Mix until ingredients are blended. Fold in cranberries, nuts, and orange rind. Pour into a greased loaf pan. Bake in slow oven (325 degrees) for about 1 hour and 10 minutes.
Holiday Hostess, 1958

CINNAMON BREAD

1 cup sugar	1 1/2 teaspoons cinnamon
1 egg	3 Tablespoons sugar
1/4 cup butter	1/4 teaspoon salt
1/2 cup milk	3 teaspoons baking powder
1 3/4 cups flour	

Cream butter and add sugar gradually. Then egg, milk, and lastly flour sifted with baking powder and salt. Put into a greased pan about 8 inches square. Mix cinnamon and 3 Tablespoons of sugar and sprinkle over the top of the mixture and bake 20 minutes. Cut into squares and serve hot.
The Savannah Cook Book, 1933

LEMON TEA BREAD

3/4 cup margarine	3/4 cup buttermilk
1 1/2 cups sugar (may decrease to 1 cup)	grated rind of one lemon
3 eggs	3/4 cup nuts
2 1/4 cups flour	juice of 2 lemons
1/4 teaspoon salt	3/4 cup powdered sugar
1/4 teaspoon baking soda	

Heat oven to 325 F. Grease and flour a 9 x 5 x 3-inch loaf pan. Cream margarine and sugar. Beat in eggs. Combine dry ingredients and add to creamed mixture alternately with buttermilk. Mix well. Stir in grated lemon rind and nuts. Spoon into prepared pan. Bake for about 1 hour and twenty minutes or until cake tester inserted in middle comes out clean. Cool 15 minutes in pan. Remove from pan and cool completely on wire rack. While the loaf is baking, prepare glaze by combining lemon juice and sugar. Let stand to allow sugar to dissolve. After removing loaf, pierce the top with a fork in a number of places and spoon glaze over loaf. Allow to cool before cutting. Makes 1 loaf

NOTE: A tart cake-like loaf. Better if allowed to season. Just delicious!!
Myrtle Harris, The Nashville Cookbook, 1977

PERSIMMON BREAD

3 ¾ cups flour	½ teaspoon nutmeg	2/3 cup Bourbon
2 teaspoons baking soda	1 teaspoon cinnamon	1 cup chopped pecans
1 teaspoon salt	1 cup margarine or	2 cups seedless raisins
1/2 cups sugar	butter, melted	
1/2 teaspoon allspice	4 eggs	

Heat oven to 350 degrees. Grease and flour two 9 x 5 x 3 loaf pans. Sift all dry ingredients together into large bowl, reserving ½ cup flour to dredge nuts and raisins. Combine butter, beaten eggs, Bourbon, and persimmon pulp. Add to dry ingredients. Mix very smooth. Dredge nuts and raisins in flour and incorporate into batter. Fill loaf pans or large stem pan ¾ full. Bake at 350 about 1 hour or until firm to touch. Cool before turning out.
Mary Buckner, The Nashville Cook Book, 1977

PUMPKIN BREAD

3 cups flour	3 teaspoons cinnamon	4 eggs, beaten
1 teaspoon baking soda	2 cups sugar	1 1/4 cups vegetable oil
1 teaspoon salt	2 cups cooked pumpkin	1/2 cups nuts (optional)

Place all dry ingredients into mixing bowl. Make a well in center and add other ingredients. Stir carefully to dampen dry ingredients. Pour into loaf pans. Bake at 350 about 1 hour.

NOTE: This bread is most delicious, can be frozen, and keeps marvelously well.
Satsuma Tea Room, More Fun for the Cook, 1974

DOUGHNUTS

2 cups brown sugar	4 cups flour
2 eggs beaten light	3 teaspoons baking flour
4 Tablespoons melted butter	1/2 teaspoon cinnamon
1 cup sweet milk	1/2 teaspoon salt

Mix in the order given (left to right) adding the dry ingredients sifted together and a sufficient amount of flour to make a dough just soft enough to handle. Do not mix any more than necessary. This will make your doughnut tough. Cover the board with flour and heat the fat for frying. Roll out a little dough at a time and cut into rings with an open doughnut cutter, cutting all the doughnuts preparatory to frying. When the fat is hot enough for the dough to rise to the top quickly, fry each batch of doughnuts 3 to 4 minutes.
The Southern Cook Book, 1939

SPICY RAISED DOUGHNUTS

2 packages of granular yeast	2 eggs, beaten
1/4 cup sugar	5 cups sifted flour
1/4 cup water	2 teaspoons salt
1/3 cup butter	2 teaspoons nutmeg
1 1/2 cup scalded milk	1/2 teaspoon cinnamon

Sprinkle granular yeast and 1 tablespoon sugar over warm (110 F) water or crumble compressed yeast and 1 Tablespoon sugar over lukewarm (85 F) water; let stand 5 minutes. Put butter and remaining sugar into large bowl; pour in hot milk, stirring until butter melts. Cool to lukewarm. Add yeast and eggs. Sift flour, salt, and spices together and stir into yeast mixture and mix well (this will make soft dough). Cover with dampened cloth and let rise in a warm place until doubled. Turn out onto lightly floured board; shape into a soft ball. Roll 1/2 inch thick and let rest 20 minutes. Cut with doughnut cutter. Fry 3 - 4 at a time in hot fat (365 F) about 3 minutes. Drain on paper towel. Sugar while warm. Makes 36.
The Farm Journal's Country Cookbook, 1959

JELLY DOUGHNUTS

Substitute 1 cup whole wheat flour for 1 cup white flour using the *Spicy Raised Doughnut* recipe above. Follow and make the recipe as below, but cut the dough with a 2 inch biscuit cutter (no hole in the center). Put a teaspoon of jelly on half of the doughnuts. Top with the other, remaining half and pinch the edges together. Fry in hot fat (365 F) about 3 minutes. Drain on paper towels. Sprinkle with confectioners' sugar. Makes 2 dozen.
The Farm Journal's Country Cookbook, 1959

SWEET POTATO PONE

2 cups grated sweet potato
1 cup butter
1 cup sugar
1/2 cup milk
1 teaspoon powdered ginger
grated rind of one orange

Blend the sugar and butter, add grated sweet potato and milk; beat well and then add the ginger and orange rind. Place in a shallow baking pan and bake in a slow oven.

NOTE: A little molasses may be used. In areas of the South, where the frost sweetens the persimmons in the fall, a delicious touch is given the pone by adding a cup or more of persimmons before cooking.
The Southern Cook Book, 1939

SOUTHERN SWEET POTATO BREAD

1/4 cup butter
1/2 cup brown sugar
2 eggs, beaten
1 cup cooked, mashed, strained sweet potatoes
3 Tablespoons milk
1 teaspoon grated orange rind
2 cups sifted self-rising flour
1/4 teaspoon nutmeg
1/4 teaspoon allspice
1/2 cup chopped nuts

Heat oven to 350 degrees. Grease and flour 9 x 5 x 3-inch loaf pan. Cream butter. Add sugar and beat until light and fluffy. Add eggs, sweet potatoes, milk, and orange rind. Mix well. Add flour, nutmeg, and allspice to sweet potato mixture with nuts. Mix until smooth. Turn batter into prepared pan. Bake for 45 minutes. Let cool in pan 10 minutes. Remove to cake rack and cool before slicing. Serve with orange cream spread.

NOTE: If using plain flour, sift 3 teaspoons baking powder and 1 teaspoon salt with flour.
Linda Thompson, The Nashville Cookbook, 1977

ORANGE CREAM SPREAD

1 Tablespoon orange juice
1 teaspoon grated orange rind
3 ounces cream cheese

Blend juice and rind into cream cheese until smooth. Spread sliced bread with cream cheese mixture. Makes 1 loaf.
Linda Thompson, The Nashville Cookbook, 1977

SWEET POTATO BISCUIT

6 potatoes
4 Tablespoons butter or lard
1 pint milk
1/2 cake compressed yeast
1 teaspoon salt
1 Tablespoon white sugar
sufficient flour to make a batter

Boil the potatoes, pare and mash them very fine through a sieve. Scald milk and add salt and sugar. Then beat until perfectly smooth. Add these to potatoes and mix well. Then add about half a cup of flour, well sifted several times, so that it will be very light. When the mixture grows tepid, add yeast which has been well dissolved in warm water and beat hard until you have a good batter. Then cover mixture with a thick cloth and put in a warm place to rise.

After 3 or 4 hours, when it is well risen, add flour sufficient enough to make a nice, soft dough. Knead very lightly and quickly for about 10 to 15 minutes. At the end of this time take up and knead lightly several times and roll the dough out. Cut into little biscuits, place them in a slightly-buttered or greased pan, about 2 inches apart, let them stand for 1/2 hour in a warm place and the bake in a quick oven for twenty minutes.

The Picayune Creole Cook Book, 1922

STUFFING

"Poultry dressings in South Carolina are of great and extensive variety. Cornbread and pecans are the most delicious, but peanuts are most commonly used. In many parts of our illustrious state these peanuts are called "goobers," and most farmers grow a patch of them. Mrs. Rhett suggests that in every one of her recipes, the flavor of pecans will be found better than that of peanuts. South Carolina and Georgia are the land of the large soft-shelled pecan and they are freely and most successfully used in delicate cooking.

Lettie Gray says the walnut, so common that it isn't fully appreciated and little used, except in Waldorf Salad, has a more telling flavor than any other nut. Although its flavor is, fortunately, not as pervasive as that of the peanut, it does retain its crisp nut-like quality even after cooking."   -200 Years of Charleston Cooking, 1930

Now, these are topics that I love to see being deliberated. I can imagine these ladies of South Carolinian society sitting around the table, each defending their personal assessment of their favorite nut to use for cooking, even as they were taking afternoon tea together. So Southern!

"In 1672, a Henry Hughes and some others surrendered land so that the town of Charleston might be built. Perhaps there is some esoteric connection between that and the fact that Mr. Edward Hughes has the most spacious garden and house in the city limits today.

Distinguished guests go back to New York and Paris and London boasting to their friends about the pressed turkey and pecan of which they partook in Mr. Hughes' house. For this is more than a mere food; it is a confection. Mr. Hughes allowed us to copy the recipe from his mother's old notebook.

A choice old Charleston recipe. We see no reason to dispute this proclamation. This stuffing is especially good for boned turkey and is, of course, only for the greatest of state occasions."

Edward H. Hughes, 200 Years of Charleston Cooking, 1930

There are about twenty ingredients to this recipe and so we have taken license not to include the massive, entire recipe. A note was appended to the recipe which read, "The most delicious stuffing that has ever been made."

CORNBREAD DRESSING

3 eggs, beaten	3 teaspoons baking powder
2 cups buttermilk	1 teaspoon baking soda
3 Tablespoons melted shortening	3 Tablespoons melted butter
2 teaspoons salt	hot water
2 1/2 cups sifted meal	onion, parsley, celery, salt, pepper

To the well-beaten eggs, add the milk, shortening and salt. Sift together the baking powder and meal and slowly stir this into the egg mixture, adding enough meal to make a medium batter. Beat well. Dissolve baking soda in 1 Tablespoon of water and add to batter. Pour the batter into a greased shallow baking pan. Bake in a hot oven (425 F) about 20 to 25 minutes or until bread begins to brown.

Allow bread to cool, then break into small pieces, crumbling the crust as well. Add the melted butter and season with onion, celery, salt and pepper or any other desired seasonings. Moisten well with hot water. Bread will sop up the moisture, so don't be afraid to add plenty of water. Cook as a side dish or fill the turkey, hen, or roast as required.
The Southern Cook Book, 1939

CORN BREAD STUFFING

Break up enough corn bread to make 4 cups and add 1 chopped onion and 1 cup of celery, and season with salt and pepper. Beat 5 eggs slightly and stir into the corn bread mixture. Mix thoroughly and stuff the chicken. Make a roll of the leftover stuffing and place in the roasting pan with the chicken. Baste the stuffing each time the chicken is basted.

NOTE: This stuffing, thoroughly cooked with the gravy outside the chicken, is considered by many the best and most tasty part of the dish. This stuffing may also be used for turkey.
William Deas, 200 Years of Charleston Cooking, 1930

CHICKEN DRESSING

NOTE: Mix 2 cups of white corn meal with 1 teaspoon salt and water sufficient to make a stiff dough. Bake in a hot griddle as you would for a hoe cake.

Using this corn bread, make a dressing using the following proportions:

3 cups corn bread	pepper
3 cups cold crumbled biscuits or toast	2 eggs
1 medium-sized onion, chopped very fine	chicken stock
3 Tablespoons butter, melted	

Mix the ingredients together, adding enough chicken stock to moisten. Half this amount will be sufficient to stuff a roasting chicken.
Mrs. I.E. Salley, 200 Years of Charleston Cooking, 1930

PEANUT DRESSING

2 cups shelled peanuts	1 egg yolk
1 1/2 cups toasted bread crumbs	broth from cooked fowl
2 Tablespoons melted butter	

The peanuts should be crisply parched, which means that they usually they need to be put into the oven and crisped somewhat before using. Grind the peanuts and add the bread crumbs, melted butter, and egg yolk. The original recipe calls for no liquid, but we found it necessary to moisten the dressing somewhat with broth obtained by cooking the neck and giblets of the fowl. We also seasoned the dressing with salt and pepper.

If the chicken is very fat, leave out the butter as there is plenty of fat in the peanuts. This recipe is a favorite in Charleston for chicken and turkey. For turkey, double the recipe.
William Deas, 200 Years of Charleston Cooking, 1930

BAKED DRESSING (Baked in pans, not in turkeys!)

1 1/2 cups butter or margarine	1 teaspoon pepper
1/2 cup turkey fat	1 teaspoon seasoned salt
1/4 cup chopped onion	2 1/2 to 3 quarts liquid (all broth or broth
2 cups chopped celery	and milk)
5 loaves bread, day old	3 eggs
2 Tablespoons salt	ground giblets

Melt butter and turkey fat (from giblet broth) in skillet. Now add onion and celery; sauté for 10 minutes. Cube bread. Add seasonings, cooked onion, celery, and fat. Add liquid, eggs, and giblets. Mix lightly. Pile lightly into large, greased rectangular pans. Bake in moderate oven (350 F) 30 to 50 minutes, depending on the quantity. Makes 50 servings (does freeze well, but everyone will opt for multiple helpings).
Farm Journal's Country Cookbook, 1959

OYSTER STUFFING

3/4 cup butter	6 cups soft bread crumbs
2 Tablespoons chopped onions	1 pint oysters, chopped
3 Tablespoons chopped parsley	salt and pepper to taste
1 1/2 cups chopped celery	

Melt the butter and in it cook the onion, parsley and celery. Add the bread crumbs and heat well. Add the chopped oysters and seasonings.

NOTE: I'm pretty sure it wasn't this recipe, but I'm positive it was an oyster dressing. My mother made this stand-alone dish at almost every holiday. I loved it! Even today, years after her death, when I think about or eat oyster dressing, I remember my mother fondly and think of our wonderful holidays as a family. I might add my mouth always starts to water! -David S.
The Southern Cook Book, 1939

PECAN STUFFING FOR TURKEY

Shell pecans and put through grinder. Mix with enough bread crumbs to hold them together and then season with melted butter, pepper, salt, and just a suspicion of chopped onion.
The Savannah Cook Book, 1933

CHESTNUT STUFFING

1 egg	1/4 cup butter	6 cups bread crumbs
1 pound chestnuts	2 cups chopped celery	parsley, chopped fine
1/4 cup chicken fat	1/2 cup chopped onions	salt and pepper

Boil the chestnuts for about 20 minutes. Remove the shells and brown skins while the nuts are still hot. Melt the chicken fat and add the butter. Cook the celery and onion in this for a few minutes, add a few sprigs of chopped parsley and the egg, bread crumbs and chestnuts; season to taste with the salt and pepper. Stir this mixture until it is thoroughly hot. Wipe the chicken or turkey dry inside, sprinkle with salt and fill with hot stuffing.

NOTE: This recipe is sufficient for a 10 pound turkey and should be reduced to about half for a 5 pound chicken.
The Southern Cook Book, 1939

DELICIOUS BREAD STUFFING

8 cups dry bread crumbs	1/2 pound bulk pork sausage
2 eggs, beaten	1/2 pound round steak, finely ground
2 cups coarsely ground carrots	1 teaspoon sage
2 small onions, coarsely ground	1/2 teaspoon marjoram
10 ½ ounce can condensed cream of mushroom soup	1/8 teaspoon nutmeg
	2 teaspoon salt

If cooking stuffing for a goose, grind the heart, liver, and gizzard together.

Blend all ingredients thoroughly in large pot or mixing bowl. Makes 12 cups of stuffing or enough for a 10-12 pound goose.

NOTE: This is an unusual stuffing at any time, but it is an ideal stuffing when cooking goose.
Farm Journal's Country Cookbook, 1959

BREAD STUFFING

Soak 1 quart of stale bread in cold water and squeeze dry. Season with the following ingredients: 1 teaspoon salt, 1/8 teaspoon black pepper, 1/4 teaspoon poultry seasoning, 1 teaspoon chopped parsley, 1/2 teaspoon onion, chopped fine (onions may be omitted if desired. Add 2 Tablespoons melted fat and mix thoroughly. Beat 1 egg lightly and add to the above mixture. Then add the giblets of the fowl or use pork or liver sausage chopped fine and partially boiled.
The Southern Cookbook, 1939

CRUMBLY BREAD STUFFING

Heat 1 1/8 cup butter or margarine in deep pot; sauté 3/4 cup minced onions until soft and tender. Combine with 4 1/2 quarts day old bread crumbs, 1/4 cup diced celery, 1 1/2 teaspoons poultry seasoning, 1/2 cup snipped parsley (optional), 1/4 teaspoon pepper and 2 1/4 teaspoons salt. Heat well without browning, stirring frequently. Makes enough to stuff neck and body cavity of a 10 pound ready to cook turkey.
Farm Journal's Country Cookbook, 1959

APPLE STUFFING

1 small onion	4 cups chopped apples
6 Tablespoons butter	2 Tablespoons chopped parsley
1 cup chopped celery	4 Tablespoons seeded raisins
3 cups stale bread crumbs	salt and pepper

Chop onion and brown in butter; add celery, bread crumbs, apple and parsley; season with salt and pepper and then add raisins.
The Southern Cook Book, 1939

CELERY STUFFING

7 cups dry bread crumbs	1/2 teaspoon poultry seasoning
1 cup chopped onion	2/3 cup melted butter or margarine
2 cups finely chopped celery	1 1/3 cup milk
2 teaspoons salt	1 1/4 cups turkey/chicken broth
1/2 teaspoon pepper	2 eggs, slightly beaten
1 1/2 teaspoons sage	

Combine bread crumbs, onion, celery and seasonings. Add melted butter, milk, broth and eggs. Toss lightly to blend. Stuff loosely into cavities of bird. Makes 6 1/2 cups stuffing; enough for 12 pound ready to cook turkey.
Farm Journal's Country Cookbook, 1959

NOTE: During the Holiday seasons at *Satsuma*, we made tons and tons of dressing to sell to the public for their holiday meals. We sold it in one pound plastic bags, which had all the seasonings added, dried chicken stock by the handfuls, ground celery and onion, and bread (both corn bread and white bread which we would freeze months ahead knowing the holidays were coming).

All the purchaser had to do was add liquid (water or broth or milk). Lots of liquid was added (very runny) because the bread absorbed the liquid as the stuffing baked. It was always recommended that the dressing be prepared as a side dish to assure the eggs were safely cooked. Although it could be used to stuff the bird in the traditional way.

CRANBERRY-ORANGE STUFFING (For roast chicken)

8 ounce package seasoned bread stuffing
1 cup cranberry orange relish
1/3 cup melted butter
1/2 teaspoon salt
1/4 teaspoon nutmeg
1 Tablespoon sugar

Combine ingredients. Toss. Make enough stuffing for one roasting chicken or small turkey.
Easy-on-the-Cook Book, 1960

ORANGE STUFFING

2 cups chopped celery
1 cup boiling water
1/4 chopped green pepper (optional)
1/3 cup chopped onion
1/3 to 1/2 cup butter or shortening
2 cups peeled, diced oranges with juice
2 teaspoons grated orange rind
3/4 teaspoon poultry seasoning
1 teaspoon salt
1/4 teaspoon pepper
7 to 8 cups lightly packed soft bread crumbs

Simmer celery in water until tender, about 10 to 15 minutes. Drain. Sauté green pepper and onion in butter until tender, but not brown. Combine oranges, seasonings and crumbs; add cooked vegetables (celery and onion) and toss together lightly. Makes enough to stuff one 5 pound duck.
Farm Journal's Country Cookbook, 1959

ALMOND HERB STUFFING

2 quarts soft bread cubes
1 cup slivered blanched almonds
1 1/2 teaspoons salt
1 teaspoon thyme
1/2 teaspoon tarragon
1/4 teaspoon savory
1/4 teaspoon pepper
1/3 cup butter or margarine
3/4 cup minced onion
2 cups warm chicken broth

Empty bread cubes into large bowl. Add almonds, salt, thyme, tarragon, savory, and pepper. Melt butter in saucepan. Add onion and cook about 5 minutes, stirring frequently. Pour the onion mixture and broth over bread cubes. Toss lightly, mixing thoroughly, until bread is well moistened. Turn into a buttered 1 1/2 quart casserole; cover. Bake at 350 F for 35 minutes. Uncover and bake 15 minutes longer. If desired, stuff a large chicken or small turkey with the stuffing. Makes 6 servings.

NOTE: Instead of chicken broth you may use two chicken bouillon cubes dissolved in two cups boiling water.
Easy-on-the-Cook Book, 1960

SPARERIBS WITH ORANGE STUFFING

2 (1 1/2 pounds) pieces of spareribs	1/3 cup chopped whole orange
2 teaspoons salt	1 teaspoon grated orange rind
1/4 teaspoon pepper	1 cup diced celery
1 1/2 cups dry or toasted bread cubes	1 egg, beaten
2 Tablespoons melted butter or margarine	1/4 teaspoon salt
	dash of pepper
1/4 cup hot water	1/8 teaspoon poultry seasoning

Rub the spareribs with salt and pepper. Place one piece in baking pan, fat side down. Toss remaining ingredients together lightly; pat this mixed stuffing firmly over ribs. Place second piece of meat over stuffing, fat side up; skewer or tie the two pieces together. Brown in a hot oven (450 F) 1/2 hour; reduce heat to moderate (350 F) and bake 1 hour longer. Cut between each 2 ribs to serve. Makes 6-8 servings.

NOTE: Good meat juices and the oranges flavor this stuffing.
Farm Journal's Country Cookbook, 1959

MAPLE GINGERBREAD

1 cup maple syrup	1 teaspoon baking soda
1 cup dairy sour cream	1 1/2 teaspoons ginger
1 egg, well beaten	1/2 teaspoon salt
2 1/3 cups sifted flour	4 Tablespoons melted butter or margarine

Blend syrup with cream and egg. Sift dry ingredients and stir into the syrup mixture. Add butter and beat thoroughly. Pour into an 8 x 12-inch baking pan, lined with greased brown paper. Bake in moderate oven (350 F) for 30 minutes. Makes 8 servings.

NOTE: Feast of the gods; warm squares of this gingerbread accompanied by bowls of applesauce.
Farm Journal's Country Cook Book, 1959

DESSERTS
SWEET AS HEAVEN

"How sweet are your words to my taste, sweeter than honey to my mouth!"
Psalm 119:103

"Life is short and our futures are unknown, so eat dessert first."
-Unknown

Southerners tend to like, love, lust over their sweets. Why this fact is true would cause volumes to be written by sociologists and historians attempting to dissect and explain this phenomenon. John T. Edge along with Ellen Rolfes, in their *A Gracious Plenty*, wrote in trying to explain sweets in the South "Eat right, act right and you will receive your reward hereafter - or at least after you finished your liver."

Hospitality is known to be one of the foundations of being Southern and what better way to express your hospitality than to serve your welcomed guests a wonderful piece of cake, pie, or other form of confection. "Greetings, really glad you all are here!"

Dessert is the happiest of conclusions for any meal. You want your family and your guests to continue raving about your wonderful dinner as they leave the table. That's why it is best to choose a dessert best fit for your meal. After a luncheon or light dinner, or at a dessert party, you'll make a hit with a rich, glamorous treat. A light, simple dessert is a natural follow-up to an elaborate dinner. Your guests will eat the special desserts with much delight and gusto; not just out of a sense of duty.

In many ways, this is how we think of Southern cooking at its absolute best and, in our estimation, the finest examples of all Southern cooking are the desserts. The pleasing sweetness that we find in honey, maple and cane syrups, caramelized, and hot brown biscuits with amber honey, a stack of hot pancakes drenched with maple or cane syrup, a frosted caramel layer cake, a luxuriously rich butterscotch pie, and a big plate filled with wavy, wrinkled sugar-topped molasses cookies are examples. Sugars and molasses are only half the story. The rest of the story are the delicious flavors that also make these unparalleled old-time dishes totally to die for and treasured.

In the period before readily accessible sugar; figs, dates, and nuts were mixed with honey to satisfy our "hankering" for sweets. With time, molasses and cane syrup became more available and popular in the South; befitting the confection of choice as a stand-alone bit of "sweet" or as a sugar alternative used in cooking. Natural maple syrup and maple sugar are not nearly so abundant across our country and our Southern region as honey because they are produced and more readily linked with the Northeast and New England, where most of the harvesting of the syrup takes place. Sugar cane syrup, sugar cane sugar, and blackstrap molasses, better known as "cane syrup", "cane sugar", and just 'lasses" enjoy equal honor in the South.

Most of the recipes that are found among these pages have been adapted for our modern-day enjoyment in our never-ending quest for something sweet.

PIES AND TORTES

Pie for dessert is as American, and by default as Southern, as the Grand Ole Flag and the Fourth of July; just a good warm piece of apple pie is all that's necessary. Serve it by itself or choose an accepted accessory, such as a big scoop of vanilla ice cream, slices of sharp cheese, or spoons of whipped cream, to take a pie from ordinary to an out of this world. Why not cut and serve your pie at the table? It is your masterpiece and it deserves to be center stage. All eyes will be focused on you as you cut through the crust, tender and flaky, perfectly crimped and browned into the delicious filling. Feel your mouth watering? I do, just thinking about it.

ALABAMA PECAN PIE

3 eggs, beaten lightly
1 cup sugar
1 cup corn syrup, light
3 Tablespoons margarine
1 teaspoon vanilla
1 cup broken pecans
1 pie shell (9 inch), unbaked

Heat oven to 400 degrees. Mix all ingredients together and pour into pie shell. Place in oven, cook for 10 minutes and reduce to 350 degrees and cook for 35-40 minutes more or until firm. Serves 8.

NOTE: A Graves' family favorite from 'way back'.
Aileen Graves, The Nashville Cookbook, 1977

PECAN PIE

1/2 cup sugar
1/2 cup dark corn syrup
3 eggs
1/2 cup butter melted
1 dash salt
1 cup pecans
9 inch unbaked pie shell

Beat eggs and remaining ingredients. Blend well and pour into the pie shell and bake at 350 for 45 minutes. Serves 8.

NOTE: Want to know the secret of pecan pie? It is not the thousands of recipes or the multitude of great cooks. The difference is the pecans. Buy pecans that have been refrigerated since they were harvested and keep them refrigerated. Once, in an emergency, we used pecans off the grocery rack and wondered what went wrong with our pies. Our guests asked if we had a new recipe or cook. The nut oils had become rancid.
David Hazelwood, Cortner Mill Restaurant cookbook, 2009

WHITE HOUSE PECAN PIE

1 cup unbroken pecan meats
1 cup dark table syrup
2 Tablespoons butter
2 eggs
1 cup sugar
1 teaspoon vanilla

Cream butter and sugar, add table syrup, beaten eggs, pecans and vanilla. Beat together well. Put into unbaked pie shell and bake in a slow oven (275 F) for about 30 minutes. Serve with whipped cream.
The Southern Cookbook, 1939

CARAMEL PECAN PIE

1/2 pound (28) caramels	3/4 cup sugar	2 eggs, slightly beaten
1/2 cup water	1/4 teaspoon salt	1 cup pecan halves
1/4 cup margarine	1/2 teaspoon vanilla	

Place caramels, water, margarine in top of double boiler. Heat, stirring frequently, until caramels are melted and mixture is smooth. Combine sugar, salt, vanilla, and eggs. Gradually add caramel sauce, mixing well. Add pecan halves. Pour into pastry lined pie pan. Bake in 400 F. oven 10 minutes; reduce heat to 350 F and continue baking 20 minutes.

NOTE: The pie filling appears to be very soft while it is hot, but as it cools it becomes firm.
Easy-on-the-Cook Book, 1960

KENTUCKY DERBY PIE

4 eggs	1 teaspoon vanilla
1/2 cup melted margarine	1/2 cup chocolate chips
1 cup corn syrup	1/2 cup nuts

Beat eggs well. Add the other ingredients. Mix chocolate chips and nuts- put on the bottom of the unbaked pie shell. Pour over these the egg mixture. Bake at 325 degrees for 45 minutes or until set. Cool before serving.

NOTE: Kentucky is known as the "Bluegrass State" and racehorse country. The premier horse race in the country is the Kentucky Derby, which is held the first Saturday of May every year. As you enjoy the Derby with friends at a Derby-watch party, place your bet on the favorite horse as you take pleasure in a warm slice of Kentucky Derby pie, topped with a small scoop of vanilla ice cream.
Satsuma Tea Room, Pies, Pies, Pies, Satsuma's Easy on the Cook Pie Supplement

KENTUCKY PIE (Idle Hour Farm recipe)

3 cups brown sugar	1/2 cup butter	1 teaspoon vanilla
3 eggs	1/2 cup cream	1 pinch salt

Cream the butter, eggs, and sugar together and then add the balance of the ingredients. Fill a pie shell and bake in a moderate oven (350 F) for 30 minutes.
The Southern Cookbook, 1939

CHESS TARTS

2 cups sugar	1/2 cup cream	12 tart shells (unbaked)
4 eggs	1 Tablespoon vinegar	
1/2 cup butter	1 teaspoon vanilla	

Heat oven to 350 F. Beat the eggs until light. Add the other ingredients. Cook slowly in shells until filling sets (45 or 50 minutes). Serves 12.
Elnora Culbert, The Nashville Cookbook, 1977

CHESS PIE

1/2 cup butter, melted
3 eggs, beaten
1 1/2 cups sugar
1 Tablespoon vinegar
1 teaspoon vanilla
1 teaspoon yellow cornmeal
1-9 inch unbaked pie shell

Melt butter and combine with sugar. Add mixture to beaten eggs. Add remaining ingredients individually, stirring well between each. Pour mixture into pie shell and bake at 325 for 55-60 minutes. Cook until set.

NOTE: Nashville and Middle Tennessee are quite famous for their chess pie and there are as many recipe variations of this pie as there are stars in the sky. There is not a wrong or right, better or best, recipe for chess pie. Each one tastes amazing. Chess pie is often mistaken for Buttermilk Pie, Buttermilk Chess Pie, Egg Pie, Egg Custard Pie, or the very popular Lemon Chess; which are all celebrated variations to this iconic pie. These pies are made from the same general recipe as chess; only with slight variations.
Claudia Hazelwood, Cortner Mill Restaurant cookbook, 2009

MERINGUE CHESS PIE

6 eggs
1 cup granulated sugar
1/2 cup brown sugar
1 Tablespoon cornmeal
1 Tablespoon flour
1/4 cup milk
1/4 cup butter, melted
1/2 teaspoon vinegar
1 teaspoon vanilla
9 inch pastry shell, unbaked

Heat oven to 400 degrees. Slightly beat 1 whole egg and 5 egg yolks. Gradually add sugars and blend. Stir in the mixture of flour and cornmeal, then the butter, milk, vinegar, and vanilla. Pour into pastry shell. Bake at 400 degrees about 10 minutes; lower the heat to 325 degrees and bake 35 minutes.

MERINGUE

Add a pinch of salt and 1/2 teaspoon cream of tartar to 5 remaining egg whites. Beat until stiff peaks are formed. Gradually add 10 Tablespoons sugar, beating until it dissolves. Cover pie with meringue, sealing completely. Bake at 375 degrees for 7-8 minutes. Serves 6.
Louise Reynolds, The Nashville Cookbook, 1977

WALNUT CHESS PIE

1 stick butter
1 cup sugar
3 Tablespoons flour
1/3 teaspoon salt
1/2 cup chopped walnuts
3 egg yolks
2/3 cup evaporated milk
1 teaspoon vanilla

Prepare pastry shell. Chill. Beat butter and sugar until well mixed. Add flour, salt, egg yolks and milk. When well mixed, stir in vanilla and walnuts. Pour into unbaked shell. Bake on lower shelf of oven until center is almost set. Bake at 375 degrees about 45 minutes. Cool thoroughly before slicing.
Satsuma Tea Room, Pies, Pies, Pies, Satsuma's Easy on the Cook Pie Supplement

MOLASSES

Molasses is another one of those sweeteners associated with Southerners and I would say rightly so. As a sweetener, we could have discussed it in several categories, because it was used in breads, pies, cakes, cookies, candy, confections, dessert sauces, and even meat curing.

In order to make molasses, sugar cane is harvested and the stalk's leaves are removed. Cane juice is then separated from the cuttings by crushing or mashing the cane stalks. The juice from the cane obtained from this process is then boiled almost to the point of being sugar. Syrup that is the subsequent product of this first boiling is known as the first syrup or cane syrup; the resulting cane syrup assures a much higher sugar content.

Second molasses is produced after a second boiling and second sugar extraction of the cane syrup product derived after the first boiling. Molasses has a different flavor and is said to have a slightly bitter taste. I don't perceive the taste as being bitter, just less sugary. In fact, I prefer the taste of molasses over the taste of cane syrup. My favorite of all molasses sweeteners is sweet sorghum molasses, which we identify in the South as just plain old sorghum molasses. The production method is the same as with sugar cane, just with sorghum stalks instead of sugar cane stalks. Many don't realize that molasses is the major component in the making of fine brown sugar, both light and dark brown sugars. I always wondered why if given a choice, all things being equal, I'd choose a brown sugar over a white or cane sugar any day. Now I think I know why that's the case. Molasses!

A variety of the sorghum plant grown in Middle Tennessee, as elsewhere in the South, provides the sweet juice for making sorghum molasses. Making this sweetener was once a very common activity in rural areas, but the interesting process of cooking the golden syrup to the right stage of thickness is now a fast disappearing art. The mule-powered mills, known for extracting the juice from the cane in the early days of settlement, are now sparse in number, but the existing mills still attract many visitors during the fall weeks. Sorghum molasses is much enjoyed as a syrup and as a natural sweetener.

MOLASSES PIE

| 1 1/4 cups molasses | 1 Tablespoon flour | 2/3 cup sugar |
| 3 eggs | 1 Tablespoon butter | 1 unbaked pie shell |

Place molasses and butter in a saucepan and let come to a boil. Beat the eggs until light and fluffy. Mix the flour and sugar and add to eggs. Add this mixture to the molasses mixture. Pour into shell and bake at 325 F for 30 minutes.
Ann Bellamy Hendon, Miss Lizzie's Heirlooms, 2009

SHOO FLY PIE

| 2/3 cup brown sugar | 2 cups sifted flour | 2/3 cup dark molasses |
| 2/3 cup shortening | 1/2 teaspoon baking soda | unbaked pastry shell |

Mix brown sugar and shortening to make crumbs. Add flour. Mix well. Mix water and baking soda, and add to molasses. Place layer of crumbs in unbaked pastry shell, then cover with molasses mixture, and next a layer of crumbs. Continue until all are used. Bake in moderate oven (350 F) 35 to 45 minutes.

NOTE: This is a dessert that deserves its fabulous reputation. All molasses lovers enjoy this unforgettable, rich gingerbread baked in a plain pie crust. Work rapidly with the molasses mixture so you don't lose the leavening power of the baking soda before it is in the oven.
What to Cook for Company, 1953

BUTTERSCOTCH OR CARAMEL?

Although caramel and butterscotch are words interchanged often, they do not mean the same thing. These words denote two totally different creations; similar yet different. Caramel is made by heating white sugar in an iron skillet slowly over low heat until it browns. Butterscotch is the marriage of two ingredients, butter and brown sugar, and when these two ingredients come together, wonderful things happen to a dish. Butterscotch is exalted as being among the most pleasurable foods and desserts around. Calorie counters just may brandish their senses when a slice of butterscotch pie is set in front of them, because very few Southerners can resist raising their forks and delighting in this great dessert.

BUTTERSCOTCH PIE

1 cup brown sugar
1 cup milk
1 egg white beaten well
2 Tablespoons butter
2 generous teaspoons flour
1 egg yolk

Boil the sugar and butter together until soft. Beat the egg yolk well and add it to the flour, then add the milk. Beat this until very smooth. Mix this well into the sugar and butter and cook until it thickens. Lemon or vanilla can be used for flavoring. Pour this into a pie pan lined with the baked pie crust. To the beaten egg white add 1 Tablespoon sugar, spread over the top of pie and brown in the oven.
Farm Journal's Country Cook Book, 1959

CARAMEL PIE/PUDDING

3 cups milk, heated in a double boiler

Caramelize 1 cup sugar by heating sugar in iron skillet over very low heat until sugar melts. Add cautiously 1/4 cup hot water (a quick addition of water could cause trouble). Stir with care until it makes a smooth syrup.

Pour gradually into hot milk and heat to boiling. Mix 1/4 cup cornstarch with 1 cup cold milk. Put this mixture in the double boiler cook 10 minutes. Beat 2 eggs well and add a little of the hot milk mixture. Add the whole to double boiler and cook, stirring constantly for two minutes. Remove from heat; add 1 teaspoon vanilla, 1/2 cup butter. This can be used as pie filling. Our customers love both our caramel custard and our caramel pie. The caramel pie consists of the caramel pudding in a pie pan with a cooked bottom crust and topped with peaks of cooked meringue.

NOTE: This is an old favorite with a true caramel flavor. The flavor will depend upon skill in caramelizing the sugar. The longer the sugar is browned, the deeper the flavor and color. Sugar burns easily so use caution.
Satsuma Tea Room, More Fun for the Cook, 1974

TRANSPARENT PIES (Tarts)

1/2 cup butter	2 cups sugar
2 cups sugar	1/2 teaspoon nutmeg or juice of 1 lemon
5 eggs	pastry

Cream the butter and sugar and add the slightly beaten eggs and the chosen flavoring. Line individual cake pans with pastry and pour in the mixture. Bake in a moderate oven (325 F.) for 20 minutes. This makes 15 tarts).
200 years of Charleston Cooking, 1930

BUTTERMILK PIE

2 cups sugar	3 eggs
3 Tablespoons flour	1 cup buttermilk
1/4 teaspoon nutmeg	juice and grated rind of 1 lemon
1/2 cup melted butter or margarine	

Mix sugar, flour and nutmeg. Add melted butter. Beat well until creamy. Add eggs and beat milk and lemon juice and rind. Beat well until blended. Put unbaked pie shell into a 9 inch pan and bake at 400 for 10 minutes. Reduce heat and bake at 325 about 30 minutes longer.

NOTE: This pie is not as rich as chess pie due to the fact that there is more acid. Some people really prefer it and I just love the lemon flavor.
Satsuma Tea Room, More Fun for the Cook, 1974

RAISIN PIE

1 cup seeded raisins, washed	1 egg, well beaten
2 cups water	juice of a lemon
1 1/2 cups sugar	2 teaspoons grated lemon rind
4 Tablespoons flour	pinch of salt

Soak raisins 3 hours. Mix sugar, flour and egg, then add seasoning, raisins and liquid. Cook over hot water for 15 minutes, stirring occasionally. When the mixture is cool, empty into pie dough lined pie plate. Cover pie with narrow strips of dough crisscrossed and bake in hot oven (450 F) for 20 minutes and in a moderate oven (350 F) for 10 minutes.
The Southern Cook Book, 1939

COBBLERS

Cobbler pies are a traditional favorite with Southern cooking. This was a great way to use the fruit that was picked fresh during growing season and then canned or "put up" in the cellar to be used all year long. Cobblers are easy to make and, when served warm with a little sweet cream or ice cream, you feel as if your taste buds have died and gone to heaven.

PEACH COBBLER

2 cups peaches, chopped
3/4 cup sugar
1/2 cup butter
3/4 cup flour
1 cup sugar
2 teaspoons baking powder
3/4 cup buttermilk

Combine peaches with 3/4 cup sugar in mixing bowl. Melt butter in 8x8 shallow baking dish. Mix the flour, 1 cup sugar and baking powder in separate bowl. Stir buttermilk into this bowl and then pour the flour mixture into the baking dish and top with peaches. Do not stir. Bake in 300 degree oven for 1 hour. Serves 6.
David Boswell Hazelwood, Miss Lizzie's Heirlooms, 2009

BLACKBERRY COBBLER

2 cups fresh blackberries
3 cups water
1 1/2 cups sugar
1/2 cup flour
1/4 cup butter
1/4 cup sugar
1/4 cup flour
1/4 cup butter
pastry for two crusts

Gently wash the berries and combine blackberries and water in a saucepan. Bring to a boil and boil until the blackberries are tender, stirring occasionally. Combine 1 1/2 cups sugar, and 1/2 cup flour in a bowl and mix well. Add a small amount of the berry liquid to the sugar mixture, blend well and pour into the blackberries. Cook until thickened, stirring occasionally. Line a deep baking dish with a pastry shell. Pour the blackberries into the pastry. Dot with 1/4 cup butter. Top with the remaining pastry. Sprinkle with a mixture of 1/4 cup sugar and 1/4 cup flour. Dot with 1/4 cup butter. Bake at 350 until brown and bubbly. Serves 6-8.
David Boswell Hazelwood, Miss Lizzie's Heirlooms, 2009

APPLE POT PIE

1/2 dozen baking apples
1/2 cup butter or other shortening
4 cups flour
1/4 teaspoon salt
1/4 teaspoon cinnamon
1/8 pound butter

Make a pie dough of flour, shortening, and salt. Add sufficient water to form dough. Roll thin on a floured board and cut into two-inch squares. Peel and core apples and cut into small pieces. Place apples into a kettle and sprinkle liberally with sugar and cinnamon. Alternate layers of dough and apples. Place butter on top. Fill kettle half full of water, cover and cook until apples are done. Serve with fresh milk or cream.
The Southern Cook Book, 1939

CHERRY COBBLER

| 12 buttermilk biscuits | 1 cup flour or cornstarch | 1/4 teaspoon salt |
| 4 cups tart cherries | 1 1/2 tsp lemon juice | 2 Tablespoons butter |

Prepare biscuit dough and place half of it in bottom of 8x8 greased pan. Pit cherries and combine all other ingredients, except butter, in a saucepan. Bring fruit to a boil and pour into baking pan over dough. Dot with butter. Cover with remaining dough and seal edges. Bake in a 350 oven for one hour.
David Boswell Hazelwood, Miss Lizzie's Heirlooms, 2009

FRIED APPLE PIES

1 cup dried apples	1 Tablespoon butter	1/2 cup milk
1/2 cup sugar	2 cups flour	1/2 cup vegetable oil
1/4 teaspoon cinnamon	1 teaspoon salt	

Rinse apples and place in a sauce pan covered with water. Cook covered over medium heat about 45 minutes. Make pastry dough while apples are cooking. Drain excess water off apples. Add sugar, butter, and cinnamon. Cook over medium heat until thickened, stirring occasionally. Spoon 2 1/2 Tablespoons of apple mixture onto each pastry circle. Fold pastry over and press edges with fork. Fry in 1 inch of 375 degree oil until golden brown on each side, turning once. Remove from oil and cool on paper towel. Makes 8-10 pies.

NOTE: Miss Lizzie's June apples were for eating fresh, making apple butter, or apples with red hots, but the favorite use was using the dried apples in the winter for fried apple pies.
David Boswell Hazelwood, Miss Lizzie's Heirlooms, 2009

APPLE CAKE PIE

5 large apples, cored and thinly sliced	1 egg, beaten
1 teaspoon lemon juice	1/2 cup sifted flour
3/4 cup sugar	1/2 teaspoon baking powder
1/4 cup butter or margarine	1/8 teaspoon salt

Place apples in well-greased 10 inch pie pan; sprinkle with lemon juice, then cover with 1/4 cup sugar. Cream together butter and remaining 1/2 cup sugar. Add egg and mix. Sift together flour, baking powder and salt then mix with creamed mixture. Spread over the fruit. Bake in a moderate oven (350 F) for 45 minutes. Serve hot or cold with either a thin custard sauce or whipped cream. Makes 8 servings.

CUSTARD SAUCE

Combine 3 beaten egg yolks, 1/4 cup sugar and dash of salt. Stir in 2 cups scalded milk. Cook over hot water, stirring constantly until mixture coats spoon. Add 1 teaspoon vanilla. Chill. Makes about 2 1/2 cups.

NOTE: Is this a cake or is it a pie? Who cares! It is so good!
Farm Journal's Country Cook Book, 1959

FRESH APPLE PIE

7 Granny Smith apples (tart cooking apples)
1 cup sugar
1 teaspoon cinnamon
2 Tablespoons flour
3 Tablespoons butter
1 unbaked double crust pastry

Peel, core, slice apples. Mix together flour, sugar, and cinnamon and sprinkle mixture over apples and mix well. Pour apples into pie shell. Dot apples with butter and cover with top crust. Seal and flute crust and cut slits in top crust. Sprinkle sugar on top of crust. Bake at 425 for 40-45 minutes until crust is brown and juice begins to bubble. Serves 8.
David Hazelwood, Cortner Mill Restaurant cookbook, 2009

FRESH GRAPE PIE

Start with 1 quart blue concord grapes. Pulp and then cook the pulp. Put pulp through strainer to remove seeds. Add seedless pulp to skins. (Pulp means to separate the skin from the grape insides. Basically, squeeze the grape.)

3/4 cup sugar
1 1/2 Tablespoons lemon juice
1 Tablespoon quick cooking tapioca

Mix all the ingredients together and put into unbaked pastry shell. Place either plain or lattice crust on top. Bake at 450 for ten minutes and lower heat to 350 and bake twenty minutes longer. We make this pie as often as we can manage when grapes are in season (a narrow window but the grape filling does freeze well after prepared). We also use the filling to make fresh grape sherbet and fresh grape ice cream in addition to our grape pie. So many people remark "My grandmother used to make that pie. I love it, but I have not eaten any in years."

NOTE: A more modern take on this traditional recipe is to add the juice and zest of one orange (chopped) to the above ingredients. It really gives a punch of flavor to the filling.
Satsuma Tea Room, Fun for the Cook, 1968

HOT BLACKBERRY PIE

1/4 cup flour
4 cups blackberries
1- 9 inch pastry, double crust
1 cup sugar
1 1/2 Tablespoons lemon juice
1 Tablespoon butter
1/4 teaspoon salt

Combine all ingredients except butter. Pour into unbaked pie shell. Dot with butter. Arrange solid or lattice cover over pie. Bake at 350 for 50-55 minutes.

NOTE: Cobblers are nice, but in my opinion with emphasis on the fruit, this pie tops the cobbler. Serving with fresh-churned vanilla ice cream is a must.
David Hazelwood, Cortner Mill Restaurant cookbook, 2009

COLD BLACKBERRY PIE

3/4 cup sugar
2 1/2 Tablespoons cornstarch
1 cup water
4 cups fresh blackberries

3 1/2 Tbl. blackberry gelatin (1 1/2 oz.)
1- 9 inch baked pie shell
whipped cream

Combine sugar, cornstarch, and water in saucepan and cook over medium heat, stirring constantly until thickened. Remove from heat and stir in gelatin until dissolved. Gently stir in blackberries. Pour mixture into pastry shell and chill in refrigerator until firm. Slice and garnish each slice with a dollop of whipped cream. Serves 8

NOTE: This is my favorite Fourth of July dessert. Blackberries have just ripened in Tennessee and this pie is so refreshing on a hot summer day. I view it as a suitable prize for picking the berries among the thorns and chiggers.
David Hazelwood, Cortner Mill Restaurant cookbook, 2009

RASPBERRY APRICOT PIE

10 ounces raspberries
32 ounces apricot halves
1/4 cup flour
3/4 cup sugar

1/8 teaspoon salt
2 Tablespoons butter
1/2 teaspoon almond extract
2- 9 inch unbaked pie crusts

If raspberries are frozen, defrost and drain, saving 1/2 cup of the juice. Place drained apricots in pie crust. Spoon raspberries over apricots and pour juice over top. Mix sugar, flour, and salt and sprinkle over berries. Dot berries with butter and sprinkle with extract. Cover with top crust and sprinkle with sugar. Bake at 400 for 50-60 minutes. Serves 8.

NOTE: The first time I had this pie was in 1992. The Iroquois Steeplechase is run the second Saturday in May each year in Nashville. It was often preceded by a Steeplechase Brunch at the Hazelwood home. Bill Cox made this pie and it has been one of my favorites ever since. I have used the recipe as a basis for trying other combinations of fruit, like blueberry-peach and blackberry peach. Increase the sugar to 1 cup while using 1 1/2 cups of these fresh fruits.
Bill Cox, Cortner Mill Restaurant cookbook, 2009

FRESH PEACH PIE

5 cups fresh peaches, sliced
1 teaspoon lemon juice
1 1/4 cups sugar

1/3 cup flour
1/4 teaspoon cinnamon
3 Tablespoons butter

Prepare a two-crust pastry and set aside. Mix peaches and lemon juice. Sift together flour, sugar, cinnamon and mix with peaches. Pour peaches into pastry lined pan. Dot peaches with butter and cover top crust. Seal and flute crust and cut slits in top crust. Sprinkle sugar on top of crust. Bake at 425 for 40-45 minutes or until crust is golden brown and juice begins to bubble through slits of crust. Serves 8
David Hazelwood, Cortner Mill Restaurant cookbook, 2009

CHERRY PIE

2 lbs. pitted tart red cherries (water pack)
1/4 teaspoon salt
1/4 teaspoon almond extract
2 1/2 Tablespoons quick-cooking tapioca
1 teaspoon lemon juice

4 drops red food color
1 1/4 cups sugar
Rich Pastry
1 Tablespoon butter

Drain cherries, putting 1/3 cup liquid in mixing bowl. Add tapioca, salt, almond extract, lemon juice, and food color; then cherries and 1 cup sugar. Mix and let stand while making pastry (store bought 10 inch top and bottom crust will work).
Fit pastry into the bottom of a 9 inch pie pan. Trim 1/2 inch beyond outer rim of pan. Fill with cherry mixture. Dot with butter. Sprinkle with remaining sugar. Moisten rim with water. To make a crisscross top, interlace 14 strips, pressing ends against moistened rim. Moisten rim again and circle with 4 remaining strips. Press down firmly and sprinkle top with sugar. To keep the higher pie pan rim from browning faster than crisscross strips, circle pie with stand-up foil cover. Fold foil over rim and leave on during entire baking.
Bake in hot (425 F) oven for 40-45 minutes. Serve warm.
Farm Journal's Country Cookbook, 1959

STRAWBERRY PIE

16 ounce package frozen strawberries
2 egg whites

1 cup sugar
2 Tablespoons lemon juice

Put the fruit (frozen), egg whites and lemon juice into large mixing bowl. Break up the frozen fruit with a fork. Beat 15 minutes with electric beater at high speed. Fold in the whipped cream. Pile into the crust and freeze.

NOTE: Delicious and tastes best the day it is made.
Satsuma Tea Room, More Fun for the Cook, 1974

AUTUMN PEAR PIE

2 Tablespoons lemon juice
4 cups sliced pears
1/3 cup granulated sugar
1/3 cup packed brown sugar, sieved
2 Tablespoons cornstarch

1/4 teaspoon salt
1/4 teaspoon nutmeg
pastry for a 2 crust pie
butter or margarine

Add the lemon juice to sliced pears. Combine the sugars, cornstarch, salt and nutmeg. Divide the dough in half. Roll 1/2 of the dough to a circle of 1/8 inch thick and fit it into a 9 inch pan. Roll the remaining 1/2 of the dough for the top crust. Arrange 1/2 of the sliced pears in the bottom crust. Sprinkle 1/2 of the sugar mixture over the pears. Add the remaining pears. Sprinkle with the remaining sugar mixture. Dot with butter. Arrange the top crust over filling. Trim and flute the edge. Prick or slash pastry to allow steam to escape. Bake at 425 F for 35 to 40 minutes. Makes 1- 9 inch pie.
Easy-on-the-Cook Book, 1960

NANNIE'S PINEAPPLE CUSTARD PIE

3/4 cup sugar	2 Tablespoons corn starch
1 cup grated pineapple, drained	3 eggs
1 cup milk	

Mix the corn starch, sugar, and milk together and put into a double boiler. Separate the eggs and place the yolks in with the sugar and milk. Cook until thick. Remove from over the hot water and add the pineapple and the beaten egg whites. Put in baked pie shell and, when cool, cover with unsweetened whipped cream.
The Southern Cookbook, 1939

PUMPKIN PIE

1 cup canned or baked and strained pumpkin	1/4 teaspoon mace	1/4 teaspoon ginger
	1/4 teaspoon cinnamon	2 beaten eggs
1/4 cup sugar	1/2 teaspoon vanilla	1/2 cup milk
1/2 teaspoon salt	1/2 teaspoon cloves	1/2 cup cream

Mix dry ingredients. Add pumpkin, eggs, milk and cream gradually. Bake in a pie pan with a plain pastry bottom crust at 450 for 15 minutes and then for 25 minutes in a moderate oven (350).

NOTE: To bake pumpkin for pie, wash and cut pumpkin in half crosswise. Scrape out seeds and stringy parts. Place in a dripping pan, shell side up, and bake until it begins to fall apart and is tender. Scrape the pulp from shell and strain.
The Southern Cookbook, 1939

TIPSY PUMPKIN PIE

9 inch unbaked pie shell	1 teaspoon cinnamon
2 eggs	1/2 teaspoon ginger
16 ounces solid pack pumpkin	1/4 teaspoon ground cloves
3/4 cup sugar	12 ounces skimmed evaporated milk
1/2 teaspoon salt	1/4 cup Tennessee whiskey

Beat eggs and stir into remaining ingredients in order given. Pour mixture into pie shell and bake at 425 for 15 minutes. Reduce temperature to 350 and bake 40-45 minutes longer. Cool on wire rack. Serves 8.

NOTE: This pie was my sister-in-law's contribution to our 1989 Thanksgiving dinner. It's been my favorite pumpkin pie ever since. I'm sure the whiskey has nothing to do with it, but I have tried vanilla extract and it just doesn't measure up. I wonder why everyone at the church suppers wants the recipe? -David H
Kitty Manson, Cortner Mill Restaurant cookbook, 2009

SWEET POTATO CUSTARD PIE

1 1/2 cups cooked, mashed sweet potatoes	2 eggs, beaten	1 teaspoon allspice
	1/2 teaspoon salt	1 1/2 cups milk
1/2 cup dark brown sugar	1/2 teaspoon salt	1 unbaked 9-inch pastry,

Heat oven to 350 degrees. Mix all ingredients. Pour into shell. Add topping. If using fresh sweet potatoes, strain the mashed sweet potatoes for strings and lumps.

SWEET POTATO CUSTARD PIE TOPPING

1/2 stick butter, melted
1/4 cup dark brown sugar
3/4 cup pecans, chopped

Combine all ingredients. Sprinkle on pie and bake until pie is set and golden brown, about 25 minutes.
Serves 6-8
Bebe King, The Nashville Cookbook, 1977

FROZEN PUMPKIN PIE WITH CARAMELIZED ALMONDS

1 pint vanilla ice cream, softened	1/2 teaspoon ginger
1 baked 10- inch pie shell	1/4 teaspoon cloves
2 cups (1 pound can) pumpkin	1 teaspoon vanilla
1 1/2 cups sugar	1 1/2 cups whipping cream
1/2 teaspoon salt	1 cup slivered almonds
1 teaspoon cinnamon	1/4 cup sugar

Spread softened ice cream in cooled pie shell, place in freezer. Mix pumpkin with 1 1/2 cups sugar, salt spices, and vanilla. Whip 1 cup cream until stiff; fold into pumpkin mixture. Pour mixture over ice cream in shell. Cover with foil; freeze about 4 hours.
Meanwhile, caramelize almonds and 1/4 cup sugar in small skillet. Place over low heat stirring constantly and rapidly until the sugar begins to turn color. Remove from the heat when the almonds become caramel colored; spread on a greased cookie sheet. Break apart when cool. Before serving pie, whip remaining 1/2 cup cream, spread over top of pie; garnish with almonds. Makes 1 (10-inch) pie.

NOTE: If a 9-inch pie pan is used, freeze the extra cup of pumpkin filling in paper cupcake pan liners and serve topped with maple nut or vanilla ice cream.
Easy-on the-Cook Book, 1960

SWEET POTATO PIE

1 stick margarine	2 cups sweet potatoes	1/2 teaspoon nutmeg
1 1/2 cups sugar	(mashed and strained)	4 teaspoon flour
1/2 cup sweet milk	3 eggs	1/4 teaspoon salt
	1/2 teaspoon cinnamon	

Mash the cooked potatoes and then measure (having learned from years of working with sweet potatoes, in order to get the smoothest filling, strain for strings and lumps after cooking and before measurement). Cream the margarine and sugar, beat the eggs and add this to the sweet potatoes. Mix all the dry ingredients and add to mixture. Stir in the milk. Pour in an unbaked shell and bake at 375 degrees for 40-45 minutes.
Sally Washington, 200 Years of Charleston Cooking, 1930

SWEET POTATO PIE

NOTE: This sweet potato pie is a mouth-watering affair in a big round dish, oozing with brown richness.

3 large sweet potatoes	1/4 teaspoon ground	4 Tablespoons sugar
2 eggs, separated	spice	pastry
1/2 teaspoon vanilla	1/2 teaspoon salt	

Boil sweet potatoes until tender, then peel and mash until soft and creamy. Add egg yolks, vanilla and spice (we chose cinnamon), salt, and sugar. Mix well and spread about an inch deep on top of pastry which has been used to line a pie tin. Bake in a quick oven (425 F) until crust is brown, about 25 minutes.
Make a meringue of egg whites and the remaining sugar and spread over top of the and return to oven, which should be slow (300 F) until meringue is brown. This pie should be served hot.

NOTE: This can be baked as a pudding without the pastry.
Sally Washington, 200 Years of Charleston Cooking, 1930

COCONUT PIE

1/2 cup shredded coconut	2 cups scalded milk
3 eggs, separated	pinch of salt
1/2 cup sugar	

Beat yolks with sugar and pinch of salt. Add egg whites, well beaten. Stir in scalded milk and at last mix in the coconut. Bake only the bottom crust in a deep pie pan in a hot oven of 475 for the first 15 minutes and then a moderate oven (350) for another 30 minutes.
The Southern Cookbook, 1939

BOSTON CREAM PIE

1 egg
1/4 cup sugar
1 1/8 cup cake flour
1/2 cup sugar
1/2 Tablespoon baking powder

1/2 teaspoon salt
3 Tablespoons vegetable oil
1/2 cup milk
3/4 teaspoon vanilla
1 cup heavy cream

Beat egg white until soft peaks form. Gradually add 1/4 cup sugar and beat until stiff peaks form. Sift together remaining dry ingredients into another bowl. Add oil, half of the milk, and vanilla. Beat 1 minute at medium speed with mixer, scraping bowl often. Add remaining milk and yolk. Beat 1 minute and scrape bowl. Gently fold in egg whites. Bake in greased and lightly floured 9" round cake pan in 350 oven for about 25 minutes. Cool for 10 minutes and remove from pan. Cool completely. Slice cake layer in half horizontally. Remove top half and set aside. Cover bottom half with a layer of chocolate cream filling. Place top half on top of cream filling and add another layer of chocolate cream filling on top. Top with whipped cream.

CHOCOLATE CREAM FILLING

1/4 cup Ghirardelli cocoa
1/2 cup sugar
3 Tablespoon flour
1/4 teaspoon salt

1 1/4 cups milk
1 egg
5 teaspoons butter
1 teaspoon vanilla

Combine sugar, cocoa, flour, and salt in a saucepan. Gradually add milk and mix well. Cook and stir over medium heat until mixture thickens and boils. Cook and stir 2 minutes longer. Very gradually stir the hot mixture into the beaten egg and return to saucepan. Cook and stir until mixture boils. Stir in butter and vanilla. Spoon over cake layer and top.
David Hazelwood, Cortner Mill Restaurant cookbook, 2009

CREAM PIE

1 1/2 cups milk
1/2 cup sugar
1/4 teaspoon salt
3 Tablespoons flour
2 eggs

1 Tablespoon butter
1/2 teaspoon vanilla
1- 9 inch baked pie shell
1 cup heavy cream, whipped

Scald 1 cup of milk in double boiler. Mix dry ingredients. Add remaining 1/2 cup of milk to dry ingredients and mix to a smooth paste. Pour into hot milk; stir slowly until thick and there is no starchy flavor. Beat eggs; add some of hot mixture slowly to beaten eggs and return to double boiler, cooking 3 to 5 minutes longer. Add butter and vanilla. Cool. Pour into baked pastry shell. Spread whipped cream on pie. If desired, meringue may be used instead of whipped cream.
What to Cook for Company, 1953

EGG CUSTARD PIE

4 eggs, separated	1 cup milk
1 Tablespoon flour	1 teaspoon vanilla extract
1 cup sugar	1/8 teaspoon nutmeg
1/2 stick butter or margarine, melted	1 pie shell (9-inch), unbaked

Heat oven to 325 degrees. Beat egg yolks until frothy. Blend flour into sugar and add to eggs. Add butter and stir well. Add vanilla and nutmeg to milk and stir gradually into egg mixture. Blend mixture and pour into shell. Bake until custard is set. Top with meringue.

MERINGUE

Heat oven to 350 degrees. Beat egg whites until very stiff. Fold in 8 Tablespoons sugar, two at a time. Add 1 teaspoon vanilla and 1/4 teaspoon baking powder. Gently spread meringue over baked custard. Being sure to seal edges. Brown in oven. Serves 6-8.

NOTE: This pie has been popular in our family for four generations. A modern hint: cover edge of pie shell with aluminum foil to prevent over browning.
Ruby Major, The Nashville Cookbook, 1977

BANANA CREAM PIE FILLING

Use four ripe bananas. Fill pastry with alternate layers of sliced bananas and cooled *Cream Pie Filling*.

CHOCOLATE CREAM PIE FILLING

Add 2 ounces melted chocolate and 1/4 cup sugar before adding hot mixture to egg in *Cream Pie Filling*.

COCONUT CREAM PIE FILLING

Stir 1 cup shredded coconut into cooled *Cream Pie Filling*. (page 372)

STRAWBERRY TARTS

Mash fresh berries; add a little sugar. Fill individual tart shells with *Cream Pie Filling* and top with a Tablespoon of crushed strawberries. Garnish with whipped cream.
What to Cook for Company, 1953

EGGNOG PIE

4 eggs, separated	1/8 teaspoon nutmeg
1 cup sugar	1 Tablespoon rum flavoring
1/2 teaspoon salt	1/8 teaspoon almond extract
1/2 cup hot water	1 cup heavy cream, whipped
1 tablespoon unflavored gelatin	9 inch baked pie shell
1/4 cup cold water	1/2 cup chopped toasted almonds

Beat egg yolks slightly; add 1/2 cup sugar, salt, hot water. Cook in double boiler until thick. Soften gelatin in cold water; add to hot custard and stir until dissolved. Cool. Beat egg whites until foamy; add the remaining 1/2 cup of sugar gradually and beat to soft peak. Add nutmeg and flavoring. Fold meringue mixture into cooled cooked mixture. Turn into baked pie shell. Chill. Spread whipped cream over pie. Top with toasted almonds. Serves 6-8.
What to Cook for Company, 1953

BANANA BLUEBERRY PIE

1 baked pie shell
2 medium sized bananas
3 ounces cream cheese
1 envelope Dream Whip
1/2 cup sugar
1/2 can blueberry pie filling

Soften cream cheese. Blend in sugar. Prepare the Dream Whip according to the directions on the package. Slice the bananas and line in the pie shell. Pour dream whip mixture. Chill 3 hours and top with blueberry pie filling.
Satsuma Tea Room, More Fun for the Cook, 1974

CREAM CHEESECAKE PIE

CRUST

1 cup graham cracker crumbs
1/4 cup nuts, chopped
1/4 cup butter, melted

Mix together and press evenly over buttered pie plate. Bake at 450 for 5 minutes. Cool.

FILLING

2 eggs
9 ounces cream cheese
1/2 cup sugar
1/2 teaspoon vanilla

Beat eggs until thick. Beat cream cheese, sugar, and vanilla together and blend with beaten eggs. Pour into crust and bake in slow oven at 325 for 20 minutes.

TOPPING

1/2 pint sour cream
5 Tablespoons sugar
1/2 teaspoon vanilla

Stir together and spread over top of pie after baking. Return to slow oven for 5 minutes. Cool and chill before serving. Serves 10.

NOTE: The very best cream cheese pie I know. Delicious with fresh strawberries, peaches, or blueberries. Nuts on top are very good also. Will freeze well. One of our favorite customers gave us this recipe. We love it.
Satsuma Tea Room, Fun for the Cook, 1968

EASY CHEESE CAKE PIE

8 ounces cream cheese
1/2 cup sugar
2 eggs beaten
1 cup whipping cream, whipped
1 teaspoon lemon juice

Soften cheese. Add remaining ingredients, except whipped cream, and beat hard. Fold in the whipped cream. Pour into graham cracker crust. Chill. Top with cherry or blueberry pie filling.

NOTE: This pie is so easy and so good.
Satsuma Tea Room, More Fun for the Cook, 1974

REFRIGERATOR CHEESECAKE

1 1/2 pounds cottage cheese
1 Tablespoon vanilla
2 Tablespoons lemon juice
1/4 teaspoon salt
2 Tablespoons unflavored gelatin
1/2 cup cold water

3 egg yolks, beaten
2 Tablespoons milk
1 cup sugar
2 cups heavy cream
3 egg whites

Rub cottage cheese through a wire sieve. Add vanilla, lemon juice and salt. Soak gelatin in cold water. Combine eggs, sugar and milk, and cook in double boiler until thickened. Add gelatin and stir until dissolved. Remove from heat. Cool slightly and stir in cheese mixture. Whip cream and fold in. Turn into a 9 inch spring form pan lined with graham cracker crust. Chill at least 8 hours.

GRAHAM CRACKER CRUST

1 1/2 cups graham cracker crumbs, 1/2 cup powdered sugar, 1/2 cup melted butter. Mix well. Line pan. Part of the crumbs may be sprinkled on top.
Satsuma, Fun for the Cook, 1968

PINEAPPLE CREAM CHEESE PIE

8 ounces cream cheese
1 cup cream (whipped)
1/2 cup sugar

1 can crushed pineapple
pinch of salt
lemon juice to taste

1 graham cracker crust

Cream the cheese. Add well drained pineapple, salt and lemon juice. Whip cream and gradually add sugar. Fold into cheese mixture and pour into crumb shell. Refrigerate several hours before serving.

GRAHAM CRACKER CRUST

1 1/4 cups graham cracker crumbs
1/3 cup melted butter

1/2 teaspoon cinnamon if desired

Blend ingredients. Press on bottom and sides of pie plate. Chill 45 minutes, add pie filling.
Satsuma Tea Room, Pies, Pies, Pies, Satsuma's Easy on the Cook Pie Supplement

FROZEN LEMON PIE

3 egg yolks, beaten
1/3 cup lemon juice
2 teaspoons grated lemon rind
1/2 cup + 1 Tablespoon sugar

1/8 teaspoon salt
3 egg whites, beaten stiff
1 cup heavy cream whipped
1/2 cup graham cracker crumbs

Mix egg yolks, sugar, lemon juice, rind, and salt. Cook in double boiler until thickened. Cool, fold in egg whites and then whipped cream. Line pie pan with graham cracker crumbs. Pour in mixture and freeze. Serves 6-8.

NOTE: Do not keep in freezer longer than 1 week as it will start to lose lemon flavor.
Satsuma Tea Room, Fun for the Cook, 1968

LEMON MERINGUE PIE

1 1/4 cups sugar	1 cup boiling water	1/4 cup lemon juice
1/3 cup pastry flour	1/4 teaspoon salt	2 tsp. grated lemon peel
3 egg yolks, beaten	1 Tablespoon butter	1-9 inch baked pie shell

Sift sugar, flour, salt together. Add butter and boiling water. Cook over low heat or in double boiler stirring slowly until thick, about 8-10 minutes. Add some of cooked mixture to beaten egg yolks, combine both mixtures and cook about 3 minutes longer. Blend in lemon juice and peel. Cool. Pour into baked pie shell. Top with meringue. Serves 6

MERINGUE

3 egg whites	1/4 teaspoon salt	6 Tablespoons sugar

Beat egg whites until frothy; add salt and generally add sugar. Beating constantly to soft peak stage. Spread on pie. Brown in moderate oven (350) 12 to 15 minutes.
What to Cook for Company, 1953

LEMON SPONGE PIE

4 eggs- beaten separately	3 Tablespoons flour	1/2 teaspoon lemon rind
1 1/4 cups sugar	1/3 cup lemon juice	1 1/2 cup milk
3 Tablespoon butter	1/4 teaspoon salt	

Using soft butter, cream with sugar, add beaten egg yolks and other ingredients. Lastly fold in stiffly beaten egg whites. Pour into an unbaked pie shell. Bake at 350 degrees for 15 minutes. Reduce heat to 300 degrees and cook 45 minutes.

NOTE: This is a new recipe for us at the restaurant, but it is the best one we have found for an easy pie that tastes like the old-fashioned one mom used to make.
Satsuma Tea Room, Pies, Pies, Pies, Satsuma's Easy on the Cook Pie Supplement

HEAVENLY LEMON PIE
MERINGUE CRUST

4 egg whites, beaten	1 cup sugar	1 1/4 tsp. cream of tartar

Sift sugar and cream of tartar together, adding gradually to the beaten egg whites. Beat 10 minutes. Use to line the pie tins. Bake at 250 for about 1 hour.

FILLING

4 egg yolks	1/4 cup lemon juice
1/2 cup sugar	1/3 quart cream

Beat the egg yolks. Add sugar and lemon juice. Cook in double boiler until thickened. Chill and fold into 1/3 quart of cream, whipped. Put in meringue crust. Chill for several hours.
Satsuma Tea Room, Fun for the Cook, 1968

LEMON-CRANBERRY MERINGUE PIE

1 baked 9-inch pie shell

FILLING

1/3 cup cornstarch	1 teaspoon grated lemon peel
1/4 cup sifted flour	7 Tablespoons lemon juice
1 1/2 cups boiling water	2 cups (1 pound can) jellied cranberry sauce
3 egg yolks, slightly beaten	
1 1/2 Tablespoons butter or margarine	

For the filling, mix the cornstarch, flour, sugar, and salt. Add the boiling water gradually, stirring constantly to prevent lumping. Place over direct heat. Cook slowly until thickened throughout, stirring constantly. Cook, uncovered, over simmering water for about 10 minutes or until clear and thick. Stir 2 or 3 times. Stir a small amount of hot mixture into egg yolks. Combine with remaining hot mixture. Continue cooking over simmering water about 5 minutes stirring constantly. Remove from heat. Add butter, lemon peel and juice. Blend thoroughly. Cool about 5 minutes. Pour 2/3 of filling into cooled pie shell; spread filling up the side to the fluted edge to prevent cranberry sauce from touching pastry. Spread with 3/4 of the cranberry sauce (1 1/2 cups) that has been finely broken apart with a fork. Top with the remaining filling.

MERINGUE

3 egg whites   1/8 teaspoon salt   6 Tablespoons sugar

Beat egg whites and salt until frothy. Add sugar gradually, beating constantly until peaks form when beater is withdrawn. Cover filling with meringue. Bake in a 350 F. oven 12 to 15 minutes or until tops of the irregular surface are golden brown. Best served the same day the pie is made.

NOTE: Use the remaining cranberry sauce (1/2 cup) as accompaniment for a meat meal.
Easy-on-the-Cook Book, 1960

LIME PIE

1-3 ounce package lime gelatin	13 ounce can evaporated milk
1/2 cup boiling water	2/3 cup sugar
4 teaspoons lemon juice	

Dissolve gelatin in boiling water. Add lemon juice and chill until thickened. Chill milk, using cold bowl, until icy. Whip milk until stiff. Beat in sugar. Fold thickened gelatin into milk. Put into 11 inch crumb crust or two 8 inch pastry crusts. Chill several hours. Serves 8 or 12.

NOTE: A very pretty pie. Especially good after a heavy meal. Easy to make and very economical.
Satsuma Tea Room, Pies, Pies, Pies, Satsuma's Easy on the Cook Pie Supplement

LIME CREAM PIE

1/2 tablespoon gelatin	4 egg yolks	3/4 cup whipping cream,
1 Tablespoon water	2 cups milk, scalded	2 teaspoons sugar
7/8 cup sugar	2 2/3 Tablespoons butter	1/2 teaspoon vanilla
1/4 cup cornstarch	7/8 cup lime juice	German sweet chocolate
1/3 teaspoon salt	1/3 tsp. grated lime peel	
2/3 cup cold milk	green food coloring	

Hydrate the gelatin in water. Combine sugar, cornstarch, and salt. Add cold milk and egg yolks. Blend thoroughly. Gradually stir mixture into the scalded milk and cook over low heat until thickened. Remove from the heat. Add butter, lime juice, lime peel and food coloring to tint mixture a pale green. Pour into a prebaked 10-inch graham cracker pie shell. Refrigerate several hours or until set. Blend cream, sugar, and vanilla. Spread on top of pie. Garnish with shredded chocolate.
Helen House, University of Illinois Home Economics Faculty Favorites, 1965

MANDARIN ORANGE CREAM PIE

2/3 cup sugar	1/2 teaspoon orange extract
1/2 cup sifted flour	1/3 cup sugar
1/2 teaspoon salt	11 ounce can mandarin orange sections, drained
1 1/2 cups scalded milk	1 baked 9-inch pie shell
3 eggs, separated	2 teaspoons grated orange peel
2 Tablespoons butter or margarine	

In the top of a double boiler, combine 2/3 cup sugar, flour, and salt. Add milk gradually, stirring constantly. Cook over direct heat until thickened, stirring constantly. Remove from heat. Beat egg yolks slightly. Blend a small amount of the hot mixture into egg yolks. Then blend egg mixture back into the mixture. Cook over boiling water about 5 minutes, stirring frequently. Stir in butter and orange extract. Cool slightly.
For meringue, beat egg whites until frothy. Add 1/3 cup sugar gradually, beating until stiff, glossy peaks are formed. Arrange orange sections over bottom of cooked pie shell. Pour the filling over oranges. Top with meringue. Sprinkle orange peel around edge of meringue. Bake at 350 F for 10 to 15 minutes to brown meringue. Makes one 9-inch pie.
Easy-on-the-Cook Book, 1960

JELLY PIE

1 unbaked pie shell	1/2 cup strawberry jelly	1 teaspoon lemon juice
4 egg whites, well beaten	1/2 cup butter	
4 egg yolks, well beaten	1 1/2 cups sugar	

Cream butter adding sugar slowly and beat well. Add yolks and jelly and fold in the whites of the eggs. Mix in the lemon juice and pour into the pie shell. Bake in a moderate oven (350 F) for about 30 minutes.
The Southern Cookbook, 1939

RICE AND PEACH GINGER PIE

1/2 cup uncooked rice	3/4 teaspoon nutmeg
2/3 cup water	2 eggs
3/4 teaspoon salt	1 cup diced peaches
2 1/2 cups milk	2 Tablespoons butter or margarine
1/2 cup heavy cream	1/2 teaspoon vanilla
2 sticks cinnamon	1 baked, 9 inch gingersnap crumb crust
1/2 cup sugar	sweetened whipped cream, optional
1 1/2 Tablespoons cornstarch	gingersnap crumbs, optional

Bring rice, water, and salt to a boil in top part of a double boiler. Lower heat to simmer; cover and cook until water is absorbed, about 5 minutes. Add milk, cream, and cinnamon sticks and bring to a boil. Place over boiling water; cover and cook until rice is tender, about 40 minutes. Remove cinnamon sticks. Combine sugar, cornstarch, and nutmeg. Beat eggs. Gradually add sugar mixture and beat thoroughly. Add to rice and milk mixture; cook until thickened, stirring constantly. Add diced peaches, butter and vanilla. Cool before pouring into crust. If desired, decorate with a ruff (collar) of sweetened whipped cream sprinkled with gingersnaps crumbs. Makes 1- 9 inch pie.
Easy-on-the-Cook Book, 1960

FRESH RHUBARB PIE

2 cups rhubarb	2 Tablespoons flour
1 cup sugar	1 egg

Cut rhubarb into ½-inch pieces. Measure and add egg slightly beaten, sugar and flour. Bake between two crusts in 450 oven for 10 minutes. Lower to 350 and bake 20 minutes.
Satsuma Tea Room, Fun for the Cook, 1968

HONEY-LEMON RHUBARB PIE

4 cups rhubarb, cut into ½-inch pieces	1/3 cup strained honey
1 1/4 cups sugar	4 to 5 drops red food color
6 Tablespoons flour	2 9-inch pie pastries
1/4 teaspoon salt	2 Tablespoons butter or margarine
2 teaspoons grated lemon rind	

Combine rhubarb, sugar, flour, salt, and rind; mix well. Blend in honey and food color. Let stand while making pastry. Line the 9-inch pan with pastry. Fill with rhubarb mixture; dot with butter. Adjust top crust and seal edges. (For a glistening top to the pie, brush top with milk and sprinkle with sugar). Bake in a very hot oven (450 F) 10 minutes; reduce heat to moderate (350 F) and bake 35 to 45 minutes more.

NOTE: For a variation to this pie, use pastry for an unbaked pie shell. Sprinkle filling top with crumbly crust, made by blending together 1/2 cup brown sugar, 1/3 cup flour, 1/4 teaspoon cinnamon; cut in 1/4 cup butter or margarine. Cover top with foil until last 20 minutes, then uncover.
Farm Journal's Country Cook Book, 1959

BLACK BOTTOM PIE (One of my favorites.)

1. Bake a single 9- inch pie crust.
2. Put a layer of Richmond Chocolate Icing over the bottom and sides of the crust.
3. Fill crust with Spanish Cream. Put into the refrigerator until set and ready to serve.
4. Bake a single 9- inch pie crust.
5. Put a layer of Richmond Chocolate Icing over the bottom and sides of the crust.
6. Fill crust with Spanish Cream. Put in the refrigerator until set and ready to serve.
7. Add whipped cream on top with grated bitter chocolate shaved/sprinkled on when ready to serve.

RICHMOND CHOCOLATE ICING

1/2 cup sugar	one oz. chocolate square	1 1/2 Tablespoons butter
2 Tablespoons cornstarch	dash of salt	1/2 teaspoon vanilla
	1/2 cup water	

Combine all the ingredients except vanilla. Cook, stirring constantly, until mixture thickens. Cook 2 minutes longer. Add vanilla. You may spread either hot or cold.
Satsuma Tea Room, Fun for the Cook, 1968

CHOCOLATE FUDGE PIE

4 eggs	1 cup chopped nuts
2 cups sugar	1 teaspoon vanilla
3 squares bitter chocolate	1- 9 inch pie tin lined with unbaked pastry shell
1/3 cup melted butter or margarine	

Beat eggs until thick and lemon colored. Gradually add sugar, beating continually. Combine melted chocolate and butter. Cool slightly. Pour into egg mixture. Stir to combine. Add nuts and vanilla. Pour mixture into pastry lined pan. Bake at 350 for 40 minutes.

NOTE: Yummy! Serve with whipped cream, hard sauce, or ice cream. In my opinion though, ice cream melting on a warm pie is the best way to appreciate this delicious pie.
Satsuma Tea Room, Fun for the Cook, 1968

GERMAN CHOCOLATE COCONUT PIE

1/4 cup butter	3 eggs
3/4 cup sugar	1 teaspoon vanilla
2 ounces sweeten cooking chocolate	1/2 cup coconut
1/3 cup evaporated milk	1/3 cup chopped nuts

Prepare pastry shell and chill. Heat butter, sugar, and chocolate. Stir constantly until melted. Cool and add milk, eggs, and vanilla. Beat well. Combine coconut and nuts, and sprinkle over bottom of unbaked shell. Pour in the mixture. Bake on lower oven shelf at 375 degrees for 45 minutes. Cool thoroughly before serving.
Satsuma Tea Room, Pies, Pies, Pies, Satsuma's Easy on the Cook Pie Supplement

CHOCOLATE MINT PIE

2 ounces melted chocolate
1/2 cup softened margarine
1 cup powdered sugar
2 egg yolks
2 egg whites
1 cup powdered sugar
1/2 teaspoon mint flavoring

Mix the first four ingredients well. Beat 2 egg whites and beat in 1 cup powdered sugar. Add this to the first mixture. Add mint flavoring. Pour all into crumb crust made of chocolate mint cookies. Refrigerate.

CHOCOLATE COOKIE PIE CRUST

1 1/3 chocolate cookie crumbs
1/3 cup melted butter

Crush cookies, add butter, blend well. Pat into bottom and side of pie pan. Bake 10 minutes at 300 degrees. Cool before filling with pie contents.
Satsuma Tea Room, Pies, Pies, Pies, Satsuma's Easy on the Cook Pie Supplement

SPANISH CREAM

1 Tablespoon gelatin
1/4 cup cold milk
1 1/3 cups scalded milk
1/2 cup sugar
2 egg yolks, slightly beaten
1/2 teaspoon vanilla
2 egg whites stiffly beaten
dash of salt

Put gelatin into cold milk and let stand at least 3 minutes. Scald milk in double boiler and mix with gelatin. Beat egg yolks slightly with sugar and salt. Pour hot milk from double boiler onto yolks stirring constantly. Return milk egg mixture to double boiler. Cook until mixture coats spoon, stirring constantly. Remove from heat. Cool, stirring until slightly thickened. Fold in stiffly beaten egg whites.
Satsuma Tea Room, Fun for the Cook, 1968

RUM PIE

1 1/2 cups milk
3/4 cup sugar
1/4 cup flour plus
1 Tablespoon cornstarch
5 egg yolks, lightly beaten
1/2 cup milk
1/2 cup butter, softened
2 to 3 Tablespoons dark rum
one 9-inch graham cracker pie crust
whipped cream
chopped pecans (optional)
1/4 cup grated semi-sweet chocolate

Heat 1 1/2 cups milk in top of a double boiler. Mix sugar with flour and cornstarch. Stir into hot milk and cook while stirring until slightly thickened. Add egg yolks to remaining 1/2 cup milk, stirring part of the hot milk mixture into the egg yolk and milk mixture before returning all to the double boiler. Cook, while stirring, until thick and smooth. Do not let mixture boil. Remove from heat and cool slightly before adding softened butter. Flavor with rum, mix, and pour into prepared pie crust. Chill. Just before serving top with whipped cream and sprinkle with chopped nuts and grated semi-sweet chocolate.
Helen Bratcher, The Nashville Cookbook, 1977

IRISH COFFEE PIE

1 Tablespoon unflavored gelatin
3/4 cup sugar
1/4 teaspoon salt
1 Tablespoon powdered instant coffee
1 egg yolk
3/4 cup milk
1/4 cup Irish whiskey

1 egg white, beaten stiff
1 1/2 cups cream, whipped
1/2 cup slivered almonds, blanched and toasted
1-10 inch baked pie shell

Topping: 1 1/2 cups sweet whipped cream

Combine gelatin, sugar, salt, and coffee in top of double boiler. Beat egg yolk and milk slightly; add to double boiler. Cook, stirring occasionally, until gelatin is melted and sugar is dissolved. Chill until thick and syrupy. Add Irish whiskey; beat until light and frothy. Fold in egg white, whipped cream and almonds. Heap into cooled pie shell; chill until set. Spread topping over pie. Makes 1-10 inch pie.
Easy-on-the-Cook Book, 1960

CHOCOLATE CREAM MINT PIE

1/2 cup soft butter
1 cup sifted confectioners' sugar
2 unbeaten eggs
1 teaspoon vanilla extract

2 ounces unsweetened, melted and cooled
1 teaspoon peppermint extract
1 baked 8-inch graham cracker crust
2 cups cream, whipped

Cream the butter. Add sugar; cream until light and fluffy. Gradually add chocolate. Add eggs, one at a time, stirring well after each addition. Stir in extracts. Pour into the crust. Refrigerate 4-6 hours. Just before serving, whip the cream and spread over the top of the pie. Makes 1-8 inch pie
Easy-on-the-Cook Book, 1960

GRASSHOPPER PIE (Crème de menthe)

20 large marshmallows
2/3 cup milk
2 Tablespoons crème de menthe

1 cup cream, whipped
1 Chocolate Wafer Crust

Melt marshmallows in milk in double boiler. Add crème de menthe. Cool. Fold in whipped cream. Pile into chocolate wafer crust. Put grated chocolate or chocolate crumbs on top. You may want to use more crème de menthe depending on individual preference. Serves 8

CHOCOLATE WAFER CRUST

1 1/3 cups crushed chocolate cookie crumbs
1/3 cup melted butter

Crush cookies, add butter, blend well. Pat firmly into bottom and side of pie pan. Bake 10 minutes at 300. Cool before filling.
Satsuma Tea Room, More Fun for the Cook, 1974

CRÈME DE MENTHE PIE

1 envelope unflavored gelatin	4 Tablespoons crème de menthe
1/4 cup cold water	2 to 3 drops green food coloring
4 egg yolks	1 1/2 cups heavy cream, whipped
3/4 cup sugar	

Soak gelatin in cold water for 5 minutes. Dissolve over hot water. Set aside to cool. Beat egg yolks with sugar until light and fluffy. Add gelatin and stir until blended. Stir in cream de menthe and coloring. Fold in whipped cream and pour mixture into prebaked crust. Chill for at least 8 hours.
Elizabeth Nyholm, University of Illinois Home Economics Faculty Favorites, 1965

PEPPERMENT ICE CREAM MERINGUE PIE WITH CHOCOLATE CRUST
(Our Baked Alaska at Satsuma)

CRUST

14 crisp chocolate cookies, crushed
5 Tablespoons butter or margarine, melted
1/4 cup finely chopped pecans

Mix crushed cookies, butter, pecans. Press mixture on bottom and sides of 9 inch pan. Bake at 300 for 8 minutes. Cool.

FILLING

1 quart peppermint ice cream, softened

Spoon softened ice cream into cold crust. Place in freezer or refrigerator compartment until ready to serve.

MERINGUE

At serving time, make meringue topping. Beat egg whites with cream of tartar until frothy. Gradually add sugar, beating until glossy and very stiff. Cover ice cream with meringue, spreading meringue to rim of shell. Bake at 450 for 3 to 5 minutes or until delicately browned. Serve immediately.
Easy-on-the-Cook Book, 1960

BAKED ALASKA RASPBERRY FLUFF PIE

3 egg whites	1 pint vanilla ice cream
3 Tablespoons sugar	1 pint chocolate ice cream
1/2 teaspoon lemon juice	1 baked 9- inch pie shell (pastry or
1/2 cup red raspberry preserves	crumb) chilled

Beat egg whites until foamy. Add sugar gradually, continuing to beat until very stiff. Gradually beat in lemon juice and preserves. Spoon ice cream into pie shell. Cover with meringue. Bake at 450 F for a few minutes until lightly browned.
Easy-on-the-Cook Book, 1960

BAKED ICE CREAM PIE

Fill the cooled pie shell with slightly softened ice cream. Cover with freezer wrapping and keep in freezer until ready to use. At serving time make meringue topping by beating egg whites with cream of tartar until frothy. Gradually add sugar, beating until glossy and very stiff.

Cover ice cream in pie shell with berries, then cover with meringue. Spread meringue to rim of shell to completely cover berries and ice cream. Bake in 450 F oven 3 to 5 minutes or until delicately browned. Serve immediately.
Easy-on-the-Cook Book, 1960

CHOCOLATE ALMOND PIE

3 small Hershey bars with almonds
18 marshmallows
1/2 cup milk
1 cup cream, whipped
1/2 teaspoon salt
1 teaspoon vanilla
1 crust, graham cracker, chocolate or ginger snap

Place first 3 ingredients in double boiler over hot water to melt. When cool, fold in whipped cream, ½ teaspoon salt, 1 teaspoon vanilla. Pour into graham cracker, chocolate or ginger snap crust. Refrigerate at least 4 hours. Serves 7.

NOTE: Can be served with whipped cream.
Satsuma Tea Room, More Fun for the Cook, 1974

MACAROON PIE

12 soda crackers
1 cup sugar
1/4 teaspoon baking powder
12 dates cut fine
1/2 cup chopped nuts
3 egg whites
1 teaspoon almond extract

Roll crackers fine with rolling pin. Mix crackers with sugar, baking powder, dates and nuts. Beat egg whites stiff. Fold into other mixture with almond extract. Pour into well-greased 8-inch pie pan and bake at 325 for 30 minutes. Serve with whipped cream or ice cream.

NOTE: Coffee ice cream is especially good with this pie!
Satsuma Tea Room, Fun for the Cook, 1968

PEAR LOVE LETTERS

15-ounce can pear halves
9-inch pie crust
2 Tablespoons raspberry jam
1/2 cup vanilla yogurt

Drain pears. Cut circle of pie crust into 4 wedge pieces and place pear half, cut side up, onto each piece. Top with jam and fold pastry to make envelope. Place on baking sheet and bake in 375 oven for 20 minutes. Remove from oven and top each with yogurt and serve immediately. Serves 4.
Bill Cox, Cortner Mill Restaurant cookbook, 2009

ANGEL TORTE

12 egg whites
2 teaspoons vanilla
1 1/2 teaspoons vinegar
3 cups sugar
1/2 cup slivered almonds

1 cup crushed pineapple
1/2 cup Maraschino cherries
1 cup heavy cream
1/2 cup powdered sugar

Add vanilla and vinegar to unbeaten egg whites. Beat until soft peaks form. Add sugar slowly and beat until very stiff. Spread in three 9-inch layer pans, lined with paper. Bake at 300 for about 1 1/2 hours. Cool, remove from pans. Take off paper. Whip cream stiff, add drained pineapple, chopped cherries and sugar and almonds. Spread between layers. Refrigerate overnight. Before serving, whip 2 cups additional cream and frost top and sides. 12-16 servings.
Satsuma Tea Room, Fun for the Cook, 1968

COCONUT OATMEAL PIE

3 eggs
2/3 cup white sugar
1 cup brown sugar

1/4 cup melted margarine
2/3 cup chopped dates (optional)

2/3 cup coconut
2/3 cup quick oatmeal
1 teaspoon vanilla

Beat the eggs until light, gradually add the mixed sugar. Beat well and add the rest of the ingredients. Pour into unbaked pie shell. Bake at 350 degrees for 35-40 minutes.

NOTE: Do not over bake.
Satsuma Tea Room, Pies, Pies, Pies, Satsuma's Easy on the Cook Pie Supplement

STRAWBERRY TARTS

1 quart fresh strawberries
1 cup sugar
1/4 teaspoon salt
4 Tablespoons cornstarch
1 cup water

red food coloring (optional)
9-inch baked pie shell
 or 6 baked individual tart shells
1 cup heavy cream, whipped
2 Tablespoons confectioners' sugar

Pick over the berries. Crush 1/2 of the berries and combine with the sugar. Add the salt, cornstarch, and water; cook over low heat until thick and clear, stirring constantly. Add a small amount of red food coloring (again, optional) to intensify the red color of the strawberries. Cut the remainder of the berries in half and put into the baked shells. Pour cooked mixture over the berries. Chill. Spread with whipped cream to which confectioners' sugar has been added. Garnish with additional berries if desired.

NOTE: One gets the full, fresh strawberry flavor when the preparation of the dessert is this way. This is a wonderful sweet dessert for that exceptional springtime meal!
Lenore Sullivan, What to Cook for Company, 1952

HUNGARIAN NUT TORTE

1/4 cup butter	1/4 cup flour
3/4 cup sugar	1/4 cup bread crumbs/pieces
2 teaspoons vanilla	3/4 cup ground nuts
1 1/2 ounces grated bitter chocolate	8 egg whites

Cream butter and sugar. Stir in other ingredients and mix well. Beat eggs, not too stiff. Fold carefully into bread crumbs/pieces mixture. Put into two greased 8-inch round cake pans. Bake at 325 for 30-35 minutes. Let stand 10 minutes. Remove from pan. Cool. Put together with filling.

FILLING

1/4 cup butter, soft	1/4 teaspoon salt
1 cup powdered sugar	1/2 teaspoon vanilla
2 Tablespoons cream	1/2 cup chopped nuts
1 Tablespoon cocoa	

Cream butter, add sugar, cream, cocoa, salt and vanilla. Mix until smooth and add chopped nuts. Spread between layers of torte. Serve with whipped cream and with grated chocolate on top. Serves 8.
Satsuma Tea Room, Fun for the Cook, 1968

FORGOTTEN TORTE

6 egg whites at room temperature	1/4 teaspoon salt
1 1/2 cups sugar	1 teaspoon vanilla extract
1/2 teaspoon cream of tartar	1/4 teaspoon almond extract

Turn on oven and set for very hot (450 F) and butter the bottom only of a 9 inch tube pan. Beat egg whites with the cream of tartar and salt until they are foamy. (If you use an electric beater turn it to medium speed.) Gradually add in the sugar, beating the mixture well as you do, and beating until the meringue forms stiff, glossy peaks. Beat in the vanilla and almond extracts. Spread the mixture evenly in the oven on the center rack and turn off heat immediately. Let stand with the door closed, of course overnight. Forget the torte. Don't get curious and peak in oven fewer than 4 or 5 hours!!! Remove from the oven next morning. Next morning the torte will be done. Loosen the sides with a sharp knife and unmold it onto a serving platter. It will settle a bit. Serve the torte frosted with whipped cream. If you wish, flavor it with cocoa and sprinkle it with chocolate curls or slivered almonds or a lemon custard may be made with four egg yolks as in the recipe for Heavenly Pie. There are many possibilities. The center may be filled with any fruit you choose mixed with whipped cream, or ice cream, or berries. Serves 8-10.

NOTE: Delicious and fun to do! But do not look inside the oven for 4 or 5 hours!!
The Holiday Hostess, 1958

PINEAPPLE TORTE

24 graham crackers
1 stick butter
1 cup sugar
1 cup milk
2 egg yolks

1/3 cup nuts
1 teaspoon vanilla
1/2 teaspoon baking powder
2 egg whites, beaten

Roll graham crackers into crumbs. Cream butter, mix with sugar, milk, egg yolks, nuts, vanilla, and baking powder. Fold in beaten egg whites. Bake in 9-inch square pan for 30 minutes at 325. Remove from the oven. Pour over following topping.

TOPPING

1 small can crushed pineapple
1 cup sugar

Mix pineapple and sugar and cook for 15 minutes on top of stove.

NOTE: This dish can be served hot or cold with whipped cream.
Satsuma Tea Room, Fun for the Cook, 1968

ELEGANT TORTE/PEACH CREAM FILLING

3 cups sifted cake flour
2 cups firmly packed brown sugar, sieved
1/2 teaspoon salt
1 cup shortening
1 egg, slightly beaten

1 cup buttermilk or sour milk
1 teaspoon baking soda
1/2 cup chopped nuts
sweetened whipped cream
or peach cream filling

Combine flour, sugar, and salt. Add shortening and blend using pastry blender until crumbly. Set aside 1 cup of this mixture. Combine the egg, milk, soda. Add to the dry ingredients; stir well. Pour into two paper-lined, greased round 9-inch pans. Sprinkle one cup crumb mixture, combined with nuts, over the top of each layer. Bake at 375 F for 25 to 30 minutes. Serve with sweetened whipped cream or peach cream filling between the layers.

PEACH CREAM FILLING

1 cup heavy cream, whipped
1/2 cup mashed peaches
1 Tablespoon lemon juice

2 Tablespoons sugar
sliced peaches

Combine whipped cream, mashed peaches, lemon juice, and sugar. Place between torte layers. Garnish with sliced peaches. Serve immediately.
Easy-on-the-Cook Book, 1960

APPLE DUMPLINGS

2 cups flour	1 cup milk
4 teaspoons baking powder	6 apples, pared (peeled) and cored
1 teaspoon salt	sugar and cinnamon
4 Tablespoons shortening	

Sift flour, baking powder and salt; cut-in shortening, add milk and mix to smooth dough. Turn onto floured board and divide into six portions. Roll each section large enough to cover one apple. Place apple on each piece of dough....fill with cinnamon and sugar....wet the edges of the dough and fold over apple. Place on greased baking pan and bake in moderate oven (350) until apples are tender (about 1/2 hour)
The Southern Cookbook, 1939

OLD-TIME APPLE DUMPLINGS

2 cups sifted flour	6 baking apples
2 teaspoon baking powder	1/2 cup sugar
1/2 teaspoon salt	1/4 teaspoon cinnamon
1/2 cup shortening	1 Tablespoon butter or margarine
2/3 cup milk	milk

Sift together flour, baking powder and salt; cut in the shortening. Stir in milk; mix until soft dough is formed. Turn out and knead lightly. Roll 1/8 inch thick then cut into six squares. Core the apples, peel; place on each square. Combine sugar and cinnamon and sprinkle this into center of each apple. Add 1/2 teaspoon butter to each. Moisten edges of dough, press corners up over apples; brush with milk. Place in a greased baking pan. Bake in moderate oven (350 F) for 30 minutes. Serve with Sweet & Tart Sauce. Makes 6 servings.

SWEET & TART SAUCE

2 cups water	1 cup sugar
1/3 cup vinegar	1 teaspoon cinnamon
1/3 cup butter	1/8 teaspoon nutmeg
1/3 cup flour	

Heat the water, vinegar, and butter together. Combine the remaining ingredients; mix thoroughly. Stir into the hot mixture, cook over low heat, stirring until thickened. Pour warm over apple dumplings. Makes 2 1/2 cups sauce.

NOTE: The Sweet & Tart Sauce accentuates the fruity flavor of apples.
Farm Journal's Country Cook Book, 1959

OATMEAL PIE

2/3 cup sugar
1/4 cup and 1 Tablespoon soft margarine
2 eggs
1/2 cup chopped dates
2/3 cup dark corn syrup
2/3 cup uncooked oatmeal
1 teaspoon vanilla
1 cup grated coconut

Beat the margarine and sugar. Add eggs. Beat well. Stir in the remaining ingredients. Bake at 325 for 40-45 minutes. Ice cream or whipped cream excellent on this pie. Serves 6.

NOTE: We have tried this pie without the dates and coconut, but it is much better with them.
Satsuma Tea Room, More Fun for the Cook, 1974

NOTES

PASTRIES & ICINGS

"A gourmet who thinks of calories is like a tart that looks at her watch."
-James Beard (1903-1985)

"A house is no home unless it contains food and fire for the mind as well as for the body."
-Margaret Fuller (1810-1850)

ALMOND CREAM FILLING

A delicious almond and cream filling is made by mixing 1 cup of whipped cream with 1/2 cup sugar and 1 pound of almonds; blanched and chopped fine.
The Savannah Cook Book, 1933

LEMON CHEESE FILLING FOR CAKES AND PIES

This is a very old "receipt" and, as this mixture will keep indefinitely, it is a wonderful item to have available.

1 pound sugar	grated rind of 2 lemons
6 eggs	juice of 3 lemons.
1/4 pound butter	

Put all together in a double boiler. Cook slowly over fire until the consistency of custard is reached.
The Savannah Cook Book, 1933

CARAMEL FILLING

3 cups brown sugar	1 1/2 cups cream
1 cup butter	8 squares (1/2 pound) chocolate, grated

Put the ingredients into a large saucepan and cook, stirring constantly, until the sugar is dissolved and the chocolate is melted. Let the mixture continue cooking until the temperature is 234 degrees F or a little of the filling dropped in cold water will form a soft ball. Remove from the fire and beat until thick and creamy, usually until the filling is cool and it will hold its shape.

NOTE: This recipe makes enough to ice a large three layer cake. This filling, as might be imagined, is very rich but the flavor is marvelous. Its keeping qualities, if allowed to remain uneaten long enough for one to test them, are remarkable. At the end of a week, the filling was quite good, as if it was the day it was made. The butter kept it soft and it seemed even more mellow than at first.
Mary Leize Simons, 200 Years of Charleston Cooking, 1930

MARSHMALLOW FILLING

1 cup sugar	2 egg whites
1/2 cup water	1/2 pound marshmallows

Boil the sugar and water together until they will spin a long thread or until 246 F is reached. Remove from the fire and, when the bubbling stops, pour in a thin stream over the stiffly beaten egg whites, beating constantly. When the syrup is all in, add the marshmallows which have been cut fine and beat the filling until stiff and cold.

NOTE: The original recipe used powdered white gum Arabic, but later marshmallows were substituted.
Mrs. Lanier Eason, 200 Years of Charleston Cooking, 1930

BOILED ICING

2 cups sugar	3 egg whites
1/2 cup water	1 Tablespoon lemon juice

Put the sugar and water into a saucepan and stir until the sugar is dissolved. Cover and let boil for 2 or 3 minutes. Then remove the cover and boil without stirring. Have the egg whites stiffly beaten and pour the syrup onto them in a thin stream, beating constantly. Continue the beating until the frosting is thick and holds its shape; add the lemon juice toward the end of the beating.

NOTE: This makes for a very fluffy icing and the lemon juice not only flavors it, but increases the whiteness of the frosting.
200 Years of Charleston Cooking, 1930

BUTTER ICING

1/2 cup butter	cream to moisten
2 cups sifted 4x sugar	flavoring

Cream the butter until soft and add sugar, blending well. Moisten with cream to the consistency desired. Any type of flavoring may be used.
The Southern Cookbook, 1939

CARAMEL ICING

3 cups sugar	1 cup milk	3 Tablespoons butter

Place 1/2 cup sugar into a small iron skillet on low heat to melt. Do not stir until almost melted. At the same time, mix 2 1/2 cups sugar and milk in heavy skillet and bring to a boil. Pour this caramelized sugar into milk mixture, stirring carefully. Cook until a few drops of mixture form soft ball in cold water (238 F.). Remove from the heat and add butter. Beat until it reaches the consistency for spreading.
Jeanne Webb, The Nashville Cookbook, 1977

QUICK CARAMEL FROSTING

1/2 cup butter	1 3/4 cups powdered sugar (or a bit more)
1/2 cup brown sugar	1 teaspoon vanilla
1/4 cup milk	

Melt butter in sauce pan. Add brown sugar and cook until sugar melts. Add milk and beat in powdered sugar until thick enough to be spread.
Satsuma Tea Room, Fun for the Cook, 1968

BUTTERMILK CARAMEL ICING

1 cup buttermilk	1/2 cup firmly packed	1/2 cup butter
2 cups sugar	dark brown sugar	1 teaspoon vanilla extract
	1/2 teaspoon baking soda	

Combine buttermilk, sugars, and soda in a saucepan. Stir over medium heat until sugars are dissolved; allow to boil, without stirring, to soft ball stage (238 F.). Add butter; remove from heat and cool 10 minutes without stirring. Add vanilla and beat until thick and creamy. If mixture is too thick, thin it with cream until it reaches spreading consistency.
Christine Alexander, The Nashville Cookbook, 1977

CARAMEL ICING WITH BROWN SUGAR

1 pound light brown sugar	1 stick butter or margarine
3 Tablespoons flour	1 teaspoon vanilla extract
3/4 cup cold water	

Mix brown sugar, flour, water, and butter. Dissolve thoroughly and cook to 238 F, (just under soft ball stage. Cool without stirring for 10 minutes. Add confectioner's sugar and vanilla and beat until spreading consistency. A few drops of hot water may be added if icing becomes too stiff.

NOTE: This icing remains creamy, never brittle, after being on the cake several days.
Doris Tate, The Nashville Cookbook, 1977

BROWN SUGAR FROSTING

1 cup brown sugar	1/2 cup water
pinch cream of tartar	2 egg whites, beaten stiff

Combine sugar and cream of tartar (a little vinegar may be used instead of cream of tartar if preferred) with the water in a saucepan. Place pan over medium flame and stir mixture until the sugar dissolves. Cover the pan and allow syrup to boil about 4 minutes. Uncover and continue cooking until syrup will form a firm ball when tried in cold water. Remove pan from flame; when all bubbling has ceased, then slowly pour syrup into a large bowl in which the egg whites have been placed, beating the mixture constantly. Continue beating the mixture 5 to 6 minutes until reaches the right consistency to spread.
The Southern Cookbook, 1939

NEVER FAIL ICING

1 cup sugar	1 Tablespoon vanilla
3 Tablespoons water	1/4 teaspoon cream of tartar
2 egg whites	pinch of salt

Put all ingredients in top of a double boiler. Have water boiling in lower part. Beat with egg beater consistently for seven minutes. Remove from fire and spread on cake.
The Southern Cookbook, 1939

RICHMOND CHOCOLATE ICING

1/2 cup sugar	1 oz. square chocolate	1 1/2 Tablespoons butter
2 Tablespoons cornstarch	dash of salt	1/2 teaspoon vanilla
	1/2 cup water	

Combine all the ingredients except vanilla. Cook, stirring constantly, until mixture thickens. Cook 2 minutes longer. Add vanilla. You may spread either hot or cold
Satsuma Tea Room, Fun for the Cook, 1968

CHOCOLATE ICING

2 cups confectioner's sugar	1 Tablespoon butter
1/4 cup cocoa	1 teaspoon vanilla
1/4 cup hot coffee	

Mix the confectioner's sugar and cocoa. Pour the hot coffee over the butter and, when it melts, beat this into the dry ingredients, adding the vanilla. When of the right consistency, spread on the cake. If the icing becomes too stiff, add a little more coffee; if too thin, add more sugar.

NOTE: This icing is not boiled and failure seems to be impossible with this particular recipe for chocolate icing, which is certainly a recommendation to any cook! Miss Anita de Saussure tells us it cannot fail. This is sufficient icing for a two layer cake.
Anita de Saussure, 200 Years of Charleston Cooking, 1930

FUDGE FROSTING

1 square (1 ounce) unsweetened chocolate	1 egg, well beaten
2 Tablespoons butter or margarine	1 teaspoon vanilla
1 1/2 cups confectioners' sugar	

Melt chocolate and butter in saucepan over low heat. Remove from heat; blend in sugar and egg. Add vanilla; beat until frosting is of spreading consistency. Enough frosting for brownies or an 8 inch or 9 inch square cake.
Easy-on-the-Cook Book, 1960

BUTTERSCOTCH CHOCOLATE FROSTING

In a saucepan, combine 3 (1 ounce) squares unsweetened chocolate, 1/4 cup butter or margarine, 1/2 cup light cream, 2/3 cup brown sugar, packed, and 1/4 teaspoon salt. Bring all to a boil, stirring constantly. Cook until the chocolate is melted. Remove from heat; add vanilla and enough confectioner's sugar for good spreading consistency (about 3 cups). Spread over the sides and top of cake.

NOTE: For a variation using sour milk, substitute sweet milk with 1/4 teaspoon cream of tartar or 1 Tablespoon lemon juice, or vinegar added.
The Farm Journal's Country Cookbook, 1959

MOCHA ICING

2 cups heavy cream
1 cup sifted powdered sugar
1/2 cup cocoa

2 Tablespoons instant coffee powder
1/8 teaspoon salt

Mix all ingredients and beat with electric beater until mixture is stiff.
Satsuma Tea Room, Fun for the Cook, 1968

MOCHA ICING

1/4 cup butter
3 teaspoons cocoa

2/3 cup confectioner's sugar (or more)
1 Tablespoon strong, clear coffee

Cream the butter, add cocoa, and sugar and moisten with coffee to the consistency you desire for icing.
The Southern Cookbook, 1939

CREAM CHEESE FROSTING

1 1/2 cups powdered sugar
1 egg white, slightly beaten

1/4 cup cream cheese
1/2 teaspoon vanilla

Beat cheese until soft, add other ingredients and beat well.
Satsuma Tea Room, Fun for the Cook, 1968

CREAM CHEESE ICING

1 package of cream cheese
1 Tablespoon warm water

1 1/2 cups confectioner's sugar
1 teaspoon vanilla

NOTE: Mash cheese. Add sugar, water and vanilla. Beat until creamy.

At the Satsuma, we were partial to Cream Cheese Icing for the prune cakes we made. Many prefer caramel icing. There is no wrong or right way.
Satsuma Tea Room, More Fun for the Cook, 1974

VANILLA CREAM CHEESE FROSTING

3 ounces cream cheese
1 Tablespoon milk

3 cups confectioners' sugar
1/2 teaspoon vanilla

Blend cream cheese and milk. Add sugar gradually, blending well. Add vanilla; mix again. Makes sufficient frosting to frost 2 dozen Empire Biscuits or to fill and frost a two layer, 8-inch cake.
Easy-on-the-Cook Book, 1960

CHOCOLATE CREAM CHEESE FROSTING

6 ounces cream cheese, softened
8 ounces sweet cooking chocolate
3 Tablespoons light cream

2 cups confectioners' sugar
1 teaspoon vanilla extract

Soften cream cheese. Melt the chocolate over hot water. Blend with the cream cheese, cream, sugar, and vanilla. Whip until smooth. Spread on a slightly warm cake.
Mary Frances Purnell, The Nashville Cookbook, 1977

HONEY CREAM-CHEESE FROSTING

3 ounces cream cheese
1 Tablespoon honey

2 1/2 cup sifted confectioners' sugar

Blend cheese with honey, gradually add sugar; beat until smooth.
Farm Journal's Country Cook Book, 1959

ROYALE FROSTING

2 egg whites
1 1/2 cups sugar
1 Tablespoon light corn syrup

1/2 cup water
1 1/2 teaspoons vanilla

Combine egg whites, sugar, corn syrup and water in top of double boiler. Mix until well-blended. Cook over boiling water, beating constantly until mixture forms stiff, glossy peaks (about 7 minutes). Beat in vanilla. Makes enough frosting for a 10- inch cake or a 3 layer cake.
Easy-on-the-Cook Book, 1960

LEMON BUTTER FROSTING

3/4 cup butter
3 1/2 cups sifted confectioners' sugar

1 Tablespoon milk
2 Tablespoons fresh lemon juice

2 Tablespoons grated lemon peel

Cream butter and sugar together. Add milk, lemon juice and peel; beat until smooth.
Easy-on-the-Cook Book, 1960

LEMON BUTTER

2 eggs
1 cup sugar
2 Tablespoons butter
2 lemons

Beat the eggs and sugar together. Add the butter and then the grated rind and the juice of the lemons. Bring to a boiling point and cook until thick, stirring constantly or, better yet cook in the upper part of a double boiler. Spread on the cake.

NOTE: Although jelly is traditional for rolled cake, this lemon butter is a Charleston suggestion which almost surpasses the jelly! If you feel however that lemon butter would be out of place in a "jelly roll," then try it as a cake filling. The amount of this recipe will cover two layers.
Miss Mitchell, 200 Years of Charleston Cooking, 1930

BROWN BUTTER FROSTING

1/2 cup butter or margarine
3 cups sifted confectioners' sugar
1/4 cup boiling water

Melt butter over medium heat until light golden brown. Add sugar, the water. Beat until frosting holds its shape. Spread and swirl about 2 teaspoons on each cookie you wish to frost. Makes about 2 1/2 cups.
Farm Journal's Country Cook Book, 1959

THIN CONFECTIONERS' SUGAR ICING

1 cup confectioners' sugar, sifted
2 Tablespoons milk
1/4 teaspoon vanilla

Mix together sugar, milk, vanilla. Beat until smooth. Spread or drizzle over coffee cake or rolls. Makes sufficient icing for one large coffee cake.
Easy-on-the-Cook Book, 1960

ORANGE ICING

2 egg whites, unbeaten
1 1/2 cups sugar
5 Tablespoons cold water
1 1/2 teaspoons light corn syrup
juice and grated rind of 1/2 orange

Put egg whites, sugar, water and corn syrup in upper part of a double boiler. Beat with egg beater until thoroughly mixed. Place over rapidly boiling water, beating constantly with beater and cook 7 minutes, or until frosting will stand in peaks. Remove from fire, add orange juice and rind and beat until thick enough to spread. This mixture will cover two 9-inch layers.
The Southern Cookbook, 1939

ORANGE CREAM FILLING AND FROSTING

FILLING

1 cup sugar	1 Tablespoon lemon juice
3 Tablespoons flour	1 Tablespoon grated orange rind
1 egg, beaten	1 teaspoon grated lemon rind
1/4 cup fresh orange juice	1 cup cream, whipped

Mix all the ingredients, except the cream. Cook over low heat, stirring constantly, until thickened. Cool and fold into whipped cream. Spread between layers of sponge cake.

FROSTING

2 to 3 cups confectioner's sugar	2 teaspoons lemon juice
1/4 cup butter, softened	2 or more Tablespoons cream
2 Tablespoons orange juice	

Mix all ingredients until smooth, using cream as needed to make spreading consistency.

NOTE: Delicious for filling and frosting sponge cake, split into layers.
Sandra C. Fleming, The Nashville Cookbook, 1977

ORANGE BUTTER CREAM FROSTING

1/3 cup soft butter or margarine	1/4 cup orange juice
1 egg yolk	1 1/2 teaspoons lemon juice
4 1/2 cups sifted confectioners' sugar	

Cream butter and egg yolk until soft and fluffy. Add sugar gradually, beating well. Combine the juices; blend in amount of the combined juices necessary to make a spreading consistency. This is sufficient to frost and fill a two layer, 9-inch round cake.
Easy-on-the-Cook Book, 1960

MERINGUE SHELLS

3 egg whites (room temperature)	dash of cream of tartar
1/8 teaspoon salt	3/4 cup sugar

Beat egg whites in mixer bowl until frothy; add salt and cream of tartar. Continue beating until soft peak stage. Very gradually add half of the sugar; beat 5 minutes longer. Add other half of the sugar, continuing to beat for 10 to 15 minutes or until all the sugar is completely dissolved. Swirl meringue shells with pastry tube or spoon into 1 1/2 inch rounds on brown or parchment paper; depress center of each with back of spoon.
Bake at 250 F for about 45 minutes to 1 hour or until thoroughly dry and crisp, but not browned at all. Makes about 15 party-size meringues.

NOTE: Meringues are delightful additions to party trays. Top with a dollop of whipped cream and one strawberry or other colorful fruit. Larger dessert meringues are perfect for ice cream shells and other fillings. May be stored in freezer in air-tight container.
Sue Umbarger, The Nashville Cookbook, 1977

SEVEN MINUTE FROSTING & SEAFOAM ICING

3/4 cups sugar	1/8 teaspoon cream of	1 egg white
2 Tablespoons water	tartar	pinch of salt
	flavoring as desired	

Mix all the ingredients except flavoring in double boiler. Stir to dissolve the sugar. Set over boiling water and beat until stiff- about 4 minutes with electric beater. It should stand in peaks. Remove from heat and beat until thick enough to spread.

NOTE: Use brown sugar instead of white when making *Seafoam Icing*.
Satsuma Tea Room, Fun for the Cook, 1968

MAPLE PIE TOPPING

1 cup heavy cream   1/4 cup maple syrup

Whip the cream until it stands in soft peaks. Drizzle the syrup over the top and carefully fold into the cream. Variation: Substitute molasses for maple syrup.

NOTE: Perfect on cold squash or that pumpkin pie you want to dress-up!
Farm Journal's Country Cook Book, 1959

BROILED COCONUT-HONEY CAKE TOPPING

2 Tablespoons soft butter   1 teaspoon grated lemon rind
2/3 cup flaked or shredded coconut   1/8 teaspoon salt
1/4 cup honey

Spread the top of the cake with butter. Combine coconut, honey, lemon rind and salt. Then blend well. Spread over the cake. Broil just long enough to toast coconut lightly, 2 to 4 minutes.

NOTE: This topping glamorizes any cake.
Farm Journal's Country Cook Book, 1959

GERMAN PASTRY

6 cups all-purpose flour   2 e 2 eggs
1/4 cup sugar   2 T 2 Tablespoons vinegar
1 Tablespoon salt   10 10 Tablespoons water
1 pound lard

Blend the first 4 ingredients; set aside. Beat the eggs, vinegar, and water. Combine two mixtures and mix. Chill for at least 2 hours before rolling. May be kept 2 weeks in covered dish in refrigerator. May also be kept in the freezer. When ready to use, roll out, place in pie pan. Flute the edges and bake at 425 until browned. Makes six 8-inch pastry shells.
Ruth Faye Kilgore, The Nashville Cookbook, 1977

SOUTHERN PASTRY

2 cups flour

1/2 teaspoon salt

1 cup butter or other shortening

1/2 cup ice water

Mix flour and salt, work butter lightly into the flour, add ice water and mix to make a stiff dough but do not knead. Roll flat and line pie plate.
The Southern Cookbook, 1939

PLAIN PASTRY

1 1/4 cups flour

1/2 teaspoon salt

6 Tablespoons shortening

3 Tablespoons cold water (or less)

Combine flour and salt: cut in shortening until particles are like very small peas or coarse meal. Sprinkle water over mixture and stir with a fork until mixture is moist and holds together when pressed between hands in a very brief kneading motion. Form into ball and chill slightly before rolling on a floured board to 1/8 inch thickness, about 1 inch larger than the pie pan. Fit rolled dough closely into the pan; use the 1 inch overhang to make a fluted standing edge around the shell. For baked crust, prick bottom and sides of crust carefully before baking at 425 F for about 10 minutes or until delicately browned. Makes one 9 inch pie shell.

NOTE: Double the ingredients for 2 shells or for double crust.
The Nashville Cookbook, 1977

PIE CRUST

1 1/2 cups quick oats

1/2 cup brown sugar

1/2 cup melted butter or margarine

Preheat oven to 350 F. Combine oats and sugar. Add butter. Mix until crumbly. Press firmly onto bottom and sides of an 8 inch pan. Bake about 8 minutes. Cool.
Elizabeth Nyholm, University of Illinois Home Economics Faculty Favorites, 1965

PASTRY: THE PASTE METHOD

1 1/2 cups flour,
sifted with 1/2 teaspoon salt

1/2 cup vegetable shortening

3 Tablespoons ice water

Take out 1/4 cup flour and cut fat into the remaining flour until the mixture is crumbly. Make a paste with 1/4 cup flour and 3 Tablespoons ice water. Add to the first mixture. Roll into a ball and cover with plastic wrap. Place in refrigerator 30 minutes.

NOTE: Pastry will make two single pie shells or one double pie crust
Evelyn Deal, The Nashville Cookbook, 1977

VODKA PIE CRUST

2 cups flour
1 teaspoon salt
2/3 cup shortening
2 Tablespoons butter
2 Tablespoons vodka
2 to 3 Tablespoons ice water

In a food processor combine shortening, butter, flour and salt. Process using on and off pulses, until the dough resembles coarse meal. Gradually add vodka and water with the machine running until the dough is moist and gathers into a ball. Makes two 9-inch crusts.

NOTE: This is not a misprint. The vodka is for the dough, not the cook. Sounds crazy, but when you think about it, it makes sense. The vodka increases the flakiness of the crust because, just like the water, it creates air spaces in the crust when it cooks away. This explanation may not convince the folks at the church picnic. David H.
Bill Hall, Cortner Mill Restaurant cookbook, 2009

CHOCOLATE COOKIE PIE CRUST

1 1/3 cups chocolate cookie crumbs
1/3 cup melted butter

Crush cookies, add butter, blend well. Pat into bottom and side of pie pan. Bake 10 minutes at 300 degrees. Cool before filling with pie contents.
Satsuma Tea Room, More Fun for the Cook, 1974

JUST-RIGHT EGG PASTRY

3 cups flour
2 Tablespoons sugar
1 1/2 teaspoons salt
3/4 cup shortening
1 large egg
1 Tablespoon lemon juice
1/4 cup plus 2 Tablespoons milk

Sift flour, sugar and salt together. Cut in the shortening until the texture is like coarse meal. Slightly beat whole egg. Add lemon juice and milk to egg; stir the liquid into flour mixture. Blend well, roll thin, line pastry tins. Prick lightly and bake for 20 minutes at 425, or as directed if using uncooked filling. Makes two 8-inch pie shells.
Nelle Stewart, The Nashville Cookbook, 1977

CREAM CHEESE PASTRY

1 cup butter or margarine, softened
8 ounces cream cheese, softened
2 1/4 cups flour
1/2 teaspoon salt

Cream butter and cheese together. Gradually blend in flour and salt. Knead lightly until the dough clings together. Wrap in wax paper and chill for ease in handling. Roll on floured board to about 1/8 inch thick for making tartlets, turnovers, or other desired forms for small party pastries. May also be used for larger pie crusts. Makes about four dozen small pastries.
Sue Umbarger, The Nashville Cookbook, 1977

BASIC CRUMB CRUST

1 1/2 cups finely crushed graham crackers
1/3 cup sugar
1/3 to 1/2 cup butter or margarine, melted

Combine crumbs with sugar and blend with melted butter. Press firmly onto bottom and sides of a 9 inch pie pan. Chill for 1 hour or bake at 350 F for about 10 minutes to set the crust. Baked crust is firmer.

FILBERT GRAHAM CRUST

Substitute 1 cup ground filberts for 1/2 cup cracker crumbs. Mix remaining 1 cup graham cracker crumbs with nuts and sugar and blend in melted butter. Bake at 350 F for about 10 minutes to toast lightly.

COCONUT GRAHAM CRUST

Same as the filbert substitution except substitute 1 cup coconut for filberts.

ZWIEBACK CRUST

Substitute Zwieback crumbs for graham cracker crumbs and use powdered sugar instead of granulated. Add a teaspoon of cinnamon if desired.

PREPARED CEREAL CRUST

Substitute crushed corn flakes, crisp rice cereal, or flaked wheat cereal for cracker crumbs.
Mildred Ann Smith, The Nashville Cookbook, 1977

GRAHAM CRACKER PIE SHELL

18 graham crackers, crushed
1/3 cup butter, melted
1/4 cup sugar

Preheat oven to 375 F. Blend cracker crumbs, butter and sugar. Press mixture into 10-inch pie plate. Bake about 7 minutes. Cool. Yield: One 10-inch pie shell.
Helen House, University of Illinois Home Economics Faculty Favorites, 1965

CAKES

"A party without cake is just a meeting."
-Julia Child (1912-2004)

A cook's reputation is often simply established with just a beautiful cake; a high, light, and wonderful cake with an eye-catching frosting gently swirled. It is a Southern custom for a good hostess to serve a delightful cake. Guests' first impressions are important; so be sure to decorate your cake. You don't have to go through lots of extra effort. Cheerful swirls, a sprinkle of coconut, shaved chocolate, chopped nuts, or tiny candies will turn a basic cake into one of beauty.

ANGEL FOOD CAKE

"Angel Food Cake is all that the name implies and is as difficult of accomplishment as any other angelic performance. Only practice makes perfect. You cannot attain it by the hit and miss method, as you can with so many other things, but it is the easiest thing in the world to eat when once it is well made."

"To begin with, an expert cake maker tells me that she measures the whites of the eggs instead of counting them, since they are as temperamental as to size, and temperamental does not go in Angel Cake as an ingredient."
Therefore:

1 1/4 cups of egg whites	1 teaspoon vanilla
1 cup flour	1 teaspoon cream of tartar
1 1/2 cups sugar	pinch of salt

"Put the salt and cream of tartar in the whites of the eggs and beat until stiff, but not too stiff or the cake will be tough. Then put the sugar in, a Tablespoon at a time, still beating until it "peaks" and, very slowly, add the flour, then the vanilla, and put into a deep ungreased pan. Cook slowly, and when done, turn pan upside down and do not touch until cold. Then cut around the sides of the pan with a knife to "disengage" it, as the old cookbooks say, and here's hoping it will be angel's food indeed."
-Harriet Ross Colquitt quoted in *The Savannah Cook Book*, 1933

BRIDE'S ANGEL FOOD CAKE

whites of 18 eggs	3/4 pound butter	1 teaspoon vanilla
1 pound sugar	1 teaspoon baking soda	
1 pound sifted flour	2 tsp cream of tartar	

Sift flour 3 times and add baking soda and cream of tartar, then cream butter and sugar until very light and add to the stiffly beaten egg whites gradually. Add flour, beating it lightly, flavor with teaspoon of vanilla. Place in angel food pan. Bake in slow oven (250 F).
The Southern Cookbook, 1939

SPONGE CAKE

"This sponge cake is famous in Savannah and the proportions given below make two large cakes. It seems enormous, so if you think your family will be satisfied with just one cake, divide the receipt proportions in half. The problem is that it will have to be done all over again a few days later after the one cake is eaten".

10 eggs
1/2 pound Swans Down cake flour

1 pound granulated sugar
juice and rind of 2 lemons

The art of a good sponge is in the making, so follow the directions verbatim:
- Separate eggs and put yolks into a large bowl and whites on a large platter.
- Grate rind of lemons and set aside in strained lemon juice to "steep."
- Sift flour 3 times
- Grease two large "stove-pipe" pans and then proceed.
- Beat egg yolks until very light, adding sugar gradually then the lemon juice and peel.
- Beat whites until stiff and dry. The old-fashioned flat egg beater is highly recommended instead of the more new-fangled electric life savers, as it makes the egg dryer. You'll get too stiff and dry before they do, but no matter….
- Stir the beaten whites into the beaten yolks and into this custard-like mixture sift again the already thrice-sifted flour, folding it in very lightly.

Harriet Ross Colquitt, The Savannah Cook Book, 1933

ANGEL FOOD CAKE

1 cup cake flour
1/2 cup powdered sugar
1 1/4 cups egg whites
1/4 teaspoon salt

1 teaspoon cream of tartar
1/2 teaspoon vanilla
1/4 teaspoon almond extract
1 cup sugar

Sift together flour and powdered sugar. If egg whites are cold, let them warm to room temperature. Beat egg whites with cream of tartar until foamy, but not stiff. Continue beating and add granulated sugar, 2 Tablespoons at a time. Beat until stiff enough to form peaks, but not until dry. Gradually fold in salt and extracts with a wire whisk. Gently fold in flour and powdered sugar 1/4 cup at a time. Turn batter into an ungreased tube pan. Bake at 300 for one hour. Remove from oven and invert pan to cool.

NOTE: We like to keep this angel food or a pound cake on hand, because they are the basis for a lot of quick desserts, when topped with fresh fruit and one of our sauces.

David Hazelwood, Cortner Mill Restaurant cookbook, 2009

POUND CAKE

Pound cake was so named for the one pound each of the major ingredients of: butter, sugar, eggs, and flour and did not originate in this country, but continued with wide acceptance among the settlers in the New World for its versatility, preserving qualities, and the ready convenience of the basic ingredients. Early pound cakes had no liquid other than egg and no leavening other than the air integrated with the other ingredients through long blending. Later recipes of pound cake include milk and small amounts of leavening. Pound Cake's many flavorings include brandy, rum, orange or lemon juice, vanilla, almond, nutmeg, and mace.

OLD FASHIONED POUND CAKE

1 pound butter
3 cups sugar
4 cups cake flour sifted with:
2 teaspoons baking powder

10-12 eggs
pinch of salt
1/4 cup orange juice

Cream butter and sugar well. Add flour and baking powder. Beat in eggs one at time until well blended. Add salt and orange juice. Beat 10 minutes with electric mixer. Bake in tube pan one hour in a 325 degree oven.

NOTE: Before the day of electric mixers, this cake had to be beaten (stirred hard) several hours by hand.
Satsuma Tea Room, Fun for the Cook, 1968

POUND CAKE

2 cups (1 pound) butter
2 cups (1 pound) sugar
10 eggs, separated

2 Tablespoons brandy
1 teaspoon vanilla extract
4 cups (1 pound) flour

1/2 teaspoon salt
(optional)

Thoroughly cream the butter; gradually add sugar and whip together until light and fluffy. Whip the egg yolks and add to creamed mixture, beating until very light. Stir in flavorings and flour; blend well. Beat egg whites until they form soft peaks, but that are not dry, and then fold into the batter until well blended. Turn into two 9 x 5 x 3 inch loaf pans which have been greased and lightly dusted with flour (a 10 inch stem pan may be used). Bake at 325 F for about an hour or until center of cake springs back when lightly pressed. Cool about 10 minutes in pans before turning out onto a rack.
Commentary, The Nashville Cookbook, 1977

STRAWBERRY DE LUX

Pound Cake is so perfect with fruits such as the dish Strawberry De Lux. The following is a recipe from the Fairvue Plantation by Mrs. Wemyss, a matriarch of Nashville high society.

Wash 3 pints of strawberries. Hull and drain. Whip 1 pint of cream and sweeten with 1 cup sugar. Add 1/2 cup sherry. Fold strawberries into the cream mixture. Serve topped with macaroon crumbs.
Mrs. Wemyss' sharing her Fairview Plantation recipe in The Nashville Cookbook, 1977

COCONUT POUND CAKE

2 sticks butter or margarine	1 cup milk
1/2 cup vegetable shortening	dash of salt
3 cups sugar	1/2 teaspoon almond flavoring
6 eggs	1/2 teaspoon coconut flavoring
3 cups flour	1 can (3 1/2 ounces) grated coconut

Cream butter, shortening, and sugar. Add eggs, one at a time, beating a total of 2 minutes after each egg. Add flour and milk alternately. Add the salt and other flavorings. Fold in the coconut; pour into tube pan lined on the bottom with waxed paper. Bake at 350 F for 1 hour and 15 minutes. Start with a cold oven. Serves 16 to 20.

TOPPING FOR COCONUT POUND CAKE

1 cup sugar	1 teaspoon coconut flavoring
1 cup water	

Boil all together for 1 minute and pour over the cake while hot.
Mary Neal Alexander, The Nashville Cookbook, 1977

STRAWBERRY SHORT CAKE

Make a rich pie crust of 1 pint of flour, 1 teaspoon baking powder, 1 Tablespoon of butter or lard. Roll out thin and bake in pie pan. When done, split with sharp knife and butter well. Spread between a strawberry mixture made of 1 quart of strawberries mashed with 1 cup of sugar. Spread another layer of the mixture on top. Serve warm with whipped cream, slightly sweetened.
The Savannah Cook Book, 1933

PEACH SHORTCAKE

2 cups sifted all-purpose flour	1 egg, beaten
3 teaspoons baking powder	2/3 cup half and half
1/2 teaspoon salt	1 1/2 cups sweetened, sliced fresh peaches
1/4 cup brown sugar, firmly packed	or frozen peaches drained
1/2 cup shortening	1 cup heavy cream, whipped
1/2 cup pecans, chopped	

Preheat oven to 425. Grease two 8-inch cake pans. Sift flour, baking powder and salt together. Cut in brown sugar and shortening until the mixture resembles corn meal. Combine egg and half and half. Make a well in dry ingredients, add the liquid ingredients and mix only until dry ingredients are dampened. Spread batter in cake pans. Bake about 12 minutes or until the cake springs back when lightly touched.
Remove from pan. Cool. Place 3/4 cup peaches on one layer; cover with 1/2 cup whipped cream. Top with other layer. Frost cake with remaining whipped cream. Decorate with peach slices. Yields 6 servings.
Mrs. Frances LaFont, University of Illinois Home Economics Faculty Favorites, 1965

BEST CHOCOLATE CAKE

1/2 cup cocoa
1/3 cup sugar
1/4 cup water

Combine ingredients above and cook in double boiler until smooth. Cool.

1 cup butter
1 cup powdered sugar
1 cup sugar
1 cup milk
4 eggs
2 1/2 cups cake flour
1/2 teaspoon salt
1 teaspoon baking soda
1 teaspoon cream of tartar

Cream butter and sugars together until very light. Beat in eggs. Add cooked cocoa mixture (above). Sift dry ingredients (flour, soda, salt, and cream of tartar) together. Add alternately with milk. Bake at 350 until done.

NOTE: We particularly like this recipe and think it is one of the best chocolate cakes we know.
Satsuma Tea Room, Fun for the Cook, 1968

BEST WHITE CAKE

1 cup butter
2 cups sugar, sifted
3 1/2 cups cake flour
5 teaspoons baking powder
1/8 teaspoon salt
1 cup milk
1 teaspoon vanilla
1/4 teaspoon almond flavoring
8 egg whites
1/8 teaspoon salt

Cream the butter and then add the sifted sugar gradually. Beat until light and creamy. Sift cake flour before measuring. Now resift the flour with baking powder and salt. Add milk alternately with the sifted flour. Beat until smooth. Beat in flavoring. Beat egg whites stiff with salt. Fold them lightly into cake batter. Bake in three greased 8 inch layer tins at 375 F for about 25 minutes.
Satsuma Tea Room, Fun for the Cook, 1968

BEST YELLOW CAKE

1 cup butter
2 cups sugar
4 egg yolks
1 1/2 teaspoons vanilla
1/2 teaspoon salt
2 2/3 cups sifted cake flour
2 teaspoons baking powder
1 cup milk
4 egg whites
1/4 teaspoon salt

Beat the butter and add sugar gradually. Beat until light and fluffy. Beat in one egg yolk at a time. Add vanilla—Sift flour, 1/2 teaspoon salt and baking powder together. Add sifted ingredients alternately with milk. Whip egg whites stiff, but not dry, with 1/4 teaspoon salt. Fold them lightly into batter. Bake in layers in a 350 F oven for 30-35 minutes.
Satsuma Tea Room, Fun for the Cook, 1968

LADY BALTIMORE CAKE

1 cup butter
1 cup sugar
1 cup milk
3 1/2 cups flour
2 teaspoons baking flour
1 teaspoon vanilla
6 eggs, whites only

Cream the butter and sugar, add gradually the milk and flour (into which the baking powder has been sifted) and lastly the well-beaten egg whites. Bake in shallow tins and put this filling between the layers. The filling is what made this cake famous.

LADY BALTIMORE CAKE FILLING

3 cups of sugar boiled with 1 cup of water until stringy. Pour this over 3 well-beaten egg whites and add 1 cup of chopped pecans, 1 cup seeded raisins and 1/2 cup of chopped figs.
The Savannah Cook Book, 1933

DOLLY VARDEN CAKE

2/3 cup butter
2 cups sugar
1 cup milk
3 cups flour
3 eggs
1 teaspoon baking powder
flavoring

Cream butter and sugar, add eggs and then the flour (into which the baking powder has been sifted) and milk and flavoring. Divide in half and bake 1/2 of batter in two layers. Saving the remaining batter to mix with the following ingredients:

1 Tablespoon molasses
2 cups raisins
some nuts or citron
1 teaspoon. each of cinnamon,
cloves and nutmeg

Bake two layers of this mixture also and put the dark and light layers together alternately with the following white icing.

DOLLY VARDEN CAKE ICING

Boil 2 cups of sugar in 2/3 cups of water until stringy. Pour gradually over the well-beaten whites of two eggs beating constantly until thick enough to spread. Flavor as desired.
The Savannah Cook Book, 1933

GOVERNOR NORTHERN'S GREAT WHITE CAKE (Recipe used since 1880)

8 egg whites
1 cup sweet milk
1 cup white butter
2 cups sugar
2 Tablespoons baking powder
2 cups flour
1 cup corn starch

Cream the butter and sugar, add the milk, then flour (into which the baking powder has been sifted) and the corn starch. Add the whites that have been stiffly beaten and bake in cake pans about 1 inch deep. Put together with white icing.
The Savannah Cook Book, 1933

PLAIN LAYER CAKE

1 1/2 cups sugar
1/2 cup butter
3 cups flour
1 cup water

2 eggs
2 teaspoons baking powder
1 teaspoon flavoring;

Sift dry ingredients. Bake in shallow tins about 20 minutes.

ICING FOR PLAIN LAYER

4 ounces of chocolate
1/2 cup milk

1 cup sugar
1 teaspoon of vanilla

The Savannah Cook Book, 1933

CREAM CAKE

1 pint flour
1 cup sugar
1/2 cup butter

1 cup of milk and water mixed
2 eggs
2 teaspoons baking powder

Cream the butter and sugar. Add eggs (unbeaten), flour, milk, and vanilla, if desired. Bake in two layers and put the following filling between them:

FILLING FOR CREAM CAKE

1 pint of milk

4 Tablespoons flour
(moistened in a little cold milk)

Mix together and cook until very thick. Put aside to cool and when it is cool, spread between layers of cake and serve with cream.
The Savannah Cook Book, 1933

NO-NAME CAKE

1 cup and 1 Tablespoon butter
2 cups very fine sugar
5 eggs, separated
3 cups flour

2 teaspoons baking powder
1 cup milk
1 1/2 teaspoons vanilla

Cream together the butter and sugar. (Confectioners' sugar was suggested for this cake, but since this tends to make a dry cake, we sifted our granulated sugar through a very fine sieve instead and still had a delicate cake.) Add the beaten egg yolks and beat well. Mix and sift the dry ingredients and add alternately with the milk to the first mixture. Add the vanilla and last of all fold in the stiffly beaten egg whites. Bake in layer cake pans in a moderately hot oven (375 F) for about 25 minutes or bake in a large shallow loaf pan for about 45 minutes in a moderate oven (350 F).

NOTE: While this cake is apparently nameless, that in no way interferes with its goodness either as a layer or loaf cake.
Mary Leize Simons, 200 Years of Charleston Cooking, 1930

PAN CAKE

1 pint of milk, 1/2-pound sifted flour, 2 eggs, 1/4 pound of butter. Beat eggs and add 1 gill (quarter of a pint) of milk. Stir the flour with this until it becomes a very smooth paste then add the rest of the milk. Stir in the butter, warmed to be soft, and if lumpy, strain. Put a small lump of butter in a pan-cake pan. When hot, pour in 2 Tablespoons of the batter and spread it so as to cover the whole pan. Fry until a light brown on both sides. Roll the cakes and sprinkle with soft sugar. Serve hot and eat along with sherry wine.
The Savannah Cook Book, 1933

SOUR CREAM CAKE

Sift together 1 1/2 cups flour, 1 teaspoon baking powder, 1/2 teaspoon salt. Beat 3 eggs until thick and then gradually beat in 1 cup sugar. Alternately add dry ingredients and 1 cup sour heavy cream with 1 1/2 teaspoon vanilla added. Pour batter into greased 9 inch square pan. Bake in moderate oven (350 F) 35 to 40 minutes. Frost with:

PEANUT FROSTING

Stir together 1/4 cup chunk-style peanut butter, 3 cup sifted confectioners' sugar, 1/4 to 1/3 cup milk, until creamy and of spreading consistency.
Farm Journal's Country Cookbook, 1959

ONE-TWO-THREE CAKE

The batter for the famous one-two-three cake, which is the foundation for all simple layer or individual cakes, is made of 1 cup of butter, two cups of sugar, three cups flour (with 3 teaspoons of baking powder), 4 eggs and enough milk or water to make the batter the right consistency.

Cream the butter and sugar, add the egg yolks, then alternately add the milk and flour. Lastly add the egg whites and flavoring.
The Savannah Cook Book, 1933

CHOCOLATE CAKE

2/3 cup shortening	2 1/4 cups sifted cake flour
1 1/2 cups sugar	1 teaspoon baking soda
3 eggs	1 teaspoon salt
2 1/2 squares unsweetened chocolate	1 1/4 cups buttermilk

Preheat oven to 350 F. Combine shortening, sugar, and eggs. Beat 5 minutes at high speed. Blend melted chocolate into creamed mixture. Sift together the flour, soda, and salt. Add together alternately with the buttermilk. Pour into two greased 9-inch layer pans or one 9 x 13 x 2 inch pan. Bake 30 to 35 minutes. Yields 15 servings.
Home Economics Cafeteria Specialty, University of Illinois, Home Economics Faculty Favorites, 1965

CHOCOLATE ROLL

NOTE: This recipe is from my husband's grandmother's cookbook, long out of print.
Anne Foster Caldwell's, Book of Southern and Creole Home Cooking, 1929

5 eggs	1 pint whipping cream	1/2 teaspoon vanilla
1/2 cup sugar	2 Tablespoons cocoa	pinch of salt

Beat egg yolks until lemon colored; add sugar, cocoa, and salt. Fold into the mixture stiffly beaten whites of eggs. Butter and dredge lightly with flour a shallow aluminum baking pan, 15 x 12, one end of pan open. Spread the batter about 1/3 of an inch thick on the pan and bake in a hot oven for 15 minutes or a slow oven for 20 minutes. Turn out onto a damp cloth and spread on a table or biscuit board, and lay a damp cloth over the cake.

FILLING

Beat 1 pint of whipped cream stiff with scant 1/2 cup of sugar and 1/2 teaspoon vanilla. Remove the damp cloth and spread cream mixture well over the cake and gently roll into a roll with the aid of the under cloth. Slip onto a silver platter. Serve from this platter with hot chocolate sauce poured over the roll.

CHOCOLATE SAUCE

1 scant cup of sugar	2 Tablespoons cold water
1/2 teaspoon vanilla	2 squares Baker's unsweetened chocolate, melted
1 whole egg	

Cook all the ingredients for about 10 minutes, stirring constantly. Add a little cream to make custard thinner.

NOTE: This old recipe for such an elegant dessert is a chef-d'oeuvre all its own!
Shared by Betty Caldwell, Food Editor of The Tennessean, The Nashville Cookbook, 1977

DEVIL'S FOOD CAKE

2 cups sugar	1 teaspoon salt
3/4 cup shortening	1 cup buttermilk
1/4 pound chocolate, melted	1 teaspoon vanilla
5 eggs	1 teaspoon baking soda
2 cups flour	

Heat oven to 325 F and line two 9-inch pans with waxed paper and grease. Cream the sugar and shortening until light. Add the melted chocolate. Add eggs, one at a time, beating well after each addition. Mix the flour and salt. Add the flour mixture and 1/2 cup buttermilk, alternately. Add vanilla. Mix soda with the remaining buttermilk and stir into the batter. Pour the batter into the prepared pans. Bake 1 hour. Spread caramel icing between layers, on the top, and on the sides. Serves 12 to 16.
Jeanne Webb, The Nashville Cookbook, 1977

RED VELVET CAKE

1/2 cup butter	1 cup buttermilk
1 1/2 cups sugar	2 1/4 cups cake flour, sifted
2 eggs	1 teaspoon baking soda
2 ounces red food coloring	1 Tablespoon vinegar
2 Tablespoons cocoa	1 teaspoon vanilla
1 teaspoon salt	

Cream butter and sugar, add eggs. Make paste of red food color and cocoa. Add to butter and sugar mixture. Add salt. Add buttermilk, alternating with flour. Add soda which has been mixed with vinegar. Then add vanilla. Do not beat hard. Use low speed on mixer. Pour mixture into two greased 9-inch pans and bake at 350 for 30 minutes or until toothpick comes out clean. Let cool and split each layer in half making 4 layers. Top with frosting.

FROSTING FOR RED VELVET CAKE

5 Tablespoons flour	2 sticks butter	1 teaspoon vanilla
1 cup milk	1 cup sugar	

Mix flour with milk until smooth. Cook over low heat until thick. Be sure it is cool. Cream 1 stick butter with sugar until fluffy. Add the cooked flour and milk mixture and beat until consistency of whipped cream. Add vanilla and frost each layer.
Dorothy Tice, Fruit of the Spirit, Mt Bethel United Methodist Church Cookbook, Marietta

CHOCOLATE ICE BOX CAKE

3/4 pound German sweet chocolate	10 egg yolks
2/3 cup sugar	8 egg whites
1/2 cup water	

Melt chocolate and add sugar and water. Add egg yolks add one at a time beating constantly. Beat egg whites until stiff and fold into yolk mixture. Put between layers of angel food or sponge cake. Chill overnight. Serve with whipped cream to which a little cinnamon has been added. This is a large recipe and will make 2 cakes.
Satsuma Tea Room, Fun for the Cook, 1968

SPICED DEVIL'S FOOD CAKE

2 cups brown sugar	1 1/2 Tablespoons cinnamon
1 cup butter	1 teaspoon allspice
2 eggs	1 teaspoon cloves
1 cup buttermilk	1 teaspoon baking soda dissolved into
3 cups flour	1/2 cup boiling water
4 squares melted cooking chocolate	1 teaspoon vanilla

Cream brown sugar and butter and add to well-beaten eggs; then add milk, chocolate, and beat flour in slowly, adding a teaspoon of vanilla and the spices. Add soda dissolved in boiling water. Bake in layer cake tins in a moderate oven (350 F) about 30 minutes.
The Southern Cookbook, 1939

BLACK CHOCOLATE CAKE

3/4 cup of shaved chocolate
1 cup milk
1 cup sugar
yolk of 1 egg

butter, size of an egg
1 1/2 cups flour (scant)
3 scant teaspoons baking powder

Put chocolate, egg yolk and 1/2 the milk into a saucepan and cook until thick, stirring constantly. When thick, remove from stove and add butter, sugar, the rest of the milk and flour, into which the baking powder has been sifted; and lastly the well-beaten egg white. Bake in 3 layers and put together with White Icing.

NOTE: Be very careful not to get too much flour. It must be very soft and bake quickly.
The Savannah Cook Book, 1933

GERMAN CHOCOLATE CAKE

1 cup butter
2 cups sugar
4 eggs yolks
2 1/2 cups cake flour
1 cup buttermilk
1/4 pound German chocolate dissolved in
1/2 cup hot water

1 teaspoon baking soda
1/2 teaspoon salt
1 teaspoon vanilla
4 egg whites beaten stiff

Cream butter and sugar. Beat in egg yolks. Sift remaining dry ingredients. Add dissolved chocolate to butter and sugar mixture. Then add dry ingredients alternately with buttermilk. Finally fold in beaten egg whites. Bake in layer cake tins at 350 for 40 minutes.

PUT LAYERS TOGETHER WITH THE FOLLOWING FILLING:

1 large can evaporated milk (12 oz.)
3 egg yolks
1 cup sugar
1/4 pound margarine

1 cup coconut
1 cup chopped nuts
1 teaspoon vanilla

Make a custard of first 4 ingredients. When cool, add remaining ingredients. This filling may also be used on top of cake or Mocha Icing may be used. This is a most delicious cake, but expensive. We prefer icing on top of cake to filling.
Satsuma Tea Room, Fun for the Cook, 1968

JAM CAKE

Store-bought sugar was, more times than not, very scarce and prohibitively expensive in the rural South. People often just made do for the holiday season and it truly was a Southern custom. Many believed that it wasn't an authentic holiday without enjoying this wonderful tradition of cooking and eating jam cake. Every family in the South has multiple narratives that are linked to their own respective, festive holidays with close neighbors and family; and in some form or fashion they will invariably be attached to some lore or highpoint involving food. Although, I must personally admit that jam cake is always great any day or time of the year.

JAM CAKE

3 cups flour
2 cups sugar
1 cup jam (any kind)
1 cup chopped nuts

2/3 cup butter
4 whole eggs
1 cup buttermilk
1 teaspoon baking soda

1 teaspoon each of allspice, cloves, mace, cinnamon and nutmeg

Cream butter and sugar, add yolks, a little flour, then jam, more flour, whites of eggs, nuts, spices, and lastly buttermilk into which the baking soda is dissolved just as ready to use. Place in greased layer-cake pans and cook for 20 minutes in a rather hot oven.

NOTE: White icing is better with this cake than any other, as it is rich enough without a heavy frosting.
The Savannah Cook Book, 1933

JAM CAKE (Known by many as Blackberry Jam Cake)

3 cups flour
2 cup sugar
2 cups blackberry jam
2 cups buttermilk

1/2 cup butter, softened
2 teaspoons nutmeg
2 teaspoons cinnamon
2 teaspoons cloves

1 teaspoon allspice
6 eggs, separated

Sift together all dry ingredients and blend in remaining ingredients. Beat egg whites until stiff. Fold into batter gently. Pour into three 9 inch cake pans. Bake at 350 for 30 minutes.

QUICK CARAMEL FROSTING

1 1/2 cups butter
3/4 cup milk
1 1/2 cups brown sugar

5 1/4 cups powdered sugar
1 Tablespoon Tennessee whiskey

Melt butter in a saucepan. Add brown sugar and cook until sugar dissolves. Add milk and whiskey and beat in powdered sugar until thick enough to spread.

NOTE: While this is not my grandmother's recipe, jam cake was a favorite at Grandmother Hazelwood's on Christmas Eve. My great grandmother made her jam cake weeks before Christmas, wrapped it a whiskey soaked cloth, and stored it in a tin.
David Hazelwood, Cortner Mill Restaurant cookbook, 2009

STRAWBERRY JAM CAKE

1 cup butter	1/4 teaspoon cloves
1/2 cup sugar	3 eggs, separated
1 cup strawberry jam	2 1/2 cups flour
1/2 cup strong black coffee	1 teaspoon baking soda dissolved into....
1 teaspoon cinnamon	4 Tablespoons sour cream

Cream butter well, add sugar gradually and beat well. Add jam and coffee to which spices have been added. Beat yolks of eggs and blend with first mixture. Sift flour and add alternately with sour cream in which soda has been dissolved. Fold in stiffly beaten egg whites. Bake in layers in moderate oven (350 F) for 45 to 55 minutes. Ice with your favorite icing.
The Southern Cookbook, 1939

SPICE CAKE

1 cup sugar	1 cup sour milk
1 cup molasses	1 2/3 teaspoons baking soda
1 cup butter	1 teaspoon each of mace, cinnamon,
3 eggs	allspice, nutmeg
1 heaping cup flour	1/2 teaspoon cloves

Cream butter and sugar and add egg yolks. Stir 2/3 teaspoon of soda into molasses and add to sugar and egg mixture. Dissolve 1 teaspoon of soda in sour milk and add this slowly, alternating with flour, then add spices and lastly the egg whites. Bake in layer pans and put together with white icing.
Gate City Cook Book, 1915 recipe as recounted in The Savannah Cook Book, 1933

SPICE CAKE

1/2 cup butter	1/4 cup milk	1/2 teaspoon mace
1 cup sugar	2 cups flour	1 1/2 teaspoons cloves
3 eggs	1 teaspoon baking soda	
1 cup molasses	1 teaspoon nutmeg	

Cream the butter and sugar together, add beaten eggs and beat well. Add molasses and milk and then the mixed and sifted dry ingredients. Bake in a shallow loaf cake pan in a moderately hot oven (375 F) for about 30 minutes.

NOTE: Mace gives this spice cake a somewhat unusual flavor. It is moist and keeps well (under lock and key from being eaten.)
This recipe was signed on the original recipe sheet as "Grandma's Own, Birdfield Plantation, South Carolina."
200 Years of Charleston Cooking, 1930

MAPLE GINGERBREAD

1 cup maple syrup
1 cup dairy sour cream
1 egg, well beaten
2 1/3 cups sifted flour

1 teaspoon baking soda
1 1/2 teaspoons ginger
1/2 teaspoon salt
4 Tablespoons melted butter

Blend syrup with cream and egg. Sift dry ingredients and stir in the syrup mixture. Add butter and beat thoroughly. Pour into an 8 x 12-inch baking pan, lined with greased brown paper. Bake in moderate oven (350 F) for 30 minutes. Makes 8 servings.

NOTE: Feast of the gods; warm squares of this gingerbread accompanied by bowls of applesauce.
Farm Journal's Country Cook Book, 1959

SOFT GINGERBREAD

Put 2 cups molasses (sorghum syrup is the best) and 2/3 cup shortening into a large bowl or pan. Heat to a boiling point and then add 3 full teaspoons baking soda and beat hard. Add 2 well-beaten eggs and 1 cup of sour milk. Then add the following dry ingredients previously mixed together- 4 cups flour, 1 Tablespoon ginger, 1 Tablespoon cinnamon and any other spices you wish, 1 teaspoon salt. Bake in a moderate oven 10-15 minutes. The batter should be rather thin in the pan. As it rises it is very light. The quantity of this receipt will make a large biscuit pan full.
The Savannah Cook Book, 1933

MISS ROSA'S GINGERBREAD

1 cup molasses
1 cup brown sugar
1/2 cup melted butter
2 eggs
1 teaspoon cinnamon

1 teaspoon ginger
1 teaspoon cloves
1 teaspoon baking powder
1 cup boiling water

3 cups flour

Stir brown sugar into melted butter and add the unbeaten eggs. Beat well. Dissolve baking soda in the boiling water and add the spices. Beat well and add the flour. Pour into a large pan (8 x 8) and bake in a moderate oven (350 F) until thoroughly baked, about 25 minutes.
The Southern Cookbook, 1939

FAIRY GINGERBREAD

1 cup butter
1 cup milk
2 cups sugar

4 cups flour
1 teaspoon baking powder

1 Tablespoon ginger

Beat butter to a cream, add sugar gradually. When very light add the ginger, then the milk and lastly the flour in which the baking powder has been sifted. Spread very thin on bottom of upside down cake tin and bake.
The Savannah Cook Book, 1933

GINGERBREAD (Especially good with warm lemon sauce)

3 eggs	1 teaspoon cinnamon
1 cup sugar	1/2 teaspoon salt
1 cup oil	2 teaspoons baking soda
1 cup molasses (sorghum preferred)	2 Tablespoons hot water
1 teaspoon cloves	2 cups flour
1 teaspoon ginger	1 cup boiling water

Heat oven to 375 F. Grease and flour rectangular 9 x 13 x 2 inch pan. Place eggs, sugar, oil, molasses, cloves, ginger, cinnamon, and salt in large bowl and beat well. Dissolve soda in 2 Tablespoons of hot water and add to the beaten mixture. Sift in flour and beat well. Add 1 cup boiling water. Beat lightly and quickly. Pour batter into prepared pan. Do not add more flour. Bake 45 minutes. Serves 10-12
Mabel Yates, The Nashville Cookbook, 1977

LEMON SAUCE FOR GINGERBREAD

1 cup sugar	3 Tablespoons butter
4 Tablespoons flour or	3 Tablespoons lemon juice
2 Tablespoons cornstarch	2 teaspoons grated lemon rind
2 cups boiling water	

Mix sugar, flour (or cornstarch); add while whisking into boiling water. Cook until thick and rather clear, stirring as needed to make smooth, about 10 minutes. Remove from heat and add butter, lemon juice, and rind. Blend well. Makes about 2 1/2 cups.

NOTE: This quickly made dessert sauce really enhances warm gingerbread, plain cakes, or puddings. It is best served warm.
Milton Starnes, The Nashville Cookbook, 1977

HOT FROSTED GINGERBREAD

1/2 cup butter	1/2 cup molasses
1/2 cup strong hot coffee	2 teaspoons baking powder
2 eggs	1 teaspoon ginger
1/2 cup sugar	1 1/2 cups flour

Melt butter with hot coffee. Beat eggs and stir in sugar and molasses. Combine this with the warm mixture. Sift in flour and ginger to make a soft batter. Stir in baking powder and spread batter ½-inch thick on greased and floured dripping pan. Bake 25 minutes in moderate oven (350 F). While hot, frost this with 1 cup confectioners' sugar, stirred with 4 Tablespoons of cream. Flavor with vanilla.
The Southern Cookbook, 1939

SOFT GINGER CAKE

1 cup ginger, 1 cup molasses, 1 cup butter, 2 1/2 cups flour, 3 eggs, 2 1/2 Tablespoons ginger, 2 Tablespoons cinnamon, 1 lemon-juice and rind, 1/2 teaspoon nutmeg, 1 teaspoon baking soda, dissolved in 1/2 cup hot water.

Mix butter and sugar, rub together and add spices and lemon, eggs, then molasses, 1/2 cup of hot water with soda. Stir quickly and add sifted flour last. Bake in greased pan in moderate oven.
The Savannah Cook Book, 1933

THIN GINGERBREAD

1/2 pound flour, 1/4 pound butter, 1/4 pound sugar, 3 eggs, 1 ounce ginger. Mix well together and roll, as thin as possible, on tin sheets and bake quickly.
The Savannah Cook Book, 1933

SOUR CREAM GINGER CAKE

1 cup sour cream	2 cups flour	1 teaspoon soda
1 cup black molasses	1 teaspoon ginger	pinch salt

Mix molasses and cream and add flour, soda, and salt. Beat until well mixed. This should be about the consistency of cake dough. Now milk or flour may be added if necessary. Bake slowly about 1 hour and serve with whipped cream.
The Savannah Cook Book, 1933

GLORIFIED GINGERBREAD

2 cups sifted all-purpose flour	2 Tablespoons molasses
1 cup sugar	1 cup sour milk
1/2 cup shortening	1 teaspoon baking soda
1/2 teaspoon cinnamon	1/2 cup confectioners' sugar
1/2 teaspoon ginger	nuts
1 egg, beaten	1/2 cup heavy cream, whipped (optional)

Preheat oven to 350 F. Combine flour, sugar, shortening, cinnamon, and ginger. Remove 1/2 cup of this mixture. Add egg, molasses, sour milk and baking soda to the dry ingredients and mix until well blended. Spread in a 7 x 11 x 2 inch or 9 inch square pan. Add confectioners' sugar and nuts to the 1/2 cup reserved dry mix. Sprinkle over the top. Bake about 25 minutes. Cut into squares while warm. Serve with whipped cream if desired.

NOTE: May be used as a dessert or morning coffee cake.
Collene King, University of Illinois Home Economics Faculty Favorites, 1965

RAW APPLE CAKE

2 cups sugar	1 teaspoon cinnamon
3 eggs	1/2 teaspoon ground cloves
1 1/2 cups vegetable oil	1 teaspoon vanilla
3 cups flour	3 cups finely chopped raw apples
1 teaspoon salt	1 cup pecans
1 teaspoon baking soda	1/2 cup grated coconut

Heat oven to 350 F and grease and flour a 12 cup Bundt pan. Cream the sugar, eggs, and vegetable oil until well mixed. Sift together flour, salt, soda, cinnamon and cloves. Add dry mixture to creamed mixture. The batter will be very stiff. Add vanilla, apples, nuts, and coconut and stir until thoroughly mixed. Pour batter into a prepared pan. Bake 1 hour and 15 minutes or until done. Serves 12 to 16.

NOTE: This apple cake will keep two weeks, if kept in a covered container. The cake may be decorated with a sugar glaze, pecan halves, and cherries. This cake is especially eye-catching at the holiday season.
Cherry Lane von Schmittou, The Nashville Cookbook, 1977

FRESH APPLE CAKE

3 cups apples, peeled, chopped	3 eggs	1 cup nuts
2 cups sugar	2 cups self-rising flour	1 cup raisins
1 cup butter or oil	1 teaspoon cinnamon	1 teaspoon vanilla
	1/2 teaspoon nutmeg	

Heat oven to 350 F and then grease two 8 or 9- inch cake pans. Place chopped apples into a bowl; add sugar and mix, let stand 10 minutes. Add the melted butter and eggs, beat with a wooden spoon. Sift dry ingredients together and add to cake mixture. Stir in nuts, raisins, and vanilla. Pour into prepared pans. Bake for 55 minutes. Serve with sauce. Serves 8 to 10.

FRESH APPLE CAKE SAUCE

1 cup sugar	1 teaspoon vanilla	1/2 cup evaporated milk
1/4 cup butter		

Bring first 3 ingredients to boil, stirring constantly. Remove from heat. Add vanilla. This sauce is good either warm or cold spooned over the cake.
Eva Redmon, The Nashville Cookbook, 1977

DRIED APPLE CAKE

2 1/2 cups sugar	2 eggs
1 cup shortening	2 1/2 cups cooked dried apples
4 cups flour	1 cup jam, blackberry
4 teaspoons baking powder	1 cup raisins
1/2 teaspoon salt	1 cup walnuts
4 teaspoons baking soda	1 cup candied cherries
1/4 cup water	

Heat oven to 350 F and grease a 10 inch tube pan and line the bottom of the pan with waxed paper. Cream the sugar and shortening until light. Resift flour with baking powder and salt. Stir soda into water. Add flour to creamed mixture alternately with the soda water. Beat in the eggs one at a time. Blend in the dried apples, jam, raisins, walnuts and cherries. Pour batter into the prepared pan and bake 2 1/2 hours.

NOTE: 1/2 the recipe makes a sheet cake. Bake at 350 F about 45 minutes. This cake is really good with caramel icing.
Zona Sears Jones, The Nashville Cookbook, 1977

APPLE SAUCE CAKE

2 1/2 cups flour	2 cups sugar
2 Tablespoons cocoa	2 teaspoons baking soda
1 teaspoon cinnamon	2 cups applesauce
1 teaspoon cloves	1/2 to 1 box (7 1/2 to 15 ounces) raisins
1 teaspoon nutmeg	1/8 teaspoon salt
3 Tablespoons butter	

Heat oven to 375 F and grease and flour a 10 inch Bundt pan. Sift together flour, cocoa, and spices. Cream butter and sugar. Add to flour mixture. Add soda to apple sauce and combine with other ingredients. Mix in raisins and salt. Pour into a prepared pan and bake about 1 hour. Serves 8 to 12.

NOTE: This recipe had been handed down through several generations of the Goodwin family. So Southern.
Jane Goodwin, The Nashville Cookbook, 1977

CARAMEL

Natural maple syrup and sugar are not nearly so abundant as honey in our Southern region, because maple sugar and syrup are produced and more readily linked with the Northeast and New England, where most of the harvesting of the syrup is made. For our purposes, sugar cane syrup and sugar cane sugar, better known as "cane syrup" and "cane sugar", enjoy equal honors in the South and in regions where maple sugar and maple syrup are unavailable or too expensive to afford on a frequent basis.

When flavors become less interesting, good cooks say it's time to bring out a heavy iron skillet and melt or caramelize sugar. These cooks would add some water to dissolve the light golden-brown sugar in a skillet to make a syrup for flavorings in candy, cakes, cookies, ice creams, puddings, etc.

Grandma called these dishes "burnt-sugar", but that's a misleading statement, because scorching and burning spoils the flavors. This is something careful cooks and "grandmas" try to avoid, but when a Southerner hears "burnt-sugar" they start to drool. Why is that the case?

Caramelizing granulated sugar in a heavy iron skillet is an old art; deriving the "right (color of) brown" from the sugar without scorching or burning. I do think it is in the Southern DNA that everyone knows how to stir the sugar as it liquefies and to watch for the light golden-brown hue. Southern cooks have long considered the" burnt-sugar" or caramel cake one of the world's best cakes; adding another charming custom, lore, to Southern cooking. I concur with this statement with every bone in my body, but at this juncture, I would also throw in a jam cake with caramel icing. Equal time is given because the holidays are just not the holidays without these.

CARAMEL CAKE

1 cup butter, 2 cups sugar, 2 1/2 cups flour- sifted twice, 4 eggs beaten together until light and foamy, 1 1/2 teaspoons baking powder, vanilla. Bake in moderate oven in three round or 2 square pans.

FILLING FOR CARAMEL CAKE

3 cups granulated sugar, 1 cup cream, 1 scant cup butter; mix well and then put on stove and boil until clear. While the above is boiling, melt 1 cup sugar over a slow fire until dark brown. Add the sugar to the above and let it boil up well together. Remove from fire and beat until thick and won't run off cake.

The Savannah Cook Book, 1933

CARAMEL CAKE

2 1/4 cups sifted cake flour
1 Tablespoon baking powder
1 teaspoon salt
1 cup sugar
1 cup milk

1/3 cup caramelized syrup (next page)
1 teaspoon almond extract
1/2 cup shortening
2 eggs, unbeaten

Sift cake flour, baking powder, salt, sugar into a mixing bowl. Blend the milk, caramelized syrup and almond extract. Add 2/3 of this mixture to dry ingredients; then add shortening. Beat about by hand or with mixer on medium speed, until the batter is well blended and glossy, scraping down the sides of the bowl frequently. Add the rem (color obtaining liquid). Add the eggs. Beat 2 minutes or until batter is very smooth. Pour into 2 greased 8 inch layer cake pans lined with wax paper. Bake in moderate oven (350 F) for 30 minutes.

Farm Journal's Country Cook Book, 1959

CARAMELIZED SYRUP

2 cups sugar
1 cup boiling water

Pour sugar into heavy skillet that heats uniformly. Melt over low heat, stirring constantly with wooden spoon to prevent scorching (don't worry about the lumps, they'll melt away). When the sugar becomes a clear, brown syrup, remove from the heat. Stir in the boiling water slowly so it does not splatter. Return to low heat and stir until syrup is smooth again. Cool. Pour into clean pint jar, cover tightly and store at room temperature. Keeps 6-8 weeks and makes 1 1/3 cups.

NOTE: Because there are so many flavorful uses for this syrup, you would be well served to double this recipe.
Farm Journal's Country Cook Book, 1959

CARAMEL CREAM FROSTING

6 Tablespoons soft butter or margarine
1 egg yolk, beaten
5 Tablespoons caramelized syrup
4 cups sifted confectioners' sugar
1 teaspoon almond extract
2 Tablespoons cream

Cream together the butter and egg yolk. Beat in alternately caramelized syrup and confectioners' sugar. Add almond extract and cream. Beat until smooth and creamy enough to spread. Frosts two 8-inch layers.
Farm Journal's Country Cook Book, 1959

CHOCOLATE PISTACHIO CAKE

18 1/2 ounces white or yellow cake mix
3 1/2 ounces pistachio pudding mix
1/2 cup orange juice
1/2 cup water
4 eggs
1/2 cup oil
3/4 cup chocolate syrup

Heat oven to 350. Grease and flour Bundt or 10-inch tube pan. Combine cake mix, pudding mix, orange juice, water, eggs, and oil in large mixing bowl. Blend to moisten the cake mix. Beat 2 minutes at medium speed with electric mixer, scraping the bowl occasionally. Pour about 3/4 batter into prepared pan. Add chocolate syrup into remaining batter. Mix well. Pour over batter into baking pan. Bake about 1 hour or until done. Cool in pan on wire rack for about 10 minutes. Remove from pan. Spread with icing.

ICING FOR PISTACHIO CAKE

1/2 cup butter
3 1/2 Tablespoons cocoa
1/2 cup milk
1 pound powdered sugar
1 teaspoon vanilla
1 cup chopped nuts

Place butter, cocoa and milk in saucepan. Bring to boil. Add sugar, vanilla, and nuts. Pour over warm cake. Serves 12-16.
Ann C. Cox, The Nashville Cookbook, 1977

COCONUT CAKE

3 1/2 cups cake flour
4 teaspoons baking powder
1 teaspoon salt
1 cup shortening
2 cups sugar
8 egg whites
1 cup milk
1 teaspoon vanilla extract
1/4 teaspoon almond extract
2 fresh coconuts
1/4 cup coconut water
1/3 cup sifted powdered sugar

Heat oven to 350 F, then grease three 9-inch cake pans. Sift flour, measure, and place in sifter, add baking powder, and salt; sift again and set aside. Cream shortening until fluffy, add sugar a little at a time until all is used. Add egg whites one at a time and beat until fluffy. Add dry ingredients alternately with milk, a little at a time, beginning and ending with dry ingredients. Add extracts and beat 2 minutes on medium speed. Divide into prepared pans and bake 25 to 30 minutes. Grate the fresh coconuts; save the water for brushing cake layers. Brush cake layers with mixture of coconut water and powdered sugar. (Plain coconut water will make the cake soggy!) Stack the cake with Boiled Icing.

BOILED ICING

1/2 cup water
3 cups sugar
1/4 cup white corn syrup
4 egg whites
1/2 teaspoon cream of tartar
1 teaspoon almond extract
1 teaspoon vanilla extract

Stir together water, sugar, and syrup until sugar is dissolved. Wipe crystals from sides of pan with damp towel. Cook to 238 F. Beat egg whites until frothy. Add cream of tartar; beat whites until stiff. Pour syrup over whites gradually and beat until smooth. Add extracts and enough sifted powdered sugar (about 1 cup) to make desired consistency. Pile icing onto cake layers and finish with swirls on top and side. Sprinkle fresh grated coconut onto each layer after icing and sprinkle more generously onto top and side of cake.

NOTE: The beautiful boiled icing recipe came from Mary Katherine Hammer. The cake and icing are a prize winner among cakes! This cake is delicious with boiled custard, eggnog, hot tea, or coffee. Serves 16 to 20.
Valeria Smithson, The Nashville Cookbook, 1977

HOLIDAY CAKE

1 1/4 cups sugar
2 1/2 cups all-purpose flour
1 1/4 teaspoons baking powder
5 eggs, beaten slightly
1 1/4 teaspoons vanilla
1 pound English walnuts
1 pound Brazil nuts
1 (10 ounce) bottle green maraschino cherries, drained
1 (10 ounce) bottle red maraschino cherries, drained
1 pound dates, chopped

Preheat oven to 300 F. Sift together sugar, flour and baking powder. Blend in eggs and vanilla. Add nuts, cherries and dates. Mix well. Pour into two greased 5 x 9 x 2 3/4 loaf pans or one 10-inch tube cake pan. Bake for 1 hour.
Marian Jackson, University of Illinois, Home Economics Faculty Favorites, 1965

HOLIDAY CAKE

1/2 cup instant potato flakes	4 eggs
1 1/2 cups boiling water	3 cups sifted self-rising flour
2/3 cup butter or margarine	1 tsp. each of cloves, cinnamon, allspice
1 cup sugar	1 cup chopped candied cherries
1 cup blackberry jam	1 cup chopped candied pineapple
1 cup cherry preserves	2 cups chopped pecans

Heat oven to 325. Grease a 10-inch tube pan and line bottom with heavy greased paper. Put potato flakes into boiling water and stir. Allow to cool. Cream butter and gradually cream in sugar. Stir in jam, preserves, and cooled potato flakes. Beat in eggs, one at a time. Sift spices with flour and stir into batter. Sift spices with flour and stir into batter. Fold in fruits and nuts. Turn batter into prepared pan and bake 1 1/2 hours. Let cake cool completely in pan. If desired, frost with thin layer of caramel icing.
Serves 16-20

NOTE: If using plain flour, add 1/2 teaspoon soda, 2 1/2 teaspoons baking powder and 1 teaspoon salt to flour.
Alice Jarman, The Nashville Cookbook 1977

ICE BOX FRUIT CAKE

1/2 pound candied cherries	2 pounds nuts
1 pound coconut	1 box graham crackers, rolled fine
1 box white raisins	
1 can Eagle Brand condensed milk	

Cut fruit and nuts into very small pieces. Add to crackers. Add milk. Mix well together. Pack into loaf cake pans lined with waxed paper. Put into refrigerator and let stand until it can be sliced like any other cake. Will keep weeks. This is an easy cake, but I don't think it is quite as good as the baked fruit cake.
Satsuma Tea Room, More Fun for the Cook, 1974

NUT CAKE

1 pound butter, softened	1/4 teaspoon salt
2 cups sugar	1 pound candied cherries
6 eggs	1 pound candied pineapple
4 cups flour	4 cups broken pecans
1 teaspoon baking powder	2 teaspoons vanilla extract

Heat oven to 250 F and then grease a 10-inch tube pan. Cream the butter and sugar; add the eggs one at a time, beating well after each. Add 3 cups flour which has been sifted with baking powder and salt. Mix the remaining cup of flour with the cherries, pineapple, and nuts. Stir this mixture into the batter. Add vanilla and pour into the prepared pan. Bake for 3 hours. Cool and turn out of pan. Serves 16 to 20.
Martha Radford, The Nashville Cookbook, 1977

WHITE FRUIT CAKE (Baked)

1 cup butter	1 cup blanched sliced almonds
1 cup sugar	1 cup citron
2 cups flour	1 cup candied pineapple
8 eggs	1 cup candied cherries
1 teaspoon baking powder	1 cup white raisins
1 teaspoon vanilla	1/2 pound fresh coconut

Cut all fruits fine. Dredge with part of the flour. Sift flour and baking powder. Cream butter and sugar. Add eggs one at a time, beating well. Add flour by hand. Fold in fruits, nuts, and coconut. Bake in greased tube pan lined with paper at 250 F about 3 hours until done when tested with a straw. Chill in refrigerator before serving.
Satsuma Tea Room, More Fun for the Cook, 1974

CHRISTENING CAKE

7 eggs	3 teaspoons nutmeg
3/4 pound butter	1 cup sherry
4 cups flour	1 cup chopped pecans
4 cups sugar	1/2 pound raisins
2 heaping teaspoons baking powder	

Cream butter and sugar together until well blended. Separate the eggs and beat yolks until light and lemon colored, then add to butter and sugar and mix thoroughly. Sift flour, baking powder and nutmeg together. Add alternately with the sherry wine. Add raisins and pecan meats. Fold in the stiffly beaten egg whites and bake in a large well-buttered cake pan in slow oven (300 F) for 4 hours.
The Southern Cookbook, 1939

PECAN NUT CAKE

3 cups nutmeats, finely chopped	1 teaspoon baking powder
6 eggs	1/2 teaspoon salt
1 Tablespoon flour	1 teaspoon vanilla
1 1/2 cups sugar	boiled orange icing

Beat the egg yolks until very light, add the sugar gradually, and beat well. Sift together the flour, baking powder and salt; add the nuts and then combine with egg mixture. Beat well. Stir in stiffly beaten egg whites and vanilla and bake in two layer cake tins. Cook in a moderate oven (350 F) for 30 to 40 minutes. When cool, ice with boiled orange icing (in the Pastry/Icing section) and cover top with whole pecans.

NOTE: Whipped cream may be substituted for icing on top.
The Southern Cookbook, 1939

BROWN AND WHITE CAKE

1/2 cup butter	1 teaspoon cloves
1 1/2 cups sugar	1 teaspoon nutmeg
4 eggs, separated	1 teaspoon mace
2 cups pastry flour	1 1/2 Tablespoons cocoa
2 teaspoons baking powder	1/2 cup milk
1 teaspoon cinnamon	

Cream the butter and sugar, add egg yolks, and beat well. Sift flour and baking powder and add to sugar and butter alternately with the milk. Beat the egg whites until stiff and add. Divide this mixture into two equal portions and to the one part add the spices and cocoa. Into a well-greased loaf cake pan (8 x 8) drop alternating spoonful of each mixture. Bake in a moderate oven 30 minutes.
The Southern Cookbook, 1939

MARBLE CAKE

NOTE: This Marble Cake is very unusual, a combination of lemon cream and spice cake; and this recipe makes a very large cake. However, it keeps moist for some time after making. We have yet to hear any objections to our making the whole amount.

FOR THE WHITE PART OF THE CAKE

1/2 cup butter	1/2 teaspoon baking soda
1 1/2 cups sugar	1/2 teaspoon cream of tartar
1 cup sour cream	2 teaspoons lemon extract
2 1/2 cups flour	4 egg whites

Cream the butter and sugar well together. Mix and sift the dry ingredients and add to the first mixture alternately with the sour cream. Flavor with the lemon extract and fold in stiffly beaten egg whites.

FOR THE BROWN PART OF THE CAKE

1/2 cup butter	2 1/2 cups flour
1/2 cup brown sugar	1/2 teaspoon baking soda
4 egg yolks	1/2 teaspoon cream of tartar
1 cup molasses	1/2 teaspoon cinnamon
1/2 cup sour cream	1/4 tsp. each of mace, nutmeg, and cloves

Cream the butter and sugar, add the beaten egg yolks, and beat well. Add the molasses. Mix and sift the dry ingredients and add to the first mixture alternately with the sour cream. Bake in layers, putting first a spoonful of light and then a spoonful of dark batter into the pan. About 1/2 hour in a moderately hot oven (375 F) will be required for baking. This cake may also be baked in a shallow loaf pan if preferred. It will of course require a longer time to bake.
Mary Leize Simons, 200 Years of Charleston Cooking, 1930

PLANTATION MARBLE CAKE

2 cups sifted cake flour	2/3 cup milk
2 teaspoons baking powder	1 teaspoon cinnamon
1/4 teaspoon salt	1/2 teaspoon cloves
1/2 cup butter or other shortening	1/2 teaspoon nutmeg
1 cup sugar	2 Tablespoons molasses
2 eggs, well beaten	

Sift flour once. After measuring, add baking powder and salt, and sift together three times. Cream the butter thoroughly, add the sugar gradually. Cream together until light and fluffy. Add the eggs; then flour, alternating with milk- just a small amount at a time. Beat after each addition until smooth. Divide the batter into two parts. To one part add spices and molasses. Drop by Tablespoons into greased loaf pan, alternating light and dark mixtures. Bake in moderate oven (350 F) 1 hour 15 minutes or until done. Spread butter frosting on top and sides of cake.
The Southern Cookbook, 1939

SWIRL CAKE

1 package Duncan Hines Butter Cake mix (yellow)	1 cup sour cream
	1 cup chopped nuts
2/3 cup Wesson oil	2 teaspoons cinnamon
1/2 cup sugar	2 Tablespoons brown sugar
4 eggs	

Beat all the ingredients except cinnamon and sugar 4 minutes. Pour 1/2 batter into greased and floured tube pan. Mix together 2 Tablespoons brown sugar, 2 Tablespoons cinnamon. Sprinkle 1/2 brown sugar and cinnamon mixture over the batter in the pan. Swirl. Put rest of the batter into the pan. Sprinkle the remaining sugar on top. Swirl again. Bake for 1 hour at 350.
Satsuma Tea Room, More Fun for the Cook, 1974

MAPLE UP-SIDE DOWN CAKE

3 Tablespoons butter or margarine	1/4 cup milk
1 cup maple sugar	1 teaspoon lemon extract
1 cup pineapple chunks	1 cup sifted flour
3 eggs, separated	1/2 teaspoon salt
1 cup sugar	1 1/2 teaspoons baking powder

Melt butter in bottom of an 8-inch round cake pan. Mix in maple sugar; arrange pineapple chunks to cover bottom of pan. Mix beaten egg yolks with sugar; add milk and extract, then dry ingredients sifted together. Fold in stiffly beaten egg whites and pour the batter over the pineapple. Bake in a moderate oven (350 F) about 45 minutes. Invert and serve cut into wedges. Garnish all this with unflavored whipped cream. Makes 6 servings.
Farm Journal's Country Cook Book, 1959

UPSIDE DOWN PINEAPPLE CAKE

1 cup butter	1/2 cup sugar
1 cup flour	1/2 cup milk
2 eggs	1 cup brown sugar
2 teaspoons baking powder	1 can pineapple

Cream together the butter and sugar add the eggs, then the milk and flour alternately (the baking powder having been sifted with the flour). Put in the bottom of a cake pan, 2 Tablespoons of butter, 1 cup of brown sugar and then melt. Then lay on this the cut-up fruit from 1 can of pineapple. Pour the cake batter over this. Bake about 20 minutes and then turn upside down onto cake platter. Serve with whipped cream.
The Savannah Cook Book, 1933

PINEAPPLE UPSIDE DOWN CAKE

1/2 cup butter	1 medium sized can sliced pineapple
1 cup brown sugar	2 Tbl. whole pecans (refrigerated fresh)

Melt butter, in large baking pan. Spread the brown sugar evenly over the pan and arrange the slices of pineapple on the brown sugar, dropping the pecans in the open spaces. Cover this arrangement with the following cake batter:

3 eggs, separated	5 Tablespoons pineapple juice	1 teaspoon baking flour
1 cup sugar	1 cup pastry flour	1 pinch salt

Beat egg yolks until light color and cream in sugar. Add pineapple juice and flour which has been sifted with baking powder and salt. Fold in the stiffly beaten egg whites and pour batter over pineapple, baking in a moderate 375 degree oven for about 1/2 hour. Turn out, upside down, and place onto a cake plate. This cake may be served with unsweetened whipped cream or ice cream if desired.
The Southern Cookbook, 1939

PUMPKIN CAKE (Excellent recipe for dairy-free diet)

3 1/2 cups self-rising flour	1 teaspoon cinnamon	2 cups pumpkin
3 cups sugar	1 cup cooking oil	1/2 cup nuts
1 teaspoon nutmeg	1/2 cup water	1 cup raisins
	4 eggs	

Heat oven to 350. Grease and flour one 10-inch cake pan. Sift dry ingredients together. Mix the sifted dry ingredients with cooking oil and water. At medium speed add eggs, one at a time. Lightly add pumpkin, nuts and raisins. Pour batter into prepared pan. Bake for 55 minutes or until cake tester comes out dry. Serves 10-12.
Martha Bell White, The Nashville Cookbook, 1977

CARROT CAKE

1 cup sugar	1/2 teaspoon salt
1/2 cup vegetable oil	1 teaspoon cinnamon
1 1/2 cups flour	1 cup grated carrots- raw
2 teaspoons baking powder	2 eggs
1/2 teaspoon baking soda	1 cup chopped nuts

Mix sugar, oil, sifted dry ingredients and carrots. Add eggs one at a time and beat well after each egg. Add nuts. Put into pan and bake 55- 60 minutes at 350. Good with cream cheese frosting. This cake keeps very well.

CREAM CHEESE ICING

8 ounces cream cheese	1 teaspoon vanilla
1 stick (1/2 cup) butter, softened	1 cup pecans, chopped
2 cups confectioners' sugar	

Let cream cheese and butter soften; mix with a spoon until creamed. Then gradually add sugar and mix well, until smooth. Add nuts, vanilla and stir. Spread onto cooled cakes. Frosts three layers
Satsuma Tea Room, Fun for the Cook, 1968

PRUNE CAKE WITH GLAZE

1 1/2 cups sugar	1 cup vegetable oil
2 cups all-purpose flour	3 large eggs, beaten
1 teaspoon baking soda	1/2 cup buttermilk
1 teaspoon ground nutmeg	1 teaspoon vanilla extract
1 teaspoon ground cinnamon	1 large jar prune baby food
1 teaspoon salt	

In a large bowl, combine the first 6 ingredients. Add oil, eggs, buttermilk and vanilla; mix well. Fold in prunes and nuts. Pour into ungreased 13 x 9-inch baking pan. Bake at 350 F for 45 minutes.

GLAZE TOPPING

1/2 cup butter, cubed	1/2 teaspoon baking soda
1/3 cup buttermilk	3/4 cup sugar
1 teaspoon vanilla extract	

Combine the topping ingredients in a saucepan, bring to a boil, and boil 2 minutes. Pour over the hot cake.

NOTE: This cake recipe was given to me years ago, by a friend who in turn got it from her mother before her. I'm now 82 and still very much enjoy baking this cake.
https://www.tasteofhome.com/recipes/prune-cake-with-glaze.

BUTTERNUT CAKE

1 cup (2 sticks) butter	2 1/2 cups plain flour	1 Tablespoon butternut
2 cups sugar	1/2 cup self-rising flour	flavoring
4 whole eggs	1 cup milk	

Heat oven to 350. Grease and flour 10-inch tube pan. Cream butter and sugar; add eggs one at a time, mixing well after each addition. Sift together plain and self-rising flour and add alternately with milk. Add flavoring and mix well. Pour into prepared pan and bake 1 hour. Cool in pan several minutes; then turn out. When thoroughly cool, spread with icing.

BUTTERNUT CAKE ICING

2 cups powdered sugar   5 Tablespoons evaporated milk
1/2 cup (1 stick) butter   pecan halves

Place all ingredients, except pecans, into small saucepan and slowly bring to boil. Remove from heat, beat a few minutes, and spread on cake. Top with pecan halves. Serves 12-16
Louise Reynolds, The Nashville Cookbook 1977

LEMON CAKE

1 package lemon or yellow cake mix   juice of 1 lemon
1 package of lemon Jell-O (8 ounces)   4 eggs
1 cup apricot nectar or water   1 cup powdered sugar
3/4 cup vegetable oil

Mix cake mix and Jell-O well. Gradually add nectar or water, oil, and lemon juice. Add eggs one at a time to mixture. Bake in tube pan in a 350 degree oven for 1 hour or more.

GLAZE FOR LEMON CAKE

Immediately top with a glaze made with 1 cup powdered sugar and the juice and rind of one lemon. Punch cake with fork creating many holes while the cake is warm, (wipe fork regularly to eliminate cake sticking as you punch holes), before pouring on glaze. The glaze will fill up holes. After the glaze cools, put a second coat of glaze on to fill up remaining holes that can still be seen.

NOTE: Of all the various recipes in existence using cake mixes, I consider this one of our best and easiest. We cooked this cake in cake pans at the *Satsuma* restaurant. This enabled us to slice and serve with some sort of topping. The size of cake cooked in these cake pans also allowed us to sell individual cakes to the public. This is an amazing cake to give for gifts.
Satsuma Tea Room, More Fun for the Cook, 1974

HONEY LEMON LAYER CAKE

1/2 cup shortening	2 cups sifted flour	1/4 cup milk
1 cup honey	3/4 teaspoon baking soda	2 Tbl lemon juice
2 eggs	1/2 teaspoon salt	

Cream together shortening and honey. Add eggs, one at a time, beating well after each addition. Sift together flour, baking soda and salt. Sour the milk with lemon juice. Add sifted dry ingredients alternately with sour milk to egg mixture. Pour into two greased 8-inch layer cake pans. Bake in a moderate oven (350 F) 25 to 30 minutes. Frost with Honey Cream-Cheese Frosting.
Farm Journal's Country Cook Book, 1959

ORANGE CAKE

5 eggs	juice of 1/2 orange
1 1/4 cups sugar	1 teaspoon baking powder
1 1/4 cups flour	

Beat well egg yolks, add sugar, and beat until smooth. Add orange juice and mix well. Add flour and baking powder, that have been sifted together. When thoroughly mixed, fold in stiffly beaten egg whites and bake in two layers in a moderate oven (350 F) for 40 minutes. Put together with orange filling.
The Southern Cookbook, 1939

SCRIPTURE CAKE

1 Tablespoon honey	1 teaspoon cinnamon
1 cup butter	3/4 teaspoon mace
2 cups sugar	3/4 teaspoon nutmeg
6 eggs	1/2 teaspoon cloves
1 cup water	1 cup chopped almonds
3 1/2 cups flour	1 cup chopped figs
2 teaspoons baking powder	2 cups raisins
1/2 teaspoon salt	1 teaspoon almond extract

Cream butter and sugar, add egg yolks and beat well. Add honey and then alternately the mixed and sifted dry ingredients and water. Then add almonds, figs, and raisins, almond extract and last of all stiffly beaten egg whites. Turn into a well-greased, shallow pan and bake in a moderate oven (350 F) for about 50 minutes.

NOTE: Fortunately, for most of us, this scripture cake recipe is translated into more straight forward language than "1 Tablespoon Judges 14:8."
Miss Emmie Bellinger, 200 Years of Charleston Cooking, 1930

PREACHER CAKE

3 cups all-purpose flour
2 teaspoons baking soda
1 teaspoon salt
1/2 teaspoon cinnamon
2 cups granulated sugar
3 eggs
1 cup vegetable oil

2 teaspoons vanilla bean paste or vanilla extract
20 ounces crushed pineapple with juice (do not drain)
1 1/2 cups finely chopped walnuts divided
1 cup flaked sweetened coconut

NOTE: This light, moist, and tropical preacher cake is the easiest dessert ever! You mix it together with a wooden spoon and two bowls. No mixer needed.

Preheat oven to 350 F. Spray a 13 x 9-inch baking pan with non-stick spray and set aside. In a mixing bowl, whisk together dry ingredients (flour, baking soda, salt, and cinnamon). In a larger mixing bowl combine granulated sugar, eggs, vegetable oil, and vanilla. Use a whisk or wooden spoon to combine well. Mixture will be creamy. Sprinkle in dry ingredients and stir together until just incorporated (when no more streaks of flour remain).
Mixture will be very dry and sticky. Add in crushed pineapple, walnuts, and coconut and mix until combined. The liquid from the pineapple will transform the mixture into a normal batter consistency. Pour batter into prepared pan and bake 45 to 50 minutes. When done, cake should be set in the center and a toothpick inserted into the center comes out clean or with only a few moist crumbs. Set cake pan on cooling rack and cool the cake in the pan until completely cool.

NOTE: My wife and I took this cake to a party. Not only did we receive rave reviews for the cake, we were also inundated with the question of why it was called a preacher cake; a noted question due to the fact our host was an ordained preacher. Neither of us knew the answer so upon looking up the answer later, we discovered that this cake was so easy to make that every time the preacher dropped in to visit a cake could be made quickly and easily.

CREAM CHEESE FROSTING

8 ounces cream cheese, softened
1/2 cup butter, softened, (1 stick)
1 teaspoon vanilla bean paste or vanilla extract

2-4 Tablespoons heavy cream (amount depends on personal preference heat, humidity. Start with 2 and go from there.
2 cups powdered sugar sifted or whisked to remove lumps.

In a large mixing bowl, add cream cheese, butter, and vanilla. Whisk or beat with electric mixer until light and fluffy. Alternate drizzling heavy cream and adding powdered sugar, whisking/beating after each addition until all the sugar is incorporated into the frosting. If the frosting is a little thick, add a bit more cream; to thin add a little more powdered sugar. Spread frosting on top of the cake with an offset spatula. Sprinkle the top with the remaining 1/2 cup walnuts and a bit of flaked coconut if desired.
https://www.thechunkychef.com/preacher-cake/

TIPSY PARSON CAKE

NOTE: This cake is frequently served in the South. Another version of this cake was the *Tipsy Squire* often made with broken pieces of sponge cake.

3 cups milk	1 angel food cake (16 ounces)
6 egg yolks	sherry wine
2/3 cup sugar	1 cup toasted slivered almonds
1 Tablespoon flour	1 cup whipping cream
1 teaspoon vanilla	

Scald milk. Beat egg yolks until light; add sugar and flour and whip until smooth. Pour the hot milk into the egg mixture, stirring constantly. Cook over low heat or in a double boiler until custard thickens and coats a spoon. Remove from heat, add vanilla, and chill the custard.

TO ASSEMBLE

Slice angel food cake horizontally into three sections. Place bottom slice in a shallow bowl and sprinkle generously with sherry. Pour chilled custard around and over the top of this first layer. Add another layer and repeat the addition of sherry and custard. Add the last layer of cake; sprinkle with sherry. Whip cream until it holds shape; sweeten lightly and cover lightly and cover the top and sides with whipped cream making swirls on top. Sprinkle toasted almonds generously over the whole cake. Pour remaining custard into the center and around the cake. Serve chilled. Serves 8 to 10.

NOTE: This cake tastes so good and with the convenience of purchasing angel food cakes already baked at the local supermarkets and bakeries; it is so easy. The store-bought cakes soak up the custard and all tastes like homemade heaven.
Cookbook Committee, The Nashville Cookbook, 1977

ICE BOX CAKE

Melt 3 squares of Baker's chocolate. Beat the yolks of 9 eggs until creamy. Add 1 cup of sugar and pour the hot chocolate into this. Then add the well-beaten whites of the eggs and 1/2 cup of powdered sugar and 1 teaspoon of vanilla.
Line a mold with lady fingers; pour in this mixture and let stand several hours. Serve with whipped cream.
The Savannah Cook Book, 1933

OLD-FASHIONED BLACKBERRY ROLLS

Wash berries carefully and put into round pan with sugar. Let this cook for a few minutes until very hot and the sugar is well dissolved. Make a pastry. After sifting together 1 heaping cup of flour, a pinch of salt, 1 teaspoon baking powder, cut in a heaping Tablespoon Snowdrift (shortening). Then stir in enough milk to make a very stiff batter.

With a large spoon drop this into pan of hot berries and juice. This will float on top. Bake until the crust is very nice and brown, sprinkle with a little sugar and serve in deep saucers. Hard sauce should be used on top of this dessert.

NOTE: Other fruits may be used in place of blackberries.
The Savannah Cook Book, 1933

BLACKBERRY ROLL

2 quarts blackberries	2 cups sugar	ice water
1 pint flour	2 Tablespoons butter	1/4 teaspoon salt

First, mix flour and salt into which is cut 2 Tablespoons butter. After mixing well, add enough ice water to make a stiff dough. Clean berries thoroughly and set them to soak with 2 cups sugar. Roll dough very thin (on floured board) into an oblong sheet. Pour berries on one end of pastry dough, roll over and pour more berries, roll again and so on until all the berries are all used. Place in a buttered baking pan. Bake in a moderate oven (350 F) about 30 to 35 minutes. When the roll has baked this length of time, begin basting with the following mixture every 5 minutes for another 1/2 hour: 1 Tablespoon butter, melted 1/2 cup sugar. Serve with powdered sugar or favorite sauce in dish in which it has been baked.
The Southern Cookbook, 1939

NONE-SO-GOOD JELLY ROLL

5 eggs, separated	grated rind of 1 lemon
1 cup sugar	2 Tablespoons lemon juice
1 cup flour	

Beat yolks well and add sugar; beat until thick, add lemon rind and juice and half of the flour and half of the stiffly-beaten egg whites, then the rest of the eggs and flour. Pour into large well-greased pan, not more than 1/4 inch thick. Bake in a moderate oven (375 F) between 10 and 15 minutes. Turn onto a sheet of heavy paper or damp cloth. Beat jelly with a fork and spread on cake. Trim off crusty edges and roll while warm. Wrap in paper or cloth and set aside to cool.
The Southern Cookbook, 1939

PALM BEACH POINCIANNA CAKE

1 pound sugar
1 pound flour (3 1/4 cups)
1 pound butter
juice and rind of 1 lemon

9 eggs, separated
2 cups chopped blanched almonds
1/2 pound citron, chopped fine
1/2 pound raisins chopped fine

Cream butter and sugar and add to well-beaten egg yolks. Then add alternately flour and egg whites, beaten stiff. Dredge fruits and nuts with flour and add to batter. Bake in layer tins in a slow oven (300 F) from 40 to 50 minutes.
NOTE: Dainty, delectable, delicious.

POINCIANNA CAKE FILLING

2 cups sugar
1 cup boiling water
juice and grated rind of 2 lemons

1 Tablespoon corn starch
2 cups grated coconut

Boil first three ingredients and add corn starch, which you have dissolved in a little cold water. Cook until it spins a thread and then beat until creamy. Add coconut and spread between layers.
The Southern Cookbook, 1939

BANANA CAKE WITH CARAMEL ICING

2 cups flour
1 tsp. baking soda
1/4 teaspoon salt
3/4 cup shortening
1 1/2 cups sugar

2 eggs
2 medium sized bananas, mashed
1/4 cup buttermilk
1 teaspoon vanilla

Heat oven to 350 F and then grease two 9-inch cake pans. Sift flour with salt and soda. Cream shortening and sugar gradually adding 1 egg at a time, beating after each addition. Add the mashed bananas to buttermilk and add alternately with flour, beginning and ending with flour. Add vanilla. After mixing all thoroughly, turn into prepared pans. Bake 30 to 35 minutes. Cool in pans a few minutes, then turn onto racks to cool.

CARAMEL ICING

3/4 cup milk
2 1/2 cups sugar

2 Tbl. butter
1/2 cup half and half

1 teaspoon vanilla
cream

Combine milk and 2 cups sugar in saucepan over low heat. Do not boil. Caramelize 1/2 cup sugar in iron skillet over low heat. Stir constantly until sugar is melted and straw colored. Remove pan from heat. Pour caramelized sugar into hot milk and sugar. Add 1 Tablespoon butter and cream. Cook and stir until sugar melts and mixture comes to a soft ball stage. Add 1 Tablespoon butter and 1 teaspoon vanilla. Cool and beat to a creamy state and spread onto cake. Should the mixture get too stiff, add a little cream. Serves 8 to 10.
Dorinda Gibson, The Nashville Cookbook, 1977

CURRANT CAKE

1 pound sugar	6 eggs
1 pound butter	2 1/4 cups flour
1/2 pound currants (mixed with some of the flour)	pinch of salt
	rind and juice of 1 lemon

Work butter and sugar together to smooth cream, then slowly work in whole eggs, one at a time. Add a little flour, lemon juice, and salt. Work in slowly the rest of flour and currants. Drop by spoonful onto large buttered pans, pressing out from the center, because cakes are better very thin. A good plan is to heat the pan a bit and allow cakes to melt as much as possible before putting them into oven to bake. Be sure to butter pans thoroughly, otherwise thin cakes will be difficult to remove. Bake in a moderate oven 350 F 10 minutes.

NOTE: This recipe was for *Old-Fashioned Christmas Drop Cakes* popular at Christmas.
The Southern Cookbook, 1939

OLD-FASHIONED STRAWBERRY SHORTCAKE

2 cups flour	1 pinch of salt	1/2 cup milk
4 teaspoons baking powder	2 large Tablespoons butter	

Add salt and baking powder to flour and lightly blend butter into flour, adding milk last. Place onto floured board and pat into 2 large cakes. Place one upon the other and bake in hot oven (450 F) 15 to 20 minutes. Crush strawberries and sweeten. Cut cake into six equal sections as you would a pie. Break each section horizontally in half and spread the center liberally with butter and crushed berries. Good topped with berries and whipped cream.

NOTE: Other fruits such as peaches or raspberries may be substituted for the strawberries.
The Southern Cookbook

CARAMEL ALMOND SPONGE

1 cup sugar	3/4 cup scalded milk	1 teaspoon vanilla
1 Tablespoon gelatin	1/2 teaspoon salt	2 cups heavy cream
1/2 cup cold water		1 cup almonds

Caramelize 3/4 cup sugar. Soften gelatin in cold water. Add caramelized sugar to hot scalded milk. Add gelatin and stir until dissolved. If mixture curdles, put on ice and beat until smooth. Add remaining sugar, salt, and vanilla. When mixture is jelly-like (after being chilled), whip until frothy. Whip cream and fold into mixture. Chop and brown almonds. Add 1/2 of almonds. Garnish with whipped cream and other half of almonds. Serves 8.
Satsuma Tea Room, Fun for the Cook, 1968

PUDDINGS & SOUFFLES

"The proof of the pudding is in the eating."
-Cervantes (1547-1616)

"A good cook is the peculiar gift of the gods.
He must be a perfect creature from the brain to the palate
and from the palate to the fingers end."
-Walter Savage Landor (1775-1864)

AMBROSIA

First brought to light in the ancient mythologies of earliest Greece, ambrosia was called the food and drink of the gods. Consuming ambrosia conferred immortality on anyone who ate or drank this dish. I don't know about immortality, but I do know Ambrosia is simply delicious. It is a holiday and also an "any day", Southern favorite. Just chill and serve. Ambrosia needs no embellishment, but many making this dish also add pineapple, bananas, diced apples and serve with whipped cream, boiled custard, and/or cake. What a way to become immortal? This is a true delicacy of the gods!

"Syllabub and Ambrosia always marked red letter days in my childhood and were invariably the signs of company coming to dinner; so, they (the dishes) shall headline the lists of desserts, although one seldom meets them nowadays. Here's hoping for a revival of these simple and delectable dishes!"

-Harriet Ross Colquitt, The Savannah Cook Book, 1933

AMBROSIA

A layer of sliced oranges, a layer of shredded fresh cocoanut, a layer of sugar, and so on, ad infinitum, depending on the size of your dish and your company. What could be simpler and more delicious? Of course, if a little wine could be poured over all, it would be so much the better.
The Savannah Cook Book, 1933

AMBROSIA

6 oranges
1 1/2 cups sugar

1 1/2 cups freshly grated coconut
sherry wine

Peel and divide oranges into sections, arrange pieces on bottom of glass dish and sprinkle generously with sugar and coconut, repeat until all ingredients are used. Pour over a wine glass of sherry wine. Chill in the ice box.
The Southern Cookbook, 1939

AMBROSIA

6 oranges
8 ounces pineapple, diced (1 cup)
3/4 cup coconut, flaked
1 banana (1 cup)
1/4 cup confectioners' sugar

Peel, de-seed and dice oranges with scissors. Mix oranges with pineapple, coconut, banana, and sugar. Chill until ready to serve. If made more than one hour before serving, add the bananas just before serving to keep them from turning brown.
Jennine Boswell Shaw, Miss Lizzie's Heirlooms, 2009

AMBROSIA

6 oranges
8 ounces pineapple, diced (1 cup)
3/4 cup coconut, flaked
1 banana (1 cup)
1/4 maraschino cherries
1/4 cup sugar

Peel, de-seed, and dice oranges. Mix oranges with pineapple, coconut, cherries, and sugar. Chill until ready to serve. Before serving, add sliced bananas. Serves 8.

NOTE: This was a holiday favorite at my grandmother Boswell's. Of course, she never had a recipe, but all of her eight children seemed to have a similar version close enough to satisfy all the family of the absence of a true recipe. (David H.)
Jeanette Hazelwood, Cortner Mill Restaurant cookbook, 2009

FROZEN AMBROSIA

4 cups orange juice
1/2 cup lemon juice
3 cups sifted confectioner's sugar
2 cups heavy cream
2 Tablespoons sugar
2 teaspoons vanilla

Mix together the orange juice, lemon juice and confectioner's sugar. Whip cream, blend in sugar and vanilla. Pour fruit juice mixture into two refrigerator trays. Spoon whipped cream over the top, but do not mix together (juice and cream will be separate layers. Freeze firm. Spoon into sherbet dishes or a compote. Top with slivered salted almonds or with peanuts. Makes 8 to 10 servings.

NOTE: A light dessert perfect for following a heavy meal such as Thanksgiving dinner with all the trimmings.
Farm Journal's Country Cookbook, 1959

SYLLABUB

To 1 pint of cream add a gill (quarter of pint) of white wine, the grated rind of 1 lemon, the whites of 3 eggs and 4 Tablespoons of powdered sugar. Whip until stiff, turn into sherbet glasses and chill.
The Savannah Cook Book, 1933

BOILED CUSTARD

Boiled custard spans the beverage-dessert classification. Its name is a bit confusing for it is decidedly not "boiled", although it is delicious! Winter holidays demand boiled custard, the delicately cooked mixture of rich milk, egg, sugar, and flavoring choice. As is found to be the rule, not the exception, with most Southern cooking, every cook has her own special preferences as to preparation, proportions of ingredients, flavoring, and manner in which it is served. It may be thin for drinking or thick enough to be eaten with a spoon. But oh, it is so good! No matter whether your region is rural or urban; regardless of the ingredients used or the consistency derived, boiled custard remains a special "go-to" dessert/beverage of the Middle Tennessee region and throughout the South.

GENERAL RULES FOR CUSTARDS

Eggs should be slightly beaten and thoroughly mixed with sugar and salt. Add hot milk slowly, stirring all the time. Custards must be cooked over moderate heat, over water in the oven if baked, or in a double boiler. When thick enough, the custard coats the spoon. Be careful and observant. Custard curdles if cooked a minute too long. If it does curdle, separate, or becomes lumpy, put it immediately into another dish over a pan of cold water and beat it smooth.

BOILED CUSTARD

1 1/2 cups milk
1 Tablespoon sugar
1 teaspoon vanilla
2 eggs

Beat eggs slightly and add sugar and mix. Slowly add scalded milk and pour all into top of a double boiler and cook until mixture coats spoon (about 10 minutes). Remove from fire and add flavoring.
The Southern Cookbook, 1939

COUNTRY BOILED CUSTARD

Take 4 eggs and beat; mix with 2 cups sugar. Put in enough milk to make the mixture thin (about 6 cups). Flavor with vanilla flavoring. Cook in a double boiler until barely thick. "Put this somewhere to keep it cold. Hang it in the well or take it to the spring, then cook a good cake to go with it!"

NOTE: This old recipe for Country Boiled Custard is a "passed-down" recipe shared with The Nashville Cookbook, 1977. The recipe had been passed to Marilyne Burgess by her grandmother, Maria Hunter, of Cumberland Furnace, Tennessee. How Southern!

BOILED CUSTARD

1 quart whole milk
3 eggs
3/4 cup sugar
1/2 teaspoon of vanilla

Put milk and sugar into double boiler over medium heat. Beat eggs and add to mixture. Stir constantly over heat and bring mix to 180 degrees. Add vanilla. Refrigerate until chilled.
Barbara Troxler, Cortner Mill Restaurant cookbook, 2009

OLD FASHIONED BOILED CUSTARD

6 cups milk
6 egg yolks
3/4 cup sugar
1 cinnamon stick
flavoring

Heat 5 cups milk with cinnamon stick in double boiler. Beat egg yolks while adding sugar; add 1 cup of cold milk and continue beating for two minutes. Remove cinnamon stick; pour egg-milk mixture into hot milk. Stir frequently with wooden spoon while cooking until it thickens enough to form coating on spoon. Remove from heat and chill several hours. Flavor and serve plain or with whipped cream, maybe even a little coconut.
The Nashville Cookbook, 1977

BOILED CUSTARD POINTERS

I want to interject a few pointers I have found to make cooking boiled custard easier. At our *Satsuma* restaurant, every Tuesday, we made boiled custard for the week. We made it for a stand-alone menu dessert item topped with real whipped cream. We made it for the base for of many of our homemade pie fillings and our other desserts (banana pudding, etc.). We often used the custard to really give our homemade ice creams a full, rich flavor. As we have mentioned, there are hundreds of variations in preparing boiled custard. Ours was similar to the ones WE have offered. I really can't share ours because it involved 2 double boilers, 2 gallons of whole milk, 21 whole eggs, 7 cups sugar, etc. Get the picture? Our recipe doesn't really translate to replication for the home kitchen.

The four recipes above, that we have offered for Boiled Custard, do translate to the home kitchen. I think that some salt should be added to the recipes, up to 1/4 teaspoon at least. I would also add 3/4 Tablespoon of cornstarch. I would mix all the dry ingredients in a separate bowl combining everything with a fork until totally blended. It saves heat-ache (lumps) as the cooking progresses. I would then include the eggs in that separate bowl of dry ingredients and mix all thoroughly with an electric mixer. All this time your milk has been cooking in a double boiler. When the milk starts to skim on top it is ready, add the other ingredients you have just mixed whipping the ingredients constantly with a whisk as you add them to the milk. You should stir periodically until you have your desired thickness. This speeds the cooking, helps the custard thicken quickly, and really helps the custard not curdle.

As the custard is cooling, again keep whisking to keep the texture smooth as you stop curdling and beat out the lumps. At the restaurant, we always did our flavoring for the custard after it cooled and we always used vanilla. The custard works with many different flavors, so don't think you have to use vanilla. The custard is also really good spiked with a little Tennessee whiskey or Kentucky Bourbon. Before the custard is used for the finished product, always strain with a tight strainer. -David S.

SOFT CUSTARD

1 quart milk	yolks of 8 eggs	1 teaspoon vanilla or
1 scant teacup butter	whites of 2 eggs	lemon or 1/2 teaspoon
1/2 teaspoon salt		almond extract

Beat sugar and egg and add 1 cup of milk. Let rest of milk boil and pour into beaten mixture. Put into double boiler and cook, stirring constantly, until thick. Then add salt and cool. Then add flavoring.

NOTE: The rest of the beaten egg whites, slightly sweetened, may be used on top of custard as a meringue.
The Savannah Cook Book, 1933

BREAD PUDDING

Beat together yolks of 4 eggs and 1/4 cup sugar. Pour this mixture into 1 pint of hot milk, add a pinch of salt, 1/2 teaspoon of vanilla and 1/2 teaspoon of almond extract.
Put into a baking dish or individual ramekins. Butter slices of stale bread, put on top of custard, buttered side up. Cook in a pan of hot water about 15 minutes.

NOTE: Delicious served with caramel sauce!
The Savannah Cook Book, 1933

BREAD PUDDING

2 beaten eggs	1/2 cup sugar
1 1/2 cups sour milk	1 teaspoon vanilla
1/3 teaspoon soda	1/4 teaspoon salt
2 Tablespoons strained honey	2/3 cup dry, stale bread pieces crumbled
(no comb to be included)	1/4 cup raisins (optional)

Mix all except the last two ingredients and pour over the crumbs, broken pieces of stale bread, and raisins which have been placed in a greased baking dish. Bake in a moderate oven (350) 30 to 40 minutes. Serve cold with cream. Serve 4-6.

CHOCOLATE BREAD PUDDING

For chocolate bread pudding mix 2 Tablespoons cocoa with the bread crumbs and omit raisins.
Cooking with Magic, 1952

ORANGE MARMALADE BREAD PUDDING

2 cups stale large bread crumbs
2 cups scalded milk
1/2 cup sugar
2 Tablespoons melted butter

3 eggs, slightly beaten
2 teaspoons vanilla
1 glass orange marmalade
1 teaspoon nutmeg

Soak the bread crumbs in milk; when cool add sugar, butter, eggs, flavoring and marmalade. Place into a buttered baking dish and bake in a slow oven (250 F) 1 hour.
The Southern Cookbook, 1939

RICE PUDDING

2 cups milk
2 (1 inch) sticks cinnamon
1/4 cup butter
1/3 cup sugar

4 eggs
1/2 cup soft boiled rice
3/4 cup raisins

Scald milk with cinnamon. Remove the cinnamon and add butter and sugar. Add the milk slowly to slightly beaten eggs and stir in other ingredients. The raisins may be omitted, if preferred, but most persons think they improve the pudding. Turn mixture into a buttered pudding dish and bake in a slow oven (300 F) until custard is firm and top is browned, about 45 minutes. The pudding will serve 6 and is (a seeming paradox) both delicate and substantial.
Mary Leize Simons, 200 Years of Charleston Cooking, 1930

RICE PUDDING

1/2 cup long grain rice
1 pint water
1 egg separated
1/2 cup sugar

1/2 teaspoon vanilla
6 ounces evaporated milk
1/2 cup pineapple, crushed
1 dash nutmeg

Boil rice in water for 15 minutes. Mix together sugar, egg yolk, and vanilla and add to rice. Blend in milk and pineapple. Beat egg white and add to rice mixture. Pour into 9 x 13 baking pan and bake in 350 oven for 30 minutes or until top has browned.
Cortner Mill Restaurant cookbook, 2009

RICE CUSTARD

1/2 cup brown sugar
2 cups cooked rice
3 Tablespoons butter

1 cup milk
3 eggs
1/2 cup raisins

1/2 teaspoon vanilla
dash of nutmeg

To the rice add the sugar, butter, milk and slightly beaten eggs. Place in deep dish and bake in moderate oven (350 F) for 1 hour. When half cooked remove from oven and add the raisins and vanilla and sprinkle with nutmeg. Replace in oven and continue baking.
The Southern Cook Book, 1939

HEAVENLY RICE PUDDING

1 cup heavenly cream
3 cups cooked rice

maple syrup

Whip the cream and fold into cooled rice. (Rice should be seasoned with salt but no other seasonings) Chill. Serve in dessert glasses with maple syrup as the sauce. Makes 6 servings.

NOTE: Maple syrup makes a superior topping for vanilla ice cream as a true treat or a yummy adornment for basic baked custard.
Farm Journal's Country Cook Book, 1959

MOLASSES PUDDING

1 egg
2 Tablespoons sugar
1/2 cup molasses
2 Tablespoons melted butter
1 1/2 cups flour

1/2 cup boiling water
1 pinch salt
1 teaspoon baking soda dissolved in hot water

Beat egg and sugar, add butter, water, soda, and molasses and then beat in flour and a little salt. Put into a double boiler and let steam for 1 hour.
The Southern Cookbook, 1939

FOAMING SAUCE FOR FRUIT PUDDING

1 cup butter
2 cups powdered sugar

1/3 cup sherry wine
2 egg whites

1/4 cup boiling water

Beat butter to a soft substance and gradually cream the sugar into it. Add the unbeaten whites of eggs gradually and then wine. Beat well. When this is a light smooth mass, gradually add boiling water, beating all the while. Place the bowl into a basin of hot water and stir almost two minutes, until you have a frothy foaming sauce.
The Southern Cook Book, 1939

BURNT CREAM

3/4 cup sugar
1 pint milk

yolk of 1 egg
1 1/2 Tablespoons cornstarch

Caramelize the sugar in a little water on the stove. Heat milk and stir into the melted sugar. Rub {stir] the cornstarch smooth in a little cold milk and add to the egg yolk, well beaten. Add this to the milk and sugar mixture and cook until thick. Let cool and, before serving, cover with whipped cream and ground burnt almonds.
The Savannah Cook Book, 1933

CARAMEL PUDDING

3 cups milk, heat in a double boiler

Caramelize 1 cup sugar by heating sugar in iron skillet over very low heat until sugar melts. Add cautiously 1/4 cup hot water (a quick addition of water could cause trouble). Stir with care until it makes a smooth syrup.

Pour gradually into hot milk and heat to boiling. Mix 1/4 cup cornstarch with 1 cup cold milk. Put this mixture into the double boiler and cook 10 minutes. Beat 2 eggs well and add a little of the hot milk mixture. Add the whole to double boiler and cook, stirring constantly for two minutes. Remove from heat; add 1 teaspoon vanilla, 1/2 cup butter.
This can be used as pie filling. Our customers love both our caramel custard and our caramel pie. The caramel pie consists of the caramel pudding in a pie pan with a cooked bottom crust and topped with peaks of cooked meringue.

NOTE: This is an old favorite with a true caramel flavor. The flavor will depend upon the skill in caramelizing the sugar. The longer the sugar is browned, the deeper the flavor and color. Sugar burns easily, so use caution.
Satsuma Tea Room, More Fun for the Cook, 1974

CARAMEL CUSTARD

3 eggs	1 pint scalded milk
1 Tablespoon water	1 teaspoon vanilla
1 cup brown sugar	

Melt sugar and water stirring constantly, and then add boiling milk. Add eggs and flavoring and bake in buttered dish in quick oven. Serve cold.
The Savannah Cook Book, 1933

CARAMEL FLAVORED CUSTARD

3 cups milk, scalded	1/2 teaspoon salt
1/3 cup caramelized syrup	1 teaspoon vanilla
4 eggs, well beaten	1 Tbl. coarse pieces dry cake or cookies
1/3 cup sugar	

Blend together milk and caramelized syrup. Combine eggs, sugar, salt, and vanilla. Slowly stir liquid into egg mixture. Pour into eight 6-ounce custard cups. Break or crumble cake over the top of each custard. Set custards in pan of hot water. Bake in moderate oven (350 F) 40 minutes, or until knife inserted in center comes out clean. Cool before turning out. Makes 8 custards.

NOTE: This recipe is for a world-wide famous French dish that has been adapted by many areas in the South and has become a Southern classic.
Farm Journal's Country Cook Book, 1959

BATTER FOR CARAMEL DUMPLINGS

2 cups sifted flour	1/2 cup sweet milk
1/2 cup sugar	1 Tablespoon melted butter
1 Tablespoon baking powder	1 teaspoon vanilla

Sift dry ingredients together and stir milk, butter, and vanilla into them to make drop batter. Add a pinch of salt. Drop by teaspoons into hot syrup. Bake 25 minutes in 400 degree oven to golden brown. To serve takeout of skillet with spoon. Turn dumplings upside down on plate. Pour syrup over them and serve with whipped cream. Serves 8.
Arlene Ziegler, The Nashville Cookbook, 1977

CARAMEL DUMPLINGS

2 1/2 cups sugar	2 Tablespoons butter	1 teaspoon vanilla
2 1/2 cups boiling water	pinch of salt	

Caramelize 1/2 cup sugar in iron skillet. Add boiling water while stirring constantly until lumps are dissolved. Add 2 cups sugar, butter, salt and vanilla. Let this syrup simmer.
Arlene Ziegler, The Nashville Cookbook, 1977

BROWN SUGAR DELIGHT

1 cup brown sugar	1 1/2 cups broken pecans	1 cup whipping cream
1 egg, beaten whole	1/2 teaspoon baking soda	
1/3 cup flour sifted	1 1/2 teaspoons vanilla	

Mix all the ingredients, except cream. Bake in a 350 degree oven for about 25 minutes. Remove from the pan and crumble in bowl. Cool. Fold in whipped cream. Chill and serve very cold. Delicious and full of calories. Serves 6.
Satsuma Tea Room, Fun for the Cook, 1968

TYLER PUDDING

Cook these ingredients in double boiler until thick:

1 1/2 cups granulated sugar	yolks of 4 eggs
1 1/2 cups brown sugar	3/4 cup of butter
1 cup heavy cream	

Cook until thick and add vanilla and the wee-beaten egg whites. Pour into pans, which have been lined with rich pastry, and sprinkle with nutmeg. Bake in a moderate oven until custard is set. If it does not get thick enough in the cooking, add a little cornstarch.
This pudding is to be served very cold and is excellent with vanilla ice cream. Rich? Of course, but was it not presidential fare?

NOTE: It was presidential fare. This "receipt" belonged to President Tyler's family and was given by Miss Mary Lee Tyler to a friend in Hay Market, Virginia many, many years ago.
The Savannah Cook Book, 1933

QUEEN OF PUDDINGS

3 Tablespoons butter	1 quart milk
1 1/2 cups granulated sugar	1 teaspoon vanilla
5 eggs, separated	1/2 cup jelly
2 cups fine, dry bread crumbs	1/2 cup sugar

Cream butter and sugar together and then add well-beaten egg yolks. Beat well and add bread crumbs, which have been soaked in milk, then add vanilla. Stir well and turn into a large pudding dish, well buttered. The dish should be about 2/3 full.
Bake in a moderate oven (350 F) until the custard is set, about 35 to 40 minutes. Then spread top of pudding with jelly, jam, or any preserved fruit and cover with a meringue made of egg whites and 1/2 cup of sugar. Bake in a slow oven (300 F) until meringue is brown. Serve cold with cream or custard sauce.

NOTE: This custard is worthy of its name. It will serve about 10 and may be varied by using fresh fruit instead of the preserves.
Mrs. Bennett, 200 Years of Charleston Cooking, 1930

QUEEN OF TRIFLES PUDDING

1/2 pound of lady fingers	3 cups boiled custard
8 macaroons	1 cup whipped cream
1/4 pound blanched almonds	1/2 cup sherry
1/4 pound crystallized fruit	

Break lady fingers and macaroons into small coarse pieces and cover with sherry; add chopped nuts and fruit, that have been cut into small pieces. Mix together and pour boiled custard over all. When ready to serve, top with sweetened whipped cream.
The Southern Cookbook, 1939

BARBARA FRITCHIE PUDDING

3/4 cup granulated sugar	2 egg yolks	nutmeg
1/2 cup whipping cream	2 egg whites	1/2 teaspoon vanilla
3/4 cup brown sugar	2 Tablespoons butter	

In a double boiler put sugar, cream, brown sugar, egg yolks, and butter and cook until thick. Remove from fire, add vanilla and well-beaten egg whites. Pour into unbaked pie shell, sprinkle with nutmeg, and bake in a slow oven (275 F) for about 45 minutes or until custard is set. Serve very cold.
The Southern Cookbook, 1939

SERENE PUDDING

1 pint milk	a little salt	1/3 box gelatin
1 cup sugar	4 eggs	

Cook milk, sugar, egg yolks, and salt together until they begin to boil. Then add the gelatin, which has been soaked in 3/4 cup of cold water. When cold, stir in well-beaten egg whites, add vanilla, and let congeal.
The Savannah Cook Book, 1933

COTTAGE PUDDING

1/2 cup sugar	1 1/2 cups flour
1 1/2 Tablespoons butter	2 teaspoons baking powder
2 eggs	1/4 teaspoon salt
1/2 cup sweet milk	

Cream butter and sugar together and add well-beaten eggs. Mix and sift dry ingredients and add alternately with milk to first mixture. Turn into a well-greased cake pan and bake in a moderate oven (350 F) for about 35 minutes. Serve hot with a sauce. This serves 6 generously.
Bossis Plantation recipe, 200 Years of Charleston Cooking, 1930

PAULINA'S DELICIOUS COTTAGE PUDDING

2 cups sifted cake flour	1/2 teaspoon salt	1 cup milk
2 teaspoons baking powder	3 Tablespoons butter	1/2 teaspoon vanilla
	1 cup sugar	

Sift flour once. After measuring, add baking powder and salt, then sift again. Cream butter, add sugar gradually, and cream all together well. Add flour, alternately with milk, a small amount at a time, beating after each addition until smooth. Add vanilla. Bake in a greased pan, 8 x 8 x 2 inches in a moderate oven (350 F) about 1 hour. Serve hot with chocolate or lemon sauce.

NOTE: Second helpin's, please!
The Southern Cookbook, 1939

SOUTHERN BATTER PUDDING

3 eggs	3/4 cup milk	1/4 teaspoon salt
2 Tablespoons sugar	1 teaspoon melted butter	
1/4 cup flour	1/2 teaspoon vanilla	

Add sugar to well-beaten egg yolks and beat again. Mix butter, salt, and vanilla into the above and then add the flour and milk alternately. Lastly, fold in stiffly-beaten egg whites. Pour into a well-buttered mold. Place mold into pan of water and steam about 1 hour or until firm; serve the pudding hot with chocolate or favorite pudding sauce.
The Southern Cookbook, 1939

BOILED BATTER PUDDING

2 Tablespoons sugar	1/4 cup flour	1/4 teaspoon vanilla
3 egg yolks	1 cup milk	
2 egg whites	1/4 teaspoon salt	

Beat egg yolks well and add sugar. Then add flour, salt, and, when mixed, milk. Flavor with vanilla and, last of all, fold in stiffly beaten egg whites. Turn into a wee-buttered pudding mold and steam for 1 hour. This will serve 6.

NOTE: This pudding should be eaten while hot. Hard sauce, particularly chocolate hard sauce, is a good accompaniment.
Miss Harleston's Notebook, 200 Years of Charleston Cooking, 1930

PUFF PUDDING

5 eggs separated	2 cups milk
3/4 cup flour	1/2 teaspoon salt

Beat egg yolks well and add gradually flour, which has been mixed to a thin paste with milk. Stir in salt and add some flavoring if desired. Turn into a casserole and bake in a moderately hot oven (375 F) for 1/2 hour. Serve with any preferred sauce.

NOTE: A cherry sauce is fantastic with this pudding or the more customary chocolate sauce may be used.
Mary Leize Simons, 200 Years of Charleston Cooking, 1930

TAPIOCA CREAM

1/3 cup instant tapioca	1/2 cup sugar	3 egg whites
1 quart milk	1 teaspoon lemon or	6 Tablespoons sugar
3 egg yolks	vanilla extract	

Scald the milk, add the tapioca and cook in the top of the double boiler for 15 minutes, stirring frequently. Beat egg yolks well, add sugar and beat again. Combine gradually with milk and tapioca mixture and return to the fire until eggs are cooked and mixture slightly thickened; about 2 minutes. Flavor and turn into a pudding dish and cover with a meringue made of egg whites and sugar. Bake in a slow oven (300 F) for 12 minutes to brown the meringue. This will serve 8.

NOTE: We found that adding 1/2 teaspoon of salt to the scalded milk improved the flavor of the pudding.
Mary Leize Simmons, 200 Years of Charleston Cooking, 1930

TAPIOCA CREAM

1/2 cup quick tapioca	1 egg separated	1 teaspoon vanilla
1 pint milk	1/4 teaspoon salt	1/3 cup sugar

Add tapioca to the milk and cook in double boiler until the tapioca is clear. Beat the yolk of the egg, add salt and sugar and hot milk mixture and cook until it thickens, like soft custard. Remove from fire, fold in egg whites, beaten stiff. Flavor when cold. The whites may be put on top, mixed with 2 Tablespoons powdered sugar and browned in oven a few minutes.
The Settlement Cookbook, 1940

TIPSY SQUIRE

Put sponge cake in bottom of a deep dish. Blanch and split half a pound of almonds (or use the modern day convenience of already-split packaged almonds) and stick about within the cake. Mix in a tumbler some sherry wine and water; sweeten to taste. Pour this mixture over the cake. Make a custard of 1 quart milk and 6 eggs. Pour custard over all this.
The Savannah Cook Book, 1933

APPLE SNOW

6 apples	1/2 teaspoon lemon juice
3 egg whites	custard sauce
sugar	

Pare, core, and slice the apples and cook them in as little water as possible until soft. Cool, strain, and add to well-beaten egg whites. Sweeten to taste and whip well until eggs and apples are thoroughly blended and pudding holds up in "points" (peaks). Then flavor (cinnamon or nutmeg may be substituted for the lemon juice if preferred.) Pour in sherbet glasses and serve with a soft custard sauce. This recipe will serve 8 generously.
Mary Leize Simons, 200 Years of Charleston Cooking, 1930

SNOW CREAM

sponge cake	2 Tablespoons powdered	1 pint heavy cream
wine flavoring	sugar	
3 egg whites	1 cup sweet wine	

Put thin slices of sponge cake in the bottom of a dish and moisten with wine. Beat the egg whites stiffly and add remaining ingredients. Beat all well and pour over cake. Allow to stand for a short time in refrigerator before serving

NOTE: The recipe calls for wine flavoring. Remember the era of Prohibition was in full swing during the writing of this recipe and, thus, this was a substitute ingredient. This popular whipped cream dessert of Charleston served from 10 to 15.
200 Years of Charleston Cooking, 1930

SNOW EGGS

4 cups milk	1 1/2 cups heavy cream	2 pints strawberries
6 egg whites	3/4 teaspoon vanilla	1 ounce unsweetened
1 1/4 cups sugar	6 egg yolks	chocolate
3/8 teaspoon salt	1 1/2 Tablespoons flour	

The day before, or early in the day, make meringue-eggs as follows: Scald milk in a large skillet. Beat egg whites till frothy, then gradually add 3/4 cup sugar and 1/4 teaspoon salt all while beating stiff. Onto hot milk drop 3 large mounds of meringue, 1 inch apart; cook 5 minutes, turning once with a slotted spoon; drain on paper towel. Repeat, then refrigerate meringues. Meringues will keep overnight.

For the custard, scald cream with vanilla and 1 1/2 cups of milk used for meringues. Meanwhile, beat egg yolks till light, then beat in 1/2 cup sugar, 1/8 teaspoon salt, flour, then a little of the cream-milk mixture. Stir the egg-mixture into the cream-milk mixture and cook over hot (not boiling) water, while stirring until sauce coats spoon. When the custard is cool, assemble as follows: Hull, wash, and slice strawberries into a deep serving dish or individual sherbet dishes. Place the meringues over the strawberries and top with custard sauce. Lastly, shave chocolate over all the dish.

NOTE: This is one of the most divine and beautiful desserts possible and it is made even more special when the fresh Tennessee strawberries are in season.
Lalah Gee, The Nashville Cookbook, 1977

CHARLOTTE RUSSE

1 1/2 Tablespoons unflavored gelatin	1/8 teaspoon salt
1/2 cup cold water	2 egg whites, beaten
2 egg yolks	1 cup cream, whipped
3/4 cup sugar	1 teaspoon vanilla
1 1/2 cups milk, scalded	

Soak gelatin in cold water for 5 minutes. Beat egg yolks, sugar, and milk together and cook in a double boiler; dissolve softened gelatin and salt in the hot mixture. When thick, remove from heat and cool. Fold in beaten egg whites, whipped cream, and vanilla. Pour into a 1 quart mold. Chill
and serve.

NOTE: This sweet delicacy appeared on many, very early Nashville menus. Absolutely wonderful with fresh fruit.
The Nashville Cookbook, 1977

CHARLOTTE RUSSE

1 Tablespoon gelatin
1 cup milk
1 pint cream

1/2 pint sugar
whites of 4 eggs

vanilla, or better, if possible, hard liquor

Soak the gelatin in a little cold water and dissolve in warm milk. When cold, add cream, well-whipped, sugar, and lastly stiffly beaten egg whites and flavoring.
The Savannah Cook Book, 1933

PINEAPPLE CHARLOTTE

A simple and very good dessert is made by lining sherbet glasses with lady fingers and then filling with a mixture made of pineapple cut in blocks and mixed with sweetened whipped cream. Chill and serve.
The Savannah Cook Book, 1933

ORANGE CHARLOTTE

1 Tablespoon gelatin
1 cup sugar
2/3 cup water
3 Tablespoons lemon juice

1 cup orange pure pulp
or 1-small can orange concentrate
1 cup whipped cream
3 egg whites

Combine gelatin, sugar, and water and stir mixture over low heat until gelatin dissolves. Cool and add lemon juice, orange pure pulp or 1 orange concentrate. Chill until it begins to thicken. Fold in egg whites beaten stiff, then whipped cream. Serves 6.
Satsuma Tea Room, More Fun for the Cook, 1974

CHOCOLATE CHERRY DESSERT

2 cups vanilla wafers, finely crushed
1/3 cup butter, melted
1/2 cup butter
1 1/2 cups sifted confectioners' sugar
2 eggs
1/4 cup sugar

2 Tablespoons cocoa
1 cup heavy cream
1 banana, mashed
1 cup walnuts, chopped
1/4 cup maraschino cherries

Mix wafer crumbs and melted butter together. Remove 2 Tablespoons of mixture and reserve for topping. Press remaining mixture into a 9-inch square pan. Cream 1/2 cup butter with confectioner's sugar. Add eggs and beat 2 minutes. Spread crumbs on top. Beat sugar, cocoa and cream together until stiff. Fold in banana, walnuts and cherries. Spread on confectioner's sugar mixture. Sprinkle reserved wafer crumbs over top. Chill 24 hours. Yield 9 to 12 servings.
Mrs. Vivian Larsen, University of Illinois, Home Economics Faculty Favorites, 1965

CHOCOLATE PUDDING

1/4 cup butter
1/2 cup sugar
1/2 cup milk
1 1/3 cups flour
1 1/2 teaspoons baking powder
1 egg
1 square melted chocolate
1/2 teaspoon vanilla

Cream butter and sugar and add well-beaten yolks of eggs. Then stir in, alternately, milk and flour. Set aside until ready to bake. Then stir in baking powder and melted chocolate together, adding the vanilla and well-beaten whites of the eggs. Bake in a ring and serve cold with whipped cream in the center.

NOTE: Don't forget the hot chocolate sauce with this dish!
The Savannah Cook Book, 1933

FUDGE SAUCE CAKE (Fudge Pudding)

1 cup sifted flour
3/4 cups sugar
2 Tablespoons cocoa
2 teaspoons baking powder
1/4 teaspoon salt
3/4 cups chopped nuts
1/2 cup milk
2 Tablespoons melted butter
1 teaspoon vanilla
1 cup- firmly packed- brown sugar
1/4 cup cocoa
1 3/4 cup hot water

Grease 8 x 8 x 2 inch square cake pan. Sift together flour, sugar, 2 Tablespoons cocoa, baking powder, and salt. Add nuts and toss lightly. Blend together milk, melted butter, and vanilla. Add to flour mixture, blend into batter and pour all into pan. Mix together brown sugar and 1/4 cup cocoa. Spread this on top of batter. Pour hot water on top of this. Bake in 375 degree oven about 1 hour. Remove from oven. Turn cake upside down on cake plate. Can be served with whipped cream or ice cream.
Satsuma Tea Room, Fun for the Cook, 1968

BANANA PUDDING

1 1/2 cups sugar
4 Tablespoons flour
1/2 teaspoon salt
4 cups milk
6 eggs, separated
2 teaspoons vanilla
1 box vanilla wafers
6 medium ripe bananas, sliced

In a thick saucepan combine sugar, flour, and milk. Cook over medium heat, stirring constantly until thickened. Beat egg yolks and pour 2 Tablespoons of hot mixture into them. Return egg yolks to saucepan mixture. Cook 5 minutes, stirring occasionally. Remove from heat and add vanilla. Line bottom of a 9 x 13 baking dish with wafers. Top wafers with a layer of sliced bananas then a layer of custard. Repeat layering, ending with custard on top. Make a meringue by beating egg whites with 1 teaspoon vanilla, until soft peaks form. Slowly add 1/2 teaspoon sugar and beat until glossy. Spread meringue over pudding and bake at 350 until meringue is delicately brown.
Bettie Bean, Cortner Mill Restaurant cookbook, 2009

BROWN BETTY

2 cups apples, peeled and sliced
1/2 cup sugar
2 Tablespoons butter
1 teaspoon cinnamon
toasted or very stale bread

Line a buttered pan with a layer of apples, then a layer of toasted or stale bread. Sprinkle with sugar and a little cinnamon, and small pieces of butter. Repeat until pan is full. Cover pan so it will steam and then bake in oven about 3/4 hour. Remove cover and allow to brown. Serve with hard sauce.
The Savannah Cook Book, 1933

MONTICELLO PANDOWDY (Spiced Apple)

6 apples
1 1/2 cups molasses
1 teaspoon nutmeg
2 teaspoons cinnamon
1/2 teaspoon ground cloves
pie crust

Peel and core the apples and cut into small pieces. Cover with cold water and let stand 10 minutes. Remove apples from the water and drain. Into a buttered baking dish, place the apples and cover with the molasses and spices. Cover the top with a pie crust and bake in a moderate oven (350 F) until done, about 1 hour. When cold, break crust into apple mixture and place on the fire to simmer for a few minutes. When well cooled, serve with cream.
The Southern Cook Book, 1939

VIRGINIA APPLE PUDDING

1/2 cup butter or margarine
1 cup sugar
1 cup sifted flour
2 teaspoons baking powder
1/4 teaspoon salt
1/4 teaspoon cinnamon
1 cup milk
2 cups cooked or canned apple slices

Melt butter in 2-quart casserole. Combine next 6 ingredients to make a batter; pour on butter. Drain apples and pile apples in center of batter. Bake in a moderate oven (375 F) until batter covers fruit and crust browns, about 30 to 40 minutes. Makes 4 to 6 servings.

NOTE: This dessert treat originated in the apple growing area of the Shenandoah Valley. Unusual in the fact that the pudding is mixed and baked in the same dish with the batter forming a chewy, brown crust over the apples. This pudding is perfect served with different members of the cream family, plain pourable cream, whipped cream, and ice cream. It also is often enjoyed with lemon sauce. The hardest piece of this pudding recipe is choosing the right complement.
Farm Journal's Country Cookbook, 1959

BAKED APPLE NUT PUDDING

1 egg, beaten
3/4 cup sugar
1/2 cup flour
1 1/2 teaspoons baking powder
1 teaspoon vanilla
1/8 teaspoon salt
1 cup chopped raw apples (peeled)
1 cup chopped nuts

Beat egg and sugar together. Mix together flour, salt, and baking powder. Add to egg mixture. Fold in apples, nuts and vanilla. Bake 25 minutes at 350. Serve warm with whipped cream or hard sauce.
Satsuma Tea Room, More Fun for the Cook, 1974

WHITE COMPOTE OF APPLES

6 large apples
2 cups water
1/2 cup sugar
juice of 1/2 lemon
cream cheese

Cut apples in half, peel them and take out the seeds. Make a syrup of the water, sugar, and lemon juice. Stew apples gently in it, until they are tender. When the apples are soft, but unbroken, remove them from the syrup and arrange in a dessert dish. Let syrup keep on boiling until it is clear and rich; then pour it over apples. Cool and serve with soft cream cheese.

NOTE: This dish makes a dessert that is an excellent finish to a hearty meal.
Madame de Genlis' recipe recounted in 200 Years of Charleston Cooking, 1930

CRANBERRY CRISP / APPLE CRISP

CRANBERRY CRISP

1 cup uncooked rolled oats
1/2 cup sifted flour
1/4 teaspoon salt
1 cup light brown sugar
1 teaspoon grated orange peel
1/3 cup butter
pound can (1 2/3 cups) cranberry sauce
1 pint vanilla ice cream

Mix together rolled oats, flour, salt, brown sugar, and orange peel. Add butter and mix until crumbly. Place 1/2 of mixture in greased 8 inch square pan. Cover with cranberry sauce. Sprinkle with remaining crumb mixture. Bake in moderate oven (350) 40-45 minutes. Cut into squares and serve warm with vanilla ice cream. Serves 9.

APPLE CRISP

Use 1 1/2 cups thick applesauce instead of cranberry sauce.
What to Cook for Company, 1953

APPLE MERINGUE

Sweeten to taste 2 cups of stewed apples and flavor with a teaspoon of vanilla. Put into baking dish and cover with a stiff meringue made of the whites of two eggs whipped up with nearly a cup of sugar (not powdered sugar) and another teaspoon of vanilla. Bake until the meringue is a light brown. The well-beaten yolks of the 2 eggs may be added to the apple mixture if desired before the meringue is put on. This makes the dish a little more delicate and not so rich without it. Serve cold with cream.

NOTE: Delicious!
The Savannah Cook Book, 1933

BAKED CRANBERRY PUDDING

2 cups sifted all-purpose flour
1 cup sugar
2 1/2 teaspoons baking powder
3 Tablespoons shortening, melted

2/3 cup milk
1 egg
2 cups cranberries

Preheat oven to 350. Sift dry ingredients into the mixing bowl of an electric mixer. Add shortening, milk, egg. Beat 2 minutes. Fold in cranberries. Pour into a greased 9-inch square baking pan. Bake about 40 minutes. Serve with hot butter sauce.

BUTTER SAUCE

1/2 cup butter or margarine
1 cup sugar

3/4 cup light cream or half and half

Melt butter in a double boiler. Add sugar and cream and mix well. Cook in boiler over hot water for 5 minutes, stirring occasionally. Serve hot. Yield is 9 servings.
Bette Schaffner, University of Illinois Home Economic Faculty Favorites, 1965

BLACKBERRY PUDDING

Mix 6 Tablespoons flour gradually in 1 pint milk and stir in a little salt, 1 egg, the yolks and whites beaten separately, and 1 quart blackberries. Cook this mixture on top of stove until it begins to thicken. Then put into a buttered dish and bake 1/2 hour. Serve with hard sauce.
The Savannah Cook Book, 1933

BLACKBERRY PUDDING

2 cups blackberries
1 1/2 cups flour

1/2 teaspoon baking soda
1/4 teaspoon salt

1/2 cup New Orleans molasses

Mix and sift the dry ingredients, stir in the berries and add the molasses. Mix well and turn into a buttered pudding dish and bake in a moderate oven (375 F) for about 1/2 hour. This serves 6. A hard sauce is suggested to be used with this dessert.
Mary Leize Simons, 200 Years of Charleston Cooking, 1930

PEACH MOUSSE

Mash 1 can of peaches through colander and sweeten with 1 cup sugar. Add 1 teaspoon lemon juice and a little almond extract. Heat juice from can and pour it over 2 Tablespoons gelatin, which has been soaked in a little cold water. Cool and mix with fruit pulp. Put into mold and, when firm, serve with whipped cream.
The Savannah Cook Book, 1933

BAKED ORANGE FLUFF

4 eggs
1 cup sugar
grated rind and juice of one orange

Beat egg yolks very lightly; slowly add sugar, beating constantly. Flavor with juice and rind. When well mixed, fold in stiffly beaten egg whites. Pour into buttered baking dish and bake in moderate oven (350 F) for about 35 minutes. Serve immediately with whipped cream.
The Southern Cook Book, 1939

LEMON (PUDDING) MERINGUE

2 cups bread crumbs
juice and grated rind of
   1 1/2 lemons
1/2 cup water
2 eggs separated
3/4 cup sugar
1/3 cup butter

The bread should be fresh and only the inside of the loaf used. Break the bread into small pieces and measure two cups. Pour cold water over grated lemon rind and let stand while butter and sugar are creamed together and egg yolks are beaten in. Mix lemon juice with grated rind and water and either add to the bread crumbs or add alternately with the crumbs to the butter mixture.

In either case, the liquid must be carefully added to avoid a separation of the butter into little particles. If this happens it does not in any way spoil the pudding, even if it does occur. Turn into a buttered pudding dish and bake in a moderate oven (350 F) for about 25 minutes. Remove from the oven, cover with a meringue made of the egg whites, beaten stiff with 4 Tablespoons sugar and return to a slow oven (300 F) for 12 minutes to brown the meringue. Serve cold. This is a very rich pudding although the amount of butter given in this recipe is less than is called for in the original recipe.

NOTE: In reading this recipe, one might think it was a recipe for bread pudding, but after tasting it, such a suspicion would never occur!
200 Years of Charleston Cooking, 1930

LEMON PUDDING

1 dozen lady fingers	1 cup granulated sugar	3 egg yolks
2 lemons	2 Tablespoons butter	2 egg whites

Crumble sponge cake, grate rinds of 2 lemons into it, and add the juice of 1 1/2 lemons. Mix butter, sugar, and egg yolks (do not beat them), adding them to the crumbled cake. Bake in a moderate oven (350 F) until light brown and set aside to cool. Beat two egg whites and flavor with juice of 1/2 lemon, adding gradually 1 1/2 cups powdered sugar. Ice [icing] over the pudding and bake in a slow oven (300 F) till it reaches a buff color. This will take about 12 minutes. This amount of sugar makes a very sugary and sweet meringue. This pudding will serve 6 and is delicious in flavor.

NOTE: This recipe has been in Miss Georgia Porter's family for 75 years; carry that forward and it becomes 165 years to my time.
Miss Georgia L. Porter, 200 Years of Charleston Cooking, 1930

LEMON CHIFFON PUDDING

2 Tablespoons flour	2 egg yolks
3/4 cup sugar	1/4 cup lemon juice
1/4 teaspoon salt	1 cup milk
1 Tablespoon grated lemon rind	2 egg whites
1 Tablespoon soft butter	

Beat egg yolks light and lemon colored. Mix flour, sugar, salt, lemon rind, and butter together. Add to egg yolks. Add lemon juice and milk. Beat egg whites stiff, but not dry, and fold into lemon mixture. Pour into buttered casserole. Place in pan of hot water and bake uncovered in 325 oven for 40-45 minutes. Chill or serve warm, plain or with whipped cream. Serves 6.
Satsuma Tea Room, Fun for the Cook, 1968

LEMON CAKE PUDDING

3/4 cup sugar	2 egg yolks, well beaten
2 Tablespoons flour	1 cup milk
1 Tablespoon grated lemon peel	1/4 cup lemon juice
1 Tablespoon butter	2 egg whites
1/8 teaspoon salt	

Heat oven to 325 degrees. Butter a 1 1/2 quart casserole dish. Set aside. Combine sugar and flour. Add lemon peel, butter, salt, and beaten egg yolks. Mix well; add milk and lemon juice (mixture will appear curdled). Beat egg whites until stiff and fold into mixture. Turn into prepared dish. Place in a pan of hot water. Bake for 40-45 minutes or until lightly set. Serve warm or chilled, with whipped cream or plain. Serves 6.

NOTE: This is a very easy dessert. The mixture separates during baking, forming a custard-like bottom and cake topping.
Faye House, The Nashville Cookbook, 1977

CHERRY DUMPLINGS

1 pound can red cherries
1 cup sugar
7/8 cup flour
1 teaspoon baking powder
1/4 teaspoon salt
1/3 cup milk
2 teaspoons melted butter

Place cherries, juice and 3/4 cup sugar in deep skillet. Bring to boil. Sift 1/4 cup sugar, flour, and baking powder. Add remaining ingredients. Mix lightly. Drop from a tablespoon into boiling cherry mixture making 4-6 dumplings. Cover and cook gently 20 minutes.
Satsuma Tea Room, More Fun for the Cook, 1974

PEACH MELBA

canned peach halves, drained
vanilla ice cream
pure seedless black raspberry preserves

For each serving place a peach half in a dish. Top with a scoop of vanilla ice cream. Spoon preserves over the ice cream.
Holiday Hostess, 1958

PEACH CREAM

Twelve peaches peeled, stoned and cut in halves, 3 eggs, and the white of 1 more, 1/2 cup of powdered sugar, 2 Tablespoons of cornstarch moistened with a little cold milk.

Scald milk, stir in cornstarch, and take from fire when it begins to thicken. Stir in the butter. When lukewarm, whip in the beaten yolks until all is very light.

Put a thick layer of peaches into a baking dish, strew (scatter and cover) thickly with sugar and pour the cream compound overall. Bake in a quick oven 10 minutes. Cover with a meringue made of the whites of 4 eggs whipped stiff with a little powdered sugar. Brown slightly.
The Savannah Cook Book, 1933

RASPBERRY FROST

12 ounces frozen raspberries
16 marshmallows
1/4 cup sugar
1/2 cup pecans or walnuts, chopped (optional)
1/2 cup heavy cream

Thaw raspberries and drain. Cut marshmallows with wet shears (so they don't stick). Combine raspberries, marshmallows, sugar, and nuts (if desired). Let mixture stand 1/2 hour; stir occasionally. Fold in whipped cream and chill. Serves 4 to 6.
Sarah S. Miller, The Nashville Cookbook, 1977

APRICOT BAVARIAN CREAM

1 Tablespoon gelatin
1/2 cup apricot juice
1/2 cup sugar
1 Tablespoon lemon juice

1 #2 can apricots, drained
1 1/3 cups creamed whipped
1/4 teaspoon salt
3 egg whites, beaten

Soak gelatin in apricot juice for 5 minutes. Dissolve over hot water. Press apricots through a sieve. Combine all ingredients except cream and egg whites. When mixture begins to set, fold in whipped cream and egg whites. Serves 6.
Satsuma Tea Room, More Fun for the Cook, 1974

DELICATE DATE NUT PUDDING

1 cup pitted dates, chopped
1/2 cup chopped nuts
1 cup sugar

1 teaspoon baking powder
pinch of salt
4 egg whites, beaten

Mix dates, nuts, sugar, baking powder, and salt. Fold into beaten egg whites. Bake in buttered pan at 300 for 20 minutes. Cool. Serve with whipped cream. Serves 8

NOTE: So easy and so good!
Satsuma Tea Room, Fun for the Cook, 1968

HONEY

Honey is the most commonly used natural sweetener the world over. Every corner of the planet has its own distinct identifiable characteristics for its particular kind of honey. Honey's fragrance and flavor vary with locality depending largely on the flowers and pollen that attract the producing bees. In my area of Middle Tennessee, clover honey is quite widespread in its production. Sourwood is a favorite type of honey found in the Southern Appalachians; tupelo honey is often found in Florida, etc. Honey is different everywhere and because of this fact, baked foods containing honey have a wonderful but a slightly varying taste; but let it be known that foods made with honey as the sweetener also stay fresh and moist much longer. Honey has stood the test of time as a sweetener, from the ancients who decidedly prized it, all through time to this very day.

BAKED HONEY CUSTARD

4 eggs
1/2 cup honey
2 1/2 cups milk

1/2 teaspoon salt
1/2 teaspoon almond extract

Beat eggs slightly with a fork. Add honey, milk, salt, and almond extract. Strain. Pour into custard cups. Place into a pan and pour boiling water around the cups to a depth of 2 inches. Bake in a moderate oven (350 F) 40 to 50 minutes, or until center is firm. Remove from water to cool. Chill. Unmold or serve in cups plain or with favorite sauce. Serves 6.

NOTE; Flavorful change for a favorite dessert.
Farm Journal's Country Cookbook, 1959

QUICK HOT WEATHER DESSERT

To the yolks of 3 eggs, beaten lightly; add gradually 2/3 cup sugar and grated rind of 1/2 lemon. Soak a Tablespoon of gelatin in a little water and melt in hot water. Add 4 Tablespoons of lemon juice and stir into egg mixture. Then add the well-beaten egg whites. Chill and serve with slightly sweetened whipped cream.
The Savannah Cook Book, 1933

MOONSHINE PUDDING

This is a very simple hot weather dessert. Beat the whites of 6 eggs with 2 cups of sugar until very stiff. Then fold in a heaping Tablespoon of preserved fruit or jelly. Set on ice to chill thoroughly and serve with cream.
The Savannah Cook Book, 1933

BAKED STRAWBERRY PUDDING

1/2 cup butter	1 teaspoon baking soda	1 teaspoon vanilla
1 cup sugar	1/4 cup nuts	1 cup flour
2 eggs	1/2 cup sour milk	1 cup strawberry jam

Cream sugar and butter. Add eggs. Beat well. Stir soda into sour milk. Add to creamed mixture. Add remaining ingredients in order given. Bake 45 minutes at 300 degrees. Serve hot with hard sauce or whipped cream. The mixture, before baking, can be kept weeks in refrigerator. Serves 12
Satsuma Tea Room, More Fun for the Cook, 1974

PRUNE PEACHY

1/2 pound uncooked prunes	1/2 cup cornstarch
1 1/2 pounds prune juice	1 1/2 cups cold water
1/2 cup sugar	1 Tablespoon lemon juice
1 stick cinnamon	cream

Pick over and wash prunes. Soak 1 hour in cold water and cook prunes until soft in the same water. There should be 1 1/2 cups of prune juice after boiling. Remove the stones from prunes, add the sugar, cinnamon and prune juice and boil for 10 minutes. Mix cornstarch with cold water, add prunes and boil for 5 minutes. Remove cinnamon stick, add lemon juice and turn into mold. Let cool and chill thoroughly in refrigerator. Serve with cream; either whipped or plain. Sufficient for 6 servings.

NOTE: If there is any difficulty persuading the family to eat their allotment of prunes, serve them in this fashion and we predict those prunes will all disappear.
Mary Heyward, 200 Years of Charleston Cooking, 1930

PINEAPPLE PUDDING

1/3 cup butter	2 eggs, separated	1 cup grated pineapple
1/2 cup sugar	1 cup bread crumbs	

Cream butter and sugar, add beaten egg yolks, then bread crumbs and fruit. Lastly, fold in stiffly beaten egg whites. Turn into a buttered pudding dish and bake in a moderate oven (325 F) for 35 minutes. Canned pineapple may be used for this dessert in place of fresh fruit, but then the sugar should be decreased. 6 small servings.
200 years of Charleston Cooking, 1930

ORANGE CHIFFON DESSERT

1 pkg orange or lemon chiffon cake mix	2 cups orange juice
2 cups sugar	3 Tablespoons lemon juice
1 teaspoon salt	1/4 cup butter
1/2 cup cornstarch	2 cups heavy cream, whipped

Blend cake mix as directed. Bake in a 9 x 14 x 2 inch pan at the temperature suggested on the package. Cool. Slice into 3 layers. Mix sugar, salt, and cornstarch. Gradually add orange juice. Cook until thickened. Add lemon juice and butter. Cool. Spread on first layer of cake. Add a layer of cream. Repeat until all layers of cake are used. Decorate the dessert with mandarin orange sections or fresh strawberries and mint leaves.
Chill 2 hours or longer. Yields 15 to 18 servings.
Mrs. Vivian Larson, University of Illinois, Home Economics Faculty Favorites, 1965

CHERRIES JUBILEE

2 cups dark sweet pitted cherries, drained	1/2 cup orange Curacao
1/2 cup cherry syrup, drained from the can	1/2 cup Cognac
1/4 cup brandy	1 quart vanilla ice cream

Heat cherries and cherry syrup in a chafing dish over boiling water until hot. Add the cherry brandy, orange Curacao and Cognac. Continue heating until warm. Ignite, stirring constantly. Serve over ice cream. The ice cream may be spooned into dessert dishes and placed in the freezer until serving time. 6 servings.

NOTE: David Hazelwood's *Cortner Mill Restaurant's* two most popular and most ordered desserts by his customers were *Cherries Jubilee* and *Bananas Foster Flambé*. The main reason I chose to use this recipe for *Cherries Jubilee*, instead of his, is this recipe has more liqueur. Sorry David.
Easy-on-the-Cook Book, 1960

BLUEBERRY ICEBOX DESSERT

1 lb. vanilla cream-filled sandwich cookies	2 eggs, separated
1/2 cup butter	#2 can blueberry pie filling
1 cup confectioner's sugar	1/2 cup nuts, chopped
	1 cup heavy cream, whipped

Crush cookies and spread 1/2 of crumbs in bottom of an 8 x 10 x 2 inch pan. Cream butter and sugar. Add egg yolks and beat thoroughly. Beat egg whites until stiff. Fold into mixture and spread over cookie crumbs. Add in succeeding layers, blueberry filling, nuts, whipped cream, and top with remaining cookie crumbs. Let set in refrigerator several hours or a day before using. Yields 12
Mrs. Vivian Larson, University of Illinois, Home Economics Faculty Favorites, 1965

COCONUT PUDDING

1/4 cup butter	1 Tablespoon finely cut citron
1 cup sugar	grated rind and juice of 1/2 lemon
1 Tablespoon water	4 eggs
1 cup grated coconut	

Mix the butter, sugar, and water in a saucepan and boil for 2 minutes. Let this cook, then add the coconut, citron and grated rind and juice of 1/2 lemon. Add well-beaten egg yolks and, last of all, fold in stiffly beaten egg whites. Bake in paper cases or individual dishes in a moderate oven (350 F) for about 25 minutes. Do not allow this mixture to stand, but bake at once.
Recipe from The Southern Cookbook recounted in 200 Years of Charleston Cooking, 1930

DANISH PUDDING

1 cup butter	1 orange rind, grated
1 3/4 cups sugar	1 package of dates, cut fine
3 eggs, beaten	1 cup pecans
1 1/2 teaspoons salt	1 cup coconut (optional)
1 cup buttermilk	3 cups flour
1 Tablespoon orange juice	1 1/2 teaspoons baking soda

Mix in order listed. Bake 1 hour in tube pan in 350 degree oven.

SAUCE FOR DANISH PUDDING

1 grated orange rind	one cup sugar	1 1/2 cups orange juice.

Stir until dissolved. Pour over pudding as soon as taken from the oven.
Satsuma Tea Room, Fun for the Cook, 1968

RASPBERRY GINGER

30 ounces frozen raspberries
1 1/2 pints heavy cream
1 cup brown sugar
1/2 teaspoon powdered ginger

Thaw and drain raspberries. Whip cream and fold in brown sugar and ginger. Carefully fold drained raspberries into cream mixture. Chill at least 1 hour. Stir gently just before serving. Good with paper-thin wafers or as a sauce on party cake squares. Serves 12-18.
Ruby D. Chancellor, The Nashville Cookbook, 1977

CHOCOLATE SOUFFLE

1 ounce chocolate
1 cup milk
2 Tablespoons butter
1 Tablespoon flour
1/3 cup sugar
3 egg yolks
1 teaspoon vanilla
3 egg whites
1/8 teaspoon salt

Melt butter in double boiler, add flour and milk, and stir until blended. When sauce is smooth, add sugar and chocolate. Beat egg yolks light, beat part of sauce into them, and then add this to remaining sauce in double boiler. Cook until mixture is slightly thickened. Cool. Add vanilla. Beat egg whites stiff with salt. Fold into chocolate mixture. Put soufflé into baking dish and put into pan of hot water. Bake at 325 about 30 minutes or until firm. Serve at once with Hard Sauce. Serves 4.

HARD SAUCE

1 1/4 cups butter
1 cup powdered sugar
1 egg
2 Tablespoons sherry

Beat butter and sugar until light. Beat in egg and add sherry.

NOTE: On my top ten list of favorite desserts.
Satsuma Tea Room, Fun for the Cook, 1968

PINEAPPLE SOUFFLE

Start with 1/2 cup butter
Cream with 3/4 cup sugar
Beat in 5 egg yolks
Add 1/4 cup dry bread crumbs,
Along with 1 cup drained crushed pineapple, add 1 Tablespoon lemon juice,
     3 egg whites, beaten stiff with 1/8 teaspoon salt

Fold beaten egg whites into mixture and bake in pan of hot water 30 minutes at 325 F. This soufflé will not fall and can be served hot or cold. Serves 4.
Satsuma Tea Room, Fun for the Cook, 1968

ORANGE SOUFFLE

Dissolve 1/2 box of gelatin in 1/2 cup of cold water. Add 1 pint of orange juice, yolks of 6 eggs, and 1 pound of sugar. Beat well together. Place bowl in a larger vessel of cracked ice and stir mixture until it begins to thicken. Then add 1 pint of whipped cream and put it in the Frigidaire (refrigerator) or pack in ice and salt.
The Savannah Cook Book, 1933

COFFEE SOUFFLE

1 1/2 cups coffee	1/4 teaspoon salt	1/2 teaspoon vanilla
1/2 cup milk	3 eggs separated	
2/3 cup sugar	1 Tablespoon gelatin	

Soften gelatin in two Tablespoons of cold milk. Mix coffee, remainder of milk, salt, and half of sugar to egg yolks, slightly beaten. Add carefully to the scalding liquid and cook, stirring constantly until the mixture thickens. As soon as custard starts to coat spoon, remove it from fire because it needs to thicken only slightly. Add softened gelatin and stir until dissolved. When cold and beginning to stiffen, add egg whites, beaten until stiff. Add vanilla, turn into a mold or put into individual sherbet glasses. Chill thoroughly and serve with whipped cream. Serves 6 generously.
Anita De Saussure, 200 Years of Charleston Cooking, 1930

LEMON SOUFFLE

5 egg yolks	2 teaspoons grated lemon rind
3/4 cups sugar	5 egg whites
1/4 cup lemon juice	1/8 teaspoon salt

Beat egg yolks very light and beat sugar in gradually. Add lemon rind and juice. Beat egg whites stiff with salt. Fold into yolk mixture. Place in baking dish. Put dish in pan of hot water and bake at 325 about 50 minutes until firm. Serve at once upon removal. Serves 4.

NOTE: This is a great favorite when we have guests. The baking dish is always scraped clean, no matter how much is made.
Satsuma Tea Room, Fun for the Cook, 1968

CHESTNUT SOUFFLE

1 pound chestnuts	1/2 cup of milk	3 eggs
1/4 cup sugar	1 Tablespoon butter	vanilla

Boil and shell chestnuts. Then boil them in sweetened milk and butter until tender. Put chestnuts through a sieve and let cool. Separate the yolks from the whites. Beat each separately. Add chestnut puree and vanilla to egg yolks. Fold in egg whites and pour into a buttered dish. Place in a moderate oven (350 F) until the soufflé is a light brown.
The Southern Cook Book, 1939

SWEET POTATO MARSHMALLOW PUDDING

3 large sweet potatoes
1 egg
2 Tablespoons butter
1 cup milk
1/2 cup seeded raisins
4 Tablespoons sugar
12 marshmallows

Boil sweet potatoes until done. Peel and mash until creamy. Add beaten egg, butter, milk, raisins, and sugar. Put into a buttered baking dish and top with marshmallows. Bake for about 10 minutes in a moderate oven (350 F) or until the marshmallows brown. Serve at once. This makes from 6-8 servings.
Leize Dawson, Villa Margherita, 200 Years of Charleston Cooking, 1930

SWEET POTATO PUDDING (a very old recipe)

1 1/2 cups milk
2 1/2 cups finely grated sweet potatoes
2 cups sugar
1 stick butter, melted
2 eggs, slightly beaten
1/4 teaspoon ginger
1/4 teaspoon cinnamon
1/4 teaspoon nutmeg
1/4 teaspoon salt

Heat oven to 350 degrees. Grease a 1 1/2 quart baking dish. Place grated potatoes in prepared dish and pour in milk. Mix remaining ingredients and add to milk-potato mixture. Bake 1 hour 15 minutes. Stir occasionally while baking. Serves 8-10.
Ruby McKeel Rives, The Nashville Cookbook, 1977

LEMON SWEET POTATO PUDDING

NOTE: This sweet potato pudding, unlike others of the same name, is really a dish to accompany meat instead of being a dessert. The flavor of lemon and orange is delicious with the sweet potatoes and is so simple to prepare that it soon will become a real favorite. Another point in its favor is that it can be prepared for the oven in the morning and merely reheated for dinner just before serving time.

6 medium-sized sweet potatoes
6 Tablespoons butter
6 Tablespoons brown sugar
2 teaspoons grated lemon rind
1 cup orange juice

Boil, peel and mash sweet potatoes. Add butter and brown sugar and stir in well. Then add lemon rind and orange juice and beat until fluffy. Turn into a well-buttered baking dish and put into a moderate oven (350 F) for half an hour. The potatoes should be in peaks on top so that they will brown. Serves 8.
Leize Dawson, Villa Margherita, 200 Years of Charleston Cooking, 1930

SWEET POTATO PONE (A ginger dessert)

1 cup grated raw sweet potato	1/4 cup molasses
2 eggs	1/2 cup milk
1/2 cup sugar	1/2 Tablespoon ginger

Add eggs to sweet potato and beat well; add remaining ingredients and beat until thoroughly mixed. Turn mixture into a buttered baking dish and bake in a moderate oven (350 F) for about an hour.

The eggs and lack of butter give this pudding a firmer and less buttery rich texture. This should be an especially popular pudding with ginger devotees.

William Deas, 200 Years of Charleston Cooking, 1930

PUMPKIN DELIGHT

1 cup flour	3 cups whipped topping, divided
1/2 cup butter, softened	2 1/2 cups milk
3/4 cup pecans, chopped	2 packages white chocolate (or vanilla)
8 ounces cream cheese (softened)	instant pudding mix (3.4 ounce)
1 cup powdered sugar	15 ounce can pumpkin puree

STEP 1: Mix flour, butter, and 1/2 cup pecans together. Press into a sprayed 9 x 9 or 9 x 13 pan. Bake for 15 minutes at 350 F. Remove and let cool. If using a 9 x 13 pan or want a thicker crust, add an additional 1/2 cup flour, 1/4 cup butter and 1/4 cup chopped pecans.

STEP 2: Blend cream cheese and powdered sugar, add 1 cup of whipped topping, then spread over cooled crust.

STEP 3: Mix milk, pudding mix, canned pumpkin, pumpkin spice and 1 cup whipped topping until smooth. Spread over top of step 2.

STEP 4: Spread remaining 1 cup of whipped topping and sprinkle pecans. Let chill for 3 hours or until set. Serve chilled and enjoy!

NOTE: With a buttery pecan crust, a whipped cream cheese layer, light and fluffy pumpkin spice pudding, and more whipped cream topped off with chopped pecans, this pumpkin delight dessert is absolutely irresistible!

https://lilluna.com/pumpkin-delight-dessert/

MARRON (large chestnut) MOUSSE

3 eggs	1 can marrons (large chestnuts)
1 scant cup sugar	lady fingers
1 pint cream	

Whip whites of eggs stiff. Ditto yolks, along with sugar. Whip cream and flavor with juice from marrons. Line a mold with lady fingers and marrons. Pour in the mixture and freeze 3 hours.

The Savannah Cook Book, 1933

ALMOND ICE BOX PUDDING

At Satsuma we were known and famous for all our desserts. The collective customer reaction for any dessert eaten at Satsuma was, "This is to die for." We had one dessert item that could be ordered any day of the week at the restaurant, but it was never found on the menu, nonetheless we sold a lot of this dessert to the enlightened restaurant customer, that had an awareness as to the existence of this gem. The name of this dish was Almond Ice Box Pudding.

I never made this recipe. For that matter, I don't even know if a recipe now survives. I do know this pudding came into existence in the early 1940's, and was formulated by the food experimentation research department at the University of Illinois, a department of which my grandmother (David S) was the professor-in-charge.

I knew of only three people who ever made this dessert. Louella Johnson head cook at Satsuma, Truman Smith my father, and Dan Smith my brother. I felt upon my completion of assembling this chapter on puddings, that in some way I needed to pay homage to this delicious and famous pudding. Two of the three people who made this delight are now gone. My brother, Dan is one of the top five best cooks I have known in my life, so I figured he could help me. I asked him if he remembered how the Almond Ice Box pudding was made. His answer was:

"Good question. I guess there is a recipe somewhere! I have made it a few times over the years since we closed the restaurant. I'm not sure if Louella or Dad went by the recipe either. I used to watch them when they made it. First take margarine or butter and cream till fluffy. Add egg yolks slowly, then powdered sugar, beat till creamy and fluffy again. Sorry, but I just go by feel and sight. Remove from the mixer and wash and dry the mixer well. Add egg whites to the clean mixer and begin whipping. About 1/2 to 3/4 way through, slowly add the powdered sugar and continue to whip till very thick and fluffy. Add vanilla and almond flavoring while still continuing beating. I then just go by taste.

After a good while, when you know, it is going to stay up and stay fluffy, take off the mixer and fold in the whites by hand along with the butter portion. Again of course, taste as you go. If you need to add more flavoring, do it slowly. The mixture should remain very fluffy. Put this mixture in aluminum pans with graham cracker crumbs on the bottom and of course on top. Put in the freezer. Don't ask me for measurements or how many eggs, I don't know what they are or would be. Again, I just use my senses."

-Dan Smith

I want to thank my brother Dan. This conversation was helpful even with the absence of ingredient measurements and the number of eggs needed. This is a good thing because most people at home will not come close to needing the quantities of the ingredients he would have recounted to me as he discussed making this dessert for the restaurant. What is helpful is the awareness of the ingredients themselves. In my estimation, the most important ingredient is the scoop of homemade vanilla ice cream that was always served with each slice of this Almond Ice Box pudding.

ICE CREAM, SHERBET, & SORBET

"Bless the Food before us, the Family beside us, and the Love between us."
-Amen

We offer a number of ice cream recipes that call for freezing in a refrigerator. Not everyone owned a "cranking" machine to freeze ice cream in the old days, but most had access to a mechanical refrigerator and the refrigerator generally had a freezer. To freeze ice creams successfully in a refrigerator a thickened base is desired. This base may be made with flour, cornstarch, eggs, tapioca, gelatin, junket or marshmallows, with whipped cream added.

Mix ingredients and place in the ice trays of the freezer, freeze to a mush, mix with a fork or remove to a chilled bowl, beat with an electric or hand beater until light. Then pour mushy mixture back into the tray, return to the freezer until it holds its shape. Ice creams should be frozen at the fastest speed. Where there is no cold control, or if the ingredients should separate, stir in the tray with a fork or spoon until well blended, then finish freezing. Confectioner's sugar should always be used in uncooked mixtures; use granulated sugar only when cooked to a syrup or in a custard.

To obtain a smoother texture, use 1/3 corn syrup and 2/3 sugar instead of sugar only. Where whipped cream is called for, beat only until it holds its shape, not too stiff. To avoid separation, all ingredients should be about the same temperature when combined. If recipes intended for an ice cream freezer are to be used in a mechanical refrigerator, reduce the amount of sugar called for in the recipe by one-fourth.

Here are some pointers for making or "cranking" ice cream in a freezer from a 1940 instruction book: "Not much has changed with today's technology but it is still best to follow manufacturer's directions with the ice cream freezer you own. Chill the can, cover the can and adjust the dasher before beginning. Adjust the can in the tub. Have the chilled mixture in the can no more than 3/4 full because as the ice cream becomes solid from a liquid it will expand. Have the salt and ice come a little higher on the outside of the can. Adjust and make sure dasher is secure and then cover the can with the ice and salt. Use 3 parts ice to one part rock salt. Measure carefully before packing and pack freezer 1/3 full of ice before adding any salt. Then add salt and ice in alternate layers until full.

Turn the crank slowly at first for about 5 minutes or until mixture begins to stiffen; then turn as quickly as possible until it is very difficult to crank, which takes about 6 minutes. If necessary, add more ice and salt using the same proportions. Pour off saltwater, but don't let it flow over the top of can. Push down ice and salt and wipe the top of can and dasher with cloth. Now remove dasher and uncover the can and then scrape down the frozen mixture along the paddles and the side of the can with a wooden spoon. Place heavy paper over the mixture in the can and then recover. Plug the dasher hole and repack the freezer with ice on sides and top. Cover with newspaper. Let the ice cream stand several hours to ripen."

"If you open a restaurant and can make only one thing yourself, make ice cream. First, you already have everything you need, except some rock salt. Second, everyone will notice the difference immediately between store-bought ice cream and fresh churned. I owe this discovery to Satsuma Tea Room's daily, fresh churned ice creams. This insight struck me like a lightning bolt as I ate lunch every day at Satsuma for 20 plus years."

-David Hazelwood- Cortner Mill Restaurant cookbook, 2009

NOTE: David H must have taken the above statement to heart, because many of the recipes for ice cream found in this section came from his cookbook, *Cortner Mill Restaurant cookbook, 2009*.

THREE TYPES OF ICE CREAM

There are three general types of ice cream; French Ice Cream, which is a rich egg yolk custard and heavy. American Ice Cream, which is less rich custard with or without flour or cornstarch, and cream or cream and milk. Philadelphia Ice Cream, which is a thin cream or cream and milk and no eggs.
Chef's Cook Book, 1939

VANILLA ICE CREAM

2 1/2 cups sugar
1 quart half and half
1 quart heavy cream
3 eggs, beaten
1 1/2 Tablespoons vanilla
1 dash of salt

In a large bowl combine sugar, beaten eggs, and salt. Stir in half and half. Blend well. Stir in cream and vanilla and pour into a 4-5 quart ice cream freezer. Freeze according to manufacturer's directions. Makes about 3 quarts.
David Hazelwood, Cortner Mill Restaurant cookbook, 2009

CHOCOLATE ALMOND ICE CREAM

2 cups sugar
2 envelopes unflavored gelatin
1 quart half and half
1 quart heavy cream
2 eggs, beaten
2 teaspoon vanilla
6 ounces unsweetened chocolate squares
1 cup toasted almonds, chopped

In a large saucepan, combine sugar, gelatin, and salt. Stir in half and half. Cook and stir over medium heat until mixture almost boils and sugar dissolves. Stir 1 cup of the hot mixture into the beaten eggs and return to saucepan. Cook and stir 2 minutes more and add melted chocolate squares. Beat with a rotary beater. Cool and add cream and vanilla. Stir in almonds. Pour mixture into 4-5 quart ice cream freezer and freeze according to manufacturer's directions. Makes about 3 quarts.

NOTE: The chocolate almond ice cream was one of my many favorite flavors at Satsuma restaurant. Truman Smith was the ice cream maker, but he never passed his recipe along to me, so I came up with this recipe honoring the spirit of the original. It is good, but not as good as Truman's. (David H.)

NOTE: Truman Smith was my (David S.) father and wow could he make some ice cream! Every day he would make, and then have churned on premise, homemade vanilla ice cream, some additional flavor of ice cream, such as the above recipe, different from vanilla, and some sort of sherbet. David Hazelwood is correct about Dad not sharing his recipe for this ice cream or any other flavors for which David had requested "how do I make this?". It wasn't to protect trade secrets that Dad never gave him the ice cream recipes. It was just, as with many Southern food recipes, that a recipe did not and never did exist. Dad made his ice cream before cranking totally by taste, look, and smell. It is so Southern.
David Hazelwood, Cortner Mill Restaurant cookbook, 2009

HOMEMADE ICE CREAM

6 eggs
1 cup sugar
4 Tablespoons white corn syrup
14 ounces sweetened condensed milk
1 teaspoon vanilla
milk to fill a gallon freezer container to within 4 inches of the top

Beat eggs and sugar with an electric mixer, then add other ingredients. Pour into container and freeze by hand or electric cranking immediately according to freezer directions. After freezing, let set packed in ice for 30 minutes to 1 hour before serving.
Evelyn Holloway, The Nashville Cookbook, 1977

CHOCOLATE CHIP
Use the basic recipe above (Homemade Ice Cream) and add: 1 large bar (8 ounces) of slivered chocolate candy.

MAPLE NUT
Use the basic recipe above omitting the vanilla and adding: 2 teaspoons maple flavoring and 1 1/2 cups toasted chopped pecans.

PINK PEPPERMINT
Use the basic recipe above omitting the vanilla and adding: 1/2 teaspoon peppermint flavoring, 1 large stick (6 ounces) peppermint candy crushed, and dash of red food coloring.

FRUIT
Add about 1 quart of any sweetened fruit to the basic recipe.

DADDY'S SPECIAL
Use the basic recipe above omitting the vanilla and adding: 1 large slivered chocolate candy bar, 1 stick crushed peppermint candy, 1/2 teaspoon peppermint flavoring, 1 cup coconut, 1 cup miniature marshmallows and dash of red food coloring. Makes 1 gallon
Evelyn Holloway, The Nashville Cookbook, 1977

LIZZIE'S ICE CREAM

2 eggs
2 cups sugar
1/4 teaspoon flavor
milk

No instructions were written, so here are mine. Beat eggs and sugar until creamy. Add 2 cups milk and vanilla flavoring. Heat in saucepan until sugar dissolves and mixture is smooth and thick. Pour into the can of a 1 gallon freezer. Add 3 cups milk (I use half and half.) One quart of fresh strawberries or peaches can be added. Freezer should not be more than 2/3 full. Churn until ice cream is firm.

NOTE: Shelby says that when the Boswells didn't have a hand crank freezer, they would put ice in a bucket and put the ice cream mix into another smaller metal bucket. The small bucket was put down into the larger bucket of ice. The mix was stirred occasionally as it froze. Where there is a will, there is always a way. Southern ingenuity!
Lizzie Boswell's recipe shared by her grandson, David Hazelwood in his Miss Lizzie's Heirlooms, 2009

STRAWBERRY ICE CREAM

2 cups sour cream
1 teaspoon baking soda
2 cups crushed, fresh strawberries
4 cups milk
2 cans condensed milk

Combine sour cream and soda. Beat well. Add milk and condensed milk. Beat well. Either freeze in the freezer or freeze in refrigerator trays. Beat once while freezing. Makes 3 quarts. Serves 12-14. Frozen berries can also be used. Surprising how good this is, and how smooth.
Satsuma Tea Room, More Fun for the Cook, 1974

STRAWBERRY SNOWBALLS

1/2 gallon vanilla ice cream
1 1/2 cups (3 1/2 oz. can) flaked coconut
2 pounds frozen whole strawberries

Using a small scoop to make balls of ice cream. Set each ball as shaped on tray in freezer. Spread coconut on large sheet of waxed paper. Roll ice cream balls in coconut to coat lightly. Return to freezer. When firm, package and keep in freezer. Makes 10 to 12 servings.

NOTE: To serve, partly thaw strawberries in a large shallow serving dish. Top with the snowballs; garnish each with a berry.
Farm Journal's Country Cookbook, 1959

BANANA ICE CREAM

3 eggs
1 1/2 cups sugar
1 1/2 Tablespoons vanilla
1 dash salt
1 quart half and half
1 quart heavy cream
7 bananas ripe

Beat eggs with mixer and add sugar, vanilla, and salt. Stir until mixed well. Add half and half and mix well. Add cream and mashed bananas and stir. Pour into 4-5 quart ice cream freezer and freeze according to manufacturer's directions.
Irene Hazelwood, Cortner Mill Restaurant cookbook, 2009

NOTE: This is not my Grandmother Hazelwood's recipe. I listed her as the contributor. It was her favorite ice cream. She made it many summer Sunday afternoons -David H.

FREEZER ICE CREAM CUSTARD

1/2 gallon milk
8 eggs
2 1/2 cups sugar
2 Tablespoons flour
1/2 pint whipping cream
1 teaspoon vanilla
flavoring

Scald milk. Beat eggs, sugar and flour. Gradually add to milk and cook until slightly thickened or spoon coats. Cool. Add whipping cream and flavoring. Freeze. Makes 1 gallon.
Mary Jo Work, The Nashville Cookbook, 1977

FROZEN CUSTARD

1 quart milk	1 cup sugar
3 eggs	2 teaspoons vanilla

Scald milk, add slightly beaten eggs, which have been mixed with sugar, being very careful that they do not curdle. Cook until the mixture coats spoon, stirring constantly. Let cool, add vanilla, and freeze using 3 parts of ice to one part salt.
Mary Leize Simons, 200 Years of Charleston Cooking, 1930

NOTE: While this custard is not rich enough to take the place of ice cream, it is smooth in texture and is an excellent base for ice cream sauces, far better in fact than the richer creams. This is a tradition that continued at Satsuma Tea Room, as we made gallons of custard weekly to be used as the base for many different dishes.

PEPPERMINT ICE CREAM

1 1/2 cups sugar	1 dash salt
1 quart half and half	2 Tablespoons peppermint extract
1 quart heavy cream	1/2 cup peppermint candy, chopped
3 eggs, beaten	

Mix sugar, eggs, and salt. Stir in half and half, cream, and peppermint flavoring. Pour into 4-5 quart ice cream freezer canister and freeze according to manufacturer's directions. After freezing is complete, stir in peppermint candy pieces. Keep cold. Makes 3 quarts.

NOTE: Don't wait until the Christmas holidays to serve this ice cream. Claudia Hazelwood, Charles Roselle, and David Smith are among the many who say they can eat this ice cream any time of the year, especially with fudge pie!
David Hazelwood, Cortner Mill Restaurant cookbook, 2009

FRESH PEACH ICE CREAM

3 eggs	1 teaspoon vanilla
3 cups sugar	1 quart half and half
dash of salt	1 quart heavy cream
6 cups fresh peaches	

Beat eggs and stir in sugar, salt, vanilla, and half and half. Puree the peaches and stir into the mixture. Pour into the freezer canister and stir in the cream. Freeze according to manufacturer's directions. Makes 1 gallon.

NOTE: Cortner Mill was owned and operated as a grist mill by Andy and Jane Cortner from 1907 to 1960. This peach ice cream recipe was Jane's and was located in some of their old papers.
Jane Cortner, Cortner Mill Restaurant cookbook, 2009

CHOCOLATE ICE CREAM

2 1/2 cups sugar	1 1/2 Tablespoons vanilla
1 quart half and half	1 dash salt
1 quart heavy cream	4 cups Ghirardelli chocolate syrup
3 eggs beaten	

In a large bowl combine sugar, beaten eggs and salt. Stir in half and half. Add cream, vanilla, and chocolate. Freeze in 4-5 quart ice cream freezer according to the manufacturer's directions. Makes about 3 quarts of ice cream.
Cortner Mill Restaurant cookbook, 2009

CHOCOLATE MOCHA ICE CREAM

2 1/2 cups sugar	1 1/2 Tablespoons vanilla
1 quart half and half	dash of salt
1 quart heavy cream	2 cups Ghirardelli chocolate syrup
3 eggs, beaten	3 Tablespoons instant coffee granules

In a large bowl combine sugar, beaten eggs and salt. Stir in half and half. Add cream, vanilla, coffee granules, and chocolate. Freeze in 4 to 5 quart ice cream freezer according to manufacturer's directions. Makes about 3 quarts of ice cream.
David Hazelwood, Cortner Mill Restaurant cookbook, 2009

MARIE LOUISE ICE CREAM

Make a strong, stiff, very sweet wine jelly as follows:
Soak 1 envelope of gelatin in 1/2 cup of cold water, and then dissolve in 1 cup of boiling water. Add 1 and 1/2 cups of sugar. When cold, add 2 cups sherry and set aside to get firm. Break jelly into small pieces with fork and add 1 pint cream whipped stiff. Mix thoroughly, put into mold which has been dipped in cold water, pack in salt and ice for three or four hours.
The Savannah Cook Book, 1933

CHERRY ICE CREAM

2 1/2 cups sugar	1 1/2 Tablespoons vanilla
1 quart half and half	1 dash salt
1 quart heavy cream	2 cups maraschino cherries, chopped
3 eggs	1/4 cup cherry syrup

In large bowl combine sugar, beaten eggs, vanilla, and salt. Stir in cream, cherry syrup, and half and half. Beat with an electric mixer one minute on high speed. Add cherries. Freeze in 4-5 quart ice cream freezer according to manufacturer's directions. Makes 3 quarts
Cortner Mill Restaurant cookbook, 2009

CHERRY NUT ICE CREAM

1 1/2 cups sugar
2 envelopes unflavored gelatin
1 quart half and half
1 quart heavy cream
2 eggs, beaten

4 teaspoons vanilla
1 cup maraschino cherries, chopped
3 Tablespoons cherry juice
1 cup walnuts, chopped
1/8 teaspoon salt

In a large saucepan combine sugar, gelatin, and salt. Stir in half and half. Cook and stir over medium heat until mixture almost boils and sugar dissolves. Stir 1 cup of hot mixture into beaten eggs and return all to saucepan. Cook and stir 2 minutes more and add cherries, juice, and nuts. Beat with a rotary beater. Cool and add cream and vanilla. Pour mixture into a 4-5 quart ice cream freezer and freeze according to manufacturer's directions. Makes about 3 quarts.
Cortner Mill Restaurant cookbook, 2009

PEACH CHERRY ICE CREAM

1 1/2 cups sugar
2 envelopes unflavored gelatin
1 quart half and half
2 eggs, beaten
4 teaspoons vanilla

1/8 teaspoon salt
3 cups peaches, fully ripe
1/2 cup sugar
2 cups cherries, fresh dark, sweet
1/2 tsp. almond extract or ground mace

In a large saucepan combine sugar, gelatin, and salt. Stir in half and half. Cook and stir over medium heat until mixture almost boils and sugar dissolves. Stir about 1/2 cup of the hot mixture into beaten eggs and return to saucepan. Cook and stir two minutes more. Remove from heat and cool. Add vanilla. Peel and mash peaches and combine with 1/2 cup sugar. Add peaches to half and half. Pit and chop cherries and add to half and half. Stir in almond extract. Pour mixture into freezer canister and freeze according to manufacturer's directions. Makes about 3 quarts.
Cortner Mill Restaurant cookbook, 2009

BUTTER-PECAN ICE CREAM

3/4 cup chopped pecans
3 Tablespoons butter
1/8 teaspoon salt
1/3 cup light corn syrup

2 Tbl. cornstarch
1/4 cup sugar
1/2 cup brown sugar
1/2 teaspoon salt

2 1/2 cups milk
2 eggs, beaten slightly
1 1/2 teaspoons vanilla
1 cup light cream

Combine pecans, butter and salt and toast in 350° oven about 10 minutes, stirring once or twice. Combine corn syrup, cornstarch, sugar, salt, and milk in top of double boiler. Mix in eggs. Cook over boiling water, constantly stirring until mixture is slightly thickened, about 5 minutes. Chill, add vanilla and light cream. Add toasted pecans. Freeze with automatic ice cream freezer following manufacturer's directions. Makes two quarts.

NOTE: Better double the recipe. There is never enough. The toasted, buttered, and salted pecans make the difference.
Lalah Gee, The Nashville Cookbook, 1977

COFFEE ICE CREAM

1 rennet tablet to coagulate milk
1 Tablespoon cold water
2 cups light cream
1/2 cup cream
1/2 cup sugar
2 Tablespoons instant coffee

Crush rennet tablet and dissolve in water. Pour cream into top of double boiler. Sift together sugar and coffee; stir into cream. Heat slowly to lukewarm. Add rennet; stir quickly for a few minutes. Pour into refrigerator trays. Let stand at room temperature until set (about 10 minutes); then freeze firm.
Turn into a chilled bowl; break into chunks with a wooden spoon; beat fluffy and smooth with an electric or rotary mixer. Return to the cold tray; freeze firm. Makes 6 to 8 servings.
Farm Journal's Country Cookbook, 1959

LEMON ICE CREAM

juice of 5 lemons
1 lemon, sliced paper thin
1 quart sugar
1 quart milk
1 quart light cream

Mix all ingredients until thoroughly blended. Pour into 1 gallon-size freezer can and freeze. Makes 1 gallon.
Barbara Mullins, The Nashville Cookbook, 1977

HONEY COCONUT ICE CREAM

1/2 cup flaked or shredded coconut
1 cup honey
1 envelope unflavored gelatin
2 Tablespoons cold water
1/4 cup brown sugar
2 eggs
3 cup light cream
1 teaspoon coconut extract

Heat the honey, but do not boil. Soften gelatin in water; add to honey along with sugar, eggs, cream and coconut extract. Beat about 2 minutes. Pour into refrigerator tray. Freeze until firm, but not hard. Turn mixture into a chilled bowl. Beat until fluffy. Pour back into refrigerator tray and freeze until firm. Toast the coconut; sprinkle over each serving. Makes 6 servings.
Farm Journal's Country Cookbook, 1959

APRICOT ICE CREAM

41 ounces sweetened apricot halves
2 bananas
1 cup coffee cream
1/2 cup sugar
1/2 cup maraschino cherries

Press apricot halves and juice through a colander. Add mashed bananas, cream, sugar, and cut-up cherries. Freeze in two ice trays. Remove and place in bowl, allow to soften, beat until smooth. Re-freeze.
Serves 6-8
Mary Jo Work, The Nashville Cookbook, 1977

RHUBARB ICE CREAM

2 cups cubed rhubarb
3/4 cup sugar
2 egg yolks, beaten
1 cup heavy cream
1 Tablespoon lemon juice
2 egg whites, unbeaten

Combine rhubarb and 1/2 cup sugar. Cook in covered pan 15 minutes over low heat (do not add water); cool.
Combine egg yolks, cream, lemon juice, rhubarb; mix well. Pour into refrigerator tray. Freeze until firm. Turn into a bowl; break in chunks. Beat until fluffy, but not melted. Beat egg whites and 1/4 cup sugar; fold into ice cream. Return to refrigerator tray. Freeze. Makes 6 servings.
Farm Journal's Country Cookbook, 1959

GOLDEN GLOW ICE CREAM

1/4 cup grated orange rind
2 cups milk
1 cup sugar
1 cup light corn syrup
1/2 teaspoon salt
8 egg yolks beaten
2 cups light cream
4 cups fresh orange juice

Place orange rind in small cheese cloth bag. Scald rind with milk in top of double boiler. Add sugar, syrup, and salt to egg yolks which have been mixed with some hot milk. Cook stirring constantly, until mixture coats spoon. Cool. Remove cheese cloth bag. Stir in cream and orange juice. Freeze. Makes 1 gallon.

NOTE: I can't think of a better use for the egg yolks left after baking an angel food cake.
Farm Journal's Country Cookbook, 1959

ORANGE FLOWER ICE CREAM

1 quart of cream
3/4 pound of sugar
1 ounce candied orange flowers
yolks of 3 eggs

Bruise the orange flowers (orange blossom nectar/ orange blossom honey can be used instead) and mix and stir them with the boiling cream. Take them from the fire, add the sugar and dissolve well. Then add beaten egg yolks. Mix all well. Freeze as indicated.
The Picayune Creole Cook Book, 1922

FIG AND PEACH ICE CREAM

Mix 1 pint custard and 1 pint cream and freeze. When 1/2 is frozen, add 1 large cup peaches, and 1 large cup figs, that have been mashed through colander, then finish freezing.
The Savannah Cook Book, 1933

FRESH FIG ICE CREAM

1 pint of cream
1 pint of milk
6 eggs, separated
1 cup sugar
2 Tablespoons sherry
1 quart fresh figs, peeled

Scald cream and milk together. Beat egg yoks and sugar until very light. Then beat egg whites to a stiff froth. Pour hot milk over sugar and egg yolks, stirring continuously. Then add stiffly beaten egg whites, mix all thoroughly, and add sherry. Last of all, stir in figs. Cool and freeze.

NOTE: The amount of sugar required will vary with the sweetness of the figs and also if sweet sherry is used. Less sugar will be needed if sweet sherry is used.
Mrs. L.D. Simonds, 200 Years of Charleston Cooking, 1930

ORANGE PEKOE TEA ICE CREAM

2 1/2 cups milk, scalded
6 whole cloves
1 Tablespoon grated orange rind
2 Tablespoons orange pekoe tea
1 envelope unflavored gelatin
1/3 cup cold water
1/4 teaspoon salt
3/4 cups sugar
4 egg yolks, slightly beaten
3/4 cup honey
4 egg whites, stiffly beaten
3 cups light cream

Scald milk with cloves and orange rind. Add tea; let stand 5 to 8 minutes over hot water. Soften gelatin in water. Strain milk; return to double boiler top. Add salt, sugar, and egg yolks, which have been mixed with some hot milk. Cook stirring constantly, until thickened. Remove from heat, add softened gelatin; blend thoroughly. Add honey. When cold, fold in egg whites and cream. Freeze with ice cream freezer. 1 gallon.
Farm Journal's Country Cookbook, 1959

PINEAPPLE MILK SHERBET

1 1/2 teaspoons gelatin, unflavored
2 Tablespoons cold water
2 cup buttermilk or sour milk
3/4 cup sugar
1 cup pineapple, crushed
1 teaspoon vanilla
1 egg white
1/4 cup sugar

Soften gelatin in cold water and dissolve over hot water. Combine buttermilk, 3/4 cup sugar, pineapple, vanilla, and gelatin. Mix well. Pour into ice cube tray or cake pan. Freeze until firm. Break into chunks and pour into chilled bowl. Beat until smooth. Beat egg white to soft peaks and gradually add 1/4 cup sugar. Continue beating until stiff peaks form. Fold egg white into pineapple mixture. Return to cold tray and freeze until firm. Serves 4 to 6.

NOTE: No one probably has ice cube trays with removable sections anymore. You may even ask, "What is an ice tray?" This has always been my favorite ice cream. In 1954, when grandmother wasn't pulling a tray out of the freezer compartment of her refrigerator, we were walking to Bryant's Grocery to buy a nickel cup for me. Tell that to Baskin-Robbins!
David Boswell Hazelwood, Miss Lizzie's Heirlooms, 2009

PINEAPPLE SORBET

| 1 fresh pineapple | 2 cup sugar |
| 1 Tablespoon lime juice | 2 cup water |

Peel and core pineapple and cut into cubes. Puree pineapple in food processor. Add lime juice and set aside. In a large saucepan combine sugar and water over medium heat. Bring to a boil and stir for five minutes until sugar dissolves. Remove from heat and add pureed pineapple. Chill thoroughly. Pour into canister of 1 quart ice cream freezer and freeze according to manufacturer's directions. Makes 8- four-ounce servings.
Cortner Mill Restaurant cookbook, 2009

THREE OF A KIND SHERBET

juice of 3 oranges	3 bananas, sliced
juice of 3 lemons	3 egg whites
3 pints water	
3 cups sugar	

Combine orange and lemon juice with water. Add sugar and stir until dissolved. Add bananas. Place in freezer until ice begins to form. Beat egg whites until stiff. Fold into partially frozen fruit juices. Continue freezing. Makes about 2 quarts sherbet.
Holiday Hostess, 1958

PINEAPPLE ICE

| 4 cups water | 1 cup orange juice |
| 2 1/2 cups sugar | 1 cup grated pineapple (juice and pulp) |

Heat two cups of water to boiling and turn over the sugar, stirring until the sugar is dissolved. Add orange juice and pineapple together with 2 cups ice cold water. Cool and freeze, using 3 parts ice to 1 part salt.

NOTE: This ice is cream color with flecks of yellow pineapple. The pineapple gives the predominant flavor, but the elusive taste of orange makes this dish out of the ordinary. Makes about 2 1/2 quarts of ice.
Mary Leize Simons, 200 years of Charleston Cooking, 193

BUTTERMILK SHERBET

4 cups buttermilk	1/2 cup sugar
1 1/2 cups light corn syrup	2 Tablespoons grated lemon rind
1/2 cup lemon juice	few drops green food coloring (optional)

Combine all ingredients. Pour into 2 refrigerator trays and freeze until mushy. Pour sherbet into chilled bowl and beat until smooth. Return sherbet to trays and freeze again until mushy. Beat and freeze twice more in the same manner. Freeze until firm. Serve garnished with mint leaves. Makes 1 1/2 quarts.
Lucy Dye, The Nashville Cookbook, 1977

LIME-PINEAPPLE SHERBET

1 cup sugar	1 Tablespoon lemon juice
2 cups water	9 ounces crushed pineapple
3 ounce package lime flavor gelatin	few drops green food coloring (optional)
6 ounce can, frozen limeade concentrate	1 1/2 cups milk

Mix sugar and water in saucepan; bring to a boil. Remove from heat and add gelatin. Stir until it dissolves. Add limeade concentrate, lemon juice, pineapple, food color (optional) and milk. Mix together. Pour into refrigerator tray; freeze firm. Remove to a mixer bowl, break into pieces. Beat until light and fluffy. Fill the trays again and freeze. Makes 2 quarts.

NOTE: This can be made a day ahead and frozen. Beat light and fluffy the day it is to be eaten.
Farm Journal's Country Cookbook, 1959

FRUIT SHERBET

1 1/2 cups sugar	juice of 2 oranges
1 1/2 cups water	2 bananas peeled and mashed
juice of 2 lemons	

Make a syrup of sugar and water. Boil for 3 minutes. Cool. Add juices and fruit at once with cool syrup. Pour into two freezer trays. Freeze at once. Serves 8. Easy and excellent!
Satsuma Tea Room, More Fun for the Cook, 1974

CRANBERRY SHERBET

2 cups cooked sweetened cranberries, strained	1 cup sugar
juice of two oranges	3 cups water
juice of 1 lemon	

Combine all ingredients. Freeze in freezer or freeze in refrigerator trays stirring several times. Serves 8.
Satsuma Tea Room, More Fun for the Cook, 1974

GRAPE ICE

2 cups water	1/2 cup orange juice
1 cup sugar	2 Tablespoons lemon juice
1 cup grape juice	1 egg white

Combine water and sugar and boil gently for 15 minutes. Add grape, orange, and lemon juice. Pour into ice cube tray and freeze until about 1 inch thick around edge. Turn into a large bowl. Add egg white and beat with a mixer until light and fluffy. Return to ice cube tray and freeze firm.
Holiday Hostess, 1958

LEMON SHERBET

1 envelope unflavored gelatin
2 1/2 cups milk
1 cup sugar
1/2 cup lemon juice
1 teaspoon grated lemon rind
1/8 teaspoon salt
2 egg whites

Soak gelatin in 1/2 cup milk. Add sugar to the remaining milk; scald. Dissolve gelatin mixture in scalded milk; cool. Add lemon juice very slowly; add rind. Freeze in refrigerator tray until mushy. Add salt to egg whites and beat. Beat in lemon mush. Return to refrigerator tray; freeze thoroughly, stirring occasionally. Makes 6 servings.
Farm Journal's Country Cookbook, 1959

LEMON SORBET

4 1/2 cups sugar
6 cups water
3 large egg whites
2 1/4 cups fresh lemon juice

Combine sugar and water in saucepan over low heat until sugar dissolves. Raise heat and boil syrup for 1 minute. In large mixing bowl beat egg whites until foamy. Slowly beat in hot syrup mixture. Add lemon juice and mix well. Cover and refrigerate overnight. The mixture will have a foam on top, but this will incorporate into the sorbet as it freezes. Pour into a canister of 4-5 quart freezer and freeze according to manufacturer's directions. Makes 3 quarts.

NOTE: We always serve a sorbet between the salad and entrée course. In addition to adding a touch of elegance to the meal, the sorbet cleanses the palate between courses. Not accustomed to sorbet, some of our guests have thought it was dessert served too small and too soon.
Cortner Mill Restaurant cookbook, 2009

LEMON OR LIME SHERBET

3 ounce package lemon or lime gelatin
1 cup boiling water
1 cup sugar
1/4 cup lemon or lime juice
1 teaspoon grated lemon or lime rind
1 quart light cream

Pour boiling water over gelatin. Stir until dissolved. Add sugar, lemon or lime juice and rind, stir to dissolve sugar. Add cream. Chill. Pour slowly into refrigerator tray. Freeze to mush. Beat with a rotary beater. Freeze firm. Makes 6 servings.
Satsuma Tea Room, More Fun for the Cook, 1974

GINGER LEMON SHERBET

3 cups milk
3/4 cup sugar
3 Tbl. finely chopped candied ginger
1/4 cup lemon juice
1 Tablespoon grated lemon peel
3 Tablespoons lime juice

Combine milk and sugar. Add ginger, lemon juice, lemon peel, and lime juice. The mixture may have a curdled appearance, but this will not affect the outcome of the texture. Freeze. Serve in sherbet glasses with garnish of a mint leaf. Serves 4-6.
What to Cook for Company, 1952

ORANGE FROST

2 mashed bananas
2 cups orange juice
juice and grated rind of 1 lemon
1 small can crushed pineapple
1 cup sugar
1/2 teaspoon salt
2 cups whole milk

Mix orange, lemon, crushed pineapple, bananas, and salt with the sugar. Very slowly beat milk into the mixture. Freeze in two ice trays. Beat once or twice while freezing. Serves 8.
Satsuma Tea Room, More Fun for the Cook, 1974

ORANGE MOUSSE

1 pint heavy cream, whipped
6 ounce can frozen orange juice
1 pint coffee cream
sweeten to taste

Mix and freeze in refrigerator. Makes 6 servings
Satsuma Tea Room, More Fun for the Cook, 1974

AVOCADO ORANGE SHERBET

1 1/2 cups mashed avocado pulp
1/4 cup pineapple juice
1 cup fresh orange juice
1/2 cup lemon juice
1 1/4 cups sugar
1 cup milk
2 teaspoons grated lemon rind
1/8 teaspoon salt

Combine avocado and juices. Add sugar, milk, rind, and salt. Blend well and freeze in ring mold. Fill the center with large strawberries or orange sections. Garnish with mint leaves. Serves 8-10.

NOTE: A tangy, pretty sherbet!
Nell F. Pinkerton, The Nashville Cookbook, 1977

CRÈME DE MENTHE ICE

1 2/3 cups sugar	1/2 cup lemon juice
3 cups water	1/2 cup crème de menthe

Cook sugar and water together for 5 minutes. Cool. Add lemon juice and crème de menthe. Pour into refrigerator trays. Freeze, stirring several times. Serves 8.
Satsuma Tea Room, More Fun for the Cook, 1974

CRÈME DE CACAO BAVARIAN

1 Tablespoon unflavored gelatin	1/4 pound marshmallows
1/4 cup cold water	1 cup whipping cream
2 cups crème de cacao	shaved sweet chocolate

Soften gelatin in cold water. Heat crème de cacao over low heat. Do not boil. Add the marshmallows to hot crème de cacao. Remove from heat, when marshmallows are melted. Add softened gelatin; stir until gelatin is dissolved. Pour into a 2-quart mixing bowl and set bowl in pan of ice. Whip cream. Fold into gelatin mixture, when mixture starts to congeal. Keep refrigerated until serving time. Garnish with shaved chocolate. Serves 8.

NOTE: Bavarian Cream was one of Satsuma's customer's favorite ice creams. We would have different variations of Bavarian Cream as stand-alone puddings topped with whipped cream. We would then freeze what we didn't sell that was left over from lunch that day and then make Bavarian Cream Ice Cream as the opportunity arose.
Easy-on-the-Cook Book, 1960

ICE CREAM AND FRUIT COMPOTE

1 quart pistachio ice cream	3 1/2 cups blueberries, drained
20 ounces frozen sliced peaches, slightly thawed and drained	1 quart vanilla ice cream
1 quart strawberry ice cream	20 ounces frozen red-raspberries, slightly thawed and drained

Chill your favorite big, deep, impressive glass dish (4 quart size). Put pistachio ice cream into bottom of dish. Arrange peaches over ice cream. Add strawberry ice cream, then blueberries over. Over blueberries put vanilla ice cream. Top with raspberries. Serve immediately. 12 Servings.
Easy-on-the-Cook Book, 1960

ELIZA'S DESSERT

1 pint of cream, 1/2 pound of marshmallows (each cut into 4 pieces), 1 teaspoon of vanilla. Beat until stiff. Add 1 large cup pecans, and 1 small cup maraschino cherries, 1/2 dozen chocolate kisses, or lady fingers broken up. Put all on ice.
The Savannah Cook Book, 1933

INDIVIDUAL ALASKAS

4 egg whites
1/4 teaspoon vanilla
1/4 cup confectioners' sugar

1 pint ice cream
6 individual sponge cake shells

Beat the egg whites until stiff, not dry. Add vanilla. Add sugar gradually; continue beating until meringue stands in peaks. Divide ice cream into 6 portions; place a portion in the center of each cake shell. Spread meringue over cake and ice cream so they are completely covered. Place on cookie sheet. Brown in 450 F oven about 5 minutes. Serve immediately. Makes 6 servings.

NOTE: Individual Alaska's may be frozen before baking.
Easy-on-the-Cook Book, 1960

PARFAIT D'AMOUR

Put some peach ice cream in a glass. Pour over this a Tablespoon of raspberry or fruit syrup and let the syrup trickle through. To this add a Tablespoon of whipped cream and serve.
The Savannah Cook Book, 1933

NOTES

DESSERT SAUCES

"Stressed spelled backwards is desserts"
-Unknown

"Don't spill this sauce onto the top of your head.
Your tongue will beat your brains out trying to get to it."
-David Hazelwood

HARD SAUCE

1 1/4 cups butter
1 cup powdered sugar

1 egg
2 Tablespoons sherry

Beat butter and sugar until light and fluffy. Beat in egg and add sherry. Mix well. Put into refrigerator and serve very cold on steamed pudding or baked apples.

NOTE: Vanilla may be used in place of sherry, if you so wish. 1 1/2 teaspoons of vanilla.
Satsuma Tea Room, Fun for the Cook, 1968

BRANDY SAUCE FOR FRITTERS (For puddings also)

3/4 cup water
1/2 cup sherry, brandy, or both

sugar to taste
1/2 teaspoon grated nutmeg

Mix the ingredients and bring to a boiling point, serve very hot.
The Southern Cook Book, 1939

EGGNOG SAUCE (Old-style)

2 egg whites, well-beaten
2 egg yolks, well beaten
2 Tablespoons whipped cream

3 Tablespoons sugar
1 teaspoon rum
2 teaspoons whiskey or Bourbon

Beat egg yolks until thick and lemon color. Add whites, then sugar, and beat again, so that they form a meringue. Next add rum and whiskey to the above and beat into this mixture the whipped cream.

NOTE: Serve with hot pudding.
The Southern Cook Book, 1939

KENTUCKY EGGNOG SAUCE

7 Tablespoons Oleo (margarine)
4 egg yolks
2 1/3 cups powdered sugar
4 egg whites
1/3 cup sherry

Beat egg yolks with sugar until lemon colored. Add melted Oleo and blend well. Cook in double boiler, while stirring, until thick. Cool and add sherry. Chill and serve over sponge cake. Makes 3+ cups. Serves 8

NOTE: It's hard to choose, but this was one of my (David H.) favorites of Satsuma's desserts. Somehow, I got Truman Smith to share the recipe. I probably sweet talked his wife Betty to get it. It made 2 quarts and served 20, so this is my reduced version. They admitted they economized by using sherry (and a lot more of it than other recipes), instead of Kentucky Bourbon, but it still made this Kentucky boy happy every week.
Truman Smith, Satsuma Tea Room, unpublished

KENTUCKY EGGNOG SAUCE

3 egg yolks
1/3 cup sugar
1 cup light cream
1 Tbl rum or Bourbon

Beat egg yolks with sugar until lemon colored. Add cream and blend well. Cook, while stirring, over hot water until thick. Cool and add flavoring. Chill and serve over ice cream and/or sponge cake.

NOTE: Perfect sauce for a basic dessert that needs a little pizzazz.
The Nashville Cookbook, 1977

FOAMY BUTTER RUM SAUCE

1/4 cup butter or margarine
1 cup sifted confectioners' sugar
1 egg, separated
1/2 cup whipping cream
2 Tablespoons (or more) rum

Cream butter or margarine and sugar until light. Add well-beaten egg yolk and blend. Cook over boiling water (double boiler) until thickened, stirring constantly. Beat egg white until stiff and stir in. Continue cooking over boiling water until smooth and thick (about 3 minutes). Remove from heat and chill. When cold, fold in stiffly beaten cream and rum. Sauce keeps well in refrigerator for several days. Stir well before serving. Makes 8 servings.
Holiday Hostess, 1958

SHERRY SAUCE

2 cups milk
6 egg yolks
1/4 cup sugar
1/8 teaspoon salt

1 cup whipping cream
3 Tablespoons sherry wine
1/2 teaspoon vanilla extract

Scald milk. Beat egg yolks slightly and add sugar and salt. Gradually stir in milk. Cook over boiling water, stirring constantly until mixture coats spoon. When cool, whip cream and fold into mixture with sherry and vanilla extract. Makes 8 generous servings.

NOTE: Wonderfully light and fluffy, and so good!
Holiday Hostess, 1958

WINE SAUCE FOR SPONGE CAKE

1/2 cup butter
1 cup sugar
1 cup sweet port wine flavoring

1/2 cup boiling water
1/4 teaspoon nutmeg

Cream the butter and sugar together well and add the other ingredients. Stir all well together and serve over the sponge cake.

NOTE: The original recipe calls for 2 cups of sugar, but in these Prohibition days (cook book published in 1930) of sweetened wines, this made far too sweet a sauce. Prohibition also dictated the use of port wine flavoring.
Mary Leize Simons, 200 Years of Charleston Cooking, 1930

SAUCE FOR COTTAGE PUDDING

1 cup sugar
1 Tablespoon flour
1/2 Tablespoon butter
2 egg yolks

1 cup boiling water
2 Tablespoons wine flavoring
1/4 teaspoon nutmeg

Mix sugar and flour well, cream in butter and add eggs, beating well. Then add boiling water gradually, stirring all the time, and cook until the mixture thickens. Remove from fire and add wine flavoring and nutmeg. Serve hot with cottage pudding.

NOTE: Remember, this recipe was written during Prohibition, hence wine "flavoring."
Mary Leize Simons, 200 Years of Charleston Cooking, 1930

RASPBERRY ROYALE SAUCE

1 Tablespoon butter
1 cup raspberries
2 Tablespoons sugar

1/2 Tablespoon rum
vanilla ice cream

Melt butter in saucepan. Add sugar and stir until dissolved. Stir in raspberries gently and remove from heat. Stir in rum and serve over ice cream.
David Hazelwood, Cortner Mill Restaurant cookbook, 2009

CRÈME DE MENTHE SAUCE

3 parts honey

1 part crème de menthe

Combine and blend with a spoon. Serve as a sauce on ice cream.
Holiday Hostess, 1958

VANILLA SAUCE

1/2 cup sugar
2 teaspoons cornstarch
or 4 teaspoons flour

1 cup water
2 to 3 Tablespoons butter
1 teaspoon vanilla

Mix sugar and cornstarch and then add to boiling water. Cook, while stirring, for about 10 minutes. Add butter and vanilla. Serve hot.

NOTE: A plain sauce remembered for its use on dried fruit rolls and steamed puddings.
Nashville City Schools Centennial Cookbook, 1852-1952

FUDGE SAUCE

2 cups white sugar
1 cup brown sugar
1 cup cocoa

3 Tablespoons flour
1/4 cup butter
1 1/2 cups water

1/2 teaspoon vanilla

Mix dry ingredients thoroughly and add butter and water. Bring to a boiling point and cook until thick; about 10 minutes. Add vanilla.

NOTE: This sauce is good served hot or cold over ice cream or cake.
Anita De Saussure, 200 Years of Charleston Cooking, 1930

CHOCOLATE SAUCE

1 cup Ghirardelli cocoa	1/2 cup hot water	1 pinch salt
1 3/4 cups sugar	1/2 cup milk	1 teaspoon vanilla

Mix sugar and cocoa in saucepan. Stir in hot water until smooth. Add milk and salt. Heat to boiling. Cook 2 minutes. Cool and then stir in vanilla. Makes two cups.

NOTE: Serve hot or cold over ice cream, fudge cake, pie or pudding.
David Hazelwood, Cortner Mill Restaurant cookbook, 2009

MOCHA SAUCE

1 1/2 cups evaporated milk	4 ounces (4 squares) unsweetened chocolate	1 teaspoon vanilla
2 cups sugar	1/4 cup (1/2 stick butter)	2 Tablespoons strong coffee

Mix milk and sugar and bring to a rolling boil; boil 1 minute. Add chocolate, reduce heat, and beat as the chocolate melts. Add butter, vanilla and coffee. Whip until well-blended and creamy. Serve warm on ice cream or desserts.
The Nashville Cookbook, 1977

BUTTERSCOTCH SAUCE

1 1/4 cups light brown sugar	1/2 cup undiluted evaporated milk
2/3 cup light corn syrup	1/2 teaspoon vanilla
1/2 stick margarine	

Mix first three ingredients and cook to 242 degrees. Add milk and vanilla. Cool. Serve over cake or ice cream. Makes about 2 cups sauce.
Virginia Kendall White, The Nashville Cookbook, 1977

HOT BROWN SUGAR SAUCE

1 cup sugar	2 Tablespoons flour	1 1/2 Tablespoons butter
1 cup light brown sugar	1 1/3 cups half and half	

Combine sugars and flour in saucepan. Stir in milk and bring to a boil. Remove from heat and whisk in butter.
Bill Hall, Cortner Mill Restaurant cookbook, 2009

CARAMELIZED SYRUP

The start for many marvelous dishes.

2 cups sugar   1 cup boiling water

Pour sugar into a heavy skillet that heats uniformly. Melt over low heat, stirring constantly with a wooden spoon to prevent scorching (Don't worry about the lumps, they'll melt away). When sugar becomes a clear, brown syrup, remove from the heat. Stir in boiling water slowly, so it doesn't splatter. Return to a low heat and stir until syrup is smooth again. Cool. Pour into a clean pint jar, cover tightly, and store at room temperature. Keeps 6 to 8 weeks. Makes 1 1/3 cups.

NOTE: Because there are so many flavorful uses for this syrup, you may prefer to double the recipe.
Farm Journal's Country Cookbook, 1959

CARAMEL SUNDAE SAUCE

1/4 cup hot water
1/2 cup caramelized syrup (recipe above)

1/4 cup chopped nuts
1/4 cup candied ginger, minced, or orange or lemon peel

Combine all ingredients. Chill. Serve over vanilla ice cream. Makes enough for 8 sundaes.

NOTE: Makes ice cream a royal dessert.
Farm Journal's Country Cookbook, 1959

LEMON SAUCE FOR FRITTERS (and puddings)

1/2 cup sugar
3 teaspoons cornstarch

1 cup boiling water
1/2 lemon

1 Tablespoon butter

Mix sugar and cornstarch in a pan, stir in boiling water; add butter, lemon juice, and grated lemon rind. Boil and stir until mixture is transparent. Serve on fruit fritters or puddings.
The Southern Cookbook, 1939

LEMON SAUCE

1 cup sugar
4 Tablespoons flour or
2 Tablespoons cornstarch

2 cups boiling water
3 Tablespoons lemon juice
2 teaspoons grated lemon rind

Mix sugar, flour (or cornstarch); add, while whisking, to boiling water. Cook until thick and rather clear, stirring as needed to make smooth, about 10 minutes. Remove from heat and add butter, lemon juice and rind. Blend well. Makes about 2 1/2 cups.

NOTE: This quickly made dessert sauce enhances warm gingerbread, plain cakes, or puddings. Best served warm.
Milton Starnes, The Nashville Cookbook, 1977

RATIFIA CREAM

NOTE: Although the basis for this dessert, as of so many Charleston ones, is heavy cream, the result is so unusual. It is a very rich custard with a distinct flavor of bitter almonds. Not too rich wafers should be served with it. You must accent ratifia on the third syllable (ratifi'a) and eat a small portion.

3 egg yolks
2 cups heavy cream
2 Tablespoons powdered sugar
2 Tablespoons cream

3 bitter almonds (laurel leaves may be used in place of the bitter almonds if desired)

Beat egg yolks, add two cups of cream and almonds in a double boiler, and bring slowly to the boiling point. Then remove almonds and add egg mixture. Stir constantly, always stirring the same way, until the mixture has become quite thick. Remove from fire and turn into sherbet glasses. This will serve 6.

NOTE: Really good atop sponge or similar cake too!
200 Years of Charleston Cooking, 1930

HONEY ORANGE SAUCE

1 cup honey
1/4 cup finely chopped orange peel

1/8 teaspoon salt

Combine all the ingredients. Heat 5 minutes, but do not boil. Makes about 1 cup.

NOTE: Perfect when served on ice cream, waffles or pancakes.
Farm Journal's Country Cook Book, 1959

WHIPPED BUTTER

Whip 1/2 pound of softened butter with 1 cup of sugar until fluffy. Add 2 Tablespoons grated orange rind, 1/4 cup chopped almonds, and two Tablespoons brandy. Stir in 1/2 cup crumbled macaroons.

NOTE: Whipped Butter may top desserts or toasted breads.
The Nashville Cookbook, 1977

HONEY (MAKE-BELIEVE)

60 white clover blossoms
40 red clover blossoms

3 roses (pink petals)
3 cups water

5 pounds sugar
1 teaspoon alum

Boil sugar, water, and alum for 20 minutes or until syrup threads. Drop in blossoms and let stand 45 minutes. Drain through cheesecloth. Seal or freeze.

NOTE: Intriguing recipe for a substitute ingredient. Try it for fun!
Lavelle Wood, The Nashville Cookbook, 1977

TENNESSEE WHISKEY SAUCE

1 cup powdered sugar	2 teaspoons Tennessee whiskey
2 Tablespoons butter, melted	2 Tablespoons milk

Combine sugar, butter, and milk in saucepan and stir over medium heat until sugar dissolves. Remove from heat and stir in whiskey.

NOTE: This is a great, quick sauce to serve over angel food or any cake not iced.
David Hazelwood, Cortner Mill Restaurant cookbook, 2009

SPICY VANILLA SAUCE (Extra good with apple fritters)

1 cup sugar	1 cup cold water
2 Tablespoons flour	2 Tablespoons butter or margarine
1/4 teaspoon nutmeg	1 teaspoon vanilla
1/8 teaspoon allspice	

Mix together in a saucepan the sugar, flour, nutmeg, and allspice. Stir in water; simmer until clear and thickened.
Blend in butter and vanilla. Serve warm over hot apple fritters. Makes about 1 1/2 cups.
Farm Journal's Country Cookbook, 1959

RHUBARB SAUCE

1 pound (4 cups) rhubarb	1 cup sugar or more	1/3 cup boiling water

Cut rhubarb into 1-inch pieces. Drop into saucepan of boiling water and cook until barely tender. Add sugar; stir and cook until tender (about 4 minutes longer) Can be served cold, making a delicious dish with whipped cream Makes about 2 cups.

NOTE: Rhubarb, enjoyed as piquant (having a pleasantly sharp taste or appetizing flavor) sauce to accompany a meal, or turned into cobbler or other type of pie, is often called "pie-plant" in the South.
Katherine Nichols, The Nashville Cookbook, 1977

COOKIES, CANDIES & CONFECTIONS

*"A good life starts with sugar as sweet as love,
but life can be boring if you don't spice it up.
Adding a little zest, even sweet and sour
helps us to appreciate the sweet even more."
-David Hazelwood*

*"Health and appetite impart the sweetness to sugar, bread, and meat."
-Ralph Waldo Emerson (1803-1882)*

BOURBON BALLS

1 cup vanilla wafer crumbs
1 cup finely chopped pecans
1/4 cup Bourbon

2 Tablespoons cocoa
1 cup powdered sugar
1 1/2 Tablespoons white corn syrup

Mix all ingredients, except sugar. Roll into balls size of large marble. Roll in powdered sugar. Keep cool and will keep well.
Satsuma Tea Room, Fun for the Cook, 1968

BOURBON BALLS

8 ounce package semi-sweet chocolate morsels
3 Tablespoons light corn syrup
1/3 to 1/2 cup Bourbon

2 1/2 cups crushed vanilla wafers
1 cup powdered sugar (reserve 1/2 cup)
1 cup finely chopped nuts

Melt chocolate morsels over hot water; add corn syrup and Bourbon and mix well. Combine wafer crumbs, 1/2 cup of the sugar, and nuts. Add to chocolate mixture and mix until well moistened. Let stand for 30 minutes before forming into 1-inch balls. Roll balls in remaining sugar. Store in tightly covered container and let "season" several days before serving. Makes 4 dozen.
Jean McGaw, The Nashville Cookbook, 1977

COOKIES

2 cups flour, 1 cup sugar, 1/2 cup butter, 1 egg, 2 Tablespoons milk, and heaping teaspoon baking powder. Flavor with lemon. Make a dough, roll and cut, and bake in biscuit pan.
The Savannah Cook Book, 1933

To store fresh cookies: pack them lightly in a cookie jar or container with a loose-fitting cover. If they soften, heat in a slow oven (300 F) about 5 minutes before serving.

COLONIAL COOKIES

Mix 1 cup butter and 2 cups sugar. Add 2 well-beaten eggs and 1/2 cup milk, in which 1 teaspoon baking soda has been dissolved. Stir in gradually 1 1/2 cups flour. Roll out, cut into shapes, and bake 10 minutes at 350 F.
The Savannah Cook Book, 1933

OLD FASHIONED SUGAR COOKIES

1/2 cup butter or Crisco
1 cup sugar
1 egg or 2 egg yolks, well beaten
1 Tablespoon cream or milk
1/2 teaspoon vanilla
1 1/2 cups all-purpose flour
1/4 teaspoon salt
1 teaspoon baking powder

Cream butter or Crisco. Beat in sugar, egg, cream or milk, and vanilla. Add flour, salt, and baking powder sifted together. Mix well. Arrange by teaspoon on a buttered cookie sheet, 1-inch apart. Bake about 8 minutes at 375. Makes about 50 to 60 cookies. To emphasize the butter flavor, brush the cookies lightly with melted butter while they are still warm.

NOTE: Plain sugar cookies need the distinctive flavor of butter but you may substitute successfully if you are making one of the variations. For richer cookies, use more butter (up to 1 cup). To deepen the color, add an extra egg yolk.
My Better Homes and Gardens Cookbook, 1938

ROLLED SUGAR COOKIES

Mix sugar cookie dough (recipe above). Add just enough flour to make the dough stiff enough to roll out about 1/4 cup. Be careful not to add too much flour or the cookies will be hard and tough. Chill 1 hour or more.
Flour board lightly or dust with confectioners' sugar and roll dough 1/4 inch thick. Cut out with cookie cutters. Arrange on cookie sheet.
Bake at 375 until delicately brown (5 to 8 minutes)

SUGAR COOKIE VARIATIONS:

For the variations below, use the Old-Fashioned Sugar Cookie recipe that is printed above.

- ALMOND COOKIES

Add to the Old-Fashioned Sugar Cookies recipe, 1/3 cup almonds, blanched and finely chopped, 1/2 teaspoon, each, cinnamon, clove, and nutmeg and the grated rind of 1/2 lemon.

- BUTTERSCOTCH COOKIES

Use brown sugar in place of white. Melt butter, add sugar, and heat slowly until ingredients well-blended. If desired, add 1/4 cup chopped nut meats. (Black walnuts are especially good).

- **CHOCOLATE COOKIES**

Add 1/2 cup dry cocoa or 2 squares melted chocolate before adding flour. Bake at (325 F). If desired, frost with chocolate frosting.

- **COCONUT COOKIES**

Add 1/2 cup shredded coconut, chopped fine.

- **DATE COOKIES**

Add 1/2 cup dates, cut fine with wet scissors.

- **LEMON SUGAR COOKIES**

Omit the vanilla. Add 1/2 teaspoon lemon extract and 2 teaspoons lemon rind.

- **MAPLE COOKIES**

Use maple sugar, crushed fine, in place of white.

- **MARMALADE COOKIES**

Reduce sugar to 2/3 cup. Add 6 teaspoons marmalade.

- **NUT COOKIES**

Add 1/2 cup chopped nut meats.

- **ORANGE COOKIES**

Use orange juice in place of milk. Add grated rind of 1/2 orange. To enhance the color, use 2 to 4 egg yolks in place of a whole egg.

- **RAISIN COOKIES**

Add 1/2 cup chopped seedless raisins.

- **SEED CAKES**

Add 1 1/2 Tablespoons caraway seeds.

- **SPICED SUGAR COOKIES**

Add 1/4 teaspoon nutmeg or cinnamon.

- **MERINGUE LAYER COOKIES**

Spread sugar cookie mixture evenly in a buttered tin, about 9 x 9.
Beat 1 egg white, add 1 cup brown sugar and 1/2 teaspoon vanilla. Spread this mixture over the cookie mixture. Sprinkle with 3/4 cup chopped nut meats and press lightly. Bake 30 minutes at 325. Cut in squares or strips.

- **JELLY LAYER COOKIES**

Spread sugar cookie mixture with a thin layer of tart jam or jelly. Beat an egg white stiff, add 5 Tablespoons sugar, 1 teaspoon cinnamon, and 6 Tablespoons chopped walnut meats and spread over the jelly. Bake 30 minutes at 325.

COOKIE SHELLS

Cut out into 4-inch rounds. Press onto outside of scallop baking shells or fluted baking tins. Bake. Serve filled with ice cream or fruit.

COOKIE STARTER (A Master Recipe)

2 1/4 cups sifted flour   3/4 teaspoon salt   1 cup butter or margarine

Sift flour and salt into bowl. Cut in butter (room temperature) until mixture resembles coarse bread crumbs. Store in clean jar with tight fitting lid. Makes 3 to 4 cups.

TIPS ON USING COOKIE STARTER

- Let crumbs reach room temperature before adding other ingredients. Loosen with fork, if mix is too compact. Your electric mixer can help you make cookie dough from the mix.
- To short-cut cookie making, shape dough into a roll; wrap and chill thoroughly. Slice and bake cookies as desired. When dough is cold, allow more time for baking. To get a thicker cookie, shape multiple teaspoons of dough with fingers and roll in palms of hands into balls; stamp with flat bottomed glass and bake.
- When you bake and then freeze, wrap cookies in foil or plastic film or store them in freezer containers.

Farm Journal's Country Cook Book, 1959

SWEET WAFERS

3 eggs, beaten lightly
1/2 large cup sugar
2 Tablespoons butter

1 cup flour
1/2 teaspoon vanilla

Mix into thin batter and put teaspoon in waffle iron one at a time.
The Savannah Cookbook, 1933

SWEET WAFERS

4 ounces butter
4 ounces sugar
3 eggs

1 1/2 teaspoons cinnamon
6 ounces flour

Cream the butter and sugar together thoroughly. Add eggs, well-beaten, and gradually stir in flour and cinnamon, sifted together. Drop on a well-greased cookie sheet and bake in a moderate oven (350 F) for about 10 minutes. This recipe will make about 3 1/2 dozen cookies.
Miss Harleston's Notebook, Bossis Plantation recipe recounted in 200 Years of Charleston Cooking, 1930

CHOCOLATE CHIP OATMEAL COOKIES

1/2 cup shortening	3/4 cup sifted flour
1/2 cup firmly-packed brown sugar sieved	1/2 teaspoon baking soda
1/2 cup granulated sugar	1/2 teaspoon salt
1 egg	1 and 1/2 cups rolled oats, uncooked
1 Tablespoon water	6 ounces semi-sweet chocolate pieces
1/2 teaspoon vanilla	1/4 cup chopped nuts

Beat shortening until creamy; add sugars gradually; beat thoroughly. Beat in egg until fluffy. Add water and vanilla. Sift together flour, baking soda and salt; add to creamed mixture. Add rolled oats, chocolate pieces and nuts. Drop from teaspoon onto greased baking sheet. Bake at 375 F about 12 minutes. Makes 3 1/2 dozen.
Easy-on-the-Cook Book, 1960

CRISP OATMEAL COOKIES

3 cups brown sugar	1 Tablespoon baking soda
3 cups butter or margarine	3 cups flour
6 cups oatmeal	

Put all this in a huge bowl and mash, knead, squeeze. Then form it into small balls, midway between a marble size and golf ball size, on an ungreased cookie sheet. Butter bottom of a small glass, dip it in granulated sugar and mash the balls flat. Keep doing it. Re-dip the bottom of the glass in sugar for each ball. Then bake at 350 for 10-12 minutes. These are crisp for several days, but I like to keep dough in the refrigerator and bake them fresh when I want them.
Satsuma Tea Room, More Fun for the Cook, 1974

ORANGE-CARROT COOKIES

1 cup shortening	1 teaspoon vanilla
3/4 cup sugar	2 cups sifted flour
1 cup cooked, mashed carrots	2 teaspoon baking flour
1 egg unbeaten	1/2 teaspoon salt

Cream shortening and sugar until fluffy. Add carrots, egg, and vanilla; mix well. Sift together flour, baking powder and salt; add to carrot mixture; mix well. Drop batter by the teaspoon onto greased baking sheet. Bake at 350 F. about 20 minutes. Makes 5 dozen. While warm, frost with Golden Glow Frosting.

GOLDEN GLOW FROSTING

Combine juice of 1/2 orange; grated rind of 1 orange, 1 Tablespoon butter or margarine and 1 cup sifted confectioners' sugar.
Farm Journal's Country Cookbook, 1959

SHORT'NIN' BREAD

*"Oh, Mama's baby loves short'nin
Oh, Mama's baby loves short'nin'
Oh, Mama's baby loves short'nin' bread*

*The short'nin' bread is always the thing to have, the thing to have,
ah-da-dah, They must have their bread"*

*"Put on the skillet, Slip on the lid, Mama's gonna make a little shorten' bread.
That ain't all she's going to do, Mama's going to make a little coffee too."*

*-Music by E.C. Perrow (1880-1968)
-Poem by James Whitcomb Riley (1849-1916)*

SHORT'NIN' BREAD

4 cups flour
1 cup light brown sugar
1 pound butter (very soft)

Mix flour and sugar. Add butter. Place on floured surface and pat to ½ inch thickness. Cut into desired shapes and bake in a moderate oven 325-350 degrees F for 20 to 25 minutes.

SCOTCH SHORT BREAD

1 cup butter (no substitute)
1/3 cup dark brown sugar, sifted
1/3 cup light brown sugar, sifted
2 1/2 cups flour

Cream butter and sugars together, work in flour and chill. Roll dough into a large sheet to 1/2 inch thick and cut lengthwise into strips 1 1/2 inches wide, then diagonally, 1 1/2 inches apart to form diamond shapes. Bake at 325 F for about 30 minutes until slightly browned. Store in cool place. Makes about 5 dozen.
Peggy Pennington, The Nashville Cookbook, 1977

ALMOND TEA CAKES (Cookies)

1/2 cup butter or margarine
1 1/4 cups sugar
3 eggs, separated
1 cup sifted flour
1 teaspoon baking powder
3 Tablespoons milk
1 cup chopped almonds
1 Tablespoon sugar
1/2 teaspoon cinnamon

Cream butter and 1/2 the sugar. Add well beaten egg yolks, flour, baking powder, and milk. Mix well; spread in 11 x 7 x 1 1/2-inch greased baking pan. Beat egg whites until stiff; beat in remaining sugar gradually. Fold in almonds; spread on top of dough. Mix together sugar and cinnamon. Sprinkle over egg whites. Bake at 350 F for about 30 minutes. Cool and cut into strips. Yields 9.
Easy-on-the-Cook Book, 1960

Tea cakes are less often made today than they were 100 to 150 years ago. Back then, the large rounds, cut from rolled sweet dough, produced warm, freshly baked tea cakes to welcome drop-in kitchen guests, one and all. There are as many family tea cake recipes that exist in the South as grains of sand on the beach. All are as good as the next.

CHOCOLATE COCONUT DREAMS

1 cup condensed milk	1 teaspoon vanilla
2/3 cup chopped semi-sweet chocolate	4 cups shredded dry coconut
1/8 teaspoon salt	

Mix all ingredients well. Drop from teaspoon onto greased cookie sheet. Bake at 325 for 10-12 minutes. This makes about 60 cookies.

NOTE: Easy, quick, delicious. Especially delicious for teas.
Satsuma Tea Room, Fun for the Cook, 1968

COCONUT KISSES

4 egg whites	1 teaspoon vanilla
1/4 teaspoon salt	2 1/2 cups moist, shredded coconut
1 1/3 cups sugar	

Beat egg whites and salt until frothy. Add sugar gradually, beating until mixture forms stiff peaks. Beat in vanilla. Fold in coconut. Drop from teaspoon onto well-greased baking sheet. Bake at 325 F for 18 to 20 minutes. Makes 4 dozen.
Easy-on-the-Cook Book, 1960

COOKIE BONBONS

	2 teaspoons vanilla
2 cups sifted flour	2 1/2 cups finely chopped pecans
1/4 cup sugar	nut halves (optional)
1/2 teaspoon salt	confectioners' sugar
1 cup butter or margarine	

Sift flour, sugar, and salt into mixing bowl. Blend in butter and vanilla with pastry blender. Add 2 cups nuts. Shape half the dough into 1/2 inch balls. Roll in remaining nuts or flatten balls and press a nut half in top of each. Bake in moderate oven (350) 15 to 20 minutes. Roll remaining dough into logs; bake. Roll in confectioners' sugar.

NOTE: Pecans inside and pecans on top. Everyone raves!
Farm Journal's County Cookbook, 1959

DATE MACAROONS

4 egg whites	1 teaspoon vanilla
1 1/2 cups sugar	1 pound pitted dates, chopped
1/8 teaspoon salt	1 cup pecans chopped

Heat oven to 350 F and butter cookie sheets. Beat egg whites until stiff, but not dry. Add sugar and salt gradually; continue beating until mixture holds shape. Blend in vanilla. Fold in dates and nuts. Drop from teaspoon onto cookie sheet. Bake for 20 minutes. Makes 7 to 8 dozen.

NOTE: Delicious served immediately or may be kept in freezer for 3 to 4 weeks.
Sarah S. Miller, The Nashville Cookbook, 1977

DOUBLE CRUNCHERS

COOKIES

1 cup flour	1 egg
1/2 teaspoon baking soda	1/2 teaspoon vanilla
1/4 teaspoon salt	1 cup corn flakes crushed
1/2 cup vegetable shortening	1 cup quick cooking rolled oats
1/2 cup sugar	1/2 cup grated coconut
1/2 cup brown sugar	

Heat oven to 350 degrees. Grease large cookie sheet. Sift together the flour, soda, and salt. Combine shortening, sugar, and brown sugar and beat until fluffy. Add flour mixture to creamed mixture and blend well. Stir in egg and vanilla. Add corn flakes, oats, and coconut. The batter will be very stiff. Remove 1/3 of batter; make remaining 2/3 of batter into balls using level teaspoons. Put balls onto a greased cookie sheet and flatten with a glass. Bake for 10 minutes or until done. Shape remaining 1/3 of the batter into smaller balls using 1/2 teaspoon. Flatten slightly and bake for 8 minutes. Cool.

CHOCOLATE FILLING

1 cup semi-sweet chocolate morsels	1 Tablespoon water
1/2 cup confectioners' sugar	3 ounces cream cheese

Melt chocolate morsels, sugar, water, and cream cheese in double boiler over hot water. Beat until creamy and then cool.

Put cookies together in following manner:
Spread the filling over the larger cookies and top with the smaller cookies. Makes 3 1/2 dozen.
Cherry Lane von Schmittou, The Nashville Cookbook, 1977

SALTED PEANUT COOKIES

2 eggs, beaten	1 teaspoon baking soda
2 cups brown sugar, firmly packed	1 teaspoon baking powder
1 1/2 cups butter or margarine, melted	1/2 teaspoon salt
1 1/2 cups salted peanuts chopped	3 cups rolled oats
2 1/2 cups sifted flour	1 cup corn flakes

Beat eggs; add sugar and mix well. Stir in butter, then peanuts, and mix. Stir together flour, soda, baking powder and salt. Combine this with rolled oats and corn flakes. Combine with egg mixture and stir well into mix. Drop dough by the Tablespoon onto a greased baking sheet. Bake in hot oven (400 F) for 8 to 10 minutes. Makes 6 dozen.

NOTE: Tablespoons are used to drop dough for family sized cookies, but for dainty tea or coffee-sized treats use a teaspoon.
Farm Journal's Country Cookbook, 1959

LEMON COOKIES

1 cup butter or margarine	1/8 teaspoon salt
1/2 cup sugar	1 Tablespoon lemon juice
1 egg, beaten	1/2 teaspoon grated lemon rind
2 cups sifted flour	
1/2 teaspoon baking powder	

Cream together butter and sugar; add egg and mix well. Sift flour, baking powder, and salt; combine with sugar mixture. Add lemon juice and rind. Form into rolls; wrap in waxed paper or pack into frozen juice cans; chill. Slice very thin. Bake on greased baking sheet in moderate oven (375 F) 8 to 10 minutes. Makes 5 to 6 dozen.
Farm Journal's Country Cookbook, 1959

GINGER SNAPS

3/4 cup shortening	2 1/2 cups flour	2 teaspoons cinnamon
1 cup sugar	2 teaspoons baking soda	about 1/2 cup sugar
1 egg unbeaten	2 teaspoons cloves	
4 Tablespoons molasses	2 teaspoons ginger	

Cream shortening; add sugar gradually, creaming until light. Add egg; beat thoroughly. Stir in molasses. Sift together flour, soda, cloves, ginger, and cinnamon; add this gradually to creamed mixture, mixing thoroughly after each addition. Chill dough. Heat oven to 350 F. Grease cookie sheet. Shape dough into balls the size of walnuts. Dip each ball in sugar; place sugar side upon prepared cookie sheet. Press flat. Bake about 15 minutes. Do not stack or store cookies until cool. Makes 3 dozen medium cookies.
Mabel Yates, The Nashville Cookbook, 1977

EMPIRE BISCUITS (Cookies)

1/2 cup margarine	1 teaspoon baking powder
1/2 cup sugar	red raspberry preserves
1 egg, slightly beaten	chopped nuts
2 cups sifted flour	vanilla cream cheese frosting
2 teaspoons cinnamon	

Cream margarine and sugar. Blend in the egg. Add flour sifted with cinnamon and baking powder; mix well. Roll thin; cut with a 2-inch round cutter. Place onto ungreased baking sheet. Bake at 350 F for 12 to 15 minutes. Cool. For each biscuit, spread preserves between 2 rounds. Frost top with vanilla cream cheese frosting. Makes 2 dozen.

NOTE: Decorate with chopped nuts and red raspberry preserves.
Easy-on-the-Cook Book, 1960

PECAN COOKIES (Crescents)

1/2 cup butter	1 teaspoon vanilla	1 cup sifted cake flour
2 Tablespoons sugar	1 cup chopped pecans	

Blend butter and sugar until creamy. Mix flour and nuts, and stir into butter mixture. Roll into small crescents. Place onto greased baking sheet. Bake in 300 oven for 45 minutes. While hot, roll in powdered sugar. When cool, roll again in powdered sugar. This is another cookie that will keep a long time.
Satsuma Tea Room, Fun for the Cook, 1968

BLACK WALNUT COOKIES

6 cups sifted flour	1/2 cup sugar
1 teaspoon salt	2 eggs, beaten
1/2 teaspoon baking soda	2 teaspoons vanilla
1 teaspoon cream of tartar	1 1/2 cups black walnut meats
1 3/4 cups butter or margarine	1 1/2 cups flaked or shredded coconut
2 1/4 cups brown sugar, firmly packed	

Sift together flour, salt, soda, and cream of tartar. Cream butter, add sugars gradually. Beat until fluffy. Add eggs and vanilla. Grind the nuts and coconut together in food chopper using medium blade or use blender. (Most people today would use food processor.) Add to creamed mixture; add flour mixture. Blend well. Chill. Shape into 4 rolls about 2 inches in diameter. Wrap in waxed paper or foil. Chill. Cut rolls into 1/8 inch slices and place onto ungreased baking sheet. Bake at 350 F 10 to 12 minutes. Makes 8 to 9 dozen.
Farm Journal's Country Cookbook, 1959

PECAN PATTIES

1/2 cup butter	1/2 cup flour
1 cup sugar	1/4 teaspoon salt
1 egg	2 cups chopped pecans

Cream butter, add sugar gradually, and then beat in well-beaten egg yolk. Fold in the well-beaten egg white and add sifted flour and salt together; then put in pecans. Drop from a spoon onto well-greased cookie pan and bake in moderate oven (350 F) 15-20 minutes. This makes about 4 dozen cookies, very rich in pecans. These are useful in the cookie box, as they keep fresh a long time.

NOTE: The idea is to use just enough other ingredients to make the pecans stick together.
Helen Whaley Simons, 200 Years of Charleston Cooking, 1930

MOLASSES SNAPS

1 1/3 cups sifted flour	1/3 cup shortening
1 teaspoon baking soda	2/3 cup sugar
3/4 teaspoon ginger	1/3 cup light molasses
1/2 teaspoon salt	1 egg

Sift together flour, baking soda, ginger and salt. Cream shortening, sugar, and molasses thoroughly. Add egg and beat until fluffy. Blend in dry ingredients. Drop by teaspoons onto greased baking sheet, allowing 2 inches between cookies. Bake in 350 degree oven about 15 minutes or until delicately browned. Makes 4 1/2 dozen. Delicious. Dough will keep in refrigerator. They are so good just baked. Bet you can't eat just one.
Satsuma Tea Room, More Fun for the Cook, 1974

MOLASSES COOKIES

1 cup sugar	1/2 teaspoon salt
1 cup shortening	1 teaspoon baking soda
1 cup light molasses	1/2 teaspoon baking powder
1 Tablespoon vinegar	1 teaspoon ginger
6 cups sifted flour	1 teaspoon cinnamon
2 eggs, beaten	

Combine sugar, shortening, molasses, and vinegar in a saucepan. Bring to a boil and cook 2 minutes. Cool. Sift together flour, salt, soda, baking powder and spices. Add eggs to cooled molasses mixture. Add dry ingredients; mix well. Chill. Roll out on lightly floured board, about 1/8 to 1/4 inch thick. Cut; put onto greased baking sheet. Bake in a moderate oven (375 F) 8 to 10 minutes or until done. Makes about 12 dozen, 2 ½-inch cookies.
Farm Journal's Country Cookbook, 1959

CRISP MOLASSES COOKIES

1 cup shortening
1 cup molasses
2 eggs, slightly beaten
1 cup sugar

3 1/2 cups sifted flour
1/2 teaspoon salt
1 teaspoon baking powder

1/4 teaspoon cinnamon
1/4 teaspoon ginger
1/2 teaspoon cloves

Heat shortening and molasses in a saucepan until shortening is melted; stirring constantly. Slowly pour this mixture over the eggs. Add sifted dry ingredients; mix thoroughly. Chill overnight. Roll 1/16 inch thick on floured board or pastry cloth; cut with 2-inch cookie cutter. Place onto baking sheet. Bake at 350 F for 10 minutes. Makes 10 dozen 2-inch cookies.
Easy-on-the-Cook Book, 1960

MOLASSES WHOLE WHEAT COOKIES

1/2 cup non-fat dry milk
1/2 teaspoon baking soda
2 teaspoon baking powder
1/2 teaspoon salt
1/3 cup shortening

3/4 cup molasses
1 teaspoon vanilla
2 eggs beaten
1 cup plus 2 Tbl. whole wheat flour
1/2 cup raisins

Sift together dry milk, soda, baking powder, and salt. Cream together shortening, molasses, and vanilla; add the eggs, blend well. Add sifted ingredients and wheat flour; stir until thoroughly mixed. Add raisins (whole, chopped, or ground). Drop by teaspoons onto lightly greased baking sheet. Bake in moderate oven (350 F) 10 to 12 minutes, until lightly browned. Makes 4 dozen 2-inch cookies.
Farm Journal's Country Cookbook, 1959

BUTTER COOKIES

2 cups sweet butter
1/2 cup sugar
2 egg yolks
1 small glass of brandy
8 cups flour

1 teaspoon baking powder
1 teaspoon vanilla
1 teaspoon ground cloves
16 ounces powdered sugar

Heat oven to 350 F. Lightly grease cookie sheet. Cream butter and sugar in a large bowl; add egg yolks, brandy, flour, baking powder, vanilla, and cloves. Knead by hand to form a stiff dough. If the dough becomes too stiff, add a little more brandy; too soft, add a little more flour. Mix well and shape into small balls about 3/4 inch in diameter or into a cylindrical shape formed in 2-inch half-moons. Place onto prepared sheet and bake for 12 to 15 minutes or until set, but not brown. Let stand for a few minutes and remove to a large platter, arrange in layers and dust each layer with powdered sugar. Pile (stack) the layers to form a mound. Makes about 80 cookies.
Donna Lee Padis, The Nashville Cookbook, 1977

PLANTATION GINGER COOKIES

1 cup dry bread crumbs	1 teaspoon ginger	1 teaspoon butter, melted
1/2 cup brown sugar	1/2 teaspoon baking soda	1 teaspoon vanilla
1/8 teaspoon salt	2 eggs, beaten	1/4 cup molasses

Combine dry ingredients, add eggs, butter, vanilla and molasses. Drop from spoon 2 inches apart onto buttered baking sheet. Bake in hot oven (400 F) 15 to 20 minutes until brown.
The Southern Cookbook, 1939

PEANUT BUTTER COOKIES

1 cup shortening	2 eggs	2 teaspoons baking soda
1 cup granulated sugar	1 cup peanut butter	1/2 teaspoon salt
1 cup brown sugar	3 cups flour	1 teaspoon vanilla

Heat oven to 375 F. Cream together shortening, sugars, eggs, vanilla. Beat thoroughly. Stir in peanut butter (creamy). Sift together flour, soda, and salt; stir into creamed mixture. Form into small balls; place onto ungreased cookie sheet. Press with tines of a fork and crisscross. Bake about 10 minutes. Makes 6 dozen.
Mabel Yates, The Nashville Cookbook, 1977

CHOCOLATE FUDGE COOKIES (Boiled)

2 cups sugar	1/2 cup peanut butter
1/2 cup milk	2 1/2 to 3 cups quick-cooking oatmeal
1 stick margarine	1 to 2 teaspoons vanilla
3 to 4 Tablespoons cocoa	½ to 1 cup chopped nuts

Boil sugar, milk, margarine, and cocoa for 1 to 1 1/2 minutes (start timing after the mixture reaches a full rolling boil). Remove from heat, add peanut butter, oatmeal, vanilla, and nuts. Beat until blended and then drop onto waxed paper (by the teaspoon). Coconut or dates may be added if desired. Yields 24-30
Satsuma Tea Room, More Fun for the Cook, 1974

NUT DROP COOKIES

1 1/2 cups brown sugar	3 cups flour
1 cup butter	1 cup seeded raisins, chopped fine
3 eggs	1 cup English walnuts, chopped fine
1 Tablespoon cinnamon	1 cup currants, chopped fine
1/2 teaspoon salt	1 teaspoon vanilla
1 teaspoon baking soda	

Beat eggs well and add sugar and butter, which have been creamed; then add salt, cinnamon, 2 ½ cups sifted flour, and baking soda dissolved in 4 Tbl. hot water. Dredge fruit and nuts with the remaining flour and add to mixture. Then add vanilla and drop by the spoonful onto greased cookie pan. Bake in moderate oven (350 F) for 10 to 12 minutes.
The Southern Cookbook, 1939

CATHEDRAL COOKIES

12 ounces chocolate chips	1 teaspoon vanilla	10 1/2 ounces colored
1/2 stick margarine	1 cup chopped nuts	miniature marshmallows
2 eggs, beaten		

Tear off 4 squares of aluminum foil and sprinkle each heavily with confectioners' sugar. Melt the chocolate chips and margarine in top of double boiler over hot water. Add beaten eggs and cook as the mixture thickens. Add vanilla and cool. Fold in nuts and marshmallows quickly, so as not to soften marshmallows. Divide cookie mixture into 4 equal parts. Shape into a roll and place onto foil. Roll tightly, closing ends carefully. Freeze. When ready to serve, slice rolls into 1/2 inch slices. Makes 48.

NOTE: Beautiful, tasty cookies.
Ruby Major, The Nashville Cookbook, 1977

BUTTERSCOTCH COOKIES

1/2 cup shortening	1/8 teaspoon salt
2 cups brown sugar	1 teaspoon soda
2 eggs, beaten	1 teaspoon cream of tartar
1 teaspoon vanilla	4 cups flour

Tear off 4 rectangles of aluminum foil or waxed paper. Cream shortening with sugar. Add eggs and vanilla. Sift salt, soda, and cream of tartar with flour and gradually add to mixture. Divide dough into 4 equal parts. Shape into a roll about 1 1/2 inches in diameter. Roll tightly in foil or waxed paper, closing ends carefully. Chill overnight. When ready to bake, heat oven to 350 F and grease baking sheets. Slice dough about 1/4 inch thick and place onto baking sheet. Bake until very light brown, about 8 to 10 minutes. Makes 6 dozen.
Evelyn Holloway, The Nashville Cookbook, 1977

PUMPKIN COOKIES

1 stick (1/2 cup) margarine	1/2 teaspoon salt
1 cup sugar	1 teaspoon cinnamon
2 eggs, well-beaten	1/2 teaspoon allspice
1 cup cooked, sieved or pureed pumpkin	3 cups flour
1 teaspoon baking soda	1 cup golden raisins
1 teaspoon baking powder	

Heat oven to 350 degrees. Grease a large baking sheet. Cream margarine and sugar. Add beaten eggs and pumpkin. Add dry ingredients which have been mixed together. Blend to make smooth batter. Stir in raisins. Drop by Tablespoon onto baking sheet. Bake for about 15 minutes until golden brown. Baking time will depend on the size of the cookie. Makes about 3 dozen.

NOTE: This cookie is a fun way to help children learn about cooking.
Helen Minns, The Nashville Cookbook, 1977

FLORIDA ORANGE COOKIES

1/4 cup butter	1/4 cup orange juice
3/4 cup sugar	2 teaspoons baking powder
1 egg	3 cups flour

Cream butter and sugar. Add juice and the grated rind of 1 orange. Gradually add well-beaten egg and flour to which baking powder has been added. Place onto a floured board and roll thin. Cut with a cookie cutter and bake in moderate oven (350 F) for 12 minutes.
The Southern Cookbook, 1939

GRAHAM CRACKER COOKIES

1 cup white sugar	32 graham crackers
1 cup margarine	1 cup chopped nuts

Cook sugar and margarine together for 10 minutes. Split 32 graham crackers and lay flat on a cookie sheet. Pour sugar and margarine mixture on top of crackers. Sprinkle with nuts and bake in a 350 degree oven for 10 minutes.

NOTE: For the little work these require, they are amazingly good.
Satsuma Tea Room, More Fun for the Cook, 1974

UNBAKED CHOCOLATE MARSHMALLOW COOKIES

2 eggs beaten, beaten stiff	1 teaspoon vanilla
1 1/4 cups powdered sugar	1 cup salted peanuts
6 ounces chocolate chips, melted	1 small package marshmallow bits

Mix together the eggs, sugar, and chocolate. Add vanilla, peanuts, and marshmallow bits. Stir until mixture is coated. Drop onto wax paper and let stand until firm. Yields 3 dozen.
Satsuma Tea Room, More Fun for the Cook, 1974

CINNAMON FAVORITES

1/2 cup butter or margarine	1 teaspoon baking powder
1 cup sugar	1/4 teaspoon salt
1 egg, unbeaten	1/2 cup finely chopped nuts
1 teaspoon vanilla	1 Tablespoon cinnamon
1 1/4 cups sifted flour	1 Tablespoon sugar

Cream together butter and sugar. Add egg and vanilla; beat well (with electric mixer, 2 minutes at medium speed). Sift flour together with baking powder and salt; add to creamed mixture; chill. Mix nuts, cinnamon and 1 Tablespoon sugar. Mold dough into walnut-size balls; roll each in nut mixture. Place balls 2 1/2 inches apart on greased baking sheet. Bake in moderate oven (350 F) 12 to 15 minutes. Yields 20.
Farm Journal's Country Cookbook, 1959

LEMON COCONUT COOKIES

1 cup butter or margarine	1/2 teaspoon lemon peel	1 cup flaked coconut
1 1/2 cups sugar	2 cups sifted flour	
1 egg	1/4 teaspoon salt	

Cream butter. Add sugar and continue creaming until light and fluffy. Add egg and lemon peel. Beat well. Sift together flour and salt. Stir this into creamed mixture. Blend in coconut. Drop by teaspoon onto ungreased baking sheet. Bake at 325 F until lightly browned around edges, 15 to 20 minutes. Makes 6 dozen 2-inch cookies.
Easy-on-the-Cook Book, 1960

CHOCOLATE MACAROONS

1/2 cup vegetable shortening	2 cups sugar
4 squares unsweetened chocolate	4 eggs, unbeaten
2 cups sifted flour	2 teaspoons vanilla
2 teaspoons baking powder	confectioners' sugar
1/2 teaspoon salt	

Melt together shortening and chocolate. Sift together flour, baking powder, and salt. Add sugar to chocolate, stirring until smooth. Add eggs singly, beating well after each; add vanilla. Add flour mixture; blend thoroughly. Chill dough 2 to 3 hours. Dip out rounded teaspoons of dough; form into small balls. Roll each into confectioners' sugar. Bake in moderate oven (375 F) about 10 minutes. (Do not overbake. Cookies should be soft when taken from the oven.) Cool on rack. Makes 5 to 6 dozen.
Farm Journal's Country Cookbook, 1959

ICE CREAM WAFERS

1 cup cookie starter (page 474)	1/3 cup sugar
1/2 teaspoon vanilla	1/2 teaspoon baking powder
1 egg yolk	

Mix all ingredients. Chill dough thoroughly. Sprinkle board and rolling pin with confectioners' sugar. Roll small amount of dough 1/8 inch thick. Cut cookies and place 1 inch apart on greased baking sheet. Bake in moderate oven (350 F) about 6 minutes, until cookies are lightly browned. Dust with confectioners' sugar. Makes 3 dozen.

NOTE: What better accompaniment for that favorite flavor of ice cream.
Farm Journal's Country Cookbook, 1959

LACE COOKIES

1/2 cup butter or margarine	1 teaspoon baking soda (dissolved in
1 Tablespoon light corn syrup	2 Tablespoons boiling water)
1 cup sugar	1 cup coconut
1/2 cup sifted flour	1/2 cup rolled oats
	1 cup chopped nuts

Combine the ingredients in the order given. Drop 4 inches apart onto greased baking sheet. Bake in a moderate oven (350 F) about 20 minutes. Let cool slightly before removing from pan. Makes about 4 dozen cookies.
Holiday Hostess, 1958

MACAROONS

3/4 pound sweet almonds	3 cups sugar
3/4 pound bitter almonds	6 egg whites

Blanch the almonds and chop them as fine as possible. Beat egg whites until they are very stiff and fold in sugar and finely chopped almonds. Drop onto buttered paper and bake in a slow oven (300 F) for 15 to 20 minutes. This recipe makes about 9 dozen macaroons.

NOTE: The bitter almonds give these macaroons their fine flavor.
Mrs. Ball, a Commingtee Plantation recipe recounted in 200 Years of Charleston Cooking, 1930

CORN FLAKE MACAROONS

2 egg whites, beaten stiff	2 cups corn flakes
1 cup sugar	1/2 teaspoon almond flavoring
1 cup shredded coconut	1/2 teaspoon vanilla
1/4 teaspoon salt	

Mix in the order given. Drop by the teaspoon onto buttered cookie sheet. Bake about 20 minutes at 350
Satsuma Tea Room, Fun for the Cook, 1968

PEANUT COOKIES

1/2 cup butter	1 egg	1/4 teaspoon salt
1 cup sugar	1/2 cup flour	2 cups chopped peanuts

Cream butter, add sugar gradually, and beat in well-beaten egg. Sift flour and salt together and add with peanuts. Drop from a spoon onto a well-greased cookie sheet and bake in a moderate oven (350 F) from 15 to 20 minutes. This makes about 4 dozen cookies which are very rich in peanuts. In fact, the idea is to use just enough of the other ingredients to make the peanuts stick together!
Helen Rhett Simons, 200 Years of Charleston Cooking, 1930

BUTTER PECAN COOKIES

1 cup butter	1 egg yolk, beaten	2 Tablespoons milk
1/2 cup brown sugar	2 1/2 cups sifted flour	1/2 cup pecan halves
1/2 teaspoon salt	1/2 teaspoon vanilla	

Combine butter, sugar, and salt, and mix until light and fluffy. Add egg yolk. Stir in flour and blend well. Add vanilla. Roll into balls ¾ inch diameter. Place 2 inches apart onto greased cookie sheet. Add milk to beaten egg and dip fork into this mixture. Press fork down on each cookie until ¼ inch thick. Place pecan in center. Bake in moderate, 350 degree, oven 10-12 minutes or until cookies are golden brown. Makes 4 dozen.
What to Cook for Company, 1952

PEANUT BUTTER COOKIES

1/2 cup sugar	1 cup peanut butter
1/2 cup white syrup	5 cups cereal (corn flakes)

Heat sugar and syrup just to boiling. Remove from heat, stir in peanut butter. Pour over cereal and spread in pan. Cut into pieces of the sizes desired. Yields 25-35.
Satsuma Tea Room, More Fun for the Cook, 1974

GUMDROP COOKIES

1 cup shortening	1 cup coconut	1/2 teaspoon salt
1 cup brown sugar	1 teaspoon vanilla	1 cup of same or different flavor gum drops, cut into small pieces
1 cup granulated sugar	2 cups sifted flour	
2 eggs	1 teaspoon baking powder	
2 cups quick-cooking oats		

Thoroughly cream shortening and sugars. Add eggs and beat well. Sift dry ingredients and add to creamed mixture. Blend. Add oats, coconut, and gumdrops; mix with spoon until well blended. Roll dough into small balls. Place onto greased cookie sheet. Press each ball with a fork. Bake in moderate oven, 350-375, for about 10 minutes. The flavor improves if stored for a few days. Yields 3-6 dozen
Satsuma Tea Room, More Fun for the Cook, 1974

TENNESSEE COCONUT ALMOND COOKIES

1/2 pound butter	2 cups coconut
1 pound confectioners' sugar	4 teaspoons almond extract
2 cups graham cracker crumbs	4 teaspoons vanilla
2 cups almonds (roasted and ground)	pink coloring

Cream butter, add sugar and mix well. Add graham cracker crumbs, almonds, coconut, almond extract, vanilla, and coloring to the butter mixture. Mix well. Spread on a greased baking pan and place in refrigerator. When firm, cut into squares and serve with ice cream.
Satsuma Tea Room, More Fun for the Cook, 1974

PLANTATION SOUR CREAM COOKIES

2 cups brown sugar
1 cup rich sour cream
1 cup butter
3 teaspoons baking soda

3 eggs
1 teaspoon nutmeg
1 teaspoon vanilla

4 cups flour (or enough so that it drops from the spoon nicely)

Cream butter and sugar and add sour cream in which baking soda has been dissolved. Beat eggs well and add. Add the vanilla, nutmeg, and then the flour. Drop from a spoon onto a well-greased cookie pan and bake in a moderate oven (350 degrees) until well browned, about 12 minutes.
The Southern Cookbook, 1939

CORN FLAKE COOKIES

2 cups sifted flour
1 teaspoon baking soda
1/2 teaspoon salt
1/2 teaspoon baking powder
1 1/4 cups shortening
1 cup white sugar

1 cup brown sugar, firmly packed
2 eggs, well beaten
1 teaspoon vanilla
2 cups flaked or shredded coconut
2 cups corn flakes

Sift flour, soda, salt and baking powder. Cream shortening; add sugars gradually; beat until light. Add eggs and vanilla. Combine dry ingredients and creamed mixture; add coconut and corn flakes. Drop by small teaspoons onto greased baking sheet, 1 1/2 inches apart. Bake in a moderate oven (350 F) for 8 to 10 minutes or until delicately browned. Makes 8 dozen.

NOTE: As a child, I can remember with great fondness and anticipation my mother making these cookies. An unusual coconut delicacy.
Farm Journal's Country Cookbook, 1959

HONEY WAFERS

1/2 cup butter
1/2 cup honey
2 cups sifted flour

1 teaspoon baking soda
1/2 teaspoon cinnamon
1/4 teaspoon cloves

1/4 teaspoon allspice
1/4 cup crushed bran flakes

Cream together butter and honey. Sift together flour, baking soda, cinnamon, cloves, and allspice. Mix with bran flakes. Combine dry ingredients with honey and butter. Chill 1 hour or until firm enough to roll easily. Roll 1/8 inch thick on lightly floured board. Cut with floured cookie cutter. Bake on greased baking sheet in moderate oven (350 F) for 8 to 10 minutes. Makes 3 dozen.

NOTE: Crisp, dainty, and delicious.
Farm Journal's Country Cookbook, 1959

BENNE SEED

"Benne is an East Indian herb called sesame in the Orient, which is supposed to be a charm with which to secure entrance and exit through any portal. It was this magic which Ali Baba employed to open the doors of the treasure cave; his 'Open Sesame!'

The slaves brought benne to this country from Africa and it is found today (written in the very early 1930's) in many of the Negro's gardens. They use it to make benne candy and benne cakes from the seed to sell in the market and they are said to pound the bean into a kind of paste which they eat on their hominy. But, most interesting of all, is the fact that although they never heard of Ali Baba and his magic words; they sprinkle it on their doorsteps to bring them luck and to ward off ha'nts!"

-Harriet Ross Colquitt on Benne in The Savannah Cook Book, 1933

Benne seeds according to folklore and tradition contain the secrets of health and good luck. Southern cooks have long used these spicy seeds to improve their culinary treats. Little Benne Cakes were reported to be one of Andrew Jackson's favorite confections.

LITTLE BENNE CAKES

3/4 cup butter
1/2 cup sugar
1 egg
1/2 cup milk
3 cups flour

2 teaspoons baking powder
1/2 teaspoon salt
1/2 teaspoon nutmeg
grated rind of 1 orange

Heat oven to 350. Grease cookie sheet. Blend butter and sugar. Beat egg slightly and mix with milk. Sift dry ingredients and add alternately with liquid to butter and sugar. Add orange rind; mix well. Flour hands and roll a Tablespoon of dough into a ball; place on prepared cookie sheet. Repeat using all the dough. Flatten and bake about 10 minutes or until golden brown. Cool on rack, then glaze with:

3/4 cup honey   2 Tablespoons butter   3 Tbl. benne seeds, toasted

Cook honey, butter, and benne seed to hard ball stage. Cool slightly, then spoon over top of each cookie, working quickly as the glaze hardens fast. Reheat over hot water if necessary. Stir to keep the seeds from rising to the top. Nice with syllabub!
Commentary, The Nashville Cookbook, 1977

BENNE CANDY

Boil together:
1 pound brown sugar
small lump of butter

1/2 cup milk
1 Tablespoon of vinegar

When beginning to thread (comes out in strings from a spoon), take off the stove and beat into this mixture 1 1/2 cups of benne seed, which have been carefully picked and parched. Drop one teaspoon at a time on a buttered dish or paper and let cool.
The Savannah Cook Book, 1933

BENNE BRITTLE

2 cups sugar	1/2 teaspoon lemon extract
1/2 teaspoon vanilla extract	2 cups parched benne seeds

Add extracts to sugar. Melt sugar in saucepan, stirring constantly just as you would for peanut brittle. When sugar is melted, add benne seed, stirring it in quickly. Pour at once onto a marble slab to cool or pour into a lightly buttered pan. Mark into 1-inch squares, while still warm, and break into pieces along these lines when cold.
Mrs. Rhett, 200 Years of Charleston Cooking, 1930

GROUND NUT CAKES (In spite of its name, this is candy.)

1 quart molasses	1/2 cup butter
1 cup brown sugar	4 cups peanuts, parched and shelled

Combine first three ingredients and boil for 1/2 hour over a slow fire. Then add roasted and shelled peanuts and continue cooking for 15 minutes. Pour onto a lightly greased shallow pan and allow to harden. Break into pieces. This makes a somewhat chewy candy similar to taffy.

NOTE: Benne cakes are made using this recipe and substituting benne seed for the peanuts, which was much better known in Charleston than in the North.
Recipe found in Carolina Housewife as recounted in 200 Years of Charleston Cooking, 1930

MOLASSES CANDY

2 cups sugar	1/4 cup butter	1/8 teaspoon baking soda
2 cups sorghum molasses	1/4 teaspoon salt	
2/3 cup water	1/4 teaspoon vinegar	

Combine first three ingredients in a large saucepan. Cook over medium heat to 265 degrees. Remove from heat and add last four ingredients. Mixture will foam and then settle. Pour onto large platter or marble cooking board which has been greased lightly. Let cool. As soon as candy can be handled, dip fingers in butter and then in flour, and pull candy until it becomes light in color. When candy is light as desired, drop onto greased surface.
Farm Journal's Country Cookbook, 1959

CHOCOLATE BITS

6 ounce package chocolate	1 small can salted peanuts
6 ounce package butterscotch bits	1 can Chinese fried noodles

Melt packaged chocolate and butterscotch bits over hot water (double boiler). Add peanuts and noodles. Drop by teaspoons onto waxed paper. Chill until set.
Satsuma Tea Room, More Fun for the Cook, 1974

MILLION DOLLAR FUDGE

4 1/2 cups sugar	2 cups chopped nuts
dash of salt	12 ounces semi-sweet chocolate pieces
2 Tablespoons butter	4 squares unsweetened chocolate
1 2/3 cups evaporated milk	1 pint marshmallow cream

Mix sugar, salt, butter, and evaporated milk in large saucepan. Bring to a boil. Boil 6 minutes. Meanwhile, place remaining ingredients into a large mixing bowl. Pour the boiling syrup over the ingredients into large mixing bowl and beat until chocolate is all melted. Pour into a 9 x 14 x 2-inch buttered pan. Let stand a few hours before cutting. Store in tin (today a plastic) box. Makes 8 dozen.
Satsuma Tea Room, More Fun for the Cook, 1974

CHOCOLATE CARAMELS

1 cake of Baker's chocolate	1 stick butter
1 cup brown sugar	1 teaspoon vanilla
3 light cups granulated sugar	pinch of salt
1 cup milk	

Cook until thick and let cool somewhat before beating till smooth. Pour onto a buttered dish and cut into squares.
NOTE: Like velvet!
The Savannah Cook Book, 1933

CARAMELS

2 cups sugar	2 Tablespoons butter
4 squares chocolate, grated	1 teaspoon vanilla
1/2 cup milk	

Put all ingredients into a saucepan, stirring until sugar is dissolved and chocolate is melted. Then let boil without stirring until firm ball stage (246 F) is reached. Remove from the fire and turn at once into a lightly buttered square pan. Do not scrape the saucepan, as the last of the caramel mixture will probably sugar. If that is added to the rest, the whole may become granular. 24 very chocolaty caramels are produced with this recipe.
Anna Gray Cart, 200 Years of Charleston Cooking, 1930

GRANDMOTHER'S CARAMELS

3 cups brown sugar	1/2 cup milk
1 cup melted butter	3/4 cup scraped chocolate

Combine all the ingredients and cook slowly until a hard ball forms in water. When done, add one teaspoon vanilla and pour into greased pan. When cool, cut into squares.

NOTE: This candy is very apt to burn, if not watched closely.
The Southern Cookbook, 1939

COCONUT FUDGE

3 cups granulated sugar	3 Tablespoons of butter	1 teaspoon lemon extract
1 cup milk	1 cup grated coconut	

Put first four ingredients into a saucepan and stir until the sugar is dissolved. Cook until a soft ball is formed when a little of mixture is tested in cold water or until 236 F is reached. Add lemon extract, but do not stir. When mixture is lukewarm (110 F), beat until thick and creamy. Turn onto a buttered pan and mark with diamonds.
Mary Leize Simmons, 200 Years of Charleston Cooking, 1930

AUNT SARAH'S FUDGE

2 cups sugar	1 Tablespoon butter
2 squares unsweetened chocolate	1 teaspoon vanilla
1 cup table cream	

Cook ingredients together without stirring until they form a soft ball when dropped into water. Cool and beat until creamy. Add chopped nuts and vanilla. Pour into a buttered dish and cut into 1 inch squares when cool.
The Southern Cookbook, 1939

DIVINITY FUDGE

2 cups sugar	2 egg whites	1 Tablespoon vanillas
1/2 cup white corn syrup	1/16 teaspoon salt	extract
1/2 cup water		1/2 cup broken pecans

Combine sugar, corn syrup, and water in saucepan. Place over medium heat and stir until dissolved. Boil without stirring to a hard ball stage, when tested in cold water, or 265 degrees. While syrup is cooking, beat egg whites until stiff but not dry. Add salt and hot syrup, pouring slowly at first, and then faster, beating constantly. When mixture is stiff, beat with wooden spoon until creamy. Add nuts and extract. Pour onto a greased dish. Mark into 1-inch squares. Makes 24 squares.

NOTE: This candy has a melt in your mouth goodness. Chopped candied cherries and pineapple may be added instead of nuts. Almond extract may replace vanilla.
Nellie Stewart, The Nashville Cookbook, 1977

NO-COOK CANDY

1 cup honey	1 cup peanut butter
1 cup dry milk powder	chopped peanuts (optional)

Mix ingredients together and shape into small balls. Roll in chopped nuts or chocolate sprinkles. Makes 36 balls, 1 1/2 inch in diameter.

NOTE: This is a perfect recipe and a treat for kids to make.
Farm Journal's Country Cookbook, 1959

CREOLE KISSES

Beat egg whites of three eggs, very stiff, with 1/2 pound pulverized sugar, 1/2 teaspoon cream of tartar, and 1 teaspoon vanilla. Old receipts say, beat 1/2 hour, but if using an electric beater, 20 minutes. This time frame gives you just enough time to be getting your pecans cut up (today most people would buy pecans already chopped) and your pans lined with brown paper and well-greased.

When egg mixture is stiff enough to "peak," beat in a cup of pecan meat and drop a teaspoon at a time onto well-buttered brown paper (parchment) and bake in a very slow oven about 1/2 hour.

If the oven gets too warm, open the stove door or turn heat off until it cools. The meringues should really dry out and not cook quickly. If you want them a golden brown, turn up the heat a few minutes.
This amount makes about 3 dozen kisses.
The Savannah Cook Book, 1933

FRENCH CANDY

1 pound powdered sugar	1 teaspoon vanilla
2 egg whites, unbeaten	figs, nuts, dates

Mix sugar with egg whites and flavor with vanilla. Roll out on a sugared board, as you would any dough, and cut into pieces to cover the nuts or dates. Figs should be cut into small pieces before covering.
This uncooked candy may also be used for centers for stuffing dates and prunes and is very good for this purpose. These candies will keep for several days, if placed in an airtight tin box. Makes about 3 dozen candies.
Bossis Plantation recipe recounted in, 200 Years of Charleston Cooking, 1930

PECAN NUT CANDY

Boil together 1 can Eagle Brand condensed milk (no other brand will do), 2 cups brown sugar, 1 lump butter, and 1 teaspoon vanilla. When done, beat thoroughly and add 1 cup pecans.
The Savannah Cook Book, 1933

PEANUT CANDY

2 cups shelled peanuts	2 cups granulated sugar

Chop peanuts fine. Put sugar into a skillet and stir constantly until it is all melted. Then add peanuts and pour at once. When cold, break into pieces. Makes about 1 pound of candy.

NOTE: The finely chopped peanuts make a much more uniformly nutty candy than the usual peanut brittle.
Mary Leize Simons, 200 Years of Charleston Cooking, 1930

PEANUT BRITTLE (Also known as Goober Brittle)

2 cups shelled raw peanuts
2 cups sugar
1 cup white corn syrup
1 cup water

1/4 teaspoon salt
1 teaspoon butter
1/4 teaspoon baking soda

Remove coating from peanuts by blanching 3 minutes in boiling water and cooling under cold water. Drain thoroughly. Generously butter a marble cooking slab or two large platters. Combine sugar, syrup, and water in a heavy skillet. Cook slowly until sugar dissolves. Increase heat and cook to soft ball stage (238 degrees). Remove from heat while testing.

Add nuts and salt to syrup. Cook to hard crack stage (290 degrees). Stir constantly. Remove from heat; add butter and soda; stir to blend. Pour onto platters or slab. Pour very thin. Cool partially by lifting around edges with spatula. Keep spatula moving so it will not stick.

When firm, but still warm, turn over. In order to make thin brittle, pull while still warm. The thinner it is the better. When cool, crack into desired size pieces. Store at once in a tightly covered container. Makes about 2 pounds.
Chole Anne Yates, The Nashville Cookbook, 1977

RASPBERRY KISSES

3 egg whites
1/8 teaspoon salt
3 1/2 Tablespoons raspberry gelatin

3/4 cup sugar
1 Tablespoon vinegar
1 cup chocolate bits

Beat 3 egg whites with salt until foamy. Gradually add 3 1/2 Tablespoons raspberry gelatin and 3/4 cup sugar. Beat to stiff peaks, making sure sugar is well dissolved or your kisses will be sticky. Mix in Tablespoon of vinegar and fold in 1 cup of chocolate bits. Drop by teaspoons onto ungreased cookie sheets. Bake 25 minutes at 250. Turn off oven, but leave the kisses in the oven for another 20 minutes. Makes 7 dozen kisses.
Satsuma Tea Room, More Fun for the Cook, 1974

ORANGE SUGARED WALNUTS

3 cups sugar
1/2 cup water
1/2 cup orange juice

1 teaspoon grated orange peel
1 pound walnut halves

Cook sugar, water, and orange juice together to soft ball stage (238 degrees). Remove from heat, add orange peel and walnuts; stir until syrup begins to look cloudy. Before the mixture hardens drop from spoon onto waxed paper or buttered surface. Separate into smaller pieces. Makes about 3 1/2 dozen.
Easy-on-the-Cookbook, 1960

GRAPEFRUIT CANDY

Soak peel of three grapefruit in water and salt overnight. Drain off next morning. Cover with cold water and cook about two hours, changing water three times. Take out of water and slice into small strips. Put 1 1/2 cups sugar with 1/2 cup cold water to boil. Put fruit peels into this and let boil slowly until all the syrup boils away. Roll in granulated sugar while warm and let stand until cold.
The Savannah Cook Book, 1933

ENGLISH TOFFEE

1/2 pound milk chocolate
2 cups salted almonds
2 cups butter or margarine
2 cups sugar
2 Tablespoons light corn syrup
6 Tablespoons water
1 teaspoon vanilla extract

Cut chocolate fine. Melt in a double boiler over warm water, stirring occasionally. Slice 1 cup almonds into halves lengthwise; coarsely chop remaining nuts. Melt butter or margarine in heavy frying pan; add sugar, almond halves, corn syrup and water. Stir until sugar is dissolved. Cook very slowly to soft crack stage (290 degrees F); stir occasionally to prevent burning. Add vanilla extract. Pour to ¼-inch thickness into buttered pans or individual molds. When cool, spread melted chocolate evenly over the top and sprinkle with remaining chopped almonds. When hard, break into pieces. Makes about 3 pounds.
Holiday Hostess, 1958

PEACH LEATHER

"Let 'er rain! And if crops are suffering from lack of rain and you feel constrained to do your bit by your country; plan to make peach leather. You will bring down rain on the just and the unjust. Making peach leather is as good as a garden party or a county fair to ensure a downpour, since it is the sun that is the essence for making."
　　　　　　　　　　　　　　　　-Harriet Ross Colquitt, The Savannah Cook Book, 1933

"It is amusing that anything so delicious should bear so dull a name. Peach leather is the most famous confection of the old plantation days. It is dependent on the sun for making and if possible, select a week when there is likely to be hot sunshine to make it. If the sun is contrary and refuses to shine, more time must be allowed for exposure of peach juice to the sun's rays."
　　　　　　　　　　　　　　　　-Miss Rutledge, 200 Years of Charleston Cooking, 1930

PEACH LEATHER

1 peck peaches peeled and mashed through a colander. For each gallon of peach pulp add 3/4 pound sugar and let come to a boil. Remove from fire and spread onto tin pie plates and put in the sun to dry. Old receipts (recipes) say the pie plates should stay in the sun 3 or 4 days, being brought in at night. When the mixture is dry enough to peel away from the plate, it is done. Sprinkle top of leather with sugar. Cut into strips and roll into wafer-like pieces of any length preferred. It will keep indefinitely in a tin.
The Savannah Cook Book, 1933

PECAN PRALINES

1 pound brown sugar
1/2 pound freshly peeled and cut pecans
1 spoon butter (literal)
4 Tablespoons water

This recipe comes from an old New Orleans newspaper, but any type of pecan will work. Just make sure fresh pecans or refrigerated-fresh pecans are used. Set sugar and water to cook. In using the water, just add enough to melt the sugar sufficiently. As it begins to boil, add pecans which have been well-shelled and cleaned. Cut some into fine pieces, others into halves, and others again into quarters. Let all boil until mixture begins to bubble. Be careful to stir the mixture constantly until syrup begins to thicken and turn to sugar. Take it off the stove at once and spread it out to dry, cool, using a marble slab, marble cooking board, candy board or buttered parchment cooking paper. These pecan pralines are absolutely delicious.
The Picayune Creole Cook Book, 1922

NEW ORLEANS PRALINES

Put 1 cup sugar into a saucepan with just enough water to cover well. Cook until it ropes slightly. Add about 1 teaspoon of butter, 1 teaspoon of vanilla and 2 cups pecans, chopped. Stir hard until creamy and drop or roll into balls.
The Savannah Cook Book, 1933

FLORIDA COCONUT PRALINES

2 cups sugar
2 cups freshly-grated coconut
1/2 cup water

Cook the sugar and water together until it makes a syrup. Take from fire and add coconut. Cook again, stirring constantly, until it forms a soft ball when put into cold water. Drop onto buttered platter and set aside to cool and harden.
The Southern Cookbook, 1939

OLD FASHIONED OATMEAL COOKIES

3/4 cup butter
1/2 cup granulated sugar
1 cup firmly packed brown sugar, sieved
2 eggs
1 1/2 cups sifted flour
1 teaspoon baking soda
1 teaspoon salt
1 1/2 teaspoons cinnamon
1/2 teaspoon nutmeg
1/4 cup milk
3 cups rolled oats, uncooked
1 cup raisins

Cream butter; add sugar; cream thoroughly. Beat in eggs, one at a time, beating well after each addition. Sift dry ingredients together and add alternately with milk. Stir in oats and raisins; mix well. Drop rounded Tablespoons of dough onto ungreased baking sheet. Flatten slightly. Bake at 375 F for 10-12 minutes. Makes about 3 1/2 dozen cookies, 3 inches in diameter.
Easy-on-the-Cook Book, 1960

LOUISIANA CREAM PRALINES

1 pound light brown sugar
dash of salt
3/4 cup evaporated milk

1 Tablespoon butter
2 cups (1/2 pound) pecan halves

Cover a baking sheet with aluminum foil or butter a baking sheet slightly. Mix sugar, salt, evaporated milk and butter in medium-size saucepan. Stir over low heat until sugar is dissolved to 234 degrees. Add pecans, stirring constantly. Remove from heat and let cool 5 minutes. Stir rapidly until mixture begins to thicken and coat pecans lightly. Drop rapidly from a teaspoon onto baking sheet to form patties. (If candy becomes too stiff to handle easily towards the end, stir in a few drops of hot water). Let pralines stand until cool and set.
Satsuma Tea Room, More Fun for the Cook, 1974

DELUXE FUDGY BROWNIES

4 squares unsweetened chocolate
1/2 cup margarine
4 eggs
2 cups sugar

1 cup sifted flour
1 teaspoon vanilla
1 cup coarsely chopped nuts

Melt chocolate and butter together over hot water. Cool slightly. Beat eggs until foamy, gradually add sugar, beating it thoroughly after each egg addition. Add chocolate mixture and blend. Stir in flour. Then add vanilla and nuts. Spread in greased 9 x 9 x 2-inch pan. Bake at 325 degrees F for 40-45 minutes. Cool in pan, then cut into squares or bars.

NOTE: Delicious served straight from the freezer or warmed with vanilla ice cream or whipped cream.
Satsuma Tea Room, More Fun for the Cook, 1974

PEANUT BUTTER BROWNIES

1/3 cup margarine
1/2 cup peanut butter
1 cup sugar
1/4 cup firmly packed brown sugar
2 eggs

1 cup sifted flour
1 teaspoon baking powder
1/4 teaspoon salt
6 ounces semi-sweet chocolates
1/2 teaspoon vanilla

Beat margarine and peanut butter together until light. Gradually add sugar and brown sugar, creaming well. Add eggs, one at a time, beating well after each addition. Add flour, baking powder, and salt; mixing well. Add chocolate bits and vanilla. Spread mixture in well-greased, 9-inch pan. Bake at 350 for 30-35 minutes. Cool and cut into squares.

NOTE: These are so good, but care must be taken not to bake them too long or they will be too hard.
Satsuma Tea Room, More Fun for the Cook, 1974

BROWNIES

4 squares unsweetened chocolate
1 1/3 cups margarine
5 eggs
2 2/3 cups sugar

1 1/3 cups cake flour
2 teaspoons vanilla
1/2 cup chopped nuts

Preheat oven to 350 F. Melt chocolate and margarine. Cool. Beat eggs until light. Blend in sugar and flour. Add chocolate mixture and vanilla. Mix thoroughly. Fold in nuts. Pour into a greased 9 x 14 x 2-inch baking pan. Bake about 35 minutes. Yields 3 1/2 dozen brownies (1 1/2 x 2 inches).
Specialty of the Home Economics Cafeteria, University of Illinois, Home Economics Faculty Favorites, 1965

FUDGE TOPPED BROWNIES

1 cup sifted flour
1 teaspoon baking powder
1/2 teaspoon salt
4 ounces unsweetened chocolate
1/2 cup butter or margarine

2 eggs well beaten
1 cup sugar
1 cup chopped pecans
2 teaspoons vanilla
fudge frosting

Sift together flour, baking powder and salt. Melt chocolate and butter over low heat. Remove from heat. Add eggs, then sugar and beat well. Blend in flour mixture; mix thoroughly. Stir in pecans and vanilla. Spread batter in well-greased 9-inch square pan. Bake at 350 F about 35 minutes. When cool, frost with fudge frosting and cut into squares. Yields 16 brownies.
Easy-on-the-Cook Book, 1960

BROWNIES-CHOCOLATE INDIANS

2/3 cup sifted flour
1/2 teaspoon baking powder
1/4 teaspoon salt
6 1/2 Tablespoons butter or shortening
2 squares unsweetened chocolate, melted

1 cup sugar
2 eggs, beaten well
1 teaspoon vanilla
1/2 cup walnut meats, broken

Sift flour once. After measuring, add baking powder and salt. Sift again. Then add butter to melted chocolate and blend. Cream sugar and eggs; add flour, vanilla and nuts. Bake in a greased pan, preferably 8 x 8 x 2 inches in a moderate oven (350 F) for 35 minutes. Before removing from pan, cut into squares. This recipe will make 2 dozen brownies.
The Southern Cookbook, 1939

GEORGIA PECAN BROWNIES

2 egg whites
1 cup brown sugar
1/2 teaspoon maple flavoring
1 cup pecans, chopped
1 cup fine dry bread crumbs

Beat egg whites stiff, add sugar and flavoring. Stir well. Combine nuts and crumbs. Fold in egg whites. Shape into small balls on buttered baking tin, bake in 325 F oven until brown
The Southern Cookbook, 1939

CONGO SQUARES

3/4 cup margarine
2 1/4 cups (1 pound) brown sugar
3 eggs
2 3/4 cups flour
1/2 teaspoon salt
2 1/2 teaspoons baking powder
1 cup broken nut meats
6 ounces semi-sweet chocolate morsels

Melt margarine in a large saucepan. Add brown sugar and mix well. Cool slightly. Add eggs one at a time, beating well after each addition. Sift together flour, baking powder and salt. Add flour mixture to mixture in the saucepan. Mix well. Add broken nut meats and chocolate morsels. Pour into 2 greased pans (7 1/2 x 11 x 4 1/2). Bake at 325 F to 350 F for 25-30 minutes. When almost cool, cut into squares. Yields 48.
Satsuma Tea Room, More Fun for the Cook, 1974

CHOCOLATE COCONUT BARS

2 cups graham cracker crumbs
1/2 cup sugar
1/2 cup melted butter
1 can Eagle Brand milk
1 cup sweet chocolate chips, melted
1 Tablespoon peanut butter

Mix crumbs, sugar, and melted butter. Pat into pan. Bake 10 minutes at 350. Mix Eagle Brand milk and coconut. Spread over crust. Bake 15 minutes. Spread melted chocolate mixed with peanut butter on top.
Satsuma Tea Room, Fun for the Cook, 1968

SUGAR BISCUITS

2/3 cup sugar
2 Tablespoons butter
1 egg
1 1/3 cups flour
1/2 teaspoon cinnamon

Despite the lack of baking powder and liquid, this recipe is correct! The result is a cinnamon-flavored sugar cookie which compares favorably with more expensive ones.
Cream butter and dry ingredients, mixed and sifted together. Roll in waxed paper and place roll in ice box to chill for several hours or overnight. When ready to bake, cut into thin slices and lay onto a well-greased baking sheet. Bake in a quick oven (425 F) for about 12 minutes. Makes two dozen cookies.
Miss Harleston's Notebook, Bossis Plantation recipe recounted in 200 Years of Charleston Cooking, 1930

CHOCOLATE-NUT DROPS

1/2 cup butter or margarine	1/2 teaspoon salt
6 Tablespoons brown sugar	few drops hot water
6 Tablespoons honey	1/2 teaspoon vanilla
1 egg, unbeaten	6 ounces semi-sweet chocolate pieces
1 1/4 cups sifted flour	1/2 cup chopped walnuts
1/2 teaspoon baking soda	

Cream butter; gradually add sugar and honey, mixing well. Beat in egg. Sift together flour, soda, and salt. Add to creamed mixture. Add water and mix to blend. Add vanilla, chocolate pieces and nuts. Drop from teaspoon onto greased baking sheet. Bake in a moderate oven (375 F) 10 to 12 minutes. Cool slightly before removing from sheet. Makes about 3 dozen.
Farm Journal's Country Cookbook, 1959

FAVORITE HONEY BAR

1/2 cup shortening	1/2 teaspoon baking powder
1/2 cup sugar	1/4 teaspoon salt
1/2 cup honey	1 cup quick-cooking rolled oats
1 egg, well beaten	1 cup flaked coconut
2/3 cup sifted flour	1 teaspoon vanilla
1/2 teaspoon baking soda	1/2 cup chopped nuts

Cream shortening, sugar and honey until light and fluffy. Add egg and blend. Sift flour with soda, baking powder and salt; add to creamed mixture. Add oats, coconut, vanilla and nuts. Spread in greased 10 1/2 x 15 pan; bake in moderate oven (350 F) for 20 to 25 minutes. When cool, cut into bars, about 1 1/2 x 2 1/2 . Makes 36 bars. Variation: Sprinkle confectioners' sugar over tops of the bars before serving.

NOTE: Better double this recipe because of the cookie jar raiders eating these chewy cookies.
Farm Journal's Country Cookbook, 1959

APRICOT SQUARES

1/2 cup butter or margarine	12 ounce can apricot filling
1 1/2 cups sugar	2 egg whites
1/4 teaspoon vanilla	1/4 cup chopped nuts
2 egg yolks, well beaten	

Cut butter into flour with a pastry blender as for a pie crust. Add 1/4 cup sugar, vanilla, and egg yolks. Mix well. Press like a crust into a shallow 8 x 12 x 1-inch pan. Spread apricot filling over the dough. Beat egg whites stiff; beat in remaining 1/4 cup sugar gradually. Spread meringue over filling. Sprinkle with chopped nuts. Bake at 350 F for 30 to 35 minutes. When cool cut into 2-inch squares. Makes 24 squares.
Easy-on-the-Cook Book, 1960

APRICOT BARS

3/4 cup margarine
1 teaspoon baking powder
1 cup brown sugar

1 1/2 cups quick-cooking rolled oats
1 1/2 cups, sifted flour
1 cup apricot or strawberry jam

Mix flour, baking powder, brown sugar, and oats. Cut into butter until crumbly. Press 2/3 of oat mixture in 13 x 9 1/2 x 2-inch baking pan. Spread with jam. Cover with remainder of crumbs. Press down slightly. Bake at 350 for 30 minutes or until lightly brown on top. Cool; cut into bars. Yields 2 dozen bars.
Satsuma Tea Room, More Fun for the Cook, 1974

APRICOT BALLS

12 ounces dried apricots
juice of 1/2 lemon

2 cups coconut
1/2 cup condensed milk

Grind apricots, add coconut and liquid together with condensed milk. Add lemon juice and knead all together. Form into small balls and roll in powdered sugar. Chill. Makes 20 balls.
Satsuma Tea Room, More Fun for the Cook, 1974

DATE NUT BALLS

1/2 cup butter
1 cup sugar
2 eggs

1 1/2 cups chopped dates
3 cups Rice Krispies
2 teaspoons vanilla

1 cup chopped almonds

Mix butter, sugar, eggs, and dates. Cook over low fire in skillet 15 minutes, stirring constantly. Remove from fire, add vanilla, Rice Krispies and chopped almonds. Do not bake. Roll into balls the size of a walnut while still warm and roll in powdered sugar.

NOTE: These will stay crisp and delicious for months.
Satsuma Tea Room, Fun for the Cook, 1968

DIVINITY CANDY WITH JELL-O

3 cups water
3/4 cup light corn syrup
3/4 cup water

3 ounces gelatin, any fruit flavor
whites of 2 eggs
1 cup chopped nuts, optional

Bring all ingredients, except gelatin and eggs, to a boil over low heat. Keep cooking, stirring occasionally, until hard ball stage (250 degrees). In the meantime, beat 2 egg whites. Keep beating until stiff but not dry. Add a 3-ounce package of fruit gelatin powder (any flavor) a Tablespoon at a time. Beat until it stands in stiff peaks. Pour syrup over egg whites, slowly, keep beating about 10 minutes until it holds shape and loses gloss. Add 1 cup chopped nuts. Can be either poured into well-greased pan or dropped by the spoonful onto waxed paper. Can also be cut into strips and rolled in grated coconut.
Satsuma Tea Room, More Fun for the Cook, 1974

CARAMEL APPLES

2 cups brown sugar
1/2 cup water
1/2 cup evaporated milk
2 Tablespoons corn syrup
1 Tablespoon vinegar
12 medium apples, washed

Remove stem from apple and stick skewer upright into stem end. Cook first 5 ingredients together and boil until a few drops poured into cold water form a hard ball (245-248 degrees F) Proceed by dipping the apple to coat with mixture and cool in cold water. Cool on wax paper.
The Settlement Cook Book, 1940

MARSHMALLOW NUT BALLS

1/2 cup sugar
2 cups sugar
2 Tablespoons hot water
1 cup milk
1 cup white Karo (corn) syrup
1 teaspoon vanilla
2 Tablespoons butter
1 pound large marshmallows
pecan pieces

Put 1/2 cup sugar in iron skillet to caramelize. Add hot water. Cook 2 cups sugar, milk, Karo (corn) syrup to soft ball stage. Do not stir. Add the caramel syrup, butter, and vanilla. Beat until creamy. Dip each marshmallow in with 2 forks. Then dip as a covering in broken pecan pieces. If mixture hardens during the process, put over hot water to melt.
Satsuma Tea Room, More Fun for the Cook, 1974

LEMON LAYER SQUARES

NOTE: A crunchy crust cookie square with a tart lemon filling.

1/2 cup butter
1 cup flour
1/4 cup confectioners' sugar

Heat oven to 350 F. Blend butter into flour and sugar until mixture clings together. Spread over the bottom of a 9-inch square pan (ungreased). Bake 10 minutes. Add filling and bake 20 minutes longer.

FILLING

2 eggs, beaten lightly
1 cup sugar
2 Tablespoons fresh lemon juice
2 Tablespoons flour
1 teaspoon lemon rind

Mix filling ingredients and pour over pre-baked mixture. Bake about 20 minutes longer until set, but not brown. Sift confectioners' sugar over warm top. Cool and cut into squares. Serves 10 to 12.

NOTE: Squares can be frozen, but are best returned to room temperature, slightly warm, before serving.
Jean Sharp, The Nashville Cookbook, 1977

JUMBLES

1/2 cup shortening	1 teaspoon vanilla	1/2 teaspoon salt
1 cup sugar	2 cups sifted flour	1/2 cup buttermilk
1 egg	1/2 teaspoon baking soda	

Cream shortening; add sugar gradually, creaming thoroughly. Add egg and vanilla; beat well. Sift dry ingredients together; add alternately with the buttermilk to the creamed mixture. Turn onto greased and floured 10 x 15-inch baking pan.

TOPPING

1/2 cup chopped nuts   1/4 cup sugar   1 teaspoon cinnamon

Sprinkle with opping made by mixing the nuts, sugar, and cinnamon. Bake in a 400 F oven 15 minutes. Cut into squares while still warm.

NOTE: Jumbles can be frozen.
Easy-on-the-Cook Book, 1960

DIAMOND DAINTIES

3/4 cup butter or margarine	1 teaspoon grated lemon peel
1 1/4 cups sugar	2 1/2 cups sifted flower
2 eggs	1/2 cup corn meal
1 teaspoon vanilla	gumdrops or flaked coconut

Cream butter. Gradually add sugar and beat until light and fluffy. Add eggs, vanilla, and lemon peel. Sift together flour and corn meal; add to creamed mixture, blending well. Chill dough several hours. Roll out on lightly floured board or pastry cloth to 1/8-inch thickness. Cut dough into diamond-shaped cookies. Place gumdrop or a little coconut in center of each. Place on greased baking sheets. Bake at 375 F 6 to 8 minutes. Makes 10 dozen small cookies.
Easy-on-the-Cook Book, 1960

COCONUT ORANGE SQUARES

1 1/2 cups flour	2 eggs
1/4 teaspoon baking powder	2 teaspoons orange rind
1 teaspoon salt	1/4 cup orange juice
1/2 cup butter	1 1/2 cups coconut
1 2/3 cups sugar	

Heat oven to 350 F. Grease and flour a 9 x 9 x 2-inch pan. Sift flour, baking powder, and salt together. Cream butter and sugar together until crumbly. Add eggs, orange rind, orange juice, and 2 cups coconut. Add the sifted dry ingredients and mix well. Spread in prepared pan. Top evenly with mixture of 1/2 cup coconut, 2 Tablespoons melted butter, 2 Tablespoons sugar. Bake for 25 minutes. Makes 24 squares.
Edna T. Matthews, The Nashville Cookbook, 1977

ALMOND CRESCENTS

1 cup margarine	4 cups flour
2/3 cup Crisco	1 cup blanched almonds, ground
1 teaspoon salt	1 teaspoon vanilla extract
3/4 cup sugar	1 teaspoon almond extract

Mix the ingredients. Form into crescents. Place onto ungreased cookie sheets. Bake in a moderate oven (325 degrees). While hot, roll, coat with powdered sugar. Cool on raised cooling racks.

NOTE: This recipe comes from my wife (David S.); passed to her by way of her mother and grandmother, etc. No Christmas or Thanksgiving goes by without marathon cookie-making. The spotlight cookie of her baking so many different and assorted cookies is the almond crescent. They are that good. This cookie is another prime example of Southern cooking or the tradition that is associated with Southern cooking. This recipe has been handed down and used by four generations of her family, which is supported by known evidence, but I would have no problem at all going out on and a limb and saying that this recipe goes back even further in her family tree; generations handing down the recipe of this wonderful cookie orally, not written down.
Lisa Atkinson & Florence Atkinson

SPICE PECANS OR WALNUTS

1 cup pecans or walnuts	1/8 teaspoon allspice
2 Tablespoons butter or margarine	salt
1/8 teaspoon cinnamon	

Melt butter. Add nuts; heat slowly 5 minutes or until nuts are thoroughly heated, stirring occasionally. Drain on absorbent paper. Shake in bowl with spices. Return to absorbent paper to drain. Sprinkle with salt
Easy-on-the-Cook Book, 1960

BUTTERSCOTCH

1 cup molasses	1 cup sugar	1/2 cup butter

The original recipe's sole directions are *"Boil until done"!*

Put all ingredients into a saucepan and cook until crack stage, or 270 F is reached. Turn at once into a lightly buttered pan and mark into squares while still warm. When candy is cold, it can be broken into pieces. This amount makes 3 dozen squares of butterscotch with a decided molasses flavor and rather darker than the usual butterscotch, but excellent in taste.
Mary Leize Simons, 200 Years of Charleston Cooking, 1930

PEANUT CLUSTERS

2/3 cup condensed milk
1 1/2 cups Spanish peanuts, salted
6 ounce package chocolate chips
1 teaspoon vanilla

Melt chocolate chips over a double boiler and remove from heat. Add condensed milk, vanilla, and peanuts. Mix and drop by teaspoon onto a buttered cookie sheet or on wax paper. Makes 1 ½ dozen.
Satsuma Tea Room, More Fun for the Cook, 1974

MERINGUE GLACES

2 egg whites
2/3 cup sugar
1/2 teaspoon vinegar
1/2 teaspoon mint extract
1/2 teaspoon vanilla extract
few drops green food coloring

Beat egg whites until stiff, but not dry. Gradually add sugar, beating continually with rotary beater. Beat in vinegar, flavoring extracts and coloring. Drop from Tablespoon onto greased baking pan, allowing room for glaces to spread. (Drop onto sheet from teaspoon if smaller glaces are desired). Bake in slow oven (300 degree F) 20 to 25 minutes. Serve with ice cream or mousse between glaces or on top. Top with a fruit sauce and whipped cream. Makes about 12 large glaces.

NOTE: Especially pretty dessert and *extra* good topped with strawberries or raspberries.
Holiday Hostess, 1958

PUMPKIN BARS

BAR MIXTURE

4 eggs
1 2/3 cups granulated sugar
1 cup cooking oil
16 ounce can pumpkin
2 teaspoons baking powder
2 cups flour
2 teaspoons cinnamon
1 teaspoon salt
1 teaspoon baking soda
nuts, chopped (your choice)

Beat eggs, sugar, oil, and pumpkin until light and fluffy. Sift together baking powder, flour cinnamon, salt and baking soda and add to pumpkin mixture. Spread in an ungreased 15 x 10 x 1-inch baking pan. Bake at 350 F. for 25 to 30 minutes. Cool cake and then frost with cream cheese icing. Put chopped nuts on top. Very moist bars.

CREAM CHEESE ICING

8 ounces cream cheese, softened
1/2 cup butter, softened
1 teaspoon vanilla
2 cups powdered sugar, sifted

Beat cream cheese and butter together until light and fluffy. Add vanilla, then powdered sugar. Frost the bars.
Donna Decker, Fruit of the Spirit, Mt. Bethel United Methodist Church, Marietta, GA, 2006

ORANGE SLICE BARS

1 pound candy orange slices
2 cups sifted flour
1/2 teaspoon salt
1 pound light brown sugar

4 eggs, slightly beaten
1 cup chopped nuts
1 teaspoon vanilla

Cut orange slices with scissors dipped into water and add flour and salt in mixing bowl. Toss lightly to coat. Add remaining ingredients and mix well. Spread in a greased 13 x 9 x 2 pan. Bake at (350 F) for 40-45 minutes. Cut into bars or squares and roll in granulated sugar. Yields 24.
Satsuma Tea Room, More Fun for the Cook, 1974

PECAN SQUARES

Beat 4 eggs light with 1 pound of medium brown sugar. Cook this in a double boiler for 20 minutes. Take off stove and add 1 1/2 cups flour (in which 1 1/2 teaspoons baking powder have been sifted), 1 teaspoon vanilla, and 1 1/2 cups chopped pecans. Spread one half-inch thick in greased, floured pan and cook 12 minutes. Cut into squares.
The Savannah Cook Book, 1933

PECAN FONDANT

3 cups sugar
1 cup water
1 1/2 Tablespoons butter

1 teaspoon vanilla
1/8 teaspoon salt
2 cups chopped pecan meats

Cook sugar and water until it forms a soft ball when tried in cold water. Remove from fire and beat until creamy; add the butter, vanilla, salt, and nut meats and pour into a buttered dish to cover bottom 1/2 inch deep. When set, cut into squares.
The Southern Cookbook, 1939

CANDIED ORANGE OR GRAPEFRUIT PEEL

3 grapefruit or 6 orange peelings
1 teaspoon salt

3 cups sugar
1 cup water

Wash fruit and peel carefully, removing all the pulp. Cut into strips about 1/4-inch wide, add 1 teaspoon salt to peel and cover with water. Boil for 15 minutes, then pour off the water and add fresh water. Boil for about 20 minutes. Change the water again and boil for another 20 minutes. After the third boiling cover with 2 1/2 cups of sugar and 1 cup water. Boil, stirring occasionally until the syrup has boiled away. Spread on crumpled paper and, before it is entirely cold, roll the peel strips in the other 1/2 cup of sugar.
The Southern Cookbook, 1939

BREAKFAST & BRUNCH

"Some Southern homes make quite an event of the 'Guest Breakfast', which frequently consists of fruit, chicken hash, hot cakes, sausage, corn bread, pie, and coffee. And then there is that celebrated ritual known as the 'Kentucky Breakfast,' which is said to consist of a big beefsteak, a quart of Bourbon and a hound dog. The dog eats the beefsteak."
-The Southern Cookbook, 1939

CORN MEAL MASH

1 cup corn meal
2 quarts boiling water
1 teaspoon salt

Moisten corn meal with enough cold water to make a paste. Stir this paste into boiling salted water, beating thoroughly. Let cool over a slow fire stirring almost constantly for 1 hour. Put into a double boiler and cook 3 hours longer. Serve hot with sugar and cream.

TO FRY: Pack hot into well-greased baking pan and let stand until cold and solid. Cut into 1/2 inch strips, roll in flour and fry on buttered griddle until brown on both sides. Serve with syrup and sausage.
The Southern Cookbook, 1939

RICE FLOUR TODDLES

NOTE: Since there was no indication on the receipt as to how the toddles were to be cooked, we were forced to do a bit of experimenting before we concluded that the best thing to do was to bake them as we would griddle cakes. They are good served with butter and jelly or butter with maple syrup.

1 cup cooked hominy
1/2 cup rice flour
1 egg
1 teaspoon salt
1/2 cup milk (about)

Mix rice flour and salt with hominy and add beaten egg which has been combined with milk. Drop onto a well-greased griddle and bake until each side is brown. This makes about 12 small cakes.

NOTE: Wheat flour, used in place of rice flour, brings out the taste of the hominy more prominently.
Miss C. Blanche Moodie, 200 Years of Charleston Cooking, 1930

FRENCH GRIDDLE CAKES

1 1/2 pints sifted flour	1 ounce (2 Tablespoons) sugar
6 eggs	1 cup milk
1 Tablespoon butter	

Beat yolks of eggs and sugar until very light. Then add flour and melted butter. Then add the warm milk. Beat all until very light. Add a half teaspoon baking powder, then add whites of eggs, beaten to a stiff froth. Beat all till very smooth. Drop a Tablespoon at a time upon the hot griddle; turn quickly and bake on the other side, allowing about two minutes in all. Place on a hot platter, butter well and spread with jelly, then roll up and dust with powdered sugar and serve very hot.
The Picayune Creole Cook Book, 1922

FRENCH PANCAKES

3/4 pound (7/8 cup) flour	1/2 pint cold milk
4 eggs	4 ounces (1/2 cup) powdered sugar

Sift flour into a bowl. Break in eggs; beat well and add 1 ounce powdered sugar. Mix thoroughly with a spatula and then add the cold milk, pouring it in gradually. Mix well for 6 minutes. Have ready at hand a clean griddle buttered lightly. When hot, drop onto it about 2 large spoons of the batter at a time.

Let the cakes bake 2 minutes on each side by turning and bake 2 minutes on the other side. Lay pancakes onto a dish; sprinkle generously with powdered sugar. Continue baking the cakes, as fast as possible, until all batter is used. Sprinkle each in turn with powdered sugar. This will make 1 dozen pancakes.
The Picayune Creole Cook Book, 1922

APPLE GRIDDLE CAKES

2 cups sifted flour	2 cups sweet milk
5 teaspoons baking powder	6 Tablespoons melted shortening or oil
2 teaspoons salt	2 eggs, beaten
3 Tablespoons sugar	1 cup finely chopped unpeeled apples
1 teaspoon cinnamon	

Sift together flour, baking powder, salt, sugar and cinnamon. Add milk, shortening and flour mixture to eggs; beat until smooth. Fold in apples. Heat griddle or heavy frying pan slowly until moderately hot. Test the temperature by sprinkling a few drops of water on it. If the drops "dance," temperature is right. Grease griddle very lightly before baking. Pour in about 1/4 cup batter for each cake. Bake until top is bubbly and edges dry. Flip and brown on other side. Makes 2 1/2 dozen cakes 4 to 5 inches in diameter or 1 dozen 6 to 7 inches in diameter.
Farm Journal Country Cookbook, 1959

FLANNEL CAKES

2 eggs	1/2 teaspoon salt
1 1/2 cups milk	2 teaspoons sugar
2 cups flour	2 Tablespoons melted butter
3 teaspoons baking powder	

Sift baking powder, salt, sugar, and flour. Beat the egg yolks well and add to the milk. Pour this into flour, add melted butter and lastly well beaten egg whites. Drop by spoonful onto hot, greased griddle. Brown on both sides and serve hot with syrup. Pork sausage goes well with flannel cakes.
The Southern Cookbook, 1939

GREEN CORN GRIDDLE CAKES

1 quart finely-grated green corn	1/2 teaspoon salt
1 pint milk	1 cup flour
4 eggs	1 Tablespoon melted butter

Beat eggs separately (yolks and whites), then add well-beaten yolks to the corn. Add salt, melted butter, and milk and mix well. Then add sufficient flour to make a thin batter and finally, the egg whites beaten to a stiff froth. Bake on a hot griddle, butter generously and serve very hot. This is a great Creole cake and very delicious.
The Picayune Creole Cook Book, 1922

SOUR MILK GRIDDLE CAKES

1 1/2 cups flour	1 teaspoon baking soda
1 cup sour milk or buttermilk	1 Tablespoon sugar
1 Tablespoon melted butter	2 eggs
1/2 teaspoon salt	

Sift flour and sugar; dissolve soda in buttermilk and add to flour. Drop in the unbeaten eggs, beat well and lastly add melted butter. Drop by spoonful onto a hot greased griddle and brown on both sides.
The Southern Cookbook, 1939

GRIDDLE CAKES

2 cups flour	2 Tablespoons melted butter
2 eggs	1 heaping Tablespoon sugar
2 teaspoons baking powder	1 1/2 cups milk
1/2 teaspoon salt	

Sift flour, salt, sugar, and baking powder, add milk and egg yolks, beat well and then add melted butter. Beat egg whites to a stiff froth and add last. Bake on a hot griddle greased lightly.
The Southern Cookbook, 1939

CREPES SUZETTE NEW ORLEANS

2 eggs	1/4 teaspoon salt
1 1/2 cups milk	1 cup cake flour
grated rind of 1/2 lemon	1 Tablespoon powdered sugar

Beat eggs until light and lemon colored; gradually stir in milk, lemon rind, and salt. Sift powdered sugar with flour and slowly beat milk mixture into flour. Drop batter by large Tablespoons onto a hot greased griddle. The batter should be thin enough to spread very easily. Fry slowly on one side; turn and fry until other side is golden brown.

SUZETTE SAUCE

1 wineglass champagne, white wine, or brandy	1 juice of an orange and grated rind
12 lumps sugar	1/2 cup melted butter

Pour a wineglass of champagne, white wine, or brandy into a chafing dish. Crush lumps of sugar in orange juice and add to champagne, which has been heating in the chafing dish. Add a little of grated orange rind and 1/2 cup melted butter. Cover and cook until a thick, smooth sauce results. Dip each pancake as it is prepared into the sauce; lift it out and roll it; sprinkle with powdered sugar and serve immediately.
The Southern Cookbook, 1939

GRIDDLE CAKES (A Master Recipe)

2 cups sifted flour	2 eggs, beaten
5 teaspoons baking powder	2 cups milk
2 teaspoons salt	6 Tablespoons melted shortening or oil
3 Tablespoons sugar	

Sift flour along with baking powder, salt and sugar. Beat eggs in a mixing bowl. Add milk, shortening and flour mixture. Stir until blended. Heat griddle or heavy frying pan slowly, until moderately hot. Test temperature by sprinkling a few drops of water onto it. When the drops stay round and bounce about, the temperature is right. If you use an electric griddle, set temperatures according to instructions.
Grease very lightly before baking each batch. Ladle or pour about 1/4 cup batter for each cake onto hot griddle. Bake until top side is full of bubbles that begin to bake and edges are dry. Turn (flip) and brown on other side. Makes about 2 1/2 dozen cakes 4 to 5 inches in diameter or 1 dozen 6 to 7 inches in diameter.

NOTE: To make sour milk griddle cakes, substitute 2 1/4 cup sour milk or buttermilk for the sweet milk. For leavening use 1 teaspoon baking soda and 1 Tablespoon baking powder.
Farm Journal's Country Cookbook, 1959

SOUR MILK/BUTTERMILK GRIDDLE CAKES

Substitute 2 1/4 cups buttermilk for sweet milk and add 1 teaspoon baking powder.
Farm Journal's Country Cookbook, 1959

GRIDDLE CAKES VARIATIONS

- **APPLE GRIDDLE CAKES**
  Add 1 cup finely chopped unpeeled raw apples and 1 teaspoon cinnamon.

- **BLUEBERRY GRIDDLE CAKES**
  Add 1 cup frozen sweetened blueberries, thawed and drained.

- **BANANA GRIDDLE CAKES**
  Add 2 mashed, ripe bananas.

- **DATE GRIDDLE CAKES**
  Add 1 cup chopped dates.

- **PINEAPPLE GRIDDLE CAKES**
  Add 1 cup well-drained crushed pineapple.

- **PECAN GRIDDLE CAKES**
  Add 1/2 cup chopped pecans.

- **CORN GRIDDLE CAKES**
  Add 1 cup cream style corn.

- **RICE GRIDDLE CAKES**
  Add 1 to 2 cups leftover rice.
  1/2 teaspoon cinnamon or nutmeg peps up the flavor.
  Add a little milk if the batter needs thinning.

- **CHEESE GRIDDLE CAKES**
  Add 1/2 cup grated Parmesan cheese.
  Farm Journal's Country Cookbook, 1959

GEORGIA FLAPJACKS

2 cups flour
1 1/2 teaspoons baking soda
1/2 teaspoon salt
1 Tablespoon sugar

2 eggs
2 cups sour milk
1 1/2 Tablespoons melted butter

Sift flour and measure two cups. Sift again. Add soda, salt, and sugar. Mix well and sift once more. Beat eggs lightly, add milk and gradually add these ingredients to the flour mixture. Beat until smooth and free from lumps and then add butter. Pour batter into a pitcher. Heat a griddle or a heavy fry pan and butter it. Pour enough batter onto the fry pan to make a cake about 5 inches in diameter. Cook until porous and brown underneath and then brown on the other side.
The Southern Cookbook, 1939

WAFFLES: SOME TECHNIQUES USED BY THE CHEF

- "Waffles are only a pancake batter cooked on a honey-comb iron. What the well-dressed waffle will wear (the accessories that may be served with it) is a food fashion statement that any chef can do well to make. The waffle batter, depending on the flour used, can be rich or plain, floury like bread, or lighter in texture, like cake.

- There is one, no two, waffle tricks which I have acquired over the course of time. The first is, always to separate the eggs and fold in last the stiffly beaten (but not dry) egg whites. This gives a foamier batter, fuller of air and produces a lighter waffle. The second trick was learned from an old Southern cook years ago while I was chief steward at the Jefferson Davis Hotel, Montgomery, Alabama.

- What I learned was to have the shortening sizzling hot, and to pour it onto the batter just before the final hard beating. This sizzling fat (especially hot sizzling bacon fat) cooks into the batter and gives it the best of all flavor.

- Don't forget that electric appliances are not supposed to be greased. This will not be necessary if you put plenty of shortening in your mixtures. This allows smokeless cooking. Preheating is necessary for a few minutes according to the type of iron used. The batters should not be too thick. A good trick for knowing when the iron is ready, hot enough, is to put a teaspoon of water in the iron, close the lid, and when the steam ceases coming out, the iron is ready for the batter.

- Remember, tenderness in waffles depends upon the amount of fat in the recipe and the mixing, instead of the liquid in the batter. A fluffy waffle however, does require more liquid than a close-grained one. The liquid can be adjusted to obtain the type of waffle desired. If the batter is baked quickly on a very hot iron, a soft waffle results, while a crisp one follows baking for a longer time on a less hot iron."

L.P. DeGouy, Chef's Cook Book, 1939

WAFFLES

"Waffles may be made of flour, rice, hominy, or corn meal. In all recipes for waffles, if you do not have milk, substitute lukewarm water and if you have no butter, you can use instead a half spoon of lard. Certainly, the taste of the waffles is improved by the butter and milk, especially the butter. Half milk and half water boiled and grown tepid may also be used in the specified proportions indicated."

"The test of a waffle in the old days was that you could pick it up with a pin. Why anyone should want to do just that has never been explained, but someone was always sure to mention it when the waffles were complimented! Even when they had to be brought across the yard from the kitchen annex, they always arrived in this crisp condition."

-The Picayune Creole Cook Book, 1922

WAFFLES

2 1/2 cups flour
1 1/2 cups milk
4 Tablespoons Wesson oil
1 teaspoon sugar
1 teaspoon salt
2 eggs
3 teaspoons baking powder

Sift together flour, salt and sugar; then add milk, then oil, then eggs, which are well-beaten. Lastly, add baking powder.

NOTE: Do not put too much in the iron as the batter spreads a great deal.
The Savannah Cook Book, 1933

MORE WAFFLES

2 eggs
1 cup Wesson oil
1/2 cup milk
1 cup water
2 cups flour
4 scant teaspoons baking powder
1 teaspoon salt
1 teaspoon sugar

Beat eggs well. Add oil, then milk and water. Sift together dry ingredients and then add them to wet ingredients. Bake in ungreased waffle irons.
The Savannah Cook Book, 1933

POTATO WAFFLES

1 pint Irish potatoes
4 eggs
1 pint flour
1 1/2 pints milk
1/2 cake compressed yeast

Mash boiled, left-over potatoes through a sieve and then add milk and sifted flour. Add yeast, which has been well-dissolved, in a little warm water and set the whole to rise for 2 hours. At the end of that time, add eggs, beaten separately, and mix well. Set to rise again for 1/2 hour, till light, and then proceed to bake about 2 minutes in a well-greased waffle iron.
The Picayune Creole Cook Book, 1922

SWEET POTATO WAFFLES

2 cups mashed sweet potatoes
1 cup melted butter
1/2 cup of sugar
1 pint milk
2 eggs
4 Tablespoons of flour

Mash potatoes through a sieve and add eggs, beaten separately. Mix well and add sugar and beat till very light. Then add butter and beat again. Add milk mixing thoroughly. Now add flour, using sufficient flour to make a thin batter that will bind the potatoes. Grease waffle irons well and bake about 2 minutes or till a delicate brown.
The Picayune Creole Cook Book, 1922

LOUISIANA WAFFLES

2 cups flour
4 teaspoons baking powder
1/2 teaspoon salt
5 Tablespoons melted butter
1 1/2 cups milk
3 eggs

To beaten egg yolks, add milk and all other ingredients with the exception of stiffly-beaten whites of eggs which are to be added last. Pour a spoonful of batter into each section of a hot waffle iron and bake until rich golden brown.
The Southern Cookbook, 1939

VIRGINA WAFFLES

1/2 cup white corn meal
1 1/2 cups milk
3 cups flour
3 Tablespoons sugar
3 teaspoons baking powder
1/2 teaspoon salt
2 eggs
3 Tablespoons melted butter

Cook corn meal in 1 1/2 cups boiling water for 30 minutes; add milk, dry ingredients, well-beaten egg yolks, butter, and well-beaten egg whites. Put one Tablespoon of waffle mixture into each compartment near the waffle iron center. Cook on greased hot waffle iron or ungreased electric waffle iron, until well-puffed and a delicate brown.
The Southern Cookbook, 1939

RICE WAFFLES

1 cup cooked rice
2 cups flour
2 eggs
1 teaspoon salt
3 teaspoons baking powder
2 Tablespoons melted butter
a little milk

After beating yolks of eggs, add rice, butter, flour, baking powder, and salt and then well-beaten egg whites. A little milk may be added if necessary. Cook on greased hot waffle iron or ungreased electric waffle iron.
The Southern Cookbook, 1939

RICE FLOUR WAFFLES

1 cup cooked, cold hominy
2 eggs
1 cup rice flour
1/3 cup wheat flour
1/4 teaspoon salt
1 cup milk
1/3 cup water
2 Tablespoons melted butter

Beat the cold hominy into eggs until it is smooth. Mix and sift dry ingredients, then add milk and water and mix to a batter. Then add egg and hominy mixture and lastly the melted butter. Bake in a hot waffle iron a little longer than is usual for plain waffles. Serve piping hot with lots of butter.
The Southern Cookbook, 1939

SOUR CREAM WAFFLES

3 eggs, separated	3/4 teaspoon salt	1 teaspoon baking soda
1 cup plain flour	1 Tablespoon sugar	1 Tbl. boiling water
2 teaspoons baking flour	1 pint sour cream	

Beat egg yolks until thick and lemon colored. Beat egg whites until stiff and dry. Sift flour, baking powder, salt, and sugar together. Combine sifted dry ingredients with beaten egg whites. Add baking soda dissolved in boiling water and stir lightly to combine ingredients. Bake in heated waffle irons. Serve with choice of syrup. Serves 4.
Jeanne Webb, The Nashville Cookbook, 1977

CRISPY WAFFLES (A Master Recipe)

2 cups sifted cake flour	3 eggs, separated
1 Tablespoon baking powder	1 1/2 cups milk
1 teaspoon salt	1/2 cup oil
2 Tablespoons sugar	

Sift all dry ingredients together. Beat egg yolks. Mix in the milk and oil. Then add dry ingredients and stir. Beat egg whites stiff and fold into batter. Bake in hot waffle iron to desired crispness. Makes 3 waffles.
Farm Journal's Country Cookbook, 1959

FIG WAFFLES

Add 1/2 cup ground or chopped figs before folding in egg whites. Serve with ice cream and lemon sauce.

BLUEBERRY WAFFLES

Use 1 cup of milk in regular waffle recipe. Add 1 cup drained, sweetened blueberries before folding in egg whites.

ORANGE WAFFLES

Substitute 1/2 cup orange juice for 1/2 cup milk in regular batter. Add 2 teaspoons grated orange rind.

FLUFFY ORANGE SAUCE FOR ORANGE WAFFLES

1/2 cup orange juice	1 egg
2 Tablespoons grated orange rind	1 cup heavy cream
1 cup sugar	

Cook everything, but the cream, over low heat, stirring constantly until thickened. Whip cream until stiff and fold into cooled orange mixture.
Farm Journal's Country Cookbook, 1959

HOMINY WAFFLES

NOTE: A good many of Charleston's favorite hot breads are made with hominy, as is this old recipe for waffles. These waffles are crisp on the outside and moist within. They are delicious and at the same time very economical waffles. They also go farther, for one of these waffles is as satisfying as two of the usual ones.

1 cup hominy	2 cups milk
2 cups flour	1 cup water
1 teaspoon salt	2 Tablespoons butter, melted

Mix the cooked hominy with sifted flour and salt. Add milk and water (any type of milk may be used) and stir in melted butter. Bake in hot waffle iron for about 4 minutes.

NOTE: A point to remember in baking hominy waffles is that they do not spread as easily as the regular waffle batter. It is well to put a Tablespoon of batter into each division of the waffle mold with an additional spoonful in the center of the iron.
Mary Leize Simons. 200 Years of Charleston Cooking, 1930

WAFFLES MARNIER

1 cup butter	16 ounces blueberries
1 pound dark brown sugar	1 pint strawberries
1 Red Delicious apple	3 bananas
16 ounces pineapple tidbits	1 cup Grand Marnier

Dissolve brown sugar in melted butter. Dice apple and add to sugar and butter. Sauté over medium heat about 10 minutes. Add remaining drained fruit, except bananas, and cook until the fruit is hot. Add sliced bananas and Grand Marnier and cook 10 minutes. Serve over crisp waffles. Serves 14.

NOTE: Fourteen people don't have to sit down at one sitting and have this dish. Leftovers can be refrigerated and reheated.
David Hazelwood, Cortner Mill Restaurant cookbook, 2009

PUMPKIN NUT WAFFLES

2 cups sifted cake flour	3 eggs separated
4 teaspoons baking powder	1 3/4 cups milk
1 teaspoon salt	1/2 cup melted shortening
3/4 teaspoon cinnamon	1/2 cup canned pumpkin
1/4 teaspoon nutmeg	3/4 cup chopped pecans

Sift together all dry ingredients. Beat egg yolks. Combine with milk, shortening, and pumpkin. Add to dry ingredients. Beat egg whites stiff. Fold into batter. Pour onto a hot waffle iron. Sprinkle with 3 Tablespoons nuts.

NOTE: Ready to be spread with butter and ready to pour on the maple syrup.
Farm Journal's Country Cookbook, 1959

Here is a thought. When guests arrive and you have no exciting dessert planned, bake waffles at the table. Such fun, terrifically entertaining, and so very unusual.

GINGERBREAD WAFFLES

2 cups sifted flour
1 teaspoon salt
1 1/4 teaspoons baking soda
2 1/2 teaspoons ginger
1 1/4 teaspoons cinnamon
1/4 teaspoon cloves

1 cup dark molasses
1/2 cup sour milk
1 egg, slightly beaten
1/3 cup oil
1 egg white, stiffly beaten

Sift dry ingredients together. Combine molasses, milk, and beaten egg. Add this to dry ingredients, then add oil. Mix well. Fold in beaten egg white. Pour onto a moderately hot waffle iron. Bake 3 minutes. Makes 5 to 6 servings.

NOTE: Serve with vanilla ice cream.
Farm Journal's Country Cookbook, 1959

SPONGE CAKE WAFFLES

5 eggs, separated
1 cup sugar
1 cup sifted cake flour

1 teaspoon baking powder
1/2 teaspoon salt
1 1/2 cups chopped dates

1/2 cup chopped nuts
1/2 cup oil
1/2 teaspoon lemon rind

Beat egg yolks until light. Add sugar gradually; beat after each addition. Sift dry ingredients together. Add dates, nuts, yolks, oil, lemon rind. Mix well. Beat egg whites until stiff. Fold into batter. Pour 1 Tablespoon batter onto each section of a moderately hot waffle iron. Bake 4 minutes. Makes 4 servings.
Farm Journal's Country Cookbook, 1959

CHOCOLATE NUT WAFFLES

1 1/2 cups sifted flour
2 teaspoons baking powder
1/2 teaspoon salt
1 cup sugar
2 eggs, separated

3/4 cup milk
1/2 cup oil
4 squares chocolate, melted
1 cup chopped nuts
1 teaspoon vanilla

Sift dry ingredients together. Beat egg yolks. Combine with milk and oil. Add chocolate. Pour liquid into dry ingredients. Add nuts and vanilla. Beat egg whites until stiff. Fold into batter. Pour onto moderately hot waffle iron. Bake 3 minutes. Makes 4 servings.
Farm Journal's Country Cookbook, 1959

OVEN FRENCH TOAST

2 teaspoons sugar
1/4 teaspoon salt
2 eggs, unbeaten
1 cup milk
1/4 cup salad oil
8 slices bread

Add sugar and salt to unbeaten eggs in shallow dish and stir until well mixed. Stir in milk and melted fat (oil). Dip bread into mixture, both sides, and place onto well-greased pan. Bake in 450 degree oven for about 10 minutes until brown.

NOTE: This is so much easier than French toast fried and not nearly as fattening. Also, the taste is even better.
Satsuma Tea Room, Fun for the Cook, 1968

BAKED FRENCH TOAST

1/2 cup butter
1 cup brown sugar
2 Tablespoons corn syrup
5 eggs
1 loaf French bread
1 1/2 cups milk
1 teaspoon cinnamon

Combine butter, sugar and corn syrup in small saucepan. Heat over medium heat to melt. Boil for 1 minute, stirring constantly. Pour into an 8 x 11-inch baking dish. Slice French bread 3/4 inch thick and place in one layer to cover syrup mixture. Flip slices over so both sides are coated. Whisk together eggs, milk, and cinnamon and pour over bread. Cover and refrigerate overnight. Bake uncovered at 350 F for 35-40 minutes or until firm and spongy in the middle.

NOTE: Can be made ahead.
Susan Peterson, Fruit of the Spirit, Mt Bethel United Methodist Church, Marietta, GA

PEACH FRENCH TOAST

6 eggs
1 cup heavy cream
10 slices sourdough bread
1/2 teaspoon peach schnapps
1/2 teaspoon vanilla
1 1/2 teaspoons cinnamon
powdered sugar

Beat eggs and add cream, vanilla, schnapps, and cinnamon. Blend well. Soak in batter the number of bread slices that will fit onto your griddle in one cooking. After about two minutes of soaking gently remove the bread from the batter and place on 400 degree griddle. Cook on both sides until golden brown. Cut each slice into triangles and place on plate. Sprinkle with powdered sugar and serve hot with warm maple syrup. Serves 5.
David Hazelwood, Cortner Mill Restaurant cookbook, 2009

COFFEE CAKE

The best summons to come to breakfast on a Sunday morning, or any other morning for that matter, is the delightful aroma of a coffee cake baking drifting through the house. You can stir up a quick coffee cake in less time than it takes a hungry family to gather together around the table. The secret for the fast cooking of a coffee cake is to keep the shortening and dry ingredients, mixed and covered in the refrigerator; just ready to add the toppings for variety.

SOUTHERN COFFEE CAKE

1/2 cup butter
1 cup sugar
3 eggs
1 1/2 cups flour

1/2 cup milk
2 teaspoons baking powder
nutmeg, cinnamon,
chopped almonds, walnuts, or pecans

Cream sugar and butter, add milk and unbeaten eggs and mix well. Sift flour and baking powder and blend with sugar and butter, adding a dash of nutmeg. Pour into well-greased loaf cake pan and sprinkle top with nutmeg, cinnamon, nuts and granulated sugar. Dot well with butter and bake in a moderate oven 20 minutes.
The Southern Cookbook, 1939

ORANGE CLUSTER COFFEE CAKE

1 package granulated dry yeast
1/4 cup warm water
1 1/4 cups milk, scalded and then cooled
4 1/2 to 5 cups all-purpose flour
4 egg yolks or two eggs, well-beaten
1/2 cup sugar
1/2 cup melted butter

1 teaspoon salt
3/4 cup sugar
2 Tablespoons grated orange rind
2 teaspoons grated lemon rind
3/4 cup finely chopped pecans
1/2 cup melted butter

Soften yeast in water for 5 minutes. Add milk and one cup flour. Beat thoroughly. Let mixture stand for 20 minutes or until light and bubbly. Blend eggs, 1/2 cup sugar, 1/2 cup butter and salt. Add to yeast mixture, mixing well. Work in much of the remaining flour as necessary to knead smooth, satin-like, elastic dough. Place in a greased bowl, cover and let rise until doubled in bulk. Turn out onto a well-floured surface and divide in halves. Form each half into a long roll and slice into 24 pieces. Blend sugar, orange rind, lemon rind, and nuts. Roll each piece of dough into a ball. Dip into melted butter, then into the nut mixture. Place into greased 10-inch tube pan close together and in layers. Let rise in a warm place about 45 minutes or until double in bulk. Preheat oven to 350 F. Bake about 45 minutes. Turn out of pan onto cake rack to cool. Yield 20 servings.
Dr. Shirley Clark, Home Economics Faculty Favorites, University of Illinois, 1965

COFFEE CAKE MIX (A Master Recipe)

8 cups sifted flour	2 teaspoons cream of tartar
4 Tablespoons baking powder	2 cups shortening or 1 2/3 cup lard
1 Tablespoon salt	

Sift together flour, baking powder, salt, and cream of tartar into a large bowl. Cut in shortening with pastry blender or use electric mixer at a low speed 1 to 2 minutes. Overmixing will cream flour and shortening together. The mixture should be dry and crumbly, like coarse cornmeal.

Store in tightly-covered container at room temperature or in refrigerator, if lard is used. Will keep 4 to 6 weeks. Makes about 12 cups (enough for 6 coffee cakes. Each cake uses 2 cups of the mix).

Farm Journal's Country Cookbook, 1959

PLAIN COFFEE CAKE

2 cups mix (stored from coffee cake mix master recipe)	2/3 cup sugar
	3/4 cup milk
2 eggs	

Measure mix into a bowl (pile lightly into measuring cup; level it with a spatula). Beat eggs until fluffy; gradually add sugar. Combine egg mixture with the mix; beat 2 minutes until light and fluffy. Add milk, 1/4 cup at a time, beating well after each addition. Spread batter in buttered 8 x 8 x 2-inch baking dish. Put on the topping. Bake in moderate oven (350 F) for 35 minutes or until toothpick inserted in center comes out clean. Makes 6-8 servings.

Farm Journal's Country Cookbook, 1959

BAKE-ON COFFEE CAKE TOPPINGS
Farm Journal's Country Cookbook, 1959

PEACH-CINNAMON TOPPING

3/4 teaspoon lemon extract	1 cup canned, cling peach slices
3/4 teaspoon almond extract	1/2 teaspoon cinnamon
1/2 cup sugar	

Add extracts to cake batter. Drain peaches and arrange over batter in pan and bake. Mix sugar with cinnamon. Sprinkle over warm coffee cake just before serving.

BROWN SUGAR-CINNAMON TOPPING

1/4 cup butter or margarine	1 1/2 cups chopped nuts
1 cup brown sugar	1/2 teaspoon cinnamon
1/4 teaspoon salt	1/2 teaspoon nutmeg
3 Tablespoons flour	

Blend with a fork butter, sugar, salt, flour, and nuts. Add cinnamon and nutmeg to mix before adding liquids. Sprinkle topping over batter in pan and bake.

APPLE-CHEESE TOPPING

1/4 cup red cinnamon candies
1 cup water
1/4 cup sugar
3/4 cup brown sugar
1 large apple, peeled and cored

1/2 cup grated, sharp cheese
3/4 cup sifted flour
1/2 cup quick-cooking rolled oats
1/4 cup butter or margarine

Combine in a sauce pan cinnamon candies, water, sugar, and 1/4 cup brown sugar. Cut apple into rings and cook in syrup until clear and shiny; drain. Add the cheese tossed with 1/2 cup flour to the coffee cake mix. Mix rolled oats, 1/4 cup flour, 1/2 cup brown sugar and butter. Sprinkle over batter in pan. Top with candied apple rings and bake.

CRANBERRY-ORANGE TOPING

2 cups cranberries, drained
1 cup sugar

2 Tablespoons grated orange rind
3/4 teaspoon orange extract

Butter 8 x 8 x 2 baking dish. Cover bottom with cranberries. Sprinkle with sugar and orange rind. Add orange extract to batter. Spread batter over cranberries and bake. Cool 15 minutes. Turn onto platter.

HONEY-PECAN COFFEE CAKE VARIATION

Use 1/2 cup brown sugar instead of 1 cup in recipe above and omit the nuts. Sprinkle topping over batter as above; then arrange 1 cup pecan halves over that. Pour 1 cup honey over all the cake. Bake.

TOASTED COCONUT TOPPING

1 cup flaked or shredded coconut
1/2 cup sugar
1 teaspoon cinnamon

1/4 cup light cream
1/2 teaspoon nutmeg

Toss together coconut, sugar, 1/2 teaspoon cinnamon, and cream. Add 1/2 teaspoon cinnamon and nutmeg to the coffee cake mix. Sprinkle topping over batter in pan and bake.

PINEAPPLE-APRICOT TOPPING

3 Tablespoons butter or margarine
1/2 cup brown sugar

4 pineapple slices, drained
6 apricot halves, drained

Melt butter in 8-inch round pan; sprinkle with sugar. Arrange pineapple and apricots on top of sugar. Spread batter over pineapple mixture and bake. Cool 15 minutes. Turn onto plate.
Farm Journal's Country Cookbook, 1959

EGGS FRICASSEE

3 hard-cooked eggs	1 cup white sauce	salt and pepper
2 Tablespoons butter	6 slices bacon or boiled ham	
2 slices toast		

Slice eggs and brown them in butter. Cook bacon or use small slices of boiled ham and arrange on toast. Lay browned eggs on top of meat and pour well-seasoned white sauce over all. This makes an excellent luncheon dish. Serves 2.

NOTE: "The name of Heyward rings down through the history of South Carolina. Thomas Heyward was a signer of the Declaration of Independence. By a curious coincidence, this recipe is given to us by a Heyward whose plantation was burned by the British, who then married a Grimball, whose plantation was burned by the Spanish."

Panchita Heyward Grimball, Wappaoolah Plantation, Cooper River in a recipe recounted in 200 years of Charleston Cooking, 1930

EGGS PONCE DE LEON

6 hard cooked eggs	1 Tablespoon butter
2 cups tomato juice	1/2 onion diced
1/2 cup chopped celery	1/2 teaspoon Worcestershire sauce
1/4 cup chopped green peppers	1/2 cup white sauce
1/2 cup mushrooms	salt and pepper to taste
1 Tablespoon flour	

Chop egg whites, and mash yolks. Brown onion in butter, add flour and blend well. Put in tomato juice and peppers and cook slowly until done. Add mushrooms, seasoning and Worcestershire. When this is all done, add white sauce, egg yolks, and chopped egg whites. Place into buttered casserole. Sprinkle with cracker crumbs, dot with butter, and brown in the oven. Serve hot.
The Southern Cookbook, 1939

EGGS NEW ORLEANS

2 1/2 cups tomatoes	1/2 cup celery
1 small onion, chopped	4 eggs
1/2 green pepper, chopped	1/2 cup American cheese, grated
1 teaspoon sugar	salt, pepper, and bay leaf
3/4 cup bread crumbs	

Cook tomatoes, pepper, onion, and seasoning together for 10 minutes, remove bay leaf, add bread crumbs and place in casserole. Break eggs on top and sprinkle with salt and pepper and cover with grated cheese. Bake in a moderate (350 F) oven until eggs have set and cheese has melted.
The Southern Cookbook, 1939

POACHED EGGS

1 or 2 eggs per person
water to cover

1/2 teaspoon of salt
1/2 teaspoon vinegar or lemon juice

Use a shallow saucepan or skillet, because it is easier to slip eggs into such a pan. Put in enough water to cover eggs, add salt and lemon juice (or vinegar) and bring just to a boil. Meanwhile, break each egg into a saucer or soup bowl, then slip one at a time into boiling water. The vinegar or lemon juice will help the whites coagulate, but the real secret of keeping the egg compact, lies in the amount of "boil" in the water. Never put eggs into rapidly boiling water. The rolling water in a strong boil will whip the white away before it can set. Lower the heat or remove from the stove and return when the boil dies down. An egg will poach to firm white and soft yolk in about 2 1/2 minutes, but you can tell by looking. When the white is all white and firm, the egg is done.

Eggs may also be poached in milk, tomato juice, or broth. If these liquids are used, omit the vinegar or lemon juice. Serve these eggs in soup bowls with the broth poured over them.

To poach eggs hard, cook them for 4 1/2 minutes. These poached eggs are often served cold in aspic or as a garnish for salads. If this is your purpose, trim off the ragged edges.
The James Beard Cookbook, 1959

BILTMORE GOLDENROD EGGS WITH WHITE SAUCE

3 hard-cooked eggs
1 cup white sauce

6 slices toast
parsley to garnish

Separate yolks and whites of each hard-cooked egg. Chop whites finely and add to white sauce. Pour over 4 pieces of toast. Mash yolks through a strainer and sprinkle over top. Cut remaining toast into triangular shapes and place on side of dish. Garnish with parsley.

WHITE SAUCE

2 Tablespoons butter
2 Tablespoons flour

1/2 cup milk
1/2 teaspoon salt

Melt butter without browning, add flour, and salt and cook until it is well blended. Add milk slowly stirring all the while to keep from scorching. When it reaches the boiling point, remove from fire and beat well or until creamy.
The Southern Cookbook, 1939

CREOLE OMELET

1 Tablespoon butter	2 onions	1 teaspoon salt
4 eggs	4 tomatoes	1/2 teaspoon paprika
2 Tablespoons olive oil	2 green peppers	

Beat eggs in a bowl with 4 tablespoons water. When butter is heated to a light brown, turn in eggs. As they brown, lift edges with a spatula and let uncooked part run under. When omelet is brown underneath and creamy on top, fold once and slip onto a hot platter, surrounding it with creole sauce.

CREOLE SAUCE

Heat 2 Tablespoons olive oil. Cut into this onions, tomatoes, and peppers. Add salt and paprika, cook slowly until wanted for the omelet.
The Southern Cookbook, 1939

CRAB OMELETTE

8 eggs	1 Tablespoon butter
1 pound crabmeat	1/2 teaspoon mustard
salt & pepper	

Mix crabmeat with butter, mustard, salt and pepper. Break eggs into mixture and heat lightly. Pour into hot, greased frying pan. When mixture begins to set, put pan into oven and cook until slightly browned, then fold over. Remove to platter and serve immediately.
The Savannah Cook Book, 1933

CLASSIC QUICHE LORRAINE

9-inch deep dish pie crust	2 cups half & half
12 slices bacon, cooked and crumbled	3/4 teaspoon salt
1 cup Swiss cheese, shredded	1/8 teaspoon pepper
4 eggs, beaten	

Prick bottom and sides of pie shell with a fork and bake at 425 F for 6-8 minutes (or according to package directions). Let cool on wire rack. Sprinkle bacon and cheese evenly into pastry shell. Combine eggs, half and half, salt, pepper; mix well and pour into shell. Bake quiche at 425 F for 15 minutes. Reduce heat to 300 F and bake an additional 40 minutes or until set.

SPINACH QUICHE

If you wish to make this a spinach quiche, cook one package frozen chopped spinach according to package instructions. Squeeze all water from spinach and dot spinach over bacon and cheese in shell before the filling is poured over. Use the same temperatures and times to bake.

NOTE: If you use a regular 9-inch pie crust, this filling will fill 2 crusts.
Fruit of the Spirit, Mt Bethel United Methodist Church, Marietta, GA

BASIC QUICHE

1 pastry for 9-inch pie	3/4 teaspoon salt
4 large or extra-large eggs	1/8 teaspoon ground nutmeg
1 3/4 cups heavy cream or half & half	1/4 pound natural shredded cheese
1 Tablespoon flour	

Prepare crust in 9-inch pan. Place "mixings" into crust. Then with wire whisk, beat eggs, and cream with flour (much easier to mix flour with a little cream to incorporate it into the first), salt and nutmeg. Stir in cheese and pour into crust. Bake 15 minutes at 425 F and then turn down to 325 F, baking 35 minutes more. Cooked when knife is inserted into center and comes out clean. Let stand 10 minutes before serving.

NOTE: You can combine any mixtures into one quiche. Usually, you would have two main ingredients in a quiche, i.e., spinach and mushroom quiche.

MIXINGS FOR SPINACH QUICHE

10 ounce package chopped spinach	1 Tablespoon flour

Thaw and squeeze spinach until well drained of excess water. Add flour and mix well.

MIXINGS FOR ONION/BACON QUICHE

1 medium to large onion	1 Tablespoon flour
1 Tablespoon butter	12 slices lean bacon

Thinly slice onion and sauté in 1 Tablespoon butter. Should not be liquid, when cooled. Add flour and mix well. Cook bacon until crisp. Drain. Then crumble or slice.

MIXINGS FOR MUSHROOM QUICHE

8 ounces sliced fresh mushrooms	1 Tablespoon flour
1 Tablespoon butter	

Sauté mushrooms in butter. Should not be liquidly when cooled. Add flour and mix well.
Pam Bailey, Fruit of the Spirit, Mt Bethel United Methodist Church, Marietta, GA

PARISH PATCH QUICHE

1 pie shell, deep dish	1/4 teaspoon salt
3/4 cup sugar cured ham or bacon	1/4 teaspoon salt
1 cup sharp Cheddar cheese, grated	1/4 teaspoon ground oregano
3 eggs	1/8 teaspoon cayenne pepper
1 cup half and half	

Dice ham or bacon into small pieces and cook in skillet. Drain meat and sprinkle it with cheese over pastry. Mix all dry ingredients and beat into eggs. Add half and half and blend well. Pour mixture into pastry and bake at 375 oven for 40 minutes until light golden brown. If you are making the quiche in advance, bake for 30 minutes and reheat before serving in 250 degree oven for 15 minutes. Serves 6.
David Hazelwood, Cortner Mill Restaurant cookbook, 2009

EGG PIE

NOTE: We are not prepared to say whether this most resembles a custard or soufflé. Certainly, this recipe violates the rules of egg cookery; yet it still remains delicious!

1 Tablespoon butter	5 eggs, separated
5 Tablespoons flour	1 teaspoon salt
1 quart milk, scalded	

Rub butter and flour together and pour onto this the scalded milk, taking care that it is perfectly smooth. Beat egg yolks with salt and add to milk and flour batter. Beat well and add egg whites, beaten stiff. Bake in a hot oven (though this is heresy) (400 F) for 35 minutes and serve at once, as it will fall if allowed to stand. This amount will serve 8.

NOTE: Chopped ham added to this recipe is marvelous! Allow about 1 cup ham and decrease the salt if necessary.
Marie Heyward, 200 years of Charleston Cooking, 1930

BREAKFAST BRIE CASSEROLE

8-ounce round of Brie	green onion, shaved, as a garnish
1 pound ground hot pork sausage	2 cups skim milk
1 cup grated Parmesan	1 Tablespoon fresh sage or 1 tsp. dried sage
6 white sandwich bread slices	
7 large eggs, divided	1 teaspoon season salt
3 cups whipped cream divided	1 teaspoon dry mustard

Trim the rind on the Brie and set aside. Cook sausage in skillet over high heat. Stir and crumble sausage. Then drain grease. Remove crust from bread and place in lightly greased 9 x 13-inch casserole. Layer evenly with Brie slices, sausage, bread slices being the top layer. Then cover with Parmesan cheese. Whisk 5 eggs, 2 cups whipped cream together and the next 5 ingredients. Pour over casserole. Cover and chill 8 hours. Whisk remaining 2 eggs and 1 cup cream and pour onto chilled casserole. Bake at 350 F for 1 hour.
Cindi Schock, Fruit of the Spirit, Mt Bethel United Methodist Church, Marietta, GA

CREAMY POACHED EGGS

10 ounces frozen cream of shrimp soup	1/4 teaspoon curry powder or thyme
1/4 cup milk	4 waffles
dash of Tabasco	water cress
4 eggs	pickled crab apples

Heat soup in 8-inch skillet. Add milk and seasonings; stir occasionally. When smooth and simmering, break eggs gently into soup. Cover pan and simmer until egg white is set or about 5 minutes. Place an egg and sauce on each waffle. Garnish each plate with water cress and crab apple. 4 servings.
Easy-on-the-Cook Book, 1960

SAVORY SCRAMBLED EGGS

1/4 cup butter or margarine	1/4 teaspoon salt
6 eggs, slightly beaten	dash of pepper
1/3 cup milk	3 ounces cream cheese, cut into pieces

Melt butter in skillet over low heat. Combine eggs, milk and seasonings; pour in skillet. Cook very slowly, stirring constantly until eggs begin to thicken. Add cream cheese. Continue cooking very slowly stirring occasionally until cheese is blended in.
Easy-on-the-Cook Book, 1960

HASH BROWN POTATOES

1 pound salt pork	1/8 teaspoon pepper
1/3 cup fat	salt (if necessary)
2 cups cold boiled potatoes	

Fry fat out of salt pork; cut pork into cubes and remove scraps. There should be 1/3 cup fat. Mix the boiled potatoes with fat; add pepper and salt; fry three minutes, stirring constantly. Let stand, to brown underneath, and fry as you would an omelet.
The Southern Cookbook, 1939

MAPLE SYRUP

1 1/2 cups dark brown sugar	2 1/2 cups water
1 1/2 cups white sugar	2 teaspoons maple extract

Combine sugars in large pan and add water. Bring to a boil and cook for 2 minutes. Reduce temperature and simmer for 10 minutes. Remove from heat, let cool slightly, and add maple extract. Serve warm. Makes 1 quart.

NOTE: When we bought Parish Patch, we inherited this recipe from Miss Mary, the former breakfast cook. It is so easy and good, there is no need to buy syrup at the store again. Go buy some maple extract today!
Miss Mary Hart/David Hazelwood, Cortner Mill Restaurant cookbook, 2009

WATERMELON SYRUP

1 ripe watermelon	1/2 cup sugar

Cut watermelon in half; scrape pulp from rind. Put pulp through food mill (processor), strainer or colander. Measure 1 gallon watermelon puree into a kettle. Add sugar, stirring until dissolved. Bring to a boil; cook 25 minutes, skimming often. Continue cooking until mixture is thick and clear. (This takes hours, but so worth it.) You end up with 1 pint. Pour hot into a hot sterilized jar; seal at once.

NOTE: Such a special and tasty treat on waffles, pancakes, griddle cakes.
Farm Journal's Country Cookbook, 1959

HONEY BUTTER

One pleasing use for honey is making honey butter. This butter is made by creaming 1/4 cup butter with 2 Tablespoons honey and then beating in 1/4 cup heavy cream until the mixture is fluffy and smooth as satin.

NOTE: This is a perfect butter to use for warm gingerbread, pancakes or toast. Come to think of it, it's pretty good spread on anything.
Farm Journal's Country Cookbook, 1959

CURDS AND CREAM

Set sour or raw milk in a crock or bowl until it becomes clabber. Pour slowly into a curd press until press is full. Place press in pan and let drain overnight. Turn onto a flat dish, grate nutmeg freely over the top, and serve with heavy sweet cream, more grated nutmeg and sugar.

NOTE: Honey may be used in place of sugar. A colander lined with double thickness of cheesecloth may be used in place of the curd press. This dish is known as "A Louisiana Every-Meal Dish"
The Southern Cookbook, 1939

HONEY BUNS

1/4 cup warm water	3 cups sifted flour
1 teaspoon sugar	3/4 cup water
1 package granular or compressed yeast	1 egg, well, beaten
1/2 cup shortening	1/2 cup honey
1/2 cup sugar	1/2 cup chopped nuts
1 teaspoon salt	

Combine warm water with 1 teaspoon sugar. Sprinkle granular yeast over warm (110 degree) mixture; or crumble compressed yeast over lukewarm (85 degree) mixture. Let stand 5 minutes. Cream shortening, 1/2 cup sugar and salt. Mix in 1 cup flour and 3/4 cup water. Add to yeast mixture. Stir in 2 cups flour and egg; cover and refrigerate overnight. Grease muffin pans, enough for 24 buns. In each muffin cup put 1 teaspoon each honey and nuts. Drop 1 Tablespoon of dough into each muffin cup. Let rise in warm place until doubled. Bake in moderate oven (375 F) 12 to 15 minutes. Serve bottoms up.

NOTE: If you are out of honey, these buns can be changed to butterscotch or maple buns. Substitute maple sugar or brown sugar for the honey. With maple syrup, use butternuts.
Farm Journal's Country Cook Book, 1959

BREAKFAST RUSKS

NOTE: Although the name might lead you to expect something very unusual, Charleston breakfast rusks are really only delicious muffins.

1 ½ Tablespoons butter
¼ cup sugar
1 egg, well-beaten
1 cup milk
1 ¾ cups flour
¼ teaspoon salt
3 teaspoons baking powder

Cream butter and sugar, add well-beaten egg and beat well. Mix and sift dry ingredients and add to first mixture alternately with milk. Turn into well-greased muffin tins and bake in a hot oven (400 F) for about 25 minutes. Makes about 9 muffins.
Mary Leize Simons, 200 Years of Charleston Cooking, 1930

> *"We may live without poetry, music, and art;*
> *We may live without conscience, and live without heart;*
> *We may live without friends; we may live without books;*
> *But civilized man cannot live without cooks."*
> -*Owen Meredith (Lord Lytton, 1831-1891)*

NOTES

JAMS, JELLIES, & PRESERVES

JELLIES EASILY MADE

Currant	Gooseberry	Blueberry	Red Raspberry
Sour Apple	Grape	Cranberry	Black Raspberry
Crabapple	Quince	Plum	Blackberry

KIND OF FRUIT TO USE

Fruits should be fresh, just ripe, or just a little under-ripe. Juicy fruits, currants, raspberries, should not be gathered after a rain. Currants, sour apples, crabapples, under-ripe grapes, quinces, raspberries, blackberries, blueberries, wild cherries, and green gooseberries contain pectin and make the best jellies.

Peaches, strawberries, and cherries lack pectin, but may be made into jelly by adding lemon juice and the strained juice of fruits that do contain pectin, or by adding apple or commercial pectin.

PECTIN

Pectin is the substance in some fruits that, when heated and combined with fruit acid and sugar, causes the mixture to congeal or jell. All fruits do not contain pectin. The acid and pectin may be supplied by the addition of juice of apples, plums, quince, etc. or homemade apple or commercial pectin.

WILD FRUITS FOR JELLY

Wild raspberries, blackberries, barberries, grapes, and beach plums all make good jellies. The frequent failure in making these comes from fruit not being fresh or from being over-ripe.
The Settlement Cook Book, 1940

RASPBERRY JAM

To every 1 pound of raspberries use 1 pound of sugar
Select fine ripe fruit and weigh, allowing equal weights of fruits and sugar. Proceed to boil as previously directed. When it all begins to jelly, it is ready to be turned into glasses.

NOTE: Raspberry Jam is very much improved by the addition of a glass of currant juice, cooking all together.
The Picayune Cook Book, 1922

BLACKBERRY JAM

2 quarts blackberries   6 cups sugar

Cook blackberries on medium heat for 1 hour. Stir in sugar. Cook for 2 hours or until blackberries reach their desired consistency. If using a candy thermometer, cook to about 220. The cooking time and temperature will vary depending on the natural sweetness of berries. Pour into jars and seal. Makes about 4 pints.

NOTE: I remember seeing this jam in a preserves stand in the middle of Grandmother's kitchen table. I often wonder where that stand is now. I hope it is still full of jam. A great many of the jars that were full of mom's blackberry jam ended up in her jam cake.
Billie Ruth Moss Gilliam, Miss Lizzie's Heirlooms, 2009

PLUM-RASPBERRY JAM

3 pounds prune plums, ground   10 ounces frozen raspberries
5 cups sugar

Put ripe firm plums through food chopper (processor) using medium blade. Combine fruit and sugar in a 5 to 6 quart pan. Add raspberries. Mix together. Bring all to a boil; reduce heat and simmer till thick, just about 40 minutes, stirring occasionally. Pour into hot sterilized jars. Seal at once. Makes 8 half-pints.
Farm Journal's Country Cookbook, 1959

ONE MINUTE RED RASPBERRY JAM

3 1/2 cups red raspberry puree   2 1/2 ounces powdered pectin
(about 7 cups berries)   1 cup cold water
6 1/2 cups sugar

Put 3/4 ripe and 1/4 slightly ripe berries through the food mill (processor). Add sugar and mix well. Put pectin and water into saucepan. Bring to a boil over medium heat, stirring constantly. Boil hard for 1 minute, stirring. Remove from heat and immediately add berry mixture. Stir about 5 minutes or until the sugar crystals are thoroughly dissolved and mixture begins to thicken. Pour immediately into freezer containers. Cover; let stand 24 hours in cool place, until completely jelled. Seal airtight and freeze. Makes 3/1/2 pints.

NOTE: For blackberry jam, use 3 1/2 cups blackberry puree (about 8 cups berries) and decrease sugar to 5 1/2 cups. Tastes like berries fresh from the blackberry patch.
Farm Journal's Country Cookbook, 1959

SCUPPERNONG JAM

"Pop the pulp out of the skins" starts the very descriptive and old receipt. Just in case this statement left you a little inquisitive as to what it means, try squeezing a scuppernong and you will soon find out.

Place skins into a vessel, cover with water, and let simmer until tender. Put pulp into another vessel and cook slowly, until seeds separate, then put through a colander to remove seeds. Put skins and pulp together and then put in 3/4 pound sugar to every 1 pound fruit. Cook until thick. This is a most excellent accompaniment for meats and a grand substitute for mince pie!

NOTE: I dedicate this receipt (recipe) to my wife Lisa, who is a true daughter of South Carolina, a Southern belle who lives for every August and September when our local supermarket's produce department start to carry the fresh scuppernongs. She will buy as many pints and quarts as she can put her hands on. She prizes this grape that much. Here you go Babe, a way to enjoy scuppernongs all year round.
The Savannah Cook Book, 1933

SPICED BLUEBERRY JAM

2 quarts blueberries
4 1/2 cups sugar (2 pounds)
1 teaspoon cinnamon
1 teaspoon allspice
6 ounce bottle liquid pectin

Crush berries. Add sugar and spices. Bring quickly to boil in large pot, stirring constantly. Boil two minutes. Add pectin. Skim jam carefully. Pour into hot sterilized pint jars or jelly glasses. Seal at once. Makes 3 pints or nine 6 ounce glasses.

NOTE: The spices pep up the berries.
Farm Journal's Country Cookbook, 1959

BLUEBARB JAM

3 cups finely cut rhubarb or
12-16 ounce package frozen rhubarb, thawed
3 cups crushed blueberries
7 cups sugar
6 ounce bottle liquid fruit pectin

If fresh rhubarb is used, simmer gently until tender. Combine with blueberries in large saucepan, add sugar; mix. Place over high heat; bring to full, rolling boil and boil hard 1 minute, stirring constantly. Remove from heat, add pectin. Stir and skim for 5 minutes. Ladle into hot sterilized glasses. Cover at once with thin layer of paraffin. Makes about 9 half-pints.

NOTE: The union of blueberries and rhubarb is a miracle flavor-blend.
Farm Journal's Country Cookbook, 1959

PEAR CHIPS

Eight pounds pears, sliced, seven pounds sugar, 4 lemons, sliced. 1 crystallized ginger, chopped. Make a syrup of water and sugar and boil fruit in it for 2 hours.
The Savannah Cook Book, 1933

PEAR CHIPS

4 pounds pears, sliced
3 1/2 pounds sugar
2 lemons, sliced
1/2 strip crystallized ginger, chopped
4 cups water

Make a syrup of sugar and water, add spices and pears and boil fruit for 1 hour. Pour into jelly glasses and seal.
The Southern Cookbook, 1939

PEAR JAM

9 large pears (6 pounds)
5 cups water
1/4 cup lemon juice or
3 Tablespoons white vinegar
13 cups sugar
2 1/2 ounces powdered pectin
1 cup water

To prevent pears from darkening during preparation, make a solution of water and lemon juice. Dip pears after peeling and store pears in the solution after coring and quartering. Dice pears (about 13 cups) and put into large pot over medium heat. Cook until pears can be mashed. Stir in pectin and bring to a full rolling boil. Remove from heat. Stir in the same amount of sugar as you had pears and return to boiling for one minute or until they are thickened (about 325 on the candy thermometer). Pour jam into hot sterilized jars and seal. Makes 8 pints.
David Boswell Hazelwood, Miss Lizzies Heirlooms, 2009

SPICED PEACH JAM

4 cups (about 3 pounds) ripe peaches
1/4 cup lemon juice
7 1/2 cups sugar
1 teaspoon cinnamon
1/2 teaspoon cloves
1/2 teaspoon allspice
3 ounces liquid pectin

Peel, pit, and grind or chop peaches fine. Combine peaches and lemon juice. Add sugar and spices; mix well. Place over high heat and bring to a full rolling boil. Boil hard 1 minute, stirring constantly. Remove from heat and immediately stir in pectin. Skim off foam with metal spoon. Cool slightly; stir and skim by turns for 5 minutes total. Ladle into hot sterilized jars and seal. Makes 6 half-pints. Let this jam set about 2 weeks before using.

NOTE: Add Spiced Peach Jam to cream cheese for a delicious sandwich spread or serve as a relish with cold meats, such as ham or chicken.
Farm Journal's Country Cookbook, 1959

SOUR CHERRY AND PINEAPPLE JAM

2 pounds sour cherries	2 cups sugar (1 pound)
20 ounce can crushed pineapple	

Pit cherries. Add pineapple; put through course blade of food grinder. Add sugar. Boil to 230 F. on candy thermometer or until thick and clear. Pour into hot, sterilized glasses. Seal at once. Makes about six 6 ounce glasses.

NOTE: Picture-pretty and delectable.
Farm Journal's Country Cookbook, 1959

APPLE BUTTER

8 cups apples	1 cup sugar
1 cup apple cider	1 teaspoon ground cinnamon
1 cup sugar	1/4 teaspoon ground cloves

Core and chop unpeeled apples and place into a large stock pot. Add cider and cook slowly until apples are soft, probably about 10 hours. Put apples through a strainer and return the resulting pulp to the pot. Add sugar and spices and cook over a low heat, stirring frequently, for one hour. The butter is done, when you place a small spoonful onto a plate and no liquid comes from the edge of the butter. Pour into two hot sterilized pint jars and seal.

NOTE: Jonathan or Winesap are some of the best varieties to use for apple butter.
David Boswell Hazelwood, Miss Lizzie's Heirlooms, 2009

DIRECTIONS FOR MAKING MARMALADE (This is French for jam.)

Marmalades (jams) are mixtures of fruits reduced to a consistency that they may be preserved. Ripe fruits that cannot stand the process of blanching required in preserving whole fruit are used for this purpose. The beauty and taste of marmalade (jam) depend on the fruits that are used, the quality of the sugar used, and the care bestowed on the preparation.

Always choose ripe, beautiful, luscious fruit. Cut the fruit into small pieces, and then add sugar and fruit in alternate layers in preserving kettle (pot), making sure bottom layer is a layer of fruit. Set kettle over fire. If fruit is not very juicy, add a small quantity of water to set kettle to boiling and to extract juices. As the fruit boils, shake kettle occasionally by lifting it from fire and turn it briskly to prevent it from burning at the bottom. Never stir with a spoon, as the mixture will be sure to burn. When the whole mixture begins to look very clear and you observe by testing a portion on a plate that it is growing thick, it is done. Then take it from the fire and put into jars at once. This is the mode of cooking that separates jams (marmalades) from jellies and preserves.
The Picayune Cook Book, 1922

ORANGE MARMALADE

6 large oranges	2 Tablespoons lemon juice
3 quarts cold water	4 cups sugar

Cut oranges in half, scoop out juice and pulp. Boil rind in enough cold water to cover, until tender; drain, cool, remove all the white part of the peel. Cut orange/yellow into strips, add juice, pulp, sugar, and water. Boil 2 hours or until thick. Place in jelly glasses.
The Southern Cook Book, 1939

ORANGE-LEMON MARMALADE

12 oranges	water
3 lemons	sugar

FIRST DAY: Slice fruit very thin. Add 2 cups water for each cup of fruit. Let stand.
SECOND DAY: Boil this mixture 30 minutes.
THIRD DAY: Cook all quantities using 3 cups fruit and water to 2 cups sugar. Cook about 2 hours. Pour into hot sterilized glasses; seal. Makes 24 six-ounce glasses.

NOTE: A perfect dress-up for buttered toast.
Farm Journal's Country Cookbook, 1959

LEMON-CARROT MARMALADE

12 large carrots, grated	juice of 3 lemons	1/8 teaspoon salt
9 cups sugar	juice of 1 orange	

Scrape carrots and grate coarsely; add sugar (make sure there are equal amounts of carrots and sugar) Let stand overnight. Add fruit juice and salt. Bring to boiling, then simmer 2 hours. Stir often and skim, when necessary. Seal in hot, sterilized glasses. Makes about eleven 6-ounce glasses.

NOTE: The orange and lemon peel, sliced very thin without any of the white membrane, makes a really nice addition to this marmalade/jam.
Farm Journal's Country Cookbook, 1959

GRAPEFRUIT AND PINEAPPLE MARMALADE

1 grapefruit	1 lemon
1 pineapple	sugar

Pare and shred pineapple, cut grapefruit and lemon into quarters and then into thin slices. Measure fruit and cover with water- 3 pints of water to 1 pint fruit. Set aside until next day. Let this mixture boil 3 or more hours or until rind is very tender. Set aside until next day. Measure and add an equal amount of sugar. Let this mixture boil until a drop jells on a cold plate. Place in jelly glasses.
The Southern Cook Book, 1939

AMBER GRAPE MARMALADE

1 1/3 cups Concord grapes	2 cups unsweetened applesauce
2 2/3 cups Thompson seedless grapes	3 1/2 cups sugar
1/2 cup water	2 teaspoons grated orange rind

Slip skins off Concords; add pulp to seedless grapes; add water.
Cook until soft and put through sieve or food mill. Sieve applesauce and add to mixture. Bring to a boil, stirring frequently. Add sugar and lemon rind. Simmer until thick and jelly-like (two drops of mixture should run together and also sheet from a metal spoon). Pour into hot sterilized glasses or jars. Seal immediately. Makes 2 1/2 pints.

NOTE: This is a treasure for your cupboard to have on hand to set out for company.
Farm Journal's Country Cookbook, 1959

GRAPEFRUIT MARMALADE

1 grapefruit, 1 lemon, 2 oranges, 4 pounds of sugar, 2 days. Cut fruit with scissors into small pieces, skin and all. Soak in water 24 hours and then boil for 1 1/2 hours. Take off stove and add sugar and let stand another 24 hours. Then boil hard for 1 hour or until thick. This fills 8 jelly glasses.
The Savannah Cook Book, 1933

BITTER ORANGE MARMALADE

This is a much more delicate and unusual than the average orange marmalade. Cut 12 oranges in half, across the fruit. Remove the pulp and then cut up the oranges very finely. To each pound of fruit, add 3 pints water and allow to stand 24 hours. Place pips (seeds) in basin and cover with water and let this stand 24 hours also. Strain off and add juice to fruit, which has been standing. Boil mixture two hours or until tender. Then cool and add 1 1/4 pounds sugar to each pound fruit and juice. After adding sugar, boil about 3/4 hour or until it jellies.
The Savannah Cook Book, 1933

APRICOT JELLY

To every 1 pint fruit juice, add 1 pound sugar. Choose apricots that are just ripe, and no more. Pare, cut in two, and take out stones. Boil fruit in enough water to cover; strain through a hair sieve, and pour liquid into earthen dishes. To every pint of liquid add a pound of sugar. Set onto fire and let boil 20 minutes, meanwhile skimming, then pour immediately into cups, glasses or preserve jars, and proceed to seal as directed. If the grated rind of an orange is added, this jelly will have a most exquisite flavor. To make apricot syrup, after pressing out the juice, put into glass bottles and add 1 pound of powdered sugar to every pound of juice along with a little cinnamon. Shake the bottle well until the sugar is melted. Let it stand 8 days. Then filter the juice, pour it into bottles, fasten securely, and keep in cool place.

NOTE: Cherry juice and all fruit juices are prepared in the same manner.
The Picayune Creole Cook Book, 1922

BLACKBERRY JELLY

For each quart of blackberries allow the following spices:
3/8 teaspoon cinnamon
1/4 teaspoon nutmeg
1/4 teaspoon mace
1/8 teaspoon cloves

Wash berries, add spices, and cook them gently until soft, stirring frequently to crush them and to prevent burning. Squeeze through jelly bag and then put juice again through a bag, using a flannel bag the second time. If a clear jelly is desired, the bag must not be squeezed. For each pint juice add 1 pound sugar and let this simmer over a low fire until a small amount will begin to jelly when dropped onto a cold plate. Turn into jelly glasses, cover with a thin coating of paraffin and allow to cool. When the jelly is cold, pour on another layer of paraffin, turning each glass so the paraffin will run well up the sides of the glass and insure a perfect seal.

NOTE: This spiced jelly makes an excellent accompaniment for meats and is an especially happy combination with cream cheese to serve as a dessert at the end of a hearty meal.
Miss Mitchell, 200 Years of Charleston Cooking, 1930

SHERRY WINE JELLY

2 3/4 cups boiling water
1/4 cup cold water
1 cup sherry wine
2 lemons, juice and rind
2 Tablespoons gelatin
1 cup sugar
2 sticks cinnamon

Add cinnamon sticks, lemon juice, and rind to boiling water and let stand over low flame until ready to use. Soak gelatin in cold water for 5 minutes. Then add gelatin to the hot mixture and stir well. Add sherry wine and sugar and strain through a cheese cloth. Pour into mold and place into ice box until set. Serve with whipped cream if desired.
The Southern Cookbook, 1939

WINE JELLY

2 packages gelatin
1 quart cold water
1 quart boiling water
1 quart wine
4 lemons, sliced
4 egg whites, stiffly beaten, also the shells
1 teaspoon ground mace
1 teaspoon ground nutmeg
1 teaspoon ground cloves
1 teaspoon ground allspice
2 sticks cinnamon
1 quart sugar

Boil all 10 minutes and strain through flannel.

NOTE: Old-fashioned invalids and new-fashioned epicures really like this famous recipe. Mrs. Martha Laurens Patterson's mother used to make quantities of it to give friends who were sick. In our day of Prohibition, possibly by decreasing the sugar, one could make this recipe by using sweet cooking wines.
Martha Laurens Patterson, 200 Years of Charleston Cooking, 1930

ORANGE JELLY-CREOLE STYLE

6 Louisiana oranges   sugar to taste
1/2 box gelatin

Extract juice of oranges. Soak gelatin, if prepared, and set bowl into boiling water till the gelatin melts. Then add the juice of the oranges and sugar to taste. Strain through a coarse piece of Swiss (cheese) cloth. Set into a mold to harden.

The Creoles have a pretty way of making baskets out of the oranges and serving the jelly in them. With a sharp knife trace out a basket in the skin of the orange, and then gradually loosening the pulp, cut the orange without breaking the skin. This orange meat is then used for the jelly and the baskets are thrown into ice water for an hour. This makes them stiff. When the jelly is hard, it is cut into little squares and gradually made to fit like blocks into the baskets. These baskets are then placed onto a dish, beautifully garnished with delicate buds and greenery, and the effect is charming.
The oranges are now cut open in this manner; the peel is marked off in eighths and pulled from the upper end of the stem, without separating them so that they open like a beautiful flower. The jelly is piled into this when cool, whipped cream is heaped on top. A few luscious strawberries are placed in the cream and thus are made a beautiful and delicious dessert. Try it!
The Picayune Cook Book, 1922

SPICED GRAPE JELLY

3 pounds Concord grapes	2 teaspoons cinnamon	8 cups sugar
1 teaspoon cloves	1/2 cup vinegar	1/2 cup liquid pectin

Cook grapes with cloves, cinnamon and vinegar (vinegar takes the place of water, starts grapes "juicing"). After juice forms, boil only 5 to 10 minutes. Longer boiling destroys the pectin, color and flavor.
Strain juice. (use milk filter pad in a wire strainer) Should now have 4 1/2 cups juice. Combine with sugar. Heat, stirring, and boil rapidly to the jelling stage, 219 F to 221 F on candy thermometer or when two drops run together and sheet off a metal spoon.
Add pectin. Boil hard 30 seconds; stir constantly. Skim; pour quickly into hot sterilized glasses. Seal at once. Makes about 12 six- ounce glasses.

NOTE: A deluxe jelly.
Farm Journal's Country Cookbook, 1959

JELLY MERINGUE (Something different to use other than whipped cream)

1 glass firm jelly   2 egg whites   pinch of salt

Beat 2 egg whites until quite stiff and able to stand by themselves, then add 1 glass firm jelly, pinch of salt, and beat thoroughly.

NOTE: Use this in place of whipped cream.
The Southern Cook Book, 1939

QUINCE GINGER

6 pounds ripe quince
4 pounds sugar
2 cups water
1 Tablespoon fresh ginger root
4 lemons, sliced thin

Pare and core quince; cut into small pieces. Combine sugar and water, stir to dissolve. Boil 5 minutes. Add chopped quince, ginger root and lemon slices. Simmer 2 hours, until fruit is transparent and deep red in color. Pour into hot sterilized glasses; seal at once. Makes 5 pints.

NOTE: For extra-special company! If fresh ginger root is unavailable, use a small piece of the dried root, but discard before sealing glasses.
Farm Journal's Country Cookbook

ROSE GERANIUM-HONEY JELLY

2 1/2 cups strained honey
3/4 cup water
6 or 7 rose geranium leaves
3 ounces liquid pectin
2 Tablespoons lemon juice

Combine honey, water and 2 or 3 rose geranium leaves; quickly bring to a boil. Add pectin, stirring constantly; bring to a rolling boil. Add lemon juice and remove from heat. Remove leaves from mixture carefully. Place a fresh, clean leaf in each jar and quickly pour hot jelly into hot sterilized jars (the leaves rise to the top). Seal. Makes four 8-ounce jars.

NOTE: Whether on hot biscuits or homemade bread toast, Grandma's famous geranium jelly never tasted so good.
Farm Journal's Country Cookbook, 1959

GENERAL DIRECTIONS FOR MAKING PRESERVES (The French word is conserve.)

"Use all surplus juices that exude from the berries or fruit to make jellies. Waste not Want not! The preserving of fruits is very similar to the making of jellies, only in that equal quantities of fruit and sugar are used. Fruits may be preserved either whole or otherwise. In preserving fruits whole, it is best to prick such fruits as pears, peaches and plums with a needle so as to give a vent to the juice which would otherwise escape and burst the skin. In preserving large fruits, always throw them into cold water as soon as they have been pared. Then have ready a pot of clear, boiling syrup.

In all cases jars must be entirely full so as to leave no room for air and these jars must be sealed as hot as possible. However, the best way is the old-fashioned way of paring the fruit carefully, either in halves or whole simply removing skins and cores. Then make a syrup of 1 pound of white sugar to each pound of fruit. Let the sugar boil until the fruit looks clear.

The syrup could also be made by putting it on top of the fire, allowing 1/2 pint fresh water to 1 pound of the best white sugar. Stir this well and bring it to a boil. Let it boil for 5 minutes and it will begin to bubble and froth. As the froth rises, the syrup will become clear. Skim the froth and put the syrup on a very low fire to settle, after which the fruit can be put in.

If the former method is used, take the fruit carefully out of the syrup as soon as possible, taking up as little syrup as need be and then place the fruit in the jars. Let the syrup continue to boil until it becomes very thick, and then fill the jars up with the syrup. When cool, close the jars.

The preference for a preparation utensil would be to use a porcelain-lined kettle. If you use a copper kettle, never allow the preserves, jams (marmalades) to cool in the kettle, on account of a thing called virdigris which will be sure to form. Never make preserves on a damp, rainy day and never use fruits that are over ripe or that have been picked in wet weather, as these will sour.

Set the jars in warm water before filling, and let them gradually heat before the hot preserves, jams or jellies are put in else they will crack. Let all bubbles rise to the top and if you see any in the lower part of the jar, insert a silver fork which will allow these bubbles to rise to the top. For success, the one great thing to be remembered is to expel all air.

It is absolutely necessary to keep all preserves, marmalades, and jellies in a cool (not cold) place that is perfectly free from dampness or of any possibility of heat. Heat will cause fermentation and the preserves will quickly sour. Dampness will make the preserves decompose and mold."

-*The Picayune Cook Book, 1922*

STRAWBERRY PRESERVES

1 quart strawberries
4 cups sugar

Wash and cap strawberries. In a large pot, combine strawberries and sugar and cook 5 minutes over low heat. When sugar dissolves, cook on high heat 8 minutes. Turn heat down to medium heat and cook 8 minutes more. Skim foam during the last 5 minutes. Pour into a pan and refrigerate overnight. Put into sterilized jars and seal. Makes 6 pints.

NOTE: It is best to raise your own berries, if you can, like Miss Lizzie did; but if you don't or can't, buy locally raised berries. The strawberries shipped from California, Florida or Mexico barely taste like strawberries with little or no taste at all. Equal parts berries and sugar will make a batch to have for breakfast anytime.
David Boswell Hazelwood, Miss Lizzie's Heirlooms, 2009

SOUR CHERRY PRESERVES

1 pound ripe, firm sour cherries   1 pound sugar

Pit the cherries; add the sugar. Boil to 240 F on a candy thermometer or until syrup is thick. Seal in hot sterilized pint jars. Makes about 2 pints.

NOTE: Bright, red, and tasty. Made from the fruit almost everyone likes.
Farm Journal's Country Cookbook, 1959

PEAR PRESERVES

2 heaping cups pears sliced into bite size   2 lemons sliced very thin
1 level cup sugar   2 cups water

Combine the above in a large container. Bring to a boil. Reduce heat and simmer 2 ½ - 3 hours. Stir occasionally. Makes 1 pint.

NOTE: One of our waitresses who is also a great cook in her own right, brought us pear preserves made by this recipe. I have never eaten preserves so good.
Satsuma Tea Room, More Fun for the Cook, 1974

PEACH PRESERVES

1 quart peaches, sliced   2 Tablespoons lemon juice
4 cups sugar

Mix peaches and 2 cups sugar and bring to a boil. Cook for 10 minutes, stirring occasionally. Add remaining sugar and lemon juice. Cook over medium heat for another 10 minutes, stirring constantly. Cool, stirring occasionally, then pour into sterilized jars and seal.
David Boswell Hazelwood, Miss Lizzie's Heirlooms, 2009

GRAPE CONSERVE

6 cups Concord grapes   1/2 cup water
6 cups sugar   1/2 teaspoon salt
juice of 2 oranges   1/2 pound seedless raisins
1/2 cup water   1 cup chopped walnuts

Remove pulp from skins, save skins, and cook pulp until seeds can be separated by forcing pulp through a strainer. Combine grape pulp with sugar, orange juice, water, salt and grape skins. Bring to a boil. Add raisins. Simmer 20 minutes or until thick. Add nuts; cook a few minutes more. Pour into hot sterilized jars. Seal at once. Makes 5 pints.

NOTE: Juicy purple grapes and oranges get together with grapes and nuts.
Farm Journal's Country Cookbook, 1959

TOMATO PRESERVES

5 pounds firm, red or yellow tomatoes
5 pounds sugar
1 lemon, sliced thin
small piece ginger root or
1 teaspoon ground ginger

Skin and cut up tomatoes. Add remaining ingredients. Simmer slowly until thick, stirring frequently (about 45 minutes). If ginger root is used, remove it now. Pour into hot sterilized glasses. Seal at once. Makes about four 6 ounce glasses.
Farm Journal's Country Cookbook, 1959

PEACH CONSERVE

4 pounds peaches
1 pound sugar
1 grated lemon
1 grated orange, skin and all
1/2 pound English walnuts

Peel peaches and boil until pulpy. Add sugar, lemon, and orange; and cook until thick. Then stir in chopped-up nuts. Put into jars and seal.

NOTE: This makes a delicious mixture for peach ice cream in winter. Mix about 1 1/2 pints conserve to 1 quart cream and you have a delectable dessert.
The Savannah Cook Book, 1933

PUMPKIN CHIPS

Peel and slice pumpkin into small chips about 1 1/2 inches by 1 1/16 inches thick. To each pound of chips add a pound of granulated sugar, juice of 2 large lemons and grated rind of 1/2 lemon. Boil all together until chips have become transparent. Take out chips and put into jars. Continue to boil the stiff syrup until it is thick; then pour it over chips into jars.

NOTE: I don't know whether anybody in the North ever makes preserves of pumpkins. I certainly have never seen them. Yet, pumpkin chip is as delicious a conserve as I have ever eaten. It has a sharp lemon flavor.
200 years of Charleston Cooking, 1930

PICKLES, RELISHES, & CANNING

"Summertime and the livin' is easy. Fish are jumpin' and the cotton is high."
-George Gershwin (1898-1937)

Early pioneer homemakers became skilled at the art of preserving the plentiful, locally grown food and discovered that fruits and vegetables could be eaten all year round. While present-day food preservation techniques have radically changed, delectable pickles continue to please the palate and also relishes have made resurgence as an exceptional main dish garnish.

The aromas from Southern kitchens of the past achieved their pleasurable peak during canning time, pickle-making, and putting up jams, jellies and preserves, as the pots and kettles of vinegar, fruits, vegetables and spices simmered, giving the promise of good eating throughout the year to come. While we frequently can no longer devote days on end to pickling and preserving as our ancestors did, many still bottle and can their specialties every year to preserve and add that fresh-picked taste to their dishes and meals. Melon rinds and fruits were generally turned into preserves and jams, mostly due to their high sugar content. Waste not, want not.

GENERAL RULES FOR PICKLES

Cucumbers for pickling must be fresh picked, not over 24 hours old. Dill is best when the seeds are full grown, but not so ripe that the seeds fall off the stalk. Use coarse salt, not table salt. Pickles will spoil if not kept completely under the brine (1/2 gallon brine covers about 1 gallon cucumbers.) Mix salt with small amount of water, and then add the rest of the water.
The Settlement Cookbook, 1940

BRINE SOLUTION-TO LIFT AN EGG

A salt brine that will just lift-up an egg from the bottom of the crock is a solution of 1 cup salt to 5 cups water. A weak brine, 1/2 cup salt to 9 cups water will cause quicker fermentation and pickles kept in this brine will spoil in a few weeks unless the scum that rises to the top of the jars is constantly skimmed off and the brine is clear.

When the pickles are done and all the fermentation stops, it is best to remove them to jars, cover them with their own brine, or add fresh cooled brine and seal.

Pickles will shrivel if too much sugar or salt is added at one time or if vinegar is too strong. Pickles that are already cured, salt or dill pickles may then be made into sweet, sour or mixed pickles and will not shrivel.

BRINE

For every two quarts water take two cups salt. Boil, skim until clear, then cool before use. A good vinegar is an essential ingredient in pickling and in making many salad dressings. Wine vinegar can easily be made at home.

PREPARE CUCUMBERS FROM THE GARDEN FOR FUTURE USE

Cucumbers picked fresh from the vine everyday may be preserved in strong brine for future use. The cucumbers can then be made into sweet, sour, dill, or mixed pickles. This way the short-lived cucumber growing season can be extended for pickle making. It also enables a person to take advantage of that perfect size of cucumber. Leave from 1/4 to 1/2 inch stems on the fresh picked cucumbers, wash carefully without removing the prickles, and put them as gathered, into a stone crock. Make enough brine to half fill the crock which will completely cover the pickles. When the cucumbers are ready to use to make pickles, soak them in cold water until freshened.

HOME-MADE VINEGAR

1 quart white wine
1 quart water
1 thick slice stale rye bread
1 Tablespoon well-aged vinegar

Cut stale bread into cubes. Mix all ingredients, pour into a large bottle, cork tightly, and allow to stand 2 to 3 weeks. Strain and pour into bottles for everyday use.

NOTE: Wine that has turned sour and is no longer fit to drink is still perfectly good to be used for vinegar. Again, waste not, want not.
Cooked to Your Taste, 1945

NOTE: David H- But, don't cook with bad wine. If it's bad to drink, it's bad for cooking too.

SWEET CRISP CUCUMBER PICKLE

2 gallons sliced cucumbers
2 cups non-iodized salt, dissolved in boiling water to cover
2 Tablespoons alum
2 1/2 pints distilled vinegar
16 cups sugar
2 Tablespoons celery seed
1 1/2 Tablespoons turmeric
2 Tablespoons pickling spices

Place cucumbers into crock jar and cover with boiling salt water. Let stand 2 days. Pour off; rinse with hot water. Put cucumbers back into jar. Cover again with boiling water in which the alum has been dissolved. Let stand 1 day. Rinse with hot water and drain. Combine remaining ingredients and boil 5 minutes. Pack cucumbers in sterilized jars and cover with hot syrup. Seal; store in cold dark place. Makes 8 quarts.
Virginia Peden, The Nashville Cookbook, 1977

QUICK SWEET PICKLE

1 quart store bought dill pickles
1 quart store bought sour pickles
4 cups sugar
2 Tablespoons whole allspice
2 or more garlic cloves, sliced

Drain and slice pickles. Place alternate layers of pickles and mixture of sugar and spices in jars. These pickles make their own syrup. Store in the refrigerator. Makes 2 1/2 quarts.
Ann Eaden, The Nashville Cookbook, 1977

BREAD AND BUTTER PICKLES

1 gallon firm, clean cucumbers
8 small white onions
2 green peppers
2 red peppers
1/2 cup salt
1 quart cracked ice

5 cups sugar
1 1/2 teaspoons turmeric
1/2 teaspoon ground cloves
2 teaspoons mustard seed
1 teaspoon celery seed
5 cups white vinegar

Slice cucumbers, onions, green and red peppers into paper thin rounds. Place into stone crock. Mix salt and ice and pack around sliced vegetables. Cover crock with weighted lid and allow to stand 3 hours, then drain. Combine sugar, spices, and vinegar. Pour over vegetables in large enamel or aluminum kettle. Bring to boil over low heat. Pour into hot sterilized jars and seal immediately. Makes 7 pints.

NOTE: This recipe is a must have in all worthy collections of pickle recipes.
Farm Journal's Country Cookbook, 1959

SWEET-SOUR DILL PICKLES

1 quart dill pickle slices or
6 large whole dill pickles
3 Tablespoons salad oil

1/2 clove garlic, sliced
2 cups sugar

Drain liquid from pickles. (You will be using previously prepared dill pickles.) If using whole pickles, cut ends off and discard. Cut pickles into one-inch chunks; place them in a jar and add garlic, and oil. Shake until the pickles are well coated with oil; add sugar and let stand about 3 hours. Shake well. If jar did not hold all the sugar, add remainder at this time. Let stand two days; shake the jar occasionally. Store in refrigerator. Makes about 1 quart.

NOTE: These pickles are exceptionally crisp and quite delicious.
Ruby Chancellor, The Nashville Cookbook, 1977

GREEN TOMATO PICKLES

4 pounds green tomatoes, sliced
4 medium onions, sliced
4 Tablespoons salt
1 teaspoon whole cloves
1 teaspoon mustard seed

1 teaspoon dry mustard
1 teaspoon whole allspice
1/4 teaspoon black pepper
2 cups vinegar
1 cup sugar

Add 2 Tablespoons salt to tomatoes and remaining 2 Tablespoons salt to onions. Let stand overnight; drain well. Tie spices loosely in a cheesecloth bag and put in kettle with vinegar and sugar. Heat to a boiling point; add tomatoes and onions and let simmer slowly 20 minutes. Pack into clean hot jars and seal immediately.
Makes 3 pints.
What to Cook for Company, 1952

SWEET DILLS

Slice 6 large dill pickles 1/2 inch thick. Boil 2 cups sugar, 1 cup water, and 1/2 cup vinegar to make a thin syrup. Add pickle slices and heat. Put into glass jars and let stand in cool place until clear.
Farm Journal's Country Cookbook, 1959

GREEN TOMATO PICKLES

1 peck green tomatoes	1/2 ounce cloves
1/2 peck onions	1/2 ounce ginger
salt	1 Tablespoon black pepper
vinegar	1 Tablespoon dry mustard
4 cups sugar	celery seed and horseradish to taste
1/2 cup salad oil	horseradish, to taste
1/2 ounce mace	

Slice tomatoes and onions. Let stand in saltwater 24 hours. Remove from saltwater and boil in fresh water for 10 minutes. Cover with vinegar. Add sugar, oil, and spices. Blend well. Store in a large crock or glass jar. It is not necessary to seal these pickles.

NOTE: This recipe was written for a young bride in 1886 and has been prepared regularly in "tomato season" ever since.
Holiday Hostess, 1958

WATERMELON RIND PICKLES

7 pounds prepared watermelon rind	1 Tablespoon mustard seed
1/2 cup lime	1/4 teaspoon oil of cinnamon
3 gallons water	1/4 teaspoon oil of cloves
5 pounds (10 cups) sugar	food coloring (optional)
2 cups vinegar	

Prepare rind by trimming away the dark green and pink portions. Cut flesh of the rind into 1-inch squares. Combine lime with 2 gallons water and soak rind overnight. Drain and wash rind thoroughly. To 1 gallon water add rind and boil until tender. Drain. Make a syrup of the remaining ingredients; drop rind into boiling syrup and cook until it appears almost transparent. At this point you may color if desired. Pack in hot jars; add syrup to cover, then seal.

NOTE: Pioneer homemakers mastered the art of preserving the abundant fruits and vegetables of the region. Though preserving techniques have drastically changed, delicious pickles and relishes continue to please the modern-day people of Nashville. A longtime favorite is the popular watermelon rind pickle. The more highly sugar-concentrated melon rind/berries became preserves, jams, and jellies.
The Nashville Cookbook, 1977

WATERMELON RIND PICKLE

Select watermelon with thick rind. Cut rind into small pieces and weigh. One melon usually makes about 5 pounds of rind and this receipt (recipe) is for that amount.
Make a syrup of 5 pounds sugar, 2 1/2 pints vinegar, 1 ounce root ginger-broken up, 1/2 ounce cloves, 1 ounce stick cinnamon, and let all come to a boil. Cover fruit/rind with hot water and boil until you can pierce it with a straw. Then drain off water and put fruit into syrup and let boil up once. Put into a stone crock and let stay covered for 3 days. Then pour off syrup, boil, and pour over fruit into jars.
The Savannah Cook Book, 1933

SQUASH PICKLES

8 cups sliced yellow squash	2 cups cider vinegar
2 cups sliced onions	3 1/2 cups sugar
1 cup diced green pepper	1 teaspoon celery seed
1 Tablespoon salt	1 teaspoon mustard seed

Combine squash, onion, and pepper. Sprinkle with salt and let stand 1 hour. Drain well but do not rinse. Add combined vinegar, sugar, and seeds. Boil gently for 3 minutes. Pack squash mixture in sterilized jars. Cover with hot syrup and seal. Process in hot water bath for 5 minutes. Makes 6 pints.

NOTE: Other spices of choice may also be added to the basic pickling solution.
Stella Bryant, The Nashville Cookbook, 1977

PICKLED BEETS

4 cups sliced cold cooked beets	3 sticks whole cinnamon
2 cups vinegar	1/2 teaspoon allspice
1/3 cup sugar	2 teaspoons white mustard seed
1/2 teaspoon salt	1 teaspoon celery seed

Combine vinegar, sugar, and salt. Tie spices loosely in cheesecloth bag; add to vinegar. Add mustard seed and celery seed. Heat to boiling. Remove cheesecloth bag. Fill clean, hot pint jars with beets and pour over hot spiced vinegar. Seal jars and let stand for 36 hours before using. Makes 2 pints.
What to Cook for Company, 1952

PICKLED CAULIFLOWER

4 heads cauliflower	2 quarts vinegar	1/4 cup mixed pickle
1 cup salt	2 cups sugar	spices

Separate flowerets of cauliflower, add salt and let stand overnight. Place in colander, rinse with cold water and let drain. Tie spices in thin bag, boil with vinegar and sugar, drop into cauliflower, boil a few minutes, and pour to overflowing into wide-mouthed bottles or jars. Seal.
The Settlement Cookbook, 1940

OKRA PICKLE

1 quart okra	1 quart white vinegar
1 each red and green hot peppers	1 cup sugar
1/2 teaspoon dill seed	1/2 cup salt
1 garlic clove	

Soak okra in ice water 4 or 5 hours before making pickle. Pack okra in hot sterile jar; place peppers, dill seed, and garlic on top of okra. Pour hot mixture of vinegar, sugar, and salt over okra. Seal jar. Store in cool dry place. Makes 1 quart.

NOTE: Excellent for the home gardener as the recipe can be made in small quantities when okra is young and tender.
Martha Bell White, The Nashville Cookbook, 1977

DILLED OKRA PICKLES

3 pounds young okra, uncut	1 quart of water
celery leaves	1 pint white vinegar
cloves of garlic	1/2 cup salt
large heads of dill and stems	

Pack scrubbed okra into hot sterilized pint jars with a few celery leaves, clove of garlic, and a head of dill for each jar. Make a brine of water, vinegar, and salt; heat to boiling. Pour over okra. Seal. Let stand 3 to 4 weeks. Makes 6 pints.
Farm Journal's Country Cookbook, 1959

ARTICHOKE PICKLES

1 peck artichokes	1 cup salt
1 gallon vinegar	1 scant Tablespoon turmeric
2 quarts onions	1/2 cup mustard
2 cups sugar	

Put salt, sugar, mustard, and turmeric into vinegar and let come to a boil. Wash and scrape artichokes and put into a crock- a layer of artichokes then a layer of sliced onions. Pour vinegar over them.
The Savannah Cook Book, 1933

CAPTAIN HENRY'S PICKLED CHERRIES

Pit cherries, place in a large crock and cover with weak vinegar; let stand 8 days, stirring twice each day. On the 9th day remove from the vinegar and drain. To each pint cherries add one pint sugar and place into crock, letting stand for 8 more days, stirring twice each day. At the end of the 8th day, place into sterile jars and seal. Serve with poultry or meats.

NOTE: Receipt (recipe) from *"A-Way Down South."*
The Southern Cookbook, 1939

CUCUMBER CINNAMON RINGS

2 gallons large cucumber rings
2 cups hydrated lime
8 1/2 cups cold water
1 cup vinegar

1 Tablespoon alum
1 small bottle red food coloring
water to cover pickles

PICKLING SOLUTION

2 cups vinegar
2 cups water
1 package Red Hot candies

10 cups sugar
8 sticks cinnamon

Peel cucumbers, slice into ½-inch slices, and remove seeds. Place into lime water to cover. Let stand 24 hours and then drain rings. Wash in cold water and soak for 3 hours; drain. Mix vinegar, alum and food coloring. Pour over cucumbers and add water to cover rings. Heat and simmer for 2 hours. Drain. Add pickling solution.

Bring pickling solution to boil. Pour over cucumber rings. Cover tightly and let stand overnight. Drain and reheat syrup and pour over rings. Repeat this step 2 more mornings. On the last morning heat rings in the liquid to boiling. Pack in sterile jars and seal.

NOTE: This recipe is a very interesting way to use large cucumbers from the garden.
Coleen Davis, The Nashville Cookbook, 1977

PEACH PICKLE

Best with Elberta peaches (one of the most popular peaches, first introduced in Georgia in 1875), not fully ripe. These are just as good as clingstones and far easier to eat. Peel fruit and stick 3 to 4 cloves into each one. To 10 pounds of fruit use 5 pounds sugar and 1 quart vinegar. Cook together until a straw can be stuck into fruit. Take peaches out and cook syrup until thick or heat syrup and pour over fruit for 3 consecutive days.
The Savannah Cook Book, 1933

PICKLED PEARS OR PICKLED CRAB APPLES

1/2 peck pears
1 cup vinegar
1 cup water
1 cup brown sugar

1 cup white sugar
1 Tablespoon cloves
1 stick cinnamon, broken into pieces

Boil 5 minutes. Add prepared fruits a little at a time. Simmer until tender. If preparing pears, peel, cut out the core and cut into quarters and halves. This is a perfect recipe for old hard tough pears. Do make sure you use firm ones though.

Pickled Crab Apples may be prepared the same way. Cut out the blossom end and prick apple with a fork. You do not have to peel the crab apples.
Satsuma Tea Room, More Fun for the Cook, 1974

PICKLED OYSTERS

1 quart oysters	1/2 cup oyster liquor	cloves
1/2 cup vinegar	whole black peppers	

Cook spices in vinegar and liquor. When hot, add oysters and cook until they curl. Keep in ice box in liquid until served.

NOTE: Makes an excellent hors d'oeuvre.
The Savannah Cook Book, 1933

HOMEMADE CHOW-CHOW

1 head cauliflower	1 teacup horseradish
1/2 head cabbage (cut as for slaw)	1 whole garlic, minced very fine
1 quart cucumbers (the very smallest)	1 pint string beans
1 quart small button onions	1 gill salad oil
2 or 3 pods green and red pepper, chopped fine	2 Tablespoons mustard seed
1/2 pound French mustard	1 cup brown sugar
1/2 teacup celery seed	1/2 ounce turmeric

Shred the cabbage as for cole slaw and cover bottom of a stone jar with cucumbers and cabbage. Then cover with a brine of salt and water, strong enough to float an egg. Let this stand for 24 hours. At the end of that time boil cauliflower, onions, and beans in separate pots till tender. Then drain off all water. Mix them with cucumbers and cabbage. Put vinegar into a porcelain-lined kettle and let it come to a boil. Add mustard seed, celery seed, grated horseradish, minced garlic and pepper pods, cut fine. Let all boil for about 5 minutes, stirring constantly till it begins to thicken. Then add sugar and make a paste of turmeric, mustard, and salad oil, moistening with a little cold vinegar, and put it into the mixture. Stir well and pour, while boiling hot, over the vegetables. Put this away into stone jars and in about 10 days it will be ready to use.
The Picayune Creole Cook Book, 1922

INDIA RELISH

1/2 peck ripe tomatoes	2 large onions
1/2 dozen sweet yellow peppers, cut fine	

Boil these for 25 minutes and drain. Add 1/2 ounce mustard seed, 2 Tablespoons salt, 1 quart vinegar, and boil. Pour to overflowing a bag and drain. Boil together 1/2 ounce celery seed, 1/2 ounce whole allspice, 1/2 ounce cloves, 1/2 teaspoon cinnamon, 3 bay leaves, 1 1/2 pounds sugar. Add tomatoes and boil all together several minutes and pour into jars while hot. This quantity will make 5 to 6 pint jars.
The Southern Cookbook, 1939

MOM'S GREEN TOMATO RELISH

1 gallon green tomatoes, ground	2 Tablespoons mustard seed
11 green peppers	2 Tablespoons celery seed
4 red peppers	turmeric powder
4 onions	1 scant quart vinegar
2 pounds brown sugar	salt

Cook the ingredients 30 minutes and seal while hot.

NOTE Good on dried beans and also with sausage.
Jeanette Boswell Hazelwood, Miss Lizzie's Heirlooms, 2009

LIZZIE'S CORN RELISH

12 ears corn	3 hot peppers	2 teaspoons turmeric
1 head cabbage	3 cups brown sugar	vinegar
6 onions	2 teaspoons mustard seed	
6 sweet peppers		

Lizzie's written cooking instructions were "cover with vinegar and boil 1 hour. Seal while hot." My additional instructions (David Boswell Hazelwood) are to cut corn from ears, chop cabbage, onions and peppers; also add sugar and spices.
Lizzie Boswell, Miss Lizzie's Heirlooms, 2009

CRANBERRY RELISH

4 cups cranberries (make sure these are clean of residual stems)	1 large orange
	2 cups sugar

Pick over, wash and drain cranberries. Grind the cranberries and unpeeled orange together. Add sugar and stir. Let stand one hour before serving. This dish will keep several weeks in the refrigerator.
Satsuma Tea Room, More Fun for the Cook, 1974

PEPPER RELISH

12 green peppers	6 white onions	1 pint vinegar
12 red peppers	1 1/2 cups sugar	salt

Put peppers and onions through meat grinder (food processor), coarse cut, sprinkle with salt, pour boiling water over them, and let stand until they turn cold. Drain water off and add vinegar and sugar. Boil 20 minutes.
The Savannah Cook Book, 1933

PEPPER RELISH

16 sweet red peppers   16 sweet green peppers   10 small onions

Chop this very fine and place into a bowl. Pour boiling water over them and let stand 5 minutes. Drain off water and again cover with boiling water and let stand 10 minutes. Pour into a muslin bag (cheese cloth) and allow draining overnight. Add 1 quart sour vinegar, 1 1/2 cups sugar, 2 1/2 teaspoons salt, and boil together for 20 minutes. While hot, pour into air-tight jars and seal.
The Southern Cookbook, 1939

HOT PEPPER RELISH

3 1/2 cups finely chopped sweet red peppers
1 tablespoon salt
3 cups sugar
1 pint vinegar

Combine peppers and salt. Let stand 3 hours. Add sugar and vinegar. Cook, stirring frequently, until thick, about 45 minutes. Pour, boiling hot, into sterilized jars, leaving 1/8 inch head space. Adjust caps. Makes about 3 half-pints.
Gladys W. Williams, The Nashville Cookbook, 1977

HOT PEPPERED JELLY

1/4 cup chopped hot green or red peppers
1 1/2 cups chopped sweet green peppers
6 1/2 cups sugar
1 1/2 cups vinegar
1 bottle liquid pectin

Mix peppers, vinegar, and sugar. Bring to boil. Boil hard for 3 minutes. Add pectin and boil 1 minute longer. Take from the stove and allow 5 minutes before putting into hot sterilized glasses. Seal.
Satsuma Tea Room, More Fun for the Cook, 1974

SPICED BEETS

1 pound fresh beets
1/2 cup vinegar
1/2 cup water
1/2 cup sugar
1 teaspoon salt
1 stick cinnamon
1/3 teaspoon allspice
3 whole cloves

Wash beets. Cut off top leaves. Cook beets in boiling water until tender. Remove skins, roots, and tops. Slice beets or, if the beets are small, they may be left whole. Tie spices loosely in a cheesecloth bag. Heat vinegar, water, sugar, salt, and spices to boiling. Add beets and boil 5 minutes. Let stand 30 minutes. Beets may be served hot or cold or sealed in a jar while hot.
What to Cook for Company, 1952

PINEAPPLE-PICKLE RELISH

1 1/2 cups sugar
1/2 cup vinegar
1/2 cup water
2 packages unflavored gelatin
1 cup cold water
16 ounces pineapple tidbits, drained
3/4 cup sweet pickles
1/2 cup slivered almonds

Mix sugar, vinegar and 1/2 cup water. Boil until it just begins to spin a thread. Dissolve gelatin, which has been softened in 1 cup water, in hot syrup; add juice from canned pineapple and enough additional water to make 1 quart liquid. Cool until mixture begins to thicken; stir in pineapple pieces, pickles, and almonds. Chill. Serve the congealed relish with meat dishes.
Jean McGaw, The Nashville Cookbook, 1977

CARROT RELISH

1 quart white vinegar
1 1/4 cups light molasses
1 Tablespoon celery seed
1 Tablespoon mustard seed
3 Tablespoons salt
3 cups coarsely ground onions
1 1/2 quarts coarsely ground carrots
2 cups coarsely ground sweet red peppers
1 cup coarsely ground sweet green peppers
1 1/2 cups coarsely ground cabbage

Combine 3 cups vinegar, molasses, spices and salt in a large pot. Bring to a boil. Boil rapidly for 5 minutes. Add all vegetables to vinegar-molasses mixture. Cook briskly 20 minutes, stirring frequently. Add remaining 1 cup vinegar and cook 5 minutes longer. Pack into hot, sterilized jars. Seal. Makes 6 pints.

NOTE: Gifts of the summer garden for winter pleasure.
Farm Journal's Country Cook Book, 1958

OCTOBER RELISH

8 carrots
6 red peppers
6 green peppers
12 small onions
2 medium heads cabbage
1/2 cup salt
2 teaspoons celery seeds
2 teaspoons mustard seeds
4 cups sugar
6 cups apple cider vinegar

With food processor on medium-coarse, grind carrots, peppers, onions, and cabbage. Place vegetables into large container, pour salt over and allow to stand for 2 hours. Drain well. To the drained vegetables add seeds, sugar, and vinegar; mix. Place into a stone crock or sterilized jars for storage. Makes 1 gallon.

NOTE: October is the month of frosts and the last of the garden harvests. After gathering the last vegetables, making a relish is an excellent way to preserve those garden vegetables. This colorful autumn relish is excellent with pork or fowl.
Sandra C. Fleming, The Nashville Cookbook, 1977

SPICED PRUNES

1 pound prunes	4 blades mace	2 peppercorns
4 cups water	2 teaspoons whole cloves	1 1/2 cups sugar
2 lemons	1 teaspoon whole allspice	1/2 cup vinegar

Wash prunes thoroughly and soak in water 3 hours or until plump; do not drain. Extract the juice of the lemons and chop peel. Tie spices in cloth bag and add, with the lemon peel, to prunes. Simmer 1 hour. Remove spice bag and add lemon juice, sugar and vinegar. Boil 5 minutes. Makes 4 cups.

NOTE: Fantastic served with roast pork or other roast meat. May be sealed in sterilized jars and used later.
What to Cook for Company, 1952

BRANDIED PEACHES/BRANDIED PEARS

9 pounds peaches or pears	1 Tablespoon stick cinnamon
9 pounds sugar	2 Tbl. whole cloves, heads removed
1 quart water	3 pints brandy

Select large clingstone peaches or perfect pears. Pare and weigh fruit. Boil sugar and water with spices tied in a bag, until clear; drop in fruit, a few at a time, and let boil until tender, but not soft. The fruit must remain whole. Repeat the process until all the fruit has been cooked. Place fruit onto a platter to drain. Continue to let syrup boil until thick, let cool, add brandy and stir well. Lift fruit and place into sterilized jars. Cover well with syrup. Seal.
The Settlement Cookbook, 1940

BRANDIED PEACHES

Although the Herald Tribune Institute was unable to test this recipe owing to the lack of corn whiskey in New York, it belongs here. Select uniform-sized peaches, not too ripe. Put them into a glass jar and cover with ripened corn whiskey. Let them steep 10 days; then take them out of whiskey and weigh them. To each pound of peaches add 3/4 pound of white sugar. Let the peaches soak in sugar until saturated. Then put all into a kettle with a few cloves and spice and boil for 1/2 hour. Pack into jars.

NOTE: Many will, after 1 day, notice the volume in the jar will have diminished (shrunk) to 1/2 their former size. Add more peaches and sugar to refill the jar. Keep this up daily for about a week, until the jar remains full. Cover but do not seal for about 6 weeks. At the end of that time, it is safe to seal the jar. Again, many will let the jar stand from 6 to 8 months for best results. This approach works, if you choose not to use corn whiskey, but let the peaches manufacture their own brandy. Spices and sugar may be added to enhance the flavor.
200 Years of Charleston Cooking, 1930

BRANDIED CHERRIES

5 pounds cherries	1 pint brandy
5 cups sugar	2 cups water

Select the dark, large sweet cherries. Boil the sugar and water 8 minutes or to a clear syrup, pour over the cherries and let stand overnight. Drain the cherries and let syrup come slowly to the boiling point, add cherries back and boil about 8 minutes. Lift out the cherries with a perforated skimmer and pack into hot, glass jars. Then cover. Boil the syrup down until quite thick and while boiling add the brandy. Pour over the cherries at once; cover and seal.
The Settlement Cookbook, 1940

BRANDIED DRIED FRUITS

Dates, figs, apricots, prunes, or any dried fruit may be brandied by adding 2 parts of strained honey to 1 part of brandy to cover. Bottle and cork. Let stand four weeks or more.
The Settlement Cookbook, 1940

BRANDIED PLUMS

Select the largest and ripest plums and wipe then well with a damp clean cloth. Prick each plum with a silver fork and place in a glass jar. Cover the plums with brandy and let them steep for 10 days. Then take the plums out of the brandy, weigh them and to each 1 pound of plums allow 3/4 pound of white sugar; let the plums lie in the sugar until they become saturated. Then put them in your kettle and boil for 1/2 hour over a slow fire.
The Carolina Housewife Magazine recipe as recounted in 200 Years of Charleston Cooking, 1930

APPLE CHUTNEY

2 quarts apples, cut into small pieces	1/2 cup strong vinegar
2 pounds granulated sugar	1/3 teaspoon ground cloves
2 cups seeded raisins	1 cup pecan meats, chopped fine
rind of 2 oranges, finely chopped	

Boil all ingredients together until apples and nuts are tender. Place into sterile jars and scald.

NOTE: It tastes even better than it reads. Delicious with chicken or game.
The Southern Cookbook, 1939

CANNING

All of us marveled at the many colorful jars of fruit and vegetables in Miss Lizzie Boswell's cellar (David Hazelwood's grandmother). It was an adventure for us to climb down into the cellar and see the many jars, potatoes, dirt floor and floating cobwebs. Climbing back out, seeing the sunshine, and breathing the fresh air was a welcome escape from the stale, musty air of the cellar. But we all knew that the great smells and tastes of the kitchen were stored down there, waiting to be released.

In the summer of 1930 Lizzie set a goal of canning 100 gallons of fruit and vegetables. It took a lot of food to feed a family of ten at the end of the Depression. In July she stepped on a nail and got blood poisoning, but the family pitched in and was successful in helping her reach the goal.

CANNING PEACHES

10 pounds ripe peaches
1/4 cup lemon juice or
3 Tablespoons white vinegar

2 cups sugar
4 cups water

Dip peaches into boiling water for 30 seconds. Combine lemon juice with 5 cups water for dipping peaches. Peel, core, and quarter peaches and dip them into lemon water solution, no longer than 20 minutes to prevent darkening. Combine sugar with 4 cups water and bring to a boil to make a hot, thin syrup. Put peaches into hot sterilized pint jars and pour syrup over peaches until covered, leaving ½-inch space at top. Seal lids and process jars in boiling water bath for 25 minutes.

NOTE: Canned peaches were a regular Sunday night dessert for Miss Lizzie's family.
David Boswell Hazelwood, Miss Lizzie's Heirlooms, 2009

CANNING PEARS

7 cups water
3 1/2 cups sugar
16 large pears (12 pounds)

10 cups water
1/2 cup lemon juice or 1/2 cup white vinegar

Prepare solution of 7 cups water and 3 1/2 cups sugar for a light syrup or increase sugar to 4 cups for medium syrup. Dip pears after peeling and store in solution of 10 cups water and 1/2 cup lemon juice after coring and quartering. Place fruit and syrup into a large pot and place on high heat until they boil (about 15 to 20 minutes). Reduce heat to medium and cook until fruit is heated through (about 5 to 10 minutes). Pack fruit into hot sterilized pint jars and pour syrup into jars until fruit is covered and syrup is 1/2 inch from top. Put tops on jars and place into water bath of boiling water for 20 minutes.
David Boswell Hazelwood, Miss Lizzie's Heirlooms, 2009

JERSEY PEACHES

Pare one peck of large peaches. Put two quarts water, 2 pounds sugar, and 1 cup vinegar into a kettle. Drop peaches in and, as soon as thoroughly heated, put them into air tight jars and pour syrup over them.
The Savannah Cook Book, 1933

LIZZIE'S CANNING OF CORN

21 pints fresh corn	1 pint sugar	1 pint salt

Cut corn off cob and scrape well. Measure corn and to 21 pints add 1 pint each of salt and sugar. Mix and let stand for 2 hours, stirring every 20 minutes. Afterwards, cook 30 minutes and seal while hot.

NOTE: With today's modern super sweet corns, you may want to reduce or even eliminate the sugar.
Lizzie Boswell, Miss Lizzie's Heirlooms, 2009

CANNING BLACKBERRIES

1 gallon blackberries	2 cups sugar

Wash blackberries and drain well. Combine berries and sugar in a large pan and cover. Bring to a boil. Pack into hot sterilized pint jars to within 1/2 inch of the top, making certain juice covers blackberries. Adjust jar lids and process for 10 minutes in a boiling water bath canner.

NOTE: Blackberries started to get ripe after the Fourth of July, so the Boswell kids were sent on a mission to pick blackberries, usually on Granny Reid's farm. She tied rags soaked in coal oil around their legs to ward off the chiggers. The smell of coal oil was many times worse than the chiggers, but the sun-warmed bath water in a wash tub made a good ending to the day.
David Boswell Hazelwood, Miss Lizzie's Heirlooms, 2009

CANNING TOMATOES

22 ripe tomatoes
salt

Blanche tomatoes for 1 minute and place into cold water to cool. Remove skins and core. Quarter tomatoes and place into a stew pot and bring to a boil. Pour tomatoes into sterilized pint jars, leaving 1/2 inch space at top. Add 1/4 teaspoon salt to each jar. Remove lids from boiling water and seal jars. Process 10 minutes in boiling water bath. Makes 18 pints.
David Boswell Hazelwood, Miss Lizzie's Heirlooms, 2009

CANNING TOMATO JUICE

1 peck tomatoes, home grown and ripe	3/4 teaspoon black pepper
1 1/2 teaspoons salt	6 Tablespoons lemon juice
3/4 teaspoon onion salt	

Wash very ripe tomatoes, cut out stem and quarter them. Heat over low temperature until mushy. Strain through a sieve. To 15 cups of juice add remaining ingredients. Reheat to boiling. Pour into sterilized jars and seal. Process for 10 minutes in boiling water bath. Makes 4 quarts.

NOTE: In August, the tomatoes seemed to come from everyone and everywhere. They appeared overnight on the front porch in baskets left by neighbors, who often had an abundance. Making tomato juice was a good way to preserve a great many tomatoes and also made a refreshing source of vitamins in the winter. It also added flavor to the soups.
David Boswell Hazelwood, Miss Lizzie's Heirlooms, 2009

PRESERVED CRANBERRIES

1 pound cranberries	1 cup water
1 pound sugar	

Pick over and wash cranberries. Make a syrup of sugar and water and boil for about 10 minutes, skimming well. Then add cranberries and boil them slowly till they are quite soft and of a fine color. The directions of this old receipt then say to "put them into warm jars and tie them up with brandy paper when cold." Since brandy paper was beyond our disposal, we turned them into jelly glasses and sealed them with paraffin, adding a thin coating as soon as the glass was filled. When cranberries were cold, another layer of paraffin was added and each glass was turned, so that the paraffin ran well up the sides of the glass to ensure a perfect seal. This makes 4 glasses of cranberry sauce.
Mary Louise Simons, 200 Years of Charleston Cooking, 1930

CANNING KRAUT (Sauerkraut)

5 pounds cabbage	4 Tablespoons salt

Shred cabbage fine and place into a large pan. Sprinkle salt over cabbage and mix well. Pack solidly into sterilized jars. Fill jars with cold water to within 1/2 inch of jar top and seal tightly. Kraut will ferment for 3 to 4 days and be ready to use in 4 to 6 weeks.

NOTE: Food had a way of being abundant, then scarce. When it was abundant, like cabbage in the spring, it had to be canned. Kraut wasn't everyone's favorite, but it did keep you from being hungry on a cold winter's day.
David Boswell Hazelwood, Miss Lizzie's Heirlooms, 2009

THIS & THAT

*"In compelling man to eat that he may live,
Nature gives an appetite to invite him, and pleasures to reward him."
Brillat-Savarin (1755-1826)*

*"Here comes Sal with a snicker and a grin,
Ground hog gravy all over her chin."*

SAUSAGE SEASONING

4 pounds pork shoulder or trimmings
4 teaspoons salt
2 teaspoons ground sage

2 teaspoons black pepper
1/2 teaspoon red pepper, crushed
1/2 teaspoon sugar

Use sausage grinder to grind pork or have your butcher do it. Blend all seasonings together thoroughly and sprinkle over ground pork. Mix thoroughly, really using your hands. Refrigerate for immediate use or freeze. Makes enough for 30 slices.

NOTE: The Boswells canned what sausage they didn't eat fresh. It was cooked partially and then put into jars with the grease and sealed.
David Boswell Hazelwood, Miss Lizzie's Heirlooms, 2009

LIZZIE'S PRESERVING MEAT

1/2 pound saltpeter
1 pound pepper

10 quarts salt
2 pounds brown sugar

Lizzie, in her notes, gave no written instructions, so here are the ones I learned from my neighbors, Paul and Estelle Smith. Use fresh country style hams that have been cooled out. A 25-30 pound ham is best. The week after Thanksgiving is about the right time to start, providing it isn't extremely warm, rainy, or below 20 degrees. If it too warm or rainy, the meat might spoil. The meat won't take the salt, if it is too cold. It takes about 30 pounds salt for each ham. Carefully rub curing mix into all crevices, hock, and around bones. Put about 1/2 inch of salt on floor of curing box. Put skin side of ham on the bottom. Hams should not touch each other or the box. Cover hams with salt. Close box and leave for 6 weeks. Take up the hams and brush off salt. Rub hams with a mixture of black pepper and molasses. Run wire through hock of ham. Cover ham with a paper sack and hang in a cool place until fall. Hams can be eaten the following spring, but flavor improves with age.
Lizzie Boswell, account given by David B. Hazelwood in Miss Lizzie's Heirlooms, 2009

POTATO AND HOPS YEAST

This recipe is taken from an old recipe collection for making a home supply of potato and hops yeast.

Peel and slice six medium size potatoes; tie a handful of hops in a square cheese cloth and boil with potatoes in 2 quarts of water. Sift together 1 pint flour and 1 pint cornmeal, adding a little salt. When the potatoes are done, scald flour and meal with water they were boiled in, stirring well. Mash potatoes through a sieve to have no lumps and stir into scalded flour. Soak 2 cakes dried yeast (or 1 cake compressed yeast) in lukewarm water; stir yeast into the mass thoroughly when the batter is lukewarm and set aside to rise overnight. In the morning, knead in enough cornmeal to make a stiff dough; roll out quite thin and cut into cakes; dry on a board in the sun or by the stove, turning every day. When dry, put into a sack and keep cool and dry. Two of these cakes should make 5 loaves.
The Nashville Cookbook, 1977

HOW TO MAKE BUTTER

Use 1 to 1 1/2 quarts heavy cream, at least 24 hours old, to churn well (heavy cream can be bought at most markets). Use cream with at least 30% butter fat. Pour cream into a glass jar, cover, and store several days in refrigerator.

Ripen the cream by letting it stand at room temperature from 4 to 6 hours. The cream will thicken and become slightly sour. This step helps give the butter a mild, good taste.

Cool cream again in refrigerator.

Pour cream into a larger bowl of the electric mixer. Use no more than 1 1/2 quarts cream to prevent splattering. Add a few drops of butter color if desired. Beat at high speed until flecks of butter begin to form. Then turn to low speed until the butter separates from the milk. Watch closely to keep the splattering to a minimum. Push down the sides of the bowl with a spatula as the cream whips.

Pour off buttermilk. Add cold water, about as much as there was buttermilk. Let beater run at lowest speed. Pour off water and repeat. Add a scant teaspoon salt and let beater mix it into butter. Remove beaters, scrape off butter with spatula, and work out water by pressing butter against side of bowl. Be sure to work out all butter.

Mold butter in a butter press or empty it into a container with tightly fitting lid. Store it in refrigerator or in freezer if for long periods of time.

NOTE: One quart cream makes about one pound butter, although it depends on how heavy the cream is.
Farm Journal's Country Cookbook, 1959

SEAWEED BUTTER

SEAWEED PASTE

5 sheets kombu, rinsed with cold water
2 Tablespoons + 1 1/2 teaspoons soy sauce
1 1/4 teaspoons sweet soy sauce

2 Tablespoons rice vinegar
2 1/2 Tablespoons mirin

In a large saucepan set over high heat, add the kombu, soy sauce, sweet soy sauce, rice vinegar, mirin and granulated sugar. Add enough water to cover the kombu completely. Bring the liquid to a simmer over high heat and then reduce heat to low and simmer gently until kombu is very tender, 2 to 3 hours. Strain mixture into a fine-mesh sieve placed over a medium bowl, reserving the cooking liquid. Blend until a thick, smooth puree forms, adding more cooking liquid as needed. Transfer seaweed paste to an airtight container and cool completely before using. Can be stored in refrigerator for one week.

SEAWEED BUTTER

1 Tablespoon granulated sugar
1/2 pound butter at room temperature
1/2 tsp. flaky sea salt, plus more for serving

1 small baguette, thinly sliced on a bias
1 bunch radishes

In a stand mixer fitted with the paddle attachment, add butter, 1/4 cup of prepared seaweed paste (or 2 Tablespoons of momoya may be substituted for the seaweed paste) and the sea salt. Beat mixture together until combined and lightly aerated, about 5 minutes. Serve seaweed butter with baguette slices, radishes, and additional sea salt. Yield: ½ pound seaweed butter, plus extra seaweed paste for additional butter.
Recipe adapted from Philip Krajeck of Rolf & Daughters Restaurant, Nashville, TN
https://www.tastingtable.com

    This recipe for seaweed butter is a very straightforward illustration of what we have been examining, but it is just one example. I personally thought at the time I tasted my seaweed butter spread on a piece of the restaurant's fresh, warm, homemade sourdough bread, that it was one of the most delicious things I had ever put into my mouth. The seaweed butter recipe is among many signature recipes of the Rolf and Daughter Restaurant in Nashville.

    Instances of new and different approaches to the classic food recipes we have come to know are endless; infinite worldwide. Boundaries and borders of food traditions are being torn down as the discriminating gourmet with their new and almost unimaginable food skills become more the norm. Foods eaten for convenience or just satisfying our basic needs for survival are being replaced by foods eaten for pleasure and enjoyment as one of our primary reasons for eating.

    I am by no means disregarding the effects of poverty, famine, mushrooming population growth, variants in food growing patterns due to climate change, etc. These consequences for the human race and its food sources are still prevalent and are realized throughout the world. They are even found in our own United States, often regarded as the richest and most powerful nation on earth. The concerns are real and alarming; quite disturbing realities for human beings in general. Life survival, mere existence for scores of people in the world is a day-to-day, hour-to-hour, minute-to-minute powerful driving force. I do think that there is a quite slow evolution towards parity and equality for all people on the way towards the goal of achieving solutions to these challenges of our survival.

It is a very slow, snail-paced evolution, and I don't think I will see the results of this parity and equality in my lifetime, nor will my grandchildren or great grandchildren see it in their lifetimes, but the trend directions are there and they are pointing in the right direction, upwards. -David S.

"Part of the secret of success in life is to eat what you like;
then let the food fight it out inside.
-Mark Twain (1835-1910)

BIBLIOGRAPHY

"After Katrina,
Cookbooks Top
the Best Seller List"
Journalist Julia Cass
Washington Post, March 22, 2006

"A Gracious Plenty":
Recipes and Recollections from the American South
by John T. Edge and Ellen Rolfes
Published by GP Putnam and Sons Adult
October 25, 1999
Contributor, University of Mississippi Center for the Study of Southern Culture

"An Ode to The Pig: Assorted Thoughts on the World's Most Controversial Food"
by Bethany Ewald Bultman

"Barbecue Sociology: The Meat of the Matter"
by John Shelton Reed
Second Collection in
"Corn Bread Nation 2"
Compiled and edited by Lolis Eric Ely
Publication published in association with
Southern Foodways Alliance
Published October 15, 2004
Chapel Hill: University of North Carolina Press

"Barbecue"
by Sylvia Lovegren
Volume 54, Issue 3
"American Heritage"
American Heritage Publishing
1949-2018   Relaunched 2018 in digital

"Betty Crocker's Picture Cook Book"
by General Mills, INC.
Betty Crocker-Tradename
Copyright 1950 by General Mills
Minneapolis, Minnesota USA

"Barbecue"
https://en.wikipedia.org/wiki/Barbecue
from Wikipedia,
The Free Encyclopedia

"Buttermilk"
https://en.wikipedia.org/wiki/Buttermilk
from Wikipedia,
The Free Encyclopedia

"Chef's Cook Book of
Profitable Recipes"
by L.P. DeGouy,
Consulting Editor
"Restaurant Management Magazine" and
"Hotel Management Magazine"
Copyright 1939, by J.O. Dahl
Published by The Dahl's, Stamford, Connecticut

"Classical Southern Cooking"
by Damon Lee Fowler
Published October 24, 1995
First Revised Edition, September 1, 2008
Gibbs Smith, INC.
PO Box 667
Layton, Utah 84041

"Cooked to Your Taste":
A Vegetable Cook Book
Compiled by Ann Williams-Heller,
Copyright 1945
by Ann Williams-Heller
Essential Books, New York
J.J. Little & Ives Company, NY

"Cooking with Magic"
by Lois Lintner Sumption and
Marguerite Linter Ashbrook
Copyright 1952 by Lois Lintner Sumption and
Margureite Lintner Ashbrook
Published by Charles A. Bennett
Peoria, Illinois USA

"Cortner Mill Circa 1825
A Community Treasure":
A Collection of Recipes by Cortner Mill Restaurant
Compiled by
David B. Hazelwood
Copyright 2009 by
Morris Press Cookbooks
P.O. 2110   Kearney, NE 68848   USA

"Cuisine of the Southern United States"
(http://en.wikipedia.org/wiki/Cuisine_
of_the_Southern_United_States)
from Wikipedia,
the Free Encyclopedia

"Easy-on-the-Cook Book"
by Chicago Home Economists in Business Members,
American Home Economics Association
Copyright, 1960
The Iowa State University Press   Ames, Iowa   USA

"Easy on the Cook: Pies, Pies, Pies":
Compiled and published
by Satsuma Tea Room
417 Union Street,
Nashville, TN 37219 USA

"Eating, Drinking, and Visiting in the South": An
Informal History
by Joe Gray Taylor
Published May 1, 1982 by
Louisiana State
University Press
338 Johnston Hall
Baton Rouge, LA 70803   USA

"Faculty Favorites":
Department of Home Economics
by Isabel Bevier
Home Economics Club
Compiled 1965
University of Illinois   Urbana, IL   USA

"Farm Journal's
Country Cook Book":
Edited by Nell B. Nichols
Copyright, 1959
by Farm Journal
Doubleday & Company, INC
Garden City   New York

"Food in History"
by Reay Tannahill
Revised Edition May 10, 1995
Published by Broadway Books
Crown Publishing Group
Random House New York, NY
Originally Published January 1, 1973
Stein and Day INC.   USA

"Foodie"
https://wikipedia.org/ wiki/Foodie
from Wikipedia,
the Free Encyclopedia

"Fruit of the Spirit":
A Collection of Recipes
by Friends in Faith Evening Circle
Mt. Bethel United Methodist Church
4385 Lower Roswell Rd,
Marietta, GA 30068
Published by Morris Press Cookbooks
Box 2110 Kearney, NE 68848

"Hog Meat and Hoecake";
Food Supply in the Old South, 1840-1860
by Sam Bowers Hilliard,
Published 1972,
University of Georgia Press
320 South Jackson
Athens, Georgia 30602
Jointly published with Southern Foodways Alliance,
April 15, 2014
USA

"Holiday Hostess Cook Book"
Compiled by
Zonta Club of Chicago
Copyright 1958 by
Zonta International
Zonta Club of Chicago   Chicago, IL
USA

"How to Grill Vegetables for Amazing Flavor"
By Allrecipes Staff
http://dish.allrecipes.com/grilling-101-grilled-vegetables/

"The James Beard Cookbook"
by James Beard, in collaboration with
Isabel E. Callvert
Copyright 1959 by James Beard
Laurel Edition. TM 674623
Dell Publishing Co.
730 Third Ave
New York, New York   USA

"Martha Logan's
Meat Cook Book"
by Beth Bailey McLean and
Thora Hegstad Campbell
Copyright 1952 by Pocket Books
Published by Pocket Books, New York   USA

"Miss Lizzie's Heirlooms":
A Collection of Recipes
Compiled by
David B. Hazelwood
Copyright 2009
by Morris Press Cookbooks
P.O. 2110 Kearney, NE 68848 USA

"My Better Homes & Garden's Cook Book":
by Better Homes & Gardens
Copyright 1930, 1937, 1938,
Fifth Edition, 1940
by Meredith Publishing Co.
Des Moines, Iowa   USA

"The Nashville Cookbook":
Specialties of
the Cumberland Region
by Nashville Area Home Economics Association
Copyright 1976, 1977
Second Edition, April 1977
McQuiddy Printing Company
711 Spence Lane Nashville, TN 37217
USA

"The Picayune Creole
Cook Book"
Compiled by The Times-Picayune Publishing
Copyright Sixth Edition, 1922
Published by The Times-Picayune Publishing CO.
New Orleans, LA
USA

"Roadfood":
The Coast-to Coast Guide to 500 of the Best
Barbecue Joints, Lobster Shacks, Ice Cream Parlors,
Highway Diners, & Much More
by Jane and Michael Stern
Copyright 2002
by Jane and Michael Stern
Broadway Books,
A Division of Random House
New York, New York 10036
USA

"Satsuma, Fun for the Cook":
110 Prized Recipes Over 50 Years
Compiled by Arlene Ziegler
Copyright 1968
by The Satsuma Tea Room
417 Union Street
Nashville, TN 37219   USA

"Satsuma, More Fun for the Cook":
A Personal Collection from Home and Tea Room
Compiled by Arlene Ziegler
Copyright 1974
by The Satsuma Tea Room
Satsuma Tea Room, 417 Union Street
Nashville, TN 37219

"The Savannah Cook Book":
A Collection of Old Fashioned Receipts
from Colonial Kitchens
Collected and edited by
Harriet Ross Colquitt
Copyright 1933
by Harriett Ross Colquitt
J.J. Little and Ives Company, New York, New York
USA

"The Settlement Cook Book":
Tested Recipes of the Settlement Cooking Classes,
The Milwaukee Public School Kitchens, The School
of Trades for Girls, and Experienced Housewives
Compiled by Mrs. Simon Kander
23RD Edition, Copyright 1940,
by The Settlement Cook Book
Printed by The Cramer-Krasselt
Milwaukee, Wisconsin
USA

The Soul of Food":
Slavery's Influence on Southern Cuisine
(http://ushistoryscene.com/article/
slavery-southern-cuisine/)
by Christina Regelski
(http://ushistoryscebe.com/author/
christiana-regelski/)
18TH Century
(http://ushistoryscene.com/century/18/)
19TH Century
(http://ushistoryscene.com/century/19/)
20TH Century
(http://ushistoryscene.com/century/20
Barbecue
(http://ushistoryscene.com/Tag
Barbeque/)
Greens
(http://ushistoryscene.com/Tag/Greens/)
Cornbread
(http://ushistoryscene.com/Tag/ Cornbread/)
Sweet Potatoes
(http://ushistoryscene.com/Tag/Sweet-Potatoes/)
Food History
(http://ushistoryscene.com/Tag/Food-History/)
African
(http://ushistoryscene.com/Tag/African)
Southern Cuisine
(http://ushistoryscene.com/Tag
Southern-Cuisine)

"The Southern Cook Book of Fine Old Recipes"
Compiled and edited by
Lillie S. Lustig, S. Claire Sondheim, and Sarah Rensel
Copyright 1939
Culinary Arts Press
P.O. Box 915   Reading, PA
USA

"Southern Cooking"
by Bill Neal
Revised Edition October 1, 1989
by University of North Carolina Press
116 South Boundary Street
Chapel Hill, NC 3808
USA

"Southern Food":
At Home, On the Road, In History
by John Egerton
Published 1987
 by Knopf   New York
Distributed by
Random House   New York
First Edition June 25, 1993
Chapel Hill Books
Published by
The University of North Carolina Press
116 S. Boundary Street
Chapel Hill, NC 27514-3808
USA

"Southern Food Primer"
 articles compiled by
Southern Foodways Alliance
Center for the Study of Southern Culture
Barnard Observatory
PO Box 1848
University, MS 38677
https://www.southernfoodways.org/scholarship/
Southern-food-primer/

"The Story of Corn"
by Betty Fussell
Reprint Edition December 15, 2004 by
University of New Mexico Press
1717 Roma Ave. N.E.
Albuquerque, NM 87106, USA
Originally Published 1992
Knopf Doubleday Publishing Group
New York   USA

"The Taste of Country Cooking:
30TH Anniversary Edition"
by Edna Lewis
Published June 27, 2012 by Knopf
Sold by Random House LLC
1ST Published May 12TH, 1976 by Knopf
New York, NY   USA

"200 Years of Charleston Cooking"
Recipes gathered by
Blanche S. Rhett
Edited by Lettie Gay
Introduction and explanatory matter by
Helen Woodward
Copyright 1930
by Jonathan Cape and Harrison Smith, INC.
Published by
Random House Publishers   New York   USA

"What to Cook for Company:
For Lovers of Good Cookery"
Compiled by Lenore Sullivan
Iowa State College
Copyright 1952
The Iowa State College Press
Published by
The Iowa State College Press,
Ames, Iowa   USA

INDEX

APPETIZERS

Apricot Sticks- 29
Avocado Canapes- 30
Bacon, Brown Sugar- 30
Balls-
    Cheese- 28
    Cheese, Parmesan- 27
    Cheese-Sausage- 28
    Date Balls- 29
    Orange Frozen- 29
    Sausage- 28
    Spinach- 29
Cheese Appetizer for Cocktails- 30
Cheese Straws- 30
Cheese Toast- 30
Cheese Wafers- 31
Chicken Liver
   Turnovers- 31

Dip-   Asparagus Surprise- 31
    Avocado- 32
    Crabmeat- 32
    Cucumber- 34
    Shrimp- 32
    Smoked Egg- 33
    Smoked Oyster- 32
    Spinach- 33
    Spinach Artichoke- 33
    West Indies- 34
Date, Warm Appetizers- 31
Fondue, Beef- 34
Goat Cheese Appetizer- 35
Macaroon Meringues- 35
Mints, Party- 35
Mushrooms, Stuffed- 35

Mushrooms, Stuffed (Variation)- 36
Olive Surprise- 36
Orange Sugared Nuts- 36
Parmesan Bits- 36
Pigs in Blankets
   (Oysters & Bacon)- 37
Pimento Cheese, Spicy- 37
Shrimp-
   Avocado Cocktail- 37
   Puffs- 37
Southern Caviar- 38
Spiced Nut Triangles- 38
Sun Dried Tomato Basil in Filo- 39
The Delicious Appetizer- 27
Water Chestnuts- 38
Water Chestnuts in Bacon- 38

BEVERAGES

Apricot Nectar, Mulled- 49
Blackberry Wine- 56
Buttermilk- 42
Chocolate- Mexican- 44
          Special Hot- 44
Cider- Homemade Apple- 49
    Mulled- 48
    Spiced- 48
Cocktail- Cranberry-Ginger Ale- 53
    Idle Hour- 47
    Plum Cordial- 48
    Sazerac- 47
    Scotch Sling- 44
    Tom and Jerry,
      Southern Style- 56
    Tomato Juice- 53
Coffee, Irish- 43
Eggnog- Charleston- 45
    Eggnog- 45
    Eggnog, Hot- 46
    Eggnog, Individual
      Portion- 54
    Eggnog with Ice Cream- 45

Float- Apple, Raw- 54
    Raspberry- 56
Julep- Mint- 39
    Orange- 40
Lemonade, David's Fresh- 41
Maple Snap- 54
Mead, How to Make- 42
Noyan- 48
Orgeat- 55
Pineapple Juice, Hot Mulled- 49
Punch-
    Apple, Hot- 46
    Chablis Orange- 52
    Champagne- 52
    Cranberry Mulled- 54
    Cranberry Spike- 54
    Fruit, Different
      Combinations- 51
    Half & Half Cooler- 52
    Heavenly Nectar- 56
    Milk- 51
    Orange- 55
    Planter's- 47
    Rum, Bacardi- 44

Punch (continued)
    Sherry, Creamy- 52
    Strawberry- 53
    Tea- 46
    Thirst Quencher- 49
    Tipsy- 55
Sangria- 45
Shrub- Cherry- 50
    Fruit Juice- 51
    Rhubarb- 50
Southern Whip- 48
Syllabub- North Carolina- 43
    Syllabub- 43
Tea- Dixie- 40
    Hot Spiced- 41
    Mint- 41
    Mint, Carolina- 41
    Southern Sweet- 40
Toddy- Hot- 44
    Plantation- 43
Tomato Cream Frosty- 55
Tomato Juice, Hot Buttered- 46
Tomato Juice, Spiced- 53

BREAD, BISCUITS & STUFFING

Biscuits-
    Angel Biscuits- 308
    Beaten Biscuits- 307
    Biscuits- 305
    Buttermilk, Miss Lizzie's-
      306
    Cheese- 309

Biscuits (continued)
    Cream- 307
    Good Morning- 306
    High- 308
    Mammy's Baking Powder- 306
    Old-Fashioned Soda- 305
    Pecan- 323

Biscuits (continued)
    Quick- 307
    Raisin- 309
    Riz- 308
    Southern- 307
    Sweet Potato- 329

BREAD, BISCUITS & STUFFING (continued)

Breads
- Banana Bread- 324-325
- Batter Bread, Mulatto Style-301
- Brown- 314
- Egg Bread (Different)- 303
- Egg Bread, Virginia Style- 303
- French Bread, Quick- 313
- Grist Bread- 307
- Hominy Bread- 297
- Lemon Bread- 325
- Lemon Tea Bread- 327
- Oatmeal Yeast Bread- 314
- Sally Lunn Hot Bread- 309-310
- Sourdough- 311
- Sourdough Starter- 311

Cornbread-
- Ash Cake- 299
- Buttermilk- 290
- Corn Bread, Owendaw- 298
- Corn Cakes, Richmond- 296
- Corn Dodgers- 299-300
- Corn Dodgers, Fried- 300
- Corn Light Bread- 294
- Corn Light Bread 1800s- 294
- Corn Light Bread, Quick- 295
- Corn Meal Batter Cakes- 293
- Corn Meal Dodger- 300
- Corn Meal Muffins- 293
- Corn Sticks- 291
- Crackling Bread- 300
- Crackling Corn Pones- 301
- Dabs- 291
- Hoe Cake- 297
- Hominy Cakes-297
- Hush Puppies- 303-304
- Hush Puppies, Self-Rising- 303
- Johnny Cake- 298-299
- Mexican- 292
- Miss Lee's Southern- 292
- Scalded Corn Balls- 292
- Spoon Bread, Southern- 295-96
- Spoon Bread, Old Virginia- 296
- Spoon Corn Bread- 295
- Tennessee- 291

Doughnuts
- Doughnuts- 328
- Jelly- 329
- Spicy Raised- 328

Fritters
- Apples, Peach, Apricot- 319
- Corn- 292
- Corn Bread- 293
- Fruit- 319
- Fruit Puffs- 320
- Fritter Batter
  -Master Recipe- 319
- Okra- 319
- Orange- 319
- Orange Puff,
  Upside Down- 321

Muffins
- A Master Recipe- 315
- Bacon- 318
- Blueberry- 317
- Buttermilk- 316
- Cranberry- 318
- Cranberry Tea- 317
- Four Weeks- 316
- Ginger- 317
- Plain- 315
- Popovers, Cream- 320
- Popovers, Good Old- 320
- Puff Pops- 320
- Pumpkin, Spiced - 318
- Quick- 315
- Southern - 337

Stuffing
- Almond Herb- 335
- Apple- 334
- Baked Pan Dressing- 332
- Bread- 333
- Bread, Crumbly- 334
- Bread Dressing, Delicious- 333
- Celery - 334
- Chestnut- 333
- Chicken- 331
- Corn Bread- 331
- Cranberry-Orange- 335

Stuffing (continued)
- Orange- 335
- Orange with Spareribs- 336
- Oyster- 332
- Peanut Dressing- 332
- Pecan Stuffing for Turkey- 336

Rolls
- Easy Breakfast- 322
- Hot Cross Buns- 322
- Light Bread Rolls- 313
- Parker House- 311
- Poppy Onion Loaf- 310
- Sally Lunn- 309-310
- Sally Lunn Sweet- 310
- Spoon- 310
- Two Hour- 313
- Yeast- 312
- Yeast Ice Box- 312

Rice
- Ashley Bread-302
- Creole Rice Cake- 301
- Rice Bread- 301
- Rice Corn Bread- 301
- Rice Griddle Cakes- 303
- Rice Muffins- 316

Sweet Breads
- Apple Bread, Fresh- 324
- Apple Nut- 324
- Apple Sauce Nut Bread- 323
- Apricot Nut Bread- 326
- Banana Bread- 324-325
- Banana Nut Bread- 325
- Cinnamon Bread- 327
- Cranberry Bread- 326
- Cream Puffs- 321
- Four O'clock Tea Scones- 321
- Gingerbread, Maple- 336
- Nut Breads- 323-324
- Peanut Tea Ring- 322
- Persimmon Bread- 327
- Pumpkin- 328
- Strawberry Nut- 326
- Sweet Potato Pone- 329
- Sweet Potato, Southern – 329

BREAKFAST & BRUNCH

Coffee Cake
- Coffee Cake Mix
  - Master Recipe- 521
- Orange Cluster- 520
- Plain- 521

Southern- 520

Coffee Cake Toppings
- Apple-Cheese- 522
- Brown Sugar-Cinnamon- 521
- Cranberry-Orange- 522

- Honey-Pecan- 522
- Peach-Cinnamon- 521
- Pineapple-Apricot- 521
- Toasted Coconut- 521

BREAKFAST & BRUNCH (continued)

Curds and Cream- 529
Eggs
- Biltmore Goldenrod-523
- Egg Pie- 526
- Fricassee- 523
- New Orleans- 523
- Poached- 524
- Poached, Creamy- 527
- Ponce de Leon- 523
- Savory Scrambled- 528

French Toast
- Baked- 519
- Oven- 519
- Peach- 519

Griddle Cakes
- Apple- 509
- Corn Meal Mash- 508
- Crepes Suzette- 511
- Flannel Cakes- 510
- French Griddle Cake- 509
- French Pancakes- 509
- Georgia Flapjacks- 512
- Green Corn- 510
- Griddle Cakes- 511
- Griddle Cakes:
  - Master Recipe- 511
  - Apple- 512
  - Banana- 512
  - Blueberry- 512
  - Cheese- 512
  - Corn- 512
  - Date- 512
  - Pecan-512
  - Pineapple- 512
  - Rice- 512
  - Rice-Flour Toddles- 512
  - Sour Milk- 510-511

Hash Brown Potatoes-528
Muffins
- Breakfast Rusks- 530
- Honey Buns- 529
- (See Also Breads- 313-320)

Omelets & Casseroles
- Breakfast Brie Casserole- 527
- Crab Omelet- 525
- Creole Omelet- 525

Quiche
- Basic Quiche- 526
- Mushroom- 526
- Onion and Bacon- 526
- Lorraine- 525
- Parish Patch- 526
- Spinach- 525-526

Syrup
- Honey Butter- 529
- Maple Syrup- 528
- Watermelon Syrup- 528

Waffles
- Chocolate Nut- 518
- Crispy Waffles-
  - A Master Recipe- 516
  - Blueberry- 516
  - Fig- 516
  - Orange Waffles- 516
- Gingerbread- 518
- Hominy- 517
- Louisiana- 515
- Marnier- 517
- More Waffles- 514
- Potato- 514
- Pumpkin Nut- 517
- Rice- 515
- Rice Flour- 515
- Sour Cream- 516
- Sponge Cake- 518
- Sweet Potato- 514
- Techniques of the Chef- 513
- Virginia- 515
- Waffles-513-514

CAKES

Angel Food Cake- 382-383
Angel Food Cake, Bride's- 382
Apple Cake, Dried- 399
Apple Cake Pie- 345
Apple Cake, Fresh- 398
Apple Cake with Sauce- 398
Apple Sauce Cake- 399
Banana Cake/Caramel Icing- 414
Blackberry Roll- 413
Blackberry Rolls,
 Old-Fashioned- 413
Brown and White Cake- 405
Butternut Cake- 409
Caramel Almond Sponge- 415
Caramel Cake- 400
Caramel Cake Frosting- 400
Carrot Cake- 408
Chocolate Cake- 389
Chocolate Cake, Best- 386
Chocolate Cake, Black- 392
Chocolate Ice Box Cake- 391

Chocolate Pistachio Cake- 401
Chocolate Roll/Chocolate Sauce- 390
Christening Cake- 404
Coconut Cake/Boiled Icing- 402
Coconut Pound Cake/Topping- 385
Cream Cake/Filling- 388
Currant Cake- 415
Devil's Food Cake- 390
Devil's Food Cake, Spiced- 391
Dolly Varden Cake w/Icing- 387
Fruit Cake, White- 404
Fudge Sauce Cake- 431
German Chocolate Cake- 392
Ginger Bread, Fairy- 395
Gingerbread, Glorified- 397
Gingerbread, Hot Frosted- 396
Gingerbread with Lemon Sauce- 396
Gingerbread, Maple- 395
Gingerbread, Miss Rosa's- 395
Gingerbread, Soft- 395
Gingerbread, Thin- 397

Ginger Cake, Soft- 397
Ginger Cake, Sour Cream- 397
Governor Northern's
 Great White Cake- 387
Holiday Cake- 402-403
Honey Lemon Layer Cake- 410
Ice Box Cake- 412
Ice Box Fruit Cake- 403
Jam Cake- 393
Jam Cake, Blackberry- 393
Jam Cake, Strawberry- 394
Jelly Roll, None-So-Good- 413
Lady Baltimore Cake- 387
Layer Cake, Plain- 388
Lemon Cake- 409
Lemon Cake Pudding- 436
Maple Up-Side Down Cake- 406
Marble Cake- 405
Marble Cake, Plantation- 406
No-Name Cake- 388

CAKES (continued)

Nut Cake- 403
One-Two-Three Cake- 389
Orange Cake- 410
Palm Beach Poinciana Cake- 414
Pan Cake- 389
Pecan Nut Cake- 404
Pineapple Upside-Down Cake- 407
Pound Cake- 384

Pound Cake, Old-Fashioned- 384
Preacher Cake- 411
Prune Cake with Glaze- 408
Pumpkin Cake- 407
Red Velvet Cake- 391
Scripture Cake- 410
Shortcake, Peach- 385
Short Cake, Strawberry- 385

Sour Cream Cake 389
Spice Cake- 394
Sponge Cake- 383
Strawberry De Lux- 384
Swirl Cake- 406
Tipsy Parson Cake- 412
White Cake, Best- 386
Yellow Cake, Best- 386

COOKIES, CANDIES & CONFECTIONS

Candies
    Benne Brittle- 491
    Benne Candy- 490
    Butterscotch- 505
    Candied Orange Peel- 507
    Caramels, Grandmother's- 492
    Chocolate Bits- 491
    Chocolate Caramels- 492
    Coconut Kisses- 477
    Coconut Fudge- 493
    Creole Kisses- 494
    Divinity Fudge- 493
    Divinity Candy with Jell-O- 502
    English Toffee- 496
    French Candy- 494
    Fudge, Aunt Sarah' - 493
    Grapefruit Candy- 496
    Ground Nut Cakes (Candy)-491
    Marshmallow Nut Balls- 503
    Meringue Glace- 506
    Million Dollar Fudge- 492
    Molasses Candy- 491
    No-Cook Candy- 493
    Peanut Brittle (Goober))- 495
    Peanut Candy- 494
    Peanut Clusters- 506
    Pecan Fondant- 507
    Pecan Patties- 494
    Pecan Nut Candy-494
    Raspberry Kisses- 495
Confections
    Apricot Balls- 502
    Apricot Bars- 502
    Apricot Square- 501
    Bourbon Balls- 471
    Brownies- 499
    Brownies-
        Chocolate Indians- 498
    Brownies, Deluxe Fudgy- 498
    Brownies, Fudge-Topped- 499
    Brownies, Georgia Pecan- 500
    Brownies, Peanut Butter- 508
    Caramel Apples- 503
    Chocolate Coconut Bars- 500
    Chocolate Coconut Dreams- 477
    Chocolate-Nut Drops- 501

    Coconut Orange Squares- 504
    Congo Square- 500
    Date Nut Balls- 502
    Diamond Dainties- 504
    Double Crunchers- 478
    Honey Bars, Favorite- 501
    Honey Wafers- 489
    Ice Cream Wafers- 486
    Jumbles- 504
    Lemon Layer Squares- 503
    Orange Slice Bars- 507
    Orange Sugared Walnuts- 495
    Peach Leather- 496
    Pralines, Florida Coconut- 497
    Pralines, Louisiana Cream- 498
    Pralines, New Orleans- 497
    Pralines, Pecan - 497
    Pumpkin Bars- 506
    Scotch Short Bread- 476
    Short'nin' Bread- 476
    Spice Pecans or Walnuts- 505
    Sweet Wafers- 474
Cookies
    Almond Crescent- 505
    Almond Tea Cakes- 476
    Benne Cakes- 490
    Black Walnut Cookies- 480
    Butter Cookies- 482
    Butter Pecan Cookies- 488
    Butterscotch- 484
    Cathedral Cookies- 484
    Chocolate Chip Oatmeal- 475
    Chocolate Cookies (Boiled)- 483
    Chocolate Macaroons-486
    Chocolate Marshmallow,- 485
    Cinnamon Favorites-485
    Colonial Cookies- 472
    Cookies- 471
    Cookie Bonbons- 477
    Cookie Shells- 500
    Cookie Starter-
        A Master Recipe- 474
    Corn Flake Cookies-489
    Corn Flake Macaroons- 487
    Date Macaroons- 478
    Empire Biscuits (Cookies)- 480

    Gingerbread, Maple- 336
    Ginger Cookies, Plantation- 483
    Ginger Snaps- 479
    Graham Cracker Cookies- 485
    Gumdrop Cookies- 487
    Jelly Layer Cookies- 473
    Lace Cookies- 487
    Lemon Coconut Cookies-486
    Lemon Cookies- 479
    Macaroons- 487
    Meringue Layer Cookies- 473
    Molasses Cookies- 481
    Molasses Cookies, Crisp- 482
    Molasses Snaps- 472
    Molasses Wheat Cookies- 482
    Nut Drop Cookies- 483
    Oatmeal Cookies, Crisp- 475
    Oatmeal Cookies,
        Old-Fashion- 497
    Orange-Carrot Cookies- 475
    Orange Cookies, Florida- 485
    Peanut Butter Cookies-483 ,488
    Peanut Cookies- 487
    Pecan Cookies (Crescents)- 480
    Pumpkin Cookies- 484
    Salted Peanut Cookies- 479
    Sour Cream Plantation-485
    Sugar Biscuits- 502
    Sugar Cookie Variations:
        Almond- 472
        Butterscotch- 472
        Chocolate- 473
        Coconut- 473
        Date-473
        Lemon- 473
        Maple- 473
        Marmalade- 473
        Nut- 473
        Old Fashioned- 472
        Orange- 473
        Raisin- 473
        Rolled- 472
        Seed Cakes- 473
        Spiced Sugar- 473

DESSERT SAUCES

Brandy Sauce for Fritters
    (for puddings also)- 463
Brown Sugar Sauce- 467
Butter Rum Sauce, Foamy- 464
Butterscotch Sauce- 467
Caramel Sundae Sauce- 468
Caramelized Syrup- 468
Chocolate Sauce- 467
Cottage Pudding Sauce- 465
Crème de Menthe Sauce- 466
Danish Pudding Sauce- 441

Eggnog Sauce, Kentucky- 464
Eggnog Sauce, Old-Style- 463
Foaming Butter Rum Sauce - 464
Fudge Sauce- 466
Hard Sauce- 463
Honey (Make-Believe)- 469
Honey Orange Sauce- 469
Lemon Sauce- 468
Lemon Sauce for Fritters
    (for puddings also)- 468
Mocha Sauce- 467

Raspberry Royale Sauce- 466
Ratifia Cream- 469
Rhubarb Sauce- 470
Sherry Sauce- 465
Vanilla Sauce- 466
Vanilla Sauce, Spicy- 470
Wine Sauce for Sponge Cake- 465
Whipped Butter- 471
Whiskey Sauce, Tennessee- 470

FRUITS

Apples
    Baked- 171-172
    Baked Butterscotch- 173
    Baked Glazed- 172
    Caramel- 173
    Caramel Candied - 174
    in Cranberry Sauce- 144
    Dried- 171
    Fried- 172
    Fried Southern- 172
    Honeyed- 174
    Poached- 179
    Plum Compote- 179
    Sauce- 173
    Sauce, Congealed- 173

Bananas
    Baked- 175
    Fried- 175
    Orange Glazed- 175
Peaches
    Broiled Peach Halves- 170
    Broiled Peaches Flamed
        w/Bourbon- 170
    Delmonico Peaches- 170
    Fried Peaches- 171
    Peach/Pear Melba- 171
    Peaches Delightful- 169
    Poached Peaches- 170
    Poached Peaches Liqueur- 170
    Stewed Peaches- 169
Other Fruits
    Apricots, Baked- 176

Other Fruits (continued)
    Cranberries, Baked- 179
    Candied Orange Peel- 176
    Cantaloupe, Spiced-176
    Cheeses Paired with Fruit- 168
    Cold Spiced Fruits- 178
    Curried Fruit Casserole- 178
    Figs, Gingered- 178
    Grapefruit, Broiled- 176
    Hot Fruit Casserole- 179
    Kumquats & Prunes-177
    Oranges, Baked- 176
    Papaya, Baked- 177
    Papaya Canapé- 177
    Pears, Poached- 168
    Pineapple, Fried- 174
    Prunes, Savannah Stewed- 175
    Rhubarb, Stewed- 178

ICE CREAM, SHERBET & SORBET

Ice Cream
- Apricot Ice Cream- 454
- Banana Ice Cream- 450
- Butter Pecan Ice Cream- 453
- Cherry Ice Cream- 452
- Cherry Nut Ice Cream- 453
- Chocolate Ice Cream- 452
- Chocolate Almond- 448
- Chocolate Chip- 449
- Chocolate Mocha 452
- Coffee Ice Cream- 454
- Daddy's Special- 449
- Fig Ice Cream- 456
- Fig and Peach Ice Cream- 455
- Freezer Ice Cream Custard- 450
- Frozen Custard- 451
- Fruit- 449
- Golden Glow Ice Cream- 455
- Homemade Ice Cream- 449
- Honey Coconut Ice Cream- 454
- Ice Cream Fruit Compote- 461
- Lemon Ice Cream- 454

Ice Cream (continued)
- Lizzie's- 449
- Maple Nut- 449
- Marie Louise Ice Cream- 452
- Orange Flower Ice Cream- 455
- Orange Frost- 460
- Peach Ice Cream- 451
- Peach Cherry Ice Cream- 453
- Pekoe Tea Ice Cream- 456
- Peppermint, Pink- 449
- Peppermint Ice Cream- 451
- Rhubarb Ice Cream- 455
- Strawberry Ice Cream- 450
- Three Types of Ice Cream- 448
- Vanilla Ice Cream- 448

Sherbet & Sorbet
- Avocado Orange Sherbet- 460
- Buttermilk Sherbet- 457
- Cranberry Sherbet- 458
- Crème de Menthe Ice- 461
- Fruit Sherbet- 458
- Ginger Lemon Sherbet- 460

Sherbet and Sorbet (continued)
- Grape Ice- 458
- Lemon Sherbet- 459
- Lemon or Lime Sherbet-459
- Lemon Sorbet- 459
- Lime-Pineapple Sherbet-458
- Pineapple Ice- 457
- Pineapple Milk Sherbet-456
- Pineapple Sorbet- 457
- Three of a Kind Sherbet-457

Not Ice Cream, Sherbet, or Sorbet, but Really Good
- Baked Alaska- 462
- Crème de Cacao Bavarian-461
- Eliza's Dessert- 461
- Orange Mousse- 460
- Parfait D' Amour- 462
- Strawberry Snowballs- 450

JAMS, JELLIES, & PRESERVES

Jams
- Apple Butter- 535
- Blackberry- 532
- BlueBarb- 533
- Blueberry, Spiced - 533
- Peach, Spiced - 534
- Pear- 534
- Plum-Raspberry- 532
- Raspberry- 531
- Red Raspberry, 1 Minute- 532
- Scuppernong- 533
- Sour-Cherry and Pineapple-535

Jelly
- Apricot- 537
- Blackberry- 538
- Fruit Used to Make Jellies- 531
- Grape, Spiced - 539

Jelly (continued)
- Hot Pepper Jelly- 553
- Jellies Easily Made- 531
- Jelly Meringue- 539
- Orange Jelly-Creole Style- 539
- Quince Ginger- 540
- Rose-Geranium Jelly- 540
- Pectin- 531
- Sherry Wine- 538
- Wine- 538
- Wild Fruits for Jelly-531

Preserves (French Conserves)
- Directions for Making Preserves- 541
- Grape Conserve- 542
- Peach Conserve- 543
- Peach Preserves- 542
- Pear Preserves- 542

Preserves (continued)
- Sour Cherry Preserves- 542
- Strawberry Preserves- 541
- Tomato Preserves- 543

Marmalades
- Directions for Making Marmalades- 535
- Amber Grape- 537
- Bitter Orange- 537
- Grapefruit- 537
- Grapefruit-Pineapple- 536
- Lemon-Carrot- 536
- Orange- 536
- Orange-Lemon- 536

Chips- (Thin Slices Made Crisp)
- Pear Chips- 534
- Pumpkin Chips- 543

MEAT & MAIN DISHES

Barbecue
- Brisket- 208
- Build an Open Pit for Barbecue- 209
- Chicken- 207-208
- Chicken, George Atherton's-279
- Chicken Breasts, Oven Barbecued- 186
- Ham- 208
- Lamb- 209

Barbecue (continued)
- Ribs- 206-207
- Ribs, Spicy Dry Rub- 206
- Sauce, Mopping- 209

Beef
- Beef Brisket, Fresh and Corned Beef- 13
- Casserole of Beef- 216
- Corned Beef and Cabbage- 214

Beef (continued)
- Corned Beef Brisket- 214
- Corned Beef Brisket, Glazed- 214
- Corned Beef Hash- 216
- Dried Beef a la Maryland- 211
- Hamburger, Bacon Roast- 214
- Hamburger, Cheese Bake- 214
- Hamburger Stroganoff- 217

MEAT & MAIN DISHES

Beef (continued)
- Hamburger Steak
  - Broiled- 215
    - Mushroom Wine Gravy 218
    - and Noodles- 215
  - Hash- 215
  - Lazy Day Stew- 218
  - Meat Loaf- 211
  - Pot Roast- 211
  - Pot Roast in Paper Bag- 212
  - Prime Rib of Beef- 210
  - Ribs of Beef a la Mission- 210
  - Sour Cream Porcupines- 217
  - Spiced Round- 210
  - Stroganoff, 216-217
  - Swedish Meat Balls- 218

Veal
- Champagne Cherries- 212
- Curry Powder- 212
- Old Dominion Fricassee- 218
- Paprika- 212

Chicken and Turkey
- Chicken a la Tartare- 188
  - with Almonds- 186
- Brandied- 188
- Breasts Baked with Sherry & Fresh Mushrooms- 189
- Broiled- 191
- Chicken Cakes- 191
- Chicken and Dumplings- 184
- Chicken on Egg Bread- 187
- Casserole, Breast- 191
- Casserole, Easy- 192
- Casserole, Rice and Chicken- 192
- Casserole with Onions- 192
- Chili Con Carne- 188
- Chinese- 290
- Cornish Game Hens- 194
- Creamed Stuffed Eggs/Chicken- 190
- Curried- 187
- Dixie Shortcake- 191
- Fried Chicken- 182

Chicken and Turkey (continued)
- Fried Chicken Batter- 183
- Fried Chicken, Creamed Gravy- 182
- Fried Chicken, Maryland- 182
- Fried Chicken Gravy- 183
- Fried Chicken, Oven- 183
- Fricassee- 189
- Ginger Glazed- 189
- Hash- 183
- Loaf- 190
- Pot Pie, Miss Cecilia's- 184
- Roasted Chicken (Turkey)- 184
- Stewed with Dumplings- 185
- Chicken Salad, Hot in Casserole- 186
- Souffle- 190
- in Sour Cream- 189
- Tetrazzini- 187
- Turkey Hash- 194

Cheese
- Cheese Molds, Individual- 227
- Cheese Pie- 228
- Cheese Souffle, Fool Proof- 227
- Fruit-Cheese Pairings- 168
- Welsh Rarebit- 227

Lamb
- Ginger Leg of Lamb- 219
- Leg of Lamb Neapolitan- 20
- Roast Leg of Lamb- 219
- Sweet Sour Lamb Chops- 219

Game
- Duck, Cold, 225
- Duck, Roasted- 193
- Goose, Roasted/Stuffing- 221
- Partridge, Roasted- 193
- Pheasant, Smothered- 223
- Possum and Taters- 223
- Possum Hunt- 224
- Quail, Sauteed, 193
- Rabbits- 223
- Rabbit, Fried- 223
- Rabbit, Onion Stuffed- 224
- Squab, Roasted with Rice- 193
- Turkey, Wild- 223
- Venison- 221

Venison (continued)
- Marinating- 222
- Roasting- 221-222
- Steaks- 222

Pork
- Chitterlings- Chit 'lings- 204
- Ham
  - Baked- 197-198
  - Baked Ham Steak- 199
  - Baked Sliced Ham and Apples- 202
  - Baked Sugar Cured Ham- 196
  - Balls with Raisin Sauce- 199
  - Barbecued- 208
  - Boiled- 200
- Country Ham
  - Baking- 198
  - Boiling- 200
  - Broiled- 200
  - Cooking- 197
  - Deviled Egg Casserole and Ham- 201
  - Frying Country Ham- 196
  - Glazing Ham- 197, 199
  - Red Eye Gravy- 196-197
  - Smithfield Ham- 198
- Loaf- 202
- Loaf, Upside-Down- 200
- Pineapple- 201
- Souffle- 201
- Pork Chops
  - Hungarian- 203
  - Italian with Herbs- 202
  - Lemon Baked- 203
  - Stuffed- 203
- Ribs
  - Barbecued- 206-207
  - Hawaiian- 204
- Sausage
  - Rice Casserole- 201
  - Seasoning- 558
  - in Wine- 202

OVER-THE-COALS COOKERY

- Angels on Wings- 289
- Barbecued Ribs- 206-207
- Barbeque Sauce- 280
- Beef Fillet, Sin- 281
- Beef Shish Kabobs- 281
  - Garlic Dressing for Beef- 282
- Mushrooms- 281
- Onions- 281
- Skewers- 281
- Tomatoes- 281
- Chicken, Barbecued- 207
- Chicken, Charcoal Broiled- 284
- Chicken, Dilly Barbecued- 285
- Chicken, Grilled Italian- 284
- Corn on the Cob- 288
- Duck, Grilled with Muscadine- 286
- Flank Steak Pinwheels w/Sauce- 282
- Fish, Foiled Fry- 286

OVER-THE-COALS COOKERY (continued)

Fish Steaks, Skewered- 285
Frankfurters, Fancy- 287
Frankfurters in Herb Buns- 286
Franks, Special (Hot Dogs)- 287
French Toast, Grilled w/ Bacon- 289
Ham, Slices-Honey Glaze- 283
             Mustard Glaze- 283
Hamburgers, Old Fashioned- 280

Lamb Kabobs- 286
Pork Chops with Balsamic Sage- 283
Pork Chops with Cherry Sauce- 282
Potatoes, Baked- 288
Potato Slices, Baked- 288
Ribs, Spicy Dry Rub- 206

Salmon, Best Grilled- 285
Sausage, Tomatoes, and Portobello
    Mushrooms, Grilled Pasta Dish- 283
Some-Mores- 289
Steak, Charcoal Grilled- 283
Tomatoes, Cheese 288
Tomatoes, Grilled w/Roquefort- 288
Vegetables, How to Grill- 287

PASTRY & ICINGS

Fillings
    Almond Cream Filling- 370
    Banana Cream Pie Filling- 353
    Caramel Filling- 370
    Chocolate Cream Filling- 352
    Coconut Cream Pie Filling- 353
    Cream Filling- 321
    Lemon Cheese Filling- 370
    Spanish Cream- 61
    Marshmallow Filling- 371
Icings
    Boiled Icing- 371
    Brown Butter Frosting- 376
    Brown Sugar Frosting- 372
    Butter Icing- 371
    Butternut Cake Icing- 409
    Butter Sauce for
        Cranberry Pudding- 432
    Butterscotch Chocolate- 374
    Caramel, Buttermilk Icing- 372
    Caramel Cream Frosting- 401
    Caramel Frosting (Quick)- 372
    Caramel Icing- 371
    Caramel Icing
        with Brown Sugar- 372

Icings (continued)
Chocolate Cream Cheese
    Frosting- 375
Chocolate Icing- 373
Chocolate Icing, Richmond- 373
Coconut-Honey Cake Topping- 378
Confectioners' Sugar Icing- 376
Cream Cheese Frosting- 374
Cream Cheese Icing- 374
Fudge Frosting- 373
Honey Cream Cheese Frosting- 375
Lemon Butter- 376
Lemon Butter Frosting- 375
Maple/Molasses Pie Topping- 378
Meringue- 340, 353, 356, 357, 363
Meringue Shells- 377
Mocha Icing- 374
Never-Fail Icing- 373
Orange Butter Cream Frosting- 377
Orange Cream Filling and
    Frosting- 400
Orange Icing- 376
Peanut Frosting- 389
Red Velvet Cake Frosting- 391
Royale Frosting- 385

Icings (continued)
    Seafoam Icing- 378
    Seven Minute Frosting- 378
    Vanilla Cream Frosting- 375
    White Icing for
        Hot Cross Buns- 322
Pastry
    Basic Crumb Crust- 381
        Filbert Graham Crust- 381
        Coconut Graham Crust- 381
        Prepared Cereal Crust- 381
        Zwieback Crust- 381
    Chocolate Cookie Pie Crust-380
    Chocolate Wafer Crust- 363
    Graham Cracker Pie Shell- 381
    Graham Cracker Crust 381
    Pastry, Cream Cheese- 381
    Pastry, Egg- 380
    Pastry: The Paste Method- 379
    Pastry, Plain- 379
    Pastry, Southern- 379
    Pie Crust- 379
    Pie Crust, Vodka- 380

PICKLES & RELISHES

Brandied
    Apple Chutney- 556
    Cherries- 556
    Dried Fruits- 556
    Peaches- 555
    Pears- 555
    Plums- 556
Canning
    Blackberries- 558
    Corn, Lizzie's- 558
    Cranberries, Preserved- 559
    Kraut (Sauerkraut)- 559
    Peaches- 557
    Peaches, Jersey- 558
    Pears- 557
    Tomatoes- 558
    Tomato Juice- 559

Pickled
    Artichoke Pickles- 549
    Beets, Pickled- 548
    Brine Solution - 544
    Cauliflower, Pickled- 548
    Cherries, Captain Henry's- 549
    Crab Apples, Pickled- 550
    Cucumber Cinnamon
        Rings-550
    Cucumber, Sweet Crisp -545
    General Rules for Pickles- 544
    Green Tomato Pickles- 547
    Okra, Dilled Pickles- 549
    Okra Pickle- 549
    Oysters, Pickled- 551
    Peach Pickle- 550
    Pears, Pickled- 550

    Squash- 548
    Sweet Dills- 547
    Sweet Pickles, Quick- 545
    Sweet-Sour Dill Pickles- 546
    Vinegar, Homemade- 545
    Watermelon Rind- 547
Relish
    Beets, Spiced- 553
    Carrot- 554
    Chow-Chow, Homemade- 551
    Corn Relish, Lizzie's- 552
    Cranberry- 552
    Cucumbers- Future Use- 545
    Green Tomato, Mom's- 552
    India- 551
    October- 554
    Pepper- 552-553

PICKLES & RELISHES (continued)

Pepper, Hot- 553
Pineapple-Pickle- 554
Prunes, Spiced- 555

PIES & TORTES

Pies
- Apple Cake, Pie- 345
- Apple Dumplings- 368
- Apple Dumplings, Old-Time w/ Sweet/Tart Sauce- 368
- Apple Pie- 346
- Apple Pies, Fried- 345
- Apple Pot Pie- 344
- Baked Alaska Raspberry Fluff Pie- 363
- Baked Ice Cream Pie- 364
- Banana Blueberry Pie- 354
- Banana Cream Pie Filling- 353
- Blackberry Cobbler- 344
- Blackberry Pie, Cold- 347
- Blackberry Pie, Hot- 346
- Black Bottom Pie- 360
- Boston Cream Pie- 352
- Buttermilk Pie- 343
- Butterscotch Pie- 342
- Caramel Pie/Pudding- 342
- Cheesecake Pie- 354
- Cheesecake, Refrigerator- 355
- Cherry Pie- 348
- Cherry Cobbler- 345
- Chess Pie- 340
- Chess Pie, Meringue- 340
- Chess Pie, Walnut- 340
- Chocolate Almond Pie- 364
- Chocolate Cream Filling- 353
- Chocolate Fudge Pie- 360
- Chocolate Cream Mint Pie- 362
- Chocolate Mint Pie- 361
- Coconut Pie- 351
- Coconut Cream Pie Filling- 353

Pies (continued)
- Coconut Oatmeal Pie- 365
- Cream Pie Filling- 352
- Cream Cheese Cake Pie- 354
- Crème de Menthe Pie- 362
- Easy Cheese Cake Pie- 354
- Egg Custard Pie- 353
- Eggnog Pie- 353
- German Chocolate Coconut- 360
- Grasshopper Pie- 362
- Grape Pie- 346
- Irish Coffee Pie- 362
- Jelly Pie- 358
- Kentucky Derby Pie- 339
- Kentucky Pie- 339
- Lemon-Cranberry Pie- 357
- Lemon Meringue Pie- 356
- Lemon Pie, Frozen- 355
- Lemon Pie, Heavenly- 356
- Lemon Sponge Pie- 356
- Lime Pie- 357
- Lime Cream Pie- 358
- Macaroon Pie- 364
- Mandarin Orange Pie- 358
- Meringue- 340, 353, 356-357, 363
- Molasses Pie- 341
- Oatmeal Pie- 369
- Peach Cobbler- 344
- Peach Pie- 347
- Pear Pie, Autumn- 348
- Pecan Pie- 338
- Pecan Pie, Alabama- 338
- Pecan Pie, Caramel- 339
- Pecan Pie, White House- 338

Pies (continued)
- Peppermint Cream Pie- Our Baked Alaska- 363
- Pineapple Cream Cheese- 355
- Pineapple Custard Pie, Nannie's- 349
- Pumpkin Pie- 349
- Pumpkin Pie,-Frozen with Caramelized Almonds,- 350
- Pumpkin Pie, Tipsy- 349
- Raisin Pie- 343
- Raspberry Apricot Pie- 347
- Rhubarb Pie- 359
- Rhubarb, Honey-Lemon- 359
- Rice and Peach Ginger Pie- 359
- Rum Pie- 361
- Shoo Fly Pie- 341
- Spanish Cream- 261
- Strawberry Pie- 348
- Sweet Potato Pie- 351
- Sweet Potato Custard Pie- 350

Tortes
- Angel Torte- 365
- Chess Tarts- 339
- Elegant Torte- Peach Cream Filling- 367
- Forgotten Torte- 36
- Hungarian Nut Torte- 366
- Pear Love Letters- 364
- Pineapple Torte- 367
- Transparent Pies (Tarts)- 343
- Strawberry Tarts- 353, 365

PUDDINGS & SOUFFLES

Ambrosia
- Ambrosia- 416-417
- Ambrosia, Frozen- 417

Puddings
- Almond Ice Box Pudding- 446
- Apple Nut Pudding- 433
- Apple Pudding, Virginia - 432
- Apple, White Compote- 433
- Apricot Bavarian Cream- 438
- Banana Pudding- 431
- Barbara Fritchie Pudding- 425
- Blackberry Pudding- 434
- Blueberry Icebox Dessert- 441

Puddings (continued)
- Boiled Batter Pudding- 427
- Boiled Custard- 418
- Boiled Custard, Country- 418
- Boiled Custard, Old-Fashioned- 419
- Bread Pudding- 419
- Bread Pudding Chocolate- 420
- Bread Pudding, Orange Marmalade- 421
- Brown Sugar Delight- 424
- Burnt Cream- 422
- Caramel Custard- 423

Puddings (continued)
- Caramel Flavored Custard- 423
- Caramel Pudding- 423
- Charlotte Russe- 429-430
- Chocolate Cherry Dessert- 430
- Chocolate Pudding- 431
- Coconut Pudding- 441
- Cottage Pudding- 426
- Cottage Pudding, Paulina's- 426
- Cranberry Pudding- 434
- Custards, General Rules- 418
- Custard, Soft- 420
- Danish Pudding with Sauce- 441

PUDDINGS & SOUFFLES (continued)

Puddings (continued)
- Delicate Date Nut Pudding- 438
- Fudge Sauce Cake- 431
- Honey Custard- 438
- Lemon Cake Pudding- 436
- Lemon Chiffon Pudding- 436
- Lemon Pudding- 436
- Lemon Pudding Meringue- 435
- Lemon Sweet Potato- 444
- Marron Chestnut) Mousse- 445
- Molasses Pudding- 422
- Moonshine Pudding- 439
- Orange Charlotte- 430
- Orange Chiffon Dessert- 440
- Orange Fluff- 435
- Orange Bread Pudding- 421
- Peach Cream- 437
- Peach Melba- 437
- Peach Mousse- 435
- Pineapple Charlotte- 430
- Pineapple Pudding- 440
- Prune Peachy- 439

Puddings (continued)
- Puff Pudding- 427
- Pumpkin Delight- 445
- Queen of Puddings- 425
- Queen of Trifles Pudding- 425
- Quick Hot Weather Dessert- 439
- Raspberry Frost- 437
- Raspberry Ginger- 442
- Rice Custard- 421
- Rice Pudding- 421
- Rice Pudding, Heavenly- 422
- Serene Pudding- 426
- Soft Custard- 420
- Southern Batter Pudding- 426
- Spanish Cream- 361
- Strawberry Pudding- 439
- Sweet Potato Pudding- 444
- Sweet Potato Pone- 445
- Tapioca Cream- 427-428
- Tipsy Squire- 428
- Tyler Pudding- 424

Souffles
- Chestnut Soufflé- 443
- Chocolate Soufflé- 442
- Coffee Soufflé- 443
- Lemon Soufflé- 443
- Orange Soufflé- 443
- Pineapple Souffle- 442

Not Pudding, Not Souffle, but Really Good
- Apple Crisp- 433
- Apple Meringue- 434
- Apple Snow- 428
- Brown Betty- 432
- Caramel Dumplings- 424
- Cherry Dumplings- 437
- Cherries Jubilee- 439
- Cranberry Crisp- 433
- Pandowdy, Monticello- 432
- Snow Cream- 428
- Snow Eggs- 429
- Syllabub- 417

SALAD & SALAD DRESSINGS

Salads
- Alligator Pear (Avocado)- 92
- Apple Chip- 94
- Apple, Cinnamon- 94
- Apple-Grapefruit- 97
- Apple, September- 994
- Apricot Nectar- 100
- Artichoke- 89
- Asparagus- 92
- Asparagus, Marinated - 91
- Asparagus Vinaigrette- 92
- Avocado- 92
- Beet and Apple- 93
- Black Cherry Wine Mold- 94
- Butter Bean Salad- 90
- Chicken & Fruit- 105
- Chicken, Jellied- 104
- Chicken Salad- 103
- Copper Pennies- 88
- Cottage Cheese, Special - 100
- Crab Salad, Mayonnaise- 103
- Cranberry, Frozen- 96
- Cranberry Gelatin Salad- 95
- Cranberry Relish, Molded- 95
- Cream Cheese Salad- 102
- Cucumber Onions Salad- 91

Salads (continued)
- Deviled Eggs- 85-86
- Dressed Eggs- 85-86
- Eggs, Stuffed- 85
- Florida Guspachy- 91
- Frozen Cream Cheese & Cranberry- 96
- Frozen Fruit Salad- 95-96
- Grapefruit Aspic- 97
- Grapefruit Salad, Jellied - 97
- Green Pepper, 90
- Guacamole- 93
- Jellied Mélange- 104
- Lime, Pineapple, and Cream Cheese- 102
- Mandarin Orange Coconut- 99
- Nut Salad w/ Dressing- 98
- Orange- 99
- Orange Sherbet- 99
- Pineapple Banana, Molded- 98
- Pineapple Cream Cheese Date- 101
- Pineapple, Overnight- 98
- Poinsettia Salad- 82
- Potato- 87
- Red Cabbage- 83

Salads (continued)
- Royal- 82
- Russian Sandwiches- 104
- Salmon- 104
- Shrimp Salad with Peas- 105
- Shrimp Salad Louis- 103
- Slaws - Buttermilk- 84
  - Broccoli- 84
  - Chinese- 84
  - Coleslaw- 83
  - Hot- 84
  - Mississippi- 83
- Snap or Wax Bean- 90
- Spinach- 81
- Spinach Salad w/ Egg & Bacon Dressing- 82
- Strawberry, Jellied - 95
- Tomato, Stuffed- 87
- Three Bean- 88
- Tomato- 87
- Tomato Aspic- 90
- Tomato and Cheese Aspic- 88
- Tomatoes, Marinated Sliced -89
- Waldorf- 93
- Waldorf Salad, Molded- 93
- Wilted- 82

Salad Dressings
- Almond Cream Cheese- 102
- Avocado Salad- 115
- Blender Salad- 114
- Bleu Cheese- 111
- Boiled, Old-Fashioned- 107
- Buttermilk- 106
- Celery Seed- 114
- Cole Slaw- 83
- Cottage Cheese- 101
- Crab Salad- 103
- Cream- 106
- Curry for Endive- 115
- Egg and Bacon Dressing- 82
- French- 109-110

Salad Dressings (continued)
- French Dressing, Creole- 110
- French Dressing for Fruit- 109
- French Dressing Variations- 110
- Fruit, Tropical- 89
- Honey Fruit Salad- 114
- Honey Mustard- 111
- Hot Bacon, Pennsylvania Dutch- 108
- Lemonade Dressing- 109
- Low Calorie- 108
- Mayonnaise- 113
- Mayonnaise, Basil- 113
- Mayonnaise -Variations- 112
- Mayonnaise, Homemade- 112
- Mayonnaise, Plain- 113

Salad Dressings (continued)
- Nut Salad Dressing- 98
- Oil Wine Vinegar Dressing- 109
- Poppy Seed- 111-112
- Russian- 109
- Salad Dressing (very old)- 106
- Savory- 115
- Shrimp Salad- 103
- Simple Salad- 106
- Sour Cream- 107-108
- Sour Cream Fruit Salad- 108
- Sour Cream, Richmond- 107
- Spinach Salad Dressing- 81
- Thousand Island- 111
- Tomatoes- 89

SAUCES

- Apple Ball Sauce for Goose or Suckling- 279
- Asparagus-Mushroom- 267
- Barbeque- 263
- Barbecue, Lemon - 184
- Barbecue, Spicy- 263
- Barbecue, Wine- 264
- Béarnaise- 259
- Blackening Spice Mix- 277
- Brown- 258
- Brown Roux- 258
- Butter- 261
- Butter, Blue Devil- 261
- Cauliflower- 273
- Cheese- 267-268
- Chili Sauce- 269
- Cocktail Sauce- 273-274
- Cranberry- 276
- Cream- 260
- Cream Cheese & Chive Sauce- 272
- Creole- 70
- Creole Red Pepper Catsup- 270
- Cucumber- 272
- Cumberland- 261
- Devil's- 264
- Dill Sauce- 268

Sauces (continued)
- Egg Sauce- 268
- Game- 278-279
- Garlic, Cold- 265
- Garlic, Hot- 265
- Green Beans- 271
- Green Pepper- 261
- Hollandaise- 259
- Hollandaise, Mock- 260
- Horseradish- 261, 264
- Horseradish, Creamy- 264
- Lemon Butter- 261
- Louis- 263
- Louisiana Poultry- 274
- Maître D' Hotel- 260
- Mint- 277
- Mornay- 260
- Mousseline- 259
- Mushroom- 266-267
- Mustard Sauce- 266
- Mutton or Lamb Sauce- 277
- Onion- 265-266
- Orange- 272-273
- Pinto Beans, Sauce- 271
- Plain Sauces- 256
- Raisin- 274

Sauces (continued)
- Raisin Sauce for Ham- 274
- Remoulade- 275
- Seafood- 276
- Seasoning- 256
- Shrimp Creole- 275
- Shrimp Sauce- 275
- Shrimp Sauce for Fish- 276
- Sour Cream Cucumber Sauce- 272
- Spinach- 271
- Steak Marinade- 278
- Steak Rub- 278
- Steak Sauce Supreme- 278
- Sweet-Sour- 263
- Tabasco a la Creole- 269
- Tartar- 275
- Texas Special- 269
- Tomato- 262
- Tomato-Cheese- 268
- Vinegar, Spiced- 271
- White Sauce- 257
- White Roux- 258

SEAFOOD

Casseroles
- Crabmeat in Casserole- 251
- Low Country Boil- 255
- Oyster Casserole- 236
- Seafood Casserole- 236
- Shrimp Curry- 237
- Tuna & Noodles- 254

Crabs, Clams, Crawfish
- Boiled Crabs- 249
- Clams a la Saint Louis- 254
- Crab Croquettes- 235-236
- Crab, Deviled- 234, 235, 250
- Crab, Deviled Norfolk- 250
- Crabmeat, Creamed- 250
- Crabmeat Peppers- 250
- Crabmeat Lorenzo- 237
- Crabs-Mushrooms- 234
- Crabs, Soft Shell- 250
- Crab Souffle- 235, 237
- Crab Stew- 251
- Crawfish, Boiled- 254

Fish
- Cakes- 231
- Fillets, Gourmet- 233
- Flounder, Baked- 232
- Flounder, Fillets- 233
- Fried Catfish- 229
- Fried Fish- 229-230
- Poached- 231
- Pompano w/ Shrimp- 234
- Salmon with Sherry Basil Sauce- 233
- Salmon, Herb-Crusted w/Tomato- 238
- Savory, Baked- 231
- Shad, Baked- 232
- Shad, Planked- 232
- Soufflé- 236

Fish (continued)
- Spanish Mackerel, Baltimore Style- 238
- Trout Amandine- 230
- Trout, Baked- 230

Frog Legs
- a la Newburg- 252
- Calvert Manor- 251
- Fried- 252
- Sautéed- 253

Lobster
- a la Newburg- 252
- Boiling Lobster- 251
- Broiled Live Lobster- 252
- Creamed Lobster- 252
- Opening Boiled Lobster- 251
- Stewed- 251
- Thermidor- 252

Oysters
- Blankets, in- 248
- Broiled- 246
- Browned- 246
- Casserole- 236
- Chesapeake Oyster Loaf- 249
- Cleaning Oysters- 245
- Creamed- 248
- Fried- 246
- Louisiane- 249
- Opening Oysters- 245
- Pie- 247-248
- Rarebit, Oyster- 249
- Rockefeller- 248
- Scalloped- 247
- Scalloped, Old Fashioned- 247
- Serving Raw Oysters or Clams- 245
- Steamed Oysters or Clams- 247
- Stew, Oyster- 246

Oysters (continued)
- Toast, on- 248

Scallops
- Fried- 254
- Scalloped- 254

Shrimp
- au Gratin, Shrimp and Crabmeat- 241
- Baked- 238, 241
- Baked with Tomatoes- 241
- Barbeque- 245
- Boiled- 239
- Caliente- 242
- Creole- 242
- Croquettes- 244
- Croquettes, Shrimp and Rice- 244
- Curry- 243
- Fondue- 243
- Fried- 239
- Fried in Tomatoes- 239
- Garlic Shrimp and Grits- 240
- Green Corn Pie with Shrimp- 132
- Paste, Shrimp- 245
- Patties, Shrimp- 244
- Peppers Stuffed with Shrimp- 243
- Pilau, Shrimp- 242
- Prawn or Shrimp Pie- 242
- Scampi- 240
- Shrimp- 238
- Shrimp with Hominy- 240
- Spicy- 243
- Stewed with Red Bell Peppers- 244

SOUPS & STEWS

- Asparagus Soup, Fresh- 63
- Bean Soup, Southern- 76
- Beef Stew, Aunt Linda's Creole- 58
- Beef Stew, Old Time- 59
- Black Bean Soup- 75
- Bouillabaisse- 71
- Brunswick Stew- 72
- Burgoo, Kentucky- 70
- Burgoo for Small Parties- 69
- Cheese Soup- 65
- Chicken Cream Soup- 78
- Chicken Custard (Hot or Cold)- 64
- Chicken or Turkey Stew- 73
- Chicken Soup, Almond - 58
- Clam Chowder- 67

- Consommé, Clear or Jellied- 74
- Corn Chowder- 67
- Corn Stew, Pioneer- 57
- Crab Soup- 64
- Crab Soup, Baltimore- 68
- Crayfish Bisque- 68
- Cream of Crab Soup, Maryland- 57
- Cream of Cucumber Soup- 65
- Cream of Potato Soup- 63
- Cream of Spinach Soup- 73
- Creamed Vegetable Soups- 80
- Creole Goulash- 78
- Creole Soup a la Madame Berge- 62
- Egg Soup- 66
- File Powder- 60

- Fish Chowder- 66
- French Onion Soup- 74
- Green Soup- 77
- Gumbo, Chicken- 61
- Gumbo, Chicken Oyster- 61
- Gumbo and File, Chicken- 62
- Gumbo, Shrimp- 61
- Gumbo, Southern- 60
- Jambalaya -135, 137-138
- Jugged Soup, Southern- 63
- Lemon Soup- 72
- Mock Terrapin Stew- 63
- Okra Soup- 77
- Onion Soup- 674
- Onion Soup au Gratin- 64

SOUPS & STEWS (continued)

Oyster Bisque- 69
Oyster Soup- 73
Oyster Stew- 246
Pioneer Corn Stew- 57
Plantation Soup- 64
Shrimp Newburg- 69
Shrimp Stew- 69
Spinach Soup- 67
Tomato Bisque Soup- 76

Tomato-Corn Chowder- 67
Tomato Soup- 58, 76
Tomato Soup, Clear- 76
Turnip Soup- 69
Vegetable Bouillon-
   (General Lee's Preferred Soup)- 75
Vegetable, Creamed- 80
Vegetable Chowder- 73
Vegetable Soup- 79

Vegetable Soup Stock- 78
Vegetable Soups, Pureed- 79
Vichyssoise- 63
Zucchini Soup- 66
Zucchini Soup, Hot or Cold- 59

THIS & THAT

How to Make Butter- 561
Potato and Hops Yeast- 561

Preserving Meat- 560
Sausage Seasoning- 560

Seaweed Butter- 562

VEGETABLES

Acorn Squash with Apple- 155
Acorn Squash- 155
Acorn Squash, Baked- 154
Apples, Baked- 167
Apple Charlotte, Vegetable- 167
Artichokes- 166
Artichokes, Jerusalem- 165
Asparagus- 150
Asparagus & Egg Casserole- 150
Asparagus, Creamed Au Gratin- 149
Asparagus, French Fried- 149
Asparagus Soufflé- 150
Beans, Best-Ever Baked- 147
Beans, Boston Baked - 146
Beans, Candied - Nuts & Apples- 166
Beans, Home-Baked- 146
Beets, Harvard- 160
Beets in Madeira Sauce- 160
Beets, Orange- 160
Beets in Orange Sauce- 160
Beets, Spicy with Apple- 160
Beets, Sweet and Sour- 160
Black-Eyed Peas- 120
Broccoli- 157-158
Broccoli and Rice- 158
Broccoli with Cheese Sauce- 158
Brussels Sprouts- 157
Brussels Sprouts, French Fried- 157
Brussels Sprouts, Sour Cream- 165
Cabbage, Creamed- 163
Carrots, Candied- 158
Carrots Glazed- 159
Carrots, Pickled- 159
Carrot Pudding- 159
Carrot, Souffle- 159
Cauliflower- 163
Cauliflower &
     Mushroom Souffle- 161
Cauliflower, Italian Style- 161
Cauliflower, Scalloped- 161
Cheese Soufflé- 150

Corn Creole- 132
Corn Custard- 131
Corn Custard, Southern- 131
Corn, Deviled- 132
Corn, Fried- 130
Corn, Fried Tennessee- 130
Corn Pie- 131
Corn Pie with Shrimp- 132
Corn Pudding- 130-131
Corn Pudding, Southern- 131
Corn Soufflé- 132
Cucumbers, Stewed- 164
Cucumbers, Stuffed- 164
Eggplant, Baked- 155
Eggplant, Broiled- 156
Eggplant Soufflé 155, 157
Eggplant, Stuffed- 155-156
Eggplant, Tomato, & Cheese- 156
Green Beans Bleu- 148
Green Bean Deluxe- 148
Green Beans, Fried- 149
Green Beans, Sweet-Sour- 148
Greens- 118
Greens Omelet- 119
Green Peas, Creamed- 163
Green Peas French Style- 163
Grits and Cheese, Baked- 129
Hominy, Fried- 129
Hominy or Grits, Baked- 128-129
Hominy, Lye- 128
Hominy, South Coast- 128
Hopping John- 119
Jambalaya- 135, 137-138
Kale and Onions, Creamed- 163
Kale with Potatoes, Baked- 119
Kale with Tomatoes- 145
Lima Bean Casserole- 140
Lima Beans, Creole- 147
Lima Beans, Fresh- 146
Lima Beans in Sour Cream- 147
Macaroni Croquettes- 162

Macaroni Pie- 167
Mushrooms in Batter- 165
Mushrooms in Cream- 165
Okra- 116-117
Okra, Corn, & Green Peppers- 133
Okra, Fried- 117
Okra, Fried & Potatoes- 117
Okra, How to Cook- 117
Okra & Tomatoes- 145
Onions Baked in Wine- 166
Onions, Shoe-String- 166
Paella (Valencian Rice)- 139
Parsnips & Salt Pork- 145
Peppers, Stuffed Creole- 166
Pilau, Carolina- 137
Pilau, Chicken- 136
Pilau, Egg- 137
Pilau, Shrimp- 242
Pilau, Tomato- 136
Pilau, Tomato-Okra- 136
Potato Croquettes- 142
Potatoes, Half Baked- 142
Potatoes, Hashed Irish- 143
Potato, Irish Pie- 142
Potato, Piedmont Croquettes- 143
Potatoes, Scalloped- 142
Potatoes, Stuffed- 143
Pot Liker- 118
Pumpkin, Ophir Plantation- 154
Rice, To Stir or Not to Stir- 135
Rice, Baked (or Rice Puff)- 135
Rice, Boiled- 135
Rice & Broccoli Casserole- 158
Rice Croquettes- 141
Rice, Croquettes, Dinah's - 138
Rice, Curried- 139, 142
Rice, Fried- 138
Rice, Mexican- 142
Rice, Mulatto- 139
Rice, Orange- 141

VEGETABLES (continued)

Rice & Pineapple- 141	Succotash, Sour Cream- 148	Sweet Potato Meringue- 126
Rice, Red- 140	Sweet Potatoes with Apple- 123	Sweet Potato Puffs- 125
Rice, Spanish- 140	Sweet Potatoes & Apples- 124	Sweet Potato, Scalloped- 123-124
Rice, Wild- 141	Sweet Potatoes, Candied- 122	Sweet Potato Snow-Balls- 124
Rice, Wild with Mushrooms- 138, 140	Sweet Potatoes, More Candied- 122	Sweet Potatoes, Stuffed- 123
Spinach Casserole- 151	Sweet Potato Casserole- 125	Tomatoes, Baked- 143
Spinach, with Egg Sauce- 151	Sweet Potatoes, Creamed- 123	Tomatoes, Broiled- 145
Spinach Souffle- 151	Sweet Potato Croquettes- 121	Tomatoes, & Bell Peppers- 145
Squash, Stuffed- 152	Sweet Potatoes with Cumberland Sauce- 125	Tomatoes, French Fried- 144
Squash Baked Stuffed- 152-153	Sweet Potatoes, Fried- 124	Tomatoes, Fried Green- 144
Squash Cakes Fried- 151	Sweet Potatoes, Georgian Style- 122	Tomato Okra Pilau- 136
Squash Casserole, Annie Laurie Atkinson's- 152	Sweet Potatoes in Honey- 122	Tomatoes, Stewed- 143-144
Squash in Cream- 153	Sweet Potatoes with Madeira Sauce- 124	To Stir or Not to Stir- 135
Squash, Summer Stuffed- 152-153	Sweet Potato Margherita- 126	Turnip Greens, Southern- 118
Squash, Summer- 154	Sweet Potatoes & Pineapple- 126	Vegetarian Stroganoff- 164
Squash Souffle- 153	Sweet Potatoes, Pineapple, Marshmallow- 126	Yam Puff- 121
String Beans and Bacon- 148		Yams, Candied- 122
		Yams, Sugared- 121
		Zucchini with Parmesan Cheese- 153

"The discovery of a new dish does more for the happiness of mankind than the discovery of a star."
-Brillat-Savarin (1755-1826)

NOTES

Made in the USA
Middletown, DE
02 April 2022